The DOS 6.0 Coursebook

Forest Lin

Tulsa Junior College

Scott/Jones Inc., Publishers
P.O. Box 696
El Granada, CA 94018

The DOS 6.0 Coursebook

Forest Lin

Copyright 1992, 1993 by Scott/Jones, Inc.

ISBN 1-881991-28-8

Book Production: Greg Hubit Bookworks
Text Design: Ideas to Images
Composition: Arizona Publication Service
Book Manufacturing: Malloy Lithographing, Inc.

W   X   5   6   7

ADDITIONAL TITLES OF INTEREST FROM SCOTT/JONES

Quickstart in Windows
by Stewart Venit

The DOS-6 Coursebook
by Forest Lin

Quickstart in DOS (120 pages)
by Forest Lin

Quickstart in C++
by William Jones

To DOS-5 Coursebook
by Forest Lin

The DOS Primer (covers versions 3 and 5)
by Dorothy Calvin

The 1-2-3 Coursebook: Beginning and Advanced Topics
by Forest Lin

Modern FORTRAN 77/90: Alternate Edition
by Gary Bronson

Assembly Language for the IBM PC Family
by William Jones

C by Discovery, Second Edition (emphasizing ANSI C)
by L. S. Foster

WordPerfect 6.0 for Windows
by Rolayne Day

Visual Basic
by Forest Lin

Contents

CHAPTER 2   **A QUICK TOUR THROUGH DOS**   41

CHAPTER 3   **MANAGING DISKS**   77

CHAPTER 4   **CREATING AND NAMING FILES**   113

CHAPTER 5   **MANAGING DIRECTORIES**   155

CHAPTER 6   **COPYING, COMPARING, AND PROTECTING FILES**   199

CHAPTER 7 **MAINTAINING FILES** 245

CHAPTER 8 **REDIRECTING FILES** 291

CHAPTER 9 **CONFIGURING THE SYSTEM** 333

CHAPTER 10 **DOS SHELL AND EDITOR**   381

CHAPTER 11 **PROGRAMMING BATCH FILES**   *437*

CHAPTER 12 **USING ANSI.SYS**

APPENDICES   *557*

INDEX

TABLES

Introduction

WHY THIS BOOK?

There are currently some 150 million PCs in use. Most of these run on DOS. That makes it by far the most popular computer program in the world. This popularity has generated a great deal of demand for DOS books.

There are two kinds of DOS books. One provides enlightenment and instructions for the general public. In this arena, a great variety is available. Most of these books, aimed at "power users," provide comprehensive coverage. They are, however, not particularly suitable for persons starting out.

The other category of books is used in the classroom. Here, the variety is limited. Most DOS textbooks are not terribly sophisticated. They rarely provide comprehensive coverage of the subject. Most of them hold your hand step by step, but never let go of it. This may be necessary as you start out, but this approach becomes a waste of time and precious book space after you learn to walk on your own.

This book aims to combine the best of the above two categories. It will hold your hand and walk you step by step when appropriate, particularly at the beginning. But it goes beyond that. Intricate points are explained in considerable detail and numerous examples are provided. Thus you find in this book a combination of structured learning environment and in-depth coverage of most topics.

WHAT IS IN THIS BOOK

There are 12 chapters in this book. Each chapter covers a function or object, or closely related ones. Related DOS commands are explained and ample examples provided. Where hands-on experience is required, you are given step by step instructions. Where you need to be aware of important points, the text explains them to you. By combining explanations and concrete steps, the book provides the optimal learning environment.

You cannot learn to use a computer program effectively by just reading a textbook; you must roll up your sleeves and literally get your fingers (and your brain) busy. Learning by doing is the best way of learning to master DOS or any other program. To that end, this book is organized to induce you to pause to digest and stop to practice. After one or a few important topics are explained and illustrated, a few Practice exercises and Drill questions will await you. The former gives you an opportunity to practice the steps you have just learned, and the latter lets you reinforce the important points explained in the text.

At the end of each chapter, the salient points are summarized and 15 essay questions are provided. You are to put in writing what you have learned so far. Writing an answer to an essay question requires you to be thoroughly familiar with the material covered in the chapter. This process should further reinforce your learning.

Appendix J provides answers to all the odd-numbered questions in each chapter. For the others, you may need to look up the section(s) preceding the questions to find answers. You can get answers to all the drill questions by running the CAI (computer-aided instruction) program included with the book; see below for details.

CONVENTIONS USED IN THIS BOOK

If you are familiar with computer books, you should have no trouble understanding the simple language used in this book. If you are not, you may need to be aware of the following words and their meanings:

Press	Use a finger to tap a key and let go.
Type	Press keys corresponding to specified letters.
Enter	Type something and end with pressing the Enter key.

For example, you may be instructed to do the following step:

1. Enter the DIR command:

   A>**dir**

Here you are asked to type DIR and press Enter. The A> notation is automatically displayed by DOS, and your commands are to be entered after it.

In the text, a DOS command name or a file name appears in uppercase (capitalized). This is done for easier reading. With some rare exceptions, you can enter a DOS command or file name in either case. Since you are most likely to enter a command in lowercase, the illustrations of actual commands which you are to enter appear in lowercase.

Learning a new subject requires you to be familiar with its special jargon. To facilitate your familiarization with pertinent terms, a list of New Terms and Symbols appears at the beginning of each chapter. These terms are arranged in the order they appear in the text. They are also bolded in the text when they appear for the first time or at crucial places. This arrangement should enable you to find new terms quickly. Appendix A (Glossary) also provides formal definitions for these terms; check it when you find a term you do not understand.

There are dozens of DOS commands. If you want to master DOS, you need to know how to use most of them. The commands to be covered in a chapter are also listed at the beginning of the chapter in the order they are to appear in the text. Some commands are covered in several chapters; they may thus be listed in several chapters.

HARDWARE/SOFTWARE ASSUMPTIONS

In the previous edition of this book, people were assumed to be using different DOS versions and a variety of hardware configurations. Times have changed since then. As versions 5 and 6 become widely accepted and hard disks are commonly used, this book has to flow with the tide and change the assumptions. Here are the new assumptions:

- You are using DOS version 6. Major features newly available in versions 5 and 6 will be pointed out. If you use an earlier version in another computer, these features are not available.

- You are using a computer that has a hard disk and two floppy drives. If you have a single floppy drive, the book will tell you how to handle a particular situation.

- DOS is booted from the hard disk, which is presumed to be drive C.

- DOS files and external commands are stored in the C:\DOS directory.

- A path command like PATH=C:\DOS is included in the AUTOEXEC.BAT file. If this is not the case, you can enter the command on the command line. This arrangement allows you to run an external DOS command from any drive or directory.

- You have at least three floppy disks for use in various activities throughout the course.

- You can write files only to your own floppy disks in drive A or B.

When you are instructed in the text to do something, the above assumptions will be followed. The book will explain how to manage a hard disk, but you will not be told to write to it or alter the existing arrangement. Ignore these assumptions if you are using your own system.

SUGGESTED WAYS OF LEARNING FROM THIS BOOK

You may be learning DOS in a short course (a single evening, perhaps), a long course (one semester, three hours per week), or any sort of arrangement in between. Here are some suggestions on how to make the most of this book.

For a short course, try the second half of Chapter 1. Start with Using the Keyboard if you are not already familiar with it. Then work from Starting and Restarting a PC to the end of the chapter. Then complete Chapter 2. These portions should give you basic knowledge from which you can expand on your own.

The book has enough material for a more comprehensive course. You can follow the chapter sequence and do all the exercises. Or you can jump from Chapter 4 to Appendix H, and then back to Chapter 5 and the remaining chapters. This will introduce to you the line editor (EDLIN) at an earlier stage and enable you to use it to write batch files sooner. Using EDLIN to write batch files is much more convenient than using COPY CON (discussed in Chapter 4). If you do not intend to write many batch files, however, you are not likely to have much use for this editor.

If you want to take advantage of the Shell, available since version 5, complete the first four chapters and then move on to Chapter 10. This chapter covers both the Shell and the Editor (EDIT). The former lets you use a graphical user interface to manage files, programs, and drives/directories. The latter can be used in lieu of EDLIN to create batch files. After completing Chapter 10, return to Chapter 5 and continue with the rest. Getting familiar with the Shell at an early stage lets you learn to use DOS from both the command line as well as from the graphical environment. If you use EDIT to create batch files, you can skip EDLIN.

If you are using this book for an advanced DOS course, concentrate on Chapter 11. This chapter has been vastly expanded from the previous edition. Every batch command is now more thoroughly discussed and many more examples have been added.

USING THIS BOOK AS A DOS REFERENCE

There are numerous DOS commands, and the number has been increasing with each new version. After you learn some new commands, you are likely to forget some of the old commands you learned earlier. You may then need to look up earlier information.

This book is designed with easy reference in mind. You can use a number of features to quickly locate any significant information in the text. Some of these are placed at the end of the book, including:

- Index
- Glossary
- DOS Commands

You can quickly find information by looking up relevant terms in the index, which is quite comprehensive.

As mentioned earlier, the beginning of each chapter lists terms and DOS commands to be discussed in the chapter. Furthermore, major points and command examples are listed under the title of Quick Start. These items may not mean much to you as you start out. But in the future, when you want to come back to find something you have forgotten, you can use them to quickly locate more related information in the chapter.

Tables and Tips & Tricks are scattered throughout the book. These are indexed in the Table of Contents. Some tables listing commands or options are most useful as quick reminders.

The quickest way to remind you how to use a command or what switches are available with it is Appendix E (DOS Commands). It provides the most vital information and examples for most DOS commands.

USING THE INCLUDED SOFTWARE

This book comes with a floppy disk, which is labeled DOS-TA (for DOS Teaching Assistant) and contains the following items:

- DRILL.EXE—CAI program
- DOSLESnn—question/answer files (e.g., DOSLES3 for Chapter 3) to be used by the CAI program
- MENU.EXE & MENUB.BAT/KEY.COM—menus for the CAI program and the question/answer files
- SAMPLE.TXT—a practice text file used in the book

The DRILL.EXE program provides CAI interactive mechanism for the drill questions appearing in each chapter of the book. To run a lesson, enter a command like this:

```
A>drill dosles1
```

This will start the drill questions for Chapter 1. If you enter the program's name alone, like this:

```
A>drill
```

you will be asked to enter a lesson after the program is started.

If you start a drill lesson with either method above, you can store the program and the lesson files in different drives. If the program is in drive A and a lesson file in B, you can enter a command like this:

```
A>drill b:dosles3
```

Once a drill lesson begins, you are given a question and prompted to supply an answer, which could be a letter, number, word, or phrase. The program will try to match your answers to those stored in the lesson file. You can give an answer in uppercase or lowercase.

A running scoreboard is displayed at the bottom of the screen. It keeps track of how many right and wrong answers you have given. If you give a right answer, some acclamation is indicated. If you supply a wrong answer, a brief explanation is displayed and you are prompted to press a key to go to the next question.

Each lesson contains 30 questions. After you finish all of them, the final score will be displayed. If you want to run the same lesson or another one, just repeat the above steps. If you want to abort a lesson, press Ctrl-C (or Ctrl-Break) at any time.

If you are a beginner, you may want to take advantage of two menu programs to simplify your access to a drill lesson. MENU.EXE is a program through which you can access any of the drill lessons. To run the program, just enter this:

    A>**menu**

When the menu screen appears, you can just press a key to select any of the available options displayed on the screen.

MENUB.BAT is a batch file comparable to the menu program explained above; KEY.COM provides interactive mechanism for the batch file. It runs rather slowly, as all complex batch files do. However, you can customize it and use it as an example for creating a similar menu batch file.

If you use MENU.EXE or MENUB.BAT to start a drill lesson, you can put it and DRILL.EXE in the same directory and the DOSLESnn files in a subdirectory named LESSON. When the user selects a file from either menu, control is transferred to DRILL.EXE, which will try to open a corresponding lesson file in the current directory; if the file is not found, it will next try the LESSON subdirectory. If it cannot find the file in either place, an error message will appear and the program will end.

ABOUT THE AUTHOR

Dr. Forest Lin is a veteran author, professor, and programmer. He has taught in various colleges for over 20 years. He has published eight other computer books—some college texts and some advanced trade books.

ACKNOWLEDGMENTS

Good books are the result of effective collaboration between authors and reviewers. Successive editions of books can become more powerful and better teaching tools because of a "feedback loop" between the author and those professors who teach out of the author's book and provide the author with classroom feedback.

One of the reasons *The DOS 6 Coursebook* is an even better book than its predecessors is because it distills classroom experiences of earlier editions of *DOS Coursebooks*. I would like to thank each "generation" of professors who have provided my publisher with feedback. They have helped this text become a successively more effective teaching tool.

The response to the *Instructor's Resource Guide* for all *DOS Coursebooks* continues to be outstanding. The author would like to thank Wesley Scruggs, Brazosport College, for his assistance in preparing this material.

Lastly, the author and publisher owe a considerable debt to Kathleen Ponti and Michael Springer for their unflagging and conscientious efforts to make this book the best it could be. They are real professionals.

Professors Helping Develop *The DOS Coursebook*

Carl Grame and Dan O'Donnell
De Anza College

Ivan Wallace
East Carolina University

Jane Varner
Montgomery College

Margaret Randall
Canada College

Dorothy Calvin
Skyline College

Jerry Martin
Ohio State University

Donna Benevich
Foothill College

Bill Barry
El Paso Community College

Mary Rasley
Lehigh County Community College

Professors Helping Develop *The DOS 5.0 Coursebook*

Bill Bechtold
Metropolitan Community College

Dave Burgett
McLennan Junior College

Peggy White
St. Johns River Community College

Christie Klozeman
Glendale Community College

Shui-Lien Huang
Mt. San Anotnio College

Sue Finch
Pima Community College

Kathy Blicharz
Pima Community College

Chris Gross-Rhode
Metropolitan Community College

Darrel Dorsett
College of San Mateo

Professors Helping Develop *The DOS 6 Coursebook*

Don Chapman
Laney College

Marvin Harris
Lansing Community College

Darrel Dorsett
College of San Mateo

Rick Logsdon
Polk Community College

Fred Cisin
Merritt College

Nancy Webb, City College of San Francisco, was especially helpful in pointing out how to refine Chapter 2 of *The DOS 5 Coursebook* and in showing the need to better delineate what students should follow step by step. . . and what they should read, but not do!

PC and DOS

T O P I C S

C O M M A N D S   C O V E R E D

DATE, TIME, CLS, VER, FASTHELP, HELP

N E W   T E R M S   A N D   S Y M B O L S

PC, DOS, mainframe, mini, micro, KB, RAM, XT, AT, CPU, clone (compatible), PS/2, math coprocessor, MCA, EISA, bus, MPC, system unit, peripheral, motherboard, ROM, firmware, BIOS, boot, expansion slot, controller card, video graphics card, MDA, pixels, Hercules, RGB, CGA, EGA, VGA, parallel port, daisy-wheel printer, dot-matrix printer, NLQ, laser printer, mouse, serial port, modem, baud, scanner, cursor, toggle, enhanced keyboard, system software (operating system), application software, CP/M, PC-DOS, MS-DOS, OS/2, UNIX, operating environment, Windows, surge protector, boot (system) disk, DOS (system) prompt, DOS command, command line, online help.

QUICK START

To distinguish different kinds of PCs:

> See Table 1.1.

To use some of the special keys and key combinations on the keyboard:

> See Table 1.2 and Table 1.3.

To boot (start) DOS:

> In a floppy system, insert a system disk in drive A and turn on the PC. If you use a hard disk, leave drive A door open and turn on the PC.

To restart DOS:

> Press the Reset button (if any) on the system unit or press this key combination on the keyboard: Ctrl-Alt-Del.

To clear the screen:

> C>cls

To show the DOS version you are using:

> C>ver

To show and/or change the current date:

> C>date

To show and/or change the current time:

> C>time

To display online help messages:

> C>fasthelp   (show a list of commands)
>
> C>help command   (help for a named command)
>
> C>command /?   (name of a command, plus /?)

To end a DOS session:

> Turn off the system unit, printer, and monitor; retrieve the disk from drive A, if any.

Lots of new terms, many of them confusing acronyms and abbreviations, will greet you in this chapter. If you are versed in **PC** (Personal Computer) technology, these should be your household words. If you are a newcomer (or have not kept up with the latest developments), you need to be familiar with this new jargon. The terms explained in this chapter will enable you to understand and use the PC and **DOS** (Disk Operating System).

PC technology changes rapidly. New terms and acronyms sprout up every week. If you want to keep up with the latest developments, the Further Reading list in Appendix I should be helpful.

This chapter introduces some commonly used PC hardware items, some software terms, and a few simple DOS commands. They will get you started on your way to mastering the PC and DOS.

PC ACRONYMS

■ *Computers can be grouped according to their sizes (from large to small) into mainframes, minis, and PCs. PCs in turn can be divided into XT, AT, PS/2, PS/1, and others.*

Computers used to be large, centrally located machines that served a lot of people. Today these mainframe computers, or **mainframes** for short, still exist, but there are other computers as well. Smaller-scale computers, serving fewer people and having less power, are called minicomputers, or **minis** for short. Next come personal computers.

When they first appeared in the mid-1970s, tiny computers were called microcomputers, or **micros** for short. The first wave of micros, for games or business uses, were generally small in size (hence the name micros) and had limited capabilities.

When IBM (International Business Machines) introduced its first micros in 1981, it chose the term **PC**. Many people began to apply this term to a computer that was supposed to do real work, not for play as micros were supposed to do. Over the years, the two terms have become blurred, and PC has mostly supplanted micro. Today, the term PC is used as a generic name referring to all small computers below minis and above game machines.

The initial IBM PC was a simple machine. It had 16**KB** of **RAM**. (RAM stands for random access memory, or simply computer memory; KB stands for kilobyte, or 1024 bytes. A byte consists of 8 bits. Appendix G explains bytes, bits, and other units of measurement in computer math.) The PC also came with one or two floppy disk drives. This arrangement soon proved to be inadequate.

In 1983, IBM produced a slightly modified model equipped with up to 256KB RAM and a hard disk (also known as Winchester disk; IBM calls it fixed disk because it is not supposed to be removed like a floppy disk). This model was named **XT** (Extended Technology).

In 1984, IBM began to market a new computer based on a new **CPU** (central processing unit, a PC's "brain" where all the calculation is done). This computer was named **AT** (Advanced Technology). Although the original PC and XT are in the same class, the AT is a much more powerful machine.

Success breeds imitation and competition. The phenomenal popularity of the PC led to a tidal wave of imitators known as IBM **clones** (exact copies) or **compatibles** (work-alikes). They can run the programs written for IBM products or accept parts and devices intended for genuine IBM machines.

Compatibles vastly expanded the PC market. Most of them cost less than half of what IBM was charging. Lower prices made PCs affordable to an increasing number of people, but drastically reduced IBM's market share.

In 1987 IBM abandoned the AT in favor of the **PS/2** (Personal System/2). This new line consists of a variety of products based on different Intel CPU chips (explained in the next section). Most of the models are equipped with a new device, an **MCA** (Micro Channel Architecture) **bus** (a circuit that carries data and allows different computer parts to communicate with one another). The MCA is protected by a wall of legal patents, which make it difficult to clone legally and technically.

IBM brought back the AT in mid-1990 by introducing a new line of computers under the label of PS/1. Like the original AT, the PS/1 featured the 286 CPU (more recent models contain 386 or 486 CPUs) and the traditional AT (not MCA) bus. The introduction of this new line marked IBM's second entry to the home market. These real computers have been much better received than the toy-like PCjr, IBM's first product aimed at the home market.

Reflecting the new market reality, the term PS/2 (or PS/1) has not replaced PC but become part of the PC terminology. Today, IBM's share of the PC market is less than one-fourth. The rest is controlled by numerous other companies such as Compaq, Dell, and Tandy. Much of the world still refers to this category of computers as PC, in which the PS/2 (or PS/1) is a subcategory of the PC.

Adding insult to injury, IBM has also lost another war—the bus war. Rival vendors formed a new group, which designed a comparable bus known as *EISA* (Extended Industry Standard Architecture).[1] Today more EISA systems are sold than MCA counterparts. Some critics are now urging IBM to abandon its proprietary MCA so that the company can become competitive again in the PC market.

---

1. Both MCA and EISA are 32-bit buses because they move data 32 bits at a time—and at a relatively high speed. In contrast to the 8 MHz, 16-bit bus of the AT (now known as ISA or Industry Standard Architecture), these new buses can move data at a much larger and faster rate.

Table 1.1

Different Kinds of PCs

Name	Meaning
PC	Personal Computer, the original IBM PC; generic term for all small-scale computers
XT	Extended Technology, the original IBM PC/XT; generic term for a PC based on the 8088 or compatible CPU
AT	Advanced Technology, the original IBM PC/AT; generic term for a PC based on the 80286 or higher CPU
PS/2	Personal System/2, the high-end PCs currently marketed by IBM; contains various models based on different CPUs; some have the new MCA bus, others have the traditional AT bus
PS/1	Personal System/1, the low-end PCs currently marketed by IBM; has the AT bus and various Intel and non-Intel CPUs.

A new bus war is heating up as of mid-1993, this time pitting CPU giant Intel (see the next section) against a group of video merchants. A new device known as a **local bus** now allows the video card and other devices to be directly connected to the CPU—instead of going through the system bus.[2] Depending on your CPU's speed, this can dramatically speed up screen display of graphics. Many PCs sold today intended to run Windows programs have motherboards equipped with local buses following the VL-Bus standard established by VESA (Video Electronics Standards Association). In the meantime, Intel has proposed a more powerful (and expensive) local bus standard. Only time can tell which standard will prevail.

The early 1990s also witnessed the arrival of a new technology and an accompanying acronym, namely **MPC** (Multimedia PC). MPC is currently at its early stage of development. In the future, it promises to combine the sound quality of a compact disk, the animation capability of a high-definition television, and the data manipulation ability of a computer into a single unit. At that point, vast educational and entertainment resources could be at our fingertips and render most current home and educational electronic gadgets obsolete.

---

2. A local bus moves data at the speed of the CPU and along a 32-bit data path, much faster than the dated AT bus still in use in most of the new systems today.

D R I L L

Select an acronym in the list to answer questions 1–6:

a. KB b. CPU c. EISA d. MCA e. RAM f. PS/2

____ 1. Computer memory.

____ 2. A line of PCs marketed by IBM.

____ 3. The "brain" of a PC.

____ 4. A unit of measurement.

____ 5. IBM's new bus structure.

____ 6. An extension of the AT bus.

DIFFERENT KINDS OF PCS

■ *Most PCs are based on a variety of CPUs made by Intel: 8088/8086, 80286, 80386, 80486, and Pentium.*

There are different ways to classify PCs. It can be done by brands, such as IBM, Compaq, Tandy, Epson, etc. It can be done by sizes, such as tower (upright, floor-mounted), desktop (sitting on top of a desk), portable (also known as luggable), laptop (can be held on a person's lap), notebook (about the size of a hardbound book), pocket (can be put in a pocket), and pen.[3] The most meaningful classification, however, is by the CPU a PC uses.

Most PCs use CPU chips made by Intel Corporation. These chips include 8088/8086, 80286, 80386, 80486, and Pentium (P5 or 586). If you intend to buy a PC, make sure you know what chip you are getting. Generally speaking, a PC based on a higher-numbered chip costs more and runs much faster.

8088 and 80286

The first IBM PC and later the IBM XT were based on the 8088 chip, operating at the 4.77 MHz (megahertz, or 1 million cycles per second) speed. Although it was

---

3. A pen computer has no keyboard. An electronic pen (stylus) is used to input commands and data. Due to the absence of a bulky keyboard, a pen computer is smaller and more portable than a laptop.

once considered a powerful chip, today it is more like a slow boat than a hot rod. A few vendors still market tiny palmtop PCs based on the 8088 or a slightly improved 8086 chip running at 10 or 12 MHz. Some also use clone chips named V20 and V30.

When IBM introduced the AT in 1984, the new model was based on the 286 chip running at 6 MHz. This was a vast improvement over the previous models. This model can run two or three times as fast the old ones. One reason for the improved speed is that this chip has an 16-bit external as well as internal data bus. Although the 8088 and the 80286 are both 16-bit chips (they process data 16 bits at a time), the 286 has a 16-bit data path and can move data 16 bits at a time—twice the rate of 8 bits for the 8088.

Compatible AT models running at 8 MHz were introduced shortly afterward. Then came 10, 12, and 25 MHz. To protect its lucrative mainframe and mini markets, IBM tried but failed to prevent its AT users from jacking up the speed. In the end, it was forced to join the competitors by increasing the speed of its AT models. By now users had a taste of more powerful personal computers at lower prices and were abandoning IBM in droves. IBM's response was to give up the entire AT line in favor of the proprietary PS/2 line in 1987. One magazine characterized this event as "The empire strikes back." The counterstrike from users, however, proved to be more potent because the PS/2 line never caught on and IBM was left further behind in the PC market. Like the Frankenstein monster, the PC market was no longer under its creator's control.

Although there are still many 286 PCs in use today, vendors are no longer selling desktop models. Here and there one can still see ads promoting cheap laptop models using this chip. They may be old models left over from the bygone era. The 16-bit chips had run their course, and the future belonged to their 32-bit heirs.

80386, 80486, and Pentium

Introduced in 1986, the 386 chip made the PC a serious computing machine. With the arrival of this chip, the PC has finally grown up and the industry has matured. Many software programs have been written to run with this and its successor chips, not those before. This is the minimum chip required to do any heavy computing today.

The first 386 chip ran at 16 MHz. Then came 20, 25, 33, and 40 MHz models. Intel still markets these chips, but at a rapidly decreasing volume. Much of the market is taken over by competitors. The fastest chip in this category, running at 40 MHz, is marketed by rival AMD (Advanced Micro Device). These chips now appear only in entry-level PCs costing $1,000 or less.

The 486 chip has at this time taken the center stage. Most mid-level PCs now use this or its various incarnations or imitations. Although it is a 32-bit chip like the 386, the 486 chip contains many more transistors than its predecessor. It can also run twice as fast as a 386 chip of a comparable clock speed. Various CPUs and the numbers of transistors in them are shown below:

CPU	Transistors
8086	29,000
286	134,000
386	275,000
486	1,200,000
586	3,100,000

If you are buying a PC today, you are confronted with a confusing array of choices in CPUs. The following table may provide the initial help you need for some chips made by Intel:

i386SX   32-bit internal bus and 16-bit external bus; math coprocessor chip[4] can be added at extra cost

i386DX   32-bit internal and external buses; math chip extra

i486SX   32-bit internal and external buses; math chip cannot be added

i486DX   32-bit internal and external buses, with built-in math chip

The confusing part is that DX and SX do no mean the same thing when applied to different chips.

If you need more confusion, Cyrix is now offering competing chips marketed as 486 clones but are more like 386s. Although they use the 486 instruction set (software code), they physically resemble the 386. You can pull out an Intel 386 chip and replace it with a Cyrix 486 chip (but not with an Intel 486 chip). You can replace a 386SX with a 486SLC (32-bit internal, 16-bit external) and a 386DX with a 486DLC (32 bits internal and external). These Cyrix 486 chips are faster than Intel 386 chips but slower than Intel 486 chips. As more clone chips appear, you can expect muddier waters ahead.

If speed is of the essence, you should pay close attention to a chip's megahertz designation. Currently, a low-end 386 system starts at 25 MHz. The 386 has reached its peak at 40 MHz and can probably go no higher. The current low for a 486 is 20 MHz and high 66 MHz. Some Intel chips run twice as fast internally as it does externally. For example, a 486DX2-50 processes data at 50 MHz but communicates with other parts at 25 MHz—in contrast to 486DX-50, which runs 50 MHz both internally and externally.

---

4. An extra chip to manipulate floating-point numbers; this chip can increase a PC's speed in handling real numbers in programs like Lotus 1-2-3.

A new generation of PC has descended on us with the arrival of **Pentium** PCs in mid-1993. Instead of 586, Intel is now giving us this Greek name. In lawsuit after lawsuit, Intel could not ward off imitators from using the 386 or 486 monikers because numbers could not be legally patented. So Intel finally decided to speak Greek by combining *pent* (five in English) and *ium* (a common ending for chemical elements such as uranium). Would Intel dare call the next chip *Sexium*?

Although the Pentium retains the 486's 32-bit internal bus, it contains more than twice the number of transistors, sports a 64-bit external path, and processes two (instead of one) instructions per clock cycle. The initial Pentium PCs can run twice as fast as the fastest 486 PCs. When the clock speed is increased, future Pentium PCs can run even faster.

The Pentium now faces competition from the even more powerful Alpha chip developed by Digital Equipment and the PowerPC chip designed by the alliance of IBM, Apple, and Motorola. The acute competition will surely bring down the current lofty prices and may even end Intel's domination of the PC's CPU market. Few players stay on top for long in this dynamic PC market; many are here today and gone tomorrow. Only the future can tell whether Intel will remain Intel or become *Outtel*, another fading star like IBM.

Other Computers

There are currently other small-scale computers that are quite capable and powerful. These include Apple Macintosh and various models produced by Atari, Commodore, NeXT, Sun and others. The more powerful models used for graphics and engineering are often referred to as workstations. Most of these are based on the 68000 line of CPUs produced by Motorola.

While they can rival the most powerful PCs based on the Intel CPUs, these computers are mostly not compatible with IBM-standard models and cannot run software packages intended for IBM clones. Most of them also use an operating system (UNIX is most commonly used) different from and not compatible with DOS.

DIFFERENT PARTS OF A PC

■ *A PC system is comprised of a system unit (which contains a motherboard, CPU, ROM, RAM, etc.), one or more disk drives, a monitor, a keyboard, a printer, and other peripherals.*

A PC system typically consists of a **system unit**, one or two disk drives (usually installed inside the system unit), a monitor, a keyboard, and a printer. These

Figure 1.1

A Personal Computer

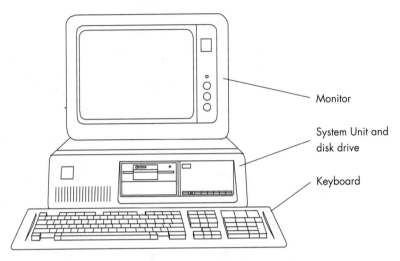

Monitor

System Unit and
disk drive

Keyboard

are the bare minimum for a complete system. For more exotic applications, a
PC could be connected to other **peripherals** like a mouse, modem, scanner, etc.

System Unit

Also referred to as the box, case, or chassis, the system unit is a rectangular
metal box whose size varies greatly. It contains the vital components of a PC.

At the bottom, inside a system unit, rests a **motherboard**. It serves as the base
for connecting all the parts, including the CPU, ROM, RAM, and expansion
slots.

A CPU is the brain of a PC. As explained in the preceding section, it determines
almost everything else in a PC.

ROM (read-only memory) is an example of **firmware**, which lies between
hardware and software. It is a hardware part containing software program
code. The code is permanently etched on the memory and stays there with or
without power. When power is turned on, the code is read and executed; when
power is off, it stays dormant.

An important component of a PC's ROM is a **BIOS** (basic input-output system)
chip. It provides the initial instructions to the PC.[4] After that, DOS is **booted**
(started) from the system files stored on disk.

---

5. Old IBM models also store a simplified BASIC language in ROM. If the BIOS cannot find
DOS to boot, this BASIC is loaded. In that case, you cannot use a disk drive.

Some laptop and pocket PCs have DOS and other programs stored in ROM. When power is turned on, DOS is automatically booted from ROM. This saves power and disk space, but reduces a machine's versatility. A newer DOS version, for example, cannot be run by such a PC—unless you replace the ROM chip.

A PC needs working space to maneuver computer code and data. This working space is **RAM** (random access memory), also called memory or dynamic memory. RAM is volatile. When power is on, it comes to life; when power is off, it is dead. Any computer code or data staying in RAM will disappear when power is off.

When you buy a PC, you need to know how much memory comes with it. Most models today come with a minimum of 1MB RAM. Some 386/486 models can be loaded with many megabytes. DOS and most application programs can handle up to 640KB. Versions 5 and 6 can convert the memory beyond 640KB to expanded memory which most programs can use; see Chapter 9 for details. Some new programs such as Windows 3.x and Lotus 1-2-3 3.x can handle the huge amount of memory your computer may have. RAM chips are getting cheaper and more programs are getting hungrier for them.

To provide an interface with an outside device, the motherboard has a number of **expansion slots. Controller cards** (also known as adapters, boards, or cartridges) with special circuitry and computer code are inserted into the slots. The controller cards in turn provide connections to a number of devices such as disk drives, monitor, printer, etc.

Disk Drives

Each PC has to have at least one disk drive. Most PCs have two floppy drives or one hard drive and one floppy drive. Most drives are installed inside the system unit, although they can be external. They are connected with cables, which are connected to a disk controller card. Some disk controller cards can control only floppy or hard disks, but others can control both.

Disk drives are used to save data to disks. There are many types of drives and storage media today. The most common are hard and floppy drives. These will be explained fully in Chapter 3.

Some systems sold today include a CD-ROM drive, together with a sound card, a pair of speakers, and some software titles on CD-ROM disks. If you have a 386 or higher PC, you can buy a CD-ROM kit for less than $500 and connect it to your PC to make it an MPC. If you want a faster CD-ROM drive and fancier features, you will have to pay higher prices.

Monitor

A monitor is used to display information entered from the keyboard or read from a disk. It is connected to the system unit via a jack in the back; the jack is in turn connected to a **video graphics card**. There are many kinds of monitors, each of which has to be matched with a compatible video graphics card.

When the first IBM-PC was introduced, buyers could choose a monochrome (one-color) monitor or a color monitor. The mono monitor was matched with the **MDA** (Monochrome Display Adapter). It could display only characters, but not graphics, which consist of a series of screen **pixels** (dots).

The **Hercules** graphics card (HGC) was soon introduced to let a monochrome monitor display both text and graphics. Besides displaying crisp characters (each formed in a 9×14 pixel matrix), it can provide a high-resolution graphics display of 720 (horizontal) by 348 (vertical) pixels. This proved to be wildly popular and widely imitated. Today, many mono monitors are equipped with this monographics card (MGA), and most graphics programs can also utilize its capabilities.

IBM's first color monitor is called **RGB** (Red Green Blue), and is paired with the **CGA** (Color Graphics Adapter) card. This combination produces poorly formed characters (8×8) and coarse graphics of 320 by 200 screen pixels in medium-resolution (color) mode and 640 by 200 in high-resolution (black and white) mode. Only 4 colors can be displayed at one time out of a palette (possible choice) of 16 colors.

The AT brought with it the **EGA** (Enhanced Graphics Adapter) card and its matching monitor. Characters become fuller (8×14) and screen pixels are increased to 640 by 350 (new ones, not produced by IBM, go up to 640×480). A total of 16 colors, out of a palette of 64, can be simultaneously displayed.

The PS/2 also appeared with a new video standard—the **VGA** (Video Graphics Array) card and monitor pair. Characters appear in 9×16 matrixes, screen graphics pixels are increased to 640×480, and 256 colors can be simultaneously displayed out of a palette of 256K (256×1024). (Low-end PS/2 models are equipped with MCGA, or Multicolor Graphics Array, which is a slimmed-down version of VGA.)

If you buy a monitor today, you are faced with a confusing array of choices. A mono monitor is most economically equipped with a Hercules-compatible card. Some mono monitors, however, can be driven by graphics cards comparable to or better than EGA or VGA; colors are displayed in different shades of gray (or brown). With color monitors, you can choose among CGA, EGA, VGA, improved EGA (SEGA, or super EGA), or improved VGA (SVGA, or super VGA) cards and matching monitors.

Monitor and graphics-card capabilities continue to advance at a rapid pace. Bigger monitors with more pixels and colors are introduced regularly. They are expensive and used for limited purposes such as desktop publishing and industrial designs.

Printer

On the back of most system units there is at least one **parallel port**, which is connected to a controller card. A printer is usually connected to this port. (Some printers are connected to serial ports.)

Various kinds of printers are available for a PC. In the beginning, the **daisy-wheel printer** was popular, highly prized, and highly priced. Like a typewriter, it can print whole characters. Although its print quality is excellent, it is slow and not very versatile. Printing characters of a different size or style requires changing the daisy wheel, or print element. Printing graphics is impossible. These printers have disappeared from the market.

The **dot-matrix printer** prints characters by putting together dots in the form of a matrix. In the beginning, 7 pins (wires) were used to form crude-looking characters consisting of a 7×7 dot matrix. Dot-matrix technology advanced rapidly. Soon, 9-pin models appeared; these inexpensive machines are still very popular today. At the high end, 24-pin models can create **NLQ** (nearly letter-quality) characters with a matrix of 24×36 dots.[5] Graphics can also be printed in 360×360 dots per inch (DPI). These printers operate at a much higher speed than daisy-wheel models. With improved print quality and continuous advance in speed, plus rapidly falling prices, they have become the most popular type of PC printers.

The **laser printer** (also known as page printer because it prints one page at a time) is the aristocrat of the printer world. Printing at 4-8 pages per minute, they are much speedier than other printers. They print good-looking text and graphics at a relatively high resolution of 300 dots per inch (dpi); professional typeset machines go beyond 1000 dpi. The most attractive attribute is probably the ability to handle different font sizes and styles. A newsletter heading, for example, can be printed in large characters of a certain style while the text in smaller characters of another style.

High prices inhibited the laser printer's widespread use. Acute competition, however, has dramatically driven down prices. Currently there are 300-dpi, 4-page-per-minute models selling for less than $600, which is less than the price of some of the high-end dot-matrix printers. If this trend continues, laser printers may eventually replace dot matrixes as standard PC printers.

Other Peripherals

A host of other peripheral devices can be connected to a PC. The most common are mouse, modem, and scanner.

Figure 1.2

A laser printer

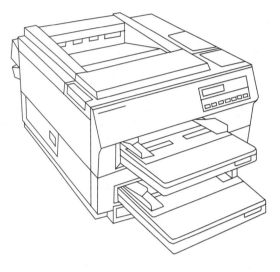

A **mouse** is an input device, which can be connected to an expansion slot (bus mouse) or a **serial port** (serial mouse). A mouse can maneuver menus and graphic objects. Many new features in version 6, such as the online help explained later in this chapter, allow you to use a mouse to move among various menu items and enter a command by clicking a screen item. The most useful task for a mouse, however, is handling graphics. Some graphics software packages are difficult or impossible to handle without using a mouse.

A **modem** (MOdulator DEModulator) is a communications device. It can convert (modulate) a computer's digital (0 or 1) signals to analog (sound wave) signals, which can be transmitted via the telephone line, and convert

Figure 1.3

A three-button mouse; some mice have two buttons

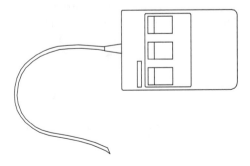

(demodulate) them back to digital signals that a receiving computer can understand. Like a mouse, a modem can be connected to an expansion slot (internal modem) or a serial port (external modem). With a proper communications software package, a modem can be used to communicate with a computer bulletin board available in many large cities, a database service provider such as CompuServe, and other properly equipped PCs.

Modems have undergone major changes. Prices have fallen while speed has increased dramatically. Only a few years ago, the 300-**baud** (bits per second or bps) modem was standard. The speed was increased to 1200, 2400, 9600, and 14,400 in rapid succession. Most of the new models also have fax capabilities.

Scanners can scan text or graphical images and feed them into a PC. With proper software, the scanned text and images can be recognized and manipulated. Scanners are most often used in desktop publishing.

D R I L L

Select an item in the list to answer questions 7–11:

a. motherboard   b. system unit   c. peripheral   d. parallel port   e. BIOS

_____ 7. A physical device connected to a computer.

_____ 8. A metal box containing a PC's vital parts.

_____ 9. A common connector (interface) for a printer.

_____ 10. Controller cards are inserted into its expansion slots.

_____ 11. Provides initial instructions to the PC.

Select an acronym in the list to answer questions 12–16:

a. EGA   b. VGA   c. NLQ   d. CGA   e. RGB

_____ 12. The latest color video graphics standard.

_____ 13. The earliest PC color video graphics card.

_____ 14. The earliest PC color monitor.

_____ 15. Introduced with the AT.

_____ 16. Print quality.

USING THE KEYBOARD

■ *The PC keyboard has gone through two changes. The current standard is called enhanced keyboard and has 101 keys.*

■ *Some single keys and key combinations allow you to do some unusual things; these are shown in Tables 1.2 and 1.3.*

A keyboard is an important peripheral device connected to the system unit via a jack (connector) in the back. It is the most commonly used device for giving your PC instructions and data. From the keyboard, you can enter a DOS command and give your PC information it can process.

Earlier Keyboards

The PC keyboard has undergone some changes. The first PC came with an 83-key keyboard. The AT has a slightly improved keyboard of 84 keys, with an enlarged Enter key and some lighted panels to show the status of various keyboard conditions. These improvements reduce the chances for making typing errors. The enlarged Enter key is most helpful. As you need to press this key to register a command to DOS, you no longer need to take your eyes off the screen and see where the Enter key is.

The 10 function keys of these earlier models are located in two columns on the left side. The right side of the keyboard features a keypad serving two purposes—cursor control and 10-key entry of numbers.

In the normal state, the keypad is used to control the **cursor** (the little blinking underscore character) in application programs such as spreadsheet or word processor. DOS normally does not recognize most of these keys. Only a few of them are used for editing a DOS command entered from the keyboard; these will be explained in Chapter 4.

The Num Lock key is a **toggle** key; it can switch between two modes. When it is pressed once, the keypad goes into numeric mode. Pressing a key on this pad displays a corresponding number on the screen. Pressing the Num Lock key another time returns the keypad to cursor-control mode. The original PC keyboard does not tell you what mode this keypad is in. Later keyboards show a lighted Num Lock panel.

The Caps Lock key toggles between uppercase and lowercase for the alphabetic keys; other keys are not affected. When Caps Lock is pressed once, pressing a letter key displays on the screen a corresponding letter in uppercase. Again, the old PC keyboard does not tell you this condition. Later keyboards show a lighted Caps Lock panel.

Figure 1.4

The PC (enhanced) keyboard

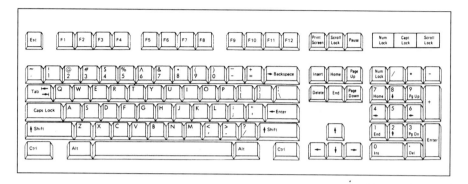

The Enhanced Keyboard

The current standard PC keyboard is commonly referred to as the **enhanced keyboard**. Altogether, it has 101 keys. Since IBM introduced the PS/2 line, this has become the only keyboard sold by the company. Most of today's PCs are sold with this keyboard.

The enhanced keyboard, as shown in Figure 1.4, has 12 function keys placed at the top row of the keyboard. The numeric keypad (with additional math operator keys) is still located at the far right. It can still be used to control the cursor and enter numbers. An extra Enter key is also added. This can speed up 10-key entry of numbers.

A cluster of extra gray-colored keys are added to the left of the keypad for the exclusive purpose of cursor control. Now you can have, if you wish, an exclusive cursor keypad and a separate numeric keypad. This is most convenient when you want to move the cursor and enter numbers, as in using a spreadsheet program.

Using Some Special Keys

Compared to a typewriter, the PC keyboard has many unusual keys. Many application programs take full advantage of them. DOS, however, normally utilizes very few of these single keys and their numerous combinations. Single keys and their functions are shown in Table 1.2.

Certain keys can be combined to perform some functions. These key combinations and their purposes are shown in Table 1.3.

When key combinations are used, hold down the first key (the first two keys if three keys are involved), press the next key, and release them.

Table 1.2

Using Single Keys

Key	Function
Backspace	Erase to the left; same as ←
Caps Lock	Toggle (switch) between uppercase & lowercase
Enter	Register a command
Esc	Abandon a command
Function keys	F1–F6 used for editing; others unused
Num Lock	Toggle keypad between number and cursor
Pause	Halt screen display
Shift	Shift to uppercase for typing a letter

Table 1.3

Using Combined Keys

Key	Function
Ctrl-Break or Ctrl-C	Terminate an action
Ctrl-Num Lock or Ctrl-S	Same as Pause; press a key to continue
Ctrl-PrtSc or Ctrl-P	Turn on/off printing; when on, whatever goes to the screen is also printed
Shift-PrtSc	Print a screen display (Shift is not required on a newer keyboard)
Ctrl-Alt-Del	Reboot DOS; same as Reset key if equipped

Most of the keys shown in Tables 1.2 and 1.3 will be more fully explained and illustrated with concrete examples in this and the next chapters.

Application programs (such as WordPerfect and Lotus 1-2-3) utilize many of the keys available on a PC keyboard and their various combinations. Different programs also use these keys for different and often conflicting purposes. You need to learn these specifics when you try to master an application program.

D R I L L

Select an item in the list to answer questions 17–20:

a. Num Lock   b. Enter   c. Ctrl-C   d. Ctrl-S.

____ 17. Registers a command.

____ 18. Halts screen scrolling.

____ 19. Terminates an action.

____ 20. Toggles between cursor and numeric modes.

SYSTEM, APPLICATION, AND ENVIRONMENT

■ *A computer program to handle hardware is known as an operating system or system software, and one that specializes in a type of task is known as application software. Between the two lies environment software.*

So far we have discussed only hardware. Hardware is useless unless there is software to make use of it. From now on we will be talking mostly about software.

Software consists of computer programs. A computer program is simply a set of instructions that a computer can understand. There are three broad categories of software: system, application, and environment. The first manages hardware (such as CPU, RAM, monitor, printer, disk drive, etc.) and provides a link between hardware and application software. **Application software** performs narrower and more specific tasks such as spreadsheet, word processing, and database management. Environment software can be used to connect the two.

System software is also known as an **operating system** (OS). Although **DOS** (disk operating system) is the best known operating system in the PC realm, two newcomers are beginning to make inroads into the market—**OS/2** and **UNIX.**

MS/PC-DOS was born with the PC. When IBM was introducing the PC, it looked for an operating system to run its new product. Digital Research, the owner of the then popular operating system called **CP/M** (Control Processor/

Micro) was uncooperative.[5] IBM decided to make a deal with an unknown startup company called Microsoft. This connection has transformed a tiny outfit into a multibillion-dollar corporation and the largest software company in the world.

PC-DOS and **MS-DOS** are in most cases identical; both are written by Microsoft. The brand marketed by IBM is called PC-DOS.[6] Other brands marketed directly by Microsoft or licensed to other vendors such as Compaq, Tandy, CompuAdd, etc. are referred to as MS-DOS. Most of today's PCs, made by IBM or anybody else, can run either brand.

Although there are minor differences between PC and MS brands, there are major changes from an earlier version to a later one.[7] While many people continue to use earlier versions, the most commonly used versions today are 5.0 and 6.0. Microsoft continues to market earlier versions, which are mostly used to operate specialized machines.

DOS is basically a single-user, single-tasking operating system. Most of the time only one person can use a computer to do one thing at a time. However, as PCs became more powerful and pervaded the corporate world, the demand for a multiuser, multitasking operating system increased.

Microsoft responded by developing OS/2 (Operating System/2) in cooperation with IBM, but eventually abandoned it to concentrate on Windows. OS/2, now developed solely by IBM, allows a properly equipped PC (8MB RAM, 386 or higher CPU) to be used to do several jobs at the same time. Although OS/2 is primarily a multitasking system, with additional hardware and software it can be a multiuser system.

OS/2 competes against UNIX, which was initially developed by AT&T. UNIX has been very popular in academia running minicomputers, which are multiuser systems. Today it is migrating to the PC world, where it can run multiple connected PCs, each of which can run multiple tasks. So far UNIX is running behind OS/2 in the number of PC users. Both are losers when compared to Windows.

Between application programs and operating systems there is another kind of software called **operating environment**. An operating environment provides an interface between a user and a number of compatible application programs. The user can switch from one program to another or move data from one

---

5. CP/M later emerged as DR DOS. Digital Research, the owner, was purchased by Novell, known for its networking software. Novell is now marketing the latest version of this system to compete against MS-DOS 6.

6. IBM is developing its own DOS 6. Future versions of MS-DOS and IBM-DOS may be more different.

7. See Appendix D for the evolution of DOS and how various versions differ from one another.

application to another without exiting any program. The Shell in DOS versions 5 and 6 is an example.

One particular package that has gained widespread acceptance in recent years is Microsoft Windows, which runs on top of DOS. Released in mid-1990, version 3.0 was extremely popular; the latest version, 3.1, has been a consistent top seller since its release in mid-1992. Used with a 386 or higher PC, it provides a graphical user interface (GUI, commonly pronounced GOO-yee) and can run several programs concurrently. A user can use a mouse to click screen objects to switch from one program to another, move data back and forth, and do many chores with little or no typing. This should make using a PC much easier for some people. Corporations like this arrangement because it cuts down the costs of training workers. Some of these features have appeared in the Shell of DOS 5 and 6.

Windows now appears in several flavors. Windows for Workgroup is a network version allowing multiple PCs to communicate with one another. Windows NT, released in mid-1993, is a 32-bit operating system like OS/2 and no longer requires DOS to run. (DOS is a 16-bit operating system because it can maneuver data only 16 bits at a time.) Microsoft continues to promote Windows as the standard interface in many new fields and, along the way, produces more new flavors. One benefit to the user is that once you are familiar with Windows, you can quickly use its various flavors because they all look similar and behave alike.

As Windows becomes more widely used and more software packages are specifically written for it, life has become a little more complicated for PC users. If you order a popular software package now, vendors will ask you whether you want a DOS or Windows version. You may also be wondering whether investing in one platform (DOS or Windows) is the right decision. Your decision now may lock you in one path which may lead to a dead end. Who says technology always simplifies our lives?

STARTING AND RESTARTING A PC

■ *Turn on the power switch to start a PC. To restart it, just press the Reset button on the front panel of the system unit. If this is not available, press Ctrl-Alt-Del.*

Depending on the model, each PC is equipped with a red lever located in various parts of the system unit. This lever can be flipped to the upward position marked ON or 1, or to the downward position marked OFF or 0. This lever, like a light switch, turns on or off power to the PC. After power is on, the fan inside the system unit will begin to blow to cool off the heat generated by electricity going through the computer. Do not block the outlet for the fan; otherwise, your computer may overheat and malfunction.

If you need to restart the computer because of "boot failure" (or a program causing the computer to freeze), you normally do not need to turn power off and then on, which takes a longer time. Instead, you can just press a red Reset button usually located on the front panel of the system unit. The fan does not stop blowing. The whole system, however, is started anew. If you press this button while running a program, the program and data residing in RAM will be wiped out.

Older PCs do not have this Reset button. To reboot your computer without turning off power, you can press this key combination:

    Ctrl-Alt-Del

Use two fingers to hold down Ctrl and Alt, and use another finger to press Del. The screen turns blank and the whole system restarts.

Some people refer to turning on power as a cold boot and pressing the Reset button (or Ctrl-Alt-Del) as a warm boot. The former will take more time than the latter, particularly in an older PC. If you have a choice, try the latter under most circumstances.

Depending on how your system is set up, you may need to turn on the monitor and printer (if you intend to print something). Some monitors have a knob you

---

T I P S   A N D   T R I C K S

S U R G E   P R O T E C T O R

If you have your own computer, you may want to invest in a device called **surge protector**. It may cost as little as $10. It can protect your PC from a sudden power surge caused by lightning and other unexpected occurrences. Without such a protection, the fragile electronic parts could overheat, rendering your computer useless.

There are many kinds of surge protectors. The more expensive models usually provide more protection against more violent power surges, but even they are not foolproof. If stormy weather is coming, the best protection is to unplug the PC's power cord.

A surge protector is usually equipped with multiple electrical outlets, to which you can connect the system unit, printer, monitor, and other peripherals you may have. When the switch on the surge protector is turned on, power is supplied to all the units that are left in the on position. This can save you the trouble of individually turning on each separate unit. When you are through, just press one single switch to shut down the whole system.

can pull out to turn on and push in to turn off. Some are equipped with a knob which you turn clockwise to turn on and counterclockwise to turn off. Newer monitors have a little panel which you press once to turn on and twice to turn off. Most monitor switches are located in the front; others, however, may be hidden in the back or below the screen. If your monitor is not on after a while, search for a knob or panel or switch to turn on (or ask a lab assistant).

D R I L L

Answer questions 21–25 with either A (for application software) or S (for system software):

____ 21. UNIX.

____ 22. WordPerfect.

____ 23. CP/M.

____ 24. Lotus 1-2-3.

____ 25. OS/2.

BOOTING DOS AND ENTERING DATE/TIME

■ *To boot DOS, you need to make available a system disk to your PC. The system files can be stored on a hard disk or a floppy disk.*

■ *If your PC calendar is backed up with a battery, the date and time data will be kept up to date. If not, you need to supply the correct numbers after DOS is booted.*

When power is supplied to a PC, the ROM BIOS inside the machine starts to work. It may send different diagnostic information to the screen. Then DOS is booted from a system disk containing hidden system files. If the system files are not available, booting fails and the screen displays an error message. You can insert a bootable disk and press a key to try again.

If you are using a hard disk, it should be set up in such a way that DOS will be booted from the hard disk. In that case, leave drive A empty or its door open.

The light on the floppy drive will turn on for a while. Then the BIOS will go to drive C to try to boot from there.

If you have no hard disk or just want to boot from a floppy disk, insert a boot disk in drive A and turn on power. A boot disk requires certain special files. You can create a boot disk by using the FORMAT command. This will be explained in Chapter 3.

If DOS succeeds in booting, a two-line message appears:

```
Current date is Sat 06-20-1993
Enter new date (mm-dd-yy): _
```

The current date read by DOS is displayed in the first line. In the second line, you are prompted to enter a correct date after the colon.

If your computer is equipped with a battery-powered calendar, a correct calendar will be maintained as long as the battery supplies the power to keep up to date. In that case, just press Enter to go to the next message. If your computer is not so equipped, the current date read by DOS may be this:

```
Current date is Tue 01-01-1980
Enter new date (mm-dd-yy): _
```

If this is the case, you need to enter the correct two-digit month, date, and year, such as:

```
Enter new date (mm-dd-yy): 06-20-93
```

Each item has two numeric digits and is separated from another item with a hyphen. Do not worry about the day of the week; DOS will take care of it.

After you enter a correct date format or just press Enter without typing a date, another two-line message appears:

```
Current time is  7:49:30.68a
Enter new time: _
```

Again, if the time is correct, just press Enter. If not, you need to enter hour, colon, minute, colon, second and optional fractions. (See the next section for more details.)

After both date and time are taken care of, a message like the following appears:

```
Microsoft(R) MS-DOS(R) Version 6.00
            (C)Copyright Microsoft Corp 1981-1993.
    C>_
```

It shows what DOS brand (PC or MS) and version number you are using. The DOS prompt (C>) appears with the cursor after it; this cursor moves as you type or do something else. DOS is now booted and ready to accept your command.

Note: If you are working with a PC in your school's lab, you could encounter the following situations:

- The hard disk contains an AUTOEXEC.BAT batch file. This file is executed as soon as the DOS is booted. In this setup, there is no need for you to enter date and time data. The DOS prompt appears immediately.

- The above batch file may contain this command:

  ```
  PROMPT=$P$G
  ```

  In this case, the DOS prompt may show one of these:

  ```
  C:\>
  C:\DOS>_
  ```

  Here C: signifies drive C, \ marks the root directory, and DOS shows the current directory. If the first prompt appears, you are in the root directory of drive C; the second example shows the current directory as C:\DOS. These terms will be explained fully in Chapter 5.

- The DOS Shell is run by the AUTOEXEC.BAT file. In that case, the screen is full of many items, as shown in Figure 10.1 in Chapter 10. If this happens, press F3 to leave this screen; the DOS prompt should appear shortly.

TIPS AND TRICKS

THE PC CALENDAR

Each PC has an internal built-in calendar. When power is on, it functions like a digital watch to keep track of date and time data. If your PC has no battery to back up this calendar, it will go back to 01-01-80 when power is turned off. If your PC has a battery-powered calendar (and as long as the battery is in good condition), it will keep track of the date and time even when power is off.

If you have a newer PC, using DATE and TIME commands will affect the calendar. The new numbers are entered into the system and kept up to date as long as the battery is working.

If you have an old IBM PC or XT, the DATE and TIME commands do not affect the system even if the calendar is powered by a battery. To change the system data, you need to use the software bundled with the hardware like the AST Sixpack multifunction card.

THE DOS PROMPT AND COMMAND LINE

■ *As soon as DOS is booted, a drive letter followed by a > (greater than) sign appears. This is the DOS prompt.*

■ *The line where the DOS prompt appears is the command line for entering a DOS command.*

■ *Use the CLS command to clear the screen, VER to show the DOS version, DATE and TIME to show and change date and time information.*

Depending on where DOS is booted from, you will see different displays after booting. If you boot from a floppy drive, this appears:

```
A>_
```

If you boot from a hard disk, you see this instead:

```
C>_
```

If the AUTOEXEC.BAT file on the boot disk contains the PROMPT PG command, the DOS prompt may look like one of these:

```
A:\>
C:\>
```

If this happens, restore the default prompt style with this command:

```
C:\>prompt
C>_
```

This is the **DOS prompt**, or **system prompt**. It consists of two elements: the drive letter and the > (greater than) sign. You are now prompted to enter a **DOS command**, which is an instruction DOS can understand and implement.

T I P S   A N D   T R I C K S

C O R R E C T I N G   T Y P I N G   E R R O R S

If you make a mistake while typing something on the command line, press Backspace or ← to move the cursor leftward and at the same time erase a typed character. After erasing an error, retype your command.

If you want to abandon a line before pressing Enter, just press the Esc key. The cursor will move down one line for you to enter a new command.

DOS uses a number of function keys as editing keys. Chapter 4 explains how to use them.

The line where the DOS prompt appears is referred to as the **command line**. Here you are to enter a command by typing something DOS understands and pressing Enter to register it. The little blinking underscore character is referred to as the cursor. It marks the position where a command is to be entered. The cursor position changes as commands are typed and entered.

Now you are going to enter some commands to instruct DOS to do some simple chores. Follow these steps:

FOLLOW
THESE
STEPS

1. Just press Enter:

   ```
   C>
   C>_
   ```

If you just press Enter without typing anything, the cursor moves down one line, and the DOS prompt is displayed again. Nothing else happens.

(If you have no hard disk, treat C> as A>. From now on, we will use C> as the default prompt where you are expected to enter a command.)

2. Clear the screen:

   ```
   C>cls
   C>_
   ```

The screen should now be cleared of everything except the DOS prompt located at the top left corner of the screen. Any time you want to clear a cluttered screen and locate the cursor at the top left corner of the screen, just enter the CLS command.

3. Find out the DOS version:

   ```
   C>ver
   MS-DOS Version 6.00
   C>_
   ```

By entering the VER command, you ask DOS to tell you what brand and version you are using. The first number signifies a major revision, the second a minor revision, and the third a special release (such as 2.11 being a 2.1 designed specifically for the PCjr) or a bug-fix release. Version 4.01, for example, is a release primarily to fix the bugs (errors) in 4.0.

4. Display the current date:

   ```
   C>date
   Current date is Sat 06-20-93
   Enter new date (mm-dd-yy): _
   ```

5. Enter month-date:

   ```
   Enter new date (mm-dd-yy): 06-21
   Invalid date
   Enter new date (mm-dd-yy): _
   ```

TIPS   AND   TRICKS

U P P E R C A S E   O R   L O W E R C A S E

Should you enter a DOS command in uppercase or lowercase? It does not matter. DOS automatically converts everything to uppercase. Thus the three commands below are treated as identical:

```
C>cls
C>Cls
C>CLS
```

There are some rare occasions when uppercase or lowercase is expected. On these occasions, you will specifically be reminded to enter the correct case.

You must enter numbers for all the three items of month (mm), date (dd), and year (yy); hyphens must also separate them. If you miss one, as shown above, DOS displays the "Invalid date" message and prompts you to enter another.

6. Enter month-date-year:

```
Enter new date (mm-dd-yy): 06-21-93
C>_
```

The new date has been accepted and the system prompt reappears. If you neglected to enter a correct date right after booting, you can use the above steps to change the current date.

7. Display the current time and enter a new time:

```
C>time
Current time is  3:37:55.39p
Enter new time: 3:40p
C>_
```

The above entry contains only hour and minute, plus the "p" for PM. Since it is not specified, the number for second will become 0.

8. Enter the current time in 24-hour format:

```
C>time
Current time is  3:42:02.71p
Enter new time: 15:43
C>_
```

9. Display the current time without changing it:

```
C>time
Current time is  3:45:02.54p
Enter new time: _
C>_
```

T I P S   A N D   T R I C K S

D A T E   A N D   T I M E   S H O R T C U T S

You can use shortcuts and various ways to enter date and time numbers. You can enter a number together with the DATE or TIME command, such as these:

```
C>date 6-3-93
C>time 9
```

When DATE is involved, you must enter three numbers. The first two numbers, however, could be a single digit. You can use 6-3-93 or 06-03-93. You can also replace a slash with a hyphen. Thus, 6/3/93 will also be accepted.

The time value also has three numbers, each separated from another with a colon. If a number is missing, it is presumed to be 0. Consider the following variations:

```
C>time 0      (midnight, 12 AM)
C>time :      (same as above)
C>time :7     (7 minutes after 12 AM)
C>time 7      (7 o'clock AM)
C>time 7p     (7 o'clock PM)
C>time 12     (noon, 12 PM)
```

In the third example, we give only the second number. The first and third numbers are set to 0, and the original numbers are lost.

If you just press Enter when prompted to enter a new time, the old time is kept.

Note: It is not vital to keep an accurate date and time for your PC. It will function even with wrong information. It is, however, a good practice to keep your PC up to date (and time). Many benefits can be derived from accurate date-time data. When you save a file, DOS saves the file's creation date and time. You can use some DOS commands to show a file's creation date-time and others to copy files marked with a specific date.

ONLINE HELP

- *Enter COMMAND /? to show the help message related to a command.*

- *Use the FASTHELP command to list commands which can provide more fast help.*

- *Use HELP to show comprehensive online help messages.*

Users of old DOS versions used to complain that DOS was hard to use because commands and switches were hard to remember. Microsoft's response was to introduce **online help** in version 5; users can enter a simple command on the command line to display helpful information related to a specific command. This welcome innovation is further improved and expanded in version 6.

Version 6's printed manual, unlike its previous counterparts, is very skimpy. Detailed information on how to use various commands and features is now stored in a comprehensive online help program. The agile electronic reference has replaced the bulky printed manual. You should get familiar with this helpful addition at this early stage so that you can take advantage of it whenever you need it.

Fast Help

To get a brief online help message related to a command, enter a command like one of these:

```
C>fasthelp command
C>command /?
```

Here *command* is the name of a command whose help message you want to display on the screen. Suppose you want to know how to use the COPY command. Enter either command below:

```
C>fasthelp copy
C>copy /?
```

(If the "Bad command or file name" error message appears, enter the CD \DOS command and try again.)

A help message may seem cryptic to a new user. As you learn to use more commands in later chapters, it will become easier for you to decipher such a message. At this point, you need to know the following conventions:

¦   Either/or; use one of the two or more available items shown

[ ]   Optional item; required under some circumstances

/   A switch

Let us use Figure 1.5 as an example. The notation [/A ¦ /B] means that this whole thing is optional. If one is needed, you use either /A or /B. In fact, the only item required after a COPY command is the source so that DOS knows where to find the file(s) to copy. All these will become clearer as you proceed with this book.

How do you know what command name is available? You can show the entire list of command names by entering this command alone:

```
C>fasthelp
```

Figure 1.5

The online help message for the COPY command

```
C:\DOS>copy /?
Copies one or more files to another location.

COPY [/A ¦ /B] source [/A ¦ /B] [+ source [/A ¦ /B] [+ ...]] [destination
   [/A ¦ /B]] [/V]

   source      Specifies the file or files to be copied.
   /A          Indicates an ASCII text file.
   /B          Indicates a binary file.
   destination Specifies the directory and/or filename for the new file(s).
   /V          Verifies that new files are written correctly.

To append files, specify a single file for destination, but multiple files
for source (using wildcards or file1+file2+file3 format).
```

A screenful of names appears, together with the --More-- message at the bottom of the screen. Press a key to display the next screen. Continue until the command prompt appears or press Ctrl-C at any time to abort.

Comprehensive Help

If you want more comprehensive help, you should use HELP instead of FASTHELP or /? as described above. If you want the initial screen to display related information about a specific command, use the command's name as a parameter, such as:

C>**help copy**

If you just enter HELP alone, the resulting display shows the initial screen as shown in Figure 1.6.

If you have used Microsoft's other products, you are in a familiar territory. If not, you should pay close attention at this early stage. Later chapters will show similar screens and arrangements. The techniques you learn here can be applied to other similar screens.

The cursor also rests at the first topic, <ANSI.SYS>. If you press Enter at this point, another screen appears to show information related to it. If you want another topic, press Esc to return to the initial screen, move the cursor to the

Figure 1.6

The initial screen of the Help command

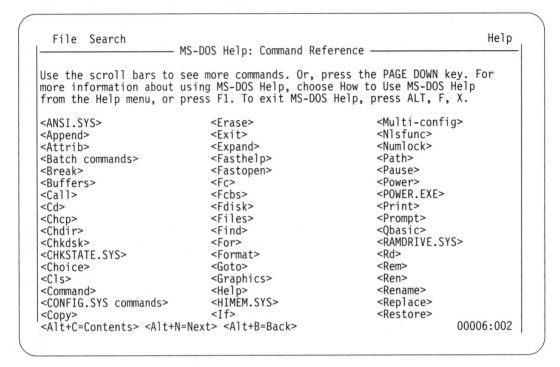

```
  File  Search                                                    Help
————————————————————— MS-DOS Help: Command Reference —————————————————————

Use the scroll bars to see more commands. Or, press the PAGE DOWN key. For
more information about using MS-DOS Help, choose How to Use MS-DOS Help
from the Help menu, or press F1. To exit MS-DOS Help, press ALT, F, X.

<ANSI.SYS>              <Erase>               <Multi-config>
<Append>               <Exit>                <Nlsfunc>
<Attrib>               <Expand>              <Numlock>
<Batch commands>       <Fasthelp>            <Path>
<Break>                <Fastopen>            <Pause>
<Buffers>              <Fc>                  <Power>
<Call>                 <Fcbs>                <POWER.EXE>
<Cd>                   <Fdisk>               <Print>
<Chcp>                 <Files>               <Prompt>
<Chdir>                <Find>                <Qbasic>
<Chkdsk>               <For>                 <RAMDRIVE.SYS>
<CHKSTATE.SYS>         <Format>              <Rd>
<Choice>               <Goto>                <Rem>
<Cls>                  <Graphics>            <Ren>
<Command>              <Help>                <Rename>
<CONFIG.SYS commands>  <HIMEM.SYS>           <Replace>
<Copy>                 <If>                  <Restore>
<Alt+C=Contents> <Alt+N=Next> <Alt+B=Back>                  00006:002
```

topic and press Enter. If you use a mouse, you can also click a desired topic (move the mouse pointer to it and press the left mouse button).

There are many ways to move the cursor to a desired topic. These are shown below:

Tab	Move forward horizontally
Shift-Tab	Reverse of Tab
↑/↓	Move vertically one line at a time
PgUp/PgDn	Scroll one screen up/down
letter	Move to the first matching topic
Shift-letter	Reverse of above
Ctrl-Home	Top of the current message
Ctrl-End	Bottom of the current message

If you press a letter key on the keyboard, the cursor jumps to the first of the group of topics whose first letter matches the key you press. For example, if you now press C, the cursor goes to <Call>. If you press C repeatedly, the cursor goes to each following matching topic and returns to the top after the bottom is reached. You can hold down Shift and press a letter key to reverse the direction.

After you go to another screen, you can always come back to the initial (table of contents) screen by pressing Alt-C or pressing Alt-B (or Esc) as many times as needed. Alt-N takes you to the next screen. You can also use a mouse to click one of the three buttons shown at the bottom of the screen—just move the mouse pointer to the item, press the left mouse button and release it. A button is an action option which you can click with a mouse or press an equivalent keyboard key. Some buttons (shown below) can also be reached by pressing Tab repeatedly; press Enter when a desired button is highlighted.

Using HELP's Menus

Notice that the top of the HELP screen shows three menus: File, Search, and Help. To activate (open) a menu, press Alt; the first (capitalized) letter of each menu is highlighted and the cursor stays at the first menu. At this time, you can press a highlighted letter (F, S, or H) to open that menu. You can also press → or ← to highlight a menu and press Enter to open it. If you have a mouse, just click a menu name without having to press Alt first.

If you do not know what a menu option is supposed to do, use the **context-sensitive help**. When an item is highlighted, press F1 to show related help message. A pop-up window appears in the middle. You can press PgUp or PgDn to show more. Press Esc or Enter to clear the message.

When you open the File menu, you are given two options:

```
Print...
Exit
```

The first item is highlighted. You can press ↑ or ↓ to highlight one of the available options. Pressing Enter executes the highlighted option; clicking a displayed item with your mouse or pressing a highlighted letter accomplishes the same goal. For example, if you now select Exit, the program ends and you are back to the DOS command line.

The Print option has an ellipsis (...) at the end. That means there are more things to come if you select this item. Selecting Print displays the **dialog box** shown in Figure 1.7. A dialog box, as shown here, lets you make selections with which you communicate with DOS.

To select or change an item in a dialog box, press Tab (forward) or Shift-Tab (reverse) to make an item current. When the cursor goes to *Printer on LPT1*, press

Figure 1.7

The Print dialog box

```
┌──────────────────────────── Print ────────────────────┐
│                                                        │
│   Print the current topic to:                          │
│                                                        │
│     ( ) Printer on LPT1                                │
│     (•) File                                           │
│                                                        │
│   Filename:  ┌──────────────────────────────────┐      │
│              │a:\help1.msg                      │      │
│              └──────────────────────────────────┘      │
│                                                        │
│  < OK >    <Cancel>    <Printer Setup...>    < Help >  │
│                                                        │
└────────────────────────────────────────────────────────┘
```

↑ or ↓ to move the bullet (•) up or down to mark the selection. If you want to print a help message, select Printer. If you want to send it to a disk file, select File.

After selecting File, the cursor goes inside the box for you to enter a file name (add a directory path if necessary). After entering a text string in the Filename box, pressing Tab moves the cursor among the buttons at the bottom row and the Filename box. What if you now want to print instead? Tab to the Filename box and press ↑; you can now shift the bullet between the two options. With a mouse, you can just click the space inside a pair of parentheses to move the bullet.

Select <Printer Setup...> if you want to change the printer port to another parallel port or serial port—depending on how your printer is connected. When you are done, select the <OK> button to print or save. Select <Help> (or press F1) if you need more information.

The Search menu has these options:

```
Find...
Repeat Last Find    F3
```

Find leads to a dialog box shown in Figure 1.8.

The topic where the cursor is located before you open this dialog box also appears inside the box. If you start typing, it will disappear. You can also move the cursor keys and edit the string. If you want a case-sensitive search or find only complete (not just a fraction) word, tab to the proper location and press the space bar to enter or clear X in the check box. Press Enter after you type a search string or select <OK> to start the search. If a matching topic is found, you are taken to the help screen of that topic. If the search string matches only a fraction of one of the available topics, the cursor moves to that topic's name

Figure 1.8

The Find dialog box

```
┌───────────────────────────── Find ─────────────────────────────┐
│                                                                 │
│   Find What:  │ANSI.SYS                                    │    │
│               └────────────────────────────────────────────┘   │
│                                                                 │
│        [ ] Match Upper/Lowercase        [ ] Whole Word          │
│                                                                 │
├─────────────────────────────────────────────────────────────────┤
│         < OK >           < Cancel >          < Help >           │
└─────────────────────────────────────────────────────────────────┘
```

instead of displaying its relevant help screen. To repeat searching for the same string, press F3.

The last menu, Help, has these options:

```
How to Use MS-DOS Help
About...
```

The second gives you a simple copyright message and the first provides details of using the HELP feature.

Steps in Using HELP

Let us now go through the following steps to find and print the help message for the COPY command:

FOLLOW
THESE
STEPS

1. Enter either command below:

   ```
   C>help
   C>help copy
   ```

   (If you enter the second command, skip step 2 below.)

2. The initial screen shown in Figure 1.6 appears. Press ↓ repeatedly (or use another method discussed earlier) to move the cursor to <Copy> and press Enter.

3. The initial help (Syntax) screen for COPY appears. The menus (File, Search, and Help) remain available. Two other options are also added near the top of the screen: Notes and Examples. If you wish, you can tab to each option and press Enter (or click it with your mouse) to show a related screen.

4. Press PgUp or PgDn to show more.

5. Open the File menu and select Print to print this message. Get your printer ready before selecting <OK>.

6. Press PgUp repeatedly until the cursor goes to Notes and press Enter. Another screen appears. Two choices, Examples and Syntax are now available. You can now select Syntax to return to the previous display.

7. Select Examples to show the third screen. You can press PgUp or PgDn to show more or select Syntax or Notes to go to a previous screen.

8. Open the File menu and select Exit. You are now back to the command line.

HELP has limited **hypertext** capability, which allows you to jump from one screen to another related topic which is usually enclosed in angle brackets (<>, in green color if you have a color monitor). You can reach a related topic by pressing Tab repeatedly to move the cursor there. In the initial Copy screen (step 3 above), if you press Tab twice, you will move the cursor to <Xcopy>. If you press Enter at that point, XCOPY's help screen will appear. You can also click a bracketed item with your mouse to do the same thing.

HELP provides much more information than FASTHELP. Use the latter if you need to find something quickly, such as available switches of a command. If you want more detailed information or information not available through FASTHELP, such as SYS files, you need to use HELP. These two can be likened to two dictionaries, one short and simplified and the other long and comprehensive. Use the one that is appropriate for the occasion.

P R A C T I C E   1 - 1

☐   1. Reboot DOS without turning off power.

☐   2. On the command line, type something and erase it.

☐   3. On the command line, type something and abandon it.

☐   4. Clear the screen.

☐   5. Show the DOS version.

☐   6. Show the current date without changing it.

☐   7. Change the current time by one minute.

☐   8. Show the fast-help message for the DIR command.

ENDING A DOS SESSION

■ *When you are through working with your PC, turn off power supply to the system unit and turn off peripherals such as monitor and printer.*

When you are done with your PC, you need to turn off its power supply. The power supply to each connected device must also be shut off. Otherwise, it may burn out or prematurely wear out. If the PC is in a lab used by others, you may leave it on for other people. (Ask a lab assistant about the lab's policy and your responsibilities.)

If you have all the peripherals connected to a multiple-outlet device, turning off the switch will shut off power to every connected device. This is the simplest and most efficient arrangement.

WARNING: Your PC may share the same power supply with another PC. In that case, do not switch off the power if the other PC is being used.

Do not forget to turn off the monitor if its power supply is not shut off. Leaving a monitor on for a long period of time will result in characters permanently etched to the screen. Such a monitor may no longer be usable or salvageable.

Do not cut off power supply in the middle of running a program. Everything in RAM will be lost. Most application programs, such as WordPerfect and Lotus 1-2-3, prescribe a procedure for an orderly exit. It is a good idea to follow such a procedure.

Generally speaking, when the DOS prompt appears, you are not running any program and can thus safely shut off power.

T I P S   A N D   T R I C K S

C O M P U T E R   R A D I A T I O N

The widespread use of computers has stirred up controversy over how much radiation is being emitted from a computer and how harmful such radiation is. Many office workers who work with computers all day have complained about cancer, miscarriages, and other harms allegedly caused by computer radiation.

The PC can emit harmful radiation from the monitor and system unit. You should take these precautions to protect yourself against potential hazards:

• When working with a PC, keep yourself as far away from the monitor and system unit as possible. The keyboard cord can be stretched for this purpose.

• Turn off the PC whenever it is not being used for a sustained period of time.

If you boot from a floppy disk, remember to remove it before or after shutting off power. After power is shut off (if you are responsible for turning on and shutting off), you can safely walk away with your own disks.

D R I L L

____ 26. If your PC has no hard disk, you need to insert a system (boot) disk in drive A to start DOS. True or false?

____ 27. A PC can maintain a correct calendar only when it is equipped with a battery. True or false?

____ 28. A DOS command must be entered in uppercase. True or false?

____ 29. The CLS command clears the entire screen, including the DOS prompt. True or false?

____ 30. The DATE and TIME commands can be used to display as well as change a PC's date and time. True or false?

S U M M A R Y   A N D   R E V I E W

Check each item as you review and understand the following highlights of the chapter.

☐ 1. Depending on sizes and capabilities, computers can be grouped into mainframes, minis, and PCs. PCs include XT, AT, PS/1, and PS/2. Many PS/2 models use IBM's new MCA bus and some new ATs are equipped with the new EISA bus.

☐ 2. A PC's capability is determined mostly by its CPU. Most CPUs used in today's PCs originated from Intel Corporation. These include 8088/8086, 80286, 80386, and 80486. The higher a CPU's number, the more powerful it is.

☐ 3. A typical PC system consists of a system unit, a keyboard, a monitor, and a printer. The system unit contains one or more disk drives and a motherboard to which a CPU, ROM and RAM chips, and peripheral devices are attached.

☐ 4. There are various types of monitors available today, each of which can be driven by a matching graphics card: Hercules for a monochrome monitor, CGA for an RGB monitor, EGA for an EGA monitor, and VGA for a VGA monitor.

☐ 5. Three common types of printers are in use today: daisy wheel, dot matrix, and laser. Daisy wheels have mostly been replaced by dot matrixes. With excellent print quality and falling prices, lasers are increasing in popularity.

6. There are two major types of PC keyboards. The first was introduced with the original IBM PC and was slightly improved when the AT was introduced. There are 10 function keys located at the left end. The keypad on the right side can be toggled between cursor and numeric modes. The enhanced keyboard that was introduced with the PS/2 has 12 function keys located at the top and an additional cursor pad in the middle.

7. There are two major categories of computer software: system and application. The former is also known as operating system, or OS for short. DOS is an OS. There are two brands of DOS—PC-DOS and MS-DOS, both written by Microsoft Corporation. The former is licensed to IBM and the latter to other PC vendors or marketed directly by Microsoft. The two are practically identical.

8. Three major operating systems are currently competing in the PC market: DOS, OS/2, and UNIX. DOS practically monopolizes the single-user and single-tasking market. The new OS/2 (originally developed by Microsoft but now completely controlled by IBM) and UNIX, which is transferred from the mini world, compete in the multiuser and multitasking environment.

9. Between an operating system and an application program lies another category of software: operating environment. There are quite a few packages available today, but the most popular is Microsoft Windows. Windows 3.x provides a graphical user interface and multitasking capability. It imitates the Macintosh's "look and feel" and is competing successfully against OS/2.

10. When you start your PC, you need to have DOS system files available before you switch on power. They could be stored on the hard disk. In that case, leave drive A empty (do not insert a disk or close the door) when power is switched on. If you have no hard disk, you need to insert a system disk in drive A and close its door (if any) before switching on power.

11. If your PC is locked up (frozen) and will no longer respond to a command from the keyboard, you need to reboot the system. Normally you do not need to switch power off and then on again. This takes a long time to restart. Instead, you can just press the Reset button. If your PC is not equipped with it, press the key combination Ctrl-Alt-Del.

12. After DOS is booted, you will be asked to enter the date and time. If they are correct, you can just press Enter to keep the old information. If your PC has a battery-backed calendar, the information will be kept up to date. If not, you need to enter the current numbers.

13. The DATE and TIME commands can be used to display as well as change the date and time information.

14. Use the CLS and VER commands to respectively clear the screen and display the DOS version.

☐   15. When you have finished using your PC, you need to shut down the whole system. Power supply to the system unit must be switched off. Other independently powered devices also need to be turned off.

R E V I E W   Q U E S T I O N S

Write an answer for each question below.

1. Briefly define these terms: PC, XT, AT, PS/1, and PS/2.

2. Explain and relate these terms: bus, MCA, and EISA.

3. Find out what CPU is used in your PC. How does it compare to the others?

4. What major components are located inside a system unit? What do they do?

5. What kind of monitor do you use? How does it compare to the other available models?

6. What kind of printer are you using? Describe its capabilities.

7. What kind of keyboard are you using? Describe its major sections.

8. What does a modem do?

9. What does the Ctrl-Alt-Del key combination do?

10. What is the difference between an operating system and an application program?

11. What are the three major operating systems for the PC today? How do they differ?

12. What is a surge protector?

13. Does your PC have a battery-backed calendar? How do you know? What purpose does it serve?

14. Discuss various ways of getting DOS online help.

15. If you neglect to enter the correct date and time right after DOS is booted, how can you change them later?

2 A Quick Tour Through DOS

T O P I C S

C O M M A N D S   C O V E R E D

DIR, TYPE, COPY, REN, DEL (ERASE), UNDELETE

N E W   T E R M S   A N D   S Y M B O L S

Files, ASCII files, executable files, batch files, current drive, directory entries, parameter, switch, source, target, syntax, path, path name, internal/external command, printout

QUICK START

To change from one drive to another:

> C>**a:**   (change the current drive from C to A)
> A>**b:**   (change the current drive from A to B)

To show directory information:

> C>**dir**   (show current directory)
> C>**dir filename**   (show a file)
> C>**dir a:**   (show drive A)

To halt (pause) screen display:

> Press Pause (if any), Ctrl-S, or Ctrl-Num Lock

To show a file's contents:

> C>**type filename**

To copy a file to another disk without a name change:

> C>**copy filename a:**

To copy a file to another disk with a new name:

> C>**copy oldname a:newname**

To copy a file to the same disk with a new name:

> C>**copy oldname newname**

To rename a file:

> C>**ren oldname newname**

To delete a file:

> C>**del filename**

To undelete a file (recover a deleted file):

> C>**undelete filename**

To print a screen display:

> Press Shift-Print Scrn (or Print Scrn alone).

To display and print simultaneously:

> Press Ctrl-P (or Ctrl-Print Scrn).

To print a disk file:

> C>**copy filename prn**

To redirect output from the screen to the printer:

```
C>dir > prn
C>type filename > prn
```

Consider this chapter a DOS survival course. It will take you, step by step, through some of the most commonly used DOS commands. These commands are rather easy to understand and use. After you become familiar with these commands, you will have built a solid foundation for further advance on DOS.

Some of these commands have more exotic details. They will be covered in later chapters. At this time, you need to concentrate on their most common applications and not get bogged down with details.

Before you proceed, you should have with you the disk labeled DOS-TA that comes with this book. The write-protect notch of the disk (a little square opening at the upper right corner) should be covered with a tab; if you have a 3.5-inch disk, slide the write-protect switch to the edge to show a see-through hole. This protects the disk and prevents you from inadvertently erasing the existing files.

You should also have two formatted floppy disks ready for use; these disks must have some space left for storing new files. If you have unformatted disks, go through the next section to format them. If your disks are already formatted, you can skip the next section for now. Formatting will be discussed more thoroughly in Chapter 3.

FORMATTING FLOPPY DISKS

■ *Use the FORMAT command to prepare floppy disks for use.*

DOS cannot store data on a brand new floppy disk. You must use the FORMAT command that comes with DOS to prepare it first.[1] Follow these steps to format two floppy disks:

FOLLOW THESE STEPS

1. Insert an unformatted disk in drive A. (If your disk matches drive B, put the disk in drive B instead.)

---

1. Some vendors sell preformatted floppy disks. If you are using such disks, there is no need for you format them.

2. Go to the DOS directory in drive C where all external commands are stored:

   C>cd \dos

3. Format drive A (change **a:** to **b:** if your disk is in drive B):

   C>format a:
   ```
   Insert new diskette for drive A:
   and press ENTER when ready...
   ```

*FOLLOW
THESE
STEPS*

4. Press the Enter key to begin. If you format a previously formatted disk, the previous format information is saved; this does not happen if a new disk is being formatted. The screen shows a message like below and begins to display a running number, showing the percentage of the disk formatted.

   ```
   Checking existing disk format.
   Saving UNFORMAT information.
   Verifying 360K
   ```

   When done, this message appears and you are prompted to enter a volume label:

   ```
   Format complete.
   Volume label (11 characters, ENTER for none)? disk1
   ```

5. Enter a label (DISK1), and a message like this appears:

   ```
   362496 bytes total disk space
   362496 bytes available on disk

   1024 bytes in each allocation unit.
    354 allocation units available on disk.

   Volume Serial Number is 0C48-19D2

   Format another (Y/N)?
   ```

6. Enter Y to format another disk.

7. Insert a new disk in drive A (or B) and repeat steps 4 and 5; enter DISK2 at step 5.

8. At step 6, enter N to discontinue. The DOS prompt reappears.

If you have followed the above steps, you will have formatted two floppy disks of the same kind. You can now use them to store files.

If you have two kinds of floppy drives and want to format a floppy disk for each, put the first disk in drive A and go through steps 1–5. Enter N at step 6. Repeat steps 1–5, except specifying **b:** instead of **a:** to format. Enter N at step 6 to end.

WHAT IS A FILE?

■ *Use file name extensions to distinguish some common types of files.*

■ *DOS executable files have three common file name extensions: COM, EXE, and BAT.*

Many DOS commands, including those discussed in this chapter, are used to maneuver files. Before you can do that, you need to be familiar with a few related terms.

A **file** is a collection of information (data), which a computer can recognize and maneuver. It can be loaded to memory or stored on disk with a unique name.

The DOS directory on your hard disk contains nearly 100 files. Each file has a file name that can be up tp eight characters in length, plus an optional extension of up to three characters placed after a period. The file name tells you the purpose of a file; the extension describes the type of file. There are many types of extensions; those you should be familiar with at this time include BAT, COM, EXE, SYS, and TXT.

ASCII Files

A file may contain nothing but ASCII characters (see Appendix B and G). Such a file is known as a text file, DOS text file, or **ASCII file**. You can use the TYPE command, as explained below, to clearly show the contents of such a file. Users commonly use file name extensions such as DOC (document) or TXT (text) to signify an ASCII file, although an extension is not mandatory. You will learn to create such files and use proper file names and extensions in Chapter 4.

A file created with a word processor usually contains formatting codes, which control text characteristics such as boldface, center, and flush right. Such a file is not a pure ASCII file. If you use TYPE to display its contents, you will find some recognizable characters and many strange-looking symbols.

COM and EXE Files

A file could contain program code that a computer could execute. Such a file is known as an **executable file** or binary file. It is created with a programming language. It can have a file name extension of COM or EXE, which is usually determined by the language you use to create such a program.

Many external DOS commands, as explained below, are separate programs. Some have COM and others have EXE extensions. When you find files with

---

T I P S   A N D   T R I C K S

R E A D M E   F I L E S

When you see a disk file named README, READ.ME, README.DOC, or README.TXT, you should try to find out what is in it. You can use the TYPE command to display its contents on the screen; you can also retrieve it to a text processor like EDLIN or the new DOS Editor. If a file is named README.EXE or README.BAT, it is a program which you can execute on the command line.

Software publishers usually prepare printed manuals long before releasing a software package. Manuals take a long time to prepare and print. After manuals are printed, programmers may add new features. Since manuals cannot be altered easily, vendors simply include a README file on disk. When you buy a package, you should try to look for such a file to learn last-minute additions or instructions.

---

these extensions on your DOS disks, you can execute them by entering their file names with or without an extension.

Batch Files

Another kind of executable file is called **batch file**. It is an ASCII file containing commands DOS can understand and execute. Batch files carry the BAT extension. Batch files are important because they can save you a lot of time. You will learn more about them starting in Chapter 4.

WARNING: If a file does not have a COM, EXE, or BAT extension, do not execute it by entering its name alone on the command line. If you do, your computer may lock up.

SYS Files

SYS files, such as ANSI.SYS and RAMDRIVE.SYS, are device drivers. When installed, they enable DOS to handle uncommon devices or add new capabilities to DOS. Chapter 9 tells you how to install these drivers.

Table 2.1 sums up the ways to distinguish the numerous DOS files by their extensions.

> **Table 2.1**
>
> *Common DOS File Name Extensions*
>
> | Extension | Purpose |
> |-----------|---------|
> | BAT | Batch file |
> | COM | Command (executable) file, binary |
> | EXE | Executable file, binary |
> | SYS | System (device) driver file, binary |
> | TXT | Text (ASCII) file |

CHANGING THE CURRENT DRIVE

■ *The DOS prompt automatically shows the letter of the current drive.*

■ *Change the current drive to a new one by entering a drive letter followed by a colon.*

When DOS is booted, the system prompt shows the letter of the current drive and the > (greater than) sign. The **current drive** (also known as default drive) is where a DOS command will look for a file—unless preceded or followed by a drive letter (as explained in the next section).

Note: Before you do the following, you must boot DOS as explained in Chapter 1.

The current drive can be changed by entering a letter, followed by a colon. Insert disks in drives A and B and follow these steps to change drives:

FOLLOW THESE STEPS

1. Change from C to B, or make B the current drive: [2]

```
C>b:
B>_
```

---

2. If your PC has only one floppy drive installed, DOS will recognize it as both A and B. You can use the drive as A or B.

You must end with a colon. If not, the current drive will not be changed and you will get this error message instead:

```
C>b
Bad command or file name
C>_
```

Here DOS interprets your move as instructing it to run a program named B (B.COM, B.EXE, or B.BAT). DOS will go to drive C (the current drive) to search for it. If such a program exists, it will be executed. If not, the above message will appear and the current drive will not change.

2. Change from B to A, or make A the current drive:

```
B>a:
A>_
```

3. Change to C:

```
A>c:
C>_
```

If you have a hard disk, the DOS prompt shows the new drive's letter. If not, you will get this error message and no change of the original drive letter:

```
A>c:
Invalid drive specification
A>_
```

4. Return to A:

```
C>a:
A>_
```

DRILL

Each file in questions 1–6 is executable. True or false?

_____ 1. README.EXE.

_____ 2. README.TXT.

_____ 3. README.BAT.

_____ 4. ANSI.SYS.

_____ 5. COMMAND.DOC.

_____ 6. COMMAND.COM.

_____ 7. DOS interprets this command as meaning that you want to:

A>c

a. go to drive C
b. run an executable file
c. cancel an action
d. copy a file

_____ 8. If a file named B.COM exists on the disk in the current drive, this command will:

A>b:

a. make B the current drive
b. execute B.COM
c. display an error message
d. do nothing

DISPLAYING DIRECTORY ENTRIES

■ *Use DIR alone to display the current drive's directory entries.*

■ *Use DIR with a drive letter to display another drive's directory entries.*

■ *Use DIR with a specific file name to display the file's directory information.*

■ *Use DIR with /P or /W switch if there are many files.*

The DIR command is used to display on the screen the **directory entries** of a disk or directory. These entries include subdirectories, if any, and file names. Directories and subdirectories will be explained in Chapter 5. Here we only demonstrate the use of DIR. Follow these steps:

FOLLOW THESE STEPS

1. Insert the DOS-TA disk in drive A. Make A the current drive:

   ```
   C>a:
   A>_
   ```

2. Show the directory entries of the disk in the current drive:

   ```
   A>dir
   ```

Figure 2.1 shows a typical directory resulting from the use of the DIR command.

Figure 2.1

The components of a disk directory

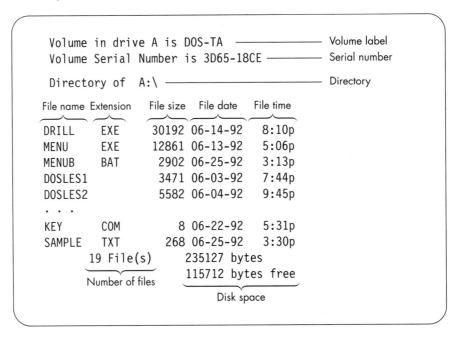

There are three distinct parts in this display. At the top is disk information. The first line shows the volume label for this disk; you will learn to create and change volume labels in Chapter 3. The second line shows the serial number, which is available only for a disk formatted with version 4 or later; this will also be explained in Chapter 3. The third line shows the current drive's letter and the current directory, which will be covered in Chapter 5.

The middle part displays files in five columns: (1) file name, (2) file name extension, (3) file size in bytes, (4) file creation date, and (5) file creation time.

The last part, containing two lines, shows the total number of files, their total bytes, and the amount of available disk space.

FOLLOW THESE STEPS

3. Go to drive B:

    A>**b:**
    B>_

4. Show the directory entries of the disk in drive A:[3]

   `B>`**`dir a:`**

The drive letter after the DIR command tells DOS to act on that particular drive rather than the current drive. If this drive parameter is omitted, DOS will act on the current drive, as shown in step 2. From now on, when you want a DOS command to act on a drive other than the current drive, just specify a drive letter after the command.

5. Show the directory information of a file in another drive:

```
B>dir a:sample.txt
 Volume in drive A is DOS-TA
 Volume Serial Number is 3D65-18CE
 Directory of  A:\
SAMPLE   TXT        268 06-25-92    3:30p
        1 File(s)            268 bytes
                         115712 bytes free
```

The top and bottom portions are the same, but the middle portion shows only one file.

6. Go back to drive A:

   `B>`**`a:`**
   `A>_`

7. Show the directory entries in the current drive in the wide format by specifying the /W switch:

   `A>`**`dir /w`**

```
 Volume in drive A is DOS-TA
 Volume Serial Number is 3D65-18CE

 Directory of  A:\
DOS      EXE    DRILL   EXE     MENU    EXE     MENUB   BAT     DOSLES1
DOSLES2         DOSLES10        DOSLES11        DOSLES12        DOSLES3
DOSLES4         DOSLES5         DOSLES6         DOSLES7         DOSLES8
DOSLES9         KEY     COM     SAMPLE  TXT
       19 File(s)       235127 bytes
                        115712 bytes free
```

---

3. If you have only one floppy drive, this message appears:

   `Insert diskette for drive B: and press any key when ready`

   If you want to show another disk, put in a new one and press a key to continue. Otherwise, just press a key.

The top and bottom portions remain the same as using DIR alone. The middle portion, however, shows only file names and extensions in five columns. File size, date, and time data are omitted.

8. Specify the /P switch:

    A>`dir /p`

DIR has two common switches, /P (pause or page) and /W (wide). They are useful if you have a lot of files to display. If there is a long list of files, the /P switch displays this message:

    `Press any key to continue...`

T I P S   A N D   T R I C K S

W H A T   I S   A   P A R A M E T E R ?

Some DOS commands require one or more **parameters** to complete a job. A parameter is a qualifier or argument (command-line argument) that defines the way a command is to do its job. Anything that comes after a command name is treated as a parameter. If you have two or more parameters, separate them with a delimiter such as a space, comma, or semicolon.

You must provide parameters as expected. If a wrong parameter is used, you will get the "Invalid parameter" message. If more parameters than expected are entered, you will get another error message, like this:

    A>`dir a: b:`
    `Too many parameters - b:`

In some cases, a parameter can be omitted. DOS then uses certain default values. Consider this example:

    A>`dir a:`

The parameter a: can be omitted. If so, the current drive is acted on. If you want the DIR command to act on another drive, you will have to specify a parameter, such as:

    A>`dir b:`

A parameter must not be separated by a space; otherwise DOS will treat it as two parameters. Consider this:

    A>`dir b: filename`
    `Too many parameters - filename`

Without a space, B:FILENAME is treated as a single parameter. The extra space makes it two parameters. Since DIR expects one parameter, the error message results.

TIPS AND TRICKS

WHAT IS A SWITCH?

A **switch** is an option that can be used with a specific DOS command. Some commands have no switch, while others have more than a dozen.

A switch enables a command to do something extra or behave in a slightly different manner. In order to make full use of a complex command, you need to know all of its available switches.

As a special kind of parameter, a switch is placed after a command and immediately preceded by a slash. A space before the slash is advisable. A lack of such a space may cause a problem under some circumstances. A space after the slash is not permitted. Consider the following:

```
A>dir / p
Invalid switch - /
```

The error message is caused by the space between the slash and the switch letter. The space makes DOS interpret your command as using a switch consisting of a single slash, which is not a valid switch.

With some exceptions, a switch can normally be placed anywhere after a command name. Both arrangements below are legal:

```
A>dir /w b:
A>dir b: /w
```

Upon pressing a key, another screen appears, and so on until the end of the display. If you press Ctrl-C (or Ctrl-Break; hold down Ctrl and press either C or Break) after this message appears, the screen shows ^C and further display of directory entries is terminated. So, if you have found what you are looking for and want no more display, just press Ctrl-C so as not to waste any more time.

PRACTICE 2-1

☐ 1. Go from drive A to B and back to drive A.

☐ 2. Display the directory entries of the disk in the current drive based on the directory order.

☐ 3. With A as the current drive, display in the wide format the directory entries of the disk in drive B.

☐ 4. With B as the current drive, display the directory information of a single file in drive A.

■ TIPS AND TRICKS ■

DRIVE FAILURE

If DOS cannot access a disk, you will be given a number of options. Suppose you leave the drive B door open (or insert no disk) and enter this command:

```
A>dir b:
Not ready reading drive B
Abort, Retry, Fail?_
```

If you want to abort the command, just press A; the DOS prompt reappears. If you want to retry, fix the drive and press R. If you press F, DOS displays a message showing the cause of the failure.

Under some circumstances, the Ignore option may appear, like this:

```
Abort, Retry, Ignore, Fail?_
```

The Ignore option tells DOS to ignore the encountered error and move forward.

---

5. With A as the current drive, display the TXT files in the C:\DOS directory according to size from small to large.

6. With A as the current directory, display all the files (including hidden and system files) in drive C's root directory according to date from the latest to the earliest. The display should pause when the screen is full.

DRILL

9. When the /W switch is used with DIR, the screen shows:
    a. each file's date and time
    b. 5 columns of file names with extensions
    c. the total number of files
    d. both b and c

10. In the command below, "b:filename" is known as:
    A>dir b:filename
    a. a switch
    b. an extension
    c. a parameter
    d. a tail

HALTING A SCREEN DISPLAY

■ *Press the Pause key to halt a screen display. If your keyboard lacks this key, use Ctrl-S or Ctrl-Num Lock. Press the space bar or another key to continue scrolling (showing more).*

When you use a command to display something that is longer than one screen length, the display quickly scrolls out of sight. To stop the scrolling so that you can examine it, try one of the following: the Pause key, the Ctrl-S combination, or the Ctrl-Num Lock combination.

The 101-key enhanced keyboard has a special key named Pause that can be used to halt the screen display. Follow these steps:

FOLLOW THESE STEPS

1. Insert the DOS-TA disk in drive A (if it is not already there).

2. Display the directory entries:

    A>**dir**

3. Press Pause.

If you press the Pause key before everything is displayed, the scrolling is suspended.

4. Press the space bar (or any other key) to continue.

If you press Ctrl-C (or Ctrl-Break), the display is terminated and the DOS prompt reappears.

If you have an older keyboard without the Pause key, you can use Ctrl-S or Ctrl-Num Lock instead (hold down Ctrl and press either key).

The Pause key is especially useful when you use the TYPE command to display a long text file, as explained below.

DISPLAYING A FILE'S CONTENTS

■ *Use TYPE followed by a file name to display a file's contents on the screen.*

■ *Use a path name when you want TYPE or another DOS command to act on a file located in another drive.*

The TYPE command is used to display on the screen a text file stored on a disk. Follow these steps to use TYPE:

1. Insert the DOS-TA disk in drive A (if it is not already there).

2. Show the contents of a file in the current drive:

    `A>`**`type sample.txt`**

    `This is a sample text file. It is to be used for
    demonstrating some DOS commands.`

    `This file has no importance. It can be copied,
    altered, and deleted after you have made use
    of it.`

    `You will learn in later chapters how to create
    and alter a file like this.`

    `A>_`

The entire contents of the text file is now displayed on the screen.

3. Halt scrolling by pressing the Pause key (or Ctrl-S) after entering this command:

    `A>`**`type c:\dos\readme.txt`**

This command displays the README.TXT file stored in the C:\DOS directory. When you press the Pause key, the writing of the text lines to the screen is halted. When you press a key again, scrolling and writing to the screen continues.

4. Terminate the display by pressing Ctrl-C. The command prompt reappears.

TIPS AND TRICKS

P A T H A N D P A T H N A M E

When you want a DOS command to act on a file located in the current drive, you need to specify only the name of the file after the command, such as:

`A>`**`type sample.txt`**

If you want a command to act on a file located somewhere else, you need to precede the file name with a **path or path name** (drive/directory) prefix so that DOS knows where to find the file, such as:

`A>`**`type b:sample.txt`**
`A>`**`type c:\dos\readme.txt`**

If a path contains several directory names, they must be separated with \. A path can be no more than 66 characters long.

Notice that every time you use TYPE, you have to specify a single parameter. This parameter must be a file—unlike DIR, for which you can specify a drive letter or a file. If you specify a drive letter alone, you will get an error message. Consider the following:

```
B>type a:
File not found - A:
```

You are now telling DOS to display a file named "a:". This is an illegal name. As you will see in Chapter 4, DOS does not allow a colon to be part of a file name. When you instruct DOS to check a file with an illegal name, it simply rejects your command without even bothering to access a disk.

COPYING FILES

- *Use COPY to copy individual files from one disk to another, or make a duplicate (with a different name) on the same disk.*

- *COPY expects two parameters, source and target.*

- *A target file name can be the same as or different from that of the source file.*

- *When only one parameter is specified, it is presumed to be the source; the current drive (directory) is assumed to be the target.*

Copying files is a vital part of using a computer. Although Chapter 6 will provide much more detail, this section gives you some simple examples so that you can start using this function as soon as possible.

Follow these steps to create copies of a file:

FOLLOW THESE STEPS

1. Insert in drive A the DOS-TA disk and in drive B a practice (formatted) disk.[4]

2. Copy a file from A to B:[5]

```
A>copy sample.txt b:
           1 File(s) copied
```

---

4. If you have a single floppy drive, put the DOS-TA disk in it first and follow the steps below. DOS will instruct you to swap disks.

5. If you have only one floppy drive, replace the DOS-TA disk with your own after the message below appears; swap disks in the future in similar situations:

```
Insert diskette for drive B: and press any key when ready
```

■ *T I P S   A N D   T R I C K S* ■

S O U R C E   A N D   T A R G E T

Some commands, including COPY, expect two parameters, source and target (sometimes referred to as destination). **Source** is where a file is read, and **target** is where a new file is written. Normally, such a command has a **syntax** (grammatical structure) like this:

A>`copy source target`

If only one parameter is specified, it is presumed to be the source, such as:

A>`copy b:sample.txt`

Here SAMPLE.TXT is read from drive B and written to drive A. The omitted second parameter is presumed to be the current drive. The above command is thus the abbreviated version of the one below:

A>`copy b:sample.txt a:`

If the source has no drive prefix, it defaults to the current drive, and a target is expected, such as:

A>`copy sample.txt b:`

If the target drive (b:) is omitted in this example, DOS assumes that you want to copy a file onto itself and will not let you do that.

Notice that the message tells you that one file has been copied. If there is a file in drive B with the exact name, its contents and date-time data will be replaced with the copy coming from drive A. This will be done without any warning.

3. Show the new directory entry:

A>`dir b:sample.txt`

You should see, among other things, this item:

`SAMPLE    TXT        268 06-25-92    3:30p`

This proves that a new file has been created after you used the COPY command.

Now remove write protection from the DOS-TA disk (peel off the write-protect tab or slide the write-protect switch to cover the hole). We will put it back later. We are going to write to this disk for now.

4. Copy a file without a target:

A>`copy b:sample.txt`

This command tells DOS to use COPY to copy the specified file from drive B to the omitted current drive, namely A. This command is the same as the one below:

A>**copy b:sample.txt a:**

The original copy in drive A matching the specified name is now replaced with the one from drive B.

   5. Go to drive B:

   A>**b:**
   B>_

   6. Copy from B to A:

   B>**copy sample.txt a:**

This does the same thing as step 4, namely copying a file from drive B to drive A. In this example, the target parameter of "a:" is required. Without it, an error message will appear, as shown below in step 7.

   7. Create a duplicate file on the same disk:

   B>**copy sample.txt sample.txt**
   File cannot be copied onto itself
         0 File(s) copied

DOS does not allow you to create a duplicate file of the same name on the same disk. This makes sense; having two files of the same name on the same disk definitely creates confusion. You may be able to tell them apart by file lengths and contents, but DOS cannot; it distinguishes files by their names only. However, if you divide a disk into various directories, you can store in each an identical copy of the same file without causing confusion. Directories are covered in Chapter 5.

   8. Create a duplicate file with a different name:

   B>**copy sample.txt sample1.txt**
         1 File(s) copied

There are now two identical files on the same disk under different names, SAMPLE.TXT and SAMPLE1.TXT. The single-digit difference in the two names enables DOS to treat them as two distinct entities.

   9. Copy a file to another drive and change the name of the target file:

   B>**copy a:sample.txt sample1.txt**

This copies a file named SAMPLE.TXT from drive A (source) to drive B (target) and changes the target file name to SAMPLE1.TXT. The original SAMPLE1.TXT in drive B, if any, is replaced with the contents of SAMPLE.TXT from drive A.

TIPS AND TRICKS

DISK DRIVE WARNING RED LIGHT

When DOS reads data from or writes data to a disk, the red (or green) light on the front panel will light up and you can hear the spinning noise coming out of the drive. Do not disturb the drive by opening the door or taking out the disk. If you do, you could cause reading or writing failure and possible damage to your disk. If you want to take out a disk and exchange it, do so after the light goes off and the spinning stops.

On some rare occasions, you may encounter an out-of-control situation of perpetual disk spinning. You can try to stop it by pressing Ctrl-C (or Ctrl-Break; hold down Ctrl and press either key). If this does not work, you may need to take out the disk and reboot DOS.

Notice that the drive prefix in the target is omitted. It could be specified as below and the result would be the same:

    B>**copy a:sample.txt b:sample1.txt**

10. Show the directory entries in B:

    B>**dir**

You should see two files of the same date, time, length, but different names:

    SAMPLE   TXT   268 06-25-92   3:30p
    SAMPLE1   TXT   268 06-25-92   3:30p

You can now restore the write-protection to the DOS-TA disk to prevent inadvertent erasure.

PRACTICE 2-2

☐ 1. Copy SAMPLE.TXT from the DOS-TA disk to your practice disk and use MYFILE.DOC as the file name on your disk.

☐ 2. Copy MYFILE.DOC to the same disk with the new name of FILE2.TXT.

☐ 3. Use TYPE to show FILE2.TXT.

☐ 4. Repeat #3, but press Ctrl-C before the entire file is displayed.

D R I L L

____ 11. This command will copy a file:
A>copy filename b:
a. from A to B
b. from B to A
c. either a or b
d. nowhere; it's illegal

____ 12. This command will copy a file:
B>copy a: filename b:
a. from A to B
b. from B to A
c. either a or b
d. nowhere; it's illegal

____ 13. Which command below is legal?
a. A>b:type filename
b. A>a:copy filename b:
c. A>type filename b:
d. B>copy b:filename a:

____ 14. Assuming file A exists in drive A, which command below is illegal?
a. B>dir b:
b. A>type b:
c. A>copy a b:
d. B>dir a: /w

RENAMING FILES

■ *Use REN to change a file's name to a new one. The new name must not
match a file already in existence on the same disk.*

A file name can be changed with the REN (RENAME) command. REN, like
COPY, is used with two parameters:

```
REN source target
```

Here you give the source (an existing file) a new name. The target file is the same file, except with a new name. If the source does not exist or the target already exists, this error message appears:

```
Duplicate file name or File not found
```

With B still the current drive, follow these steps to change file names:

FOLLOW
THESE
STEPS

1. Change a file name to that of another existing file:

   ```
   B>ren sample.txt sample1.txt
   Duplicate file name or file not found
   ```

Since SAMPLE1.TXT already exists on the same disk, you are not allowed to change SAMPLE.TXT to SAMPLE1.TXT.

2. Change to a different name:

   ```
   B>ren sample.txt sample
   B>_
   ```

The drive is activated and the DOS prompt reappears, but no message is displayed. That means the renaming has been successful.

3. Show the contents of the file:

   ```
   B>type sample
   ```

The screen should show the same text file as SAMPLE.TXT.

DELETING FILES

■ *Use DEL (or ERASE) to delete a file or group of matching files.*

■ *Use DEL with caution. You may not successfully bring it back.*

When you no longer need a file, you can delete it. If a disk runs out of space for storing new files, you can delete some existing files to make room. To delete a file, simply use the DEL or ERASE command.

DEL and ERASE are interchangeable. Either one can be used to remove from disk a file or a group of matching files stored there. DEL is more commonly used because it is shorter.

If you have not changed the setup from the previous section, you are ready to practice deleting files. Follow these steps to delete one file at a time:

FOLLOW
THESE
STEPS

1. Delete a file in the current drive:

   ```
   B>del sample1.txt
   ```

Drive B should light up and hum for a while. But no message tells you that one file has been deleted.

2. Use DIR to see whether the file still exists:

    B>**dir sample1.txt**
    File not found

The message tells you that DOS can no longer find the file.

3. Go to drive A:

    B>**a:**
    A>_

4. Delete a file in another drive:

    A>**del b:sample**

5. Use TYPE to see whether a file exists:

    A>**type b:sample**
    File not found - SAMPLE

The two files created by COPY in the previous section are now deleted from your practice disk in drive B. Later in the text, you should use similar steps to delete files created in various practice exercises. This will free disk space for future use. When files you create are to be kept for future use, you will be so instructed.

You can delete all the files on one disk with a single DEL command or delete a group of files matching the specified name. You do so by using DEL with certain wild card characters. These will be explained in Chapter 4.

When you use DEL or ERASE to delete a file, DOS does not actually erase a file from disk; it merely marks the disk space as available for future use. If you have not written to the same disk space, you can use UNDELETE to restore the file.

UNDELETING FILES

■ *Use UNDELETE to undelete a file you have inadvertently deleted.*

■ *UNDELETE is an external command. You must tell DOS where to access this program.*

If you have inadvertently deleted a file, you can bring it back with the UNDELETE command available since version 5.

UNDELETE is an external command (see below). You need to tell DOS where to access such a command. You can usually go to the DOS directory in drive C to do it. Follow these steps to practice deleting and undeleting:

FOLLOW
THESE
STEPS

1. Insert in drive B the disk used in the previous section (if it is not already there).

2. Undelete the SAMPLE.TXT file:

    B>**c:\dos\undelete sample1.txt**

This command goes to the C:\DOS directory to execute UNDELETE to undelete SAMPLE1.TXT in the current drive.

3. Press Y when you are asked Y/N.

4. Press S when you are asked to supply the first character of the file name. After the procedure is completed, the screen appears as shown below:

    B>**c:\dos\undelete sample1.txt**

    ```
    Directory: B:\
    File Specifications: SAMPLE1.TXT
        Deletion-tracking file not found.
        MS-DOS directory contains    1 deleted files.
        Of those,    1 files may be recovered.
    Using the MS-DOS directory.
        ?AMPLE1  TXT     268 11-25-92  5:20p ...A  Undelete (Y/N)?y
        Please type the first character for ?AMPLE1 .TXT: s
    File successfully undeleted.
    ```

5. Show the file's existence:

    B>**type sample1.txt**

6. Delete the file:

    B>**del sample1.txt**

UNDELETE has other details, which will be discussed in Chapter 6.

PRACTICE 2-3

☐ 1. Rename the MYFILE.DOC file on your practice disk NEWDOC.

☐ 2. With A as the current drive and your practice disk in drive B, delete NEWDOC on the practice disk.

☐ 3. Go to drive B and delete FILE2.TXT.

☐ 4. Use DIR and TYPE to verify the nonexistence of MYFILE.DOC, NEWDOC, and FILE2.TXT.

D R I L L

____ 15. Which command below is legal?
   a. A>ren file1 b:file2
   b. A>ren b:filename
   c. A>ren b:filename newfile
   d. A>a:ren file1 file2

____ 16. This command will cause DOS to erase from disk all the information related to FILENAME. True or false?

   A>del b:filename

____ 17. Which command will succeed in transferring and renaming a file?
   a. A>copy file b:text
   b. A>ren file b:text
   c. A>type file b:text
   d. A>dir file b:text

____ 18. Which command has a required parameter missing?
   a. A>copy filename b:
   b. B>dir
   c. A>del filename
   d. B>ren filename

INTERNAL AND EXTERNAL COMMANDS

■ *Internal commands are included in the COMMAND.COM file and loaded to RAM. They can be used regardless of what the current drive is.*

■ *External commands are individual programs stored on a disk. To use an external command, you need to guide DOS to where the program is stored, unless it is in the current drive.*

There are two kinds of DOS commands, internal and external. **Internal commands** can be used anywhere, regardless of the drive you are in. They are included in the COMMAND.COM file, which is loaded to RAM when DOS is booted.

External commands are separate program files stored on different disks in the DOS package. These files have the COM or EXE file name extension. These programs can be run by entering correct file names on the command line. The extensions are not necessary when you want to run such a program.

External commands are not included in COMMAND.COM. To keep COMMAND.COM small so that it will not take up too much memory, infrequently used DOS commands are intentionally left out. A small operating system is considered a virtue because there is more memory left for application programs and data files.

To use an external command in a floppy system, put the matching program on the disk in the current drive; if DOS cannot find this program to run, it will display an error message:

```
A>undelete sample.txt
Bad command or file name
```

If the program is not located in the current drive, you can add a drive letter to tell DOS where to load this program, such as:

```
A>b:undelete sample.txt
```

This command tells DOS to go to drive B to run the UNDELETE.EXE program and restore SAMPLE.TXT in the current drive (A).

If you have a hard disk, you can store most or all DOS external commands in a directory named DOS. When you want to run an external command, you can make that directory current. When you run an external command, DOS goes to the current directory to find the command.

Another way is to precede a command with a directory path, like this:

```
A>c:\dos\undelete sample.txt
```

This command tells DOS to go to the directory named DOS in drive C to run the UNDELETE.EXE program stored there and restore the file in the current drive.

Still another way of using an external command is to use the PATH=C:\DOS command to direct DOS where to search for executable files in the specified directory. This will be explained in Chapter 5.

PRINTING A SCREEN DISPLAY AND DISK FILE

■ *Use the Shift-Print Scrn key combination to print what is displayed on the screen.*

■ *Use Ctrl-P or Ctrl-Print Scrn to display as well as print what is displayed on the screen.*

■ *Use COPY to copy a disk file to the printer.*

■ *Use the redirection symbol > with DIR and TYPE to print directory entries and a file's contents.*

There are a number of ways to produce a **printout**—putting text on paper. You can display text lines on the screen and then print the screen display. You can display and print simultaneously. You can redirect a screen display to the printer. You can also send a file stored on a disk to the printer.

Printing a Screen Display

Follow these steps to print a screen display:

FOLLOW
THESE
STEPS

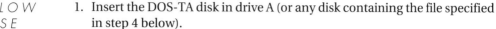

1. Insert the DOS-TA disk in drive A (or any disk containing the file specified in step 4 below).

2. Turn on the printer and roll in paper to the proper position.

3. Clear the screen:

   `A>cls`

4. Display text on the screen:

   `A>type sample.txt`

5. Print the screen display by pressing the following key combination:

   `A><Shift>-<Print Scrn>`

Here you are to hold down a Shift key and press the Print Scrn key (Prn Scn on an older keyboard); on a newer keyboard, pressing Shift is not necessary. The screen display should be sent to the printer.

If your printer does not print, it may be offline and not accepting messages. If that happens, turn the printer off and on again, and repeat step 5.

Simultaneous Displaying and Printing

Another way to get a hard (printed) copy of what is shown on the screen is to echo each text line to the printer. The steps below demonstrate how to do it:

1. Put the DOS-TA disk in drive A and get the printer ready.

2. Press Ctrl-P (or Ctrl-Print Scrn)—hold down Ctrl and press either key.

3. Display text on the screen and print it at the same time:

   `A>type sample.txt`

4. Press Ctrl-P again to disable the echo effect.

Like other toggle keys, Ctrl-P toggles between printing and nonprinting modes. In printing mode, what goes to the screen also is sent to the printer. In nonprinting mode, commands and their outputs go only to the screen.

If you have a daisy-wheel printer, whatever you type in printing mode, including the command in step 3, is displayed on the screen and sent to the printer; the printer produces an exact copy of what is shown on the screen.

TIPS AND TRICKS

PRINTING SCREEN GRAPHICS

DOS can print characters displayed on the screen without any trouble. However, when there is a graphics image (which is basically composed of numerous dots), you need to load a program named GRAPHICS.COM first. Without this extra step, a blank image will be sent to the printer and the printer will not print anything.

When you are ready to print a screen image (do not do this at this time), follow these steps:

1. Load GRAPHICS.COM:

   C>\dos\graphics

2. Run your application program and display the graphics on the screen.

3. Print the screen display by holding down Shift and pressing the Print Scrn key (pressing Shift is unnecessary on a newer keyboard).

If you do some unusual printing, such as printing color graphics, check the details after running HELP GRAPHICS.

On a dot-matrix printer, typed characters are not printed until Esc, Enter, or Backspace is pressed. If you do not want a command to be printed, type the command first (without pressing Enter), then press Ctrl-P, and finally press Enter. If you enter the command in step 3 by using this method, only the text (and the DOS prompt) will be printed.

Copying a File to the Printer

If you already have a file containing only ASCII text, you can use COPY to print it. Follow these steps:

FOLLOW THESE STEPS

1. Get the printer ready.

2. Copy a file from disk to the printer:

   A>copy sample.txt prn

PRN is a DOS device name. DOS recognizes it as a printer. You can also use LPT1 and produce the same result, such as:

   A>copy sample.txt lpt1

The text file is now printed. And the screen shows only this message:

   1 File(s) copied

Redirecting Output to the Printer

Another technique is to redirect output from the screen to the printer. Whatever normally goes to the screen can be redirected to the printer. Follow these steps:

FOLLOW
THESE
STEPS

1. Insert the DOS-TA disk (or any disk) in drive A.

2. Send its list of directory entries to the printer, which should be left on:

    A>**dir /w > prn**

All the directory entries of the disk in drive A will be printed in the wide format. Notice that the screen does not show the output of the command; it is redirected to the printer instead.

If you want to print another disk's information, put it in drive A and repeat the same command. After you finish printing, you can cut out the printout and tape it on a pertinent disk. This technique allows you to quickly locate a file on a disk without having to use the DIR command again and again.

You can also use TYPE to print a disk file by entering a command like this:

    A>**type sample.txt > prn**

This redirects output from the screen to the printer. The text is printed but not displayed.

If you find an online help message useful and want to make a hard copy, a command like this will do it:

    A>**dir /? > prn**

This redirects the help message for the DIR command from the normal screen output to the printer.

The techniques of redirecting output will be covered more thoroughly in Chapter 8.

PRACTICE 2-4

☐ 1. Use DIR to display the directory entries of a disk and then print the screen display.

☐ 2. Repeat the above, but simultaneously display and print the output.

☐ 3. Use the TYPE command to send the SAMPLE.TXT file to the screen and printer. Your command should not be printed.

☐ 4. Repeat the above without displaying text on the screen.

☐   5. Use the COPY command to send the SAMPLE.TXT file to the printer.

☐   6. Print the online help message for the UNDELETE command.

D R I L L

Each command in questions 19–22 is internal. True or false?

____ 19. COPY.

____ 20. UNDELETE.

____ 21. GRAPHICS.

____ 22. TYPE.

____ 23. If the UNDELETE.EXE file is stored on the disk in drive A (and the PATH command has not been used), this command will work. True or false?

    B>undelete sample.txt

____ 24. Which command below will NOT print?
    a. A>copy filename prn
    b. A>dir b: > prn
    c. A>type filename > prn
    d. A>ren filename > prn

DIR'S NEW SWITCHES (ADVANCED OPTIONAL TOPIC)

■   *Use DIR with /A to display files of certain attributes and /O to specify the order to display files.*

Version 5 added five switches to the DIR command; version 6 has given it yet another. So the command now has 8 switches altogether. In addition to the old /P and /W switches discussed earlier in this chapter, the six newer switches are shown below:

/A: Attributes; to show files with certain attributes, including A (archive files only), D (directories only), H (hidden files only), R (read-only files only), S (system files only); use /A alone to show all files, including hidden ones; Chapter 7 discusses file attributes.

/B   Bare format; file and directory names only; will negate /W if used together

/C   Compression ratio; see Chapter 7 for file compression

/L   Lower case used to show information

/O: Order (what order to display) according to D (date/time in ascending order), N (names of files and directories mixed and sorted in alphabetic order), E (extensions in alphabetic order), G (group directories before files, both unsorted), or S (size in ascending order); use – before each value to reverse the default order; default: /O is the same as /O:GN

/S   Subdirectories' files are also displayed

The /O: switch is most useful because DIR normally displays directory entries based on the order that each is saved in the directory. This order makes it difficult to find a specific item in a long list. You can more easily spot an item from a long list when it is arranged in a more meaningful order.

In the /A: and /O: switches, you can use a – (minus) sign to signify the opposite attribute or order. For example, /A:–R means not read-only; all the files, except those read-only, will be displayed. /O:S displays files according to their size from smaller to larger; /O:–S, on the other hand, shows larger files first.

The : (colon) after /A: and /O: is optional. Thus /AH, /A:H, /OE, and /O:E are all legal. However, adding a colon makes a switch more readable.

You can use two or more switches in one command. In /A: and /O:, you can also supply one or more values. For example, /O:ES shows files and subdirectories sorted by extension from small to large.

/A and /O can be used without any accompanying value. To do so you must not add a : (colon) at the end. Used alone, /A shows all files, including the normally invisible hidden and system files; without /A, hidden and system files are not shown. /O alone displays directory names on top and file names at the bottom, each separately sorted in alphabetical order.

The commands below illustrate how these switches can be used in various situations:

`C>dir /b`	Only files and directories
`C>dir b:\*.txt /s`	All directories in drive B matching *.TXT files
`C>dir /b /l`	Display in bare format and lower case
`C>dir \ /a:d /s`	Directories only in entire drive C
`C>dir /o /p`	Directory/file names in alphabetical order, pause
`C>dir /a /o`	Directories and all files in alphabetical order

C>dir /o:-d /w	Most recent dates first, wide
C>dir /o:-s /p /w	Largest files first, pause, wide
C>dir a: /o:e	Drive A, sort extensions small to large

These switches can also be preset in the DOS environment. See Chapter 9 for details.

It is hard to remember so many switches and attributes. But don't forget there is an online help. You can display the available switches with this simple command:

C>dir /?

You can also print the help message, as demonstrated in the preceding section.

DRILL

Use the list below to answer questions 25–30:

a. C>dir /b /p   b. C>dir /a:d   c. C>dir /o /a   d. C>dir \ /s /p   e. C>dir /o:d /w

____ 25. Displays files sorted by date in ascending order.

____ 26. Displays directories only.

____ 27. Displays all of drive C's directories and visible files.

____ 28. Displays only directory and file names.

____ 29. Displays directories and all files (including hidden ones) sorted by name in alphabetical order.

____ 30. Displays all visible files in wide format.

SUMMARY AND REVIEW

Check each item as you review and understand the following highlights of the chapter.

☐ 1. A file is a collection of information that DOS can maneuver. DOS can recognize files by their file name extensions. The four common extensions are COM (command), EXE (executable), BAT (batch), and SYS (system).

2. Text files, commonly called ASCII files, usually carry the optional extensions of TXT or DOC. When you buy a software package, pay attention to a file named README. It usually contains information not available in the printed manual.

3. When DOS is booted, the system prompt automatically displays the letter of the current drive. The current drive is where DOS will look for a file when instructed to do so.

4. If a command is to act on a file not in the current drive, you need to add a parameter after the command, specifying which drive or file the command is to act on.

5. The current drive can be changed. To do so, simply enter a letter followed by a colon.

6. The DIR command can display directory information related to a file or an entire disk. You can find out useful information such as file names, sizes, creation dates, etc.

7. DIR has seven switches, four of which are commonly used: /P (pause), /W (wide), /A (attributes), and /O (sort order). A switch is an option that can cause a command to behave in a slightly different manner.

8. When a command such as DIR displays more than a screen of information, the display normally continues to scroll until the end is reached. If you want to halt the scrolling at any point, just press Pause. If your keyboard lacks this key, use Ctrl-S or Ctrl-Num Lock.

9. When you want to see what is in a file, use the TYPE command to display its contents on the screen. TYPE can clearly display all the characters of a pure ASCII file. Other files will display strange characters.

10. You can use COPY to create duplicates of individual files. COPY expects two parameters, source and target. If only one is provided, DOS treats it as the source and the current drive as the target.

11. COPY can copy a file from one disk to another with the same or a different name. It can also make a duplicate file with a different name on the same disk. Two files of the same name, however, cannot be stored on the same disk (in the same directory).

12. REN allows you to change a file's name. The new name must not be the same as that of another file on the same disk (in the same directory).

☐   13. Use DEL or ERASE, followed by a file name, to delete a particular file. Use UNDELETE, followed by a file name, to recover a deleted file.

☐   14. Internal commands such as DEL, COPY, and REN can be used from any drive or directory because they are loaded to memory when DOS is booted. External commands like FORMAT and UNDELETE, however, must be stored in the current drive or directory or have a path provided so DOS can find them to execute.

☐   15. To create a printout, use one of the following methods:
    a. Press Shift-Print Scrn to print a screen display.
    b. Press Ctrl-P to simultaneously display and print.
    c. Use the COPY command to copy a file to the printer.
    d. Use > with DIR or TYPE to redirect output to PRN.

REVIEW QUESTIONS

Write an answer for each question below.

1. What is a file? What do these file name extensions mean: COM, EXE, BAT, SYS?

2. What is the significance of a README file?

3. What does the current drive mean? How do you change it?

4. If you use DIR without any parameter, what does it do? What are the items displayed?

5. DIR has four commonly used switches, namely /P, /W, /A, and /O. What does each do?

6. How can you halt a long screen display?

7. How do the terms switch and parameter differ?

8. How many parameters does COPY expect? What happens if only one is specified?

9. Can you make a duplicate of a file with the same name and on the same disk? Explain.

10. If both A.TXT and B.TXT exist on the same disk (directory), explain the consequences of these two commands:
    a. A>ren a.txt b.txt
    b. A>copy a.txt b.txt

11. What will you be asked to do when you use UNDELETE to recover a deleted file?

12. How do internal and external commands differ?

13. Explain what each key combination does.
    a. Ctrl-P
    b. Ctrl-S
    c. Shift-Print Scrn

14. What does this command do?
    A>dir b: /p > lpt1

15. What does this command do?
    A>copy filename prn

Managing Disks

C O M M A N D S   C O V E R E D

FORMAT, VOL, LABEL, CHKDSK, FDISK, UNFORMAT

N E W   T E R M S   A N D   S Y M B O L S

CD-ROM, DAT, write-protect notch/switch, index hole (sector notch), read-write opening, track, sector, boot record, FAT (file allocation table), cluster (allocation unit), volume label, platter, cylinder, partition, virus

Q U I C K   S T A R T

To identify different parts of a floppy disk:

See Figures 3.1 and 3.2.

To understand how DOS organizes a floppy disk:

See Figures 3.3 and 3.4.

To format a disk:

C>format a:

To see a disk's volume label:

C>vol a:

To see and/or change a disk's volume label:

C>label a:

To check an entire disk:

C>chkdsk a:

To check a file's contiguity:

C>chkdsk a:filename

To check a disk's fragmentation:

C>chkdsk a:*.*

To check a disk and display all the file names:

C>chkdsk a: /v

To recover files due to a corrupted FAT:

C>chkdsk a: /f

To partition a hard disk:

A>fdisk

To recover a disk from inadvertent reformatting:

C>unformat a:

When you create a file, you may need to save it for later use. There are a wide variety of electronic media on which you can save your files. The most popular are floppy and hard disks.

A number of DOS commands can be used to manage disks. You can use them to prepare disks for use, check their contents, change their volume labels, and so on.

This chapter explains these closely related topics in this order: (1) different kinds of storage media, (2) different parts of a floppy disk, (3) ways to protect a floppy disk, (4) how DOS organizes a floppy disk, (5) different kinds and sizes of floppy disks, (6) preparing (formatting) a disk for use, (7) analysis of a formatted disk, (8) the processes of booting and storing data, (9) displaying and changing a disk's volume label, (10) checking the contents of a disk, (11) preparing a hard disk for use, and (12) recovering data from an inadvertent reformatting.

You will encounter quite a few computer numbers in this chapter. If they confuse you, consult the terms and numbers explained in Appendix G, Basic Computer Math.

DIFFERENT TYPES OF STORAGE MEDIA

■ *Many types of storage media are available today. The most common ones are floppy and hard disks.*

There is a wide variety of available media today to store computer data. As computer technology continues to advance rapidly, more variety and higher capacity can be expected.

The most common medium is the floppy disk, or diskette. It is the most versatile and economical way to save data. Every PC must have a least one floppy drive to handle floppy disks. Floppy disks come in various sizes and capacities, as explained below.

Hard disks, also known as fixed disks, are becoming more common. Their prices have fallen as fast as their capacities have increased. As more application programs require larger and faster disk drives, more and more users are finding it hard to compute without a fast and decent-sized hard disk. Only a few years ago, 10MB disks were common. Today you will have difficulty buying a hard disk smaller than 80MB. Hard disks of several gigabytes and fast access time of 10 milliseconds (in contrast to 80 ms for earlier models) are increasingly common.

CD-ROMs (Compact Disk - Read Only Memory) are increasingly used to store and distribute massive volumes of data. These disks resemble compact disks and can be handled by a specially equipped disk player. The stored data can be read but not altered. This arrangement is useful for storing and distributing permanent data. Microsoft, for example, markets a package called Bookshelf that contains a host of reference works. MPCs (multimedia PCs) are now commonly equipped with CD-ROMs.

DAT (digital audio tape) is beginning to migrate from music to computer. A DAT tape, resembling an audio cassette tape, can store vast amount (gigabytes) of data. It can be used like a floppy disk for random access, but is most useful in backing up large files.

Other types of media abound, but none has so far matched the popularity of floppy disks. In this book, we will concentrate on understanding them.

FLOPPY DISK TYPES AND PARTS

■ *On the surface, a floppy disk consists of a protective jacket, a write-protect device, an indexing device, a spinning device, and an opening for reading and writing.*

There are two kinds of floppy disks in use today: 5.25-inch and 3.5-inch. The former can be divided into 360KB and 1.2MB, and the latter 720KB, 1.44MB, and 2.88MB.

5.25-Inch Floppy Disks

The first IBM-PC was equipped with a floppy drive that could handle 5.25-inch, single-sided, double-density (SS/DD), eight-sectored (see below for the meanings of these terms) floppy disks. Each disk could store only up to 160KB of data. Double-sided (DS/DD) drives and disks soon became available, making a total disk capacity of 320KB. This disk's storage capacity was finally increased to 360KB by a new DOS version.

The AT brought with it the high-density (IBM refers to it as high capacity; others call it high density or DS/HD) drives and disks. At the same time, Microsoft released DOS 3.0 to accommodate these new disks. They could each store up to 1.2MB of data. Today many AT models come with this floppy drive.

As shown in Figure 3.1, a 5.25-inch disk has a number of parts you need to be aware of. The **write-protect notch** can be covered with a write-protect tab,

Figure 3.1

A 5.25-inch floppy disk

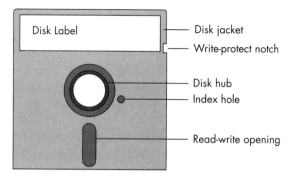

which comes with a disk package, to prevent writing to the disk. Such a disk can be read; the stored data, however, cannot be altered. When you want to write to it or delete some files there, just peel off the tab.

The disk hub (360KB disks have it, but not 1.2MB disks) is a reinforced ring, which a drive can grab to spin the disk inside the disk jacket. As the disk spins, the **index hole** regulates the timing for reading the data or writing to the disk in the **read-write opening**.

3.5-Inch Floppy Disks

The 3.5-inch drive was made popular by the Apple Macintosh. IBM made it the standard for its entire PS/1 and PS/2 lines, thus abandoning the 5.25-inch standard. Microsoft also made available DOS 3.2 to handle this new media. Depending on drives and disks, a 3.5-inch disk can be formatted to 720KB (double-density), 1.44MB (high-density), or 2.88MB (extrahigh-density) capacity. Some vendors refer to them as minidisks or microfloppies.

Figure 3.2

A 3.5-inch floppy disk (reverse side)

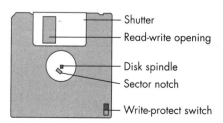

Many of today's PCs are also equipped with 3.5-inch drives. All the Tandy PCs today, for example, use only 3.5-inch drives. Most vendors, however, offer buyers a full spectrum of options. In some models, you can choose among four drives or some sort of combination; as of this writing, 2.88MB drives are not yet widely available.

A 3.5-inch disk's storage media (shown in Figure 3.2), just as floppy and fragile as that of a 5.25-inch disk, is housed in a rigid plastic case and thus much better protected. The **write-protect switch** can be pushed to the edge (showing a see-through hole) to prevent writing to the disk. This is comparable to breaking off an attached plastic piece on an audio cassette tape to prevent recording. When the hole is covered, data can be written to the disk.

The **read-write opening** is protected with a metal shutter. You can slide the shutter to expose it. When the disk is inserted in a drive, the shutter is automatically opened, thus exposing it for reading and writing.

The **disk spindle** serves the same purpose as the disk hub and the **sector notch** as the index hole of a 5.25-inch disk. They control the spinning and timing of reading and writing to the read-write opening.

Although 360KB and 1.2MB disks look alike, 720KB and 1.44MB disks differ in one important aspect. A 1.44MB disk has an extra square hole on the opposite end of the write-protect switch. Some people drill a hole on a 720KB disk so it can be used in a 1.44MB drive. It is not advisable.

CARING FOR A FLOPPY DISK

■ *A floppy disk must be treated with tender loving care.*

A floppy disk operates very much like a video or audio tape. The recording media is a piece of plastic coated with metal oxide. When recording, electric current is sent to magnetize some parts. The magnetized portions can then be read.

The media on which data is written is fragile and needs special protection. If you do not take good care of it, it could become useless and the data written on it could be lost forever. Consequently, you should take the following precautions:

- Do not touch the exposed parts. A 5.25-inch disk is not so well protected as a 3.5-inch disk. Its exposed parts require you to exercise extra care.

- Do not take a disk near high-power electric current or magnetic field. These forces can ruin your recorded data and damage your disk.

- Do not smoke near your computer. Cigarette smoke contains particles that can accumulate on a disk and cause harm.

- Do not expose a disk to dust. Put it in an envelope or enclosed storage box whenever you can.

- Do not expose a disk to extreme temperatures or strong light.

- Do not handle a disk roughly, such as bending, twisting, or putting strong pressure on it.

- Always back up (duplicate) your important files. A disk can go bad for no apparent reason. For this reason, DOS has provided various commands to back up files, including COPY, introduced in Chapter 2.

The metal oxide on a disk can lose its strength after a long period of heavy use. The disk may no longer record data reliably. It is then time to discard the disk.

A disk drive read/write head, like a tape recorder record/play head, can have an excessive accumulation of metal oxide particles, which could render the drive unreliable. There are commercial devices that can clean up the accumulation. If a drive is heavily used, you may need to give it a periodical cleanup.

If you want to protect the data on a disk, you should write-protect it (putting a tab on a 5.25-inch disk or sliding the write-protect switch to the edge on a 3.5-inch disk). This prevents data from being written to it and reduces the possibility of losing the data already there. PC users, veterans and novices alike, can make simple but disastrous mistakes. For example, you may intend to diskcopy from A to B, but end up instructing DOS to diskcopy from B to A. If disk A contains something you want to save, you may have a disaster on your hands. On such an occasion, write-protection will prevent the mistake (and could save you from a heart attack).

Most 5.25-inch disks are sold with write-protect tabs. If you do not have one handy and are not too sure what a particular command will do, use any kind of adhesive tape to cover the write-protect notch.

D R I L L

Select a disk capacity in the list to answer questions 1–4:

a. 360KB   b. 720KB   c. 1.2MB   d. 1.4MB.

_____   1. 3.5-inch double-density.

_____   2. 3.5-inch high-density.

_____   3. 5.25-inch double-density.

_____   4. 5.25-inch high-density.

____ 5. A 5.25-inch disk has better protection on the storage media than a 3.5-inch counterpart. True or false?

____ 6. When a disk is write-protected, a file stored there can still be deleted. True or false?

____ 7. A 5.25-inch disk is write-protected when the write-protect notch is covered. True or false?

____ 8. A 3.5-inch disk is write-protected when the write-protect switch is open (showing a see-through hole). True or false?

____ 9. To allow a drive to access the storage media of a 3.5-inch disk, you must manually open the read-write opening before inserting it in the drive. True or false?

____ 10. Users of a CD-ROM normally cannot alter the data stored on the disk. True or false?

ANALYSIS OF FLOPPY DISKS

■ *After formatting, a disk is divided into a number of tracks, each of which is in turn divided into a number of sectors. Each sector has 512-byte storage capacity.*

A floppy disk has two sides. Most vendors sell double-sided disks. That means both sides are certified as usable. Today some disks, though not many, are sold as single-sided at a lower price. That means that the manufacturer guarantees only one side. However, both sides are useful and are likely to perform equally well.

To understand how DOS organizes and utilizes a disk, you need to be familiar with these two terms: track and sector.

If the protective jacket is taken off, a floppy disk resembles a compact disk in size and shape. This round disk, after formatting (as explained below), is divided into concentric rings called **tracks**, as shown in Figure 3.3. The outermost ring is track 0, and the innermost track 39 on a 5.25-inch double-density disk. A high-density 5.25-inch disk has 80 tracks (0–79). A 3.5-inch disk also has 80 tracks.

Each track is divided into a number of **sectors**; each sector has a storage capacity of 512 bytes. A 5.25-inch double-density disk can be divided into 8 or 9 sectors per track by using switches available with the FORMAT command. A 5.25-inch high-density disk can have up to 15 sectors per track. A 3.5-inch disk

Figure 3.3

Dissection of a formatted disk

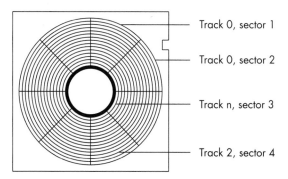

Track 0, sector 1

Track 0, sector 2

Track n, sector 3

Track 2, sector 4

can be double-density, high-density, or extrahigh-density and formatted respectively to 9, 18, or 36 sectors per track, as shown in Table 3.1.

A 5.25-inch, double-sided, double-density disk formatted to 9 sectors per track has 360KB capacity, which can be calculated with the following formula:

2 sides × 40 tracks × 9 sectors × 512 bytes = 368640

That number is the same as 360 multiplied by 1024, which is 1KB or 2 to the power of 10. (If you have trouble understanding these numbers, see Appendix G for an explanation.)

A double-sided disk drive has two read-write heads, which can handle both sides of a double-sided disk. When DOS writes to such a disk, the first free

Table 3.1

Floppy Disk Configurations

Size	Tracks per side	Sectors per track	Capacity
5.25"	40	8	320KB
5.25"	40	9	360KB
5.25"	80	15	1.2MB
3.5"	80	9	720KB
3.5"	80	18	1.44MB
3.5"	80	36	2.88MB

sector of the first track (track 0) of the first side (side 0) is filled; then the second sector, and so on. When the first track of side 0 is completely filled, DOS goes to the other side (side 1) and follows the same pattern. After that, the second track of side 0 is filled, and so on.

DISK INCOMPATIBILITY

■ *The 5.25-inch and 3.5-inch drives/disks are incompatible.*

■ *There is some degree of compatibility between 360KB and 1.2MB systems, and between 720KB and 1.44MB systems.*

Normally you need to match a floppy disk to the correct floppy drive. There are, however, some exceptions to this rule.

When you buy a floppy disk, you need to know what kind of drive you have. First, you need to know whether the drive is 3.5 inch or 5.25 inch. The two are totally incompatible. A 3.5-inch disk cannot be inserted into a 5.25-inch drive, and vice versa.

Second, you need to know whether your drive is double or high density. You need to buy disks matching the drive's capacity. These disks are specifically labeled as double density (360KB for 5.25 inch or 720KB for 3.5 inch) or high density (1.2MB for 5.25 inch or 1.44MB for 3.5 inch).

If you use a variety of floppy drives, double density at home and high density in the office for example, here are some more observations you need to keep in mind:

- A 1.2MB (or 1.44MB) drive can read and write to a 360KB (or 720KB) disk. A 360KB (or 720KB) drive, however, cannot read or write to a disk formatted to 1.2MB (or 1.44MB).

- A 1.2MB drive can format a double-density disk (360KB) to 360KB or 1.2MB capacity. In the latter case, not all the disk space is available for use. Depending on drives and disks, as much as half of the total 1.2MB capacity may be marked as "bad sectors" and thus unusable. The rest may not be too reliable.

- A 1.44MB drive can format a double-density disk to 720KB capacity. Some 1.44MB drives can format a double-density disk to 1.44MB capacity, but most cannot. The absence of an extra hole on a 720KB disk usually prevents its formatting to 1.44MB capacity.

- A 360KB disk formatted in a 360KB drive can be reliably read and written to by a 1.2MB drive.

Table 3.2

DOS Versions and Disk Capacities

DOS Version	Disk Capacity
2.0	360KB
3.0	1.2MB
3.2	720KB
3.3/4	1.44MB
5.0	2.88MB

- A double-density disk formatted to 360KB capacity in a 1.2MB drive may not be reliably read or written to by a 360KB drive. This problem is more evident in earlier drives; you are not likely to encounter any problem in later models. A 3.5-inch disk formatted to 720KB in a 1.44MB drive can be handled by a 720KB drive without any problem.

Finally, you need to be aware of the fact that not all DOS versions can handle recently available drives and disks. The earlier DOS versions were not designed for devices that did not then exist. DOS versions capable of handling a specific drive/disk are shown in Table 3.2.

If you use version 3.3 or later, you need not worry about DOS's capability. It can handle all the four types of drives/disks commonly in use today.[1] Only version 5 or later can handle 2.88MB drives and disks, but these are not yet commonly available.

D R I L L

____ 11. After formatting, a disk is divided into a number of concentric rings called _____.

____ 12. Each ring is divided into a number of subunits called _____.

____ 13. Each of the above units has a storage capacity of _____ bytes.

---

1. If you intend to buy a floppy drive to attach to your current system, you must know whether your BIOS and disk controller card can handle it. If you bought an AT-class PC in 1990, it can handle all four common types of drives. Earlier ATs and XT-class PCs may not be able to handle newer drives.

_____ 14. A double-density drive cannot format a high-density disk to its full capacity. True or false?

_____ 15. All the DOS versions since 3.0 can handle 3.5-inch drives and disks. True or false?

FORMATTING FLOPPY DISKS

■   *Use FORMAT to prepare a disk for use by DOS.*

■   *Specify the /S switch to create a boot (system) disk.*

■   *Use a variety of available switches if you want to format disks for use in incompatible drives.*

WARNING: Use the FORMAT command with great caution. Formatting a disk may destroy the existing data on that disk. If you reformat a disk inadvertently, use UNFORMAT to repair the damage before you do anything else.

Before a floppy disk can be used by DOS, it must be prepared with the FORMAT command. By formatting a disk, DOS divides it into tracks and sectors, as explained before. In addition, DOS also stores in certain sectors information used to manage the disk. This information enables DOS to find files to read and available space to store data. This section discusses how to format disks. Future sections will provide more detail as to what formatting does to disks.

Using No Switch

If you use FORMAT without specifying a switch, a disk is formatted to the default capacity of the drive. Consider the following:

    C>**format a:**

This command tells DOS to load FORMAT.COM from the current directory, which should be C:\DOS, and format the disk in drive A. Keep in mind that FORMAT is an external command, and, as explained in Chapter 2, you need to tell DOS where to access it, unless it is in the current drive.

Since no switch is specified, the above command will format the disk in drive A according to that drive's capacity. If it is a 5.25-inch double-density drive, the disk will be formatted to 360KB capacity. If it is a 5.25-inch high-density drive, you will get 1.2MB capacity, and so on.

If you have only one kind of floppy drive, you do not need to worry about FORMAT's complicated switches. By not using any switch, your disks will be formatted to their full capacity.

FORMAT'S Switches

The FORMAT command has these switches:

/1	1 side only
/4	Format 360KB disk in a 1.2MB drive
/8	8 sectors per track
/B	Blank space for later transfer of system files
/F:n	Disk capacity; n=160, 180, 320, 720, 1.2, 1.44, 2.88
/N:n	Number of sectors per track, used with /T
/Q	Quick formatting
/S	System files transferred
/T:n	Tracks per side, used with /N
/U	Unconditional formatting
/V:1	Volume label; if omitted, you'll be prompted

If you have different kinds of floppy drives, such as 1.2MB and 360KB, and need to use a disk in both drives, you may want to pay closer attention to these switches.

If you have a 1.2MB drive, you can format a double-density disk to 360KB capacity. Such a disk can be used by both 360KB drives and 1.2MB drives. To format a double-density disk to 360KB capacity in a 1.2MB drive, try this command:

```
C>format a: /4
```

The /F Switch

You can use the /F switch to specify any available capacity. If you use this switch, the other related switches are unnecessary. These are the available values you can specify with the /F switch:

160, 180, 320, 360, 720, 1.2 (or 1200), 1.44 (or 1440), 2.88 (or 2880)

These numbers are the capacities you want to format your disk to: 160KB (single sided, double density, 8 sectors), 180KB (single sided, double density, 9 sectors), 320KB (double sided, double density, 8 sectors), 360KB (double sided, double density, 9 sectors), 720KB (3.5 inch, double density), 1.2MB (5.25 inch, high density), 1.44MB (3.5 inch, high density), 2.88MB (3.5 inch, extrahigh density).

Thus, instead of using the /4 switch as shown in the preceding example, you could use this instead:

```
C>format a: /f:360
```

This will format a disk in a 1.2MB drive to the capacity of 360KB.

The /N and /T Switches

The /N and /T switches were intended in previous versions to accommodate 3.5-inch disks. Since the /F switch became available starting in version 4, they have become obsolete. To format a 720KB disk in a 1.44MB drive, you can use either command below:

```
C>format a: /f:720
C>format a: /n:9 /t:80
```

The second tells DOS to format by 9 sectors per track and 80 tracks each side. It is a more complicated way in the current version, but the only way in earlier versions.

The /S Switch

If you format with the /S switch, you ask DOS to transfer the system to the formatted disk. Three hidden files and COMMAND.COM will be transferred. This disk can then be used for booting DOS and may be called a boot disk or system disk. This switch can be used with any other except /B.

The /B Switch

The /B switch is to set aside blank space for later transfer of the system files. This reserves enough space in the beginning sectors for the system files. You can then use this disk to save the programs you have developed. The disk can then be marketed without copyright infringement. If a buyer uses the SYS command (explained in Chapter 7) to transfer the system files to this disk, it becomes bootable.

This switch is necessary only if you intend to transfer the system files of earlier versions to this disk. Those files must be located in the beginning and contiguous sectors for the disk to be bootable. Version 5 or later no longer requires the system files to be arranged that way. The new SYS command can make a disk bootable as long as there is enough disk space.

The /V Switch

The /V switch is for volume label. DOS will prompt you to enter a volume label after a disk is formatted—even though the /V switch is not specified. You can, however, use the /V switch to enter a volume label, like this:

```
C>format a: /v:practice
```

In this case, PRACTICE will be used as the volume label for the disk, and you will not be prompted to enter one.

WHAT IS ON A BOOT DISK?

When you specify the /S switch with FORMAT, DOS transfers the following four system files to the newly formatted disk:

IO.SYS

MSDOS.SYS   *Hidden files*

DBLSPACE.BIN

COMMAND.COM

The first three are hidden and the fourth is not. Some DOS commands, such as COPY and DEL, cannot "see" these hidden files. TYPE, CHKDSK, DISKCOPY, and SYS can recognize their existence. You can also use the /A switch with DIR to show hidden files.

Using the /S switch with FORMAT is not the only way to make a disk bootable. After you format a disk without using any switch, you can use SYS to transfer the hidden system files and COMMAND.COM to the new disk. This will make the disk bootable. See Chapter 7 for more details.

The /Q and /U switches

The /Q and /U switches are available since version 5. /Q does not scan bad sectors. Use it only on a disk that has been previously formatted. If /Q is not used, formatting involves rescanning every track and marking bad sectors and setting them aside so that they will not be used for storing data. /Q can speed up reformatting a used disk.

The /U switch does unconditional formatting. Existing data will be destroyed. You can no longer use UNFORMAT (see below) to recover the data. This switch should be used if you have a new disk or encountered read or write errors with a disk. If you use /Q to format a new disk, you will be prompted with Y/N to format the disk with the /U switch.

Undocumented Switches

Microsoft has been accused by some book authors of purposefully hiding some functions available in its operating systems, DOS and Windows. The purpose of this, according to the accusers, is to gain an advantage over competitors; Microsoft's own application programs such as Word and Excel can call these functions, but competitors, not knowing these hidden functions, have to write extra routines to do the same thing. In its defense, Microsoft claims that these functions are not publicized because they may not be reliable and that the company does not guarantee them.

Soon after the release of DOS 5, some users discovered the FORMAT command's two hidden switches which were not documented anywhere. These discoveries were widely publicized in PC magazines. With this much publicity, one would think that Microsoft would make these switches official and document them somewhere in DOS 6. However, Microsoft has chosen to remain silent and has said nothing so far.

The two undocumented switches are /AUTOTEST and /BACKUP. The first does not pause and displays nothing after formatting. The second will pause for a label entry unless it is supplied with the /V switch; it will also show the results. Neither can be used with the /Q switch; you will get the "Parameters are not compatible" error. If you need to format lots of disks and don't want to be bothered by numerous pauses, these two switches are most useful. As demonstrated in Chapter 11, you can use a batch file to automate the process and format many disks with minimal human intervention.

Formatting Steps

In the beginning of Chapter 2, you were given specific steps of formatting disks. These steps, with more details, are repeated here. Depending on your circumstances, you may or may not want to follow the following steps:

FOLLOW THESE STEPS

1. Go to the DOS directory in drive C where all external commands are stored:

   C>**cd \dos**

2. Format without transferring the system files:

   ```
   C>format a:
   Insert new diskette for drive A:
   and press ENTER when ready...
   ```

3. Press the Enter key to begin. If you format a previously formatted disk, the previous format information is saved; this does not happen if a new disk is being formatted. The screen shows the message below and begins to display a running number, showing the percentage of the disk formatted.

   ```
   Checking existing disk format.
   Saving UNFORMAT information.
   Verifying 360K
   ```

When done, this message appears and you are prompted to enter a volume label:

```
Format complete.
Volume label (11 characters, ENTER for none)? disk1
```

4. Enter a label (DISK1), and this message appears:

```
       362496 bytes total disk space
       362496 bytes available on disk
         1024 bytes in each allocation unit.
          354 allocation units available on disk.
   Volume Serial Number is 0C48-19D2
   Format another (Y/N)?
```

5. Enter Y to format another disk.

6. Insert a new disk in drive A and repeat steps 3 and 4.

7. At step 5, enter N to discontinue.

If you want to use FORMAT with a different switch, you must end it and then enter it with another switch.

8. Replace the disk in drive A and enter this command:

   C>**format a: /s**

9. Repeat steps 3 and 4. After step 4, enter N to end.

If you have followed the above steps, you will have formatted two disks without the system files and one with the system files for booting DOS. From now on you can use this boot disk to start DOS and the other two to store files. Whenever you need to format more disks, just follow the above steps with or without the /S switch.

If you are observant, you will have noticed that some numbers do not add up. For example, 360KB should be 368640 (360 × 1024) but a 360KB disk is formatted to only 362496 bytes, which is only 354KB (354 × 1024). Where are the missing 6KB? They are used by DOS to manage the disk, as explained in the next section.

Formatting to a Wrong Capacity

What happens if you format a double-density disk in a high-density drive without specifying any capacity-size switch? With a 5.25-inch disk, formatting will proceed and a big part of the 1.2MB capacity will be identified as unusable; the rest is usable but may not be reliable. The screen display below shows the result:

```
C>format a:
Insert new diskette for drive A:
and press ENTER when ready...

Checking existing disk format.
Existing format differs from that specified.
This disk cannot be unformatted.
```

```
Proceed with Format (Y/N)?y
Formatting 1.2M
Format complete.

Volume label (11 characters, ENTER for none)?

    1213952 bytes total disk space
     430080 bytes in bad sectors
     783872 bytes available on disk

        512 bytes in each allocation unit.
       1531 allocation units available on disk.

Volume Serial Number is 222D-15F4

Format another (Y/N)?n
```

The read-write head of a 1.2MB drive is smaller than that of a 360KB drive. It has difficulty formatting the wider tracks of a lower-density disk. To ensure the longevity of the drive, it is not advisable to do the type of formatting shown above. However, in case of emergency, such as when you need more than 360KB capacity, the above approach is one way out; just don't do it on a regular basis.

You cannot format a 3.5-inch, double-density (720KB) disk to 1.44MB capacity. DOS simply will not let you do that. If you format a 720KB disk in a 1.44MB drive without specifying a capacity-size switch, this message is displayed:

```
Invalid media or Track 0 bad - disk unusable
Format terminated
Format another (Y/N)?
```

WHAT FORMATTING DOES

Formatting a disk does more than what the numbers displayed in the preceding section tell you. Consider these acts DOS performs in doing a simple formatting:

- Saves any previous FAT and root directory for recovery (using UNFORMAT) of any data stored on the disk. See more details at the end of this chapter.

- Scans every track to detect bad sectors, which are marked as unavailable for storing data.

- Divides a disk into tracks and sectors depending on drive/disk capacity and FORMAT switch(es) specified.

- Makes the first sector the boot record.

Figure 3.4

Items created by formatting

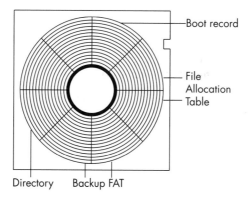

- Allocates the next few sectors for a file allocation table (FAT).
- Allocates the next few sectors for a duplicate FAT.
- Allocates a number of sectors for a directory.

The first three acts were explained in the preceding sections. The others are explained in this section.

Boot Record

The **boot record** contains information about the disk—type, size, capacity, cluster number, etc. The information enables DOS to handle each disk correctly during reading and writing. In addition, there is a short program in charge of loading DOS into memory. If it can find the system files on the same disk to load, control is passed to them. If not, this error message stored in the boot record is displayed:

```
Non-System disk or disk error
Replace and strike any key when ready
```

File Allocation Table

The **FAT** (file allocation table) is a crucial part of a disk. As the name implies, this is a table used for allocating disk space to store files and for accessing the stored files. DOS uses it to keep track of used, unused, and damaged (unusable) clusters (see below). When you read or write to a disk, DOS depends on the information stored in the FAT to carry out your command. Without this table, DOS would not know where to find a file to read or available space to write to.

Since the FAT is so important, DOS creates a backup FAT in the formatting process and keeps it up to date as files are saved or deleted. Should the original be corrupted, the backup is used.

The number of sectors set aside for each table varies with disk capacity: 2 for 360KB, 3 for 720KB, 7 for 1.2MB, 9 for 1.44MB, and 18 for 2.88MB. The larger a disk's capacity, the more space is needed to manage it.

Directory

After the boot record and two FATs, DOS creates a directory structure to manage file entries. The number of sectors used depends on the type of disk, as shown in Table 3.3.

DOS requires 32 bytes for managing each file stored on disk. Information related to file name, date-time, file size, and file attribute(s) is stored there.

Using the 32-byte number and Table 3.3, we can calculate how many files can be stored in the root directory of a disk. Below is the formula for a double-sided, double-density disk:

7 sectors × 512 bytes per sector / 32 bytes = 112 entries

That means you cannot store more than 112 files (including subdirectories and the volume label, if any) in the root directory of such a 360KB disk. This limit, however, does not apply to the number of files stored in a subdirectory. Directories and subdirectories will be explained in Chapter 5.

Cluster

When formatting is completed, DOS displays something called "allocation unit," as shown below for a 360KB disk:

```
1024 bytes in each allocation unit
354 allocation units available on disk
```

Table 3.3

Root Directory Sizes and File Limits

Disk Type	Sectors	File Entries
Single-sided	4	64
Double-sided	7	112
High-density	14	224
Hard disk	32	512

This allocation unit is commonly referred to as a **cluster.** A cluster is the smallest space DOS can work with. A file, even as short as one byte, takes up a cluster of disk space.

How much disk space is a cluster? It varies. On a 1.2MB disk, a cluster is 512 bytes, or 1 sector. On a 360KB disk, it is 1KB, or 2 sectors. On a hard disk, it may be 4, 8, 16, or more sectors; a 2GB disk has 64 sectors, or 32 KB, per cluster.

Every time you create a file or directory, a cluster is allocated. On a 360KB disk, for example, a 1-byte file takes up 1024 bytes of space. If the file is at least 1 byte longer than a cluster, the next entire cluster is also allocated. This mechanism is efficient in managing large files but very wasteful of disk space when short files are involved.

BOOTING AND MANAGING DATA

Now that you are familiar with some basic terms related to disks, they should help you understand how DOS works. Here we cover the processes how DOS gets started and how it stores data. While you do not need to know these inner workings of DOS to make it work for you, a little knowledge may help you solve some problems later.

Booting Procedure

When you turn on power supply, the BIOS in your PC is activated. The program stored on a ROM chip checks your PC hardware to make sure it is in order. Then the boot record on the boot disk starts the process of booting. This process involves loading IO.SYS, DBLSPACE.BIN, MSDOS.SYS, and COMMAND.COM to memory.

IO.SYS interfaces with the BIOS routine and augments its functions of managing hardware devices. If the boot disk's CONFIG.SYS file contains installable device drivers such as ANSI.SYS, they will also be loaded to memory so that DOS can handle more devices.

DBLSPACE.BIN is new with version 6. It resides in memory to compress and decompress data when you save a file to or retrieve it from a compressed disk. It has no effect when an uncompressed disk is encountered. See Chapter 7 for more details.

MSDOS.SYS serves as the DOS kernel, providing interface between the BIOS functions and application programs. It manages files, allocates memory, and performs other system tasks.

COMMAND.COM serves as the command processor (or interpreter). It interfaces with you the user and the lower-level functions. When you enter a command, this program determines whether it can be handled. If so, lower-level functions are called to complete a job. If not, it shows you an error message.

Data Management

When you ask DOS to save a file, it saves to the directory the name you have supplied, plus information related to date-time, file attributes, the beginning cluster's number (location), and the file size. Then it relies on the FAT to allocate unused clusters to store data.

Most of a disk consists of sequentially numbered clusters; what happens to each cluster is recorded in the corresponding FAT entry. The FAT has 12-bit or 16-bit entries, depending on disk size, to keep track of each corresponding cluster. The FAT entry for cluster 10, for example, may be a 0, which means that the space is available. It may contain a special number marking the cluster as defective (unusable) or another number to mark it as the end of a file. It may also store the number (location) of another cluster to link the current cluster to the next cluster.

If one cluster is not enough to store a file, DOS checks the FAT to find another unused cluster. The two clusters may not be next to each other because the adjacent cluster may already be used. How can DOS know that the two clusters store the related data? Each previous cluster's corresponding FAT entry stores the number (location) of the next related cluster. This mechanism allows various noncontiguous clusters to be used to store the same file. The clusters are now chained together.

When you tell DOS to read a file, such as using TYPE or COPY, it goes to the directory to find the matching file and the beginning cluster number to locate the first cluster. Since the first cluster's corresponding FAT entry has a pointer pointing to the next cluster, DOS then uses this pointer number to find the related data. This continues until the cluster's corresponding FAT entry has a number that signifies the end of the file.

When you use DEL to delete a file, DOS enters a number in the directory to replace the first character of the file name and writes 0 in the FAT entries corresponding to the clusters storing the data. The clusters are now available for reuse. The original file, however, remains—except the first character in the file name. If the clusters are not reused, UNDELETE can restore most of the original data.

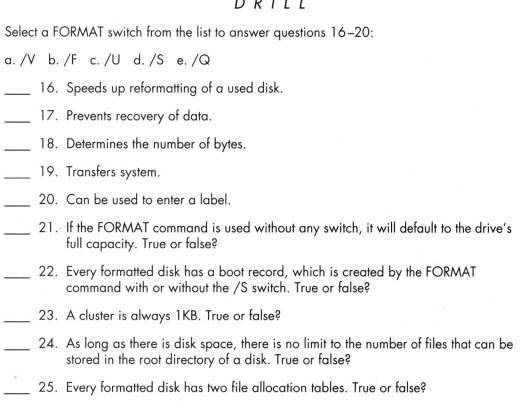

D R I L L

Select a FORMAT switch from the list to answer questions 16–20:

a. /V b. /F c. /U d. /S e. /Q

____ 16. Speeds up reformatting of a used disk.

____ 17. Prevents recovery of data.

____ 18. Determines the number of bytes.

____ 19. Transfers system.

____ 20. Can be used to enter a label.

____ 21. If the FORMAT command is used without any switch, it will default to the drive's full capacity. True or false?

____ 22. Every formatted disk has a boot record, which is created by the FORMAT command with or without the /S switch. True or false?

____ 23. A cluster is always 1KB. True or false?

____ 24. As long as there is disk space, there is no limit to the number of files that can be stored in the root directory of a disk. True or false?

____ 25. Every formatted disk has two file allocation tables. True or false?

VOLUME LABEL

■ *Use VOL to display a disk's volume label.*

■ *Use LABEL to display as well as change a disk's volume label.*

A **volume label** is a name you assign to a disk. It can be up to 11 characters long. Since you cannot easily see what data is stored on a disk, you should give it a meaningful name for easier identification.

If you have entered a volume label during the formatting process, you can use the VOL (Volume) command to display it and the LABEL command to display and, if necessary, change it.

The VOL command is internal. That means it can be used no matter what the current drive is. To display the volume label of the disk in the current drive, simply enter this command:

```
A>vol
  Volume in drive A is DISK1
  Volume Serial Number is 0C48-19D2
```

The volume label that you have previously entered is displayed in uppercase. If you used version 4 or later to format this disk, a serial number is also shown.

To display the volume label of another drive, specify the target drive after the command:

```
A>vol c:
```

If you want to give a disk a volume label or change an existing one, you can use the LABEL command. This is an external command and you must tell DOS where to access it. Make the C:\DOS directory current and follow these steps:

FOLLOW THESE STEPS

1. Show the volume label of the disk in drive A:

```
C>label a:
Volume in drive A is DISK1
Volume Serial Number is 0C48-19D2
Volume label (11 characters, ENTER for none)?_
```

The previously entered volume label is displayed, plus a serial number. You are now prompted for a response. If you enter a new name after the question mark, it will become this disk's volume label and replace the existing one, if any.

2. Press Enter:

```
Delete current volume label (Y/N)?_
```

Since your disk has a volume label, if you just press Enter, you are prompted with Y or N to delete it.

3. Enter N:

```
Delete current volume label (Y/N)?n
```

If you respond with N, the original volume label is kept and the DOS prompt is displayed.

4. Change the volume label in drive A:

```
C>label a:disk2
```

This is a shortcut to changing a disk's volume label. The original DISK1 name is changed to DISK2.

5. Display drive A's volume label:

```
C>vol a:
Volume in drive A is DISK2
Volume Serial Number is 0C48-19D2
```

The volume label is changed, but the serial number, if any, remains the same.

6. Restore the original name:

```
C>label a:disk1
```

7. Verify the change:

```
C>vol a:
```

P R A C T I C E   3 - 1

☐   1. With A as the current drive, use VOL to show the volume label of the disk in drive A.

☐   2. With A as the current drive, use VOL to show the volume label of the disk in drive B.

☐   3. Use LABEL to give a disk in drive A a volume label if it doesn't have one. If the disk already has a volume label, use LABEL to display it without change.

☐   4. With A as the current drive, print the volume label of drive C.

CHECKING A DISK

■ *Use CHKDSK with a drive as a parameter to check the disk's usage.*

■ *Use CHKDSK with a file name as a parameter to check the contiguity or fragmentation of the file's storage.*

The external CHKDSK (Check Disk) command is very important in managing both hard and floppy disks. It can display the following information:

- Volume label, if any, and date of creation
- Serial number for a disk formatted with version 4 or later
- Number of files, both hidden and not hidden
- Number of bad sectors, if any
- Lost clusters, if any, due to a corrupted FAT
- Amount (in bytes) of available disk space

- Size (in bytes) of each cluster (allocation unit)
- Number of clusters, total and available
- RAM, total and available
- File names and directories
- Contiguity or fragmentation of files

The CHKDSK command can be used in a variety of ways. You can:

- Check an entire disk
- Check a single file
- Check all the matching files
- Specify either /F or /V switch

Checking an Entire Disk

Now insert in drive A a disk to be checked, and enter this command:

```
C>chkdsk a:

Volume DOS6SYS     created 06-13-1993 9:29p
Volume Serial Number is 3D4F-1CE4

    362496 bytes total disk space
    132096 bytes in 3 hidden files
     53248 bytes in 1 user files
    177152 bytes available on disk

      1024 bytes in each allocation unit
       354 total allocation units on disk
       173 available allocation units on disk

    655360 total bytes memory
    578208 bytes free
```

There are four sections in this display. The first shows volume label and serial number. If you have not entered a volume label, neither it nor the creation date will be available. If a disk is formatted by version 3.3 or earlier, the serial number is not available.

The creation date is determined by the latest time you entered the volume label. If you use the LABEL command to change it, the creation date will be based on that. If you use LABEL to delete a volume label, neither the label nor the creation date is available.

The second section contains a series of numbers related to the disk. The first is the total disk capacity. The second and third show, respectively, the number of hidden and unhidden files.

The number for available disk space is probably the most important. It tells you how many bytes of disk space are left. If there is little or no space left, it is time to use another disk or delete some files.

The third section shows cluster (allocation unit) information. As explained earlier, a cluster can be one, two, or more sectors depending on what kind of drive/disk is involved.

Finally, the last group of numbers show total installed RAM (or the amount DOS can use) and the amount still available. If your PC has more than 640KB ($640 \times 1024 = 655360$), only 640KB is shown. As more programs are loaded and remain in memory, the amount of free bytes decreases. Before you load another program, you may need to see whether there is enough memory for it.

Checking Matching Files

Instead of checking an entire disk, you can check a single file or all the files matching a certain pattern. To check a single file, enter this:

```
C>chkdsk filename
```

This command checks a file named FILENAME in the current directory. All the numbers as displayed earlier are shown, plus this:

```
All specified file(s) are contiguous
```

This message tells you that all the contents of the file are connected and not scattered in various unconnected clusters of the disk.

If you want to check a series of files matching a pattern, try a command like this:

```
C>chkdsk file?
```

If there are files that are not contiguous, they are displayed as shown below.

Checking Disk Fragmentation

As DOS stores data to a disk, it writes to the first available space. If an adjacent area is used by another file, an expanded file is scattered in various unconnected clusters. If you work with several files and keep expanding them, they will all be divided. To find out whether all the files are contiguous or not, try this command:

```
C>chkdsk a:*.*

Volume DOSBOOK      created 11-11-1991 7:05p
 . . .

A:\DIR.05 Contains 3 non-contiguous blocks
A:\TOUR.02 Contains 4 non-contiguous blocks
A:\DISK.03 Contains 5 non-contiguous blocks
```

All the files that are non-contiguous are shown. The contiguous ones are not displayed.

The *.* notation means all the files in the specified drive. You can use the wild card characters of * and ? to find matching files. These characters will be explained in Chapter 4 (see p. 122).

The /F and /V Switches

CHKDSK has two switches, as shown below:

/F   Fix files; repair damaged files

/V   Verbose; show files and paths

The /F switch is used to fix allocation errors. Sometimes clusters of data are lost because of a corrupted FAT. The data stay on the disk, but DOS can no longer reach them. When you use CHKDSK without /F, this message may appear:

```
Errors found, F parameter not specified
Corrections will not be written to disk

    1 lost allocation units found in 1 chains.
       2048 bytes disk space would be freed
```

When this happens, you can use a command like the one below to repair the FAT and recover the lost data:

```
C>chkdsk a: /f
```

CHKDSK will prompt you for a response, like this:

```
    1 lost allocation units found in 1 chains.
Convert lost chains to files (Y/N)?y
```

If you enter Y, DOS will correct errors in the FAT and gather the lost data and save them with the name of FILEnnnn.CHK, with nnnn as four-digit sequential numbers of 0000, 0001, 0002, etc.

When you see these files, you can use the TYPE command to look into their contents. There may be ASCII characters as well as garbage. You can retrieve them into your application program and perhaps salvage them.

The /V switch displays a verbose (detailed) version, including file names and what directories they are stored in, as shown below:

```
C>chkdsk a: /v

Volume DOSBOOK     created 11-11-1991 7:05p
Directory A:\
        A:\DIR.05
        A:\TOUR.02
        A:\DISK.03

        .   .   .

  362496 bytes total disk space
  265216 bytes in 8 user files
   97280 bytes available on disk

    1024 bytes in each allocation unit
     354 total allocation units on disk
      95 available allocation units on disk

  655360 total bytes memory
  515648 bytes free
```

SETTING UP A HARD DISK

■ *Set up a hard disk by partitioning it with FDISK and formatting (using FORMAT) it with the /S switch.*

This section explains hard disks. It should not concern you unless you have your own hard disk and want to prepare it for data storage.

WARNING: Do not use either FDISK or FORMAT unless you intend to set up a hard disk. Either command, once implemented, could destroy any existing data stored on a hard disk.

There are few occasions when you need to set up a hard disk so it can store data. If you use a PC in a lab, the installed hard disk, if any, is already set up and there is no need for you to worry how it works. If you buy a hard disk from a local vendor, the vendor will set up it and get it ready for your use.

There are two occasions when you need to set up a hard disk: when you buy a hard disk in a mail order and when your hard disk is completely messed up. On such occasions, knowing how to set up a hard disk may enable you to use your PC again. This section tells you how to set it up, and Chapter 5 explains how to use directories to make efficient use of it.

Inside a hard disk drive, there may be a number of disks called platters. A **platter** is the equivalent of a floppy disk, but more rigid. Both sides of a platter are also coated with metal oxide like a floppy. By stacking up more platters together, a hard disk can increase its capacity.

DOS manages a hard disk similar to the way it does a floppy disk. Each side of a platter is divided into a number of tracks called **cylinders** and cylinders are divided into sectors. Typically, a 40MB disk has three platters. Each platter has two sides. Each side has 820 cylinders. Each cylinder has 17 sectors. Each sector, as you already know, has 512 bytes. By multiplying these numbers, you get the total of slightly more than 40MB:

$$3 \times 2 \times 820 \times 17 \times 512 = 42823680$$

Like a floppy disk, a hard disk needs to be formatted before DOS can use it. Before formatting it, however, you need to create one or more units called **partitions**. These two acts require two DOS commands, FDISK (Fixed Disk) and FORMAT.

When you want to partition a hard disk, insert in drive A a disk containing the FDISK.EXE program and enter this command:

>   A>**fdisk**

After the program is loaded, a message like this appears:

```
             MS-DOS Version 6.00
           Fixed Disk Setup Program
      (C)Copyright Microsoft Corp. 1983 - 1993
                 FDISK Options

Current fixed disk drive: 1

Choose one of the following:

1. Create DOS partition or Logical DOS Drive
2. Set active partition
3. Delete partition or Logical DOS Drive
4. Display partition information

Enter choice: [1]

Press Esc to exit FDISK
```

If you have another hard disk installed, a fifth option will appear to let you select another hard disk to partition.

If you wish to terminate, just press Esc, and the DOS prompt will reappear.

To see how your hard disk has been partitioned, press 4 and Enter. A display like this may appear:

Display Partition Information

```
Current fixed disk drive: 1

Partition Status    Type   Volume Label  Mbytes  System   Usage
 C: 1          A     PRI DOS  MS-DOS_5        40  FAT16      98%

Total disk space is   41 Mbytes (1 Mbyte = 1048576 bytes)

Press Esc to return to FDISK Options
```

The above display shows that a 41MB hard disk has been partitioned into one drive as the primary DOS partition and designated as the active partition. That means DOS can be booted from this drive if you turn on power while leaving drive A empty or its door open.

When you use FDISK, you are prompted with a series of menus, each of which has a default selection. The first menu, for example, has 1 as the default option. If you want to choose the default option at each step, just press Enter.

If you choose all the default options, DOS will create one drive out of your hard disk. The size of this drive is based on the hard disk's capacity.

If you want to partition your disk into several drives, you can give a megabyte or percentage number for each drive.

After FDISK runs its course and completes creating disk partition(s), you need to format the newly partitioned disk so DOS can use it. If you want to boot from the hard disk, you need to specify the /S switch to transfer system files. With a disk containing FORMAT.COM in drive A, enter this command:

```
A>format c: /s
```

Before formatting starts, this warning message appears first:

```
WARNING, ALL DATA ON NON-REMOVABLE DISK
DRIVE C: WILL BE LOST!
Proceed with Format (Y/N)?n
```

If you enter Y, formatting proceeds as when a floppy disk is involved.

If you purchase a hard disk, it is likely to be low-level formatted and ready for you to run FDISK and FORMAT. If not, you need to use the included program to low-level format it first and then run FDISK and FORMAT.

UNFORMATTING DISKS

Starting with version 5, formatting a used disk involves saving the directory information before the reformatting. The saved information can then be used by the UNFORMAT command to restore the contents before the reformatting. This allows you to recover data from an inadvertent formatting.

WARNING: UNFORMAT should be used to unformat an inadvertently reformatted disk as soon as possible. If you save files to the reformatted disk, the original data may not be completely recovered.

Depending on which target drive you want to recover, enter a command like the following to unformat a disk:

```
C>unformat a:
C>unformat c:
```

The first command results in a display shown below:

```
C>unformat a:
Insert disk to rebuild in drive A:
and press ENTER when ready.

Restores the system area of your disk by using the image file created
by the MIRROR command.

    WARNING !!        WARNING !!

This command should be used only to recover from the inadvertent use of
the FORMAT command or the RECOVER command.  Any other use of the UNFORMAT
command may cause you to lose data!  Files modified since the MIRROR image
file was created may be lost.

Searching disk for MIRROR image.

The last time the MIRROR or FORMAT command was used was at 09:44 on 06-12-93.

The MIRROR image file has been validated.

Are you sure you want to update the system area of your drive A (Y/N)?
```

Choose Y if you want to proceed, or N if you want to abort.

UNFORMAT has these switches:

/J	Test to see whether a disk can be recovered with a mirror file
/L	List existing files and directories
/P	Print output
/PARTN	Use PARTNSAV.FIL to restore corrupted partitions; list partition tables when combined with /L
/U	Unformat without using a mirror file
/TEST	Test to see whether disk can be recovered without using a mirror file

Mirror files and PARTNSAV.FIL are created by the MIRROR command available in version 5. This command is no longer available and some of its functions are merged into UNDELETE. UNFORMAT in version 6 can still use the earlier files, if they exist, to recover from formatting.

═══ *TIPS AND TRICKS* ═══

U N C O N V E N T I O N A L   S Y N T A X

The UNFORMAT and UNDELETE commands come from another company called
Central Point. They do not always conform to DOS conventions. With a typical DOS
command, you can put a switch anywhere after the command name. In these two
commands, however, you must put a target drive/directory parameter (if any) right
after the command name and any switch after that. If you put a switch before the
drive parameter, something may go wrong. Consider the following examples:

```
C:\DOS>unformat /test a:
Invalid or unspecified drive.
```

```
C:\DOS>undelete /list a:
Directory: C:\DOS
File Specifications: *.*
Invalid parameter specifications.
```

In both cases, the drive you specify after a switch is ignored. If you place a drive
specification right after a command name, these commands will execute your order
without any problem. Thus, the correct syntax should be:

```
C:\DOS>unformat a: /test
C:\DOS>undelete a: /list
```

If you have used the /U switch with FORMAT, UNFORMAT is not likely to fully
restore the reformatted disk.

P R A C T I C E   3 - 2

1. With A as the current drive, check the disk in drive A without showing files.

2. Repeat the above, but showing all the files stored on that disk.

3. With C as the current drive, check the contiguity of all the files in drive A, showing
   only fragmented files' names.

4. With C as the current drive, check the disk in drive A without specifying a switch
   and redirect the output to the printer.

5. Insert a practice disk in drive A and quick-format it.

6. Unformat the reformatted disk in drive A.

D R I L L

____ 26. LABEL can change a volume label, but VOL cannot. True or false?

____ 27. CHKDSK shows available RAM as well as disk space. True or false?

____ 28. This command will?

　　　　　C>chkdsk a:*.* /v
- a.　show all the files
- b.　show only fragmented files
- c.　show no file names
- d.　cause an error message

____ 29. If you use CHKDSK without any switch, DOS will actually fix a corrupted file and store recovered pieces in files named FILEnnnn.CHK. True or false?

____ 30. Before a hard disk can be formatted, it must be partitioned with FDISK (or a comparable program). True or false?

S U M M A R Y   A N D   R E V I E W

Check each item as you review and understand the following highlights of the chapter.

☐　1. The most commonly used storage media are the 3.5-inch and 5.25-inch floppy disks. While differing in size, they share common arrangements: write-protect notch (switch), indexing device, read-write opening, and protective cover.

☐　2. A floppy disk contains a fragile (floppy) piece of plastic coated with metal oxide. It should be treated with great care and protected from many harmful elements. If not, it may not reliably store data or stored data may be lost.

☐　3. DOS uses the FORMAT command to prepare a disk for use. Formatting divides a disk into a number of concentric rings called tracks, each of which is divided into a number of subunits called sectors, each of which has 512-byte storage capacity.

☐　4. The FORMAT command has many available switches. The most important is the /S switch. It transfers four system files (three hidden files plus COMMAND.COM) to the disk being formatted. This will make the new disk bootable, which means that you can start DOS with this disk.

☐   5. If no FORMAT switch is used, a disk is formatted to its full capacity. Thus, a 1.2MB drive formats a 5.25-inch high-density disk to 1.2MB capacity. If you need to format a disk to a different capacity, specify a capacity number after /F:.

☐   6. As more types of disks become available, compatibility has become a serious problem. For example, 3.5-inch and 5.25-inch drives/disks are never compatible. A high-density drive (1.2MB or 1.44MB) can read and write to a double-density disk (360KB or 720KB); the reverse is not true.

☐   7. You may use different drives in different places, 360KB at home and 1.2MB in the office, for example. If you want a disk to be usable in both drives, you need to format it to the lower capacity of the two.

☐   8. Besides tracks and sectors, formatting also creates a boot record, two FATs, and a directory. This overhead reduces each disk's capacity for storing data.

☐   9. When DOS stores data on a disk, it takes up at least one cluster for a file. A cluster may be 1 or more sectors, depending on what type of disk. Thus, a 1-byte file could eat up disk space of at least 512 bytes.

☐   10. The internal VOL command can be used to display a disk's volume label, which can be created when FORMAT is used with the /V switch.

☐   11. The external LABEL command can be used to show, create, change, and delete a volume label.

☐   12. Use the external command CHKDSK to show a variety of useful information, including RAM and disk space. Use the /F switch to fix corrupted files and the /V switch to display file names.

☐   13. A hard disk needs to be partitioned with FDISK and then formatted with the /S switch to be bootable. A large-capacity hard disk can be divided into a number of drives; one of them can be made bootable and the rest used for data storage.

☐   14. Use UNFORMAT to recover data from an inadvertently reformatted disk. If a mirror file exists, recovery may be more thorough; if not, UNFORMAT will try to recover the disk using the information saved during the most recent formatting.

R E V I E W   Q U E S T I O N S

Write an answer for each question below.

1. Explain CD-ROM and DAT.

2. Compare and contrast the different types of floppy disks in use today.

3. Explain the compatibility problems of 360KB and 1.2MB drives and disks (720KB and 1.44MB if you use 3.5-inch floppy disks).

4. Explain the different external parts of a floppy disk.

5. How does FORMAT divide a disk?

6. What items are created by FORMAT to manage a disk?

7. What is a cluster? What is its significance?

8. Explain the purposes of the /S and /Q switches of FORMAT.

9. What does FORMAT's /F switch do?

10. Explain the purposes of VOL and LABEL.

11. What items are displayed on the screen by using CHKDSK without any switch?

12. What do CHKDSK's /F and /V switches do?

13. How can you find out whether the files on a disk are contiguous or fragmented?

14. What does the UNFORMAT command do?

15. How is a hard disk organized?

4 Creating and Naming Files

C O M M A N D S   C O V E R E D

COPY (COPY CON), DIR, TYPE, DEL, REN, DOSKEY

N E W   T E R M S   A N D   S Y M B O L S

DOS device name, reserved word, CON, AUX, COM1, PRN, NUL, LPT1, wild card characters, ?, *, DOS editing keys, template, batch file, replaceable parameter (dummy variable), %, AUTOEXEC.BAT, $, macro, ¶, metastrings

QUICK START

To create a file:

    `A>copy con filename`

To append from the keyboard to an existing file:

    `A>copy filename + con`

To avoid illegal characters in file names

    See the list on page 120.

For a list of DOS device names:

    See Table 4.1

To use wild card characters of ? and *:

    See the Wild Card Characters section

To copy matching files:

    `A>copy file? b:`

To delete all the files:

    `A>del *.*`

To rename matching files:

    `A>ren file?.txt *.doc`

To use DOS editing keys:

    See Table 4.2.

To install DOSKEY with insert mode as the default:

    `C>doskey /insert`

To recycle a previously entered command:

    See Table 4.3.

To edit the command line after DOSKEY is installed:

    See Table 4.4.

To enter multiple commands in a single line after DOSKEY is installed:

    `C>command1 ¶ command2 ¶ command3...`

To create a macro:

>C>doskey macro=command1 $t command2 $t command3...

To use some special characters (metastrings) in a macro:

>See Table 4.5.

To customize a DOS command (to substitute a macro for a DOS command):

>C>doskey dir=dir /o /p
>C>doskey format=c:\dos\format a: /q

So far you have learned to use various DOS commands such as COPY, DIR, and TYPE to handle existing files. From now on, you will learn how to create your own files. Then you will use that knowledge to create batch files that DOS can execute. If you use batch files often, you can save a great deal of time and vastly increase your productivity.

While creating files, you need to observe DOS file name conventions and avoid illegal names. This chapter teaches you which file names to use and which to avoid.

While creating files, you can take advantage of DOS editing keys to avoid repetitive typing and thus simplify your work. After studying this chapter, you will know how to recycle previously entered commands.

When you handle existing files, you can utilize wild card characters (also known as global file name characters) to speed up access to the files that match certain specifications. In this chapter you will learn how and where to use these characters.

Version 5 introduced a new command called DOSKEY. It allows you to reuse and edit many previously entered commands. This arrangement can speed up entering some of the repetitive commands. You can also use DOSKEY to create macros that resemble batch files. DOSKEY is covered at the end of the chapter.

CREATING FILES WITH COPY CON

■   *Use COPY CON to create a file.*

■   *End file creation by entering the ^Z character.*

To create a short file, you can use the COPY command, combined with CON and a file name. When you are done, DOS will copy from what you have entered from the keyboard (and displayed on the screen) to the named file on disk. Follow these steps to create a file:

FOLLOW THESE STEPS

1. Place a practice disk in drive A and enter the following:

   A>**copy con chap1.txt**

2. Type the following lines and press Enter at the end of each:

   This is line one.
   This is line two.

3. Press Ctrl-Z, or F6, to display the ^Z character.

The ^Z (ASCII 26) character, which is treated by DOS as a single character, is the end-of-file marker. When DOS encounters this character, it considers a text file to have ended.

4. Press Enter to save the file.

After the above steps, the screen appears as follows:

   A>**copy con chap1.txt**
   This is line one.
   This is line two.
   ^Z
       1 File(s) copied

DOS tells you that one file has been copied. It means that the keystrokes entered from the keyboard and displayed on the screen have been copied to the disk file named CHAP1.TXT.

TIPS AND TRICKS

FILE CREATION AND EXISTING FILES

When creating a file, beware of potential conflict with an existing file or directory.

If you use the name of a file already in existence in the current directory, the new file will replace the old. You will not be warned that an existing file is to be replaced. If you are not careful, you could inadvertently wipe out an important file.

If you use the name of a subdirectory of the current directory, you will not succeed in creating a file. Suppose you have created a directory named CHAP1.TXT as a subdirectory of the root directory. If you are in the root directory and try to use COPY CON to create a file named CHAP1.TXT, DOS will redisplay your typed lines on the screen and tell you that one file has been copied. It is copied to the screen, not to disk. The existence of an identical directory name will prevent DOS from creating a file of the same name. Directories are explained in the next chapter.

5. Display the file's contents:

```
A>type chap1.txt
```

The two lines in the file should be displayed on the screen.

APPENDING TO A FILE

■ *Append lines to an existing file by using the command*
COPY FILENAME + CON.

Sometimes you want to append (add) lines to an existing file. You could use COPY CON to create a file with the same name and retype everything, plus the new lines. Or you could just add the new lines to those already in existence. To do the latter, simply follow these steps:

```
A>copy chap1.txt + con
CHAP1.TXT               (added by DOS)
CON                     (added by DOS)
This is line three.     (typed by you)
^Z
        1 File(s) copied
```

T I P S   A N D   T R I C K S

T H E   S Y N T A X   O F   C O P Y   C O N

You may be puzzled by this syntax of COPY CON:

```
A>copy con filename
```

This syntax does not seem so perplexing if you remember this syntax of COPY:

```
A>copy source target
```

When DOS encounters a command like this:

```
A>copy con filename
```

it interprets your intent as copying from CON to FILENAME. Here CON is the console (keyboard and monitor combined). What comes out of the console is copied to disk; a disk file is thus created.

Conversely, you can copy from a disk file to the console, such as:

```
A>copy filename con
```

This will display the named file on the screen. Its use will be more fully explained in Chapter 6.

The COPY CHAP1.TXT + CON (space before and after the + is optional) command tells DOS to add from the keyboard (console) to the named file already in existence. Upon pressing Enter, DOS responds by displaying the first two lines in uppercase, telling you that the second (CON) will be appended to the first (CHAP1.TXT).

If the file does not already exist, the file name is not displayed and only CON is shown. Whatever you type, after you enter ^Z, DOS will display the text on the screen but not send it to the nonexistent file. Here is an example:

```
A>copy chap2.txt + con
CON                        (added by DOS)
This line is not saved.    (typed by you)
^Z
This line is not saved.    (displayed by DOS)
        1 File(s) copied
```

If you reverse CON and the name of an existing file, the file contents will be added to the screen, as illustrated below:

```
A>copy con + chap1.txt
CON                         (added by DOS)
This line won't be saved.   (typed by you)
^Z                          (lines below displayed by DOS)
This line won't be saved.
CHAP1.TXT
This is line one.
This is line two.
This is line three.
        1 File(s) copied
```

Here DOS interprets the command as adding to the screen the contents of the existing file. It displays CON, but not the file name, at the beginning. After you type lines and enter ^Z, the new lines are repeated, plus those from the named file.

Using COPY CON to create or append to a file is, as shown above, very simple. However, you cannot edit a file with it. After Enter is pressed, a line is no longer available for modification. If a file is more than a few lines long or needs frequent changes, a better tool is EDLIN or EDIT. EDIT will be covered in Chapter 10 and EDLIN in Appendix H.

P R A C T I C E   4 - 1

☐   1. Use COPY CON to create a file named QUOTE containing this line:

      Live simply so others may simply live.

☐   2. Add this line to QUOTE:

       Learn to read so you may read to learn.

☐   3. Rename QUOTE as QUOTES.

☐   4. Display the contents of QUOTES on the screen.

DOS FILE NAME CONVENTIONS

■ *Certain characters are not allowed as part of a file name.*

■ *A DOS device name cannot be used as a file name.*

You have been asked to enter file names on many occasions. Mostly, however, you have been asked to enter the names of existing files. That posed no problem; all you needed to do was to enter the exact names. In this chapter, you are asked to enter new file names. It poses a new problem for you because you cannot just use any names. Before we proceed further, you need to know what file names are permitted.

DOS imposes a few major constraints on a file name:

- It can be no more than eight characters long, plus a maximum of three characters placed after a period for an optional extension.

- Every file name in the same directory must be unique, i.e., different from another.

- Certain characters are not permitted.

- DOS device names cannot be used as file names.

Maximum Length

A file name can be no longer than eight characters, plus an optional extension of no more than three characters; the name and the extension are separated by a period. While a file name can be as short as a single character, it cannot be longer than this maximum:

```
FILENAME.EXT
```

If you enter more than eight characters without inserting a period, those beyond the eighth character are ignored and discarded. If you have more than three characters after the period, only three are retained.

Illegal Characters

In creating a file, you cannot use as part of a file name any of the characters listed below:

(space)   ?   *   "   /   \   [   ]   : | <   >   +   =   ;   ,

These characters are used by DOS for various purposes. Most of them are shown and briefly explained in Appendix E (see the SYMBOLS item). They will be more fully discussed in later chapters.

Also excluded are the ASCII characters below 32, in addition to 127.[1] These characters, obtained by holding down Ctrl and pressing a letter key (or holding down Alt and typing a number on the numeric keypad), are used to control computer hardware and communications. See Chapters 11 and 12 for examples of their uses.

If you use any character in either of the above categories, you will get the "Invalid number of parameters" or "File creation error" message.

DOS Device Names

DOS device names are **reserved words** which have special meanings to DOS and should not be used as your file names. These are shown in Table 4.1.

If you use any of these as a file name, DOS will interpret your intent as using one of these devices, not creating a file.

Unlike the special characters, a device name can be part of a file name. For example, while CON alone cannot be a file name, it can be combined with other

---

Table 4.1

DOS Device Names

Device Name	Purpose
CON	Console (keyboard and screen)
AUX	Auxiliary device (serial port)
COM1/2/3/4	Communications (serial) ports
PRN	Printer (parallel port)
LPT1/2/3	Line printers (parallel ports)
NUL	Nonexistent (dummy) device

---

1. Entering ASCII 127 has the same effect as pressing the Backspace key.

legal characters to form a legal name. Thus, CONSOLE, AUXCON, and so on are perfectly legal names.

Extensions to Avoid

While it is possible to use file name extensions of COM and EXE, it is not advisable. These are used in executable files created by compilers or assemblers. A file created with COPY CON cannot be executable just because you add such an extension. Besides, you could unwittingly replace a program that comes with DOS. Most damaging of all, if you try to run such a file (one created with COPY CON carrying the COM or EXE extension), it will most likely lock up your computer, requiring rebooting.

If you use programs that follow special extensions in naming the files they create, such as BAS for BASIC, WK1 for Lotus 1-2-3, and DBF for dBASE, you should also avoid using these extensions in the files you create. These files carry special formatting codes recognizable by the programs that create them.

T I P S   A N D   T R I C K S

A B L A N K   I N   A   F I L E   N A M E

You cannot use a space (pressing the space bar, or ASCII 32) in a file name. You can, however, use the blank character of ASCII 255. Either character shows nothing on the screen, but DOS treats them differently. You can, for example, create a file like this:

```
A>copy con no way
There is no way a novice can peek into this file.
^Z
```

After typing NO, hold down Alt and type 255 on the numeric keypad. Then type WAY and press Enter. If you just press the space bar where the gap is shown, you will get this error message instead:

```
A>copy con no way
Too many parameters
```

When you want to use DEL, DIR, REN, COPY, TYPE, and other commands on this file, you need to supply ASCII 255 where the gap is.[2]

---

2. If your keyboard does nothing after you press Alt-255, you need to take an extra step. Use KEYB.COM to tell DOS what type of keyboard you are using, like this:

```
C:\DOS>keyb us
```

Use the /E switch if you are using an enhanced keyboard, like this:

```
C:\DOS>keyb us /e
```

D R I L L

____ 1. If there is an existing file named FILENAME located in the current directory and you enter the following command, DOS will NOT create a new file. True or false?

   A>copy con filename

____ 2. This command will create a file named CON. True or false?

   A>copy con con

____ 3. Which file name below is illegal?

   a. A–B
   b. A_B
   c. A+B
   d. A^B

____ 4. Which file name below is legal?

   a. US..$$$
   b. BR/#
   c. FRANK.|||
   d. JAN(!).YEN

WILD CARD CHARACTERS

■ *Use ? to match one single character in a particular position of a file name.*

■ *Use * to match all the characters from a particular position.*

The **wild card characters**, ? (question mark) and * (asterisk), can be used on existing file names to speed up your work. The ? is used to represent any single character, the * applies to multiple characters. They are useful because DOS will automatically find matching files when you want to do something about them. This will save you the trouble of repeatedly typing specific file names that are similar.

The ? Character

Follow these steps to demonstrate the use of the ? wild card character:

1. Create a new file:

   ```
   A>copy con chap2.txt
   This is from chapter 2.
   ^Z
   ```

2. Show matching files:

   ```
   A>dir chap?.txt
   . . .
   CHAP1     TXT
   CHAP2     TXT
   . . .
   ```

If you have not erased the file previously created, two files should show up.

When DOS encounters a ? character, it will substitute any character found in a specific position. For example, if you enter this command:

```
A>dir chap?.txt
```

DOS will display the following files, if they exist:

```
CHAP.TXT
CHAP1.TXT
CHAP2.TXT
CHAPA.TXT
CHAPB.TXT
 . . .
```

In short, any file name with the pattern of CHAP, followed by zero or one character, followed by the TXT extension, will be considered matching.

If you want to copy all the related files, you can simplify typing by entering a simplified command like this:

```
A>copy chap?.txt b:
```

This will copy all the matching files shown above from drive A to drive B. This will save you the trouble of copying each file separately.

If you have a file named CHAP12.TXT, what can you do? The single ? will not match more than one character. You can, however, use the character twice or more:

```
A>copy chap??.txt b:
```

This command will copy the following:

```
CHAP.TXT
CHAP1.TXT
CHAP12.TXT
```

In short, any file matching the fixed characters, plus zero or up to two of the missing characters, will be acted on. If there are three characters missing, such as CHAP123.TXT, the file will not be identified.

When a ? character is not placed at the end of a file name or extension, every character and position must match. Suppose you have these files:

```
CHAPTXT
CHAP1TXT
CHAP2TXT
```

The command below will list the last two, but not the first:

```
A>dir chap?txt
```

The * Character

If you use the * character, it will match anything missing. For example, if you enter this command:

```
A>dir chap*.*
```

DOS will display these files, if they exist:

```
CHAP
CHAP1.TXT
CHAP123.ABC
CHAP1234.ANY
```

In other words, any file starting with CHAP, plus zero or up to four more characters, plus zero or up to three extension characters, will all be considered matching.

When DIR is used, DOS will loosely match many files. If you omit the extension, DOS will assume that you want to include it. This command:

```
A>dir chap*
```

will do the same things as the one in the preceding example; it is treated the same as CHAP*.*.

On the other hand, if you put a period at the end, like below:

```
A>dir chap*.
```

you ask DOS to show only those matching files without extensions. Those with extensions will not be considered matching. If you enter a command like this:

```
A>dir *.
```

DOS will display all the files without extensions. However, this command:

```
A>dir .*
```

will display everything, just like DIR *.*, or simply DIR alone. The DIR command's default setting is global, meaning everything included.

The above examples will not necessarily apply to the DEL (or ERASE), REN, or COPY commands. These will require an exact match before an action is taken. For example, this command:

A>**copy chap* b:**

will copy only CHAP, CHAP1, CHAPXXXX, and so on, i.e., any file starting with CHAP, plus zero or up to four more characters. However, it will not copy any file with an extension, such as CHAP1.TXT. In short, it is treated the same as with a period added at the end. Thus the following will copy and rename only the matching files without extensions:

A>**copy chap* work***

If you want DOS to act on all the existing files in a directory, use the global specifier of *.* with a specific command (except DIR as explained earlier), such as:

A>**copy *.* b:**

This command will copy everything from drive A to drive B.

Wild card characters can be applied to REN as well. You can thus quickly rename a lot of files this way:

A>**ren chap*.txt *.doc**

All the matching files with the TXT extension will keep their original names but with the new DOC extension. Using * in the target can also save typing time when working on a single file, such as:

A>**ren longname.txt *.bak**

This can save the trouble of retyping a long file name. The above is thus a shortcut of below:

A>**ren longname.txt longname.bak**

The Danger of Using ? and * with DEL

Using a wild card character, particularly *, with DEL or ERASE is dangerous and you should use it with great caution. Consider the following:

A>**del chap***

It will delete as many files as it copies, as shown above. There are, however, two important reasons for you to be careful. First, it does not warn you that multiple files will be erased. Second, unintended files could be erased. Before you enter such a sweeping command with potentially disastrous consequences, you should make sure that you know what you are doing.

The only time DOS gives you a warning is when you want to delete everything in a directory, such as:

```
A>del *.*
All files in directory will be deleted!
Are you sure (Y/N)?_
```

This command generates the warning message and seeks confirmation from you. If you enter Y, everything in the current directory of the current drive will be erased.

An identical warning and (Y/N) prompt will also appear when you want to delete the contents of an entire subdirectory, such as:

```
A>del misc
```

If MISC is a file name in the current directory, no warning is given. If it is a subdirectory name, however, DOS interprets your order to mean to erase all the files in that subdirectory. If you Enter Y, every file there will be erased.

Realizing the potential danger of combining DEL with a wild card, Microsoft added the /P (Prompt) switch to version 4 and later. You should take advantage of it, such as:

```
A>del chap* /p
```

TIPS AND TRICKS

A PERIOD AS THE CURRENT DIRECTORY

In Chapter 5 you will learn that a period (.) alone as a parameter is interpreted by DOS as the current directory. You can use it to replace *.* where it is appropriate, such as:

```
A>copy . b:
A>del .
A>echo y ¦ del .
```

The space before the period is optional; DOS can recognize your intention even without this space.

The first command will copy every file in the current directory in drive A to the current directory in drive B.

The second command will delete everything; you will be prompted with Y/N. The third will automatically supply the Y without waiting for your response. Do NOT use this destructive command unless you know what you are doing. If you want to experiment with it, create a separate directory and some nonsense files. The ECHO command will be discussed in Chapters 8, 11, and 12.

When a matching file is found and targeted for deletion, its name and path will be shown and you will be asked to enter Y or N. Only if you enter Y will DOS delete a displayed file.

If you have inadvertently deleted files, use UNDELETE to undelete them before doing anything else. Use the same wild card characters that you have used with DEL.

TYPE and Wild Cards

You cannot use a wild card when a command can act on only one file at a time. For example, if you try this:

```
A>type chap?.txt
Invalid filename or file not found
```

DOS will refuse to oblige, and give you an error message instead. You cannot use TYPE to display the contents of more than one file at a time.

One way to bypass this limitation is to use this command instead:

```
A>copy chap?.txt con
```

This will display the contents of all the matching files one after another.

Another way is to use TYPE with the FOR...IN...DO command. This command will be covered in Chapters 8 and 11.

PRACTICE 4-2

☐ 1. Create a file named QUOTA and put this line in it:
Those who do not learn from history are doomed to repeat it.

☐ 2. Use ? character(s) with DIR to show both QUOTES and QUOTA.

☐ 3. Use DEL and * to delete both files.

☐ 4. Use UNDELETE and * to undelete both deleted files.

DRILL

____ 5. This command will delete all of the following, except:
```
A>del day??.*
```
a. DAY
b. DAYON.TRA
c. DAYNA.PAY
d. DAYSON.WK1

____ 6. This command will show all but:

    A>dir file*.

    a. FILE123

    b. FILE12.3

    c. FILE1234

    d. FILES123

____ 7. When you enter the DEL *.* command, DOS will ask you to enter Y/N before deleting everything in the current directory. True or false?

____ 8. This command will:

    A>del .

    a. delete all the files in drive A's current directory

    b. give a warning and a Y/N prompt

    c. both a and b

    d. cause an error message due to an illegal command

____ 9. This command will copy

    B>copy . a:

    a. all the files from drive B to drive A

    b. some files from B to A

    c. all the files from A to B

    d. nowhere to nowhere; it's illegal

____ 10. The DIR command alone works the same way as DIR *.*. True or false?

____ 11. This command will match a file named CHAP22.TXT. True or false?

    A>dir chap*.

____ 12. This command is legal. True or false?

    A>type *.*

DOS EDITING KEYS

■ *Use the first five function keys (F1-F5), plus the Esc, Ins, Del, and Backspace keys to save time when entering DOS commands.*

When you enter a DOS command or use COPY CON to create a file, you can take advantage of the **DOS editing keys** to simplify your work. Skillful and selective use of these keys can save you time in typing DOS commands.

The Template and Editing Keys

When you type a command and press Enter, this command is saved in a memory buffer called the **template**. When you enter a new command, it replaces the old one in the template. What is stored in the template can be copied to the screen in order to avoid repetitive typing.

Suppose you have most recently entered the following:

```
A>type chap1.txt
```

Now you want to redo the same thing. You can retype the whole line and press Enter to display the text. Or you can just press F3. The whole line reappears on the command line. If you then press Enter, you can quickly reissue that command.

Table 4.2 summarizes what you can do with these editing keys. It shows that with F3 you can copy from the template and display on the screen everything from the cursor position to the end of the template. If the cursor is at the beginning of the command line when F3 is pressed, the entire previous line is copied. If not, the portion before it is skipped.

Table 4.2

DOS Editing Keys

Key	Function
F1 (or →)	Copy one character from template to screen
F2c	Copy all characters before first typed c
F3	Copy all characters from cursor to end of line
F4c	Skip characters before first typed c (Then use F1 or F3 to copy the rest)
F5	Store the current line in the template
F6	Insert ^Z character
Esc	Abandon edited line; start anew
Ins	Insert mode on/off
Del	Skip over a character in template
Backspace (or ←)	Delete to left a displayed character

(c denotes a character)

Think of the template as an exact copy of the line you have most recently entered. If you want to recycle this line, you can use the keys in Table 4.2 to do it. In addition to using F1–F4 keys to copy the whole or portions of that line to the screen, you can insert extras at proper places after pressing the Ins key once, or skip over certain characters in the template by pressing Del an appropriate number of times. The Ins and Del keys are trickier than the rest because you do not immediately see what is done to the template.

Steps of Using Editing Keys

To practice using the DOS editing keys, let us follow these steps:

FOLLOW THESE STEPS

1. Put a practice disk in drive A and create a file by entering the following:

```
A>copy con chap1.txt
This is line one.
This is line two.
^Z
```

2. Display the contents of the file:

```
A>type chap1.txt
```

3. Type DIR and press F3:

```
A>dire chap1.txt
```

Notice that "dir" has replaced "typ", but the "e" still remains. Pressing F3 at this point copies from the template to the screen the remainder of the line, i.e., from the fourth character to the end. If you press Enter at this point, DOS will give you an error message because DIRE is not a legal command.

4. Press Esc to abandon the line:

```
A>dire chap1.txt\
```

—

A backslash appears at the end of the line and the cursor moves to the beginning of the next line. (Another alternative is to press Backspace repeatedly to erase everything and then start anew from the beginning of the same line.) You can now start anew. Any time you want to abandon an edited line, just press Esc. Nothing is changed, and the abandoned line does not replace the one still in the template.

5. Type DIR, press Del once, press F3, and press Enter:

```
A>dire chap1.txt\
  dir chap1.txt
```

By pressing Del after typing DIR, one character in the template is skipped over and the cursor is positioned at the next character; you do not see the result right away, but DOS is keeping track. Pressing F3 at this point copies only the remaining characters, those from the cursor position to the end of the line.

6. Type TYPE and press F3 (do not press Enter):

    A>**type**chap1.txt

If you press Enter now, you will get an error message. You need to insert a space between the command and the file name for DOS to recognize your intention.

7. Press Esc to abandon the edited line:

    A>typechap1.txt\

8. Press F1 until TYPE appears, press Ins once, press the space bar once, press F3, and press Enter:

    A>typechap1.txt\
      type chap1.txt

Press Ins once to turn on insert mode, another time to turn it off. When insert mode is on, characters you type are inserted at the cursor location, and the rest are pushed rightward. If insert mode is not on, characters you type replace existing ones.

You cannot tell from the screen or the keyboard whether insert mode is on or off. You basically have to feel it in the dark. Pressing Enter or another editing key returns you to the default off mode. To turn on again, press Ins once again.

9. Press F4, press the space bar once, press Ins once, type DIR, press F3 and Enter:

    A>**dir** chap1.txt

By pressing F4 followed by the space bar, the characters before the first space are skipped over. Pressing F3 after that will copy only the characters located from it to the end of the line. By pressing Ins once and typing DIR before pressing F3, you insert DIR and copy the original characters not skipped over.

10. Press F2, type c, type *, press Del four times, press F3 and Enter:

    A>dir *.txt

By pressing F2 followed by c, all the characters before the first c (lowercase) are displayed on the screen. Pressing Del each time skips over one character in the template. The screen does not show the skipping until you press F3 to copy the unskipped portion.

11. Type *.TXT and press F5:

```
A>*.txt@
```
    —

After pressing F5, the @ sign appears to mark the end of the line, and the cursor moves down to the beginning of the next line. DOS does not execute this line; it puts the line in the template instead, replacing the previously entered line.

12. Press Ins once, type DIR, press the space bar once, and press F3:

```
A>*.txt@
  dir *.txt
```

The "*.txt" string previously stored in the template is now copied to the screen after you press F3.

Using Editing Keys with COPY CON

DOS editing keys can be used with COPY CON to duplicate the whole or portions of a previous line. Let us use the file you created in step 1 to demonstrate how this can be done. First, enter the following:

```
A>copy con chap1.txt
This is line one.
```
    —

After you press Enter and the cursor moves down to the next line, the previous line is put in the template. If you want to duplicate part of this line in the new line, you can use a proper editing key to avoid retyping the whole line.

One way to do this is to press F3 to copy the previous line, then press Backspace or ← four times to erase "one.", then type "two." and press Enter.

Another way is to press F2, then press o (lowercase) to copy everything before this character, then type "two." and press Enter.

Instead of saving this file by entering ^Z, let's break it. Hold down Ctrl, press C, and release both. The ^C character (treated by DOS as a single character) appears at the end:

```
A>copy con chap1.txt
This is line one.
This is line two.
^C

A>_
```

Your effort to copy from the keyboard to a file on disk is terminated. No file is created. If there is an existing file with the same name, it remains unaltered.

Ctrl-C is often used to terminate a DOS function or a computer program in progress; you can also use it to terminate a batch file or program being executed. If it does not work, try the Ctrl-Break combination. Some programs intentionally disable either combination to prevent premature termination; they will usually provide other ways for an orderly exit.

A Mnemonic System

The function keys used for editing seem quite confusing. After using them for a long time, I have developed a mnemonic system to associate each key with a specific function:

F1   One at a time

F2   To (Two)—up to—a typed character

F3   Three's a crowd, whole bunch

F4   From (same 1st letter as Four) a typed character

F5   File (rhymes with Five) to template

This system may help you remember what to do. If not, you may have a better idea of your own.

P R A C T I C E   4 - 3

☐   1. Use COPY CON to enter this line:
       You can't be all things to all people.

☐   2. Use F2, DEL and F3 to add a second line:
       You can be all things to all people.

☐   3. Use F4, Ins and F3 to add a third line:
       Be all things to all people.

☐   4. Abort (cancel) the file creation.

D R I L L

Find an answer in the list below to match questions 13–17:

a. F1   b. F2   c. F3   d. F4   e. F5.

_____ 13. Copy all remaining characters from the template.

_____ 14. Store a line in the template without execution.

_____ 15. Copy before the first typed character.

____   16. Skip before the first typed character.

____   17. Copy one character.

CREATING AND USING BATCH FILES

■   *Put a series of DOS commands in a batch file. Run the batch file to execute the commands.*

■   *Use replaceable parameters to make a batch file more versatile.*

■   *Create an AUTOEXEC.BAT file and store it on the boot disk. The commands in this file are automatically executed after DOS is booted from this disk.*

Now that you have learned to create files, you can use the knowledge to create batch files. A **batch file** (or batch program) contains a batch (bunch) of commands which DOS will execute one after another. It is a very useful tool that can save you time and labor as you work with your computer.

Batch File Requirements

A batch file has to meet certain conditions. It must

- contain only ASCII text

- include commands DOS understands

- have a BAT extension in its file name

First, it must be ASCII text which DOS can read. What you create with COPY CON, EDLIN, or the DOS Editor is ASCII text. A file you create with your word processor may not be pure ASCII text. In that case, DOS may not recognize or follow your commands.

Second, a batch file must contain commands DOS understands. If not, error messages may be generated or intended tasks may not be performed. The DOS commands we have covered so far can all be entered into a batch file.

Third, a batch file must have the file name extension of BAT. If this extension is missing, DOS will not execute the commands in it. Do not use EXE or COM as an extension for a DOS batch file. If you try to execute such a file, you will most likely lock up your computer.

In naming a batch file, you should avoid the name of an internal or external DOS command. This can avoid confusion between DOS commands and your batch files. We will return to this topic after you know how to create and use batch files.

Batch File Examples

Let us follow these steps to create a batch file:

1. Put a practice disk in drive A and enter the following:

   A>**copy con da.bat**

This command tells DOS to create a file named DA.BAT. The file name is arbitrary, but the BAT extension is mandatory.

2. Type this command and press Enter:

   dir a: /o /p

This command is to instruct DOS to list the files in drive A one screen at a time, sorted by file name in alphabetic order.

3. Press F6 (or Ctrl-Z) and Enter to save the file. The screen now shows the following:

   ```
   A>copy con da.bat
   dir a: /o /p
   ^Z
            1 File(s) copied
   ```

4. Enter the following command to display the contents of the newly created file:

   A>**type da.bat**

5. Use the new batch file by entering this:

   A>**da**

After step 5, the directory information of drive A should be displayed on the screen. With the existence of this batch file, you can just enter DA (instead of DIR A: /O /P) to show what is in drive A.

Suppose you now repeat the above steps to create two more batch files with the names and contents shown below:

```
DB.BAT    DIR B: /O /P
DC.BAT    DIR C: /O /P
```

From now on, any time you want to know what is in a particular drive, just enter DA, DB, or DC.

Replaceable Parameters (Advanced Optional Topic)

The above arrangement requires you to maintain three separate files. Couldn't we combine them into one? Yes. To do that you need to know the concept of **replaceable parameter** (also known as **dummy variable**), which is designated as % followed by a number (0–9), such as %1, %2, and so on. A replaceable parameter is a place holder, marking a place inside a batch file for a corresponding parameter from the command line. If a parameter is entered on the command line, it replaces the corresponding replaceable parameter (now you know why this clumsy name). If no corresponding parameter is entered, the replaceable parameter is treated as nonexistent and completely ignored.

Let us illustrate this novel idea with some concrete examples. Follow these keystrokes to create a batch file:

```
A>copy con d.bat
dir %1: /o /p
^Z
```

This file differs from the others by one character. Instead of a drive letter, you find the % sign followed by 1 (parameter number 1, corresponding to the first parameter from the command line).

When you use this batch file, you need to enter the name of the file, plus the expected parameter, a drive letter to replace %1. For example, if you want to show drive C's current directory, all you need to do is to enter the following:

```
A>d  c
```

The D is for D.BAT (you can enter the entire file name if you so wish), and C is for drive C. This tells DOS to run the D.BAT batch file and put C in place of %1. DOS will treat the single command in the batch file as:

```
dir c: /o /p
```

If you want to show another directory, just enter a different parameter. Instead of C, you can enter A, B, or any other drive you may have.

The batch file name (D) and the parameter (C) must be separated. If you put them together, as in DC, DOS will execute DC.BAT instead. If the file does not exist, an error message will follow.

If no parameter follows the batch file name, DOS will fail to carry out your wish. Without a parameter, the command inside the batch file becomes:

```
dir : /o /p
```

In this case, DOS is asked to list a file named ":". Nothing will be listed because the colon character cannot be used as a file name.

If the D.BAT file is in drive A and the current drive is changed to another one such as B, you need to provide a path so that DOS knows where to find the batch file to execute, such as:

```
B>a:d  b
```

This command tells DOS to go to drive A to run D.BAT and to display the files in drive B.

One variation of this batch file is to take out the colon and keep the rest, like this:

```
A>copy con d.bat
dir %1 /o /p
^Z
```

In this case, if you specify no parameter when running the batch file, DOS will use the current drive as the target instead of giving you an error message. On the other hand, if you want to target a different drive, you must include a colon like this:

```
A>d b:
```

Without the colon, DOS will interpret your command as showing a file named B.

AUTOEXEC Batch File (Advanced Optional Topic)

An **AUTOEXEC.BAT** file is an automatic executable batch file. Every time DOS is booted, it looks for such a file and executes it if it exists.[3] Such a file allows you to instruct DOS to automatically execute many commands without any human intervention. A lot of time can be saved and a lot of work can be done automatically if you can use this device skillfully.

An AUTOEXEC.BAT file must meet certain conditions before DOS will execute it automatically:

- The name must be exact. Thus you can have only one such file on a boot disk.

- The file must be stored in the root directory of the boot disk, together with the COMMAND.COM file.

- The file must contain commands DOS can execute.

Creating an AUTOEXEC.BAT file follows the same steps as in the creation of any other file. Let us now create such a file with the following commands:

```
A>copy con autoexec.bat
date
time
path=c:\dos;a:\bat
^Z
```

---

3. You can also run such a batch file by entering the name on the command line.

An AUTOEXEC.BAT file will be created and stored on the disk in drive A.

When this file is executed, DOS will first show this:

```
A>date
Current date is Sun  6-24-1993
Enter new date (mm-dd-yy): _
```

This is the familiar scene explained in Chapter 1. If the date is correct, you can just press Enter. If not, enter a new date. Then the next command is executed:

```
A>time
Current time is 10:15:31.58
Enter new time: _
```

Give it the same treatment as the date item.

If the DATE and TIME commands are not present in an AUTOEXEC.BAT file, DOS will not pause to let you enter new information. Instead, the computer's internal time is used. If your computer has a battery-powered clock, you should take out both DATE and TIME commands. If not, they are necessary for you to enter accurate numbers.

The PATH=C:\DOS;A:\BAT command is executed after DATE and TIME commands are taken care of. It tells DOS to look in the C:\DOS and A:\BAT directories for executable files entered on the command line. This is a good arrangement if all the external DOS commands are stored in C:\DOS and your batch files in A:\BAT. With this arrangement, you can execute a batch file or external DOS command from any drive or directory; DOS will go to the specified paths to find and execute them. PATH and directories will be explained fully in Chapter 5.

If you have a hard disk and work with several software packages, you can take advantage of an AUTOEXEC.BAT file to speed up your access to a particular program. One way to handle this situation is to create a number of batch files with similar names, such as AUTOEXEC.WP for WordPerfect, AUTOEXEC.123 for Lotus 1-2-3, and so on. These files are not executable because of the absence of a BAT extension. However, when the time comes for you to work continuously with a package, all you need to do is to change the extension to BAT.

To create a batch file for WordPerfect, enter the following:

```
C>copy con autoexec.wp
cd\wp51
wp
cd\
^Z
```

The batch file for Lotus 1-2-3 may look like this:

```
C>copy con autoexec.123
cd\123r24
123
cd\
^Z
```

When the time comes to work with WordPerfect, just use the REN command to change AUTOEXEC.WP to AUTOEXEC.BAT. That way, every time the computer is turned on, the current directory will be changed and WordPerfect will be loaded. When you exit WordPerfect, the current directory will be changed to the root directory again.

The CD command is to change the current directory. Like PATH, it will be explained in the next chapter.

This arrangement is suitable if you work with an application continuously over a period of time. If you alternate among different packages, each for a short period of time, the following arrangement may be better:

```
C>copy con w.bat
cd\wp51
wp
cd\
^Z

C>copy con l.bat
cd\123r24
123
cd\
^Z
```

This way, after DOS is booted, you can just enter L to run Lotus 1-2-3, or W to start WordPerfect.

If you have quite a few packages you use alternatively, you may consider building a menu batch file to show you available options and let you press a single key to start a program. This device will be explored after you learn more batch commands in Chapter 11.

There are many uses for batch files. This chapter has given you just a hint of what is to come. Where appropriate, future chapters will exploit batch files to save you time and increase your productivity.

Batch files can be structured like computer programs. You can use certain commands to control program flow. These commands are explained in Chapter 11. They will be used to write more sophisticated batch files in Chapters 11 and 12.

Speedy Creation of Batch Files

If you create batch files often, you may want to employ a batch file to speed up your work. This batch file will do the trick:

```
A>copy con b.bat
copy con %1.bat
^Z
```

From now on, every time you want to create a batch file, just enter B, followed by a file name, minus the BAT extension. Suppose you want to create an AUTOEXEC.BAT file. You can just enter the following:

```
A>b autoexec
```

The screen will be ready for your work by showing the following:

```
A>b autoexec
copy con autoexec.bat

_
```

After you enter appropriate commands and end with ^Z, a batch file will be created. This saves you the trouble of typing a long command at the beginning.

If you forget to enter a file name, the screen will show this instead:

```
A>b
copy con .bat

_
```

Since you do not have a legal file name, you should not continue. Press Ctrl-C. You will be asked whether you want to terminate the batch job. Enter Y and rerun the B.BAT file to start anew.

If you want to automatically execute a batch file right after you finish creating it, this arrangement will do the trick:

```
A>copy con b.bat
copy con %1.bat
%1
^Z
```

Suppose you want to test a batch file again and again. You can simply run the batch file this way:

```
A>b test
copy con test.bat   (entered by the batch file)

. . .               (commands entered by you)

^Z                  (entered by you)
test                (entered by the batch file)
```

The first line is automatically displayed, and you can start entering your batch lines. After you enter ^Z at the end, the last line automatically executes the batch file (TEST.BAT) that has just been created and saved.

DOS COMMANDS AND BATCH FILES

■ *It is not advisable to use an internal or external DOS command's name as a batch file name. You have to go through extra trouble to use such a batch file.*

Earlier you were warned to avoid using a DOS command as the name of a batch file. It is possible but troublesome to access such a file. Suppose you create this file:

```
A>copy con dir.bat
dir b: /o /p
^Z
```

This will result in DIR.BAT being saved to drive A. If you issue DIR now, the internal command will be executed, preventing you from reaching the batch file saved on disk. You may consider using your batch file this way:

```
A>dir.bat
```

No use. DOS will interpret your command to mean this:

```
A>dir *.bat
```

The only way you can use this batch file is by adding a drive/directory prefix, like this:

```
A>a:dir
```

This forces DOS to go to drive A to execute an external command or batch file.

An external command's name can be used as a batch file name. However, you need careful planning to avoid confusion. For example, if you have CHKDSK.EXE and CHKDSK.BAT stored on the same disk (in the same directory), the former takes precedence. If you issue this command:

```
C>chkdsk
```

DOS will first try to execute CHKDSK.COM. If CHKDSK.COM is not available, CHKDSK.EXE is next. Only then will CHKDSK.BAT take its turn.

If a batch file and a matching external DOS command are not stored in the same directory, the batch file can be executed without any problem. Suppose you store all your external DOS commands in the DOS directory in drive C and nowhere else, you can create a batch file and save it to drive A, like this:

```
A>copy con chkdsk.bat
c:\dos\chkdsk %1
^Z
```

With A as the current drive, you can run the batch file without a parameter, like this:

```
A>chkdsk
```

This command will execute CHKDSK.BAT from drive A. The batch file will then go to the DOS directory in drive C to run the CHKDSK.EXE program and check the disk in drive A. Since no parameter is specified, the %1 is ignored and the current drive (A) is the target. If CHKDSK.BAT does not exist in drive A and the PATH=C:\DOS command has previously been entered, the above command will lead DOS to execute CHKDSK.EXE in the C:\DOS directory and check the disk in the current drive.

You can run the batch file with various parameters, like the following:

```
A>chkdsk /v
A>chkdsk filename
A>chkdsk b:*.*
```

The first will check the disk and list all the files in drive A. The second will check the contiguity of FILENAME in drive A. And the third will check the contiguity of all the files in drive B. These parameters were explained in Chapter 3 (page 101).

Note: Although it is not advisable, it is possible to store in the same directory a batch file and an external DOS command, both having the same name. When you want to execute the batch file, enter the full name, including BAT. Without the extension, DOS will give priority to a file with a COM or EXE extension.

DOSKEY, MACROS, AND BATCH FILES

■ *Install DOSKEY so that you can recycle previously entered commands.*
  Install it with the /INSERT switch if you prefer insert mode to be the default.

■ *Recycle a previous command by pressing F8, F9, ↑, or ↓. Use F7 or DOSKEY*
  /H to display all the commands in the buffer. Use →, ←, Ctrl-→, Ctrl-←,
  Home, End, Ctrl-Home, and Ctrl-End to edit the command line text.

■ *Use DOSKEY to create macros by assigning a series of commands to a name.*
  Enter the name on the command line to execute all the assigned commands.

Now that you have rudimentary knowledge of batch files, it is an opportune time to elaborate on DOSKEY and to use it to create macros (explained below) and batch files.

Installing DOSKEY

If you load DOSKEY with no switch, a buffer of 512 bytes is set aside to store your commands. Since each character you type is 1 byte, this amount is sufficient to store 40 average commands. If you need to set a different amount, use the /BUFSIZE switch, like this:

```
C:\DOS>doskey /bufsize=1024
```

This sets aside a buffer of 1024 bytes. This can be done only when you run the program the first time or concurrent with /REINSTALL.

You can use the /REINSTALL switch to install another copy with the default or a specified buffer size. This act clears any previously installed buffer. If you encounter the "Insufficient memory" message, use this switch to clear the previous buffer and set aside memory for a new buffer, such as:

```
C>doskey /reinstall /bufsize=1200
```

By default, DOSKEY is installed with typeover (overstrike or replace) mode on. To insert text on the command line, press Ins to switch to insert mode. You can also change the default by using the /INSERT switch to make insert mode the default; in that case, press Ins to switch to typeover mode. If you change your mind, run DOSKEY another time with /OVERSTRIKE. These switches can be used after installation. When Ins is pressed, the cursor is enlarged, signifying the mode opposite to the default; when Enter is pressed, the default mode will return.

Managing and Editing Stored Commands

After DOSKEY is installed and you have entered a few commands, use the keys shown in Table 4.3 to recycle and manage them. If you have entered many commands, press F7 to display a list; each command is preceded by a number. Press F9 to show a prompt for a number. Enter the desired number to recycle that command.

If you enter more commands than the available buffer memory, the earlier ones are phased out to make room for new ones. You can also clear the buffer by pressing Alt-F7.

Once a command appears on the command line, you can edit it with the keys shown in Table 4.4 (you can still use the keys shown in Table 4.2). In contrast to the original DOS editing keys, you can now press → and ← to move among the displayed characters without erasing them.

You can also enter multiple commands in a single line, with each separated by a ¶ sign (known as paragraph mark; press Ctrl-T to insert it).

Table 4.3

DOSKEY Command-Management Keys

Key	Purpose
↑	Display the previous command
↓	Display the next command
PgUp	Display the first command
PgDn	Display the last command
Esc	Clear the command line
F7	Display all the stored commands
Alt-F7	Clear all stored commands from the buffer
F8	Cycle commands upward or search for a command
F9	Prompt for a number to display that command
Alt-F10	Clear macro buffer

Table 4.4

DOSKEY Cursor-Control Keys

Key	Purpose
Home	Beginning of the line
End	End of the line
←/→	One character left/right
Ctrl-←	One word left
Ctrl-→	One word right
Backspace	Erase one character to the left
Del	Delete one character at the cursor
Ctrl-End	Delete from cursor to end of line
Ctrl-Home	Delete from cursor to beginning of line
Ins	Toggle between insert and typeover mode
Esc	Clear the command line
Ctrl-T	Insert ¶ to mark end of a command; use $T in a macro

Insert the DOS-TA disk in drive A and follow these steps to demonstrate various uses for DOSKEY:

FOLLOW
THESE
STEPS

1. Install DOSKEY with insert mode as the default:

   ```
   C>doskey /insert
   DOSKEY installed.
   ```

   This goes to the C:\DOS directory to run the program; your hard disk should make some noise.

2. Enter three commands:

   ```
   C>dir a: /o:s
   C>type a:sample.txt
   C>dir *.txt ¶ type readme.txt
   ```

   A space before or after ¶ (press Ctrl-T) is optional. While these spaces improve readability, they are not required nor will they interfere with a command. After the second command, you can press ↑ to bring back the previous command to the command line; edit it to result in the third command before pressing Enter.

3. Display all the stored commands by pressing F7; the above three commands appear, each preceded with a number.

4. Display the first command by pressing F9 and then enter 1 when prompted; the first command appears on the command line.

5. Clear the command line by pressing Esc.

6. Clear the buffer by pressing Alt-F7.

7. Press various keys shown in Table 4.3. No command is available for recycling.

The F8 key is a little tricky to use. When the command line is clear, pressing this key displays the most recent command; pressing it repeatedly will recycle previous commands one by one, just as the ↑ key. You can also type one or more characters and press F8 to fill in the rest. F8 will find the most recent matching command to display the entire string.

Creating and Using Macros (Advanced Optional Topic)

A macro is one or more commands (or keystrokes) assigned to a name. Once you use DOSKEY to make DOS recognize the commands as the equivalent of the name, you can use the name to execute the commands. This is comparable to your assigning multiple digits to a key on your phone; after making the assignment, you can just press a key to redial all the assigned digits. You can use this shortcut to instruct DOS to quickly do a series of tasks. If you work with DOS often, this device can save you lots of time and typing.

To create a macro, you simply use DOSKEY to assign a string consisting of one or more commands to a name, like this:

```
C>doskey t=type a:sample.txt
```

This long command is assigned to a single letter; the string before the = is the macro name and the string after it is the command assigned to the macro named T. You can insert a space before and after the =, but it will be ignored.

Now insert the DOS-TA disk in drive A and enter this single letter to execute the long command:

```
C>t
```

If you assign another string to the same name, the name will be identified with the new string.

If you want to delete a macro, assign nothing to it, like this:

```
C>doskey t=
```

What happens if you use a DOS command name as a macro name? The macro has priority. Consider this:

```
C>doskey dir=dir a: /o /p
```

If you now enter DIR, the macro, not the original command, will be executed. This arrangement allows you to customize a DOS command. If you want to use the original command, you must delete the macro as shown above or add a space, comma, or semicolon before the command, as in the following:

```
C> dir
C>,dir
C>;dir
```

Replaceable Parameters and Redirection (Advanced Optional Topic)

You can use replaceable parameters and redirection symbols in a macro, just as in a batch file. Instead of %, however, you must use $ before a number to designate a replaceable parameter. You also need to use metastrings to represent redirection symbols (this topic will be more fully explored in Chapter 8).

If you want to assign multiple commands to a macro, you need to separate them with $T. This is the equivalent of your pressing Enter on the command line. You use a ¶ to separate two commands on the command line, as explained earlier, but $T in a macro. Make sure you do not use them in a wrong place. If you use a ¶ while creating a macro, the command(s) before it will be saved to the macro; anything after that will be immediately executed but not saved to the macro.

Here are two macro examples using metastrings and replaceable parameters:

```
C>doskey mov=copy $1 $2 $t del $1
C>doskey kill=echo y $b del a:\temp
```

The first requires two parameters from the user, like this:

```
C>mov *.txt a:
```

DOS will then translate your macro to the following concrete commands:

```
C>copy *.txt a:
C>del *.txt
```

Our second macro will delete all the files in the A:\TEMP directory. If you store all temporary files there and need to clear the entire directory from time to time, the following command will erase all the files stored there:

```
C>kill
```

DOS will translate your macro to this specific command:

```
C>echo y ¦ del a:\temp
```

Notice that $B is converted to ¦. The first part will supply the Y needed to delete all the files in a directory. You will not be asked Yes or No. Do not use a command like this unless you know what you are doing.

Some symbols, such as ¦, >, <, and >>, have special meanings to DOS. When DOS encounters these symbols, it acts upon them immediately. If you do not want this to happen, you need to substitute them with something called **metastrings**. Chapter 5 provides more details; for now, you can use in a macro the strings shown in Table 4.5.

As explained earlier, you can use % and a number as a replaceable parameter in a batch file. In a macro, you use $ and a number to signify a replaceable parameter. When you use $ with a number, the replaceable parameter expects a single argument, which ends with a parameter delimiter (space, comma, or semicolon). If you want a replaceable parameter to accept all the arguments supplied on the command line, use $*, like this:

```
C>doskey pd=dir $* $g lpt1
```

Suppose you run this macro like this:

```
C>pd \ /o:-d /w
```

DOS executes your macro this way:

```
C>dir \ /o:-d /w > lpt1
```

Table 4.5	
DOSKEY Metastrings	

Metastring	**Command Line Equivalent**
$1–$9	Arguments 1–9 supplied by user
$*	All the supplied arguments
$l	<
$g	>
gg	>>
$b	¦
$$	$
$t	Carriage return

If you use $1 instead of $* in the macro, the macro will be executed this way:

```
C>pd \ > lpt1
```

You may supply multiple parameters, but anything after the first space will be ignored.

Saving Commands and Macros

The /HISTORY (or /H) and /MACROS (or /M) switches can be used to display and save stored commands and macros. /H acts the same as your pressing F7, except that commands are not marked with numbers. /M is the only way you can show the macros you have created.

Instead of displaying these items on the screen, you can redirect them to a file to save them (if not saved, they will be lost when the computer is shut off), like these:

```
C>doskey /h > a:history.txt
C>doskey /m > a:macros.txt
```

If you have created two macros as demonstrated earlier, the MACROS.TXT file will contain these two lines:

```
MOV=copy $1 $2 $t del $1
KILL=echo y $b del a:\temp
```

TIPS AND TRICKS

MACROS AND BATCH FILES

Instead of using a text editor to modify macros to make them executable, you can send executable macro lines to a disk file, like these two commands:

```
A>echo doskey mov=copy $1 $2 $t del $1 >> macro.bat
A>echo doskey kill=echo y $b del a:\temp >> macro.bat
```

The first command appends anything after ECHO and before >> to a file named MACRO.BAT. If this file does not exist in drive A, it will be created. The second command adds another line to the file.

If you now run the batch file, it will create two macros for you. You can then start using the macros without having to enter them from the keyboard. If DOSKEY is not installed, running this batch file will load DOSKEY and create the macros at the same time.

If you use a text editor like EDLIN or EDIT to add DOSKEY before each line and add the BAT extension to the file name, you can in the future run the batch file to load DOSKEY and automatically create the two macros. You can also use the CALL command placed in your AUTOEXEC.BAT file to call this macro file; this will save you the trouble of having to run this batch file by yourself.

Macros resemble batch files in many ways. Some batch commands can even be used in a macro. See Chapter 11 for more details of batch files and the differences between the two.

PRACTICE 4-4

☐ 1. Create a batch file named F.BAT to reduce the keystrokes normally needed to format a disk. Assume that FORMAT.COM is stored in C:\DOS and the target drive is A.

☐ 2. Alter the above batch file and change fixed target drive of A to a replaceable parameter. Use the batch file to format a disk in drive B.

☐ 3. Use B.BAT discussed in the text to create CK.BAT, which will load CHKDSK.EXE from the C:\DOS directory and check a disk specified from the keyboard as a parameter.

☐ 4. Create an AUTOEXEC.BAT file that will automatically run a computer program, such as QBASIC, as soon as DOS is booted from this disk.

☐   5. Use DOSKEY to create a macro named QL that will allow the user to enter a volume label for the disk in drive A. Use this macro to give a volume label to your practice disk in drive A.

☐   6. Use DOSKEY to create a macro named QC that will check the disk in the drive supplied on the command line; the output should show file names and be redirected to the printer. Use the macro on the disk in drive A.

D R I L L

_____ 18. An AUTOEXEC.BAT file can be placed in any directory and DOS will execute it. True or false?

_____ 19. Assuming all the files are in the current directory, this command will execute which file?

   A>prog
   a. PROG.COM
   b. PROG.EXE
   c. PROG.BAT
   d. PROG.DOC

_____ 20. A macro ceases to exist after your PC's power supply is shut off. True or false?

_____ 21. A macro named DEL can never be executed because the internal DEL command has priority over it. True or false?

_____ 22. You can never execute a batch file named COPY.BAT. True or false?

Use the list below (all related to DOSKEY) to answer questions 23–30:

a. Home   b. Ctrl-Home   c. Esc   d. Ctrl-T   e. ↑   f. PgUp   g. F7   h. F9.

_____ 23. Move the cursor to the beginning of the command line.

_____ 24. Clear the command line.

_____ 25. Display all the previously entered commands.

_____ 26. Display the most recently entered command.

_____ 27. Delete to the beginning of the command line.

_____ 28. Prompt for a number to display that command.

_____ 29. Insert a paragraph mark.

_____ 30. Display the first command in the buffer.

S U M M A R Y   A N D   R E V I E W

Check each item as you review and understand the following highlights of the chapter.

☐   1.   Use COPY CON followed by a file name to create a file. Type the lines to be saved to the file. Press F6 and Enter to end.

☐   2.   When creating a file, do not use the name of an existing file in the current directory, unless you mean to replace the old file with the new one. There is no warning that a file is to be replaced.

☐   3.   Do not use the name of a subdirectory as the name of a file to be created. If you do, DOS will not save the file you intend to create, but echo the file to the screen instead.

☐   4.   Observe DOS file name conventions when creating or renaming a file. A file name can be no longer than eight characters, plus an optional extension of up to three characters.

☐   5.   Do not use certain characters, such as ¦ and >. These are used by DOS for special purposes such as piping and redirection.

☐   6.   Do not use DOS device names as file names; also avoid DOS commands under most circumstances.

☐   7.   Do not use wild card characters of ? and * in a file name when using COPY CON to create a file.

☐   8.   Use wild card characters when acting on existing files. Each ? character represents a character of the same position in a file name. Each * represents all the remaining characters up to the end of a file name or extension.

☐   9.   Use the global specifier of *.* (can be replaced with a single period) to speed up actions on all the existing files in a specific directory, such as copying and deleting. Use it with caution when combined with DEL or ERASE. As a precautionary measure, use the /P switch when DEL is combined with a wild card.

☐   10.   Use COPY CON to create short batch files. Use batch files to save time and increase productivity. Use a batch file to speed up creation of other batch files.

☐   11.   For DOS to be able to execute it, a batch file must have an extension of BAT in the name and contain only ASCII text and commands DOS can execute.

☐   12.   Create an AUTOEXEC.BAT file and store it on the boot disk for DOS to automatically perform certain initial tasks so you do not have to do them manually.

☐   13. Install DOSKEY to recycle and edit old commands. Use the /INSERT switch if you prefer insert mode by default. Press Ins to switch between the default and the opposite modes.

☐   14. Recycle some commands by using ↑, ↓, F8, F9, and other keys. Edit the command line text by using Home, End, →, ←, Ctrl-→, Ctrl-←, Ctrl-Home, Ctrl-End, and so on.

☐   15. Create a macro by using DOSKEY to assign a list of commands to a short name. Enter the short name on the command line to issue all the assigned commands.

☐   16. Use ECHO to send macro lines to a disk file with the BAT extension. Run this batch file to automatically install DOSKEY and create some useful macros.

R E V I E W   Q U E S T I O N S

Write an answer for each question below.

1.   If you enter the COPY CON FILENAME command, what are you asking DOS to do?

2.   When you use COPY CON to create a file, how do you end?

3.   If you decide not to create a file after using COPY CON, how do you abort it?

4.   Suppose you want to add lines to an existing file named WORK. What command do you use?

5.   Name five characters which cannot be used in a file name.

6.   Can you use characters not on the keyboard as parts of a file name? How?

7.   Can you use wild card characters of ? and * in naming a file?

8.   Can you use wild card characters when deleting files?

9.   Can you use wild card characters with TYPE or RENAME?

10.   What will this command do?
        A>copy file* con

11.   What happens if you press Esc after typing a DOS command?

12.   If a batch file is stored in the C:\BAT directory, what can you do to enable you to run the batch file from any drive or directory?

13. What is the purpose of using a replaceable parameter in a batch file?

14. How do the replaceable parameters differ for macros and batch files?

15. With DOSKEY installed, can you enter multiple commands in a single line? How do you do it on the command line and in a macro?

Managing Directories

C O M M A N D S   C O V E R E D

MD (MKDIR), RD (RMDIR), CD (CHDIR), MOVE, DELTREE, TREE, PROMPT, PATH, APPEND

N E W   T E R M S   A N D   S Y M B O L S

Directory, subdirectory, parent directory, root directory, current directory, \, ., .., metastring, $, TSR, DOS environment, command path, data path

QUICK START

For examples of organizing a hard disk:

> See Figures 5.1 and 5.2

To create a subdirectory:

> A>md practice

To remove a subdirectory:

> A>rd practice

To change to a subdirectory

> A>cd practice

To change to the root directory:

> A>cd\

To change to one level above the current directory:

> A>cd..

To display a directory path:

> A>cd

To move files ABC and XYZ from drive A to B:

> A>move abc,xyz b:

To delete the MYDIR directory and all its files and subdirectories:

> A>deltree \mydir

To use metastrings with PROMPT:

> See Table 5.1.

To create a DOS prompt showing the current drive, directory, and >:

> A>prompt pg

To display a treelike structure of directories:

> C>tree a:

To be able to run external DOS commands stored in the C:\DOS directory and batch files stored in the C:\BAT directory:

> C>path=c:\dos;c:\bat

To access data files in both C:\BAT\TXT and B:\FILES:

C>append c:\bat\txt;b:\files

To show a PATH or APPEND list:

C>path
C>append

To clear a path list:

C>path;
C>append;

Computer storage media continue to be built with larger and larger capacities. Some of today's hard disks have more than 1 gigabytes (billion bytes) of storage capacity. A typical CD-ROM disc can store 680MB data (or 74 minutes of music). Even floppy disks continue to expand in storage capacity while their physical size continues to shrink. A few years ago, 5.25-inch 360KB disks were standard. Today 5.25-inch 1.2MB and 3.5-inch 1.4MB floppies are standard. More recently, 3.5-inch 2.88MB and 20MB floppies have begun to appear.

How do you handle a large-capacity disk? You divide it into smaller units and subunits, and store related information in a particular unit. Then you use an index or catalogue through which you can quickly find what you need. This is comparable to a library putting different kinds of books in different areas and using a catalogue to locate a specific book. Many things in human society are organized this way: telephone directories, a book's table of contents, and so on.

DOS follows the same idea in handling your disk. It allows you to divide a disk into many directories (units) and subdirectories (subunits). It also provides quite a few tools for you to manage these directories. These directories and the tools to manage them are discussed in this chapter.

ORGANIZING A DISK

■ *A directory structure can be created to suit your specific needs.*

■ *Using directories to store files has many advantages.*

To visualize a disk and its directory structure, think of a file cabinet. A file cabinet may have several drawers, which can be compared to a disk's directories. A drawer may be divided into several sections, which are comparable to subdirectories. In addition, each directory also serves as an index, keeping track of files stored in it; this is analogous to your putting labels in proper places to keep track of things.

The concept of directory should not be new to you. When DOS formats a disk, as explained in Chapter 3, it creates a root directory. When you save a file to the disk, the file name, extension, location, date, etc. are saved to the directory. When you use the DIR command, DOS uses the saved data to show you the files (and other related data) in a directory. When you create a subdirectory, as explained below, DOS also manages it in the same way it does the root directory.

Basic Terms

There are a few commonly used terms you need to be familiar with to better understand the concept of directories. In the beginning, there is the **root directory**. Every disk has a root directory, which is created during formatting. If you do nothing to divide up your disk, there is only one directory, the root directory.

If you divide a disk into units and subunits, you have directories and subdirectories. These are terms used to relate one directory to another. The active directory is the **current directory**; the root directory is always the current directory if a disk is not divided. The one above it (the next higher level), if any, is the **parent directory**. The one below it (the next lower level), if any, is a **subdirectory** (some people refer to it as child directory). As you go closer to the root directory, you go to higher levels. As you go further to the subdivisions, you go to lower levels.[1]

Sample Organizations

Directories and subdirectories can be organized in many ways. In a system used by several persons, the hard disk may be like the structure shown in Figure 5.1. In this arrangement, each person occupies a directory, which is a

Figure 5.1

A multiuser directory structure

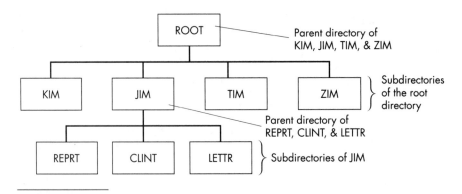

---

1. A lower level directory goes into the branches, and a higher level directory goes closer to the root. This is comparable to dangling a tree upside down, with the root at the top.

Figure 5.2

A single-user directory structure

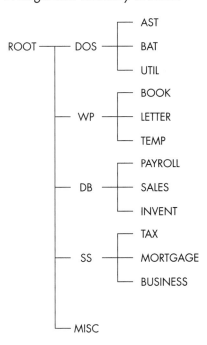

subdirectory of the root directory. In each person's directory, subdirectories can be created to store related files. This way, when Jim wants to find his correspondence, he can go to the directory bearing his name, and from there his LETTR subdirectory.

If you use a hard disk all by yourself, you may want to organize it according to functions, tasks, or software packages. Figure 5.2 could serve as a model.

In the above example, instead of lumping all the files in one directory, you divide them into five directories. In this arrangement, you can go to the WP directory to do word processing, to the SS directory to work on spreadsheets, and so on.

Advantages of Directories

Although it may take some extra time to create and move around directories, they do provide you many advantages, particularly when you have a large number of files. By using directories, you can:

- Group related files in one directory for easier remembrance and access.

- Display (using DIR) on the screen a shorter list of files each time, thus saving time and enabling you to find a file more quickly.

A   HARD   DISK'S   ROOT   DIRECTORY

When a colleague of mine first got a PC installed in his office, he copied all the files from many floppy disks to the hard disk without using any subdirectories. When he used the DIR command on the hard disk, a long, long list of files scrolled across the screen. It was a mess.

If you have a hard disk, you normally should not store any file in the root directory except these:

```
COMMAND.COM
CONFIG.SYS
AUTOEXEC.BAT
```

These, plus the hidden system files, must be in the root directory for DOS to boot from the hard disk.

The rest of the root directory should store only subdirectories. As you acquire a new software package, create a subdirectory and install the package in it. This arrangement keeps the root directory relatively uncluttered and allows you to quickly find what you need.

- Save unlimited number of files (as long as there is disk space), thus circumventing the DOS limit on the number of files in the root directory.

- Use identical file names that are stored in different directories.

- Share a large-capacity disk with other users, perhaps coworkers or fellow students, with a relatively well-defined territory for each.

- Store different software packages on one disk but in different directories. If you store them on the same disk without separating them into different directories, they may clash with one another and crash your computer.

MAKING AND REMOVING DIRECTORIES

■ *Create a directory with MD, followed by a directory name.*

■ *Remove a directory with RD, followed by a directory name.*

The first step in using directories is to create them. Once you have created them, you also need to know how to remove them when they are no longer needed. To do this, you need to use the commands MD (or MKDIR, for make directory) and RD (or RMDIR, for remove directory).

Follow these steps to create and remove a directory:

1. Put a practice disk in drive A and enter this command:

   A>**md practice**

2. Display directory entries to see what you have done:[2]

   A>**dir**

The screen shows your old files, if any, plus a directory you just created:

```
  . . .

  PRACTICE      <DIR>       6-22-93    7:22p

  . . .
```

The <DIR> notation tells you that this is a directory, which is a subdirectory of the current directory. The date and time of creation are not different from regular DOS files.

3. Remove the newly created directory:

   A>**rd practice**

4. Use DIR again to show directory entries.

The PRACTICE directory is now gone, removed by the RD command. After the removal, there is no trace of what has been done.

A directory, like a small file, takes up a cluster of disk space; a cluster, as explained in Chapter 3, can be several kilobytes long. If you have a small number of files, you may not want to waste this space for extra directories.

A directory name cannot be changed by REN. Starting in version 5, a menu option in the Shell can be used to change a directory name; this will be covered in Chapter 10. Version 6 comes with a new MOVE command which can be used to change a directory name; this will be discussed in a later section in this chapter.

DRILL

_____ 1. Before you can create a directory, you must first use MD to create a root directory. True or false?

---

2. You can show the subdirectory entries by putting the subdirectory name after DIR, like this:

   A>**dir practice**

═══ *T I P S   A N D   T R I C K S* ═══

DIRECTORY NAMES

DOS treats a directory name as a file name. In entering a directory name, you need to follow DOS file name conventions. You can have no more than eight legal characters, plus an optional extension of up to three characters. These conventions were explained in Chapter 4.

You are not allowed to use the name of a file in the current directory as a directory name. Suppose you have a file named PRACTICE located in the root directory. DOS will not let you create a subdirectory named PRACTICE from the root directory. Having two identical names, even though one for a file and the other for a directory, will create confusion and is thus illegal.

____ 2. This file should not be put in the root directory of a hard disk:
  a. COMMAND.COM
  b. CONFIG.SYS
  c. AUTOEXEC.BAT
  d. LETTER.JAN

____ 3. Suppose there is already a file named MISC in the current directory, this command will create a directory named MISC. True or false?

  A>md misc

____ 4. The REN command can be used to change a directory name. True or false?

MANEUVERING RELATED DIRECTORIES

■ *Use CD (or CHDIR) to change to a different directory.*

■ *Use \ to designate the root directory or as a directory separator.*

After you create a directory, you need to know how to get in or out of that directory or how to make use of it. The following steps illustrate some simple uses:

FOLLOW THESE STEPS

1. Create a test file:

```
A>copy con testfile
This is a test file.
^Z
```

2. Create a directory named BACKUP:

    A>**md backup**

3. Go to the new directory:

    A>**cd backup**

The CD (or CHDIR, for change directory) command is used to change to the directory specified after the command. The above command tells DOS to go to the named directory, which is a subdirectory of the current directory.

4. Display the files in the directory:

    A>**dir**

The screen shows the following:

```
Volume in drive A has no label ————— Disk volume label
Directory of  A:\BACKUP ————————— Directory path
   .        <DIR>     6-22-93   7:46p —— Current directory
   ..       <DIR>     6-22-93   7:46p —— Parent directory
       2 File(s)          0 bytes
                    198656 bytes free
```

The first line shows the volume label name for this disk. The second line indicates the location of the current directory and how it is related to the root directory. The A:\BACKUP path shows you that the BACKUP directory is a subdirectory of the root directory in drive A.

What you see here is an empty directory with no file but two directory notations. The single period (.) indicates the current directory, and the two periods (..) represent the parent directory. While there is no file stored in the current directory, DOS tells you there are two files, one for the current directory and the other for the parent directory. In counting the number of files, DOS treats a directory as a file.

5. Copy a file from the root directory to the current directory:

    A>**copy \testfile, ___**

The backslash (\) is used to indicate the root directory. The command above tells DOS to copy the named file from the root directory to the unspecified target directory (here meaning the current directory). If you want the laborious way, you can try either command below:

    A>**copy \testfile \backup**
    A>**copy \testfile \backup\testfile**

The first command tells DOS to copy a file named TESTFILE, which is in the root directory, to the directory named BACKUP, which is one level below the root directory; the name of the file is not changed. The second adds a file name to the target directory. If you want a name different from the original, you can change it here.[3]

You can also copy a file from another drive to drive A's current directory, like this:

A>`copy b:filename`

This command will copy FILENAME from drive B's current directory to drive A's current directory.

6. Display the directory entries again:

A>`dir`

This time you see the name of a new file you just copied into this directory, displayed below two directory notations.

7. Go to the root directory:

A>`cd \`

Putting a backslash (\) after the CD command always takes you to the root directory no matter where you are.

8. Try to remove the directory:

A>`rd backup`

What do you get? Does the following message surprise you?

`Invalid path, not directory,`
`or directory not empty`

The reason for this message is that the directory you want to remove is not empty.

9. Delete the file in the subdirectory:

A>`del \backup\testfile`

This command tells DOS to go to the BACKUP directory to delete the named file.

10. Try again to remove the directory:

A>`rd backup`

This time, DOS willingly obliges. The directory is gone, after the file stored there has been erased.

---

3. Although these extra entries are optional here, they may be necessary when the target directory is different from the current one.

DEL (ERASE) AND DIRECTORIES

■ *DEL or ERASE can be used only to erase files, but not directories. It can be used to erase all the files in a subdirectory.*

You cannot use the DEL or ERASE command to remove a directory; you can use it only to delete files. Suppose you are in the root directory and enter this command:

```
A>del backup
```

If BACKUP is a file, it is immediately erased. If it is a directory, you will be asked:

```
All files in directory will be deleted!
Are you sure (Y/N)?_
```

DOS assumes that you want to erase every file stored in the BACKUP directory and asks you to confirm. If you enter Y, the files are erased, but the directory remains. So, if you intend to clear a subdirectory and then remove it, enter the following commands:

```
A>del backup
All files in directory will be deleted!
Are you sure? (Y/N)y
A>rd backup
```

The above two commands produce the same results as the following four commands:

```
A>cd backup
A>del *.*
A>cd \
A>rd backup
```

WARNING: Using DEL to clear an entire subdirectory could be hazardous. You may not know what is stored in the subdirectory. If you want to be sure, go to the subdirectory and check what is in it first.

If you want to be cautious, use the /P (Prompt) switch with DEL, such as:

```
A>del backup /p
```

Each file targeted for deletion, together with its path, will be displayed and you will be asked for Y or N. If you enter Y, it is deleted and the next matching file will be shown.

On the other hand, if you know what you are doing and want to do things quickly, you can use a command like this:

```
A>echo y ¦ del backup ¦ rd backup
```

This command will delete all the files in the BACKUP directory and remove the directory with no pause or hesitation; the required Y will be piped in by ECHO. So use it with caution. See Chapter 8 for more about piping and redirection.

P R A C T I C E   5 - 1

1. Insert a practice disk in drive A and create a file named COMPUTER containing this sentence:

   Those who are low in computer skill cannot expect to thrive in a high-tech world.

2. Create a directory named TEMP and make TEMP the current directory.

3. Copy COMPUTER from the root directory to the TEMP directory.

4. Go to the root directory of drive A and delete all the files in the TEMP directory.

5. Remove the TEMP directory.

6. Use DOSKEY to create a macro named DIRECT that will do all the following:
   a. Make A the current drive.
   b. Create a directory named TEMP.
   c. Make TEMP the current directory.
   d. Start COPY CON with a file named X.BAT.
   Verify the macro's creation.

7. Run the DIRECT macro to create the X.BAT batch file that will create a macro named DIRECT (using the same name) that will delete X.BAT and remove TEMP. Show the results of running the macro.

8. Run X.BAT and verify the macro's new contents.

9. Run DIRECT and verify the result.

MANEUVERING MULTILEVEL DIRECTORIES

■ *In a multilevel directory structure, you need to provide a full path if you want to move to a desired directory. Use backslashes (\) to separate directory names.*

You can use a number of ways to create and navigate in a multilevel directory structure. The following steps show you how to create multilevel directories and move from one to another:

FOLLOW
THESE
STEPS

1. Create a first-level directory:

   A>**md \dir1**

The above command creates a directory named DIR1. The \ is optional if you are in the root directory; it could be substituted with a space, as illustrated previously. A space before \ is optional, but a space after it is illegal.

2. Create a second-level directory:

   A>**md \dir1\dir2**

This tells DOS to create DIR2, which is a subdirectory of DIR1, which in turn is a subdirectory of the root directory. DIR1 must exist before DIR2 can be created. If not, an error message appears.

Instead of the above command, you can use the CD command to go to the DIR1 directory and then create a subdirectory from there. Thus, the above command could be replaced by the following two commands:

   A>**cd dir1**
   A>**md dir2**

In the second command above, you cannot use a \. If you did, DOS would assume that you intended to create a first-level directory (a subdirectory of the root directory), not a subdirectory of the current directory.

3. Create a third-level directory:

   A>**md \dir1\dir2\dir3**

You are now creating a directory that is three levels below the root directory. All the backslashes are necessary to tell DOS where each fits in. If you go to level 2 directory, you can create a subdirectory from there as illustrated in the above alternative method.

4. Go from the root to level 2 directory:

   A>**cd \dir1\dir2**

Since you are in the root directory to begin with, you need to use backslashes to guide DOS to a specific place. In this case, you tell DOS to go to DIR2, which is a subdirectory of DIR1, which in turn is a subdirectory of the root directory. The first \ is optional here.

The above command could be replaced with the following:

   A>**cd dir1**
   A>**cd dir2**

In this alternative method, you tell DOS to go to the next (lower) level one
step at a time.

5. Display the files:

```
A>dir
```

```
Volume in drive A has no label
Directory of  A:\DIR1\DIR2

 .              <DIR>      3-22-93   8:20p
 ..             <DIR>      3-22-93   8:20p
DIR3            <DIR>      3-22-93   8:20p
      3 File(s)        0 bytes
                  133120 bytes free
```

Although there is no file stored in this directory, the screen shows three files in
existence. As mentioned earlier, DOS counts a directory as a file. The above
screen tells you that there is a subdirectory named DIR3. That plus the current
directory (designated with a single period) and the parent (marked with two
periods) make up the three files. If you go to the DIR3 directory, you will see
only two files listed—one for the current and one for the parent.

6. Display the root directory's entries:

```
A>dir \
```

Even though you are in another directory, you can always use \ to tell DOS to do
something to the root directory. This command does not change the current
directory; you are still in DIR2.

7. Display level 3 directory entries:

```
A>dir dir3
```

T I P S   A N D   T R I C K S

S P A C E   V E R S U S   B A C K S L A S H

Inserted after MD (CD or RD), a space and a backslash have different implications.
With a space, DOS assumes you want to create a subdirectory of the current
directory. If you use \ instead, DOS assumes you want to create a subdirectory of the
root directory. The two happen to have the same effect when you are in the root
directory. If you are not, they cause different consequences.

This command tells DOS to display the directory that is a subdirectory of the current directory. Do not include \ here. If you do, you tell DOS that DIR3 is a subdirectory of the root directory. This will lead to an error message in our case.

8. Go to the root directory:

    A>**cd** \

9. Display level 3 directory entries:

    A>**dir** \dir1\dir2\dir3

This command displays the files in DIR3, but it does not change the current directory. The root directory remains the current directory.

MANEUVERING UNRELATED DIRECTORIES

■ *To move between two directories not directly related, you need to provide DOS a specific and complete path.*

■ *Use CD followed by two periods (..) to move to the parent directory.*

■ *CD can change a directory, but not a drive; to change a drive, enter a drive letter followed by a colon (e.g., C:).*

■ *Use CD alone to display the directory path of a drive. Knowing the directory path of the source or target drive can save time when copying, displaying, or deleting files.*

Moving from one directory to another directory, if the two are not directly related, requires special manipulation. One way to visualize the problem is to treat directories as branches of a tree. DOS rules do not allow you to jump like a monkey from one branch to another. You must go like a sloth to where the branches meet and from there to a new branch. To travel from one directory to another unrelated directory, you need to direct DOS to the connecting point (or the root directory) and branch from there to the new directory.

In the directory structure below, you may be tempted to jump directly from REPRT to CLINT without going through the connecting point (JIM). If you did that, however, you would get an error message "Invalid directory."

Changing to Unrelated Directories

To illustrate how you can navigate among a complex directory structure, let us suppose that you have in drive C a structure like this:

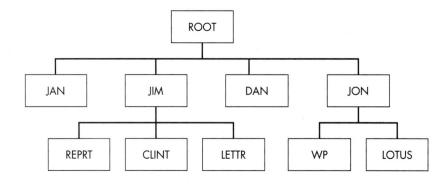

The list below provides some examples of going from one directory to another, not directly related, directory:

To go from this directory	To this directory	Enter this command
REPRT	LOTUS	C>CD\JON\LOTUS
LETTR	DAN	C>CD\DAN
JAN	WP	C>CD\JON\WP
DAN	REPRT	C>CD\JIM\REPRT
LOTUS	JAN	C>CD\JAN
JON	REPRT	C>CD\JIM\REPRT
WP	CLINT	C>CD\JIM\CLINT
REPRT	CLINT	C>CD..\CLINT

Let us examine the first and last examples. The first example shows how to get from REPRT to LOTUS. The command tells DOS to go to the root directory (the first \), then branch from there to JON, and then branch from there to LOTUS. This command could be replaced with the two below:

```
C>cd \
C>cd jon\lotus   (or cd \jon\lotus)
```

The second command above can also be replaced with these two:

```
C>cd jon
C>cd lotus
```

Two Periods as the Parent Directory

The last command in the table uses two periods (..) to signify the parent directory. This command tells DOS to go up one level and then branch from there to the CLINT subdirectory. This command could be replaced with the following two:

```
C>cd..
C>cd clint
```

You should not use \ in the second command shown above. If you did, DOS would consider CLINT to be one level below the root directory. This would generate an error message in our example.

Using two periods to move up one level is very convenient if you are deep inside a multilevel directory structure. You may not remember the parent directory's name or it may be laborious to type a long name. It is much simpler just to use two periods, such as this command:

```
C>dir..
```

This command will show the files in the parent directory; the current directory is not changed.

Now that we are in a dotty mode, let's explore more dots. What happens if you put three dots after a pertinent command? Here is an example:

```
C>cd...
```

You will get an "Invalid directory" error and no change of directory. On the other hand, there is this example:

```
C>dir...
```

This is a good command to use. It is the same as this:

```
C>dir *.
```

Both will show only the directory entries, file or directory names, that have no extensions. Since most people do not use extensions for directory names, either command can quickly show a list of directories.

Changing a Drive

Although CD can change the current directory, you cannot use it to change the current drive. For example, if you enter the command in the first line, the second line shows that the current drive is still A:

```
A>cd c:\
A>_
```

T I P S   A N D   T R I C K S

S K I P P I N G   A   D I R E C T O R Y   P A T H

Knowing the current directories of different drives may be useful when you want to copy files from one drive to another. You can skip a directory path. For example, if drive C's current directory is C:\JON\WP, the simple command below will copy a file to it:

```
A>copy filename c:
```

If drive C's current directory is not known or not the target directory you have in mind, you will need to specify it, such as:

```
A>copy filename c:\jon\wp
```

This command will copy FILENAME from the current directory of drive A to the C:\JON\WP directory.

What you have done here is to change the current directory in drive C to the root directory. You are still in drive A. To go to drive C, you need to change it with this command:

```
A>c:
C>_
```

After the above two commands, you are now in the root directory of drive C.

Showing the Current Directory

You can use the CD command alone to make DOS show you the current directory. The screen may display something like this:

```
A>cd
A:\TEMP
```

You can also specify a drive to show its current directory:

```
A>cd c:
```

This may show a result like this:

```
C:\JON\WP
```

Notice that there is no > sign. This is what distinguishes it from the display produced by PROMPT, explained in another section below.

P R A C T I C E   5 - 2

☐   1. Create on the previous practice disk a directory structure shown below:

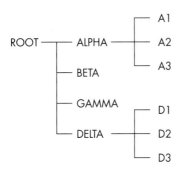

☐   2. Make A1 the current directory and copy COMPUTER (created in the preceding session) to it from drive A's root directory.

☐   3. Keep A1 as the current directory, but copy COMPUTER from there to D3.

☐   4. Change the current directory to D1.

☐   5. Display the entries in the root directory.

☐   6. Display the current directory's path.

☐   7. Use DOSKEY to create a macro named C that will allow you to enter two directory names to copy COMPUTER (which should be included in the macro) from the first to the second.

☐   8. Use the C macro to copy COMPUTER from D3 to BETA.

(Save the directory structure for the next session.)

D R I L L

___   5. If you enter the RD TEMP command, you will:
   a. remove the TEMP directory located anywhere
   b. remove the current directory if named TEMP
   c. always remove a subdirectory named TEMP
   d. not necessarily do anything

____ 6. If you enter the DEL TEMP command where TEMP is a subdirectory of the current directory, you will:

   a. erase the directory's name

   b. erase the files in that directory

   c. cause an error message

   d. remove the directory

Select from the list of commands below to answer 7–11:

a. CD\   b. CD   c. CD.   d. CD..   e. CD...

____ 7. Make the root directory the current directory.

____ 8. Not a valid command.

____ 9. Show the current directory and current drive.

____ 10. Do nothing; keep the same current directory.

____ 11. Make the parent directory the current directory.

____ 12. Used alone, the CD command will display a DOS prompt like this:

   a. A:\>

   b. A:\

   c. B:\DOS>

   d. C>

MOVING FILES AND RENAMING DIRECTORIES

■ *Use the MOVE.EXE command to move and rename a single file or multiple files and to rename a directory.*

■ *Use wildcards with MOVE as with COPY and similar commands.*

DOS 6 includes a new external command called MOVE.EXE that can do the following:

• Move and rename a single file.

• Move but not rename multiple files.

• Rename but not move a directory.

The above tasks can be done in old versions, but with elaborate steps. Moving files involves using COPY to duplicate them and then using DEL to erase the old ones. Renaming a directory can be done only with the DOS Shell available in DOS 5 or later, but not before. The new MOVE command makes these chores much easier.

Moving Steps

Let us do something to gain a little practical experience. Put a practice disk in drive A and follow these steps. (To get the prompt styles shown below, enter PROMPT PG on the command line.)

FOLLOW THESE STEPS

1. Create two directories:

   ```
   A:\>md abc
   A:\>md xyz
   ```

2. Go to \ABC and create two files:

   ```
   A:\>cd abc

   A:\ABC>copy con file1
   This is file 1.
   ^Z

   A:\ABC>copy con file2
   This is file 2.
   ^Z
   ```

3. Move FILE1 from the current directory to \XYZ and rename it FILEX; the message below shows a successful move:

   ```
   A:\ABC>move file1 \xyz\filex
   a:\abc\file1 => a:\xyz\filex [ok]
   ```

4. Move FILEX back to \ABC and restore the original name:

   ```
   A:\ABC>move \xyz\filex \abc\file1
   ```

5. Go to the root directory and move two files from one subdirectory to another:

   ```
   A:\ABC>cd\
   ```

   ```
   A:\>move \abc\file1,\abc\file2 \xyz
   ```

The two files in \ABC have now been moved to \XYZ. Notice that we have to provide a full path for each file. Each file is also separated from another by a comma; do not replace a comma with a space or semicolon. If a file is not preceded by a path, DOS will assume that you want to move a file from the current (root) directory to \XYZ. In our example, the first parameter could be shortened to \ABC\File? or \ABC*.*.

6. Move the files from \XYZ to the root directory:

```
A:\>move \xyz\f*
Required parameter missing
```

If we were using COPY, the above command would be legal and successfully executed; the missing target parameter would be the current (root) directory. But MOVE requires both parameters. In our case, ., \, or A:\ at the end would have successfully moved the matching files to the root directory.

7. Create a directory and move files simultaneously:

```
A:\>move \xyz\f* \new\one
Make directory "a:\new\one"? [yn] y
a:\xyz\file1 => a:\new\one\file1 [ok]
a:\xyz\file2 => a:\new\one\file2 [ok]
```

Since the \NEW\ONE directory does not exist, you are asked whether you want to create it. After you enter Y, the directory is created and the two files moved to it. If you enter N, this will be the result:

```
A:\>move \xyz\f* \new\one
Make directory "a:\new\one"? [yn] n
Cannot move multiple files to a single file
```

In this case, DOS assumes that you want to combine all the files matching F* to a new file named ONE in the \NEW directory. You cannot use MOVE to do that. You can, however, use COPY to do it, as explained in Chapter 6.

8. Change directory names one at a time:

```
A:\>move \new\one \new\uno
a:\new\one => a:\new\uno [ok]
```

```
A:\>move \new \old
a:\new => a:\old [ok]
```

Do not change two or more directory names at one time. If you do, this is the result:

```
A:\>move \new\one \old\uno
  a:\new\one => a:\old\uno [Unable to open source]
```

After the above steps, there are now these items on your disk:

```
\ABC
\XYZ
\OLD\UNO\FILE1
\OLD\UNO\FILE2
```

These items will be used by DELTREE later in this chapter.

MOVE, COPY, and Wild Cards

Although MOVE behaves like COPY, there are many differences, which are further accentuated when combined with wild cards. We can now summarize what you can or cannot do with MOVE and how it differs with COPY and other similar commands:

- MOVE accepts multiple source files separated by commas; COPY or REN does not permit this.

- MOVE requires both source and target parameters specified. On the other hand, if only one parameter is specified with COPY, the current directory becomes the target.

- You can move and rename a single file (but not multiple files) in one step; if the source and the target are in the same location, the file is renamed. If the target already exists, it is replaced without warning; REN does not allow replacement in this situation.

- When MOVE encounters multiple source files, it will move them to the existing target directory. If the directory does not exist, it will be created. In this situation, COPY will copy the source files to the existing directory or, if the specified target is a file or nonexisting, combine the source files and put them in the target.

- With MOVE, you can use wild cards in the source but not in the target parameter; the latter will cause confusion. COPY and REN permit wild cards in both source and target.

- A single period and double periods can be used in the target parameter with MOVE; put in the source parameter, they will confuse MOVE (see below).

- MOVE does not distinguish between a file and a directory; COPY and REN do.

You can use wild cards liberally with COPY or REN. These commands are perfectly legal:

```
A:\>copy file?.txt *.bak     (copy and rename multiple files)
A:\>ren file?.txt *.bak      (rename multiple files)
A:\>copy longfile *.bak      (copy and rename one file)
A:\>ren longfile *.bak       (rename one file)
```

MOVE cannot be used in any of the above situations. Here is the result:

```
A:\>move file?.txt *.bak
Make directory "a:\*.bak"? [yn] y
Cannot move multiple files to a single file
```

MOVE is now confused. It tries to create a directory and then tries to combine files—both without success.

The following examples provide more contrasts among the three commands:

```
A:\>copy file? total    (copy or file combination)
A:\>ren file? total     (illegal)
A:\>move file? total    (creating directory)
```

In the first example, all the matching files will be copied to the TOTAL directory (if existent) or combined to the TOTAL file. In the last example, all the matching files will be moved to the TOTAL directory if it exists. If the directory does not exist, you will be asked to supply Y or N to create a directory. If TOTAL is an existing file name, this error message appears:

```
Cannot move multiple files to a single file
```

If you specify only one parameter, COPY assumes the current directory to be the target and proceeds to copy the specified matching files, such as this example:

```
A:\ABC>copy \*.txt
```

It will copy all the matching files from the root to the current directory. In the same situation, MOVE will give you this message:

```
Required parameter missing
```

MOVE accepts a single period (.) and double periods (..) only in the target parameter. Here are two examples:

```
A:\ABC>move file? ..
A:\ABC>move \file? .
```

The first moves matching files from the current directory to the parent directory, and the second the opposite direction. Putting periods in the source parameter can confuse MOVE, such as:

```
A:\ABC>move .. .
A:\ABC>move . \xyz
```

In the first case, nothing is done, not even an error message; COPY would have copied all the files from the parent to the current directory. In the second case, the period is treated as the current directory; no action is taken and this message is shown:

```
Cannot move abc - No such file or directory
```

Both MOVE and COPY will overwrite matching target files. If the target location contains files of the same names specified by you, the new files will replace the old without warning or a prompt—unless they contain hidden or read-only attributes. This makes MOVE behave like COPY. Neither can "see" a hidden file as a source; neither can overwrite a hidden or read-only file.[4]

---

4. You can use UNDELETE to recover files written over by MOVE. To increase recovery chances, use UNDELETE before you save another file to the disk. If Delete Sentry (see Chapter 6) is on, the overwritten files are also saved to the Sentry directory.

MOVE cannot distinguish between files and directories. When COPY or REN is used with wild cards, they will identify only matching files; MOVE, however, will try to identify both files and directories. Suppose FILE1 and FILE2 are in the root directory and you want to move them to \ABC. Using wild cards leads to these peculiar responses:

```
A:\>move *.* \abc
a:\abc => a:\abc\abc [Unable to open source]
a:\xyz => a:\abc\xyz [Unable to open source]
a:\file1 => a:\abc\file1 [ok]
a:\file2 => a:\abc\file2 [ok]
```

In this case, MOVE tries to move everything, including files and directories, to the target. Although files are successfully moved, directories remain where they are.

The *.* in the above example cannot be replaced with a single period. If you do that, no action is taken—not even an error message. This can also happen in other circumstances. The error-handling routine of this program has not been perfected.

The fact that MOVE does not tell apart a file and a directory can pose an intriguing situation. Consider these two examples:

```
A:\>copy dir1 dir2
A:\>move dir1 dir2
```

Assuming that DIR1 and DIR2 are existing subdirectories, the first command will copy all the files from the first directory to the second. The second command will lead to an error—[Unable to open source]. MOVE considers your intent as renaming a directory and is unable to do so because another directory is using the name. If you intend to move all the files, you have to be specific, such as this example:

```
A:\>move dir1\*.* dir2
```

This will successfully move all the matching files from the first directory to the second; if the target directory does not exist, it will be created.

DELETING FILES AND DIRECTORIES

■ *Use DELTREE.EXE with caution to delete files and directories.*

DOS 6 comes with an new external command called DELTREE.EXE. It is a convenient and powerful tool; it is also dangerous. If you make a mistake, there may be no recourse. Use it with caution as you would any power tool.

Before we discuss this tool further, let us have some practice in using it. Use the previous disk and follow these steps:

1. Create a file in the root directory:

   ```
   A:\>copy con rootfile
   This is in the root directory.
   ^Z
   ```

2. Delete everything in drive A:

   ```
   A:\>deltree .
   Delete directory ".\abc" and all its subdirectories? [yn] y
   Deleting .\abc...
   Delete directory ".\xyz" and all its subdirectories? [yn] y
   Deleting .\xyz...
   Delete directory ".\old" and all its subdirectories? [yn] y
   Deleting .\old...
   Delete file ".\rootfile"? [yn] y
   Deleting .\rootfile...
   ```

If you have files you want to keep, enter N when prompted. If your disk contains nothing except what you did in this and previous sections, the above display shows the result. All the items, files and directories, on the disk are now wiped out.

In step 2, we ask DELTREE to delete everything in the current (root) directory. As shown above, when a matching item is found, you are asked to enter Y or N. If Y is entered, the item is deleted; if N is provided, it remains intact. If you press any other key, the cursor does not budge.

If you use no wild card, only one matching item will be deleted. In our example above, if you enter DELTREE ROOTFILE, only the file will be deleted.

DELTREE has a single switch, namely /Y. If it is used, you are not prompted to supply Y or N; any matching item is deleted as well as shown on the screen. Do not use this switch unless you know what you are doing.

DELTREE is comparable to combining DEL and RD. DEL can delete files but not directories. RD can remove directories but not files.

DELTREE is in some ways more than combining DEL and RD. DEL cannot delete hidden or read-only files. RD cannot remove a directory that is not empty. DELTREE, on the contrary, can delete hidden and read-only files, plus directories that may contain subdirectories and hidden or read-only files. It is not unlike lopping off a tree branch—with all the subbranches, leaves, fruits, and all.

DELTREE can delete almost anything that the DIR /A command shows. It is thus a good idea to use this command to show all the matching items before you resort to DELTREE. When an item slated for deletion is displayed, pay close attention before entering Y.

DELTREE behaves like DEL, not DIR, in finding matching items. Suppose you have two files named X and X.BAT in the same directory. DIR X will match both. DEL X and DELTREE X will match only X, but not X.BAT.

 Extreme caution is required when you use DELTREE with a wild card together with the /Y switch. It can delete all the matching files and directories. When a file is involved, it can carry any attribute and still be deleted. If no /Y is used, the file will at least be shown and you will be prompted to enter Y or N. If a file is in the targeted directory, it will not even be shown and the whole directory will be wiped out.

A file that is deleted with DELTREE, just like one that is erased with DEL, can be recovered with UNDELETE. Deleted subdirectories and the files in them, however, are not recoverable—unless you use Delete Sentry, which will be explained in Chapter 6.

When DEL encounters a nonexistent file, it tells you "File not found." DELTREE, however, does nothing and says nothing—just like MOVE, discussed in the previous section.

MANEUVERING THE PROMPT

- *Use the internal PROMPT command and a metastring character to display the current drive, current directory, date-time, etc.*

- *Use PROMPT alone to restore the default DOS prompt.*

One tool you can use to locate where you are in a maze of complex directories is the PROMPT command. You can use it to display the current directory as the DOS prompt. Once you know where you are, you can tell where other things are.

Metastring Characters

PROMPT is followed with a text string or a **metastring**, which consists of $ and another character. A metastring (meta means after) can transform a character to another character or an action as explained below.

When used with a regular text string, PROMPT simply displays that text string as a prompt. You could, for example, enter this command:

```
C>prompt Hello:
```

Here you just type the PROMPT command, space, and then the text string. The space can be replaced with an equal sign (=) without making any difference (this also applies to PATH and APPEND discussed below), such as

```
C>prompt=Hello:
```

Table 5.1

Prompt Metastring Characters

Character	Function
$	$ character (dollar sign)
_	(Underscore) linefeed (new line)
b	Bar; vertical bar (¦) character
d	Date; current date number
e	Esc
g	Greater than (>) character
h	Backspace; to erase previous character
l	Less than (<) character
n	Name (letter) of current drive
p	Path; Current drive/directory
q	Equal (=) character
t	Time; current time number
v	Version number

(Note: The letters can be in uppercase or lowercase.)

After the command, the new prompt becomes:

```
Hello:_
```

If you want to return to the original (default) prompt, simply enter the PROMPT command without any string attached. The familiar C> prompt reappears. Or, if you want to be more elaborate, you can use this:

```
prompt $n$g
```

The $n metastring tells DOS to display the current drive letter, and $g to show the greater than (>) sign. The characters that can be used after $ are shown in Table 5.1.

If a character in Table 5.1 is not preceded with $, it is treated as a literal string and displayed; no action is taken. For example, if you enter this:

```
C>prompt q
```

you get the letter q displayed as the prompt message, not an equal sign.

To display a nonalphabet character appearing in Table 5.1, you must precede it with $. Without $, these characters will generate error messages shown below:

━━━ *T I P S   A N D   T R I C K S* ━━━

P R O M P T   A N D   D O S K E Y   M E T A S T R I N G S

You can use metastring characters after both DOSKEY and PROMPT. Some of these characters can be used with both for the same purposes. Others, however, have different meanings or are used in only one. If you get confused, the table below should help:

$1–$9	Numbered replaceable parameters in DOSKEY only
$*	Global replaceable parameter in DOSKEY only
$t	Time in PROMPT; command separator in DOSKEY (macro)
$_	Carriage return in PROMPT only
$$	$ in both
$b	¦ in both
$g	> in both
$l	< in both

$Q is not recognized by DOSKEY. To insert = in DOSKEY, just use the sign directly. In PROMPT, you can use $Q or the = sign interchangeably, unless it is the first character after the command. Compare the following:

Command	Resulting prompt
`C>prompt===`	`C>`
`C>prompt D==`	`D==`
`C>prompt=D==`	`D==`
`C>prompt $q=$q`	`===`

```
C>prompt >
File creation error

C>prompt <
File not found

C>prompt ¦
Syntax error
```

These characters have special meanings to DOS, as explained in Chapter 8.

A character other than those listed in Table 5.1 and placed after $ is ignored by DOS, and those after the first character are displayed as a literal string. For example, you could enter this:

```
C>prompt $care
are_
```

On the other hand, you could try this:

```
C>prompt $time
19:05:26.95ime_
```

$t generates time, but others are treated as a literal string.

Useful Prompt Displays

The metastring list in Table 5.1 contains numerous ways for you to maneuver the DOS prompt. The most useful, however, is the one to show the current drive and directory:

```
C>prompt $p$g
```

This command may lead to the display of a new prompt like this:

```
C:\DOS>_
```

If you get lost in your directory maze, just use this prompt as the North Star to navigate around. Moreover, if you are a person who is easily disoriented and constantly needs a road sign to guide you, you can put the above command in your AUTOEXEC.BAT batch file.

If you want to put date and time information in the prompt, this command will do the trick:

```
C>prompt $d $t
```

Notice the space between the two metastrings. Without it, there would be no space separating the date and time numbers shown below:

```
Wed  6-24-1993 11:16:22.30_
```

If you want to display date and time in two lines, you can enter this command:

```
prompt $d$_$t
```

T I P S   A N D   T R I C K S

P R O M P T $ P   A N D   A   F L O P P Y   D R I V E

If the current drive is a floppy drive, entering the PROMPT $P command alone or in combination with other strings will activate the drive and cause the drive light to appear. If the drive is not ready for reading (e.g., no disk inserted), an error message appears. If you want to change from drive A to B in a one-floppy system, this message also appears:

```
Insert diskette for drive B: and press any key when ready
```

If PROMPT $P is not used or is negated by another metastring, the above message is not shown, nor does the drive light appear.

The prompt message now becomes:

```
Wed  6-24-1993
11:17:48.20_
```

The cursor stays at the end of the second line for you to enter a new command. Notice also that the time information has changed. Every time you make a move, including just pressing Enter, a new time appears, reflecting the latest time.

If the prompt is too long and too intrusive, you may just want to display the time data by entering this command:

prompt $t

The prompt now becomes:

```
11:19:00.58_
```

T I P S   A N D   T R I C K S

P R O M P T   A N D   D O S K E Y   S H O R T C U T S

If you use PROMPT often, you can use DOSKEY to speed up your work. And if you use DOSKEY often, you can even use a macro to save you time. The way to do it is to designate a specific alphabetic letter for a particular command and consistently use that letter as a shortcut.

Suppose you want to use K for DOSKEY and P for PROMPT. (That should be easy to remember: think of KP as kitchen police, as in KP duty.) Here is how you create the K and P macros:

```
C>doskey k=doskey $*
```

```
C>k p=prompt $*
```

The second command uses the newly created K macro to create another macro. It is the same as:

```
C>doskey p=prompt $*
```

You can now use K for DOSKEY or P for PROMPT. Suppose you want to print the DOSKEY help message. This command will do:

```
C>k /? > prn
```

And this will show you how many macros you have created:

```
C>k /m
```

You can use the same technique to manipulate the prompt, as in the following examples:

```
C>p $p$g       (path and >)
C>p            (restore default prompt)
```

Fancy Prompts

What if you want to display only hours and minutes, not seconds and fractions? You can erase the extra characters like this:

`prompt $t$h$h$h$h$h$h`

Each $h combination erases a displayed character to the left, just like pressing the Backspace key once; six of them erase six characters. What is left becomes:

`11:22_`

Let us now bring back the familiar C> prompt, combined with the current directory and time:

`prompt $t$h$h$h$h$h$h $p$g`

A new prompt appears:

`11:22 C:\DOS>_`

Now you know not only where you are, but also what time it is each time you enter a new command. From now on, you will no longer be so immersed in learning DOS or using your PC that you lose track of time.

You can put date-time display at a specific area of the screen and/or in specific colors. To do that, you need to use ANSI.SYS. That will be covered in Chapter 12.

P R A C T I C E   5 - 3

☐   1. Change the prompt setting to show the current drive, current directory, and the $ sign.

☐   2. Move to three different directories in the directory structure created in the previous Practice session. The screen should show different prompt displays.

☐   3. Change the prompt to show minutes, seconds (no fractions), and the >> sign.

☐   4. Restore the original (default) system prompt.

☐   5. Use DOSKEY to create a macro named PS (prompt style) which will allow you to enter a single metastring character to change the DOS prompt style.

☐   6. Modify the above so that the prompt style will always end with the > sign.

☐   7. Use ECHO to create a batch file named KP that contains the K and P macros discussed in the text. The file should be saved to drive A. Delete the K and P macros and verify their deletion.

☐   8. Run the KP batch file. Use the P macro to create the prompt showing the current date and the ¦ sign. Restore the default prompt.

☐   9. Create a macro named TIMEPROM that will show the prompt style containing the current time (only hour and minute, no second or fraction) and the directory path, like this:

       11:22 C:\DOS>

Run the macro to change the prompt style. Delete the macro and verify its deletion. Restore the default prompt style.

☐   10. Edit the above macro line so that an executable macro will be saved to the PROM.BAT file in drive A. Run the PROM.BAT file. Run the TIMEPROM macro.

DRILL

____ 13. Used alone, the PROMPT command will display a DOS prompt like this:
  a. A:\>
  b. A:\
  c. B:\DOS>
  d. C>

Answers for questions 14–20:

a. L b. P c. N d. G e. $ f. D g. Q

Each of these characters is used with PROMPT and placed after $ for the purpose of displaying:

____ 14. >

____ 15. <

____ 16. =

____ 17. The dollar sign

____ 18. The current directory

____ 19. The current drive

____ 20. The current date

____ 21. When you want to erase a displayed prompt character, you use $B to do it. True or false?

____ 22. The command of PROMPT T_PG will display:

      a. 9:10:22.12A>

      b. 9:10:22.12A:\DOS>

      c. 9:10:22.12A:\

      d. 9:10:22.12
        B:\DIR1>

USING TREE TO DISPLAY DIRECTORIES

■ *Use the external TREE command to display the directory structure of a
drive or a specific directory.*

The TREE command is used to show the tree structure of your directories. It is
useful when your directory structure gets complicated and confusing.

TREE, unlike PROMPT, is an external command. You need to tell DOS where to
access the TREE.COM program before you can enlist its help.

You can use it to analyze an entire disk or a specific directory. If you analyze a
directory, only that directory and its subdirectories are affected. Here is an
example:

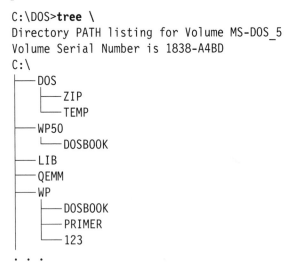

```
C:\DOS>tree \
Directory PATH listing for Volume MS-DOS_5
Volume Serial Number is 1838-A4BD
C:\
├───DOS
│   ├───ZIP
│   └───TEMP
├───WP50
│   └───DOSBOOK
├───LIB
├───QEMM
├───WP
│   ├───DOSBOOK
│   ├───PRIMER
│   └───123
│ . . .
```

In this example, we go to the current directory, C:\DOS, to load TREE.COM and
analyze the entire C drive from the root directory down.

The display clearly shows how various directories are related. In our example,
there are five directories under the root directory. Two of them have no

subdirectory and three have subdirectories. WP, for example, has three subdirectories.

You can specify a directory to show its subdirectories, such as this example:

```
C:\>\dos\tree \dos
Directory PATH listing for Volume MS-DOS 5
Volume Serial Number is 1838-A4BD
C:\DOS
├───ZIP
└───TEMP
```

Here we are in the root directory and want to load TREE.COM from the DOS directory to show the DOS directory's structure. It shows that there are two subdirectories in the C:\DOS directory.

TREE has two switches, /A and /F. The /A switch specifies using ASCII characters (instead of using graphic characters to draw lines) to connect various directories, as shown below. This switch can speed up screen display.

```
C:\>\dos\tree /a
Directory PATH listing for Volume MS-DOS_5
Volume Serial Number is 1838-A4BD
C:.
+---DOS
|   +---ZIP
|   \---TEMP
+---WP50
|   \---DOSBOOK
+---LIB
+---QEMM
+---WP
|   +---DOSBOOK
|   +---PRIMER
|   \---123
.  .  .
```

The /F switch is to display the directory structure as well as files in each directory. The files are arranged in the same order as when you use DIR without specifying a sort order. You can also use DIR /S to show the files in the current (or specified) directory and its subdirectories.

If you have a large number of directories and files, the screen display created by TREE will continue to scroll off the screen. You can use Pause (or Ctrl-S) to pause the scrolling or display one screen at a time by using this command:

```
C:\DOS>tree \ | prn
```

If you want to print the entire directory structure of drive C, enter this command:

```
C:DOS>tree \ > prn
```

ACCESSING COMMAND FILES WITH PATH

■ *Use the internal PATH command followed by a list of drives and directories to make DOS search in the list for an executable (command) file.*

■ *Use PATH alone to show an existing path list.*

Another useful DOS tool to help you navigate around a complex directory structure is the PATH command. You can use it to make DOS search in predetermined paths for an executable file (with COM, EXE or BAT extension) and then execute it.

Suppose you store all the external DOS commands in the C:\DOS directory and all your batch files in C:\BAT. You now want DOS to execute a DOS program or a batch file you have created—regardless of where the current directory is. This command will let you do that:

```
C>path c:\dos;c:\bat
```

After entering the above command, you can run a program or batch file from any drive or directory. Suppose you are in drive A and enter this command:

```
A>mybat
```

DOS will first go to the current directory in the current drive to search for MYBAT.COM, then MYBAT.EXE, and finally MYBAT.BAT—unless MYBAT is a macro, in which case it has top priority. If it fails to find a matching file, it goes to the path list, if any, and follows the order in that list. If MYBAT is not in C:\DOS, DOS will finally go to C:\BAT. If the file is found, it is executed. If not, this familiar message appears:

```
Bad command or file name
```

In that case, either the named file is not executable or not stored in the specified path list. You may then examine what paths DOS is asked to follow. To do that, simply enter this command:

```
A>path
```

DOS will respond by showing you this:

```
PATH=C:\DOS;C:\BAT
```

That is exactly what you ordered it to do.

If the whole string does not appear, one likely cause is that you have inserted a space somewhere. The existence of a space will cause DOS to terminate reading the rest. Also, do not forget to separate each path with a semicolon.

You can insert a space after the PATH command, or you can replace it with an equal sign (=). Either one will work. It is more convenient to simply press the space bar.

Each time you enter a new path, the latest path list will replace the old one. DOS remembers only the most recently entered information. You can, however, use a batch file to add new items to an existing path list. This technique will be explored in Chapter 9.

If you want to delete an existing path list, simply put a semicolon (plus an optional space) after the PATH command, such as:

A>**path;**

If you now enter the PATH command alone, DOS displays the "No Path" message.

A path list, a prompt string, and an APPEND list discussed below are stored in a memory area called the **DOS environment**. You can use the SET command to maneuver them. See Chapter 9 and 11 for more details.

ACCESSING DATA FILES WITH APPEND

■ *Use the external command of APPEND, followed by a list of drives and directories, to make DOS search in the list for a data file.*

■ *Use an available switch with APPEND to make DOS search for both data and executable files.*

When you use PATH, DOS will search for executable files (**command path**), but not data files (**data path**). You need the APPEND command to search for the latter. If you use a proper switch, it can search for both data and executable files. It can also be used on a network to access remote data files.

Unlike PATH, APPEND is an external command. But once loaded, it stays resident until power is off. It is known as a **TSR** (terminate and stay resident) or memory-resident program; you first encountered a TSR program in DOSKEY in Chapter 4.

Follow these steps to install APPEND and change its parameters:

FOLLOW
THESE
STEPS

1. Install APPEND:

   C:\DOS>**append /e**

APPEND has now entered the DOS environment.

2. Display the environment variables:

   C:\DOS>**set**

You may see other things, but not APPEND.

3. Set APPEND parameters:

   C:\DOS>**append c:\;c:\dos;c:\bat;a:\ /x**

We are including a path list, plus specifying the /X switch whose purpose is explained below.

4. Display APPEND's list:

```
C:\DOS>append
APPEND=C:\;C:\DOS;C:\BAT;A:\
```

You can now use APPEND as you do with PATH, as explained earlier. If you enter the SET command now, the above line will also appear.

5. Insert the DOS-TA disk in drive A and show a file:

```
C:\DOS>type sample.txt
```

The file's contents should be shown on the screen—even though the current directory is C:\DOS and the data file is in A:\. When this situation is encountered, DOS will search for the specified data file, SAMPLE.TXT, in the current directory and, if not found, follow the data-path list to display the first matching file. If the file cannot be found, then an error message appears.

APPEND has these switches:

/E	Store paths in DOS environment; can then be changed by the SET command
/PATH:ON	Search both command-line and environment paths
/PATH:OFF	Ignore environment path if command-line path specified
/X or /X:ON	Act like PATH, search for COM, EXE, BAT
/X:OFF	Not search for executable files
;	Placed after APPEND to clear path list

The /E switch causes APPEND to be stored in the DOS environment, like PATH and PROMPT. You can then manipulate it as an environment variable, as explained in Chapter 9. If you want to put it in the environment, you must specify this switch without any path list when you install APPEND (running it the first time). If you do it after that, you will get the "Invalid switch" message.

The /X: switches instruct DOS whether or not to search for executable as well as data files along the APPEND list. Use /X or /X:ON to turn on this feature and /X:OFF to turn it off. /X:OFF is the default.

When /X: is on, DOS will search for an executable file in the APPEND list, just as it does in the PATH list. Suppose there is no PATH list and you enter this command:

```
C:\>append c:\dos /x:on
```

You can now execute an external DOS command stored in the C:\DOS directory even though the command is not in the current directory. If /X: is off, DOS does not go through the APPEND list to search for an executable file.

When the /X: switch is on, you can use COPY to search for source files. Suppose you are in A:\ and FILE1 and FILE2 are stored in the A:\FILES directory, you can enter this command:

    A:\>**copy file? b:**

COPY will locate the source files (if the directory is included in the APPEND list). Other commands, such as DIR, XCOPY, PRINT, and REPLACE will not search the APPEND list. If /X: is not turned on, even COPY will not go through the APPEND list.

The /PATH: switches tell DOS whether or not to search for a data file beyond the path entered on the command line. If set to on (default) by this command:

    A:\>**append b:\bat /path:on**

TIPS AND TRICKS

THE HAZARD OF A TSR PROGRAM

There are many TSR programs available today. The most popular is Borland's Sidekick. They are popular with computer users, for they can perform many small but useful functions not available in major application software.

There is so far no set standard as to where each TSR program should stay in your computer memory. If you use some of these, they may claim the same memory area. If that happens, your computer will be frozen, requiring rebooting.

APPEND, like other TSR programs, could clash with other programs in the memory. If I run WordPerfect's Shell program and then run WordPerfect, I cannot go to DOS, run APPEND, and return. The computer will simply freeze. On the other hand, if I run APPEND first and then load Shell and WordPerfect, I have no problem. The order in which you run a TSR program could be a matter or life or death.

If you have a 386/486 PC, you can use the LOADHIGH command to load TSR programs like DOSKEY and APPEND to the upper memory area. So far I have successfully used this technique to load APPEND and DOSKEY without crashing my computer. The only problem is that every time I return to WordPerfect, the loaded TSR programs will be erased. It is not very convenient, but it is certainly more bearable than having my PC frozen and losing all the data. See Chapter 9 for more details of loading TSRs in the upper memory area.

and if you enter this command:

`A:\>`**type b:\sample.txt**

DOS will go to the root directory of drive B (the path specified on the command line), plus the directories specified in the APPEND list, to search for SAMPLE.TXT. If /PATH: is set to off, DOS will search only in drive B's root directory, as specified on the command line. If no path is specified on the command line, such as:

`A:\>`**type x.bat**

DOS will search all the paths in the APPEND list regardless of whether /PATH: is on or off. If a matching file is found in the current directory, it has priority over those in the list.

P R A C T I C E   5 - 4

1. Use the TREE command to show the directory structure of the disk in a drive and display the result with ASCII characters.

2. Use TREE to show the C:\DOS directory by specifying the switch that will display files.

3. Use TREE to display the directory structure of DELTA, created in Practice 5-3.

4. Enter a PATH list that would allow you to execute from anywhere a program that is stored in the DELTA directory. Display the path list on the screen.

5. Use APPEND with the switch that will make DOS search for both data and executable files in the DELTA directory. Display the APPEND path list on the screen.

6. Create a macro named AP that will allow you to enter an append list and change any switch.

7. Run AP macro three times, the first time to enter the C:\DOS;C:\BAT;A:\ path list, the second time to turn /X: on, and the third time to turn /X: off.

8. Display the APPEND list and environment variables. Use the AP macro to clear the APPEND list and verify the deletion.

D R I L L

____ 23. TREE, APPEND, and PATH are all external commands. True or false?

____ 24. The command below will:

    A>tree b: /f/a

  a. Analyze drive A
  b. Use ASCII characters and display files
  c. Display only ASCII files
  d. Cause an error message due to an illegal switch

____ 25. The /A switch can speed up the way the TREE command displays a directory structure. True or false?

____ 26. Used alone, PATH tells DOS to clear the previously entered path specifications. True or false?

____ 27. You can use PATH to search for a nonexecutable (data) file. True or false?

____ 28. If you enter PATH followed by path specifications several times, only the most recently entered information will be remembered by DOS.

____ 29. APPEND is an external command. But it stays in memory after it is used the first time. True or false?

____ 30. APPEND can be used to access both data and executable files. True or false?

S U M M A R Y   A N D   R E V I E W

Check each item as you review and understand the following highlights of the chapter:

☐   1. Every disk has a root directory. You can, if you wish, create other directories and subdirectories. The root directory is the highest-level directory. Other, lower-level directories can be structured in any way you wish.

☐   2. The current directory is the active directory, where actions can be taken without giving DOS a path. The directory above (one level higher) is referred to as the parent directory. The one below (one level lower) is referred to as a subdirectory. The granddaddy of all directories is the root directory.

☐   3. Using directories to store a large number of files has many advantages. You can better organize and find your files if you store different types in different directories. For example, letters can be in one directory and reports in another.

☐   4. Use the MD (or MKDIR) command followed by a name to create a directory that is a subdirectory of the current directory. If the directory to be created is not a subdirectory of the current directory, provide a path before the directory name to be created.

5. Use the RD (or RMDIR) command followed by a name to remove a directory. Provide a path if the directory to be removed is not a subdirectory of the current directory. A directory must be empty (not contain anything) before it can be removed.

6. Use the CD (or CHDIR) command to change the current directory. Put a name after the command if you want to move to a subdirectory. Put two periods (..) after it if you want to move to the parent directory. Add a specific path for others.

7. When actions related to the current directory are to be taken, just enter a command such as DIR. If these actions are related to other directories, you need to add a path.

8. Use the MOVE command to move files or rename directories.

9. Use the DELTREE command to remove directories, together with files in them. This is a dangerous command; it can chop off lots of files and subdirectories.

10. Take advantage of the PROMPT command to display meaningful messages. If you want the system prompt to show the name of the current directory in the current drive, use the PROMPT PG command.

11. A number of metastrings can be put after the PROMPT command to perform some useful tasks, such as showing the current time or directory path.

12. Use DOSKEY to create single-letter macros that can simplify the process of entering DOSKEY or PROMPT commands.

13. DOSKEY and PROMPT share some common metastring characters. Some, however, are exclusive to one or the other. Consult a table in the text to avoid confusion.

14. If your directory structure becomes complicated and confusing, use the external TREE command to show it. Version 3.3 or earlier shows a listing and can analyze only a whole disk. Version 4 or later shows an easier-to-read diagram instead of listing and can be used to analyze a specific directory.

15. Use the PATH command followed by drive and directory specifications to establish a command path, which can guide DOS to search for an executable file when you enter the program name to execute it. This can save the time and trouble of looking for it manually. Use the PATH command alone to display the most recently entered path list.

16. Use APPEND to establish a data path, which can guide DOS to access data files that may be stored in places other than the current directory. APPEND stays in memory after running the first time. This could conflict with other programs and crash your computer.

R E V I E W   Q U E S T I O N S

Write an answer for each question below.

1. What are some of the advantages of using directories to save files?

2. Define root directory.

3. Define current directory.

4. What happens if you enter this command:
    A>md fatcat

5. Enter a command below to create a directory named RUNNER which is a subdirectory of the root directory:
    A:\SPORTS\SHOPS>_

6. How does DOS interpret this command:
    A:\SPORTS>rd shops

7. What is the easiest way to designate the directory directly above the current one as the new current directory?

8. Enter a command below to make the root directory the current directory:
    A:\SPORTS\SHOPS>_

9. What happens if you enter the PROMPT command alone?

10. If you want the prompt to show the current directory of the current drive, plus the greater than (>) sign, what command do you enter?

11. What command do you use if you want the prompt to display the current date, followed by the default prompt in a new line?

12. What prompt message will appear if you enter this command:
    PROMPT=$Greetings, world:

13. What does the following command do:
    A>c:\dos\tree

14. What is the purpose of using PATH or APPEND followed by some directory specifications?

15. What is the purpose of using the PATH or APPEND command alone? How do you clear a path list?

Copying, Comparing, and Protecting Files

COMMANDS COVERED

COPY, VERIFY, XCOPY, DISKCOPY, FC, DISKCOMP, UNDELETE, DEFRAG, MSAV, VSAFE

NEW TERMS AND SYMBOLS

+, ^Z, _

QUICK START

To combine and copy to the last file, which will be created or replaced:

```
A>copy file1 + file2 fileall     (or)
A>copy file* fileall
A>copy /b prog* prog.all         (binary mode)
```

To append (add) to the first file, which must exist:

```
A>copy file1 + file2 + file3     (or)
A>copy file1 + file?
A>copy /b prog1 + prog2          (binary mode)
```

To change file dates:

```
A>copy file . +         (single file)
A>copy file? . +        (matching files)
A>copy . . +            (all files—ASCII mode)
A>copy /b *.exe . +     (binary files)
```

To copy to devices:

```
A>copy con prn          (from console to printer)
A>copy file prn         (from disk to printer)
A>copy file con         (from disk to screen)
A>copy file? con        (display multiple files)
A>copy /b *.exe con     (display multiple binary files)
```

To copy files and subdirectories with prompt for Y/N:

```
C:\DOS>xcopy /s /p a:file? b:
```

To compare files:

```
C:\DOS>fc file1 file2
```

To duplicate a floppy disk track by track:

```
C:\DOS>diskcopy a: b:
```

To compare two floppy disks:

```
C:\DOS>diskcomp a: b:
```

To protect against deletion:

```
C:\DOS>undelete /load
```

To defragment a disk:

```
C:\DOS>defrag a:
```

To detect and clean viruses:

```
C:\DOS>msav
```

To monitor virus activities:

```
C:\DOS>vsafe
```

Copying files is a vital part of working with a computer. The files you acquire or create need to be protected with backup copies; if one is corrupted, you still have the backup. Copies can also be distributed to other persons or used on other computers. All these options would not be possible if you could not make copies.

So far you have learned to use the COPY and DISKCOPY commands to produce duplicates. In this chapter you learn to use COPY to do more tricks, including combining files and putting a new date and time on existing files.

The XCOPY command, an improved version of COPY, is also covered in this chapter. Some of its functions related to backing up files will be explained in the next chapter.

The three commands, COPY, XCOPY, and DISKCOPY, overlap in some aspects but differ in others. You will find out how they differ and how to apply them to different situations.

After learning different ways of copying files, you will also learn to compare files and disks to find out possible variations and identify errors.

A series of new tools to protect your disks and files are also covered here. These include UNDELETE, DEFRAG (disk defragmenter), MSAV (Microsoft Anti-Virus), and VSAFE (virus monitor).

COPY COMMAND'S MANY USES

COPY's uses, explained before, are summarized here.

You have learned different ways to use the COPY command. The list below sums up what we have covered on this most commonly used command:

Command	Purpose
A>**copy filename b:**	Copy one file from A to B
A>**copy b:*.***	Copy all files from B to A
A>**copy b:.**	Same as above
A>**copy b:file?.txt**	Copy matching files from B to A
A>**copy chap*.* b:*.bak**	New extension in target files

Command	Purpose
A>`copy chap*.* *.bak`	Same directory, new extension
A>`copy con filename`	Create a file and save in A
A>`copy filename + con`	Add to an existing file in A
A>`copy filename con`	Display a file on the screen
A>`copy file?.txt con`	Display matching files

The COPY command follows this syntax:

A>`copy source target`

If there is only one parameter, as in the second to fourth examples above, it is assumed to be the source. The target is assumed to be the current directory.

These examples copy specific or matching files from the source to the target with or without changes in the file names. Duplicate files carry the date-time of the original files. What if you want the duplicate files to have different date-time, or want to combine several files into one, or want to handle binary files or copy to devices? The sections below explain these possible variations.

COMBINING (CONCATENATING) FILES

■ *Append all the files to the first by connecting all the files with a +.*

■ *Combine files with a +, and copy them to the last file, which must be separated from the rest with a space.*

The COPY command can be used to combine several files into one. Although a target file includes everything from source files, the latter files remain intact.

Let us create two separate files and try to put them into one. Insert a practice disk in drive A and follow these steps:

FOLLOW THESE STEPS

1. Create the first file:

    A>`copy con file1`
    `This is from FILE1.`
    `^Z`

2. Create the second file:

    A>`copy con file2`
    `This is from FILE2.`
    `^Z`

3. Combine FILE1 and FILE2 into FILE3:

```
A>copy file1 + file2 file3
FILE1
FILE2
        1 File(s) copied
```

Notice the absence of a + before the last file. This plus sign plays a crucial role, as you will see in the examples below. In this command, DOS treats the files connected with a + as source files and the last, not connected with a +, as the target. The space before and after a + is optional.

Note: The screen displays the "1 File(s) copied" message. This actually means that one file has been created, namely FILE3. If this file does not already exist, it will be created. If it already exists, its original contents will be replaced.

4. Display the contents of the combined file:

```
A>type file3
This is from FILE1.
This is from FILE2.
```

Notice the order: FILE1 is placed before FILE2. This order is determined by the way you arrange them in step 3.

So far both FILE1 and FILE2 remain unchanged. You can use the TYPE command to show their contents. The following steps, however, will change their contents.

5. Show the creation date-time of FILE2:

```
A>dir file2
```

Write down (or memorize) the time of FILE2's creation. This number will be compared to a new time shown later.

6. Combine all three files:

```
A>copy file2 + file1 + file3
FILE2
FILE1
FILE3
        1 File(s) copied
```

After you enter the command, three file names are automatically displayed. Again, you are told that one file has been copied, which you should interpret to mean that one file, namely FILE2, has been created.

Note: Notice the order of the files displayed on the screen. Since all the files in the command are connected with a +, you ask DOS to append to the first file. FILE2, which is placed at the beginning of the list, is the target, and the rest are sources. The target file is changed, but the source files remain intact.

7. Show the contents of the target file:

```
A>type file2
This is from FILE2.
This is from FILE1.
This is from FILE1.
This is from FILE2.
```

The first line comes from the original FILE2, the second from FILE1, and the last two from FILE3.

8. Show FILE2's creation date-time:

```
A>dir file2
```

Compare this time to the one shown in step 5. You can now safely conclude that DOS treats FILE2 as a new file with a new date-time and contents.

What about FILE1 and FILE3, placed after the first + sign? They remain unchanged, keeping the same contents and date-time data. You can prove it by using the TYPE command on them.

You can append from as many files or from as many directories as you wish. Consider the following example:

```
A>copy file1 + b:file2 + c:\dosbook\chap3 + chap4
```

After this command, FILE1 not only will keep its original contents but also will include the contents of all the other source files shown after the first +; all the latter files remain unaltered.

WARNING: If you link a series of files with a + to append to the first, you should be aware of an unusual situation. If the target (first) file does not exist, the next existing file will become the target. Consider this:

```
A>copy file0 + file1 + file2 + file3
```

If FILE0 does not exist, FILE1 will be the target and the others will be appended to it.

USING WILD CARDS TO COMBINE FILES

■ *Combine all the source files matching a pattern and copy them to a target, which must be separated with a space.*

■ *Append to a target placed before a + all the source files matching a pattern placed after the +.*

Wild card characters can be used in combining files. Several related files can be combined and put in a new file, such as:

```
A>copy file*.txt fileall.txt
```

In this example, FILE1.TXT, FILE2.TXT, etc. are copied to FILEALL.TXT. If FILEALL.TXT does not exist, it will be created. If it already exists, its contents and date-time will be replaced.

Instead of copying related files, you could append them, such as:

```
A>copy file1.txt + file*.txt
```

All the files matching the FILE*.TXT pattern will be appended to the target file (located before the +), except the target file itself. If the target file does not exist, no copying will be done; a series of error messages will appear instead.

Note: In either example above, do not use a wild card in the extension of the target file, such as FILEALL.* or FILE1.*. If you do, only the last matching source file will be copied to the target. The ending message on the screen shows multiple files, not just one, copied. When you see this message, you should know that file concatenation has not be done.

A command like the two above may generate a peculiar situation and this cryptic error message:

```
Content of destination lost before copy
```

This message may mean a loss of data. On the other hand, it may not. Let us use some concrete examples. Suppose we have these file names and their contents as shown on the right:

```
FILE1     a
FILE2     b
FILE3     c
```

Suppose also that the files' order in the directory is as shown above, namely FILE1 first and FILE3 last. The following shows each target file's contents after each command (assuming that when a command is issued, only the above three files exist):

```
A>copy file? fileall        FILEALL = abc
A>copy file? file1          FILE1 = abc
A>copy file? file2          FILE2 = ac
A>copy file? file3          FILE3 = ab
A>copy fileall + file?      FILEALL not created
A>copy file1 + file?        FILE1 = abc
A>copy file2 + file?        FILE2 = bac
A>copy file3 + file?        FILE3 = cab
```

All the commands except the first two will show the "Content of destination lost before copy" message. However, the third and fourth examples show loss of data and the fifth no creation of a file.

In the first example, all the three files' contents are put in the newly created file. If this file exists, its contents will be replaced. If FILEALL does not exist in the fifth example, a series of errors appear and no file is created.

In the third, fourth, and fifth examples, the directory order of a target file makes a big difference. If the target file is before all the other matching files, as in the second example, there is no loss of data. Since FILE2 and FILE3 are not the first matching files in the directory, the third and fourth examples show that their original contents are lost.

There is no loss of data in our last three examples. Regardless of where each target file is located in the directory, the original contents are kept and new data are added after them. If a target file does not exist in this situation, it will not be created, as in our fifth example. This is in contrast to the result in the first example.

CHANGING A FILE'S DATE-TIME

■ *Place a + after a file name to put the current date-time on the file. Use wild cards for matching files.*

The COPY command can be used to put the current date and time on an old file. This will make an old file appear to be created more recently; or earlier, if you set your computer time to an earlier date. The following is one way to do it:

```
A>copy file*.txt b:*.* +
```

This copies all the matching files to drive B, keeping the same file names but using the current date and time.

WARNING: The + should be put at the end of target files, not source files. If you put it right after the source, DOS would interpret your instruction quite differently. Consider the following:

```
A>copy file1 + b:
```

It appears that you intend to copy a file from A to B and stamp the current date and time on the new file. DOS, however, will append all the files in the current directory of drive B to the file before the +.

If there is a single file on which you want to stamp a new date and time, try this:

```
A>copy file1 + ,,
```

WARNING: The above example, appearing in IBM manuals, is hazardous. Do NOT use a wild card character in such an operation, such as:

```
A>copy file? + ,,
FILE1
File not found -
Content of destination lost before copy
        0 File(s) copied
```

FILE1, the first matching file found by DOS is now deleted. The message tells you that the file can no longer be found.

If you append an existing file to a nonexistent file, or vice versa, the existing file will also carry a new date and time while keeping its original name and contents, such as:

```
A>copy file1 + dummy
```

If DUMMY exists, it will be appended to FILE1. If not, FILE1 will carry a new date and time. The order of the two files can be reversed without affecting the outcome. Again, do not use wild cards in the target (before the +); the first matching file will also be lost as explained above.

If you have multiple files to update but want to keep them on the current disk, try the following:

```
A>copy file*.txt *.* +
```

Every time a file is worked on, the message "Content of destination lost before copy" will be displayed. Each target file is replaced with a matching source file. Thus the contents of each file remain unchanged. However, since each target file is created by this operation, new date and time data is attached to it.

T I P S   A N D   T R I C K S

CHANGING FILE DATES

There are many ways to change file dates. The simplest and safest way, which I stumbled upon while testing COPY's various combinations, is to use a single period judiciously, such as:

```
A>copy file1 . +
A>copy file*.txt . +
```

The first command will change the date-time of one file, and the second all the matching files. The space after the period is optional, but the one before it is mandatory. Without this space, DOS will consider your move to be copying a file to itself and refuse to do anything.

If you want to change all the files in one directory, try either command below:

```
A>copy *.* *.* +
A>copy . . +
```

As explained in Chapters 4 and 5, a single period can be used in lieu of *.*. The above two commands are thus identical.

SUMMARY OF COMBINING FILES

■ *Rules of combining files are summarized here.*

The rules of combining files seem complicated and confusing. Perhaps the summary examples below may help:

Append to First File:

A1.   A>`copy target + source1 + source2...`

A2.   A>`copy all.txt + *.txt`

Combine and Copy to Last File:

B1.   A>`copy source1 + source2... target`

B2.   A>`copy *.txt all.txt`

Change an Existing File's Date-Time:

C1.   A>`copy file1.txt + ,,`

C2.   A>`copy file1.txt . +`

C3.   A>`copy file1.txt + dummy`

C4.   A>`copy dummy + file1.txt`

C5.   A>`copy file*.* *.* +`

C6.   A>`copy b:file*.* +`

C7.   A>`copy *.* *.* +`

C8.   A>`copy . . +`

The A examples append all the files (listed or matching) to the file appearing before the first +. In such cases, where all the files are connected with a +, the first file is the target and all the others are sources. In A1, if the first file does not exist, the first existing file in the list is treated as the target. In A2, if the target file does not exist, no copying is done.

The B examples show all the source files connected with a +, and the target file appearing last and separated from the rest with a space. All the source files go to the target, which is created if nonexistent or completely replaced if existent.

The C examples show various ways of updating (adding new date and time to) old files. C1-C4 update a single file in the current directory. C5 updates all the matching files in the current directory. C6 copies matching files to another drive, updating the target files. C2-C5 will also generate error messages without hindering the updating. Finally, C7 and C8 let you change all the files in one directory.

━━━━━   *T I P S   A N D   T R I C K S*   ━━━━━

H A Z A R D O U S   C O P Y   P A R A M E T E R S

When used with certain parameters, the COPY command could erase your files. Consider these examples:

```
A>copy file? combo
A>copy file? + ,,
A>copy file? + dummy
A>copy file? filex
```

The first will replace the contents of COMBO if it exists. The second will delete the first matching file found and do nothing to the other files, if they exist. What the third example does depends on whether DUMMY exists. If it does, it is appended to the first matching file. If not, the first matching file is deleted, just as in the second example. In the last example, if FILEX is not the first of all the matching files in the directory, its original contents will be lost.

If you want to stamp the current date on a binary file, make sure you use the /B switch, like these:

```
A>copy /b prog.exe + ,,
A>copy /b prog*.com . +
```

Without the /B switch (the space before / is optional), your updated programs would be much shorter, only up to the first ^Z; they would most likely be ruined by such an operation. See the next section for explanation.

P R A C T I C E   6 - 1

☐   1. Create two files named TEST1 and TEST2, each containing one line of text.

☐   2. Combine TEST1 and TEST2 into a new file named TEST3.

☐   3. Append TEST1 and TEST2 to TEST3; link all three files with a +.

☐   4. Append TEST2 and TEST3 to TEST1; use wild cards.

☐   5. Change all the files to the current date-time.

☐   6. Use DOSKEY to create a macro named CPY that will allow the user to enter two parameters to do copying or file combination. The macro should include the file name TEST, which will allow the user to enter a number to do something to a file.

(Keep these test files and the macro until you are instructed to delete them.)

D R I L L

____   1. This command will copy:

A>copy file??.* *.bak

a. matching files to another disk

b. matching files to the same disk with new extensions

c. only matching source files that have no extensions

d. nothing; it's illegal

____   2. This command will:

A>copy filename + b:

a. copy a file to drive B

b. copy a file from drive B to A

c. append files from B to the named file

d. do nothing; it's illegal

____   3. Which of the following is legal?

a. A>copy *.* a:

b. A>copy *.* b:

c. A>b:copy *.*

d. A>b:copy *.* a:

____   4. This command will:

A>copy filename .+

a. append all the matching files to the named file

b. copy the file to the current drive

c. stamp the current date and time on the file

d. do nothing

____   5. This command will

A>copy file1 + file2 + file3

a. append the first two files to the third

b. create the third file if nonexistent

c. replace the third file if existent

d. append the last two files to the first

_____ 6. This command will

      A>copy file1 + file2 file3

  a. combine the first two and put in the third

  b. create the third file if nonexistent

  c. replace the third file if it exists

  d. all of the above

COPY COMMAND'S SWITCHES

■ *Use /V to verify writing, /A for ASCII mode, and /B for binary mode.*

■ *Use /B when combining binary files or putting a new date-time on binary files.*

The COPY command comes with three switches:

    /V   Verify target files

    /A   ASCII copying

    /B   Binary copying

Verifying Writing /V

The /V switch turns on VERIFY for a particular copying operation. For example, this command:

```
A>copy file1 b: /v
```

copies FILE1 from drive A to drive B and verifies the target file's writing.

The above example turns on the VERIFY function only during this particular operation. The function is off in future copying operations, unless you use the /V switch again.

You can turn on VERIFY by entering this command:

```
A>verify on
```

After this command, every copying operation will be followed by verification. Adding the /V switch after this does not change its status, but the switch is redundant.

To find out whether VERIFY is on or off, you can enter the command alone:

```
A>verify
VERIFY is on
```

DOS responds by showing the status. To turn off VERIFY, this command will do:

```
A>verify off
```

Entering VERIFY now shows the off status:

```
A>verify
VERIFY is off
```

The VERIFY function is rarely needed. The act of copying a file seldom goes wrong. If you want to be doubly sure, it causes no harm to use it. The only thing you lose is time—it takes extra time to check a target file.

ASCII or Binary Mode

The /A and /B switches tell DOS to be in ASCII or binary mode during copying or combining files.

When DOS copies a file, it operates by default in binary mode. Everything in the source is faithfully read and then written to the target.

When combining files (including any operation using a + or having wild cards in the source), however, COPY operates by default in ASCII mode. Each source file is read only before the first ^Z character encountered; the rest is ignored. The target file will in most cases also have an extra ^Z character added to the end.

The ^Z Character *identifies the end of a file*

The ^Z character is a remnant of the past. Before version 3.0, DOS used this character (ASCII 26) to identify the end of a file. Newer versions use the value stored in the disk's directory to determine each file's size. These versions can handle files without the ^Z, but still honor it when it is encountered. If a file contains no ^Z or has a ^Z at the very end, DOS knows its size and can handle it without any problem.

However, if there is a ^Z in the middle of a file, as many binary files (such as computer programs) do, this may create a problem. If you want to combine such files, you may need to use /A or /B switches selectively.

When DOS encounters COPY used with the /B switch in the source, it will read everything. But the reading will end at the first ^Z when /A is used. In case of a target file, /A causes the addition of ^Z to the end (unless it already exists), but /B does not.

Another rule to remember is that the /A or /B switch affects the file immediately preceding it and all the files after it—unless negated by a later switch.

The following examples provide ample illustrations and explanations for just about all imaginable scenarios for the rules stated above:

Command	Explanation
A>**copy fil* b:all**	Read source before ^Z, no ^Z added to ALL
A>**copy f1+f2 f3**	Read F1 & F2 before ^Z, add ^Z in F3
A>**copy f1+f2+f3**	Read F2 & F3 before ^Z, add ^Z in F1
A>**copy fil* b:**	Read all in source, no extra ^Z in target
A>**copy fil* b:+**	New date in B, ^Z added
A>**copy fil* b:+/b**	New date in B, no ^Z
A>**copy fil b:/a**	Read all in source, add ^Z in target
A>**copy fil/a b:**	Read before 1st ^Z, add ^Z in target
A>**copy fil/a b:/b**	Read before 1st ^Z, no extra ^Z in target
A>**copy con fil**	No ^Z added to FIL
A>**copy/a con fil**	Add ^Z to FIL
A>**copy fil+con**	Add ^Z to FIL
A>**copy fil+,,**	ASCII mode, Add ^Z to FIL
A>**copy/b fil+,,**	Binary mode, no extra ^Z added
A>**copy fil .+**	ASCII mode, no extra ^Z added
A>**copy fil con**	Display before 1st ^Z, same as TYPE
A>**copy/b fil con**	Display all, including ^Z

As you can see, when simple copying is involved, binary mode is the default unless you add switches. In file combination, however, ASCII mode is the default.

Whenever a + is involved, the target file usually has a ^Z added at the end. The first example has no +, so no ^Z is added. In contrast, the second example has a +, that is why F3 will have ^Z and one byte longer than F1 and F2 combined.

WARNING: Stamping a new date on an existing file requires using a + and is thus an ASCII operation; reading of a source file stops when the first ^Z is encountered. If you do not use /B with a binary file, an updated binary file would most likely be incomplete and useless.

The last items in the above list, copying to the console, will be explained more fully in the next section.

COPYING TO DEVICES

■ *Use COPY to copy data to PRN and CON. Use /B with CON to display binary files.*

The COPY command can be used to communicate with devices such as the console (keyboard and monitor), printer, modem, and so on.

In Chapter 4, you encountered the COPY CON command used to copy from the console to a file or vice versa. Other devices can be used in a similar manner. This technique can be used to communicate with the printer.

Copying to the Printer

To demonstrate how you can send data to the printer, follow these steps:

FOLLOW THESE STEPS

1. Enter the command to copy from the console to the printer:

   ```
   A>copy con prn
   ```
   –

2. Type the following line and press Enter:

   This is a test.

3. Turn on the printer, if it is not already on.

4. Enter the ^Z character (press F6 and Enter). The screen appears as below:

   ```
   A>copy con prn
   This is a test.
   ^Z
           1 File(s) copied
   ```

The single line of text is sent to the printer and the print head returns to the left margin. If ^Z is placed at the end of the text line, the print head will stay in that position rather than returning to the left margin.

When you give the COPY CON PRN command, you instruct DOS to copy from the device named CON to the device named PRN. PRN can be replaced with LPT1. If you want to send to the second printer (connected to the second parallel port), you need to use LPT2.

Another way you can use COPY to communicate with the printer is to send an existing disk file to it, such as:

```
A>copy file1.txt prn
        1 File(s) copied
```

from file to printer

If the copying is successful, DOS tells you that one file has been copied. If the file cannot be found, this message appears:

```
A>copy file5 prn
FILE5 File not found
        0 File(s) copied
```

If the printer is not on, the computer freezes and you get this response after a little pause:

```
A>copy file3 prn
Write fault error writing device PRN
Abort, Retry, Ignore, Fail? _
```

If you press A, the DOS prompt reappears and the previous command is aborted. If you turn on the printer and press R, the text is printed. If you choose I or F the temporary freeze continues until the same error message reappears.

Copying to the Console

You can use COPY to copy a disk file to the screen. That has the same effect as using the TYPE command. One major difference is that COPY can combine several files and display them on the screen. Consider this command:

```
A>copy file1 + file2 con
```

All the contents of the first file, followed by the second, will quickly scroll through the screen. At the end DOS tells you "1 File(s) copied".[1]

When used to copy from a disk file to the screen, COPY operates in ASCII mode. It stops reading when the first ^Z is encountered. This works the same as using TYPE. TYPE does not allow a switch, but you can use the /B switch with COPY CON to read an entire file, such as:

A>**copy file1 /b con**

This is the trick you can use to see whether a file contains the ^Z character. Where there is such a character, it appears on the screen as a right arrow sign (→). This sign has the value of ASCII 26, which is also the value of ^Z.

You can also use wild card characters when copying files to the screen, such as:

A>**copy file? /b con**

---

1. This technique can also be applied to PRN. Several files can be combined and sent to the printer. The /A and /B switches can be freely used. Here is an example:

```
A>copy file1/b + file2/a prn
```

The entire FILE1 will be read and combined with FILE2's contents before the first ^Z, and the combined file will be printed.

```
━━━━━  T I P S   A N D   T R I C K S  ━━━━━
```

E L I M I N A T I N G   T H E   ^ Z   C H A R A C T E R

Many files created by DOS, as shown in The ^Z Character section earlier, have the ^Z character automatically added at the end. This extraneous character can cause problem in some situations. You can get rid of it by using the following techniques:

```
A>copy filename + dummy
A>copy dummy + filename
A>copy filename . +
```

Here DUMMY is a nonexistent file. After entering any command above, the file will be reduced by one byte and free of the ^Z character. The file's date will also be changed.

If you have multiple files, the following command will do:

```
A>copy file? . +
```

This will also stamp the current date on the matching files and strip off any extra ^Z.

All the matching files will be displayed one after another until the end. You can use the Pause or Ctrl-S (or Ctrl-Num Lock) to halt the continuous scrolling.[2]

P R A C T I C E   6 - 2

☐ 1. Use COPY's binary switch to individually display the three test files created earlier, and determine which file contains the ^Z character.

☐ 2. Use COPY and wild card(s) to display all the three files one after another.

☐ 3. Combine and print TEST2 and TEST3; use a single command for both actions.

☐ 4. Use the CPY macro to send all the three test files to the null device.

☐ 5. Use the CPY macro to print TEST3.

☐ 6. Use the CPY macro to do #2 above.

---

2. While experimenting with this device, I discovered a peculiar pattern not documented anywhere. If you use the /B switch to display a binary file, you cannot break the scrolling. If you have a long file and a slow computer, this simple action could occupy the computer for a long time. On the contrary, the scrolling can be aborted (using Ctrl-C or Ctrl-Break) when no switch is used or when an ASCII file is displayed.

D R I L L

____ 7. The following command will:

B>copy file1 + file2 prn

a. combine two files and send them to the screen

b. append FILE2 to FILE1

c. append FILE1 to FILE2

d. combine two files and print them

____ 8. The following command will:

A>copy file?? fileall

a. read source files before ^Z and add ^Z to the target

b. create FILEALL if it does not exist

c. replace the contents of FILEALL if it exists

d. do all of the above

____ 9. Which of the following commands reads only up to the first ^Z before copying?

a. A>copy filename b:

b. A>copy filename /b b:

c. A>copy filename /a b:

d. A>copy a:filename b:

____ 10. The following command will:

A>copy filename +.

a. stamp the current date on FILENAME

b. append all the files to FILENAME

c. append files with no extension to FILENAME

d. generate an error message

____ 11. Which command will not add ^Z to the target file?

a. A>copy filename /a b:

b. A>copy filename b: +

c. A>copy b:filename /a

d. A>copy filename /a b: /b

____ 12. The two commands below behave exactly alike. True or false?

A>type filename

A>copy /b filename con

USING THE XCOPY COMMAND *for lrg files*

■ *Use XCOPY to speed up copying large files and duplicate subdirectories.*

The XCOPY command first appeared in version 3.2. It is an improved version of COPY. It has three major properties:

- It works like COPY, except faster on large files.
- It creates and copies subdirectories.
- It copies files with the A attribute.

The first two characteristics are covered below. The third, used for backing up files, will be covered in the next chapter. You will better understand its use after knowing file attributes, also covered in the next chapter.

Because XCOPY.EXE is nearly 16KB long, it would take too much memory to put it in the COMMAND.COM file. Consequently, to use XCOPY you need to provide the path to this external command.

need a path to use xcopy

The syntax of XCOPY is the same as COPY:

```
XCOPY source target /switch
```

The following is an example:

```
C:\DOS>xcopy a:chap*.txt b:
```

This command will load XCOPY.EXE from the current directory and then copy all the matching files from drive A to B. XCOPY first reads all the matching files to the available memory and then starts writing. The screen displays each file's name as it is being written:

```
C:\DOS>xcopy a:chap*.txt b:

Reading source file(s)...
CHAP1.TXT
CHAP2.TXT
CHAP3.TXT
        3 File(s) copied
```

XCOPY will execute your instruction without hesitation under most circumstances. However, one particular circumstance could cause confusion—copying a single file to the same directory, such as:

note

```
A>xcopy chap1.txt chap1.bak
```

There are two possibilities with this command. One is to copy the first file to the second file, creating it if nonexistent or replacing it if existent. The second is to copy the first item, which is a file, to the second item, which is a subdirectory to be created, if necessary.

When COPY encounters this situation, it will copy the first to the second, if the second is an existing subdirectory. If such a subdirectory does not exist, the second item will be treated as a file name.

Since XCOPY can create a subdirectory before copying files, it needs to know what your intention is. If the target is an existing subdirectory, the source is immediately copied to the subdirectory. If not, this question appears:

```
A>xcopy chap1.txt chap1.bak
Does CHAP1.BAK specify a file name
or directory name on the target
(F=file, D=directory)?_
```

If you press F, CHAP1.TXT will be copied to the file named CHAP1.BAK. If this file does not exist, it will be created; if it already exists, its contents will be replaced. If you press D, a subdirectory named CHAP1.BAK will be created and another copy of CHAPT1.TXT will go to the subdirectory.

Do not be surprised if DOS fails to create a subdirectory under this circumstance. If a file bearing the same name exists or if you use a DOS device name such as PRN, no subdirectory will be created and no copying will be done. The next section elaborates on this.

XCOPY COMMAND'S SWITCHES

■ *Use XCOPY's switches for various copying purposes.*

■ *Do not use XCOPY to combine files or send data to DOS devices.*

The XCOPY command has quite a few switches, as shown below:

/A	Archive; copy files marked with A
/D:mm-dd-yy	Date; copy files on or after the specified date
/E	Empty source directories are also copied; used with /S
/M	ReMove source archive bit after backup
/P	Prompt Y/N when wild cards are used
/S	Subdirectories with files are copied
/V	Verify target writing
/W	Wait for keyboard action before copying

The /V switch looks familiar. In fact, it serves the same purpose as the identical switch used with COPY—to verify target files.

Copying Subdirectories

The /S switch is not only useful but also powerful. It is used to copy matching source files in the current directory and its subdirectories. If an identical directory structure does not exist in the target, it will be created before copying. Consider this command:

```
C:\>\dos\xcopy *.bat a: /s
```

It goes to the DOS directory to load XCOPY.EXE and copies all the matching files from the current directory (which happens to be root directory in this case) down. The screen may show this:

```
C:\>\dos\xcopy *.bat a: /s

Reading source file(s)...
AUTOEXEC.BAT
DOS\DING.BAT
ARAB\NIGHT\SING.BAT
        3 File(s) copied
```

Notice that the full path of each matching file is shown on the screen. The same pattern will be duplicated in the target.

Now go to drive A and explore what the command has done. The directories, if they did not already exist, are created. And the files displayed on the screen are copied there.

The /S switch is powerful, but it cannot work magic. Suppose you have batch files located in the C:\BAT directory. Suppose you are now in the root directory and want to copy the batch files to another subdirectory (C:\DOS). You may consider using this command:

```
C:\>xcopy *.bat \dos /s
```

You expect XCOPY to search in all the subdirectories and find matching files to copy to the target subdirectory. That is asking too much of the command. Instead of obeying your order, DOS will give you this error message:

```
Cannot perform a cyclic copy
        0 File(s) copied
```

The reason for the refusal is that the target directory, namely C:\DOS, happens to be one of the source directories. Without this inhibition, files would be copied onto themselves.

The /S switch alone will not transfer an empty subdirectory in the source to the target. If you want an empty subdirectory found in the source also duplicated in the target, you need to combine /S with /E, such as:

```
A>xcopy *.* b: /s /e
```

This command will transfer everything from drive A to B. All the files and subdirectories will be transferred. Without the /E switch, only subdirectories containing files will be duplicated in B. The empty subdirectories, if any, will be ignored.

Using the /S switch is convenient. It saves you the trouble of having to create target directories first before doing any copying to individual directories. However, if you use it indiscriminately, you could give yourself more trouble. If you are not happy with an existing directory structure and you use /S, you will just duplicate the messy arrangement, thus requiring you to spend more time to clean it up.

Prompt, Wait and Backup

When you use the /P switch, DOS will show each file to be copied and prompt you for Y or N. This is most useful if wild card characters are used. This lets you decide which of the matching files to copy, as shown below:

```
A>xcopy chap* b: /p
CHAP1 (Y/N)? _
```

If you press N, this file is not copied. If you press Y, it is copied. The next matching file will be displayed and you will be prompted until the last matching file is acted on.

The /W switch instructs DOS to wait before copying. This message appears before any action, reading or writing, is done:

```
A>xcopy file??.txt b: /w
Press any key to begin copying file(s) _
```

This is useful if you want to use a drive to load the XCOPY.EXE program and then use it as a source or target drive. After the program is loaded, you can take the disk out and use the drive for copying.

The /A, /D, and /M switches are all related to backing up files. They let you copy only the files marked with the archive bit (/A), created on or after a certain date (/D), and remove the archive attribute from the source files that have been copied (/M). These switches will be explained in greater detail when we discuss file backup in the next chapter.

XCOPY's Limitations

XCOPY does not recognize DOS device names of AUX, COM1, CON, NUL, and PRN (or LPT1). If you try to copy a file to one of these devices, you will get the following response:[3]

---

3. You probably remember that if you use COPY in this situation, the named file will be printed without further ado.

```
C:\DOS>xcopy a:chap1.txt prn
Does PRN specify a file name
or directory name on the target
(F=file, D=directory)? f

Cannot XCOPY to a reserved device
        0 File(s) copied
```

If you answer D in the above example, you will get this error message:

```
Unable to create directory
        0 File(s) copied
```

Another point to remember is that XCOPY, like COPY, cannot copy to an unformatted disk. Unlike DISKCOPY, XCOPY cannot format a disk.

Finally, do not combine files with XCOPY. You will either get the "Invalid parameter" message or the result will surprise you. This is an example:

A>xcopy file1 + file2

This command will be interpreted as copying the first to the second, not appending the second to the first as in the case of COPY.

P R A C T I C E   6 - 3

☐ 1. Place the disk containing the previously created test files in drive A. Create a subdirectory with the name of TESTDIR. Copy TEST1 to this directory and delete it in the root directory.

☐ 2. Place another practice disk in drive B. Use XCOPY to copy all the test files from A to B. Make sure you use three switches: one to make DOS wait for your move before copying, one to prompt you for Y/N before copying a file, and one to copy subdirectories.

☐ 3. Go to drive B and examine the results of the above command. What items were created?

☐ 4. Use DOSKEY to create a macro named XC that will load XCOPY from C:\DOS and will let you copy files according to the parameters specified on the command line.

☐ 5. Undo the results created in #2 above by entering all the commands in a single line.

☐ 6. Use the XC macro to repeat #2 above.

D R I L L

____ 13. Which command is illegal?

    a. A>copy con prn

    b. A>copy filename prn

    c. A>copy con filename

    d. A>xcopy filename con

____ 14. When XCOPY is used with the /W switch, copying begins immediately. True or false?

____ 15. When XCOPY is used with /E alone, empty directories in the source drive will be copied to the target. True or false?

____ 16. XCOPY's /S switch will copy only the directories that contain files, but not empty ones. True or false?

____ 17. XCOPY can be used to combine files. True or false?

____ 18. A target disk must be formatted when you use XCOPY. True or false?

COPYING A WHOLE DISK WITH DISKCOPY

■ *Use DISKCOPY to duplicate a disk track by track.*

You have learned to use COPY and XCOPY to create duplicate files. You can also use the DISKCOPY command to create a duplicate disk containing the identical items as the original disk. This external command can be used only with floppies, not hard disks. It copies from source disk to target disk track by track, not file by file as in the case of COPY and XCOPY.

When you run the command, it is loaded to memory and resides there until you terminate it. This frees the drives for copying files, just as using the /W switch with XCOPY. To copy from drive A to B, put the source disk in drive A and a target disk in drive B and enter the following command, which leads to the instructions and messages below:

```
C:\DOS>diskcopy a: b:
Insert SOURCE diskette in drive A:
Insert TARGET diskette in drive B:
Press any key to continue...
```

```
Copying 40 tracks
9 Sectors/Track, 2 Side(s)

Volume Serial Number is xxxx-xxxx

Copy another diskette (Y/N) ?n
```

Make sure you do not mix up the source and the target disks. If you reverse them, you could wipe out the original and replace it with garbage. One way to protect yourself is to write-protect the source disk. This will prevent it from being overwritten with something else.

If you have one floppy drive, you can still use the above command. After DOS reads the source disk, it will prompt you to insert the target disk in the same drive. If there is not enough memory for a one-pass operation, you may be prompted to swap disks several times to copy just one disk.

The DISKCOPY command will wipe out the target disk's contents. If necessary, it will format the target disk according to the specifications of the source disk. The target disk's contents, if any, will be erased before copying.

DISKCOPY will duplicate a bootable disk. If the source disk is bootable, i.e., formatted with FORMAT/S, the target will also be bootable. This command is thus most useful when you need to duplicate an original system disk.

DISKCOPY has two switches, /1 for copying only one side and /V for verifying the target disk. The second switch is new with version 5.

Since incompatible disks have different numbers of tracks and storage capacity for each track, you cannot use one type of disk as source and another as target. If you copy from a lower capacity disk to a higher capacity disk of the same size, DISKCOPY will format the target to the lower capacity before copying. If you reverse the two, it will format to the higher capacity and may fail to copy all the data.

COMPARING COPY, XCOPY, AND DISKCOPY

■ *Differences and similarities among the commands are explained.*

■ *Use COPY or XCOPY, but not DISKCOPY, to duplicate a fragmented disk.*

COPY and XCOPY have many similarities and differences. COPY copies one file at a time; XCOPY reads source files to the available memory before writing to the target. This difference makes XCOPY work faster if you have ample RAM and copy large files.

COPY can copy files to devices, combine them, change their new date and time, and read or write files in ASCII format. XCOPY can do none of these things.

XCOPY can copy subdirectories, prompt you for Y/N before copying a matching file, wait for you to insert a source or target disk, and copy files with certain attributes. COPY can do none of these.

DISKCOPY can copy to an unformatted disk and will erase the contents of the target disk, but COPY or XCOPY requires the target disk to be formatted and will only add to the target disk's contents.

COPY and XCOPY can copy from one type of media to a different type, such as from a floppy disk to a hard disk or from a 3.5-inch disk to a 5.25-inch disk. DISKCOPY, on the other hand, is suitable for copying between two identical types of floppy disks.

While COPY and XCOPY copy each file as a unit, DISKCOPY physically duplicates a whole disk's contents. If a disk is used often, files will be fragmented. One file may be stored in different noncontiguous sectors. This could slow down access time and prematurely wear out disk drive mechanism. If you use DISKCOPY, such a disk will be exactly duplicated, fragmentation and all. COPY or XCOPY, however, can cure this problem.

If a disk is used often for writing and deleting files, it is a good idea to periodically go through a simple exercise to reintegrate each file (put together all the scattered pieces). Put the used disk in drive A and a formatted blank disk in drive B and enter either command below:

```
A>copy *.* b:          (or A>copy . b:)
C:\DOS>xcopy a:*.* b:  (or C:\DOS>xcopy a:. b:)
```

Either command will put each file together and transfer to the new disk. After that, each file will stick together physically and occupy contiguous sectors—until more writing and deleting cause new fragmentation.

COMPARING FILES FC _ filename _ filename

■ *Compare two ASCII or binary files with the FC command.*

You may have two files and wonder whether or not they are identical and, if not, how they differ. On such an occasion, you can use the external FC.EXE command to find out for you.

If the two files are identical, you get this message:

```
A>fc file1 file2
Comparing files FILE1 and FILE2
FC: no differences encountered
```

If no parameter is specified, this message appears:

```
C:\DOS>fc
FC: Insufficient number of filespecs
```

To compare two similar files, let us first create two files and then compare them. Follow these steps:

FOLLOW THESE STEPS

1. Create the first file:

```
A>copy con file1
This is file A.
^Z
```

2. Create the second file:

```
A>copy con file2
This is file B.
^Z
```

3. Compare the two files:

```
A>fc file1 file2
Comparing files FILE1 and FILE2
***** FILE1
This is line A.
***** FILE2
This is line B.
*****
```

If there is a difference, the comparable lines are displayed as shown below:

```
A>fc file1 file2
Comparing files FILE1 and FILE2
***** FILE1
This is line A.
***** FILE2
This is line B.
*****
```

The comparable sets of the two files are displayed for your view. Even if the two files are of different sizes, comparison will proceed.

If you have two large files to compare, you may want to display an abbreviated version by using the /A switch:

```
A>fc /a file1 file2
```

This displays only the beginning and ending lines for each set of differences. The screen is not cluttered with the whole text.

If you want the comparison to ignore cases and treat uppercase and lowercase the same, you can use the /C switch:

A>**fc /c file1 file2**

When binary files are encountered—those with COM, EXE, SYS, OBJ, LIB, and BIN extensions—FC uses binary mode as the default, which will result in a display of address locations and mismatched bytes. When these are not encountered, ASCII is the default. You can change the default by using the /B (binary) or /L (ASCII) switch.

So far we have illustrated the most commonly used switches. The other switches are briefly explained below:

/A	Abbreviated; only first and last lines shown
/B	Binary comparison; byte by byte; no resynchronizing
/C	Case difference ignored
/L	Line comparison; ASCII text; resynchronize; default
/LBn	Line buffer (default n=100); maximum lines of errors compared; comparison ends when buffer is full
/N	Number; line numbers displayed in ASCII comparison
/T	Tabs are not expanded to spaces for comparison
/W	White spaces and tabs are compressed for comparison
/nn	Number (default nn=2) of consecutive lines must match for the two files to be considered resynchronized.

If you use the /B switch, characters in comparable positions are compared. If we compare our two files, this is the result:

A>**fc file1 file2 /b**
Comparing files FILE1 and FILE2
0000000D: 41 42

The display shows that in the 14th position (D in hex) from the beginning of each file, FILE1 has the value of 41 in hex and FILE2 has 42 in hex.

FC can compare files of different sizes. This difference in size will not be reported by FC if you do an ASCII comparison. In a binary comparison, comparison will proceed and this message appears at the end of the report:

FC: FILE2 longer than FILE1

FC will also resynchronize the two files being compared in an ASCII comparison. By default, when two lines are identical, the files are considered in synch. When one file has extra lines, the differences will be displayed. FC will try to resynchronize the two files. If two consecutive lines are identical between the two files, the two files are resynchronized and the lines are not displayed.

Follow these steps to demonstrate the comparison of two similar files:

1. Create the first file:

   ```
   A>copy con file1
   one
   two
   three
   four
   five
   ^Z
   ```

2. Create the second file:

   ```
   A>copy con file2
   xxx
   one
   two
   three
   four
   five
   ```

3. Compare the two files:

   ```
   A>fc file1 file2 /n
   Comparing files FILE1 and FILE2
   ***** FILE1
         1:   one
         2:   two
   ***** FILE2
         1:   xxx
         2:   one
         3:   two
   *****
   ```

Notice that the last three lines are considered identical and are not displayed.

COMPARING DISKS

■ *Compare two floppy disks (not hard disks) with DISKCOMP. Comparison is meaningful only between the same kind of diskettes and between an original and a duplicate created with DISKCOPY.*

When you have two diskettes you want to compare, you can use DISKCOMP, which is an external command. You need to enter drive specifications after the command. If not, this message appears:

```
C:\DOS>diskcomp
Invalid drive specification
Specified drive does not exist
or is non-removable
```

From the message, you know that you must enter drive specifications and can compare only diskettes, not a hard disk. If you enter two floppy disk drives, the comparison will proceed as shown below:

Command → `C:\DOS>diskcomp a: b:`

```
Insert FIRST diskette in drive A:

Insert SECOND diskette in drive B:

Press any key to continue...

Comparing 40 tracks
9 sectors per track, 2 side(s)

Compare OK

Compare another diskette (Y/N) ?n
```

Can you compare two diskettes even if you have only one floppy drive? Yes. Just issue the above command. You will be prompted to insert the first diskette, then the second. The comparison will then begin.

If a comparison results in discrepancies, errors are reported like this:

```
Compare error on
side 0, track 15

Compare error on
side 1, track 15

Compare error on
side 0, track 1^C
```

To end further comparison, press Ctrl-C. If errors are found, it makes no sense to continue the comparison.

DISKCOMP compares two disks track by track. It is meaningful to compare an original and one produced by DISKCOPY. If COPY or XCOPY is used, the target's contents may be rearranged and not identical to the source. DISKCOMP may thus find discrepancies between such disks.

DISKCOMP has two switches, /1 and /8; they are intended to accommodate earlier diskettes. The first compares only the first sides of the two diskettes, and the second compares only the first 8 sectors per track.

DELETION PROTECTION

■ *Use Delete Tracker or Delete Sentry to increase chances of recovering deleted files.*

DOS 5 came with UNDELETE to recover files erased by DEL, and MIRROR to keep track of deleted files to enhance their recovery. In DOS 6, MIRROR is merged into UNDELETE and no longer exists as a separate entity. Furthermore, UNDELETE also offers a new level of protection.

Three Levels of Protection

UNDELETE now offers three levels of deletion protection: standard, Delete Tracker, and Delete Sentry. Each provides progressively more protection with more cost to your RAM and disk space.

The standard level of protection requires you to do nothing and imposes no additional overhead. When you use UNDELETE to recover a deleted file, DOS uses the directory information to show files; each recoverable file's name, minus the first character, will be shown. This works well if the erased file was stored in the contiguous clusters and the space has not been written over by another file.

The other two levels require you to use proper switches with UNDELETE to load a memory-resident portion requiring 9KB or 13.5KB RAM. Delete Tracker uses a small hidden file named PCTRACKER.DEL (the same file created by MIRROR in DOS 5) to track deletions. When you delete a file, its FAT entries and the file name's first character—items normally erased—are saved to PCTRACKER.DEL. When you try to undelete a file, PCTRACKER.DEL is used to restore it. This method can restore a file that was not saved in contiguous clusters. Recovery may be only partial if some of the space is used by another file.

Delete Sentry offers the highest degree of protection. It uses a hidden directory named SENTRY to store the files you deleted. When the directory is full, earlier files are then discarded to make room for new ones. How large is the SENTRY directory and how long are the junk files kept? The default values for these and others are kept in the UNDELETE.INI file; see another section below for details.

UNDELETE comes with 11 switches:

/ALL	Recover all files
/DOS	Use DOS directory to recover files
/DS	Use Delete Sentry to recover files
/DT	Use Delete Tracker to recover files
/LIST	List recoverable files.

Undelete switches

/LOAD	Load memory-resident portion with default values
/PURGE	Clear the contents of SENTRY directory
/S	Load memory-resident portion for Sentry
/STATUS	Show protection status
/T	Load memory-resident portion for Tracker
/UNLOAD	Unload memory-resident portion

Some of them are used for setting up the system and others to let you recover deleted files. We will first discuss these options and then ask you to do some activities.

Installing UNDELETE

If you want to use Delete Tracker or Delete Sentry, you need to load the memory-resident portion by specifying the /LOAD switch. If you want to unload, use the /UNLOAD switch to clear the memory-resident portion from RAM. Used with /LOAD, UNDELETE will use an ASCII file named UNDELETE.INI to set default values, including what level of protection and which drive(s). If this file does not exist, it will be created.

If you do not want to use the default values contained in the UNDELETE.INI file, you can specify them by using /S[drive] for Sentry or /Tdrive[-entries] for Tracker. Use /S to specify a drive to protect, such as /SC (drive C) or /SA /SC (for both drive A and drive C); if no drive is specified with /S, the current drive is used. With /T, a drive (which you want to track) is required but the number of entries is optional. You can specify 1 to 999 entries; for example, UNDELETE /TA-20 will track drive A for 20 entries. If it is not specified, the following default values are used, each in turn determining the file size of PCTRACKER.DEL:

Disk size	Entries	File size
360KB	25	5KB
720KB	50	9KB
1.2MB	75	14KB
1.44MB	75	14KB
20MB	101	18KB
32MB	202	36KB
32MB	303	55KB

You can use /STATUS to show you what kind of protection and which drive. You can also use /PURGE[drive] to delete the contents in the hidden SENTRY drive. If no drive is specified, the current drive is searched.

Recovering Deleted Files

You can specify a switch to use a particular method to recover deleted files. /DOS uses the directory to recover files, /DT the PCTRACKER.DEL file, and /DS the SENTRY directory. If no switch is used with UNDELETE, DOS will try the best method (Sentry) and if it is unavailable the next best—Tracker and finally standard.

Used alone, the above switches will prompt you for Y/N for recovering a deleted file. In the case of /DOS, you will also be asked to supply the first missing character to complete a file name. If you combine /ALL with any of these switches, you are not prompted. If you combine /DOS and /ALL, the first characters of the recovered files will use the following list:

        #%&0123456789ABCDEFGHIJKLMNOPQRSTUVWXYZ.

The first recovered file will use #, the second %, and so on.

You can combine /LIST with /DS, /DT, or /DOS to list (but not recover) all the files that can be recovered. Based on the specified method, in combination with drive and file name parameters, the recoverable files are displayed. You can thus try different combinations to see what files can be recovered. If you intend to recover a specific file, use the same parameter, minus the /LIST switch.

Using UNDELETE

We are going to take a few steps to demonstrate how to install UNDELETE and use it to recover a file. Before you do the following, copy SAMPLE.TXT (discussed in Chapter 2) to a practice disk in drive A and make sure a path is provided to C:\DOS to access external DOS commands. Now follow these steps:

FOLLOW THESE STEPS

1. Load UNDELETE to protect drive A with Delete Sentry:

        A>**undelete /sa**

2. Show status:

        A>**undelete /status**

   A message tells you that drive A is enabled.

3. Delete SAMPLE.TXT:

        A>**del sample.txt**

4. Undelete all the files protected by Delete Sentry:

        A>**undelete /ds /all**

   The file deleted in step 3 is now automatically recovered. There is no need for you to supply the first character of the file name.

5. Unload Delete Sentry:

   A>**undelete /unload**

   Confirm with Y at the prompt, and a message tells you that the program is unloaded.

6. Purge the SENTRY directory:

   A>**undelete /purge**

If you want to know what else has happened that is not evident to you, go to the C:\DOS directory and use TYPE to show the UNDELETE.INI file. Some of the parameters you specified show up here.

When you delete files with Delete Sentry on, the SENTRY directory is automatically created in the target drive. You can use DIR /A to show the name. You can use CD to go to the directory and DIR to show the file names. You may find a name like #A1B2C3F.MS; the sequential letters and numbers change as more deleted files are put in the directory. These files contain the contents of the deleted files. There is also a hidden file named CONTROL.FIL, which contains the above file names. If you run UNDELETE /PURGE in the SENTRY directory, the files will be deleted. If you do it in a higher directory, the directory will also be removed.

The UNDELETE.INI File

You can use a text editor to alter the UNDELETE.INI file created by UNDELETE. Your UNDELETE.INI may look like this:

```
[configuration]
archive=FALSE
days=7
percentage=20
[sentry.drives]
A=
C=
[mirror.drives]
[sentry.files]
sentry.files=*.* -*.TMP -*.VM? -*.WOA -*.SWP -*.SPL -*.RMG -*.IMG -*.THM -*.DOV
[defaults]
d.sentry=TRUE
d.tracker=FALSE
```

The second line deserves special attention. It means that files with archive (A) bits on will not be saved to the SENTRY directory when it is erased. If you want to protect the files you create, change this line to archive=TRUE. Change other values as you see fit. For example, days=7 and percentage=20 can be changed to days=14 and percentage=5. The new values will use up to 5% of your disk space to save your junk files for up to two weeks. After you resave the edited file over the old and run UNDELETE with /LOAD, these new values will be in effect.

To understand what the other default values such as -*.WM? in this file mean, enter HELP UNDELETE on the command line and then go to the Note screen.

DEFRAGMENTING A DISK

■ *Use DEFRAG to defragment a hard or floppy disk.*

A fragmented disk can slow down disk access and prematurely wear out a disk drive. Many PC users have for many years used Norton Utilities and similar packages to defragment their hard disks. DOS 6 now includes DEFRAG licensed from Symantec, which has purchased Norton Utilities.

DEFRAG is relatively easy to use. Just enter the command on the DOS command line. If no drive is specified, the current drive is the target. To defragment drive A, enter this:

```
C:\DOS>defrag a:
```

A screen like Figure 6.1 appears. The top portion uses different graphic characters to portray the disk condition; the purpose of each character is explained in the Legend box at the bottom right corner.

The center of the screen gives you two options, with Optimize highlighted. If you press Enter now, defragmenting will begin. If you press Esc once, the Optimize menu (top left corner) will open; the same thing happens if you select the Configure option. If you press Esc twice, the center box will disappear.

If you press F1 or click the F1=Help button at the top right corner, a pop-up window appears. You can use a cursor key to highlight an item and press Enter to show related help message. If the screen is full, press PgUp or PgDn to show more. Press Esc to exit when done.

To open the Optimize menu, click it with your mouse or press Alt. This menu shows eight items:

```
Begin optimization
Drive...
Optimization method...
File sort...
Map legend...
About Defrag...
eXit
```

To select an option, click it with your mouse or press ↓ or ↑ to highlight an option and press Enter. You can also press a letter key that corresponds to the first capital letter of each option.

Figure 6.1

The DEFRAG screen

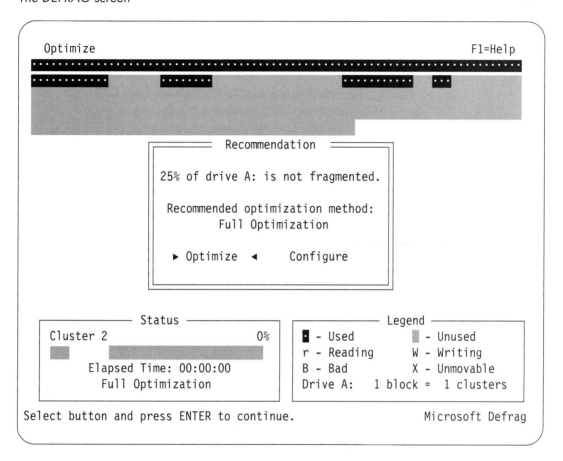

Drive lets you select a new drive. If the target disk is not fragmented to begin with, a message and the OK button appear. Press Enter to clear the message. Stick in a new disk if you wish. Open the menu and select Drive. The available drive icons appear. Select drive A and it will be read. Follow this procedure anytime you want to work on another disk.

Optimization method lets you choose between Full and Unfragment. The former, the default, will reintegrate the entire disk and take more time. The latter will put together different pieces of each file without putting all the files next to each other, thus leaving gaps between files.

File sort lets you choose among: Unsorted (based on the disk order, default), Name, Extension, Date & Time, and Size. If you choose to sort, you can also choose Ascending or Descending order. Sorting takes extra time.

Map legend shows the same thing as shown at the bottom right corner of the initial screen. The other items in the menu are either self evident or redundant.

After you settle all the options and select *Begin optimization* from the menu (or press Alt-B), the characters in the top portion begin to move around. The bottom left box also shows elapsed time and completion percentage. If you work on a large disk, this could take a long time. A floppy disk with only a few files will take a short time.

When a disk is completed, you are prompted for another drive, for more configuration, or for exit. You can always select eXit from the menu to get out and get back to the command line.

DEFRAG /? shows a series of switches. These switches let you set the configuration values before the full screen appears. You can set these values either from the command line or from the Optimize menu.

If you have used Norton Utilities, you will know that the package includes many other tools for you to fix or read a disk. The scaled-down portion bundled with DOS 6 does nothing except defragmenting disk files.

VIRUS VIGILANCE

■ *Use MSAV to detect and clean viruses.*

■ *Load VSAFE to monitor virus activities.*

If your PC has been attacked by a computer virus and you have not purchased an anti-virus program, the anti-virus feature in DOS 6 will be of great benefit to you.

Virus Overview

Computer viruses have generated considerable headline news in recent years. A computer-science graduate student was convicted of unleashing a virus to paralyze for a few days the nationwide Internet network system. The Michelangelo and Columbus Day viruses attracted worldwide attention and sent throngs of people to computer stores waiting to buy anti-virus programs. Vendors of these programs (notably Central Point Anti-Virus and Norton AntiVirus) thrived in this widespread panic. User demand finally led Microsoft to license Central Point's Anti-Virus and include it in DOS 6.

A computer virus is a computer program that hides itself in your computer system and travels via disks or networks to infect other systems. Some viruses can play harmless but annoying tricks such as making weird noises or making an image pop out on the screen unexpectedly. Others can do a great deal of harm such as erasing all or certain types of files on your hard disk or damaging some programs to render them useless.

There are all kinds of viruses, each given a unique name by those who discovered it. More are being hatched each year. You can use MS Anti-Virus to show a list of viruses it can identify and what harm they are supposed to cause.

You are vulnerable if you meet the following conditions:

- Use a networked PC.
- Run programs downloaded from bulletin boards.
- Boot your PC with an infected disk.

All in all, the more your system has contacts with the outside world, the more likely it will be infected. It is the same principle as the more you reach out and touch someone, the more likely you are to catch a flu virus.

If you belong to the susceptible category, you should take some steps to protect your hardware and software. Before DOS 6, you had to shell out big bucks to purchase an anti-virus program. Now DOS 6 can give you some protection with no extra cost. It comes with two related programs, MSAV and VSAFE. Use MSAV to detect and/or clean known viruses from disks, and load VSAFE to monitor any virus activity when the PC is on.

MSAV's Main Menu

You start MS Anti-Virus by running the program on the DOS command line:

```
C:\DOS>msav
```

The program begins to read the C (current) drive and, after a while, displays the Main Menu, shown in Figure 6.2.

The cursor also rests at the first of these options:

```
Detect
Detect & Clean
Select new drive
Options
Exit
```

As you press ↑ or ↓ to move the cursor up or down to highlight an option, the little box on the right displays the information about the highlighted option. When you press Enter, the highlighted menu option will be selected and a proper action taken.

The bottom right corner shows Work Drive, Last Virus Found, and Last Action. If you change a drive, found a virus, or take any action against a virus, proper messages will be shown here.

The bottom line of the screen shows 8 options that overlap with the menu options shown in the middle of the screen. Each of these options is preceded by a function key number to indicate that you can select it by pressing a proper function key.

Figure 6.2

MSAV's Main Menu

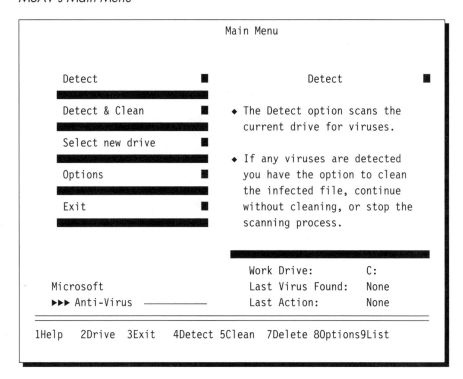

If you have a mouse, you can easily select any item shown on the screen by moving the mouse pointer there and then pressing the left mouse button. Also, in the initial Main Menu screen as well as other subsequent screens, there is an icon at the top left corner that looks like the door of a disk drive. You can use a mouse to click it to close that screen or exit MS Anti-Virus. You can also press Esc on the keyboard to do the same thing.

Getting Help

Let us follow these steps to get familiar with MS Anti-Virus:

FOLLOW THESE STEPS

1. Start the program:

       C:\DOS>**msav**

2. Press F1 (or click Help) when the Main Menu appears. The initial help screen appears, listing the topics at the top and the options at the bottom.

3. Press F1 again. A new screen appears explaining how to use the help system. Press PgDn repeatedly to show more.

4. Press F2 (or click Index). An index of topics appears. Press Enter with the first item (About Microsoft Anti-Virus) highlighted.

5. Press Esc or F3 (or click Exit). You are now back to the Main Menu.

6. Press F9 (or click List). The Virus List screen appears. Each known virus's name, type, and size are shown in one line.

7. Press PgDn or PgUp to scroll the list, or Home or End to go to the top or bottom. Altogether, 1234 viruses are listed.

8. When a virus is highlighted, press Enter to show more details; you can also click a name with a mouse.

9. Press Esc (or F3) twice to return to the Main Menu.

Detecting and Cleaning

We are going to demonstrate how to check a floppy disk and clean any virus on it. Insert in drive A a formatted and used disk, and follow these steps:

FOLLOW THESE STEPS

1. From the Main Menu, press F2 (or click Drive). The bottom of the screen shows a one-line instruction. The cursor now goes to the top left corner where drive letters and icons are shown.

2. Press Tab to highlight drive A and press Enter. You can also click the icon with a mouse. The bottom right corner shows A as the work drive.

3. Press ↑ or ↓ to highlight Options and press Enter; or click it with a mouse. The Options screen now appears.

4. With a mouse, click appropriate check boxes to enter or clear check marks in desired options; click OK when done. From the keyboard, press Tab to highlight an option and then press the space bar to enter or clear a check mark; when done, press Esc or tab to OK and press Enter.

5. Press F5 or click Clean to begin action. The screen shows a bar indicating the completion rate. When done, a new screen shows how many files checked, infected, and cleaned.

6. Press Esc to return to the Main Menu.

7. Press Esc or F3 to exit. A screen appears with a check mark marking the Save Configuration check box. Press Tab to highlight the check box and press the space bar to clear it. Click OK or tab to OK and press Enter. The DOS command line reappears.

In step 4, you can check an option to ask MS Anti-Virus to create a report. A file named MSAV.RPT containing similar information shown at step 5 will be saved to the root directory of the disk being checked. You can read this ASCII file with the TYPE command. Erase it if you do not want to keep it.

Many of the options in the Main Menu can be specified on the command line as parameters. For example, you can enter MSAV A: to scan drive A. You can also use various combinations of 25 available switches. Enter HELP MSAV to show all the available switches and their legal combinations.

Monitoring Viruses

Another way of guarding your system against a virus attack is to load VSAFE.COM to memory so that it can continuously monitor suspicious activities. This TSR (terminate and state resident, or memory resident) program can be loaded and unloaded as you wish. It takes up 44KB of your RAM.

After running VSAFE, the screen shows a message and the <Alt>-<V> hotkey. Pressing Alt-V displays its menu, shown in Figure 6.3.

You can now press a number key to toggle on/off any of the available protections. Pressing Esc returns you to the command line. If you press Alt-U instead, the program is erased from memory. VSAFE can also be unloaded with the /U switch.

WARNING: VSAFE should be loaded from the normal DOS prompt, not after a shell program is in memory. If you load VSAFE with an application such as WordPerfect already in memory, your PC may lock up because the memory

Figure 6.3

The VSAFE menu

```
 ┌─────────────────────────────────────────────┐
 │     VSafe Warning Options                    │
 │                                              │
 │   ┌───────────────────────────────┬──────┐   │
 │   │   Warning type                │  ON  │   │
 │   ├───────────────────────────────┼──────┤   │
 │   │ 1 │ HD Low level format       │  X   │   │
 │   │ 2 │ Resident                  │      │   │
 │   │ 3 │ General write protect     │      │   │
 │   │ 4 │ Check executable files    │  X   │   │
 │   │ 5 │ Boot sector viruses       │  X   │   │
 │   │ 6 │ Protect HD boot sector    │  X   │   │
 │   │ 7 │ Protect FD boot sector    │      │   │
 │   │ 8 │ Protect executable files  │      │   │
 │   └───────────────────────────────┴──────┘   │
 │                                              │
 │     Press 1-8 toggle ON/OFF                  │
 │     Press Esc to Exit                        │
 │     Press Alt-U to unload from memory        │
 │                                              │
 └─────────────────────────────────────────────┘
```

needed for your application's return may be occupied by VSAFE. If this happens, you will need to reboot your PC and lose the data in RAM.

What you do with regard to viruses depends on your circumstance. If your PC has rare contacts with the outside world, you may not want to devote 44KB of RAM to VSAFE, which also slows down your PC to check viruses. On the other hand, if you are a prime target, you may want to regularly scan new disks (using MSAV) and load VSAFE to safeguard your system.

New viruses continue to appear periodically. If they are different from the existing known strands, MSAV or VSAFE may not be able to detect or ward off. Each DOS 6 package comes with two coupons in the printed manual. You can send them to Central Point for the first two updates free.

P R A C T I C E   6 - 4

☐   1. Compare the two practice disks; cancel the comparison if error is found.

☐   2. Use FC to do an ASCII comparison between TEST1 and TEST2. Discrepancies should also be marked with line numbers.

☐   3. Use FC to do a binary comparison between TEST1 and TEST2.

☐   4. Load UNDELETE with Delete Tracker to track drive A.

☐   5. How can you tell that drive A is now protected by Delete Tracker after the above action?

☐   6. Create a file named XXX, type anything, and save it to drive A. Delete XXX. Undelete it. Besides XXX, what other file has DOS saved to drive A?

☐   7. Defragment a disk in drive A.

D R I L L

___   19. A target disk does not have to be formatted when DISKCOPY is used. True or false?

___   20. DISKCOPY duplicates tracks, but COPY and XCOPY duplicate files. True or false?

___   21. XCOPY can duplicate a bootable disk. True or false?

___   22. DISKCOPY will not defragment a fragmented disk as COPY or XCOPY will. True or false?

____ 23. Which of the following is legal:

    a. A>diskcomp a: c:

    b. A>diskcopy c: a:

    c. A>fc

    d. A>xcopy b:*.*

For questions 24–30, answer E for external command, or I for internal command.

____ 24. COPY

____ 25. XCOPY

____ 26. FC

____ 27. TYPE

____ 28. DISKCOPY

____ 29. DISKCOMP

____ 30. VERIFY

S U M M A R Y   A N D   R E V I E W

Check each item as you review and understand the following highlights of the chapter.

☐   1. Use the COPY command to create duplicate files with the same names or new names. Use wild card characters to speed up action.

☐   2. Use COPY to append files; place the target file at the beginning, followed by a plus (+) and each source file.

☐   3. Use COPY to combine files; connect source files with + signs (or wild cards), and place target at the end, separated from the rest by a space.

☐   4. Use COPY to place new date and time data on a file by putting a + at the end of the target. Make sure to use the /B switch if a binary file is involved.

☐   5. Use the /V switch with COPY to verify the target file. Use /A or /B to read or write to ASCII or binary files.

☐ 6. Use COPY to copy files to devices such as CON and PRN. Files can be combined and sent to these devices.

☐ 7. Use XCOPY to speed up copying large files. Use the /S switch to copy subdirectories, /S/E to copy even empty directories, /P to display a Y/N prompt, and /W to wait for your action.

☐ 8. Copy an original disk, particularly the system disk, with DISKCOPY. However, do not use this command to copy a fragmented disk.

☐ 9. Use COPY *.* or XCOPY *.* to reintegrate the fragmented files. File fragmentation occurs when a disk is used repeatedly for saving altered files.

☐ 10. Use FC to compare ASCII files. The comparable text lines that are not identical are displayed for your review. They are easy to read and compare.

☐ 11. Use FC with /B for a binary comparison and with /N to mark variant lines with sequential numbers in an ASCII comparison.

☐ 12. Compare diskettes, not hard disks, with DISKCOMP. If there are errors between the original supplied by the vendor and your copy, use DISKCOPY to make another copy of the original.

☐ 13. Use UNDELETE with /S to load Delete Sentry or /T to load Delete Tracker. Either will greatly enhance your chances of recovering deleted files.

☐ 14. Use DEFRAG to defragment a much used disk, hard or floppy. Different parts of the same file will be brought together. This can speed up disk access.

☐ 15. Use MSAV to detect and clean viruses. Load VSAFE to monitor any virus-like activities.

R E V I E W   Q U E S T I O N S

Write an answer for each question below.

1. 1.What does the following command do:
   A>copy b:*.doc *.bak

2. What does this command do?
   A>copy filename.ext b: +

3. What does this command do?
   A>copy filename.ext + b:

4. What does the following command do, and will the target file size be the same as the sum of all the source files?

   A>copy *.ext all.ext

5. What is the default mode of COPY when simple copying is done? What about when files are combined?

6. How can you stamp the current date and time on a single file?

7. What differences do the following commands produce?

   A>copy *.* b:
   A>diskcopy a: b:

8. What does this command do?

   A>copy filename.ext b: /a

9. Give a command that will copy a disk file named FILENAME to the printer.

10. What is the difference between the following two commands:

    A>type filename
    A>copy filename /b con

11. What does XCOPY s /S switch do?

12. What does this command do?

    A>xcopy *.* b: /s/e

13. Can you use XCOPY to combine files or copy them to a device?

14. How do UNDELETE s /S and /T switches differ?

15. What s the significance of the UNDELETE.INI file?

Maintaining Files

QUICK START

To transfer COMMAND.COM and the two hidden system files to another disk:

> A>sys c:

To replace files (replace target with source):

> A>replace source b:target

To show file attributes:

> C:\DOS>attrib a:file?

To add attributes (to remove, replace + with -):

> A>attrib +a +r +h +s file?

To use XCOPY to copy a new file and remove its A attribute:

> A>xcopy filename b: /a/m

To start MS Backup:

> C:\DOS>msbackup

To compress a hard or floppy disk:

> C:\DOS>dblspace

To mount a compressed floppy disk:

> C:\DOS>dblspace a: /mount

To send files to the print queue:

> C:\DOS>print a:file?

After using your computer for an extended period of time, you are likely to accumulate a large number of files and possibly a large number of large files. You may need to back up these files for safety. You may have to selectively replace or restore them in various storage media.

Backing up files is vital. Electronic media such as hard or floppy disks are fragile. The data stored on them could be wiped out in a flash. If you have no backup copies, you could lose your work and possibly your entire business. In the computer press, there are continuous horror stories of individuals and companies suffering immeasurable losses due to data loss.

Should you lose a file, try one of these measures:

- Use a duplicate file created by COPY, XCOPY, or REPLACE.

- Use UNDELETE to recover an accidentally deleted file or UNFORMAT to restore an inadvertently reformatted disk. UNFORMAT was discussed in Chapter 3 and UNDELETE in Chapter 6.

- Use MSBACKUP to restore the file from a backup floppy disk.

- Use the hard copy produced by PRINT.

All these measures require you to take necessary preparatory steps ahead of time. This chapter discusses these steps, except UNFORMAT and UNDELETE, in the order as shown above.

DoubleSpace, a file compression utility new in version 6, is also covered in this chapter. This program is most useful if you are running out of disk space to store your ever increasing files.

Sometimes you need to transfer system files to a disk to make it bootable. This requires using the SYS command. We start with this command.

USING SYS TO CREATE A SYSTEM DISK

■ *Use SYS.COM to transfer COMMAND.COM and the hidden system files to a disk to make it bootable.*

There are a number of ways you can create a system (boot) disk. In previous chapters you have learned the following methods:

- Formatting a disk with the /S switch. This transfers COMMAND.COM and the two hidden system files to the newly formatted disk.

- Using DISKCOPY to create a duplicate of a system disk. If the original copy is bootable, the duplicate will also be bootable.

Another method is to use the SYS.COM program to transfer the system files to a new disk. Follow these steps:

1. Put a target disk in drive A.

2. Transfer the system files to drive A:

    C:\DOS>**sys a:**

This command runs SYS.COM in drive C's current directory and transfers four files to drive A.

If you have a two-floppy system (and no hard disk), follow these steps:

1. Put in drive A a system disk; make sure the SYS.COM file is also stored there.

2. Transfer the system files to drive B:

    A>**sys b:**

You can also transfer the system files to your hard disk. Follow these steps:

1. Put in drive A a system disk; make sure the SYS.COM file is also stored there.

2. Transfer the system files to drive C:

    A>**sys c:**

SYS transfers four files—IO.SYS, MSDOS.SYS, DBLSPACE.BIN, and COMMAND.COM—from the source disk to the target disk. If there are duplicate files on the target disk, they will be replaced. If the target disk contained comparable files of an earlier DOS version, they will be replaced

---

T I P S   A N D   T R I C K S

C H A N G I N G   F R O M   P C - D O S   T O   M S - D O S

If you replace PC-DOS with MS-DOS, or vice versa, SYS.COM (or the SETUP program) will copy the hidden system files from a floppy disk to your hard disk. However, since the hidden files of the two brands do not share the same names, the old hidden files will remain and take up your disk space.

You cannot use DEL or ERASE to get rid of them. One way out is to use ATTRIB to show the hidden files' names and attributes, like this:

    C:\DOS>**attrib *.***

This will show all the files and their attributes in the root directory. You can then remove their hidden and system attributes. Once these attributes are removed, these files can be deleted without any problem.

by those from the new version. After the above steps, you can boot version 6 from the target disk, including your hard disk.

DOS is becoming smarter in each new version. Earlier versions (3.3 and before) require the two hidden system files, IO.SYS and MSDOS.SYS, to be located entirely (not fragmented) in the beginning clusters of a boot disk for the disk to be bootable. The system files of versions 4 or later must also be in the beginning clusters, but do not have to be contiguous. How can you make an old disk bootable if the beginning clusters are already occupied?

The SYS command in version 5 or 6 will vacate the first two clusters and put there the beginning portions of the two system files. These two files will thus be placed at the beginning of the directory and DOS can find them to boot. Don't be surprised that after using SYS you find these two system files located in the root directory ahead of the older files saved on the disk.

The SYS program in the earlier versions will transfer only the two hidden system files. After running SYS, you would be required to copy COMMAND.COM to the new disk to make it bootable. The SYS command in version 5 or 6 transfers all the necessary files without your doing anything else.

REPLACING OLD FILES

■ *Use REPLACE to replace or update old DOS files or your own files.*

The REPLACE command can be used to replace old files with the new ones. In its simplest form, it can behave like COPY. But when its various switches are used, it can do much more to maintain files.

The Syntax of REPLACE

REPLACE's syntax resembles COPY's:

```
C:\DOS>replace source target
```

This will replace target files with source files, or place source files in the target.

Normally, when you think of the English verb "replace," you think of replacing the first object with the second object. The situation is reversed with REPLACE. If you think of replacing the second file with the first (or placing the first file in the second), you are closer to the syntax of REPLACE.

If there is only one parameter, it is presumed to be the source, and the target is the current drive, such as:

```
A>replace b:file1
```

This will replace FILE1 in drive A with FILE1 in drive B.

The Switches of REPLACE

REPLACE has these switches:

/A	Add files which are in source but not in target
/P	Prompt for Y/N to replace old files
/R	Read-only files are also replaced
/S	Subdirectories in target; files there replaced
/U	Update old files with new ones
/W	Wait for key press before acting

In earlier versions, REPLACE was very handy in replacing the old DOS files on your hard disk with the new ones from floppy disks. The SETUP program in version 5 or 6 has made it less useful. However, there may be situations when you want to replace the old DOS files with the new ones. You can still use REPLACE for such a task.

Suppose you want to replace old DOS files on your hard disk with the new ones in drive A. You can enter a command like this:

```
A>replace *.com c:\ /s
```

This will replace all the COM files in drive C from the root directory down to all the subdirectories with files of identical names found in drive A. This is a very sweeping command. It will automatically replace and display every matching file. If you want to be prompted for Y/N before each file is replaced, try this:

```
A>replace *.com c:\ /s/p
Replace C:\DOS\DISKCOPY.COM? (Y/N)_
```

If you press Y, the displayed file is replaced. If N is pressed, it is not replaced.

You can use the /A switch to add the files to the target drive that exists in the source but not in the target, such as:

```
A>replace *.exe c:\dos /a/p
```

This will add any EXE file to C:\DOS that is found in drive A but not in C:\DOS. The old files in the target are not replaced.

You can use the /U switch to update (replace) older files with newer ones. There is no adding involved. Only files of identical names are compared and replaced. If two identical files have the same date-time, no replacing occurs. This avoids repeated replacing of identical files.

When the /A switch is used, you cannot use /U. If you did, you would get this error message:

```
Invalid parameter combination
```

REPLACE ends after the specified files on the source disk are copied to the target. If you want to replace another disk, you have to run it again. If you want to load the program from a floppy disk and then use it for copying, you can use the /W switch, such as:

```
A>replace *.com c:\dos /w/a/p
Press any key to continue...
```

You can now take out the disk containing REPLACE.EXE and insert another disk to replace your old DOS files on the hard disk.

The /R switch is used to overcome the R (read-only) attribute. When a target file is designated as read-only (explained in the next section), you must use /R to replace it with a new one. If not, the remaining replacing operation will end when such a file is encountered; the screen also shows the file's name and the "Access Denied" message. If /R is used, all the matching target files will be replaced.

Replacing Your Own Files

REPLACE can also be used to replace the files you create. To demonstrate how to use it on your own files, we will create a few and then replace some. Before you do the following, make sure the PATH=C:\DOS command has been entered. Insert a practice disk in drive A and another in drive B, and follow these steps:

FOLLOW THESE STEPS

1. Create the first file:

```
A>copy con file1
This is file 1.
^Z
```

2. Add this file to drive B:

```
A>replace file? b: /a
Adding B:\FILE1
1 file(s) added
```

This adds to drive B all the matching files found in drive A but not in drive B. If you have a single-floppy system, you will be asked to swap disks.

3. Change the contents of the file in drive B:

```
A>copy con b:file1
This is a new file.
^Z
```

4. Update the old file, with the Y/N prompt:

```
A>replace b:file? /u/p
Replace A:\FILE1? (Y/N)y
Replacing A:\FILE1
1 file(s) replaced
```

5. Show the file in drive A:

A>**type file1**
This is a new file.

The original FILE1 in drive A has been replaced with the one from drive B carrying the same name but with a later date-time.

P R A C T I C E   7 - 1

☐　　1. Create and save in drive A two simple files named TEST1 and TEST2. Use REPLACE to copy the matching files (TEST?) to drive B.

☐　　2. Delete the two matching files in drive A. Use the /A, /P and /W switches with REPLACE to copy all matching files from B to A.

☐　　3. Add a line to TEST1 in drive A. Use the /U switch with REPLACE to copy matching files to drive B.

☐　　4. Use SYS to make the disk in drive A a boot disk.

☐　　5. Use DIR to show only the two hidden system files.

☐　　6. Reboot DOS with the disk in drive A.

D R I L L

____　1. In version 6, you can use SYS to transfer the DOS system files to an old disk and make it bootable. True or false?

____　2. If you enter the command below, all the matching files in drive C (including all the subdirectories) will be replaced with the files of identical names in drive A. True or false?

C:\DOS>replace a:*.* /s

____　3. The command below will replace old files and add new files from the source to the target. True or false?

C:\DOS>replace a:*.* /a

____　4. The following command will:

C:\DOS>replace a:project?.txt b:

a. replace B's matching files with those from A

b. replace A's matching files with those from B

c. add files to B that are in A but not in B

d. add files to B that are in B but not in A

_____ 5. The following command will:

      A>replace b:project?.txt /a

    a. replace B's matching files with those from A

    b. replace A's matching files with those from B

    c. add files to B that are in A but not in B

    d. add files to A that are in B but not in A

_____ 6. If PROJECT.TXT exists in A but not in B, the following command will copy it from A to B. True or false?

      B>replace a:project.txt /u

SETTING AND REMOVING FILE ATTRIBUTES

■ *Use ATTRIB to set or remove various file attributes.*

When you have many existing files, you can set certain attributes on them. These attributes can then be used to manipulate the files. For example, you can copy or replace only the files that carry certain attributes.

As explained in Chapter 3, file attributes, if any, are stored in a directory. You can use the ATTRIB command to display them. You can also use it to set or remove these attributes. For example, to set a file to read-only, this command will do:

```
C:\DOS>attrib +r a:filename
```

You can use four attributes and one switch with ATTRIB:

A	Archive
H	Hidden
R	Read-only
S	System
/S	Subdirectories

You can use a plus (+) before an attribute to set it and a minus (-) to remove it. To demonstrate how to use ATTRIB, let us create a file and then set and remove its attributes.

FOLLOW THESE STEPS

1. Create FILE1:

```
A>copy con file1
This is file 1.
^Z
```

2. Show its attributes:

    ```
    A>attrib file1
         A          A:\FILE1
    ```

The **archive** (A) attribute is automatically set as the default when a file is created or modified. This attribute can be used by XCOPY, MSBACKUP, and RESTORE to move files.

3. Set read-only attribute:

    ```
    A>attrib +r file1
    ```

4. Show the new attributes:

    ```
    A>attrib file1
         A    R    A:\FILE1
    ```

5. Delete FILE1:

    ```
    A>del file1
    Access denied
    ```

6. Add a line to FILE1:

    ```
    A>copy file1 + con
    FILE1
    Access denied   - A:FILE1.
             0 File(s) copied
    ```

When the **read-only** (R) attribute is set, a file can only be read; but it cannot be added, deleted, or replaced. If you attempt any of these moves, you will be denied access.

7. Remove two attributes:

    ```
    A>attrib -a -r file1
    ```

8. Show attributes:

    ```
    A>attrib file1
                   A:\FILE1
    ```

9. Set archive attribute:

    ```
    A>attrib +a file1
    ```

This file has now been returned to its original state.

You can use ATTRIB with wild card characters or to process all the matching files in subdirectories, such as:

```
C:\DOS>attrib +a +r b:\file?.* /s
```

Each matching file found in drive B's root directory and all the subdirectories, if any, will be processed. Your disk will make some noise, but the files being processed are not displayed.

Attributes, like switches, can be put anywhere after the ATTRIB command. The command below is also legal:

```
C:\DOS>attrib /s b:\file?.* +a +r
```

When you have two or more attributes, each must be separated from another with a space. While DOS will accept multiple switches that are not separated with a space, it will reject attributes that are lumped together. Here is an example:

```
C:\DOS>attrib a:file1 +a+r
Parameter format not correct - +a+r
```

This problem can easily be cured by putting a space between +A and +R.

HANDLING HIDDEN AND SYSTEM FILES

The ATTRIB command's H and S attributes are available since version 5. You can use them to display invisible files or hide regular files. For example, this command shows all the files in the root directory of drive C, including the hidden files and their attributes:

```
C:\DOS>attrib \*.*
SHR     C:\IO.SYS
SHR     C:\MSDOS.SYS
. . .
```

Two files are shown as system (S), hidden (H), and read-only (R). The R attribute can be removed (or set) like the A attribute. The H and S attributes, however, must be removed as a pair. If you specify one without the other, an error message appears:

```
C:\DOS>attrib \*.sys -h
Not resetting hidden file C:\IO.SYS
Not resetting hidden file C:\MSDOS.SYS
```

The following command, however, will remove both H and S attributes:

```
C:\DOS>attrib \*.sys -h -s
```

You can set the H or S attribute individually if a file does not have either attribute. This rule does not apply when a file already has one or both of these attributes. Suppose you have a newly created file named FILE1. It has only the A attribute automatically added, as explained in the preceding section. You can add the H or S attribute or both by entering one of these commands:

```
C:\DOS>attrib a:file1 +h
C:\DOS>attrib a:file1 +s
C:\DOS>attrib a:file1 +h +s
```

However, if FILE1 already has H, S, or both, things become complicated. Suppose FILE1 now has H, which is the case if you enter only the first command above. You can no longer set S alone by entering the second command above. You will get this message instead:

```
Not resetting system file A:\FILE1
```

If you enter the third command instead, your command will be accepted and FILE1 will have both H and S. If you want to remove H and set S, this command will do:

```
C:\DOS>attrib a:file1 -h +s
```

T I P S   A N D   T R I C K S

D I R E C T O R I E S   A N D   F I L E   A T T R I B U T E S

A directory can be given file attributes with a command like this:

```
C:\DOS>attrib +h xxx
```

Regardless of whether XXX is a file name or a directory name, it will have the H attribute after the above command.

When a directory has the S and/or the H attribute, the DIR command alone cannot "see" it. However, when it is combined with the /A switch, the directory name will be displayed on the screen; the same is true when the name is specified, such as:

```
C:\DOS>dir xxx
```

DIR also "sees" a hidden directory when combined with a comma, like this:

```
C:\DOS>dir,
```

Inserting a space or using another character will not work.

A directory's attribute does not protect the files inside from deletion. You can assign R, S, or H to it and the files inside can still be wiped out by DEL or DELTREE. An individual file given the R attribute can be protected from DEL but not DELTREE.

When either or both of the H and S attributes are set, DEL, COPY, XCOPY, and REPLACE cannot see them. TYPE, however, can read and display their contents.

You can remove the H and/or S attributes of the two hidden system files on a boot disk. They will still boot even after these attributes are removed.

As explained in Chapter 2, you can also use the /A switch with DIR to show all the files, including hidden ones. This method, however, cannot show what attributes each displayed file may have.

BACKING UP FILES WITH XCOPY

■ *Use XCOPY to copy archive or dated files.*

Among the commands that can be used to back up files, XCOPY looks most familiar. We have covered some of its switches in the previous chapter. We are going to use the rest for backing up files.

As you have learned in Chapter 6, XCOPY contains, among others, these switches:

/A	Archive; copy files marked with A
/D:date	Date; copy files created on or after date
/M	Remove source archive bit after backup

We are going to demonstrate how to use them for backing up files. Follow these steps:

FOLLOW THESE STEPS

1. Set A and R attributes to FILE1, which was created earlier:

       A>**attrib +a +r file1**

2. Copy files by the date:

       A>**xcopy file? b: /d:06-25-92**

Specify the current date or earlier after the /D: switch; use the mm-dd-yy format. All the matching files on or after the specified date will be copied to the target disk.

3. Copy and remove the archive attribute:

       A>**xcopy file? b: /m**

After this operation, the source files no longer carry the A attribute. The target files, however, still have it. This arrangement can avoid duplicating backup. If you use the /A or /M switch in the future, these files will not be copied because of the lack of the archive bit. However, you can still use XCOPY (or COPY) without any switch to copy such files.

4. Show source file attributes:

```
A>attrib file?
       R     A:\FILE1
```

Notice the A attribute is gone, removed by the /M switch.

5. Copy archive files:

```
A>xcopy file? b: /a
       0 File(s) copied
```

Since the files have the A attribute removed, XCOPY cannot find any matching file to copy.

6. Show target file attributes:

```
A>attrib b:file?
   A             A:\FILE1
```

The A is automatically added regardless of whether a source file has it or not. Notice that the R attribute is not copied. This is true regardless of whether you use COPY, XCOPY, or REPLACE.

7. Copy matching archive files from B to A:

```
A>xcopy b:file? /a
Access denied  - A:\FILE1.
         0 File(s) copied
```

TIPS AND TRICKS

EXIT CODES

REPLACE, XCOPY, RESTORE and some other commands return an **exit code** in response to a particular state of execution. If a job is successfully completed, for example, each will return the exit code of 0. If an error of some sort is encountered, that particular exit code number is returned.

Exit codes can be used by the IF command in a batch file to test the state of a command's execution. If a job is successfully completed, the batch file can tell the user about that. If a specific error is encountered, the batch file can warn the user with a specific message. This will be covered in Chapter 11.

The original file in drive A carries the R attribute and thus cannot be overwritten.

8. Replace FILE1 in drive A with the same file in drive B:

    A>**replace b:file1**

    ```
    Replacing A\FILE1
    Access denied  - A:\FILE1
    ```

    ```
    No files replaced
    ```

9. Replace with the /R (read-only) switch:

    A>**replace b:file1 /r**

    ```
    Replacing A:\FILE1
    ```

    ```
    1 file(s) replaced
    ```

This time the replacing is successful. The file in drive B has replaced the file in drive A.

10. Show the new file's attributes:

    A>**attrib file1**
    ```
         A   R    A:\FILE1
    ```

The old file's attributes are not changed, only the contents are.

XCOPY, like COPY, stops copying when the target disk runs out of space. This could become a problem if you have a long file. The remedy to this situation is the MSBACKUP command explained below.

P R A C T I C E   7 - 2

1. Show the file attributes of TEST1 and TEST2 in drive A, created in the previous session.

2. Add the read-only attribute to the above files.

3. Use REPLACE to replace the two matching files in A with those from B.

4. Use XCOPY to copy the two files in A to B and at the same time remove the archive bit of each source file.

5. Delete the two files in A. Use REPLACE to add the two files in B to A. (These two files will be used in the next session.)

6. Add the S attribute to the two files in A.

☐ 7. Use DEL to delete the two files and explain what happens.

☐ 8. Remove the S attribute from the two files.

D R I L L

_____ 7. You can delete a file when the read-only attribute is set. True or false?

_____ 8. You can set or remove a file's attribute only one file at a time and one attribute each time. True or false?

_____ 9. There is no way you can make the two hidden system files visible. True or false?

_____ 10. When a file has the S attribute, you cannot use TYPE to show its contents. True or false?

_____ 11. A file with the S attribute cannot be deleted. True or false?

_____ 12. After the first command, both the second and the third commands below will succeed in replacing FILE1 in drive A with FILE1 from drive B. True or false?

    A>attrib +r file1

    A>replace b:file1 /r

    A>xcopy b:file1

_____ 13. Assuming FILE1 also exists in B and is not set to read-only, the second command below will succeed in replacing that file. True or false?

    A>attrib +r file1

    A>replace file1 b:

_____ 14. If you use the /M switch with XCOPY to copy a file, you cannot use XCOPY to copy the file again without doing something to the file first. True or false?

_____ 15. The following command will:

    A>xcopy file? b: /a

    a. add files to B that are found in A but not in B

    b. add files to A that are found in B but not in A

    c. copy only files with the archive bit

    d. remove source files' archive bit

_____ 16. The target file after the second command below will have:

    A>attrib +a +r file1

    A>xcopy file1 b:

    a. the same attributes as the source

    b. no R attribute

    c. no A attribute

    d. neither A nor R attribute

____ 17. The second command below will:

> A>attrib +r file1
> A>replace b:file1

    a. replace the file in A with the one in B

    b. replace the file in B with the one in A

    c. display "Access denied" message

    d. do nothing

____ 18. If the target disk runs out of room, XCOPY will prompt you to insert a new disk and continue copying. True or false?

BACKING UP FILES WITH MSBACKUP

■ *Use MS Backup to backup files from a hard disk to floppy disks. Use the same program to restore files if your hard disk files are ruined.*

■ *Create different setup files for different types of backups. Use a setup file to quickly do backup procedure.*

■ *Use the comprehensive help system whenever you encounter problems.*

The pair of BACKUP and RESTORE commands were available in DOS from versions 2 through 5. They can be used to back up a large number of files and restore them to their original locations. These commands, however, were rarely used and often criticized. They were slow, inefficient, difficult to use, and lacking many features available in other packages. Following the "if you can't beat them, join them" approach, Microsoft has licensed Norton Backup from Symantec and included a scaled-down version[1] in DOS 6.

Microsoft Backup (MSBACKUP), as the new feature is now called, can now be used to back up files as well as restore them. The old BACKUP is no longer included.[2] RESTORE, however, is still kept. It serves only one purpose—to restore files from the old backup files created by BACKUP. (Each previous RESTORE can restore only the files created by BACKUP of the same version. RESTORE in version 6 can restore files created by BACKUP in any version.)

---

1. Unlike the original Norton Backup, MS Backup cannot handle tape drives.

2. It should remain in the C:\DOS directory unless it has been intentionally deleted. DOS 6's SETUP program does not erase it.

The Main Screen

If you chose to install the Backup option when you ran the SETUP program, as explained in Appendix F, several related files would be copied to the C:\DOS directory. You now need to run MSBACKUP.EXE to configure it. A series of tests will follow and you will be instructed to choose a proper floppy disk type and insert a disk in the chosen drive to test the compatibility. You can use a mouse to click an option or tab to the desired choice and press Enter. If the configuration and compatibility tests are successful, a menu appears for you to do backup. A series of files with the MSBACKUP and DEFAULT names and various extensions will be created and saved to C:\DOS.

After you have set up the system, running MS Backup the second time leads to the main screen. The top of the screen shows two menus:

       File   Help

You can open a menu by clicking it with a mouse (pressing left or right button). From the keyboard, you need to hold down Alt and press F (File) or H (Help) to pull down a menu. If you follow Microsoft's convention of pressing Alt (and then releasing it), you can wait forever for a menu to open.

The middle of the main screen shows a dialog box with four options (buttons), shown in Figure 7.1.

The first option is highlighted and flanked by two triangles. The bottom of the screen shows a one-line message about this action. You can click another option with a mouse, or tab to it and press Enter. You can also press a highlighted letter to select that option.

After you choose an option, another window will appear. Each window has at its top left corner an icon that looks like the door of a disk drive (commonly

Figure 7.1

The main screen of MS Backup

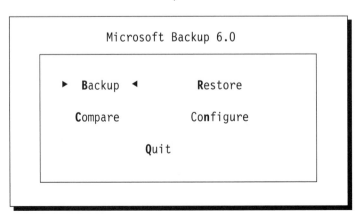

known as a control box among Windows users). You can generally double-click this icon to close a window—just move the mouse pointer there and press the left button twice in rapid succession. Pressing Esc will also do the same thing.

Getting Help

MS Backup contains elaborate and comprehensive online help (MSBACKUP.HLP is more than 300KB in size). Numerous topics, each with a title, are logically arranged and cross-linked. You can scroll through the entire system by following the prearranged sequence of topics one after another, or jump from one topic to another as you see fit. With this system, you no longer need a printed manual.

To use this help system, press F1 from the main screen. A window appears in the middle with a text frame titled BACKUP HELP TOPIC. This frame also appears when you open the Help menu and select Index.

Opening the Help menu leads to these options:

```
Index
Basic Skills
Backup
Compare
Restore
Configure
Glossary
Using Help
```

The middle group of items provides help for the four items shown in the main screen. Others add bells and whistles to this versatile system. You can go directly to a topic or start with the basics.

One way to explore the whole system is to press F1 from the main screen or select Index from the Help menu. The BACKUP HELP TOPIC appears. The bottom of the screen shows four buttons:

```
Topics     previous     Next     Cancel
```

Topics (or Alt-T) always leads to this first frame. Previous is at this time not capitalized, meaning it is not available. As you go to a subsequent frame, it will become capitalized and you can click it with a mouse or press Alt-P to reach each previous frame. Next (or Alt-N) goes to a prearranged frame. Cancel (or Esc) clears the help screen and returns you to the main screen.

At this time, you can press Alt-N repeatedly to go to each subsequent frame. Related topics that can give more information are highlighted in each frame. You can click it or tab to it and press Enter to jump to that frame; this allows you to break out of the prearranged sequence.

When a long text frame is encountered, a scroll bar appears on the right side. You can press PgUp or PgDn to scroll the text. You can also click the ↑ or ↓ or drag the scroll box with your mouse to scroll the text. Home (but not Ctrl-Home) and End (but not Ctrl-End) show the top and bottom of each frame.

After you choose an option from the main screen, Compare, for example, you can press F1 to show a context-sensitive help. A pertinent frame, Compare in our case, will appear. You can then follow the above procedure to read as much as you want.

Backup Options

By selecting Backup from the main screen, another screen appears that resembles Figure 7.2. This screen shows 8 buttons:

```
Setup File
Backup From
Backup To
Select Files
Backup Type
Start Backup
Cancel
Options
```

You can now press Tab to highlight a button and move the pair of triangles marking the current button. As you tab to a button, the bottom of the screen shows a one-line message related to the current selection. Press Enter to select the button. You can also select a button by pressing a highlighted letter or clicking it with your mouse.

To back up files, you need to do the following steps:

- Select source files if necessary.
- Change the target drive if necessary.
- Change backup type if necessary.
- Change options if necessary.
- Select Start Backup.

The default values are set by the setup file known as DEFAULT.SET. This file was created when you first ran MS Backup. We will discuss this in another section below. The above steps are necessary only if you want to change the default values.

Notice that in Figure 7.2, drive C is marked by a triangle. This is the default source drive. When you tab to this area, you can press ↑ or ↓ to move the triangle to mark one of the available drives.

Figure 7.2

The Backup screen

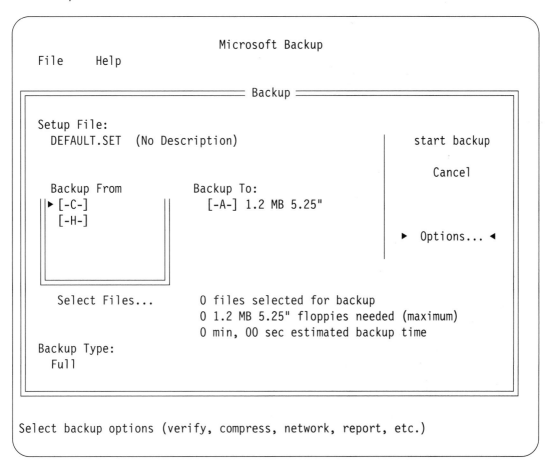

```
                         Microsoft Backup
    File     Help

                         ══════ Backup ══════
   Setup File:
     DEFAULT.SET  (No Description)                     start backup

                                                         Cancel
      Backup From          Backup To:
    ▶ [-C-]                  [-A-] 1.2 MB 5.25"
      [-H-]
                                               ▶   Options... ◀



        Select Files...      0 files selected for backup
                             0 1.2 MB 5.25" floppies needed (maximum)
                             0 min, 00 sec estimated backup time
   Backup Type:
     Full



  Select backup options (verify, compress, network, report, etc.)
```

When a drive is current, you can press the space bar (or the right mouse button) repeatedly to toggle between no file or All Files, and possibly Some Files if at least one file has been selected. As a message is shown after the drive letter, check the middle of the screen to see how many files will be backed up, and how many disks and how much time will be needed. Take these numbers into consideration before selecting Start Backup.

To select files to back up, select the Select Files button. The current drive will be read and displayed. The resulting screen may resemble Figure 7.3.

The left side of the screen shows the directory structure of the current drive (C in our case). The right side shows the files in the current directory. As you move the cursor up or down to highlight another directory, the right side changes accordingly. Each side has a scroll box. You can scroll the display with the usual

Figure 7.3

The Select Files screen

```
                          Select Backup Files
   [-C-]  [-H-]

   C:\*.*

   C:\               ↑   a       .bat        10   1-31-92   4:05p  ...a ◀↑
   ├─123                 auto    .bak       163   5-08-93   8:45a  ...a
   ├─123R23              autoexec.b         236   5-11-93   8:24p  ...a
   │  └─WYSIWYG          autoexec.bat       165   5-11-93   9:39p  ...a
   ├─123R24              autoexec.y         166   5-08-93   4:43p  ...a
   ├─BAT                 command .com    52,925   3-10-93   6:00a  r...
   │  └─X                config  .bak       465   5-12-93   9:43a  ...a
   ├─BTFONTS             config  .sys       477   5-12-93   9:44a  ...a
   ├─C                   config  .x         488   5-11-93   8:24p  ...a
   │  ├─BIN              config  .y         261   5-08-93   5:04p  ...a
   │  └─INCLUDE      ↓   io      .sys    40,470   3-10-93   6:00a  rhs. ↓

   Total Files:  1,173  [    39,085 K]   Selected Files:     0  [        0 K]

     Include      Exclude      Special      Display   ▶   OK  ◀   Cancel


   Select entire directories with right mouse button or Spacebar
```

cursor keys or with this scroll box/bar. Another technique is to press a letter, D, for example, to go to the first directory or file starting with that letter. You can use a mouse to click either side to move the cursor there; from the keyboard, use Tab or Shift-Tab to switch sides.

The bottom of the screen shows four buttons for you to use wild cards to include or exclude matching files, such as *.WK1 for all Lotus 1-2-3 files; you can also use the Edit option from Include or Exclude to change existing selections. You can use Special to handle files fitting a date range or with certain file attributes. Use Display to specify how files are to be displayed—sorted by name, extension, and so on. After selecting Display, you can check Group Selected Files. This leads to a display of selected files at the top in alphabetic order while the unselected files are listed in reverse order at the bottom. This lets you quickly find out the selected (and not yet backed up) files.

To select or deselect a file or a whole directory, move the cursor to the right item and press the space bar; you can do the same thing with a mouse by clicking it with the right mouse button. If the items to be selected/deselected are next to each other, you can drag the mouse to simplify the process; just

T I P S   A N D   T R I C K S

L I T T L E   S I G N S ,   B I G   M E A N I N G S

As you select directories or files, pay attention to the little characters added or deleted in response to your action. When a whole directory is selected, the directory name is preceded by a ▶ sign. If some files in a directory are selected, a » sign marks the directory. When a file is selected, it has a check mark (✓) before it. If a file has been backed up and not available for the next backup, a dot (.) appears instead. When the cursor goes to the right side, the current directory on the left side is marked by a ◀ sign. A directory is also highlighted if it contains selected files or if you have made changes in the current session. These connections are summarized below:

▶	Entire directory selected
»	Some files in the directory selected
✓	Selected files
.	Backed up files not available for another backup
◀	Current directory

move the mouse pointer to the first item, hold down the right button, and move the mouse pointer. Selected files are preceded by check marks; these are slated for backup.

As you select or deselect files or directories, pay attention to the changing number of files and total kilobytes. Selecting a different type of backup will also affect these numbers. If the numbers are not what you expected, recheck the selected directories and files as well as backup type. When you are done, select the OK button and you are back to the Backup screen; selecting Cancel negates all the changes.

Notice the file attributes shown at the right margin of Figure 7.3. After backing up, some of the A attributes may be removed, as explained in the next two sections.

You can now select Backup To or Backup Type. A window pops up in the middle to show available options and with one marked by a bullet as selected. You can click a new one or press ↑ or ↓ and then the space bar to select a new one. Pressing the space bar repeatedly will also move the bullet among the available options. You can also just press a highlighted letter to move the bullet there. We will discuss backup types in another section below.

If you wish, you can select Options from the Backup screen to show these available options:

```
           Disk Backup Options

    Verify Backup Data (Read and Compare)
  ✓ Compress Backup Data
    Password Protect Backup Sets
  ✓ Prompt Before Overwriting Used Diskettes
    Always Format Diskettes

  ✓ Use Error Correction on Diskettes
  ✓ Keep Old Backup Catalogs

  ✓ Audible Prompts (Beep)
    Quit After Backup
```

The default selections are check-marked. You can select or deselect (toggle between the two) an option with any of these techniques:

- Click it with your mouse.

- Tab to it and press the space bar.

- Press a highlighted key.

Some of these options do not require explanation. If you want to know what each does, press F1 and select a pertinent item. If you check the first or sixth option, you increase the backup data's reliability—at the cost of more time and/or disk space. If you specify a password and forget what it is, you cannot compare or restore the data. We will explain Catalogs later.

Backup Steps

MS Backup has many features that require a great deal of attention from the beginning user. If the above discussion has confused you with too many details, this section should help you refocus on the basic steps.

Depending on your school policy, you may or may not want to do the following; if you follow these steps, a series of files will be written to your hard disk. You also need a floppy disk that contains nothing you want to keep. Put it in drive A and follow these steps:

FOLLOW THESE STEPS

1. Start MS Backup:

    C:\DOS>**msbackup**

    The main screen appears as shown in Figure 7.1.

2. Select Backup. Figure 7.2 appears.

3. Select Select Files. If drive C is not the source drive, select it first. Drive C's directories and files are read and displayed.

4. Press D (and other cursor keys if necessary) to highlight the C:\DOS directory. Press Tab to move the cursor to the right-side window.

5. Press O (and other cursor keys if necessary) to highlight OS2.TXT. (The A attribute of this file, if any, will be removed after backup.)

6. Press the space bar or press the right mouse button to check-mark it.

7. Select the OK button to return to Figure 7.3.

8. If backup type is not Full, change to Full; if the target disk is different from what you have, select Backup To and change to your disk type and letter.

9. Select Start Backup. You are instructed to insert a disk. If your disk contains some files, you will be prompted to select an option; select Overwrite if you intend to erase the displayed files. Backup begins and, upon completion, another screen displays pertinent statistics. Press Enter or select OK. Select Quit and you are done.

The above steps create more than half a dozen files in the C:\DOS directory. List them with this command:

```
C:\DOS>dir /o-d /p
```

The newly created or modified files are displayed at the top. These files will be used to manage restoration in case of damage to the original files.

Examine your floppy disk and you will find what the program has done. The disk has been given the label DEFAULT.FUL, meaning Default setup file and Full backup type. A read-only file is also saved to drive A with a name like this:

```
CC30513A.001
```

The file name can be interpreted this way:

C	The first source drive
C	The last source drive
3	Year, 1993
05	Month, May
13	Date, 13th
A	Sequence of the day; if two or more backups are done in one day, it could be A or B (if Keep Old Backup Catalogs is off) or A to Z (if Keep Old Backup Catalogs is on)
001	The first target disk

(We no longer need this file that takes up the entire disk. You can use ATTRIB to remove the R attribute and then delete it.)

A corresponding catalog file with the same name except the FUL extension is also saved to the C:\DOS directory. The extension could also be INC (incremental) or DIF (differential) depending on the backup type selected; these are explained in the next section.

A new DEFAULT.SET file is created to save the settings you have selected, and the previous file of the same name is now changed to DEFAULT.BAK. DEFAULT.CAT (master catalog) is also created to contain the catalog(s). All these are ASCII files that can be shown with the TYPE command.

Each time you do a backup, you need at least one floppy disk. Even if you back up a small file, an entire disk is used up. You can no longer add new files to it—although you can write over it with a new backup file that will lead to the loss of the original data. So, pay close attention to the required byte size shown on the screen. If more disks are required, you will be prompted to insert a new one.

Different Types of Backup

MS Backup lets you choose one of these backup types:

Full	Backs up all the selected files (including those without A attributes) and remove their A attributes, if any, after backup.
Incremental	Backs up selected files (only those with A attributes) and removes their A attributes.
Differential	Backs up selected files (only those with A attributes) but does not remove the A attributes of the source files.

All the fancy names can be reduced to a simple archive bit. MS Backup, like the old BACKUP before version 6, depends on the archive file attribute to identify certain files to back up. When you do a full backup, all the files' A attributes are removed. The check marks, however, remain—if Full backup remains selected. If you do another full backup to a new disk, you have two identical backup copies.

If you now change to Incremental or Differential backup type, all the check marks are changed to little dots; these files are no longer selected for backup. If you change back to Full, the check marks reappear; these files are now selected again for backup.

So, after you do a full backup at the outset, you can select Incremental backup to back up only those new and changed files—files that have A attributes. The full backup copy contains the original files, and each ensuing incremental copy holds the new and modified ones. Together, they protect you from any loss to your files on the hard disk. You must keep all the disks because the new ones build on the old ones. If files are modified, each backup copy will be different from the previous one. You can thus restore an older version this way. This combination is efficient only if you create new files regularly, such as writing letters. It can be wasteful of your disk space if you work with the same files again and again because each time a file is changed it is slated for backup; many versions of the same file, with perhaps little change from one another, are taking up your disk space.

On the other hand, if you follow the initial full backup with a differential backup, you can reuse the disk holding the differential copy while keeping the full copy. A differential backup does not remove A attributes. So the same files, regardless of whether they have changed or not, remain selected for another backup. If you overwrite a disk holding the previous differential copy, you are backing up the same files, some of which may be changed and others not. There is thus no need for you to keep all the cumulative copies—just the full copy and the latest differential copy. This combination is desirable if you work with the same files again and again. Just select those active files and use Differential to back up the latest version over each previous one.

Compare and Restore

The Compare and Restore buttons shown in the main screen (Figure 7.1) can be used to compare the files in the original and those on the backup disk, and restore backup files to the original (or other) places if the original files are damaged or lost.

In both operations, you are given a similar screen and asked to specify a source and a target. You can choose to compare or restore backup files to the original or another drive or directory. The top left of the screen shows the current

---

T I P S   A N D   T R I C K S

S E L E C T I N G   A N   E N T I R E   D I R E C T O R Y

It pays to organize your files logically. It pays double if you do so and use MS Backup to back up your files.

If you select an entire directory to back up, any file with the A attribute will automatically be selected. When you add a file to the directory or modify an existing file, it is automatically check-marked, i.e., slated for back up in the future—regardless of which of the three backup types you select. If you select individual files, the unselected or new files are not affected by a backup procedure.

Suppose you work with WordPerfect to write letters for your company. You can select the C:\WP\LETTER directory for backup. Execute incremental backup periodically, perhaps once a week, to a new disk. Use a setup file (see another section below) to determine all the settings to quickly complete the job.

Backup Set Catalog. By selecting the file name, a list of available files appears for you to choose. These files—with file names containing dates and with FUL, DIF, or INC extensions—store all the backup information for file comparison or restoration. Select a proper catalog file here.

Next, you need to select the Select Files button. The available file names will appear as you highlight each directory. Select the files you want to compare or restore by check-marking them.

If you now select Start Compare or Start Restore, the action will begin. When completed, a window pops up to show a summary report.

Compare and Restore use a series of catalog files created by Backup. There is a master catalog file with the name combining the setup file name (such as DEFAULT) and the CAT extension; this is automatically created each time you perform a full backup. It contains the names of the other catalogs with the FUL, INC, or DIF extensions. These catalog files are used by MS Backup to record all the directories and file names so that they can be compared and restored.

Both Compare and Restore display a new button called Catalog. Selecting it leads to these options:

```
Load
Retrieve
Rebuild
Delete
```

Use Load to make a catalog current and Delete to delete a catalog file; either option leads to a separate window showing all the available files. Use Retrieve to load from a floppy disk and Rebuild to rebuild a damaged or deleted catalog file; a list of options, including drive letters, will appear for you to choose.

Configuration and Setup Files

The Configuration button in the main screen (Figure 7.1) lets you configure your video, mouse, and backup devices. It will also let you run a compatibility test. Use these options when you have a new device or want to change the way they are configured. Use the Save option after making the desired choices.

If your backup activities are varied, you can use a number of setup files to better manage your backup routine. At the beginning, the DEFAULT.SET file supplies all the backup settings such as selected files, target drive type, and so on. Instead of having to change these settings for a different type of backup, you can save the current settings to a setup file and open it when you want to make those settings current. This can save time and simplify backup process.

The File menu can be used to manage setup files. It has these options:

```
Open Setup
Save Setup
Save Setup As
Delete Setup
Print
Printer Setup
Exit
```

Use Open Setup to change to another setup file. The available files will appear for you to select; the selected one will replace the current.

Save Setup saves the current settings after you have made changes. The file name will remain the same but the options may change. Save Setup As lets you save the current settings to another file; you will be asked to enter a file name, and SET will be added as the extension.

Delete Setup leads to a display of all the available setup files. You can choose to delete one or more.

Print lets you send a setup file to the printer. You can use Printer Setup to change to a different port or to a disk file. The disk file will have the TXT extension. If the current setup file is named DEFAULT.SET, this file will be DEFAULT.TXT. Both are ASCII files containing identical information.

T I P S   A N D   T R I C K S

S P E E D Y   B A C K U P

Judicious use of setup files can save you lots of time—if you use a variety of backup settings.

Let us assume that you write letters for your company and work on the company's budgets as well. The former needs incremental backup while the latter is suited for differential backup. Each type also backs up the files in a different directory. If you have to change all the different settings each time you back up, you will not only be confused and error-prone, but also be spending lots of time for trivial matters.

For the letters, select the C:\WP\LETTER directory for source files (deselect all other, if any), select Incremental type, make other necessary changes, select File and Save As to save the settings as LETTER.SET (the extension is optional). Next, select the C:\123\BUDGET directory (or whatever directory you use) for source files, deselect other source files, select Differential type, make other necessary changes, and save the settings to BUDGET.SET.

At the scheduled time for backup, just open a proper setup file and select Start Backup. That's all.

After you save the current settings to a setup file, it becomes current and appears at the top left corner, under Setup File (see Figure 7.2). Selecting this file name leads to a new window showing all the available setup file names. You can select any to make it current.

DOUBLING DISK SPACE WITH DOUBLESPACE

■ *Use DBLSPACE to compress a hard or floppy disk so that more disk space will be available to store files.*

■ *Use DBLSPACE with the /MOUNT switch to make DoubleSpace recognize a compressed floppy disk.*

File Compression Overview

As application programs and user-created files become larger, disks—no matter how large they have become—are filled up more quickly than ever. Ingenious programmers came up with the idea of compressing data so that more of it can be stored on the same disk space.

The idea of data compression has been around for sometime. It involves using a token to represent repetitive characters. When a file is saved (or compressed), tokens are used to reduce space consumption. When the file is retrieved (or decompressed), the original characters are restored.

Bulletin boards have for a long time distributed a number of popular file-compression programs. These are useful for compressing your inactive files to reduce storage space or for vendors to reduce costs in distributing their packages. One problem is that DOS does not recognize them. Before you want to run a program or retrieve a data file, you must manually decompress it.

Then came two popular packages, Stacker and SuperStor, that can compress and decompress on the fly. They use a memory-resident program loaded by your CONFIG.SYS file at the beginning of each session. When you save or retrieve a file, this program will compress or decompress without your doing anything.

The popularity of these two packages led Microsoft to license a similar technology from a relatively unknown company called Vertisoft and include it in DOS 6.[3] Known as DoubleSpace, this utility can—depending on the type of files involved—approximately double the storage capacity of a disk, hard or floppy. Once it is installed, it becomes transparent, meaning that you use it without noticing it too much.

---

3. As soon as DOS 6 was released, Stacker filed a law suit against Microsoft for infringing on its patented technology.

The way DOS manages data compression and decompression is by loading a program called DBLSPACE.BIN right after IO.SYS is loaded. After your system is setup (explained in the next section), this program is loaded without your doing anything, not even tinkering with a CONFIG.SYS file. When your application such as WordPerfect or Lotus 1-2-3 saves a file, DOS compresses the data before sending it to disk. The data is also automatically decompressed when it is retrieved. Neither you nor your application will notice any difference, except a little extra time to save and retrieve a file.

Compressing a Hard Disk

To set up DoubleSpace on your hard disk, run the DBLSPACE.EXE program that was copied to the C:\DOS directory by the SETUP program (see Appendix). There is a risk in compressing your hard disk—you could lose files. You should have backup copies of your vital files in case the compression goes awry.

The following steps illustrate how to compress your hard disk (actually compress the files on your hard disk) for the first time. Depending on your PC's speed and hard disk's size, you may need hours to complete these steps. So choose a proper time before you do it. *Do not do these unless you are using your own hard disk*; you need, however, to understand the concepts and techniques discussed here. You can do similar steps later when we explain how to compress a floppy disk.

1. Run DoubleSpace:

   C:\DOS>**dblspace**

The initial screen appears. You are asked to press Enter to continue. You are then given two choices:

   Express Setup (recommended)
   Custom Setup

The first choice is highlighted; you can press Enter to proceed. (Choose Custom Setup if you do not want to compress the existing data, want to compress a drive other than C, or determine compression settings by yourself.)

2. The screen now shows the estimated time to compress the files on the hard disk. Press F1 if you need help; press PgUp or PgDn to see more. Press F3 if you want to quit. By now the program has run CHKDSK to check your hard disk. If an error is found, you will be advised to abort and run CHKDSK with the /F switch to repair the file allocation table. Restart DoubleSpace after you are through.

3. The program now restarts your system. You should not have a disk in drive A; otherwise, your PC will be rebooted from there. File compression now begins. The screen shows a running time that is needed to complete

the job; a bar also displays the percentage completed. As each file is compressed, its name is also displayed. There is nothing for you to do except wait.

4. After all the files are compressed, the program runs the DEFRAG program to defragment the hard disk. The screen displays various moving characters as fragmented files are brought together. Again, more waiting.

5. After DEFRAG runs its course, the entire process is now completed. The final screen shows the disk spaces before and after compressing, the compression ratio, and the drive (usually H, depending on the number of drives you have) created to store the compressed files. You are also instructed to press Enter to restart your system. After your PC restarts, the DBLSPACE.BIN is loaded to memory. When you save a file to your hard disk from now on, it will be compressed.

In the above steps, DoubleSpace performs these acts:

- Creates a logical drive named H

- Compresses the files that can be compressed and stores them in a huge file named DBLSPACE.000

- Moves all the data from drive C to H—including DBLSPACE.000 and the files that cannot be compressed

DOS now begins to treat H as the physical drive and C as the logical drive. When you now save files to C, DOS will shuffle data to H and put them in the DBLSPACE.000 file.

If you go to drive H (enter H:) and use DIR, you will see nothing except the drive label, which was automatically added. If you add the /A switch, this is the result:

```
H:\>dir /a

 Volume in drive H is HOST_FOR_C
 Volume Serial Number is 1A97-264E
 Directory of H:\

IO       SYS      40470 03-10-93    6:00a
MSDOS    SYS      38138 03-10-93    6:00a
DBLSPACE BIN      51214 03-10-93    6:00a
DBLSPACE INI         91 04-24-93    8:45a
DBLSPACE 000  39604224 04-24-93    8:46a
        5 file(s)    39734137 bytes
                      2596864 bytes free
```

Notice that drive H is given the volume label of HOST_FOR_C. Drive C is now compressed and H uncompressed. All the compressible files in C are stored in DBLSPACE.000; this and the uncompressible files are also moved to drive H (think of H as host). The files in drive H are not compressed because DOS needs them to manage the disk.

The DBLSPACE.000 file is known as a **compressed volume file** (CVF). This huge file contains all the compressed files in drive C—like a bag containing your compacted garbage. Most of the time you need not pay attention to it. You can proceed to use DOS and drive C as usual. When a compressed file (one stored in DBLSPACE.000) is deleted or modified, the contents and date-time numbers of DBLSPACE.000 and DBLSPACE.INI will also change. If you delete this compressed volume file, all the compressed data stored in drive C will be lost.

To protect the files in drive H from tampering, they are all given system, hidden, and read-only attributes. You can use ATTRIB to show them:

```
H:\>attrib
     SHR      H:\IO.SYS
     SHR      H:\MSDOS.SYS
     SHR      H:\DBLSPACE.BIN
     SHR      H:\DBLSPACE.INI
     SHR      H:\DBLSPACE.000
```

If you use CHKDSK on drive C now, you will see a larger number in available disk space, plus two additional lines shown below:

```
C>chkdsk

. . .

DoubleSpace is checking drive C.
DoubleSpace found no errors on drive C.
```

You can ask DOS to tell you more about a compressed file by using DBLSPACE and /INFO on a specific drive letter as a parameter. If you use /INFO and no drive letter, the current drive is acted on; if you use a drive letter, the switch is optional. Either command below shows the same result, similar to this:

```
C:\DOS>dblspace /info
C:\DOS>dblspace c:

DoubleSpace is examining drive C.

Compressed drive C is stored on uncompressed drive H in the file
H:\DBLSPACE.000.

     Space used:            39.50 MB
     Compression ratio:     1.7 to 1

     Space free:            27.27 MB
     Est. compression ratio: 2.0 to 1

     Total space:           66.77 MB
```

When you compress the first drive, DoubleSpace uses a letter, such as H, as the host drive. The next drive may be assigned G, F, and so on. In case you get confused which host drive matches which physical drive, use the /LIST switch to show them.

The DIR command is also given additional switches to show compression information:

/C	Show compression ratio
/CH	Show host drive's compression ration
/OC	Show compression ratio from small to large files
/O-C	Same as above, except from large to small files

If you use /C on a drive that is not compressed, the switch is ignored and no compression information is shown.

Compressing a Floppy Disk

You can use DoubleSpace to compress a high-density floppy disk, in effect doubling the storage capacity. If you try to compress a double-density floppy disk, an error message appears telling you that you need at least 1.1MB disk capacity to proceed.

Figure 7.4

The DoubleSpace screen and menu

```
 ╭──────────────────────────────────────────────────────────────────╮
 │                                                                    │
 │    Drive   Compress   Tools   Help                                 │
 │                                                                    │
 │                                                                    │
 │                                            Free           Total    │
 │         Drive   Description            Space (MB)     Space (MB)   │
 │        ┌──────────────────────────────────────────────────────┐   │
 │         C      Compressed hard drive      23.17         62.68  │↑  │
 │        │                                                      │    │
 │        │                                                      │███ │
 │        │                                                      │    │
 │        │                                                      │    │
 │        │                                                      │↓   │
 │        └──────────────────────────────────────────────────────┘   │
 │                                                                    │
 │    To work with a compressed drive, press the UP ARROW or DOWN     │
 │    ARROW key to select it. Then, choose the action you want        │
 │    from the Drive or Tools menu.                                   │
 │                                                                    │
 │    To quit DoubleSpace, choose Exit from the Drive menu. For       │
 │    help, press F1.                                                 │
 │                                                                    │
 │                                                                    │
 │    DoubleSpace  │  F1=Help  ALT=Menu Bar  ↓=Next Item  ↑=Previous Item │
 │                                                                    │
 ╰──────────────────────────────────────────────────────────────────╯
```

Place a proper disk in drive A and follow these steps to compress a floppy disk:

1. Run DoubleSpace:

   `C:\DOS>`**`dblspace`**

   The initial screen appears as shown in Figure 7.4. It shows that drive C is already compressed.

2. Select Compress (click it with a mouse; or press Alt, move the cursor to the menu, and press Enter. Two options appear. Select Existing Drive and, if necessary, a specific drive.

3. Your system is scanned. A new display shows drive A's capacity and the projected disk space after compression. Press Enter to proceed.

4. A new screen appears with several options. Press C to continue.

5. A new screen shows various time numbers as described in step 3 earlier when we tried to compress a hard disk.

6. Figure 7.4 reappears, except with drive A and related information inserted at the top of the box, above C.

7. Select Drive and then Exit. The DOS prompt reappears.

The disk in drive A is now compressed and mounted (explained below). Any existing files are compressed and stored in the DBLSPACE.000 in drive G (the letter before H). If you now save a file to drive A, the data goes to this compressed volume file, as explained in the previous section. If you save a file to drive G, the uncompressed data will go to the uncompressed drive, which is likely to have limited space left.

If you use another disk in drive A and then return to the compressed disk, it becomes disconnected and the compressed volume file is no longer recognized by DOS, neither is drive G. If you use DIR on drive A, you will see a file named READTHIS.TXT. If you use TYPE to read it, you will find that it tells you to mount (link it to DOS or make DOS recognize it) by making that drive current and entering DBLSPACE /MOUNT, like this:

`A:\>`**`dblspace /mount`**

If the target drive is not current, you can use it as a parameter, such as:

`C\DOS>`**`dblspace /mount a:`**

After a while, a message tells you that drive A is mounted. If DOS cannot find DBLSPACE.EXE, use a proper prefix or PATH to direct DOS to where the command is stored. When a disk is mounted, you can access drive G and can see READTHIS.TXT only in drive G but not drive A.

The idea of mounting a floppy disk can cause problems if you need to save two floppy copies of a file to the same drive. Suppose you use WordPerfect and save a file to two floppy disks, assuming both are compressed. If the first disk is mounted, there is no problem. If you take out the first disk and insert the second and save the same file again, you are likely to encounter insufficient disk space because DOS, not connected to the new compressed disk, tries to save to the uncompressed space which is likely to be very limited. At this point, the first disk is disconnected and the second is not yet mounted. If you now go back to the first disk, it is also not recognized. You have to go to the command line to mount each new floppy disk—a pain all over. This problem is less acute if you have two floppy drives and keep both mounted without changing disks.

Maintaining Compressed Disks

You can use DoubleSpace to maintain compressed disks, hard or floppy. If you examine Figure 7.4, you will find four menus at the top of the screen: Drive, Compress, Tool, and Help. Use Help the way you manage HELP as explained in Chapter 1. When a topic's window appears, you can use PgUp or PgDn to show more; you can also use a mouse to maneuver the scroll bar/box on the right side of the screen. In any particular screen, you may see a little arrow ($\rightarrow$) pointing to a line. You can highlight such a line and press Enter to show more related information. You can also press Tab to point to any other item which may give you more help. If you have a mouse, you can click any highlighted item.

As shown in Figure 7.4, the mounted drive(s) are displayed in a separate box in the middle. Drive C is automatically mounted. You have to mount the removable drives manually. If several drives are mounted, you highlight the one you want to do something to and use a proper menu to do it.

Opening a menu is by pressing Alt or clicking it with a mouse, as explained when we covered HELP in Chapter 1. Opening the Drive menu displays the options shown in Figure 7.5. As you move the cursor up or down, notice the bottom of the screen showing a one-line explanation for the current item.

You are already familiar with Mount and Unmount. The former you can do on the command line and the latter by using another disk. Format removes all the data but retains the compressed volume file; this allows the disk to store new data. Delete removes everything; you can do also use DEL after using ATTRIB to remove all the protective file attributes.

Choosing Info is the same as pressing Enter when a mounted drive is highlighted. The new screen will display information about the current drive's compression. From this screen, you can choose the Size or Ratio button; these two are the same as choosing the second and third options from the Drive menu. If you choose Size, you are asked to enter a number for the uncompressed drive. If you enter a valid number, the number for the compressed drive will go up or down to increase or decrease the size accordingly. If the number you type is not acceptable, an *invalid* message appears instead. Press Enter to accept a valid number or Esc to abort.

Choosing Ratio (or Change Ratio) leads to another screen that shows compression ratio information and prompts you to enter a new ratio num-

Figure 7.5

The Drive menu's options

```
┌─────────────────────┐
│ Info...             │
│ Change Size...      │
│ Change Ratio...     │
├─────────────────────┤
│ Mount...            │
│ Unmount...          │
├─────────────────────┤
│ Format...           │
│ Delete...           │
├─────────────────────┤
│ Exit                │
└─────────────────────┘
```

ber. Compression ratio is an estimate.[4] If the number estimated by DOS is not proper, you can change it. Keep in mind that increasing or decreasing compression ratio does not increase or decrease your disk's capacity to store data.

The compression ratio number may be important in some situations. Suppose you have a 30KB file. If this file can be compressed 3 to 1, then it takes up only 10KB disk space. If your disk has only 10KB free space left and you supply DOS the 3 to 1 ratio, this file can be successfully saved. If DOS estimates compression ratio to be 2 to 1, it will "see" only 20KB space available to save the file and issue an error message prematurely. On the other hand, if the compression ratio is set too high, DOS may proceed to save a file and then belatedly discover insufficient space.

To find out the average compression ratio of a type of files, enter a command like this on the command line:

```
C:\123>dir *.wk1 /c
```

This will show the compression ratio for each 1-2-3 worksheet file and, at the bottom, the average ratio. This last number can then be used to tell DOS what kind of compression ratio you want.

The Compress menu has two options:

```
Existing Drive
Create New Drive
```

---

4. Some types of files are more compressible than others. Compiled program files can be reduced very little but data, particularly graphic, files can be greatly reduced.

Existing Drive is used to compress any uncompressed but compressible disk. This was demonstrated earlier when we compressed a floppy disk. Create a New Drive lets you create a new compressed drive with the available disk space in the designated drive.

If you open the Tools menu, you find three options:

```
Defragment
Chkdsk
Options
```

The first runs the DEFRAG program and the second CHKDSK; both were covered earlier when we compressed a hard disk. Options lets you designate the last (highest) drive letter for a compressed drive (normally H) and change the number for available removable drives.

Most of what you can do from the DoubleSpace screen can be done on the command line, which bypasses the menus and screen displays and can thus speed up an act. When a particular menu option is highlighted, Format in the Drive menu, for example, press F1 to show help information and the option's command line equivalent. You can also enter DBLSPACE /? to find the available switches. For example, instead of choosing Format from the Drive menu, you can enter this command:

```
C:\DOS>dblspace /format a:
```

A warning message appears to prompt you for Y or N. This does not load the bulky menu and is executed quickly.

If you use a compressed floppy disk on two computers, both systems must be running DOS 6. If not, use an uncompressed disk.

Caveat Emptor

Barely one month after the Spring 1993 release of DOS 6, many users, according to the press, began to notice bugs in DoubleSpace. Some bugs were so vicious that they trashed files and crashed hard disks. In my case, after using DoubleSpace for a couple of weeks, checking my compressed hard disk always causes my PC to freeze. This does not happen if I use CHKDSK on an uncompressed floppy disk.

Some users claim that this problem is caused by SmartDrive. This disk-caching program has a new write cache which temporarily stores in RAM the data slated for saving—until when the CPU is not busy. It may not completely flush data from RAM to disk in some situations. This can corrupt files and directories. If this is true, one way to reduce risks is to delete the SMARTDRV.EXE line from your AUTOEXEC.BAT file (or add REM before the line.) If you must use SmartDrive, you should, before you shut off your PC, run SMARTDRV with the /C switch to save to disk any data remaining in the write cache.

If you are not using any compressed disk or do not plan to, you can remove DBLSPACE.BIN and DBLSPACE.SYS (the latter is a small program to get the former to load high) from your boot disk. You can use ATTRIB to take out their protective file attributes and then delete them. If you now reboot, DOS will run without DoubleSpace. This can also free up some memory for other use. When and if you want to use DoubleSpace, copy these files from the original disks to the C:\DOS directory.

If Microsoft can identify and fix these bugs, it is likely to follow its past practice by releasing a free bug-fix program to vendors and bulletin boards. If you encounter problems, you should be on the lookout for it. In the meantime, better be safe than sorry—save a copy of your most critical files to uncompressed floppy disks.

In most of Microsoft's ads, DoubleSpace was prominently touted as the most important reason for buying DOS 6. The feature proved to be quite seductive. More than three million copies were sold in the first few weeks. Now with so many irate users fuming over their trashed files and crashed disks, DoubleSpace may spell DoubleTrouble for Microsoft.

PRINTING IN THE BACKGROUND

■ *Use PRINT to print files in the background while you continue to use your computer.*

We have so far discussed a variety of ways to print files, including Shift-Print Scrn to print a screen display, Ctrl-P to echo every move to the printer, and COPY to copy a file from a disk or the screen to the printer. These acts let the printer monopolize the entire system. While the printing goes on, you cannot use the computer.

If you want to use the printer and the computer at the same time, you need to use the PRINT.EXE program. It provides a simple and crude multitasking mechanism. This program enables two devices (console and printer) to share the system. The CPU juggles between the two tasks and sometimes slows down one in favor of the other.

PRINT's Switches

PRINT has nine switches. Six can be specified only when you install the program; they set the parameters of the command. These are listed below:

/B:size	Buffer size in bytes, default 512
/D:dev	Device, such as COM1, default PRN
/M:max	Maximum number of clock ticks, 1-255, default 2

/Q:num   Queue; maximum number of files put in print queue

/S:slice   Time slices, 1–255, default 8

/U:wait   Wait clock ticks, 1–255, default 1

Three switches can be specified at any time, during and after the program is installed; they are used to manage the print queue. These are shown below:

/C   Cancel printing file(s)

/P   Print file(s), default

/T   Terminate all printing

PRINT is partially memory-resident. After running it the first time, the resident portion stays in memory until the power is off or your PC is rebooted. If you want to enter the command again, you need to provide a path to where it is stored, just as for any external command.

To load this program with all the default settings, just enter this:

```
C:\DOS>print
Name of list device [PRN]:
Resident part of PRINT installed
PRINT queue is empty
```

When you enter PRINT the first time, you are asked what device you intend to use. If your printer is connected to a parallel port, the default of PRN is what you need. You can thus just press Enter to accept it. If you have something else, such as a serial port, enter a proper device name, such as:

```
C:\DOS>print /d:com1
```

After you press Enter, a two-line message appears, telling you that the program is successfully installed and that there is no file in the print queue.

A **print queue** is a series of the names of the files you want to print. It is comparable to a series of numbers taken by people at a service counter waiting for their number to be called. You can line up files in the queue to be printed one after another. By default, the print queue size is set to 10 files. You can change it to 4 or up to 32 by using the /Q switch.

The /B switch can be used to increase or decrease the print buffer, which is set to 512 bytes by default. Increasing the print buffer speeds up printing but decreases available memory for DOS, just as increasing the value in the /Q switch does.

The /M, /S, and /U switches are used to determine how the computer and the printer share the time. When one gets more time, the other slows down. If you want the printer to work faster at the expense of the computer, increase the values of /M and /U or decrease the value of /S. Most of the time you have no need to tinker with them.

After PRINT is installed, you can use the /P, /C, or /T to manage the print queue. The /P switch is the default and is often redundant. The /C switch is used to cancel individual files and the /T switch to terminate (clear) the entire print queue.

Steps to Print Files

To demonstrate how to use the PRINT command, let us create a directory and four files with these steps:

FOLLOW THESE STEPS

1. Create a new directory and make it current:

   ```
   A>md back
   A>cd back
   ```

2. Create FILE1:

   ```
   A>copy con file1
   This is file 1.
   ^Z
   ```

3. Repeat the above step to create FILE2, FILE3, and FILE4.

4. Return to the root directory:

   ```
   A>cd\
   ```

To conserve paper, we will not actually print all of them. Keep in mind that when PRINT prints a file, it consumes a whole page regardless of how short the file may be. We will thus selectively turn the printer on and off to demonstrate printing without wasting a great deal of paper.

If you have installed PRINT.EXE as explained above, you are ready to go:

FOLLOW THESE STEPS

1. Turn off the printer if it is on.

2. Send files to the print queue:

   ```
   A>print \back\file?
   A:\BACK\FILE1 is currently being printed
   A:\BACK\FILE2 is in queue
   A:\BACK\FILE3 is in queue
   A:\BACK\FILE4 is in queue
   ```

3. Clear the print queue:

   ```
   A>print /t
   Errors on list device indicate that it
   may be off-line. Please check it.
   PRINT queue is empty
   ```

4. Show the state of the print queue:

```
A>print
Errors on list device indicate that it
may be off-line. Please check it.
PRINT queue is empty
```

5. Send files to the print queue again:

```
A>print \back\file?
```

The same message as shown after step 2 appears, plus a two-line error message as shown in steps 3 and 4.

6. Cancel three files and keep one:

```
A>print file1 /c file2 file4 file3 /p
Errors on list device indicate that it
may be off-line. Please check it.

A:\BACK\FILE3 is currently being printed
A:\BACK\FILE3 is in queue
```

In this arrangement, the /C switch affects one file before it and two files after it, and the /P switch controls a file placed before it. This command cancels FILE1, FILE2, and FILE4. The only file left in the print queue is FILE3.

7. Turn on the printer.

FILE3 is printed, sent from the print buffer to the printer. And the paper rolls up one page. Turn off the printer if you want to prevent the paper from rolling up an entire page.

The /C and /P switches follow the same rule. Each controls the file placed immediately before it and all the files after it, unless negated by the other switch. Consider this example:

```
A>print /c file1 file2 file3 file4 /p
```

The first three files are controlled by the /C switch placed before them. The control on the fourth file, however, is negated by the /P switch placed after it. This command will result in clearing the first three files while retaining the last in the print queue.

PRINT operates in ASCII mode and reads a file only before the first ^Z. If a file contains such a character in the middle, the portion after it is not printed. If a ^Z character is known to exist in a file, you can use the following to bypass the character:

```
A>copy /b filename prn
```

This will ignore ^Z and print everything that is printable.

PRINT, like APPEND and DOSKEY, is a TSR program. Once loaded, a portion of it stays in the memory until power is shut off. It may collide with other programs competing for the same memory area and freeze your computer. As a TSR, it can also be loaded to the upper memory area; see Chapter 9 for details.

P R A C T I C E   7 - 5

☐   1. Turn off the printer. Send all the TEST files to the print queue.

☐   2. Terminate the print queue.

☐   3. Send TEST1 and TEST2 to the print queue again.

☐   4. Cancel TEST1 and TEST2 but enter FILE3 into the print queue. Turn on the printer to print TEST3.

☐   5. With the printer still on, send the README.TXT file stored in the C:\DOS directory to the print queue.

☐   6. While the printing is going on, use DIR to show the C:\DOS directory one screen at a time. Explain what happens. Turn off the printer after all the directory entries are shown. Clear the print queue.

D R I L L

Match the following symbols (used by MS Backup) to the statements in questions 19-23:

a.   b. »   c. ✓   d. .   e.
▶   ◀
_____ 19. Marks the current directory.

_____ 20. Marks a directory where all the files are selected.

_____ 21. Marks a directory where some files are selected.

_____ 22. Marks selected files available for backup.

_____ 23. Marks backed up files not available for another backup.

_____ 24. In all three types of backup (full, differential, and incremental), selected files will have their archive attributes removed after backup. True or false?

_____ 25. After a differential backup, selected files are still marked as selected and available for another backup. True or false?

_____ 26. After a full backup, selected files are still marked as available for backup. True or false?

____ 27. Which file below is known as a compressed volume file (CVF)?
     a. DBLSPACE.BIN
     b. DBLSPACE.000
     c. DBLSPACE.SYS
     d. DBLSPACE.INI

____ 28. If you tell DoubleSpace to use a higher compression ratio, you will actually increase a disk's available space. True or false?

____ 29. The following command will send all the matching files to the print queue even if the printer is turned off. True or false?
     A>print test?

____ 30. The following command will:
     A>print test1 /c test2 /p
     a. cancel the first, print the second
     b. cancel the second, print the first
     c. cancel both files
     d. print both files

S U M M A R Y   A N D   R E V I E W

Check each item as you review and understand the following highlights of the chapter:

☐   1. Use SYS.COM to transfer the hidden system files and COMMAND.COM. This can make the target disk (hard or floppy) bootable.

☐   2. If you do not use SETUP to install DOS files on your hard disk, you can use REPLACE to replace the old DOS files on the hard disk with the new ones from a floppy disk. You can also use it to replace your own old files with the newer ones.

☐   3. Use ATTRIB to display, set, or remove A (archive), H (hidden), R (read-only), or S (system) file attributes. The A attribute is automatically added when a file is created or modified. The R attribute can prevent a file's deletion, modification, or replacement. The H or S attribute makes a file invisible to the human eye as well as most DOS commands.

☐   4. Use XCOPY with /M to remove the A attribute of a source file after copying it. This can prevent another copying of the files that are not modified. You can, however, still use XCOPY with no switch or other switches to copy a file without the A attribute.

☐ 5. XCOPY cannot overwrite a file that is set to read-only. REPLACE, with /R, can overwrite such a file.

☐ 6. A target file of XCOPY and REPLACE has the A attribute automatically added, but the R attribute of a source file is not copied to the target.

☐ 7. Use MSBACKUP to back up important files on a regular basis. Select the Backup option to back up files. If the files on the hard disk are ruined, run MSBACKUP and use the Restore option to restore the files from floppy disks.

☐ 8. Develop a backup strategy to protect your files. Use full backup for the first time. Selected files are backed up and their A attributes removed. They are no longer available for the other two types of backup.

☐ 9. If you keep creating new files, follow a full backup with periodical incremental backups. Keep all the backup disks to safeguard against a future hard disk disaster. An incremental backup removes the A attributes of the selected files. If you select an entire directory to back up files, those files that have been backed up are no longer selected for a future incremental backup because their A attributes have been removed. Only new and modified files, those with A attributes, are selected for the next incremental backup.

☐ 10. If you work on the same files again and again, follow a full backup with periodical differential backups. A differential backup does not remove the A attributes of the backed up files. So they remain selected for another differential backup. Since the same files are backed up again, you can overwrite a previous differential backup copy so that only the latest version will be saved. If you keep the full backup copy and the latest differential backup copy, you are in good shape.

☐ 11. To speed up a backup procedure, create a setup file for each kind of backup, together with the selected files and other settings. When you want to do this type of backup, just load this setup file and start backing up. This can save you lots of time and reduce possible errors.

☐ 12. If the original files are lost, you can use Restore option of MS Backup to restore them from a backup disk. Available files will be shown for you to select.

☐ 13. If you want to expand the storage capacity of your disks, hard or floppy, use DoubleSpace to compress them. A big file named DBLSPACE.000 will be created and existing compressible files will be put in it. You can use the disks and drives as usual. In the case of a floppy disk, you have to mount it anytime a new compressed disk is used.

☐ 14. Use PRINT to print files in the background. You can use a number of switches to determine how the printer and the computer are to share time. These switches must be specified when you run PRINT the first time. Most of the time you can just accept the default setting and do not need to tinker with these technical specifications.

☐   15. Use /C to cancel specific files, /P to print specific files, and /T to terminate all printing. You can use these switches of PRINT at will, with the printer on or off.

R E V I E W   Q U E S T I O N S

Write an answer for each question below:

1. What is the purpose of SYS.COM?

2. What does this command do?
    A>replace b:file? /a

3. What will happen if you insert a disk with DOS commands in drive A and issue this command?
    C:\>replace a:*.* /s

4. What does this command do?
    A>attrib +r *.*

5. If both A and B contain FILE1, what will happen after the second command below?
    A>attrib +r file1
    A>replace b:file1 /r

6. If both A and B contain FILE1, what will happen after the second command below?
    A>attrib +r file1
    A>xcopy b:file1

7. What does XCOPY's /M switch do?

8. What does a full backup do?

9. What does an incremental backup do?

10. What does a differential backup do?

11. Explain the meaning of this backup file: CD31213A.001

12. What does DEFAULT.SET do?

13. What is the major advantage in selecting an entire directory to back up files?

14. From the DOS command line, how do you make DoubleSpace recognize a compressed floppy disk in drive A?

15. What does this command do?
    A>print /c file1 file2 file3 /p

Redirecting Files

TOPICS

Redirecting Output

Redirecting Output with ECHO

Redirecting Input

Pipes and Filters

Using MORE

Using SORT

Using FIND

Combining Filters

Inserting Date and Time in a File

COMMANDS COVERED

ECHO, MORE, SORT, FIND, FOR..IN..DO, DIR, CHKDSK, ATTRIB

NEW TERMS AND SYMBOLS

standard input device, standard output device, redirection, pipe, >, >>, <, ¦, filter

Q U I C K   S T A R T

For piping and redirection symbols:

See Table 8.1.

To redirect directory output to a file:

A>dir > filename

To print directory entries:

A>dir > prn

To redirect file display to the printer:

A>type filename > prn

To respond to some DOS commands, redirect input from a file:

A>del *.* < filename

To print a text line entered from the keyboard:

A>echo This line is printed > prn

To display directory entries one screen at a time:

A>dir ¦ more

To display a text file one screen at a time:

A>more < filename
A>type filename ¦ more

To print a typed text line as soon as Enter is pressed:

A>more > prn

To sort the text lines of a file by first word:

A>sort < filename

To sort directory entries by extension and display the result one screen at a time:

A>dir ¦ sort /+10 ¦ more
A>dir /o:e /p

To find "Smith" lines from a file:

> A>find "Smith" filename

To find "Smith" lines but not show 1-inch line and file name:

> A>find "Smith" filename ¦ find "Smith"

To find "SMITH" files, sorted and displayed one screen at a time:

> A>dir ¦ find "SMITH" ¦ sort ¦ more

To find files and directories on a disk matching "SMITH":

> A>chkdsk /v ¦ find "SMITH" ¦ sort ¦ more

To insert date and time in a file:

> A>echo ¦ more ¦ date ¦ find "C" >> filename
> A>echo ¦ more ¦ time ¦ find "C" >> filename
> A>echo/ ¦ date ¦ find "C" >> filename
> A>echo/ ¦ time ¦ find "C" >> filename

Normally DOS works with certain presumptions. Input (raw data) is expected to come from the **standard input device**, which is the keyboard. Output (processed data) goes to the **standard output device**, which is the monitor screen. Error (what went wrong) and informational (what has been done) messages also go to the standard output device.

Anytime you want to deviate from this pattern, you must tell DOS to **redirect** input and/or output to another device. Input can be redirected from a file saved on disk or from a device such as a mouse, modem, or scanner. Output can be redirected to a number of devices, such as disk drive, printer, modem, and so on.

Besides the ability to redirect input and output, DOS provides the mechanism to **pipe** (connect) several commands together. Furthermore, three filter commands are provided, giving you more power to maneuver your files.

Redirection uses the first three symbols shown in Table 8.1. The fourth is used for piping.

This chapter first explains redirection and then connects (pipes) various versatile tools together with the filter commands of MORE, SORT, and FIND.

Table 8.1

Redirection and Piping Symbols

Symbol	Purpose
>	Redirect to a new output device
<	Redirect from a new input device
>>	Append to an output device
¦	Pipe (chain) commands

REDIRECTING OUTPUT

■ *Use > or >> with various DOS commands to redirect or append outputs to devices or files.*

This section demonstrates how to redirect output and compares output redirection with the COPY command.

Redirection Steps

Turn on the printer, insert a practice disk in drive A and another disk in drive B, and follow these steps to redirect output to new devices:

FOLLOW THESE STEPS

1. Output current directory entries to a file on disk:

    A>**dir > fildir**

Instead of the usual display on the screen, nothing shows up. Drive A is activated and a file named FILDIR is created. If this file already exists, its original contents will be wiped out.

2. Display on the screen the file just created:

    A>**type fildir**

The screen shows what you will normally see when DIR is entered and no redirection is involved.

3. Print the file (redirect it to the printer):

    A>**type fildir > prn**

The file is now printed. Normally, when you use TYPE, a file's contents appear on the screen. The above command redirects the output to the device named PRN, which could also be LPT1 (or COM1 if your printer is connected to the first serial port).

4. Append drive B's directory entries to FILDIR:

    `A>dir b:\ /w >> fildir`

This adds the wide-format directory entries of the root directory in drive B to FILDIR. Do not use a single > symbol here. If you did, the new data would replace the old.

5. Show the expanded file on the screen:

    `A>type fildir`

If you did everything correctly, the screen should show a display consisting of a long part at the beginning and a wide part at the end.

COPY and Output Redirection

The command in step 3 above could have been this instead:

    `A>copy fildir prn`

This will also print the file. The only difference is the display of this message:

    `1 File(s) copied`

If you use COPY, however, do not use the > symbol between the source file and the target device, such as:

    `A>copy fildir > prn`

This command will neither print the file nor make a duplicate of it. DOS will consider your move to be copying a file onto itself, which is illegal.

If you intend to copy a file and redirect the message—"1 File(s) copied"—to the printer, here is a legal way:

    `A>copy fildir fildir2 > prn`

If you intend to redirect a file to the NUL device, in effect not doing anything or showing any result on the screen, both commands below will work:

    `A>type fildir > nul`
    `A>copy fildir nul > nul`

The second command will copy the file to NUL and redirect any message to NUL as well. If the second NUL (together with the > symbol) is missing, the "1 File(s) copied" message will appear on the screen. If the first is missing, the copying will fail due to the absence of a target.

You already know that instead of TYPE you can use the following command to display a file's contents:

A>`copy fildir con`

This will display the file, plus the message of "1 File(s) copied," which is what distinguishes TYPE and COPY CON. You can redirect the message from the screen to the NUL device:

A>`copy fildir con > nul`

This will make COPY CON behave exactly like TYPE. You can also redirect the message to the printer:

A>`copy fildir con > prn`

REDIRECTING OUTPUT WITH ECHO

■ *Use ECHO to redirect data to a file or the printer.*

The ECHO command is normally used to echo data to the monitor screen, the standard output device. You can use it to redirect screen data to various other places. Turn on your printer and enter the following commands to see what each does:

1. A>`echo This is a test.`

2. A>`echo This is a test. > con`

3. A>`echo This is a test. > nul`

4. A>`echo This is a test. > prn`

5. A>`echo This is a test. > testfile`

6. A>`echo This is a test. >> testfile`

7. A>`echo >> testfile`

8. A>`echo < testfile`

9. A>`echo This line is ">" displayed on the screen.`

10. A>`echo This is '>' a file.`

11. A>`echo con > prn`

The first and second behave the same way, echoing the text line to the standard output device, namely the screen.

T I P S   A N D   T R I C K S

ERROR MESSAGES CANNOT BE REDIRECTED

DOS produces two kinds of messages. Informational messages tell you what has been or will be done. Error messages tell you what has gone wrong. The former can be redirected to a device. The latter, however, always go to the screen and cannot be redirected. Consider the following two examples:

```
A>copy filename
File cannot be copied onto itself
        0 File(s) copied
```

```
A>copy filename > prn
File cannot be copied onto itself
```

In the first case, both are displayed on the screen. In the second, the "0 File(s) copied" message goes to the printer, but the error message remains on the screen.

Lines 3 and 4, respectively, redirect output to NUL (discarding it) and the printer (printing it).

Line 5 creates a file and saves to it the text between ECHO and >; if the file exists, its original contents are replaced. Line 6 appends the text to an existing file, without replacing its contents. Line 7 appends the "ECHO is on" message to the named file. Line 8 displays on the screen the "ECHO is on" message, thus ignoring the input redirection.

To display a redirection or piping symbol, you need to put it in double quotes. In line 9, everything after ECHO is echoed to the screen as originally entered. In line 10, a file with a single quote (the first word located right after >) as its name will be saved, and its contents consist of this line:[1]

```
This is ' a file.
```

Line 11 sends "con" to the printer. You might interpret this line as letting you enter input on the screen and then output it to the printer. It does not work that way; ECHO does not accept input from a file (such as line 8) or device such as CON.

ECHO is commonly used in batch files and with ANSI.SYS. These are covered in Chapters 11 and 12.

---

1. The odd thing about this is that the contents both before and after the redirection symbol are sent to the file.

REDIRECTING INPUT

■ *Use the < symbol to redirect an input from a file, which may provide a necessary response to a DOS command.*

There are occasions when a DOS command needs an input before making its next move. Most of the time, you are asked to enter Y or N from the keyboard. Instead of entering these manually, you can redirect them from an existing disk file which contains a predetermined input.

Input for DEL

An example of the need to enter a Y/N input is when you use this command:

```
A>del *.*
```

As you already know, this command will lead to this response:

```
A>del *.*
All files in directory will be deleted!
Are you sure (Y/N)?_
```

If you wish to go ahead, you are supposed to type Y and then press Enter to start deleting.

If you know what you are doing, you can simplify your work with this command:

```
A>del *.* < yes
```

Here YES is a file name which is intended to supply the Y response when asked by DOS. You now need to create this file named YES, as shown below:

```
A>copy con yes
y
^Z
```

This file contains two keystrokes, Y and a carriage return. Do not forget to press Enter after Y. It is needed to get the DEL command going.

You can put the whole thing together in a batch file like this (do not run this batch file until you read the warning below):

```
A>copy con delall.bat
del *.* < yes
^Z
```

When you run this batch file, DOS automatically goes through these steps:

```
A>delall
del *.* < yes
All files in directory will be deleted!
Are you sure (Y/N)?y
```

The Y, followed by Enter, is supplied by the YES file. So DOS starts deletion without further delay.

WARNING: This batch file is a mass file killer; do not use it unless you know what you are doing. When you run it, by simply entering DELALL, all the files in the current directory will be immediately wiped out. If the batch file is also stored there, it will also disappear; as a result, the "Batch file missing" message will be displayed.

If you want to experiment with this batch file, you can create a separate directory, make it the current directory, and put some dispensable files there. Provide a path to the root directory where you store DELALL.BAT. Run the batch file and see what happens. If you make a mistake, use UNDELETE right away to restore all the deleted files.

Instead of creating two separate files as illustrated above, you could integrate the whole thing into one file like this:

```
A>copy con delall.bat
echo y > yes
del *.* < yes
^Z
```

Each time this modified batch file is run, the first line will create a new file named YES which will contain a single character of Y, plus a carriage return; if this file already exists, it will be replaced. The second line will redirect the required Y from the newly created file to delete everything, including the newly created YES file.

You may ask, why bother redirecting input? There is a simpler way, you say. Here is what you might contemplate:

```
A>copy con delall.bat
del *.* y
^Z
```

Another possibility you might have in mind is this:

```
A>copy con delall.bat
del *.*
y
^Z
```

Neither one will work. The first will generate an error message—too many parameters. The second will wait for your response and then run a program or batch file named Y, which will most likely generate an error message—"bad command or file name".

Input for FORMAT

Although supplying Y blindly is a dangerous practice and defeats the purpose of letting you exercise caution before a destructive move, supplying N could be time saving. Consider the following batch file:

```
A>copy con fmat.bat
@echo off
c:\dos\format b: < go
^Z
```

This batch file is intended to load FORMAT.COM from the C:\DOS directory and then format the disk in drive B. The required responses are input from the GO file, which is created with the following steps:

```
A>copy con go


n
^Z
```

This file has two empty lines (pressing Enter twice) and one letter N. The first Enter is to respond to this:

```
Insert new diskette for drive B:
and press ENTER when ready...
```

The second Enter is to enter no volume label. After formatting is complete, you are prompted to enter a volume label. This requires a response from you. By pressing Enter (or redirecting the required input from a file), no volume label is created, and the formatting process moves on. You can, if you wish, enter a single label here, such as ABCCORP; in that case, all the disks formatted with this batch file will carry this label.

The N in the GO file is to tell DOS to format no more. This is the last response required to complete a formatting process.

If you have lots of disks to format at one time, change the N in the GO file to Y. When a disk is done, this message will appear:

```
Insert new diskette for drive B:
and press ENTER when ready...
```

You can insert a new disk and press Enter to format another one. You can also press Ctrl-Break to end.

P R A C T I C E   8 - 1

☐ 1. Use COPY CON to create a file named FOOL; enter the following three lines of text:

A fool always finds one more foolish to admire him.

Fools rush in where angels fear to tread.

A fool and his money are soon parted.

☐ 2. Use ECHO to add a line to FOOL.

☐ 3. Use TYPE to send FOOL to NUL and then to the printer.

☐ 4. Use COPY to send FOOL to NUL and then to the printer.

☐ 5. Use COPY CON to create a file named CR, which contains a single carriage return (pressing Enter once). Create a batch file named T.BAT which will redirect CR to the TIME command and thus allow you to enter T alone to show the current time.

☐ 6. Use DOSKEY to create a macro named DT. It should allow the user to enter DT to show the current date and time without having to press Enter. (Use the CR file created in #5 for input redirection.)

D R I L L

___ 1. The following command will:

A>dir > file1

a. create a file named FILE1

b. destroy FILE1's contents if it exists

c. do neither a nor b

d. do both a and b

___ 2. The following command will:

A>dir >> file1

a. append data to FILE1, if existent

b. replace the contents of FILE1 if existent

c. create FILE1 if it does not already exist

d. do both a and c

e. do none of above

_____ 3. The following command will:
      A>type file1 > prn
   a. display and print FILE1
   b. print FILE1
   c. display FILE1
   d. do nothing

_____ 4. The following command will:
      A>copy file1 > prn
   a. print FILE1
   b. copy FILE1 to a file named PRN
   c. both a and b
   d. generate an error message

_____ 5. If your printer is turned on, this command will:
      A>echo test line > prn
   a. print two words
   b. print three words
   c. do nothing
   d. generate an error message

_____ 6. The following command will:
      A>copy file1 nul > nul
   a. copy FILE1 to a file named NUL
   b. display a message on the screen
   c. copy to device NUL and show no message
   d. generate an error message

_____ 7. If YES is not a file, the following command will:
      A>del *.* < yes
   a. delete all files immediately
   b. prompt you to enter Y/N
   c. do nothing
   d. generate a "File not found" message

_____ 8. To enable the following command to complete its job without any human
      intervention, the GO file must contain:
      C:\DOS>format a: < go
   a. a single N
   b. a blank line, followed by N
   c. two blank lines, N, followed by Enter
   d. a blank line, two Ns

PIPES AND FILTERS

■ *Use a pipe to connect two DOS commands.*

■ *Use a filter command to sort, find, or display files.*

So far you have run each DOS command by itself. Here you will learn that several DOS commands can be chained together and that an output from one command can be piped to another command.

This section explains the general principles of piping and filtering. Details of related commands will follow.

Piping

A **pipe** (¦) is a connector of two commands. Like a water pipe (or hose) that connects a faucet to a garden, a DOS pipe connects two commands or programs placed before and after it. When you turn on the faucet, the water that comes out of the faucet goes through the pipe to the garden. The output from the command before a DOS pipe is fed to the next command as input. Consider the following arrangement:

```
A>dir ¦ find "EXE" ¦ sort
```

The output of DIR is fed to FIND. When matching files are found, they are fed to SORT, which displays the found files in alphabetical order.

Pipes can be used to run one program after another, such as:

```
A>prog1 ¦ prog2 ¦ prog3
```

After you exit PROG1, PROG2 is executed, and so on.

If you pipe two DOS commands together, in which the first does not produce an output that can be used as an input for the second, the first output is not displayed and only the second is, such as:

```
A>dir ¦ path
A>path ¦ dir
```

In the first example, DIR's output is not shown and only the output by PATH is displayed; in the second, the reverse is true.

In each piping operation, DOS may create two temporary files with odd names like these:

```
BACOAJEB
BACOAJFM
```

Normally these files are automatically deleted after a piping operation is completed. On some rare occasions, they may remain on disk. You can use TYPE to show their contents and DEL to get rid of them.

Filtering

A **filter** is a device that materials go through and come out different from their original state. DOS provides three filter commands:

MORE   Display text 24 lines at a time

SORT   Produce sorted output

FIND   Display found lines

These filters process raw materials and produce outputs explained above. They can be used alone or in combination with others. Their output can go to the screen or be redirected to other devices.

USING MORE

■ *Redirect an input file to MORE to display one screen at a time.*

■ *Use MORE and redirect output to PRN to print each typed line.*

The MORE command filters from a source and redirects output to the screen one screen (page) at a time. Twenty-four lines are displayed at one time, and the bottom of the screen displays this message:

-- More --

It tells you that there is more. Pressing a key will display another page until the end. Pressing Ctrl-C or Ctrl-Break will terminate the display.

Using MORE Alone

If the command is entered alone, you may be puzzled about its behavior. The cursor moves down two lines and nothing else happens:

A>**more**

_

You might think the computer is locked up. It is not. If you press Enter alone, the cursor keeps moving down two lines each time and nothing else happens. If you enter a line, it is immediately echoed (duplicated) to the screen.

This behavior may seem puzzling to you, but it is actually logical. Without being given any direction, DOS assumes that you are inputting from the keyboard (standard input) and outputting to the screen (standard output). So every time you type something and press Enter, it is duplicated on the screen. To get out of the MORE screen, press Ctrl-C or Ctrl-Z and Enter.

Using MORE alone echoes input and output to the screen. It has the same effect as the following:

```
A>more > con
A>more < con
```

Using MORE to Display

MORE is most often used to output text lines to the screen one screen at a time. The text lines could be directory entries or input from a disk file. The syntax for each situation appears like this:

```
A>dir ¦ more
A>more < filename
A>type filename ¦ more
```

In the first case, the output of DIR is filtered by MORE. If the display goes beyond a screenful, MORE will pause and display a message. The result is comparable to using the /P switch with DIR. In the second case, the disk file is input to the MORE filter and regulated the same way. The third command produces the same result as the second; the text read by TYPE is filtered by MORE to display one screen at a time.

The symbols may look confusing. Can other symbols be used with MORE? Yes. However, each symbol produces a different result. Some make sense; others do not. The list below shows many possible variations:

```
A>more ¦ dir      Execute MORE command and then DIR command
A>more > dir      Create a file named DIR
A>more >> dir     Append to a file named DIR
A>more < dir      Input a file named DIR
A>more << dir     Same as above
A>dir > more      Create a file named MORE
A>dir >> more     Append to a file named MORE
A>dir ¦ more      Filter directory through MORE command
A>dir < more      MORE file ignored or "File not found"
A>dir << more     Same as above
```

In the first example, the MORE command is executed without any parameter. After you enter ^Z (press F6 and Enter) to end, the DIR command is then executed. If you press Ctrl-C, DIR is not executed.

In the second and third examples, MORE is executed to allow you to enter text lines. When you enter ^C or ^Z, the text lines are sent to a file named DIR (this has nothing to do with the DIR command).

The last two examples do not make sense because the DIR command does not accept an input from a disk file. If the file named MORE (not MORE.COM) exists, DIR is executed but the file input is ignored. If the file does not exist, the "File not found" message is shown and the DIR command is not executed.

MORE, TYPE, and COPY CON

You can use MORE, TYPE, and COPY CON to display files. Follow these steps to see how they differ (make C:\DOS the current directory first):

FOLLOW
THESE
STEPS

1. Show a file with MORE:

    `C:\DOS>`**`more < readme.txt`**

2. Press the space bar a few times to show several screens. Press Ctrl-C to abort.

3. Use TYPE alone and press Ctrl-C to abort:

    `C:\DOS>`**`type readme.txt`**

4. Combine TYPE and MORE:

    `C:\DOS>`**`type readme.txt ¦ more`**

5. Repeat step 2.

6. Use COPY CON and then press Ctrl-C to abort:

    `C:\DOS>`**`copy readme.txt con`**

If you use COPY CON or TYPE alone, as in steps 3 and 6, the scrolling continues until the end of the file or until Ctrl-C is pressed. When MORE is used, as in steps 1 and 4, the scrolling pauses after the screen is full.

In displaying file contents on the screen, the MORE command behaves very much like TYPE, with the exception of showing one screen at a time. They both treat a file as ASCII text and stop reading it as soon as the first ^Z (end-of-file marker) is encountered. COPY CON does the same thing, except that you can use the /B switch to read an entire binary file, like this:

`C:\DOS>`**`copy /b more.com con`**

When you use COPY, you cannot combine it with MORE, like this:

`C:\DOS>`**`copy /b more.com con ¦ more`**

It will not work. Since COPY CON produces no output that MORE can use, the MORE command is ignored.

Using a Batch File to Display Files

If you want an easy way to display file contents, the short batch file below will work well:

```
A>copy con read.bat
@echo off
c:\dos\more < %1
^Z
```

When you want to show a file, just enter a command like this:

```
A>read filename
```

This requires you to enter the name of a file to be displayed. This name is then assigned to the %1 replaceable parameter. If no file name is entered, this message appears:

```
File not found
```

If this happens, MORE is not loaded—unlike the situation when the MORE command is entered alone.

Note: MORE, like TYPE, expects only one parameter. Consequently, you cannot use wild cards on the command line or multiple replaceable parameters in the above batch file.

Using MORE to Print

MORE can be used to print text lines entered from the keyboard. This will add another printing technique to what you learned in Chapter 2. Now turn on the printer and follow these steps to see what happens. (The following description is based on an Epson; it may not apply to other printers.)

FOLLOW THESE STEPS

1. Redirect output to the printer:

   ```
   A>more > prn
   ```

2. Enter a line:

   This line goes to the printer.

What happens? The displayed line is redirected to the printer.

3. Enter a line after pressing Tab once:

   This line is indented.

The line is printed at the first tab, just as it is displayed on the screen.

4. Press Enter alone. The cursor moves down one line and the printer roller moves up one line.

5. Press F7 (to display ^@) and Enter to send a null character. The above phenomenon is repeated.

6. Press Ctrl-P, enter a line, and press Ctrl-P again. If you have a daisy-wheel printer, each letter is sent to the printer as it is typed. With a dot-matrix printer, the whole line is printed when Enter is pressed.

7. Send ASCII 12 by pressing Ctrl-L, or hold down Alt and type 12 on the numeric keypad. This is the formfeed character; it will cause the paper to advance by one page.

8. Press Ctrl-C (or F6 and Enter to enter ^Z) to terminate.

The above steps show that with MORE every line is faithfully redirected to the printer. In step 8, either method produces the same result. There is nothing left to print, and nothing is printed.

In contrast, repeat the above steps after entering this command:

> A>`copy con prn`

T I P S   A N D   T R I C K S

P R I N T I N G   F R O M   T H E   S C R E E N

If you need to print a short document you type on the screen, there are a number of ways to do that. For printing each line after Enter is pressed, use this command:

> A>`more > prn`

Instead of using the MORE command, you can use COPY CON to do the same thing:

1. Enter this command to begin:

   > A>`copy con prn`

2. Press Ctrl-P and start typing. Each line is printed after Enter is pressed.

3. Press Ctrl-P and then Ctrl-C when done.

To print after the whole document is finished, follow these steps:

1. Enter this command to begin:

   > A>`copy con prn`

2. When done, press F6 and Enter to print.

Nothing is printed until you press Ctrl-P. Entering ^Z in step 8 sends everything to the printer. Entering ^C (pressing Ctrl-C) prints nothing.

P R A C T I C E   8 - 2

☐ 1. Use MORE to type and print the following two lines of text:

He who knows others is learned;
He who knows himself is wise.

☐ 2. Use MORE to redirect FOOL (created in the previous session) to NUL.

☐ 3. Use MORE to redirect FOOL to the printer.

☐ 4. Use DOSKEY to create a macro named M. It should allow the user to enter a file name to print it. Use MORE and redirect output to the printer. Use the macro to print FOOL.

☐ 5. Modify the M macro so that it will use MORE to display the file supplied as a parameter by the user and pause (use PAUSE) when the entire file is displayed. When the user presses a key to end the pause, the macro will then print the file. Use the macro to print the FOOL file created earlier.

☐ 6. Create a macro named T. It should use TYPE and let the user enter one or more parameters. The user can enter a parameter to display a file or two parameters to print it. Use T to display FOOL and use it again to print it.

D R I L L

____ 9. The following command will:

A>path ¦ dir

a. display a path list
b. display directory entries
c. do both a and b
d. generate an error message

____ 10. The following command will display directory entries one screen at a time. True or false?

A>dir ¦ more

____ 11. The following command will do the same as Question 10 above. True or false?

A>dir > more

____ 12. If a file named MORE exists in the current directory, this command will:

   A>dir < more

   a. display the current directory all at once

   b. display the file named MORE a screen at a time

   c. create a file named MORE

   d. display a "File not found" message

____ 13. The MORE filter can display the contents of an entire binary file. True or false?

____ 14. The following command will print each text line as it is entered on the screen. True or false?

   A>more > prn

____ 15. If MORE is entered without a parameter, an error message will be displayed. True or false?

USING SORT

■ *Use SORT to sort text lines of an ASCII text file.*

■ *Use the /R switch to sort in descending order; use the /+c switch to sort by a specific column.*

■ *Use DIR with SORT and a column number to display sorted directory entries.*

The SORT filter can sort text lines that go to the screen. These text lines can include those you enter from the keyboard, those input from a disk file, or directory entries. It can handle a file up to 64KB.

Creating and Sorting a Database

Before demonstrating how the SORT command works, let us first create a database of quotations and then manipulate it in a variety of ways.

FOLLOW THESE STEPS

1. Create a database by entering the following:

```
A>copy con quotes
Confucius: He who does not economize will have to agonize.
Franklin: He who has a trade has an estate.
Lao Tse: He who knows does not speak.
Reagan: We start bombing Russia in five minutes.
```

```
        Cervantes: Be slow of tongue and quick of eye.
        ^Z
```

2. Sort the file:

```
A>sort < quotes
Cervantes: Be slow of tongue and quick of eye.
Confucius: He who does not economize will have to agonize.
Franklin: He who has a trade has an estate.
Lao Tse: He who knows does not speak.
Reagan: We start bombing Russia in five minutes.
```

To sort a file by first word, as shown above, simply input it to the SORT filter. The file is now sorted in ascending order.

3. Save after sorting:

```
A>sort < quotes > quotes.srt
```

If you want to save the sorted file, simply redirect the output to a file name, as above. The screen does not display the sorted file. Instead, it is redirected to the named file. If you use the same file name for both input and output, the sorted version replaces the original.

4. Sort in descending order and append to an existing file:

```
A>sort /r < quotes >> quotes.srt
```

The target file now contains duplicates. The top portion is in ascending order and the bottom the reverse of that.

Sorting by a Column

In addition to /R (reverse), SORT has another, /+c, switch. In this switch, you put a plus sign after the backslash and a column number, which is the position of a letter counting from the left margin.

To demonstrate how this works, let us build another database that can be meaningfully sorted according to a column number, and then sort by that column:

FOLLOW THESE STEPS

1. Create the file below; press the space bar 10 times before entering the first number and align the other numbers with the first:

```
A>copy con phones
Townsend, Skip          453-8909
Zagler, Zig             323-2121
Bumsteer, Dag           405-3216
Wane, Johnny            987-6543
Wayman, Jane            555-0101
^Z
```

2. Sort by first word (last name):

```
A>sort < phones
Bumsteer, Dag          405-3216
Townsend, Skip         453-8909
Wane, Johnny           987-6543
Wayman, Jane           555-0101
Zagler, Zig            323-2121
```

3. Sort by phone number:

```
A>sort < phones /+25
Zagler, Zig            323-2121
Bumsteer, Dag          405-3216
Townsend, Skip         453-8909
Wayman, Jane           555-0101
Wane, Johnny           987-6543
```

In step 3 we sort the database by the 25th column, which is the first digit of each telephone number. The result is that the database is rearranged according to the ascending order of the phone numbers.

4. Sort the phone numbers in reverse order:

```
A>sort < phones /+25 /r
Wane, Johnny           987-6543
Wayman, Jane           555-0101
Townsend, Skip         453-8909
Bumsteer, Dag          405-3216
Zagler, Zig            323-2121
```

5. Sort the names in reverse order:

```
A>sort < phones /r
Zagler, Zig            323-2121
Wayman, Jane           555-0101
Wane, Johnny           987-6543
Townsend, Skip         453-8909
Bumsteer, Dag          405-3216
```

Sorting Directory Entries[2]

SORT can be used to display your directory entries in a way that will enable you to find files more quickly. This command will display all files in ascending order:

```
A>dir | sort
```

---

2. The techniques discussed here were commonly used by users of earlier versions to display directory entries in more meaningful ways. The DIR command of version 5 or 6 has numerous switches that have made these techniques less useful.

If you have many files in a directory, the above command is most useful. Since all the file names are shown in alphabetical order, you can quickly locate what you are looking for. The above command can now be replaced in version 5 or 6 by this:

```
A>dir /o
```

You can also enlist the help of MORE, such as:

```
A>dir | sort | more
```

One screen of files will be shown at a time, and in alphabetical order. It works the same as this:

```
A>dir /o /p
```

Directory items of each file are arranged in a logical manner. You can use this orderly arrangement to sort by a specific column. The following and Table 8.2 show where each item is located:

```
CHAP      001         3547 09-17-91  10:30p
CHAP      002        12317 09-27-91   2:34p
CHAP      003     11101117 01-09-92   8:01p
```

To sort by extension, enter this command:

```
A>dir | sort /+10 | more
```

All the items shown, including the messages and file counts, are sorted. First come the files without extensions, the total number of which is tabulated and

---

Table 8.2

Directory Entries and Column Positions

Directory Entry	Column
File name	1
Extension	10
File size	14
Month	24
Date	27
Year	30
Hour	34
Minute	37

displayed. Then come subdirectories, if any. Finally appear other extensions in alphabetical order, with messages mixed together.

This command will sort by file size:

```
A>dir | sort /+14 | more
```

Sorting by different date/time items is not particularly meaningful. If you go by month (/+24), you will end up having this order:

```
CHAP      003  11101117 01-09-91   8:01p
CHAP      001      3547 09-17-90  10:30p
CHAP      002     12317 09-27-90   2:34p
```

Going by year (/+30) produces the least misleading order. The month and date will not be in order, but the year will be correct.

In version 5 or 6, all these deficiencies are corrected by DIR's new /O switch. You can use /O:D to sort by date-time in ascending order (earliest first) or /O:-D in descending order (latest first).

Numeric vs. Alphanumeric Sort

SORT can sort alphanumeric words accurately. The ASCII values are compared, but upper and lower cases are adjusted (placing a, rather than B, after A). To demonstrate how SORT works with entries from the keyboard, follow these steps:

FOLLOW THESE STEPS

1. Run the SORT program without entering any parameter.

2. Enter from the keyboard the items to be sorted.

3. Enter ^Z by pressing F6 and Enter.

The results of the above steps are shown below:

```
A>sort
Zip
zap
Abel
ace
able
^Z
Abel
able
ace
zap
Zip
```

SORT cannot do an accurate numeric sort. Numbers are treated as alphanumeric characters whose values are based on the ASCII table, except adjusting for uppercase and lowercase. The following is an example:

```
A>sort
111119
11118
9.999
0.2222
0.2221
^Z
0.2221
0.2222
111119
11118
9.999
```

Numbers of unequal lengths are not placed according to their numeric values. It is thus meaningless to sort such numbers. However, numbers of equal lengths, such as ZIP, license, telephone, or Social Security numbers can be sorted accurately—and quickly.

SORT's Input and Output

SORT's output can be redirected to a device such as a printer. Here are two possibilities:

```
A>sort > prn
A>sort /r < filename > prn
```

The first line will allow you to enter on the screen the items to be sorted. When ^Z is entered, the sorted lines are sent to the printer, not the screen.

The second example sorts the named file in reverse order. The output is also redirected to the printer rather than the screen.

MORE and SORT

The two filter commands of MORE and SORT can be combined, such as these examples:

```
A>more ¦ sort
A>sort ¦ more
```

The first command will load MORE and let you enter lines from the keyboard. If you enter more than 24 lines, the — More — message appears; you can press a key and continue making more entries. When you enter ^Z, the lines will be redisplayed in sorted order. The scrolling does not pause even if there are more than 24 lines.

The second example will load SORT and let you enter lines from the keyboard. When you enter ^Z, the lines are redisplayed in sorted order. If more than 24 lines are entered, the sorted screen will pause and display the — More — message.

P R A C T I C E   8 - 3

☐   1. Build a database of 12 records and name it ADDRESS. Each record should have four fields as shown below. The State field should contain four states, each of which should appear in three records.

Drake, Daffy   123 Kwack Ave., Fun City   CA   94000

☐   2. Sort the records by last name in ascending order.

☐   3. Sort by last name in descending order.

☐   4. Sort by state in ascending order.

☐   5. Sort by ZIP in ascending order and print the output.

☐   6. Use DOSKEY to create a macro named S. It should allow the user to enter one or more switches and use them to sort the ADDRESS file. Use S to sort ADDRESS by ZIP in descending order.

D R I L L

____   16. The SORT command can accurately sort numerals of unequal lengths. True or false?

____   17. SORT strictly follows the ASCII table in arranging alphanumeric characters. True or false?

____   18. The following command will:

A>sort < filename ¦ more

a. sort text lines in ascending order

b. display 24 lines and pause

c. do both a and b

d. display sorted lines without pause

____ 19. If you have a database in which the first field contains first name followed by last name, you can use SORT to accurately sort by last name. True or false?

____ 20. By default, SORT sorts by descending order. True or false?

____ 21. SORT can be used to sort directory entries by any specific column. True or false?

____ 22. The following command will:

    A>dir ¦ sort ¦ more

  a. display 24 lines, sorted

  b. display — MORE — message if there is more

  c. generate an error message

  d. do both 1 and 2

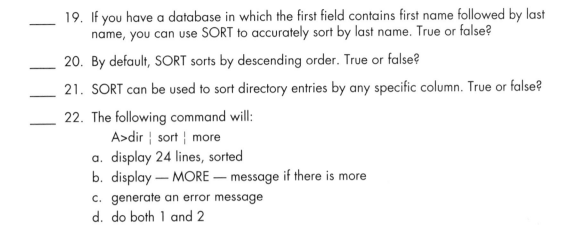

USING FIND

■ *Use FIND with a search string to find text lines in a file.*

■ *Use /V to find lines not containing a search string, /C to find the number of matching lines, /N to number and display matching lines, and /I to make a search case insensitive.*

The FIND command can be used to search for text strings in a file or directory entries. Input data going to the screen is filtered by FIND and output is displayed or redirected.

Finding Text Strings

To find a text string from a disk file, enter a command like this:

    A>`find "string" filename`

The string you want to search for has to be put inside double quotes. If the string is found, the whole line containing it is displayed on the screen.

Let us try to find a quote in the QUOTES file created earlier. Follow these steps:

FOLLOW THESE STEPS

1. Enter a word in lowercase as a search string:

    A>`find "franklin" quotes`

    ---------- QUOTES

DOS tells you that nothing matching is found. The file name is displayed, but nothing else is shown.

2. Use a different case:

```
A>find "Franklin" quotes

---------- QUOTES
Franklin: He who has a trade has an estate.
```

This time, one matching line is found. The difference this time is using uppercase for the first letter, which matches the entry in the database. So, keep in mind that a search operation is case sensitive unless you specify the /I switch.

3. Enter a phrase as a search string:

```
A>find /i "he who" quotes
```

This will catch three lines. A search string can be anything, as long as it is inside quotes. You can, as shown here, use several words as a search string.

4. Enter two search strings:

```
A>find "He" quotes | find "Confucius" quotes

---------- QUOTES
Confucius: He who does not economize will have to agonize.
```

This tells DOS to search for lines containing "He", and then search in that group lines containing "Confucius"; it will catch only one line, together with the file name, as shown above.

T I P S   A N D   T R I C K S

F I N D   W I T H O U T   L I N E   O R   F I L E   N A M E

When you use the FIND command to search for lines in a file, the screen always shows a one-inch line, followed by the file name in uppercase.

Some people go through a lot of trouble devising complicated ways to remove the distracting line and file name. If you find these items objectionable and do not want them displayed, the simplest trick is to repeat a search string without the file name, such as:

```
A>find "He who" quotes | find "He who"
```

This in effect suppresses display of the extraneous line. The extra line does not appear regardless of whether any matching line is found or not. This technique can save you a lot of paper if you redirect output to the printer, such as:

```
A>find "He who" quotes | find "He who" > prn
```

5. Omit file name in the second search string:

```
A>find "He who" quotes | find "Confucius"
Confucius: He who does not economize will have to agonize.
```

The same result appears, but the file name is not displayed.

FIND's Switches

FIND has four switches, as shown below:

/C   Count number of lines found

/I   Insensitive concerning case; A=a

/N   Number; a number precedes each found line

/V   Void; shows lines not containing search string

To find the lines not containing "He who", enter this command:

```
A>find /v "He who" quotes
```

This will show two lines.

When you want to know how many lines without actually displaying the lines, use the /C switch. If you want each line found displayed and numbered, use the /N switch, such as:

```
A>find /n "He who" quotes
```

```
---------- QUOTES
[1]Confucius: He who does not economize will have to agonize.
[2]Franklin: He who has a trade has an estate.
[3]Lao Tse: He who knows does not speak.
```

When /C is used, alone or with /V and/or /N, no line is displayed; only the total number of matching lines is shown. It in effect negates the other two switches.

If you use /I, uppercase and lowercase letters are treated the same. Consider this example:

```
A>find /i "john" filename
```

Since /I is used, DOS will consider "john", "John", and "JOHN" all matching. If /I is not specified, only "john" will be considered matching.

Note: A string that is broken up by a carriage return is not the same as the one that is not. Suppose you want to find "red rose". If the two words are separated by a carriage return, with one at the end of a line and the other at the beginning of a new line, the string will not be considered matching.

Finding Directory Entries

FIND can be used to find directory entries, such as:

```
C:\DOS>dir | find "EXE"
```

The output of DIR will be filtered by FIND in search of any line containing the search string of "EXE"; make sure to use uppercase in the search string because DIR normally displays everything in uppercase. This command will thus display all the files in the current directory with the EXE extension, plus possibly other matching files; do not put a period in the search string because no period appears anywhere on the screen produced by DIR. If you do not want subdirectories displayed, this command will do:

```
C:\DOS>dir | find /v "<DIR>"
```

The search string in the above situation could be shortened to "<".

FIND, like MORE and SORT, reads a file as ASCII text. It stops reading when the first ^Z is encountered. Consequently, it is not very useful in finding text strings in binary files.

COMBINING FILTERS

■ *Combine FIND, SORT, MORE, CHKDSK, and ATTRIB, and put them in batch files to quickly search for text lines or file names.*

Most of the data output to the screen can be filtered and redirected, including file names and text lines. This section shows how to combine various filter commands to produce outputs in specific ways.

Before file names are output to the screen, you can use a number of ways to filter them, such as this example:

```
C:\DOS>dir | find "REPORT" | sort /+30
```

This command will list all the file names carrying the letters of REPORT, such as REPORT1.TXT and NWREPORT. These files are also sorted by their 30th column, namely year. The above command can be replaced with this speedier technique in version 5 or 6:

```
C:\DOS>dir /o:d | find "REPORT"
```

A command like the above can be used to locate a file on a large disk. Suppose you remember having created many report files and buried them in various directories. A command like this can quickly find the one you need:

```
C:\DOS>dir \ /o:d /s | find "REPORT" | more
```

This command will go to all the directories in drive C to search for files containing the "REPORT" string and display them sorted by date. If more than 24 files are found, the scrolling will pause.

WARNING: When filtering file names, make sure you use uppercase in a search string because DOS normally outputs file names only in uppercase. If you were to use "report" as a search string, nothing would be shown because no file name is displayed in lowercase. On the other hand, if you use the /L switch with DIR, file names will be displayed in lowercase. In that case, you must use "report", but not "REPORT", like this:

```
C:\DOS>dir \ /o:d /l /s ¦ find "report" ¦ more
```

Since CHKDSK and ATTRIB also output file names to the screen, you can also filter the outputs. Consider the following two examples:

```
A>chkdsk /v ¦ find "SMITH" ¦ more
A>attrib /s *.* ¦ find "SMITH" ¦ more
```

Both produce file names and their directory paths. The only difference is that the latter also displays file attributes. The MORE filter is necessary only if you expect lots of SMITH files.

If you have complex directories and spend a lot of time searching for files, this batch file should be helpful:

```
A>copy con seefile.bat
@echo off
chkdsk /v ¦ find "%1"
^Z
```

When you run this batch file, make sure you use uppercase in a search string. Suppose you are now in a subdirectory in drive C, you can run your batch file stored in drive A this way:

```
C:\BAT>a:seefile SMITH
```

The last line in the batch file will be executed this way:

```
chkdsk /v ¦ find "SMITH"
```

The entire drive C will be searched and all the SMITH files (and directories), and their paths, will be displayed.

If you need to look for text lines inside various files, the batch file below should be useful (notice the double %% inside a batch file):

```
A>copy con seeline.bat
@echo off
for %%x in (%1) do find "%2" %%x
^Z
```

You need to enter two parameters when you use this batch file, the first for file name(s) and the second for search string, like these two examples:

```
A>seeline file? Smith
A>seeline *.* Smith
```

The first searches for "Smith" in files matching the FILE? pattern and the second searches in all the files. If you want the output redirected to a file named SEELINE.TXT, change the sole command line to this:

```
for %%x in (%1) do find "%2" %%x > seeline.txt
```

This batch file will not accept multiple words as a search string, for they cannot be assigned to a single replaceable parameter.

Some outputs to the screen cannot be filtered. Here are two examples (notice the single % for a command-line entry):

```
A>for %x in (file?) do type %x | find "Smith"
A>copy file? con | find "Smith"
```

Both will display entire files of all those matching FILE?. The filter is ignored.

The FOR..IN..DO command is often used in complex batch files and is thus explained more fully in Chapter 11.

P R A C T I C E   8 - 4

1. Find in ADDRESS (created in the previous session) all the records from one state.

2. Find and sort (by last name in ascending order) the records in another state.

3. Use two search strings to find matching records. (The output should show the normal line and file name.)

4. Do a search but suppress the display of this line:
   ———————— ADDRESS

5. Create a batch file named SEEADD.BAT. It should have a fixed search file name, namely ADDRESS. It should allow you to enter a single parameter to search for matching lines.

6. Use DOSKEY to create a macro named SL. It should do what SEELINE.BAT does. Use SL to search for CA lines in the ADDRESS file.

INSERTING DATE AND TIME IN A FILE

■ *Use DATE and TIME with ECHO, FIND, and MORE to insert date-time in a file.*

■ *Create a batch file that will allow you to add note or diary entries, with the current date and time automatically added after each entry.*

One of the most useful ways of using FIND is inserting date and/or time information in a file. There are occasions when you want to date a file or a piece of information. Entering date and time data can be quite time consuming. Making DOS do it automatically can be time saving.

Adding Date and Time with MORE

When you enter the DATE command on the command line, you get this response:

```
A>date
Current date is Sat 06-27-1992
Enter new date (mm-dd-yy):_
```

You can now enter new data at the cursor location. If you combine DATE with ECHO and MORE, the effect is the same as pressing Enter without entering new data:

```
A>echo ¦ more ¦ date
Current date is Sat 06-27-1992
Enter new date (mm-dd-yy):
A>_
```

This mechanism can be used to send the whole message, or one line, to a file or a device such as a printer.

Now follow these steps and see what happens (make sure there is a practice disk in drive A):

FOLLOW THESE STEPS

1. Enter the command below:

```
A>echo ¦ more ¦ date > datedata
```

Your disk drive should make a little noise. That means it is saving a file.

2. Display the file on the screen:

```
A>type datedata
```

The file just created should resemble this:

```
Current date is Sat 06-27-1992
Enter new date (mm-dd-yy):
```

3. Use FIND to save only one line:

```
A>echo | more | date | find "C" > datedata
```

4. Display the new file:

```
A>type datedata
Current date is Sat 06-27-1992
```

This time only one line is sent to the file. The FIND command searches for a line with an uppercase C and the output is redirected to a file.[3]

Adding Date-Time with an Input File

You can also insert the date/time without using MORE. To provide for a required input, you need to have an existing file. Suppose you already have a file named CR which contains a single carriage return. You can now use the batch file below to add date and time to a file:

```
A>copy con datefile.bat
@echo off
date < cr | find "C" >> notes
time < cr | find "C" >> notes
^Z
```

The CR file will supply the carriage return as required by both DATE and TIME.

Every time you run DATEFILE.BAT, the current date and time data will be appended to the file named NOTES.

To make this batch file more versatile, change "notes" to %1. Then you can use it to insert the date-time in any file, like this:

```
A>datefile report5.bud
```

Adding Date-Time with ECHO

We have saved the simplest technique to be covered last. This technique involves neither the external MORE command nor accessing a disk file. It simply uses ECHO in a batch file to echo a carriage return where one is expected.

---

3. The following command will produce the same result:
```
A>echo | more | date | find /v "E" > datedata
```
This eliminates the line with an uppercase E and sends the rest to the file.

Earlier in this chapter we used the technique of echoing Y to DEL to supply the required confirmation without a pause. Here we need to supply a carriage return. How can we supply a carriage return with ECHO?

Your first reaction may be to use ECHO alone. It does not work. If you enter ECHO alone on the command line, you get this response:

```
A>echo
ECHO is on
```

We do not need this message. Instead, we need an empty line consisting of a simple carriage return. If we add a slash, on the other hand, we get the desired result:

```
A>echo/
A>_
```

Armed with this knowledge, you can now show the current date without pressing the Enter key on the keyboard when the date is shown:

```
A>echo/ ¦ date
Current date is Sat 06-27-1992
Enter new date (mm-dd-yy):
A>_
```

If you now combine the above command with FIND, you will show only the first line:

```
A>echo/ ¦ date ¦ find "C"
Current date is Sat 06-27-1992
A>_
```

We can now modify our earlier batch file as follows:

```
A>copy con datefile.bat
@echo off
echo/ ¦ date ¦ find "C" >> notes
echo/ ¦ time ¦ find "C" >> notes
^Z
```

This batch file is simpler and more elegant than its previous version because you do not need to create and maintain a separate file to supply the required carriage return. It uses only one external command. Here you can even take out the last portion containing the external FIND command. It will still work, except that your file will contain an extra line serving no purpose.

Diary Project

As the final project in this chapter, we are going to create a batch file that will let you make diary (or note) entries and then automatically add date and time data to the end of each entry.

1. The first step is to create this batch file:

```
A>copy con diary.bat
@echo off
copy diary.txt + con
echo/ ¦ date ¦ find "C" >> diary.txt
echo/ ¦ time ¦ find "C" >> diary.txt
^Z
```

This batch file will append whatever is typed from the keyboard and displayed on the screen to an existing file named DIARY.TXT. Before you can use this batch file, you need to create a DIARY.TXT file.

2. Create the DIARY.TXT file:

```
A>copy con diary.txt
This is my new diary. I will add something everyday.
^Z
```

After these two files have been created, you are ready to make a diary entry.

3. Make a diary entry:

```
A>diary
DIARY.TXT
CON
Learned some new and neat DOS tricks. Begin to feel
confident about taming this beast.

More ethnic violence in the former USSR. Is this a
repeat of the events leading to WWI? Plus ca change,
plus c'est la meme chose.

^Z
```

The first two words are automatically displayed by DOS, telling you that what is entered from the console will be appended to the file named DIARY.TXT. If you find only CON here, which happens when the DIARY.TXT file is nonexistent or inaccessible, your entry will not be saved.

After you press F6 and Enter, what you have typed, plus two more lines, will be saved.

4. Show your diary:

```
A>type diary.txt
This is my new diary. I will add something everyday.

Learned some new and neat DOS tricks. Begin to feel
confident about taming this beast.
```

> More ethnic violence in the former USSR. Is this a
> repeat of the events leading to WWI? Plus ca change,
> plus c'est la meme chose.
>
> Current date is Sat 06-27-1992
> Current time is 8:38:21.72p

The first line came from the original DIARY.TXT file. The two ensuing paragraphs are what you just typed. And the last two lines are automatically added by the batch file.

Each time you add an entry to your diary by using DIARY.BAT, the date-time lines will be added to the end of what you enter, thus meticulously dating (and timing) each entry—all without any effort on your part. With this batch file, you no longer have any excuse for not recording your daily reflections.

As your diary grows, you can use FIND, SORT, and MORE to manage it and look for something quickly. As you are now versed in using these commands, managing such a file should be easy.

P R A C T I C E   8 - 5

1. Modify DIARY.BAT so that you can use a batch file named NOTE.BAT to create a file named NOTES. Also arrange for automatic appending of date and time without using the MORE command.

2. Use this batch file three times and add a few lines each time.

3. Create a batch file named NT.BAT so that it will create a macro named NT. This macro should execute NOTE.BAT.

4. Use SEELINE.BAT created in the previous section to search for lines in the NOTES file matching a search string entered from the keyboard as a parameter.

5. Use DOSKEY to create a macro named SM. It should allow the user to enter a file name as a parameter. The file should be sorted in ascending order and pause for every 24 lines.

6. Use the SM macro to show the README.TXT file in the C:\DOS directory.

D R I L L

___ 23. The following command is in correct syntax. True or false?
   A>find "search string" filename

____ 24. The following command will generate an error message. True or false?

      A>find "string" filename ¦ find "string"

____ 25. The following command will sort found lines. True or false?

      A>find "string" filename ¦ sort

____ 26. The following command will show the total number of found lines, and display all the lines with sequential numbers. True or false?

      A>find /c/n "string" filename

____ 27. The following command will find only the files created in January, 1990. True or false?

      A>dir ¦ find "1-" ¦ find "-90"

____ 28. If you want to search for anything other than "string," the following is a correct command. True or false?

      A>find /v "string" filename

____ 29. The following command will sort and print:

      A>find "string1" filename ¦ find "string2" ¦ sort > prn

    a. lines containing string1, plus file name

    b. lines containing string1 OR string2, no file name

    c. lines containing string1 AND string2, no file name

    d. nothing

____ 30. The following command will print the current date. True or false?

      A>echo ¦ more ¦ date ¦ find "C" > prn

S U M M A R Y   A N D   R E V I E W

Check each item as you review and understand the following highlights of the chapter:

☐   1. Use > to redirect output to a new device, and < to redirect input from a new device. Use >> to append to a target device. Use ¦ to pipe (connect) two DOS commands.

☐   2. If a DOS command requires one parameter and sends output to the standard output device, the output can be redirected to another device. For example, instead of sending the output from DIR and TYPE to the screen, you can redirect it to a new device such as NUL or the printer.

3. If a DOS command requires two parameters, source and target, either one plus the message can be redirected to a new device. For example, you can use COPY to send a file from the screen or a disk to NUL or the printer. Instead of letting the message (1 File(s) copied) go to the screen, you can also redirect it elsewhere.

4. Some DOS commands such as FORMAT and DISKCOPY require input from the keyboard before a task is completed. The required input can be redirected from a file on disk. This can save time and automate some jobs.

5. Use ¦ to pipe together related DOS commands to automate some functions. The output from the first command becomes the input for the second. If the first outputs nothing that the second can use, only the output of the second is displayed.

6. DOS provides three filter commands (external programs), MORE, SORT, and FIND. These can be used alone or piped to each other or to other commands.

7. Use MORE to display ASCII text one screen at a time. To do so, redirect a file as input to the command, such as:
   A>more < filename

8. Use MORE and redirect output to the printer to print text lines entered from the keyboard one line at a time. As soon as Enter is pressed, a line is sent to the printer. The command to do that is:
   A>more > prn

9. To sort lines entered from the keyboard, run SORT, enter lines to be sorted, and finally press F6 and Enter.

10. To sort lines of a text file, redirect it as an input to SORT, such as:
    A>sort < filename

11. Use the /R switch with SORT to sort in descending order, and /+c (where c is a column number) to sort by a certain column. The latter can be used to sort directory entries. For example, to sort by extension, enter this command:
    A>dir ¦ sort /+10

12. Use FIND to output text lines matching one or more search strings. To use FIND correctly, you need to enter a search string in double quotes followed by a file name, such as:
    A>find "string" filename

13. FIND can be used with /V to output nonmatching lines, /C to count matching lines, and /N to number and output matching lines.

☐   14. FIND automatically outputs a one-inch line and a file name. This can be eliminated by entering a second search string without a file name, such as:

A>find "string" filename ¦ find "string"

☐   15. Use FIND to insert the date and time in a file—a convenient way to keep track of records. Use the following examples to add the current date and time to a file:

A>echo ¦ more ¦ date ¦ find "C" >> filename
A>echo ¦ more ¦ time ¦ find "C" >> filename

A>echo/ ¦ date ¦ find "C" >> filename
A>echo/ ¦ time ¦ find "C" >> filename

REVIEW   QUESTIONS

Write an answer for each question below:

1. What are considered by DOS to be standard input and output devices? What do these devices do?

2. Explain the purpose of each symbol below:

    >, <, >>, ¦

3. How do the following commands differ?

    A>dir > filename
    A>dir < filename
    A>dir >> filename

4. What happens to each of the following commands?

    A>copy filename con > nul
    A>copy file1 file2 > nul
    A>type filename > prn

5. What does each of the following commands do?

    A>echo This is a line. > nul
    A>echo This is a line. > prn
    A>echo This is a line. > filename
    A>echo This is a line. >> filename

6. What happens when you run this batch file?

    A>copy con all.bat
    del *.*

    y
    ^Z

7. What happens if you enter this command?

   A>more ¦ dir

8. Compare and contrast the following two commands:

   A>more > prn

   A>copy con prn

9. What kinds of numbers can be accurately sorted by SORT? Why?

10. Explain what each of the following two commands is supposed to do.

    A>sort > prn

    A>sort /+22 filename > prn

11. Enter the command to search for all the files created in a specific month of a specific year. Explain the command.

12. Explain what each of the four switches of FIND is supposed to do.

13. Enter a command to find matching directory entries and display the items sorted by file size.

14. Enter a command to search in a file for matching lines which are to be sorted and printed without the "————————FILENAME" line.

15. Explain how this command is supposed to work:

    A>echo ¦ more ¦ date ¦ find "C" > datedata

Configuring the System

C O M M A N D S   C O V E R E D

MODE, LASTDRIVE, SUBST, CONFIG.SYS, ANSI.SYS, DEVICE, BREAK, BUFFERS, FILES, SET, RAMDRIVE.SYS, COMSPEC, SHELL, PATH, PROMPT, DIRCMD, HIMEM.SYS, EMM386, DOS, DEVICEHIGH, LOADHIGH, MEMKAKER, MEM, MSD

N E W   T E R M S   A N D   S Y M B O L S

Code page, logical drive, disk buffer, file handle, device drivers, RAM (virtual) disk, DOS environment, environment variable, %variable%, CMOS, conventional memory, expanded memory, LIM, EMS, extended memory, XMS, UMA, UMBs, HMA

QUICK START

To set the keyboard to the highest speed:

```
C>mode con rate=32 delay=1
```

To report device status:

```
C>mode
```

To set a dot-matrix printer to 132 columns and 8 lines per inch:

```
C>mode lpt1 cols=132 lines=8
```

To substitute a logical drive (Z:) for a real directory, show substitution, and then delete it:

```
C>subst z: c:\ss\central\budget\report
C>subst
C>subst z: /d
```

To increase buffers, file handles, and install a RAM disk and ANSI.SYS, include these in your CONFIG.SYS:

```
buffers=20
files=20
device=c:\dos\ramdrive.sys
device=c:\dos\ansi.sys
```

To expand the environment to 512 bytes, add this line to your CONFIG.SYS:

```
shell=c:\command.com /p /e:512
```

To use a RAM disk for copying in a one-floppy system:

Use the RAMCOPY.BAT batch file

To add path items to an existing path list:

Use the ADDPATH.BAT batch file.

To quickly set a prompt style:

Use the SETPROM.BAT batch file.

To assign a default parameter (for the DIR command) to the DIRCMD variable:

```
C>set dircmd=/w /o a:
```

To load DOS in the high memory area, make upper memory blocks available for TSR programs, and convert extended memory to expanded memory, add these lines in your CONFIG.SYS:

```
device=c:\dos\himem.sys
dos=high,umb
device=c:\dos\emm386.exe 640 ram
devicehigh=c:\dos\ansi.sys
```

To show memory use in detail, one screen at a time:

```
C>mem /debug /p
```

To use MemMaker to optimize your PC's memory:

```
C>memmaker
```

To find out more about your system:

```
C>msd
```

This chapter deals mostly with defining and modifying your hardware parts. A host of DOS commands and special files are available to control their performance or report their current status. Most of these are covered in this chapter.

In the order listed below, you will learn to:

- Use MODE to report device status, control monitor, printer, and keyboard
- Use SUBST to reroute directories
- Use CONFIG.SYS to set BREAK, BUFFERS, FILES, and LASTDRIVE values, and install device drivers
- Become familiar with the DOS environment and maneuver it with batch files
- Comprehend how DOS manages your PC memory and take advantage of the extra memory available in more powerful PCs
- Use MemMaker to optimize memory
- Use MEM to report memory use
- Use MSD to report a great deal of information about your system as well as memory use

THE MANY USES OF MODE

■ *MODE's various uses are summarized.*

■ *Use MODE CON followed by specifics to set keyboard speed.*

■ *Use MODE to set mono or color 40/80 modes on a CGA system.*

■ *Use MODE to set EGA/VGA to 25, 43, or 50 lines.*

■ *Use MODE to set printing 6/8 lines per inch and/or 80/132 columns.*

■ *Use MODE to report the status for all or a specific device.*

MODE is a jack-of-all-trades command which can be used to control many devices connected to the computer. You can use it to control the following:

- Keyboard speed

- Parallel adapter, usually connected to a printer

- Serial adapter, connected to a printer, mouse, or modem

- Video display modes

- Report status of a device

Other peripheral devices connected through a parallel port, serial port, keyboard, and monitor jack can all be controlled by using MODE.

These devices can also be instructed to accept and output certain code pages (foreign languages). These are not likely to be needed by you. We will concentrate on using American English.

Speeding Up the Keyboard

Your keyboard normally operates at a snail's pace. To test how slowly it repeats itself, hold down a letter key, "x" for example. Then hold down the Backspace key to delete them—ever so slowly.

You can improve your keyboard's speed by entering this command:

```
C>mode con rate=32 delay=1
```

Do not forget the CON. Here you are telling DOS to set a console speed.

Now, repeat pressing a key and then Backspace to see the difference. The cursor now travels more than twice the earlier speed.

You must enter both values together; otherwise, this error message appears:

```
RATE and DELAY must be specified together
```

A keyboard normally operates at the rate of repeating 20 times per second and a delay of 0.5 second. That is the same as entering this command:

```
C>mode con rate=20 delay=2
```

Each delay is 0.25 second. You are allowed to enter delay values as short as 1 (0.25 second) and as long as 4 (1 second). Rate is the speed a keystroke is repeated every second. You can go from as low as 1 to as high as 32. If you want your keyboard automatically set at a higher speed every time you begin to use it, you should include a command like the above in your AUTOEXEC.BAT file.

MODE CON may not work with your keyboard if your PC's BIOS does not support a higher keyboard speed. It does not work on an IBM keyboard connected to an original IBM PC.

Setting Display Modes

The normal monitor displays text 80 columns by 25 lines. If you have a special graphics card (adapter) installed in your computer, such as CGA (Color Graphics Adapter), EGA (Enhanced Graphics Adapter), VGA (Video Graphics Array), you can change these numbers.

If you have a CGA card and an RGB (Red Green Blue) color monitor, you can use MODE to set these values:

MONO	Monochrome (no color) display
BW40	Black and white, 40 columns
BW80	Black and white, 80 columns
CO40	Color, 40 columns
CO80	Color, 80 columns

T I P S   A N D   T R I C K S

S P E E D Y   C U R S O R

There are commercial software packages that will allow you to dramatically speed up your keyboard. The most famous is Cruise Control.

I use a package called Repeat Performance provided by WordPerfect Corporation. I use it to set a keystroke repeat rate of 120 per second and the minimum delay speed of 0.25 second. This speed is about six times the highest rate you can set with MODE.

The higher cursor speed can increase productivity. While doing word processing, I can move the cursor anywhere much more quickly. On the DOS command line, pressing a key without the slightest delay displays a whole line of the same letter. Pressing Backspace or the ← key erases them just as fast.

To disable colors, enter this:

C>**mode mono**

This is the same as BW80; both disable colors. It is the only option for a monochrome system.

This command changes to 40-column color display:

C>**mode co40**

If you have a monochrome monitor with a MDA (Monochrome Display Adapter) or Hercules (monochrome graphics) card, any option except MONO will lead to an error message, such as:

C>**mode bw80**
Function not supported on this computer

If you have a CGA system and the screen display is not centered, you can shift it left or right, such as:

C>**mode co40, r, t**

This shifts to the right by one column and tests the new display. Or you can try this:

C>**mode co80, 1, t**

This shifts to the left by two columns (each shift is by two when in the 80-column mode) and tests the result.

You cannot shift the screen with a monochrome, EGA, or VGA system. If you try, you will get a message like this:

Unable to shift screen left

Starting with version 4.0, in addition to switching between 40 and 80 columns, you can also change from 25 to 43 or 50 lines of text per screen with an EGA or VGA system. After ANSI.SYS is installed, you can try this command:

C>**mode con cols=80 lines=43**

If you do not need to reset the column number, you can just change the line number:

C>**mode con lines=43**

If the display looks unattractive, you can change it to the default 25 lines.

Setting Printer Modes

You can use MODE to control your printer to print the number of characters per line and the number of lines per inch. The syntax goes like this:

C>**mode lpt1 cols=# lines=#**

You can, if you wish, put a colon (:) after LPT1. The "cols=" and "lines=" notations are optional; if they are not used, you need to put a comma between them. Here you are supposed to supply 80 (default) or 132 in place of the first #, and 6 (default) or 8 in place of the second, such as:

```
C>mode lpt1 cols=132 lines=8 retry=p
LPT1: not rerouted
LPT1: set for 132
Printer lines per inch set
Resident portion of MODE loaded
Infinite retry on parallel printer time-out
```

Your printer should be turned on when you enter this command. If not, you will get the "Printer error" message and the printer will not be affected by the MODE command.

Notice the use of LPT1. You can put a colon at the end if you wish; it will make no difference. However, you cannot substitute PRN for LPT1. This would be the result:

```
C>mode prn cols=132
Invalid parameter - cols=132
```

The RETRY parameter is optional. It is to respond to a busy or not-ready status of the parallel port. You can enter one of these values: B (busy), E (error), N (none), P (persist), or R (ready). If no parameter is entered, N is the default.

You can enter just column and line numbers separated with a comma, such as:

```
C>mode lpt1 132, 8, p
```

If you want no change for the first value, make sure to insert an extra comma. This command will keep the original column number but change line number to 8:

```
C>mode lpt1 , 8, p
```

P is optional; it could be substituted with B. Either will continuously try to send output to the parallel port even though it may be busy or not ready. Press Ctrl-C if you want to regain control of the computer.

Now follow these steps to see how MODE affects your dot-matrix printer connected to the first parallel port:

FOLLOW THESE STEPS

1. Change to the 132-column mode (you can also add a : after lpt1):

```
C>mode lpt1 132
```

If your printer is on, the message below appears:

```
C>mode lpt1 132
LPT1: not rerouted
LPT1: set for 132
No retry on parallel printer time-out
```

2. Send a line to the printer:

> C>echo This should be printed in tiny letters > prn

The characters should be printed at the rate of 16.5 characters per inch.

3. Restore the 80-column mode:

> C>mode lpt1 80
> LPT1: not rerouted
> LPT1: set for 80
> No retry on parallel printer time-out

4. Print another line:

> C>echo This is the regular print. > prn

The line should be printed at the rate of 10 characters per inch.

The above steps should work with modern dot-matrix printers. Some older models may not work. A daisy-wheel printer is not likely to obey these commands.

Reporting Device Status

We have used MODE to control various DOS devices. We can also use it to report (display on the screen) the available devices and the status of each. To do that, simply enter the command without any parameter:

> C>mode

The screen displays a report of all the devices:

> Status for device LPT1:
> ----------------------
> LPT1: not rerouted
> RETRY=NONE
> Code page operation not supported on this device
>
> Status for device LPT2:
> ----------------------
> LPT2: not rerouted
> RETRY=NONE
> Code page operation not supported on this device
>
> Status for device LPT3:
> ----------------------
> LPT3: not rerouted

```
Status for device CON:
----------------------
COLUMNS=80
LINES=25
Code page operation not supported on this device
```

If you want to see the status of a single device, place the device name after MODE, such as:

C>**mode con**

With this command, only the last part of the above report will be displayed.

The above display shows no printer rerouted (redirected). You can redirect LPT1 to the first serial port this way:

C>**mode lpt1=com1**

```
Resident portion of MODE loaded
LPT1: rerouted to COM1:
```

You can now report the status of LPT1:

C>**mode lpt1 /status**

```
Status for device LPT1:
----------------------
LPT1: rerouted to COM1:
RETRY=NONE
Code page operation not supported on this device
```

The /STATUS switch is used to report code page information. It can be shortened to /STA. Without this switch the last line above will not be shown.

If you now want to print to the first parallel port, this command will work:

C>**mode lpt1**

Code page is Microsoft's fancy term for a number designated for one of the supported foreign languages. You can use MODE to set a value so that a printer or monitor can output symbols unique to that particular language. That should not concern most American users.

In using a serial port, you can set various values, such as:

C>**mode com1 baud=2400 stop=1 data=8 parity=none**
```
COM1: 2400,n,8,1,-
```

You can set these values for a modem or printer connected to the first serial port. The above specifies 2400 bits per second transmission rate, 1 as the number of stop bits, 8 as the number of data bits, and no parity bit to check transmission errors. Your modem or serial printer should provide instructions as to what values to set. In the case of a modem, the baud rate can be set by the communications program you use.

P R A C T I C E   9 - 1

☐ 1. Use MODE to set your keyboard to the highest possible speed.

☐ 2. If you have a color-graphics system, use MODE to set:
   a. 40-column color
   b. 80-column black and white
   c. 80-column color

☐ 3. If you have a dot-matrix printer, do the following:
   a. set to 132 columns and use ECHO to print a line
   b. set to 80 columns and use ECHO to print a line

☐ 4. Use MODE to report the status of the monitor and printer.

☐ 5. Use DOSKEY to create a macro named PM (printer mode). It should let the user enter a column and/or line number to set their values.

☐ 6. Use PM to set printing to 80 columns and 8 lines.

☐ 7. Use PM to show the printer status and restore the default values.

(The following assumes that you use an EGA or VGA monitor and have installed ANSI.SYS.)

☐ 8. Create a macro named MM (monitor mode). It should let the user enter two numbers to set monitor column and line numbers.

☐ 9. Use MM to set 40 columns and 25 lines, 80 columns and 50 lines, and 80 columns and 25 lines.

D R I L L

____ 1. If the command below is entered, the result is to:
   C>mode
   a. report the status of all devices
   b. set all devices to default values
   c. do both a and b
   d. generate an error message due to illegal use

____ 2. In setting keyboard speed, you can set RATE and DELAY separately. True or false?

____ 3. The following command will:

      C>mode lpt1 120

    a. set 120-column printing

    b. set 132-column printing

    c. do nothing

    d. generate an error message

____ 4. You can use MODE to shift screen display on any kind of monitor. True or false?

____ 5. The command below will allow you to use a printer connected to the first serial port. True or false?

      C>mode lpt1:=com1:

____ 6. The command below will:

      C>mode con

    a. display options to let you set a monitor mode

    b. report monitor status

    c. do nothing

    d. generate an error message

SUBSTITUTING DRIVES

■ *Use SUBST to substitute a real or logical drive for an existing directory.*

Note: Version 5 and before included the ASSIGN, JOIN, and SUBST commands to reroute drives. The first two are longer included in version 6. The SUBST command discussed here can do most of what the other two commands could.

Just as you use PATH or APPEND to make DOS search for a file not in the current directory, you can use the external SUBST command to make DOS treat a drive or directory in a different way. You can use SUBST to substitute a drive for an existing directory. When you specify the drive to do something, DOS will go to the associated directory to do it.

Before we discuss the finer points of SUBST, let us follow these steps to demonstrate its use:

FOLLOW THESE STEPS

1. Set a new prompt:

```
A>prompt $p$g
A:\>_
```

2. Create a new directory:

```
A:\>md level1
```

3. Go to the new directory:

```
A:\>cd level1
A:\LEVEL1>_
```

4. Create a subdirectory:

```
A:\LEVEL1>md level2
```

5. Change to the new subdirectory:

```
A:\LEVEL1>cd level2
A:\LEVEL1\LEVEL2>_
```

6. Go to the root directory:

```
A:\LEVEL1\LEVEL2>cd\
A:\>_
```

7. Substitute drive D for the subdirectory:

```
A:\>subst d: a:\level1\level2
```

8. Show the directory of A:\LEVEL1\LEVEL2:

```
A:\>dir d:
```

The directory entries of A:\LEVEL1\LEVEL2 are displayed. This can save you the trouble of typing the long path.

9. Show the SUBST list:

```
A:\>subst
D: => A:\LEVEL1\LEVEL2
```

This shows that the D drive is assigned the value pointed to by the arrow.

10. Delete the SUBST list:

```
A:\>subst d: /d
```

Before you can substitute D for another directory, you must delete its assigned value as shown above. Otherwise, this error message will appear:

```
Invalid parameter - d:
```

The SUBST command can be a time saver if you use a hard disk and a complex directory structure. Suppose your report files are located in this directory:

```
C:\SS\CENTRAL\BUDGET\REPORT
```

Suppose you now enter the command below to substitute R for this long directory path:

```
C:\>subst r: c:\ss\central\budget\report
```

Anytime you want to do something with regard to the REPORT directory, just use R: to replace the long path. For example, if you are in another directory, you can quickly go to that directory by entering its designated drive letter:

```
C:\WP\LETTER>r:
R:\>_
```

Although the DOS prompt shows the substituted letter as the current directory, you are actually in the REPORT directory.

Can you use any drive letter and substitute it for an existing directory? Yes and no. If you have one or two floppy disks and one hard disk, you normally have up to four drive letters to use, namely A to D. If you want more, which will also take up more memory, you need to specify the last drive letter with the LASTDRIVE command. Suppose you want to use up to ten drive letters. You need to add the following line to your CONFIG.SYS file and reboot:

```
lastdrive=j
```

Now you can use up to the letter J with the SUBST command.

DOS can handle a drive that has no physical existence. It is then treated as a logical or virtual (simulated) drive. A **logical drive** is one that is recognized by DOS as a legitimate drive. If your hard disk is divided into two logical drives, DOS will recognize them as two drives even though there is only one physical drive. A logical drive may be just a letter without any physical existence, but you can use SUBST to substitute it for a real thing.

SUBST requires two parameters. The first parameter must be a valid drive letter and the second an existing directory. After the substitution, you can use the first parameter to access the second. If the first parameter is an actual drive, you can no longer access the data there unless you delete or change the substitution.

Another rule to remember is that you cannot substitute the current drive for a directory. Consider this example:

```
A>subst a: c:\dos
Invalid parameter - a:
```

Since the current drive is A, DOS will not let you substitute it for another directory. On the other hand, this will work:

```
C>subst a: c:\dos
```

Since the current drive is C, drive A can be designated as the first parameter. If you now use drive A, you will access the files in the C:\DOS directory.

Keep the above rule in mind when you want to delete a substitution—you cannot delete the current drive that has been associated with another directory. The solution is to make another drive current before attempting deletion.

SUBST's second parameter must be a directory, not a drive. Consider this example:

```
C>subst a: b:
Invalid parameter - b:
```

On the other hand, this will work fine:

```
C>subst a: b:\
```

After this command, accessing drive A or B will always go to drive B's root directory; drive A, on the other hand, is no longer accessible. Suppose drive B has a directory named XXX. Can you access this directory? Yes, either command below will work:

```
C>dir a:\xxx
C>dir b:\xxx
```

If you have made multiple substitutions, you can delete them one at a time. If you try to delete several at a time, you will get the "Incorrect number of parameters" error.

WARNING: Do not substitute drive C for another directory, such as this example:

```
A>subst c: a:\
```

After the above command, every time you try to access drive C, DOS will direct you to drive A. You can no longer access SUBST.EXE stored in the C:\DOS directory. Unless you have this command in drive A or B, you can no longer use the command to change the drive. You have to reboot if you want to use drive C.

The online reference on SUBST (enter HELP SUBST and then go to the Notes screen) admonishes you not to use the following commands with SUBST because they may not work or their results may not be predictable:

ASSIGN	DISKCOMP	MIRROR
BACKUP	DISKCOPY	RESTORE
CHKDSK	FDISK	RECOVER
DATAMON	FORMAT	SYS
DEFRAG	LABEL	

Also, a compressed drive can be substituted for something else, but DOS may not correctly calculate the available disk space.

You can use a substituted drive as a target for DEL or DELTREE. The files in the associated directory will be deleted. DELTREE, however, will not delete the directory. Nor can you remove an empty directory with RD. Only after you delete the substitution can you use RD or DELTREE to remove a directory.

P R A C T I C E   9 - 2

☐ 1. Make the necessary arrangement so that DOS will accept X as the last drive letter.

☐ 2. Create an empty directory named A:\XYZ and substitute drive X for it.

☐ 3. Make drive X current. What does the DOS prompt show? If necessary, enter a command to make the system prompt show the path and the > sign.

☐ 4. Create in drive X a file named JUNK.

☐ 5. Go to drive A's root directory.

☐ 6. Use DEL to delete all the files in drive X.

☐ 7. Use RD and DELTREE to remove the A:\XYZ directory. Explain what happens.

☐ 8. Use MOVE to change XYZ to ABC. Explain what happens.

☐ 9. Delete the substitution. Show proof of deletion.

☐ 10. Change A:\XYZ to A:\ABC. Explain what happens.

D R I L L

____ 7. The second command below will produce:

      A>subst k: a:\nano

      A>subst

     a. A:\NANO => K:

     b. K: => A:\NANO

     c. A: => K:\NANO

     d. Invalid parameter

____ 8. The A:\NANO directory must exist for the command below to be implemented. True or false?

      A:\>subst k: a:\nano

____ 9. After the steps in question 7, the following command will show the directory entries of A:\NANO. True or false?

      A>dir k:

____ 10. You can use RD or DELTREE to remove a directory that is associated with a drive. True or false?

____ 11. What happens after these two commands?

        B>subst z: b:\bat

        B>subst a: z:\

    a. A:\ is associated with B:\BAT

    b. Z:\ is associated with B:\BAT

    c. both A:\ and Z:\ are associated with B:\BAT

    d. substitution will fail

CONFIGURATION COMMANDS

■ *Put configuration commands in a CONFIG.SYS file stored in the root directory of a system disk to change default values in the system.*

■ *Increase BUFFERS and FILES numbers to enhance your computer's capacity.*

CONFIG.SYS is a file created by you to define how your system is supposed to work. It can contain configuration commands that enable your hardware and software to perform specific functions, such as handling more files, which they otherwise cannot do.

CONFIG.SYS

You can put more than a dozen commands or device drivers in a CONFIG.SYS file. Here are some common ones:

```
BREAK
BUFFERS
FILES
DEVICE=ANSI.SYS
DEVICE=RAMDRIVE.SYS
```

A CONFIG.SYS file must be in the root directory of a system (boot) disk. After the system files on the disk are loaded, CONFIG.SYS takes its turn, and finally AUTOEXEC.BAT is executed. To create a CONFIG.SYS file, you may do something like this:

```
A>copy con config.sys
break on
buffers=20
files=20
device=ansi.sys /x
device=ramdrive.sys 120
^Z
```

Note: You can put REM before a line in a CONFIG.SYS file, like this:

```
rem device=ansi.sys /x
```

When your PC is booted with this new file, this line will not be executed. When you want to load ANSI.SYS again, just take out the REM command and reboot.

BREAK

The BREAK command can be put in CONFIG.SYS or entered on the command line. Follow these steps to see how it works:

FOLLOW THESE STEPS

1. Check to see whether BREAK is on or off:

```
A>break
BREAK is off
```

This is the default state. If you do nothing, BREAK is off.

2. Turn on BREAK:

```
A>break on
```

3. Check the new state:

```
A>break
BREAK is on
```

The state of BREAK determines when DOS is to check for Ctrl-Break and interrupt an activity. When BREAK is off, DOS checks for Ctrl-Break only when working with the standard input (keyboard), standard output (monitor), serial and parallel ports.

When BREAK is turned on, DOS checks for Ctrl-Break while performing any task. This allows you to interrupt a program running in RAM or a disk-accessing activity. If BREAK is off and something goes wrong, such as a program stuck in a perpetual loop, you cannot interrupt it.

To compensate for more frequent checking when BREAK is on, DOS will naturally slow down. It is thus advisable to leave BREAK off normally. When you do a great deal of program testing or disk accessing, you can temporarily turn it on.

To demonstrate how BREAK can affect the computer, first create this batch file:

```
A>copy con brktest.bat
@echo off
:LOOP
set a=aardvark
goto LOOP
^Z
```

Run the batch file after turning on BREAK. Terminate the batch file with Ctrl-Break.

Next, turn off BREAK and run the batch file. This time the computer is stuck in a perpetual loop and you cannot break out of it. You must now reboot the computer.

If the first line of the batch file is deleted, you can terminate the batch file regardless of the status of BREAK. The reason is that the batch file writes to the monitor, which DOS can intercept.

The SET command is discussed below. The looping mechanism will be explained in Chapter 11.

BUFFERS

BUFFERS and FILES are strictly configuration commands and must be entered from a CONFIG.SYS file. DOS cannot recognize them when they are entered from the command line.

BUFFERS determines the number of disk buffers. A **disk buffer** is a memory area reserved to store disk information for quick action and reduced access to the physical disk. Each buffer takes up 532 bytes of memory, which is slightly bigger than a sector.

You can set BUFFERS value 1–99. If you do nothing, DOS assumes a default value based on the available hardware as shown in Table 9.1.

For most occasions, 20–30 buffers are considered optimal. If you do frequent random (rather than sequential) disk reading and writing, you may speed up your work by having more buffers. However, more than 30 buffers will generally slow down your computer.

Table 9.1

Disk Buffers

Buffers	Hardware Configuration
2	128KB RAM, 360KB drive
3	bigger than 360KB drive
5	more than 128KB RAM
10	more than 256KB RAM
15	more than 512KB RAM

You can add a look-ahead number (secondary cache) in this syntax:

```
buffers=number,ahead
```

A look-ahead number can be 1–8, with the default value of 1. This tells DOS the number of buffers to look ahead when reading data. The more you specify, the more DOS will speed up sequential (not random) reading.

FILES

FILES specifies the number of files that can be opened at one time. If you do nothing, DOS can handle up to 8 files simultaneously. You can specify up to 255.

To enable DOS to handle a file, each file is given a **file handle**, which is a code number. Each file handle takes up 48 bytes of memory.

An application program requiring more than the default of 8 file handles will tell you how many to specify. If you encounter an error message like "Run out of file handles," you can no longer access another file. The simple remedy is to increase the value of FILES.

INSTALLABLE DEVICE DRIVERS

■ *Include RAMDRIVE.SYS and ANSI.SYS in your CONFIG.SYS file to create a RAM disk and install the ANSI driver.*

■ *Use a RAM disk to store information for quick access by DOS or to do copying in a one-floppy system.*

In the CONFIG.SYS file discussed in the previous section, we included a couple of **device drivers**. These are special files used to drive specific devices; they usually have the SYS extension in their file names. There are about a dozen such drivers in the DOS package, some of which can be used to redefine the keyboard, monitor, or printer to accommodate foreign languages. Most of these should not concern you, except two—ANSI.SYS and RAMDRIVE.SYS.

ANSI.SYS is used to enhance the keyboard and monitor. Once installed, it can be used to redefine (remap) many keys on your keyboard and set screen colors and cursor positions. To install this driver, you must include a line like the following in your CONFIG.SYS:

```
device=c:\dos\ansi.sys /x
```

This command goes to C:\DOS to install ANSI.SYS; this file must be stored in the designated directory. If your arrangement is different, you must direct DOS to the directory storing the ANSI.SYS file.

You can specify one of these two available options:

/K   Kill (ignore) the extra keys on the enhanced keyboard

/X   Extra keys on the enhanced keyboard definable

The enhanced keyboard with 101 keys can be greatly enhanced with the /X switch. With this switch, you can define or redefine F11 and F12 function keys and the extra cursor keypad in the middle. If your application program does not allow the use of the extra keys, you may need to use the /K switch to make peace with it.

ANSI.SYS can vastly increase the capabilities of DOS. Anybody who wants to master DOS should learn to take advantage of it. Chapter 12 is exclusively devoted to it. You can better utilize it after you learn to use EDIT (Chapter 10) to write programlike batch files (Chapter 11).

Creating a RAM Disk

RAMDRIVE.SYS is used to create a **RAM disk** (RAM drive or virtual disk). A RAM disk is a separate area of memory that can act as a disk drive. You can copy files to and from it. You can temporarily store files there; the files disappear when power is off. You can store there accessory files needed by an application program, such as WordStar overlay files; this can cut down access to disk and greatly speed up action.

You can maneuver a RAM disk just as a regular disk drive. You can create multiple RAM disks. In each disk, you can create directories and subdirectories. You can even use CHKDSK on it.

To create a RAM disk, you need to include a line like the following in your CONFIG.SYS file:

```
device=c:\dos\ramdrive.sys 384 256 64 /e
```

This assumes that RAMDRIVE.SYS is stored in the C:\DOS directory. If your arrangement is different, change it accordingly.

Notice there are three numbers and a switch. Actually all these are optional. If you do not specify them, certain default values apply.

The first number specifies the size of the RAM disk, which can be any number from 16 to 4096. If not specified, 64KB is the presumed size. If the value you specify exceeds the available memory, the default value will be used.

The second number is for sector size. If omitted, 512 bytes will be used. You can specify 128, 256, or 512. If you store small files in the RAM disk, specify a smaller number. Otherwise, let DOS determine the number for you.

The third number is for the number of directory entries (files and subdirectories) that can be stored in the RAM disk's root directory. If omitted, 64 is the default. The range can be from 2 to 1024.

You can use /E or /A switch; if neither is specified, conventional memory is used to create a RAM disk. The /E switch is for extended memory. You must install HIMEM.SYS before you can use /E (see Managing Memory below). Most AT (286 or higher) or PS/2 computers are equipped with a minimum of 1MB RAM. Since DOS can access only 640KB, you can use the remaining 384KB for a RAM disk. The /E switch tells DOS to use the otherwise inaccessible memory.

Instead of /E, you can use /A in version 4 or later. That tells DOS to use expanded memory conforming to the LIM (Lotus Intel Microsoft) specifications. If you have a choice, use /E rather than /A because most DOS application programs can use expanded, but not extended, memory. It is thus a waste of your resource to use expanded memory for a RAM disk.

You can set up two or more RAM disks. Just enter in your CONFIG.SYS as many lines for as many disks, such as:

```
device=c:\dos\ramdrive.sys
device=c:\dos\ramdrive.sys
```

This will set up two RAM disks using the default values.

Using a RAM Disk

If you have one floppy drive and a hard disk—which is a common configuration for many people, you are likely to encounter a great deal of inconvenience when you copy files from one floppy disk to another. If you happen to have unused RAM, you can create a RAM disk and copy files between it and the floppy drive.

After a RAM disk is created, you can create a batch file to make the job of copying much easier. The batch file below will copy files from A to F, pause for you to swap disks, then copy the same files from F to A, and finally delete the same files in F:

```
A>copy con ramcopy.bat
@echo off
rem RAMCOPY.BAT--copy from A to RAM disk and back
if .==%1. goto END
echo Insert source disk in A and
pause
copy a:%1 f:
echo Copy from A to F is complete.
echo Insert target disk in A and
pause
copy f:%1 a:
del f:%1
:END
```

Change F to your RAM disk's specific letter if it is different. This letter is determined by DOS when creating a RAM disk. It uses the letter after the letter used for the last installed drive.

With this batch file, you can specify one file or a series of matching files to copy. The following shows a sequence of events for copying matching files:

```
C:\BAT>ramcopy file?
Insert source disk in A and
Press any key to continue...

A:FILE1
A:FILE2
        2 File(s) copied
Copy from A to F is complete.
Insert target disk in A and
Press any key to continue...

F:FILE1
F:FILE2
        2 File(s) copied
C:\BAT>
```

If no parameter follows the batch file name, batch execution branches to the END label and nothing is copied.

This batch file contains label, parameter, parameter testing, and several batch commands. All will be explained in Chapter 11.

P R A C T I C E   9 - 3

1. Find out whether BREAK is on or off. Change it to the opposite state and then return it to the original.

2. Create a RAM disk with 64KB size and 512 bytes per sector.

3. Create a directory named TEMP on the RAM disk and copy RAMCOPY.BAT to it.

4. Use DOSKEY to create a macro named RC. This macro should go to the F:\TEMP directory to run RAMCOPY.BAT and let the user enter a parameter to copy specified files.

5. Use RC to copy RAMCOPY.BAT from drive A to another disk in drive A.

6. Remove the F:\TEMP directory, delete the RC macro, and erase the extra copy of RAMCOPY.BAT.

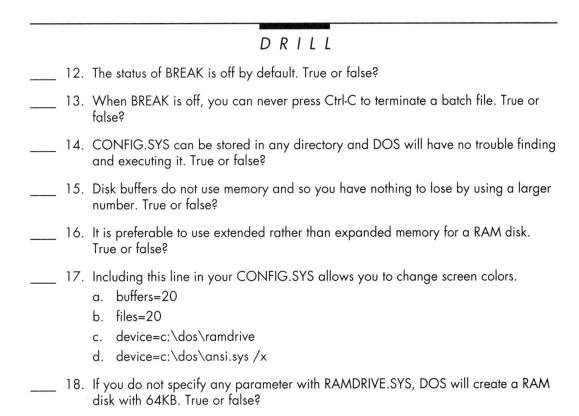

DRILL

____ 12. The status of BREAK is off by default. True or false?

____ 13. When BREAK is off, you can never press Ctrl-C to terminate a batch file. True or false?

____ 14. CONFIG.SYS can be stored in any directory and DOS will have no trouble finding and executing it. True or false?

____ 15. Disk buffers do not use memory and so you have nothing to lose by using a larger number. True or false?

____ 16. It is preferable to use extended rather than expanded memory for a RAM disk. True or false?

____ 17. Including this line in your CONFIG.SYS allows you to change screen colors.
   a. buffers=20
   b. files=20
   c. device=c:\dos\ramdrive
   d. device=c:\dos\ansi.sys /x

____ 18. If you do not specify any parameter with RAMDRIVE.SYS, DOS will create a RAM disk with 64KB. True or false?

THE DOS ENVIRONMENT

■ *Use the SHELL command to expand the environment.*

■ *Use the environment to manage APPEND, PATH, PROMPT, and DIRCMD.*

There is an area of memory which DOS sets aside to keep track of path, prompt, and other information. This is called the environment, or **DOS environment**. You can use the SET command to see what is stored in the environment:

```
A>set
COMSPEC=C:\COMMAND.COM
PATH=D:\C\BIN;D:\C;
LIB=D:\C\LIB;
INCLUDE=D:\C\INCLUDE;
INIT=D:\C\SOURCE\ME\INI;
```

These strings are put in the environment by DOS, AUTOEXEC.BAT, or other programs. The first line tells DOS to load COMMAND.COM from C:\ when necessary.[1] The remaining lines are to guide the QuickC compiler to compile and link a C program code. Your application program may add a different set of strings.

COMSPEC, PATH, PROMPT, APPEND (if installed with the /E switch), and DIRCMD are environment variables DOS can recognize. They are entered into the environment when pertinent commands are entered on the command line, from a batch/configuration file, or from a macro. Try these steps to see how you change the environment:

FOLLOW THESE STEPS

1. Enter a path:

   A>**set path=b:\bat**

You can omit SET when entering PATH, PROMPT, or APPEND into the environment. If you want to set the value of COMSPEC or DIRCMD or create your own environment variable, however, you must use SET.

2. See the environment:

   A>**set**

   . . .

   PATH=b:\bat

The earlier path list, if any, is replaced by the new one. DOS automatically displays the string before = in uppercase.

3. Display path list:

   A>**path**
   PATH=b:\bat

The display is taken right out of the environment.

4. Remove the path from the environment with either command below:

   A>**set path=**
   A>**path;**

5. See the environment again:

   A>**set**

---

1. When a large application program is loaded, a portion of COMMAND.COM will be pushed out of RAM. If you need to use a DOS command that is pushed out, DOS needs to know where to reload COMMAND.COM. If the file is in the root directory of the boot disk, DOS knows where to find it. If not, you need to have a line like the following in your AUTOEXEC.BAT file to direct DOS to the right place.

   comspec=c:\dos\command.com

TIPS AND TRICKS

EXPANDING THE ENVIRONMENT

The environment space is by default limited to 256 bytes. DOS will expand this space as needed. However, DOS cannot expand in two situations: when a batch file is being executed and after a memory-resident program occupies a memory area, thus blocking expansion to a contiguous area. You may then get this message:

```
Out of environment space
```

That means there is no more space available to store your addition. One remedy is to reserve more memory for the environment with a command like this added to your CONFIG.SYS:

```
shell=c:\command.com /p /e:512
```

This specifies the environment size of 512 bytes and instructs DOS to keep COMMAND.COM permanently in memory (instead of exiting right after loading). The /P switch is necessary, and the /E switch lets you specify 160 to 32768 bytes.

This time there is no more PATH command in the environment. If you enter the PATH command alone, you will get the "No Path" message.

In all the above steps, PATH could be replaced with APPEND with identical results. PROMPT also works in a similar manner. PATH, APPEND, and PROMPT were explained in Chapter 5. PROMPT will be covered more thoroughly in Chapter 12.

THE ENVIRONMENT AND BATCH FILES

■ *Use batch files to maneuver environment variables.*

You can enter your own **environment variables** (also known as named parameters) by using the SET command, such as:

```
A>set password=open sesame
```

After entering this command you can use the SET command alone to see the environment having this string:

```
PASSWORD=open sesame
```

DOS automatically converts the variable, which is the string before =, to uppercase and keeps the value, which is the string after =, the way you type it.

Maneuvering Environment Variables

Although you can enter a variable and its assigned value into the environment from the command line (or a macro), other actions, such as passing a value from one variable to another, must be done via a batch file. Try the following to demonstrate this point:

FOLLOW THESE STEPS

1. Set a new prompt:

   ```
   A>prompt $p$g
   A:\>_
   ```

2. Create a batch file:

   ```
   A:\>copy con testprom.bat
   set prompt1=%prompt%
   echo prompt %prompt1% > newprom.bat
   ^Z
   ```

The first line of the batch file will create a new variable named PROMPT1 and assign to it the value of the variable named PROMPT. The notation of %PROMPT% means the value of a variable named PROMPT. In our case,

---

TIPS AND TRICKS

ENVIRONMENTAL CASES

Case and spacing may play an important role in an environment variable. Consider the following examples:

```
A>set password=open sesame
A>set password = open sesame
A>set password=Open Sesame
```

They are all different from one another. They will respectively enter the following into the environment:

```
PASSWORD=open sesame
PASSWORD = open sesame
PASSWORD=Open Sesame
```

If you enter them one after another, the third will replace the first, because of the same variable name. The second, however, is treated as a different variable because of the extra space at the end.

The three values after = are treated as being different from one another. The first and third differ in case, and the second differs from the others in spacing.

%PROMPT% has the value of "pg" because of step 1. After the batch file's first line is executed, PROMPT1 will hold the value of pg.

The second line is to save "prompt" and the value of PROMPT1 to a new batch file named NEWPROM.BAT. After this line is executed, that file will contain "prompt pg". You can use the TYPE command to verify that.

3. Run the batch file:

```
A:\>testprom
A:\>set prompt1=$p$g
A:\>echo prompt $p$g > newprom.bat
A:\>_
```

Notice that both %PROMPT% and %PROMPT1% are converted to metastrings. If you display the environment now, it shows "PROMPT1=pg".

4. Delete the prompt from the environment (restore the default prompt):

```
A:\>prompt
A>_
```

5. Run the NEWPROM.BAT batch file created in step 3:

```
A>newprom
A>prompt $p$g
A:\>_
```

Notice that the system prompt has been changed. The environment now also contains "PROMPT=pg".

6. Make an assignment on the command line:

```
A:\>set prompt1=%prompt%
```

Nothing happens on the screen. If you go to the environment, you see "PROMPT1=%prompt%", not "PROMPT1=pg".

7. Delete the prompt from the environment:

```
A:\>prompt
A>_
```

8. Change the prompt:

```
A>echo prompt %prompt1%
prompt %prompt1%
A>_
```

The system prompt is not changed; only the literal string is echoed to the screen. Compared to a command entered from a batch file in step 3, the identical command entered on the command line in step 6 does not pass a value from one variable to another.

Selecting a Prompt Style

Parameters (command-line arguments) entered with a batch file (when a batch file is run) can be passed to environment variables, which in turn can pass values to other batch files or be maneuvered in various ways. We will use this mechanism to maneuver prompt styles.

In Chapter 5 you learned to use PROMPT to create a great variety of prompt styles. To create a prompt style, you have to go through laborious steps. Now that you know the environment, you can put a few styles there and use a batch file to make one of them active at a moment's notice.

We will use two batch files. The first is to quickly enter into the environment all the prompt styles you might use. A batch file like this will do:

```
A>copy con envprom.bat
@echo off
set pd=$d$g
set pt=$t$h$h$h$h$h$h$g
set pp=$p$g
set pv=$v$g
^Z
```

All of these can be individually entered from the command line, if you so wish. The four prompt styles respectively display date, time, current directory, and DOS version. Running this batch file will enter the following variables and values into the environment:

```
PD=$d$g
PT=$t$h$h$h$h$h$h$g
PP=$p$g
PV=$v$g
```

When you want to use a particular prompt style, just run the batch file below with one of the four available parameters:

```
A>copy con setprom.bat
@echo off
if %1.==d. prompt=%pd%
if %1.==t. prompt=%pt%
if %1.==p. prompt=%pp%
if %1.==v. prompt=%pv%
^Z
```

The IF batch command is used to test the parameter entered on the command line. If you enter D as the parameter, for example, the first line is tested true and the assignment is made. Chapter 11 explains this and other batch commands.

If you run this batch file with no parameter or a nonmatching parameter, nothing happens. If you enter a parameter matching one of the four available choices, the matching prompt style is activated. If you go through all four parameters one after another, this is the result:

```
A>setprom t
21:26>setprom d
Sat 06-27-1993>setprom p
A:\>setprom v
MS-DOS Version 6.0>_
```

If you use numerous and multilevel directories, you can use a technique like this to navigate among them quickly. Just enter various directory lists into the environment and use a batch file to quickly make one of them active.

Adding to a Path List

When you enter a variable into the environment, an existing variable of the same name and its assigned value will be erased—just as when you create a new file using the name of an existing file. What if you just want to add something to an existing variable? You could enlist the help of a batch file.

One occasion on which you could use addition rather than replacement is when you want to add a drive or directory to a path list already in the environment. The batch file below could do just that:

```
A>copy con addpath.bat
@echo off
set path=%path%;%1
^Z
```

This batch file will let you keep the old list and add new items to it—instead of completely replacing the old list. Every time you need to add a path, just enter an appropriate parameter after the batch file name, such as:

```
A>addpath b:\ss\acct
```

This will insert after the existing path list a semicolon and the additional path. Suppose the original list is this:

```
PATH=a:\dos\util
```

After running the batch file, use the SET command to show the new list as:

```
PATH=a:\dos\util;b:\ss\acct
```

If no path is specified after the batch file name, such as:

```
A>addpath
```

the batch file will insert an additional semicolon after the original list. This will do no harm.

If you specify the /E parameter when you run APPEND command for the first time, as explained in Chapter 5, this command enters the environment and can thus be manipulated just like PATH. What has been said about PATH can all be applied to APPEND.

The environment can serve many useful purposes when you write batch files. We will later explore the technique of providing for a password to prevent unauthorized entry to a batch file. See PASS.BAT in Chapter 11 for details.

Restoring the Original Path

Instead of adding items to an existing path list, you can temporarily assign it to another variable. That frees PATH to assign your own list. When you are done with your list, you can restore the original list. This technique can also be applied to PROMPT.

The following batch file demonstrates this technique:

```
A>copy con showpath.bat
@echo off
set path1=%path%
set path=c:\bat
echo old path is: %path1%
echo new path is: %path%
set path=%path1%
echo current path is: %path%
set path1=
^Z
```

Assuming that the existing path list is C:\DOS, running this batch file shows this result:

```
A>showpath
old path is: C:\DOS
new path is: c:\bat
current path is: C:\DOS
```

If you want to use your own list instead of the existing list, create and run a batch file containing the first two SET lines shown in SHOWPATH.BAT. When you are done, create and run another batch file containing the last two SET commands; this will restore the original path list.

DIR'S ENVIRONMENT VARIABLE

As you already learned in Chapter 2, the DIR command since version 5 has many new switches. You have now many more choices. Your life will be much simpler if you can make a particular pattern the default. Yes, you can do just that and you should definitely take advantage of it. You can use the SET command to assign to the DIRCMD variable a parameter which may consist of multiple switches and other items. After making the assignment (entering it into the environment), executing the DIR command alone will show the directory information based on the value assigned to DIRCMD.

Follow these steps:

FOLLOW THESE STEPS

1. Assign a value (parameter) to the DIRCMD variable:

   ```
   C>set dircmd=/w /o a:
   ```

2. Display the environment contents:

   ```
   C>set
   . . .
   DIRCMD=/o /w a:
   ```

The variable and the assigned value are now in the environment.

3. Use DIR with the default parameter:

   ```
   C>dir
   ```

Drive A's directory entries appear wide and sorted according to file name. Without the default parameter, you would have to enter this command:

```
C>dir /o /w a:
```

4. Override one of the default switches:

   ```
   C>dir /-w
   ```

The resulting display is no longer wide. The /W switch in the environment is negated by /–W. You can override not only a default switch but also the default drive/directory specification. For example, these commands will work just fine:

```
C>dir b:
C>dir c:
C>dir /-w \dos
C>dir \dos /-w
C>dir file?
```

In the first two cases, B: or C: replaces A:, but the other default values are kept. In the next two, /–W overrides /W and \DOS replaces A:—no matter how you arrange the command-line parameters. In the last example, FILE? replaces A:; that means the matching files in the current directory (not drive A) are shown. What if you want to show the matching files in drive A instead? Simple, just specify the drive with the file name, like this:

C>`dir a:file?`

If you have a specific parameter you like to use with DIR most of the time, add a line in your AUTOEXEC.BAT to set it as the default. This can save you the trouble of having to enter it into the environment in each new session.

DIRCMD should be distinguished from PATH, PROMPT, and APPEND. Unlike the other three, it is not a command. You cannot enter it alone on the command line. Nor can you use it alone to assign a value; you must use SET to assign a value to it just as you do with your own variables.

DIRCMD is a unique variable that DIR can recognize on the command line. When a value is assigned to this variable, DIR can use the value as the default parameter. You can assign the same value to another variable, but DIR cannot recognize it. Suppose you enter the following:

A>`set d=/w /o`

Since you did not use DIRCMD, the DIR command entered on the command line will not recognize it. On the other hand, the switches will be in effect if you put this in a batch file:

`dir %d%`

MANAGING MEMORY

This section does not concern you if you have no computer of your own. The system you are using in the lab or office should be set up to its maximum efficiency. You just use the computer as it is set up.

If you have your own computer or contemplate buying one. what is discussed here could be important. Knowing these things could let you purchase a better system or make most of it.

CMOS and Battery

Unless you have a first-generation PC or XT, your computer is likely to be equipped with a battery and CMOS (complementary metal oxide semiconductor). CMOS is a type of computer memory that uses little power. It is used to store configuration information such as date/time, monitor, drives, and other devices that you may have. A battery supplies the power to store the information.

When the battery runs out of juice, the stored information is lost. You may get the "invalid configuration" message and may be unable to use the system. It is then time to replace the battery and reconfigure the system.

After replacing the battery, you need to run a setup program stored on disk or press Ctrl-Alt-Esc to run the program stored in the BIOS. A series of menus will guide you to enter your hardware information as well as date-time numbers. The information will then keep your PC going until the battery is out of commission.

If your PC is used often, the battery can last longer; when the PC is on, the battery is not used. An infrequently used PC can have its battery drained in less than the specified time of 3–5 years. One way to prevent the unpleasant disruption is to snap on some backup batteries. Most PCs are equipped with this backup pack that uses commonly available AA batteries. A little timely preventive measure here can save you lots of trouble later.

RAM Varieties

There are three kinds of RAM: conventional, expanded, and extended. **Conventional memory** is the first 640KB RAM that DOS and all DOS-based application programs can use. **Expanded memory** is additional RAM intended to allow some applications to access more memory. **Extended memory** comes with 286 and higher CPUs; in such a PC equipped with 1MB RAM, 640KB is treated as conventional memory and 384 as extended memory.

A little history is in order because these memory varieties are the result of the events occurring at the dawn of the PC revolution.

The initial 8088 chip, which IBM chose to build its first PC with, can address 1MB (1024KB) RAM. This is divided into 16 banks of 64KB each; these are identified by their hex numbers from 0 to F. IBM set aside the top 384KB (A to F) for system use. This in turn forced DOS to limit itself to the lower 640KB (0 to 9), commonly known as conventional, lower, or base memory.[2]

The area between 640KB and 1MB is known as the upper memory area (UMA), as shown in Figure 9.1a. It is used by BIOS, video display, and other hardware devices. Different blocks of this area are not used; these are known as upper memory blocks (UMBs). DOS version 5 or later can utilize some of these blocks.

After DOS is booted, the system files are loaded in the beginning portion of conventional memory. Device drivers occupy the next memory area.

---

2. A Microsoft spokesman proudly asked this question in a conference: What's Microsoft best known for? Instead of the expected DOS, he got "the 640K limitation" and a hearty guffaw from the audience. Clearly this limitation has caused considerable embarrassment to both IBM and Microsoft and many headaches for PC users.

Figure 9.1

Memory allocation

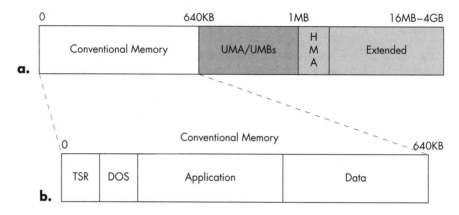

COMMAND.COM then takes the adjacent area. An application program is loaded on top of that. The rest of the memory is used to store data, as shown in Figure 9.1b.

As application programs became more powerful and user friendly, their sizes grew bigger and bigger. In the meantime, users continued to manipulate larger and larger amounts of data. The 640KB barrier soon became a real roadblock.

The drive to overcome the barrier was led by Lotus because users of its 1-2-3 spreadsheet soon ran out of RAM to manipulate their larger and larger worksheets. It was joined by Intel and Microsoft. Their **LIM-EMS** (Lotus Intel Microsoft Expanded Memory Specification) has provided, since 1983, the standard for expanded memory. Most major application programs, including 1-2-3 and WordPerfect, can access a large amount of expanded memory.

The LIM system uses a memory manager program residing in conventional memory to switch data and some program code to expanded memory which complies with the LIM rules. You can buy such EMS boards to add expanded memory. This scheme is a stopgap measure, which is relatively slow and useful in mostly PCs based on the 8088 or 8086 CPUs and some older 286 systems.

The 286 (introduced in 1984) and 386SX can address 16MB, and the 386DX and 486DX/SX up to 4GB of memory. The extra memory beyond the 1MB area is known as extended memory (XMS or extended memory specification). It is faster and can be used only by newer programs such as Release 3.x of 1-2-3 and Windows 3.x and Windows-compliant programs. Most DOS-based programs cannot take advantage of it. DOS version 5 or 6 can provide some relief for people using 286 PCs and more for 386/486 system users.

Using High Memory

Version 5 or 6 includes a number of memory-management programs and device drivers, most notably the extended-memory manager (HIMEM.SYS, for CPUs 286 or higher) and the expanded-memory manager (EMM386.EXE, for CPUs 386 or higher). These let you do the following:

- Load DOS in the first 64KB memory in the beginning of extended memory known as the high memory area (HMA). This applies to any system 286 or higher. HIMEM.SYS is used to do this.

- Move some device drivers and TSR programs from conventional memory to some unused upper memory blocks (UMBs) in the upper memory area (UMA), thus making more conventional memory available for application programs. This applies to any system higher than 286, not to 286 itself or those below.[3] It requires EMM386.EXE.

- Convert extended memory to expanded memory on a 386/486 system so that older DOS-based application programs can use the extra memory. This also requires EMM386.EXE.[4]

To run DOS in the HMA, you need to have these commands in your CONFIG.SYS file (make sure the order is as shown):

```
device=c:\dos\himem.sys
dos=high
```

The first command loads the extended-memory manager, which can see and take advantage of the 64KB additional memory in the HMA. The second instructs this manager to load DOS in the HMA.

When you install DOS, the SETUP program, if it detects your system to be based on the 286 or higher CPU, will add these lines to a CONFIG.SYS file. If you have booted your PC with this file in the root directory of the boot disk, DOS is already running in the HMA.

To place device drivers (file names with the SYS extension) in the UMA (the memory area below the HMA) of a 386 or higher PC, you need these lines in your CONFIG.SYS file:

```
device=c:\dos\himem.sys
dos=high,umb
device=c:\dos\emm386.exe ram
devicehigh=c:\mouse\mouse.sys
. . .
```

---

3. Some of the newer 286 chips have the built-in capability to manage expanded memory. Such a system usually comes with its own EMS driver. Use that driver instead of EMM386.EXE.

4. Do not use this program if you are using other EMS programs such as QEMM or 386MAX.

The second command can also be split up without making any difference, like this:

```
dos=high
dos=umb
```

The first is to load DOS high and the second to make unused UMBs available for EMM386.EXE to manage.

EMM386 and Its Switches

You can use EMM386.EXE with no switch or one of the two available switches, RAM and NOEMS. Either switch allows access to UMBs. The difference between them is that RAM converts XMS to EMS and NOEMS does not. A number can be specified with RAM or without it. This number determines the amount of XMS to be converted to EMS. If no number is specified, 256KB is presumed. You can specify any number between 16 (for 16KB) and 32768 (for 32MB). If the number specified is lower than the available XMS, the rest remains unconverted; if it is higher, all the available memory is converted.

Using RAM (in contrast to NOEMS) reduces the UMA available for loading device drivers or programs because part of it will be used to manage EMS. The NOEMS switch should be used if your program does not use EMS, such as Windows 3.x and most Windows-compliant programs.

Here are some sample configuration commands (don't forget the EXE extension) and what they mean:

```
device=c:\dos\emm386.exe          (256KB EMS, no UMBs)

device=c:\dos\emm386.exe 1024     (1MB EMS, no UMBs)

device=c:\dos\emm386.exe noems    (UMBs, no EMS)

device=c:\dos\emm386.exe ram      (256KB EMS, UMBs)

device=c:\dos\emm386.exe 1024 ram (1MB EMS, UMBs)
```

If you use the RAM or NOEMS switch, you can load device drivers or programs to the available UMBs, like this:

```
devicehigh=c:\mouse\mouse.sys
devicehigh=c:\dos\ansi.sys
```

This will place MOUSE.SYS stored in the C:\MOUSE directory and ANSI.SYS stored in the C:\DOS directory in upper memory blocks.

If neither RAM nor NOEMS is specified, the UMA is not available for loading device drivers or programs. The DEVICEHIGH command will be treated the same as DEVICE. Device drivers will be loaded in conventional memory instead.

EMM386.EXE can also be used on the command line. When used as a command (rather than a device driver), it can be accompanied with one of the five switches: ON, OFF, AUTO, W=ON, or W=OFF. ON is to activate the EMS driver, OFF to deactivate it, AUTO is to let any program use EMS when needed. W=ON and W=OFF are used with Weitek chips. If you specify no switch, the program will tell you the current status of EMS support, as shown below:

```
C>emm386
MICROSOFT Expanded Memory Manager 386  Version 4.20.06X
(C) Copyright Microsoft Corporation 1986, 1990
   Available expanded memory . . . . . . .    224 KB
   LIM/EMS version . . . . . . . . . . . .    4.0
   Total expanded memory pages . . . . . .    38
   Available expanded memory pages . . . .    14
   Total handles . . . . . . . . . . . . .    64
   Active handles  . . . . . . . . . . . .     1
   Page frame segment  . . . . . . . . . .    D000 H
EMM386 Active.
```

Loading Programs in UMBs

After EMM386.EXE is loaded with either RAM or NOEMS switch, you can try to load a program in one of the available UMBs. To run a TSR program (files with COM or EXE extensions) in the UMA, use the internal LOADHIGH (or LH) command, like this:

```
C:\DOS>loadhigh doskey
```

This loads DOSKEY.COM to the UMA. You can also do it with an AUTOEXEC.BAT by adding this line:

```
loadhigh c:\dos\doskey
```

If a TSR program, such as PRINT, APPEND, and DOSKEY, cannot be loaded in the UMA, it will go to conventional memory instead. HIMEM.SYS and EMM386.EXE, for example, cannot be loaded in the UMA. DEVICEHIGH or LOADHIGH will have no effect on these driver files or programs.

Placing a device driver or running a TSR program in the UMA is a hit-and-miss proposition. Some programs do not run properly in the UMA. Your PC may even lock up due to memory conflict. Before you load some programs in the UMA, prepare a floppy boot disk. If your PC locks up, use this disk to reboot.

Load programs in reverse order of size, from larger to smaller. The memory manager uses the largest available UMB to load each program. If you place smaller programs ahead of larger ones, some areas will be underutilized.

OPTIMIZING MEMORY WITH MEMMAKER

■ *Use MEMMAKER to analyze CONFIG.SYS and AUTOEXEC.BAT files to optimize memory for your applications.*

DOS 6 has a memory optimizer called MemMaker. It will analyze your CONFIG.SYS and AUTOEXEC.BAT files and alter them (if necessary) in an attempt to load TSR programs to the UMA so that more conventional memory can be made available for your applications.

Note: Do not do what is described here unless you are using your own computer that has a 386 or higher CPU.

Here are the steps you need to follow to use MemMaker:

FOLLOW
THESE
STEPS

1. Run MemMaker:

   `C:\DOS>`**memmaker**

   The initial message appears. Press Enter to continue.

2. You are asked to choose between Express or Custom setup. The former is highly automatic, and the latter gives you more control. Choose Express to start. You can press the space bar to change a selection. You can also press F1 for help and F3 to exit.

3. You are asked whether your applications use EMS. After you make a selection, you are instructed to remove floppy disks so that MemMaker will reboot from your hard disk.

If your PC freezes, reboot by pressing the Reset button (or Ctrl-Alt-Del). MemMaker will pick up where it left off. If it freezes again, reboot another time. You will be asked whether your system works properly. If yes, the screen shows the available memory before and after the optimization. If not, you will be asked to exit or undo changes. If the process fails, the above steps may be repeated.

Whether MemMaker succeeds or fails, examine your CONFIG.SYS and AUTOEXEC.BAT files carefully. Your original files now have UMB extensions added to them and moved to the C:\DOS directory. The new ones may have lots of commands added. If you are satisfied with the new files, boot with them from now on. If not, feel free to restore the original. You can also ask MemMaker to restore your original files with the /UNDO switch, like this:

   `C:\DOS>`**memmaker /undo**

The above steps will create in the C:\DOS directory a file named MEMMAKER.STS. Examine this ASCII file to see what the program has done. You will find lots of numbers, the results of calculating your memory and trying to match your TSRs to the available upper memory blocks. If you encounter problems, also examine the MEMMAKER.INF file in the C:\DOS directory; it comes with the DOS package.

If you choose Custom setup in step 2 above, you will be asked to set Yes or No for six questions. You can also choose Yes or No to optimize each TSR program. If you are knowledgeable about your PC, you can change the values. Otherwise, just accept the default values.

In my old system with a 386 CPU and 1MB memory, MemMaker asks me whether my applications use EMS. If I say No, my PC always freezes and displays a 8237 ERROR message. If I say Yes to EMS, MemMaker proceeds to successfully optimize the system without any problem. So, if your optimizing attempt fails, try various combinations; one of them may work.

If you have tried various ways and nothing works, you may want to give up on MemMaker. Perform a clean boot by pressing F5 when the Starting MS-DOS message appears. This bypasses the CONFIG.SYS and AUTOEXEC.BAT files (see the end of Chapter 11 for more related ideas). You can then use the /UNDO switch or whatever that is necessary to restore your original configuration.

REPORTING MEMORY STATUS

■ *Use MEM to report memory use; use it with /CLASSIFY or /DEBUG to show more details.*

If you wonder what is in the invisible world of computer memory, you can use a command to tell you. The MEM.EXE program can give you a simplified report if no parameter is entered, such as:

```
C:\DOS>mem

Memory Type        Total  =  Used  +  Free
----------------   ------    ------   ------
Conventional        640K      75K     565K
Upper                91K      60K      31K
Adapter RAM/ROM       0K       0K       0K
Extended (XMS)      293K     293K       0K
----------------   ------    ------   ------
Total memory       1024K     428K     596K

Total under 1 MB    731K     135K     596K
Total Expanded (EMS)                  448K   (458752 bytes)
Free Expanded (EMS)                     0K       (0 bytes)

Largest executable program size       565K   (578096 bytes)
Largest free upper memory block        31K    (32112 bytes)
MS-DOS is resident in the high memory area.
```

If you want to see a detailed report of what programs are in memory and how much memory each occupies, use the /CLASSIFY (or /C) switch:

C>mem /c

If you have installed PRINT and APPEND, for example, their names and sizes will also show up in the display. If you want more details (including input-output devices and locations), try the /DEBUG (or /D) switch:

C>mem /d

To pause the display after the screen is full, add the /PAGE (or /P) switch:

C>mem /d /p

The detailed information is useful to programmers, but not to most ordinary DOS users. If you are not a programmer, you need only to know what programs are already loaded and whether there is enough memory to load another program. To show just free memory, use /FREE (or /F):

C>mem /f

Instead of showing a long list with /D, you can use /MODULE (or /M) to show a single module (program), like this:

C>mem /m:command

Here you put the name of the program (COMMAND.COM in our case) after /M; the colon is optional.

SYSTEM DIAGNOSIS

■ *Use the diagnostic program MSD.EXE to get information about your computer system.*

DOS 6 includes a new diagnostic program called MSD.EXE (Microsoft Diagnostics). It will give you a slew of information about your system.

To run the program, just enter the name on the command line, like this:

C:\DOS>**msd**

A display like Figure 9.1 appears.

The middle of the screen contains various items showing how your computer is equipped, plus 8 options through which more related information is available. To select an option, just click it with your mouse or use Tab to highlight it and press Enter. Another screen appears. Click the OK button or press Enter or Esc to return to the initial screen.

Of the 8 options, Memory, TSR Programs, and Device Drivers provide lots of useful information. They show what programs are loaded in RAM, where in RAM, and how much RAM for each.

If more information is available, a scroll bar appears on the right side; this happens, for example, when you choose Memory. You can press PgUp or PgDn to scroll up or down. You can press Home (or Ctrl-Home) or End (or Ctrl-End) to go to the top or bottom of the display. You can click the ↑ or ↓ arrow shown at the top and bottom of the scroll bar; they are the equivalent of pressing comparable keys on the keyboard. You can also drag the scroll box inside the scroll bar—move the mouse pointer to the box, hold down the left mouse button, and move the box up or down to scroll the screen text.

The top of the screen in Figure 9.1 shows a menu bar with three options. You can open a menu by pressing Alt and a pertinent letter or using a mouse to click a displayed menu. Help gives no help except the program's name; this program has no help of any kind—a glaring deficiency.

Figure 9.1

The initial MSD screen

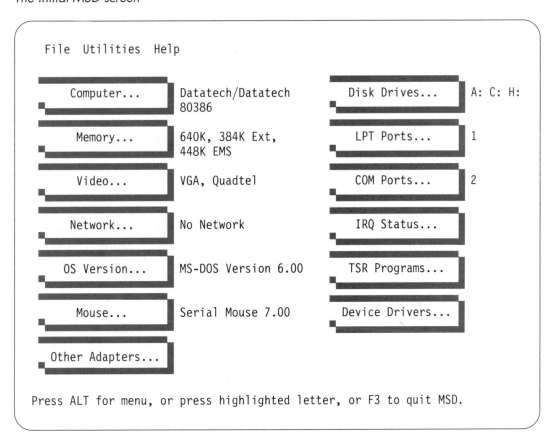

The Utilities menu gives you these options:

```
Memory Block Display
Memory Browser
Insert Command
Test Printer
Black & White
```

The last option lets you toggle between color and black-white display. If you have difficulty reading the screen, try the other option. Test Printer lets you choose a port and test your printer.

Insert Command leads to a display of the commands in your CONFIG.SYS and AUTOEXEC.BAT that can be altered, including FILES and BUFFERS. You can modify existing ones or add new ones. When you select the OK button, what you change will be saved over the original files. So do not do this unless you are using your own computer.

Memory Block Display shows memory use. Two parallel windows appear, each with a separate scroll box. The left, titled Allocated Memory, lists loaded programs; the right, titled Memory Map, shows the location of memory for the highlighted program. You can use your mouse to scroll either box. From the keyboard, press Tab to make a window active before you press PgUp or PgDn to scroll it.

Memory Browser lets you snoop at the system BIOS and video BIOS. Again, two parallel windows appear to show memory use. When you select the OK button, more information will be shown about the selected BIOS.

The File menu has these options:

```
Find File
Print Report

 . . .

Exit
```

The middle part of the menu shows a series of system files, including your CONFIG.SYS, AUTOEXEC.BAT, and files with the INI extension. You can select any to read the contents. You can read other files by using the first two options in the menu.

Selecting Find File leads to a dialog box, and the cursor goes to the first area for you to type:

```
Search for [        ]
```

After you type something, say COMMAND.COM, press Tab to move the cursor to the next area:

```
Start from [        ]
```

The current directory will also be displayed, and you can start editing by pressing a cursor key. You can also start typing a new string. The old string disappears as you start typing. Let us type \ here to start from the root directory.

You can now press Enter or select the Search button. A window appears with the matching files displayed. Since we do not use a wild card, only one file is displayed, namely COMMAND.COM. Press Enter or select the Display File button. Another screen appears to show the contents of the file. You can now scroll the screen up or down to see more. Press Esc to return to the initial screen.

Selecting Print Report leads to another dialog box. The top portion, titled Report Information, displays all the items whose reports are available. You can click inside each pair of brackets to show X or clear it. Or you can tab to each and press the space bar to enter or clear an X. The items marked with an X will have their reports generated.

The bottom portion of the screen, titled Print To, lets you choose the destination of the report. You can choose a printer port (LPT1-3 or COM1-4) or File. To make a selection, click the desired item with your mouse; it will be marked with a bullet (•). From the keyboard, tab (Tab or Shift-Tab) to this area and then use ↑ or ↓ to move the bullet to the desired option. When you are satisfied with the selections, select the OK button to print. (If you choose a nonexisting printer port or your printer is not turned on, nothing happens, not even an error message.)

If you select File in the above procedure, you will be asked to enter a file name, including a directory prefix if necessary. The default file name is REPORT.MSD and it will be saved to the current directory—unless you change either. If you have chosen Customer Information in the top half of the screen, another screen will appear for you to fill in a series of information which will be included in the printed or saved report.

If your system malfunctions and you need long-distance help from your vendor, MSD can be an invaluable tool. Just follow the above procedure to save or print a report. Then mail, fax, or transmit the report. The technicians on the other side may be able to solve your problem by reading your report. Some mail-order PC vendors have been doing this for some time. They include a modem and a diagnostic program with every system sold. If the system fails, the program will generate a report, which the modem will transmit to the vendor to solve your problem. No more long delays or shipping bulky packages back and forth!

P R A C T I C E   9 - 4

☐ 1. Install APPEND with the /E switch. Create a batch file named ADDAPPND.BAT similar to ADDPATH.BAT.

☐ 2. Enter an APPEND list into the environment. Use ADDAPPND.BAT to add to the list.

☐ 3. Modify ENVPROM.BAT and SETPROM.BAT to display the following prompt:

  Enter a command:_

☐ 4. Create two batch files named ENVDIR.BAT and C.BAT similar to the above two files and use them to move from one directory to another. *Hint:* C.BAT should use IF, and ENVDIR.BAT should contain lines like this:

  set d1=\wp\work

☐ 5. Use DOSKEY to create and run a macro named CD. It should let the user enter a parameter to go to one of the directories entered into the environment by ENVDIR.BAT.

☐ 6. Create and run a batch file named TIMEPROM.BAT. It should save the original value assigned to PROMPT and set this prompt style:

  12:25>>_

☐ 7. Create and run a batch file named OLDPROM.BAT. It should restore the original prompt style.

☐ 8. Use DOSKEY to create a macro named D. It should allow the user to enter one or more parameters to assign a value to DIRCMD and display directory entries based on the specified parameters. Use D to show the current drive's root directory with the /O and /W switches.

D R I L L

____ 19. The DOS commands that can be entered into the environment include:
   a. PATH
   b. PROMPT
   c. APPEND
   d. all the above

____ 20. To enable you to enter APPEND into the environment, you must run it with the /E switch for the first. True or false?

____ 21. The following command will:
   A>path;
   a. delete the PATH string from the environment
   b. enter the PATH= string in the environment
   c. do nothing
   d. generate an error message

____ 22. The command below will:
   A>prompt;

    a. delete the PROMPT string from the environment

    b. enter the PROMPT= string in the environment

    c. do nothing

    d. generate an error message

____ 23. The following command entered on the command line will:

    A>set p1=%prompt%

    a. assign the old prompt value to P1

    b. assign %prompt% to P1

    c. change the prompt on the screen

    d. delete an existing prompt string in the environment

____ 24. The following command from a batch file will:

    set p1=%prompt%

    a. assign the old prompt value to P1

    b. assign the %prompt% string to P1

    c. change the prompt on the screen

    d. delete an existing prompt string in the environment

____ 25. You can enter a default parameter for DIR like below. True or false?

    C>dircmd=/o /p

Use the following items to answer questions 26–30:

a. MSD b. HMA c. UMA d. HIMEM.SYS e. EMM386.EXE

____ 26. The memory area between 640KB and 1MB.

____ 27. The 64KB memory beyond 1MB.

____ 28. A program to show system information.

____ 29. A program to load DOS outside of conventional memory in a 286 or higher PC.

____ 30. A program to load programs to upper memory blocks in a newer PC.

S U M M A R Y   A N D   R E V I E W

Check each item as you review and understand the following highlights of the chapter:

☐   1. Use MODE without any parameter to report the status of all devices. To report a device's status, put the device name after MODE.

☐   2. Use MODE to set a higher keyboard speed. This will increase your productivity.

☐ 3. Use MODE to set monitor modes, including numbers of columns and lines. You need special equipment to set some of the unusual attributes.

☐ 4. Use MODE to set a dot-matrix printer to print 80 or 132 columns and 6 or 8 lines per inch.

☐ 5. Use MODE to reroute one device to another, such as rerouting printing to a printer connected to a serial port.

☐ 6. Use SUBST to substitute a drive for a directory. You can use a logical but nonexisting drive if you add the LASTDRIVE command in your CONFIG.SYS file.

☐ 7. Include BREAK, BUFFERS, FILES, and DEVICE commands in your CONFIG.SYS file to enhance your system's performance.

☐ 8. Install RAMDRIVE.SYS by including the name in your CONFIG.SYS file. This can create a RAM disk. Use it to store temporary files or copy files in a one-floppy system.

☐ 9. DOS sets aside a special memory area called environment to handle PATH, PROMPT, and APPEND (if installed with /E) commands.

☐ 10. The default size for the environment is 256 bytes. If you need more space in the environment, include the SHELL command, plus the /P and /E:bytes switches, in your CONFIG.SYS.

☐ 11. You can create your own environment variables and assign them values from the command line or a macro. To maneuver these variables and their values, you can do it with batch files, but not from the command line or a macro.

☐ 12. To take full advantage of the environment, you can enter available directory lists or prompt styles into the environment and then use a batch file to quickly activate one of them. You can also use a batch file to add paths to an existing path list.

☐ 13. Enter a default parameter for the DIRCMD variable, which is available since version 5. The value assigned to it is used by DIR on the command line to display directory information.

☐ 14. If you have a 286 or higher system, use HIMEM.SYS to install DOS in the high memory area. If you have a 386/486 system, use EMM386.EXE to put device drivers and TSR programs in the upper memory area. You can also convert extended memory to expanded memory, which, unlike extended memory, can be used by most programs.

☐ 15. Use MemMaker to optimize your memory. It will alter your CONFIG.SYS and AUTOEXEC.BAT files in order to optimize memory use. If you don't like the result, use the /UNDO switch to restore the original files.

☐ 16. Use MEM to find out memory use and availability. Use /C or /D to display detailed information about programs loaded, their sizes, and locations. Add /P to pause a long display. Use /F to show free memory and /M to show a single program.

☐ 17. Use the MSD program to sleuth on your system and memory use. Lots of information will be displayed on the screen. You can also print out a report.

R E V I E W   Q U E S T I O N S

Write an answer for each question below:

1. List the devices which MODE can control and their corresponding device names recognized by DOS.

2. What kind of monitor do you have? What functions can you set by using MODE?

3. With a dot-matrix printer, what are the legal numbers of lines and columns you can set by using MODE?

4. What items does a complete device status report contain?

5. Can you substitute a nonexisting drive for a nonexisting directory?

6. What does the LASTDRIVE command do?

7. What can MemMaker do? Can you undo what it has done?

8. What is the default status of BREAK? What difference does it make whether it is on or off?

9. What is a RAM disk? How can you create one?

10. What is the DOS environment? What is its default size? How can you increase it?

11. What DOS commands are automatically entered into the environment after they are used? How can you add variables into the environment?

12. Compare conventional memory, expanded memory, and extended memory.

13. What device drivers are available in version 5 or 6 to manage memory in a 286 or higher system?

14. What can MEM do?

15. What does MemMaker do?

10 DOS Shell and Editor

COMMANDS COVERED

DOSSHELL, EDIT

NEW TERMS AND SYMBOLS

Icons, click, double click, drag, title bar, menu bar, drive icon, Directory Tree, File List, Program List, status line, scroll bar, scroll box, context-sensitive help, hypertext, +, −, *, →, ▶, ♦, dialog box, button, program item properties, program group, clipboard, cut and paste, bookmark

QUICK START

To start the Shell:

> C:\DOS>**dosshell**

To start the Editor:

> C:\DOS>**edit**

To move from one Shell window to another:

> Press Tab to move forward or Shift-Tab to reverse. Click a window or an item in a window.

To open a Shell menu:

> Click a menu; press Tab or F10 to activate the menu bar and press a highlighted letter.

To get help from the Shell or Editor:

> Press F1 when doing something to get context-sensitive help. Open the Help menu to get hypertext help frames.

Managing directories:

> Press or click – to collapse a directory, + to expand a directory up to one-level subdirectories, * to expand all the subdirectories of the current directory, and Ctrl-* to expand all the directories.

To rename a directory:

> Highlight the directory, select Rename from the File menu, and enter a name.

To view a file's contents:

> Highlight the file and press F9.

To select multiple files:

> See Table 10.1.

To launch a program:

> Open a program (double click or highlight it and press Enter) or a data file associated with a program.

To print a file:

> Run PRINT.EXE. Highlight a file. Select Print from the File menu.

To associate a program and a data file:

Highlight a program or a data file, select Associate from the File menu, and enter a file name extension or a program name.

To switch among programs:

See Table 10.2.

To create or alter a program item or program group:

Move the cursor to the Program List window and select New or Properties.

To move the cursor in the Editor screen:

See Table 10.3.

To search for or replace strings:

Select Find or Change from the Search menu, and supply a search string and a replace string (for Change).

To select text lines:

Hold down Shift and move the cursor to highlight text.

To delete, cut, and paste:

Select text and press Del to delete, Shift-Del to cut, Ctrl-Ins to copy, and Shift-Ins to paste.

To copy or print help text:

Display a help frame, select text lines, press Ctrl-Ins to send it to the clipboard, go to the editing screen, press Shift-Ins to make a copy. To print, select text lines and select Print from the File menu.

To insert ASCII 0-31 characters:

Press Ctrl-P and a corresponding letter while holding down Ctrl.

Versions 5 and 6 include the DOS Shell[1] and the DOS Editor. The two share similar interfaces which can be manipulated with a mouse as well as the traditional keyboard. After you get familiar with one, you can quickly master the other. Their similarities are the main reason for the two to be covered in the same chapter.

---

1. The Shell first appeared in version 4.0. It had limited capabilities and, unlike the one in the current version, was avoided by most users.

This chapter explains the Shell first. Unlike in previous chapters, you will not see much action at first. Your first priority here is to get familiar with the new graphical environment. Only after you know where things are and what they are supposed to do can you perform some actions.

MOUSE AND KEYBOARD CONVENTIONS

■   *Different mouse and keyboard rules and techniques are summarized here.*

If your PC is equipped with a mouse, you can use it to manipulate **icons** (screen objects) or text in both the Shell and the Editor. To activate your mouse, you need to include this line in your CONFIG.SYS file and reboot your system:

```
device=c:\mouse\mouse.sys
```

This assumes that your mouse driver which comes with your mouse package is located in the C:\MOUSE directory.

In the following terms, the first few are pertinent to mouse users and the rest to both mouse and keyboard users:

Click	Move the mouse pointer to an object, press the left button once, and release it.
Double Click	When you are asked to double click an item, you are to move the mouse pointer to it and press the left button twice in rapid succession.
Drag	Move the mouse pointer to an object, hold down the left button, drag the object to a new location, and release the button.
Select	When you are asked to select an object, you can click it or use the cursor-movement keys to move the cursor to the object (followed by pressing Enter in some situations).
Highlight	When you are asked to highlight an object, click it or move the cursor to it. The object is highlighted.
Open	When you are asked to open an item, you need to highlight it and press Enter. With the mouse, you click a menu once to open it and double click a file, program, or a help item to open it.

The mouse is particularly adroit in handling screen objects. The mouse pointer can be moved anywhere on the screen. You can thus access any screen object more quickly than from the keyboard.

U S I N G   T H E   D O S   S H E L L

When you use the SETUP program to install version 6 (see Appendix F), it creates and stores on your hard disk a series of files with the DOSSHELL name plus various extension names. These files are used to run the DOS Shell.

The Shell is a graphical user interface (GUI), which displays on the screen various icons and objects. You can do many acts from the Shell, thus avoiding typing on the command line or entering some cryptic DOS commands and their required parameters. These are the things you can do with the Shell:

- Display information related to drives, directories, and files.

- Manage directories and files in many ways without having to type related commands.

- Launch multiple programs and switch from one to another.

STARTING AND EXITING THE SHELL

■ *Enter DOSSHELL to start the Shell; press F3 to exit.*

To start the Shell, go to the C:\DOS directory and enter this command:

```
C:\DOS>dosshell
```

If you have unusual circumstances, you may want to use one of the available switches (/B, /G, and /T); see the online help (DOSSHELL /?) for their uses. Instead of a switch, you can also use a menu option inside the Shell to alter screen appearances.

To exit the Shell and return to the command line, follow these steps:

FOLLOW THESE STEPS

1. Press Alt or F10 to activate the menu bar.

2. Press F to open the File menu.

3. Press X to choose the Exit option.

Unless you have a program loaded from the Shell, the command line should appear.

Instead of the above steps, you can also press F3 or Alt-F4 as shortcuts to get out of the Shell.

THE INITIAL SCREEN

■   *The six major parts of the Shell screen are discussed here.*

■   *Click any area or press Tab/Shift-Tab to make any window active. Inside each window, click any item or use a cursor-movement key to move to any item.*

■   *Use the mouse to maneuver the scroll bar/box. For keyboard users, use the scroll box to gauge the contents.*

After the Shell is run, it begins to read all the files and directories in the current drive. This could take some time if your system has a large hard disk and a slow CPU. Then it displays the initial screen, as shown in Figure 10.1.

Different Parts of the Shell Screen

The initial Shell screen consists of the following parts:

Title Bar	The first line showing MS-DOS Shell is known as the Shell title bar.
Menu Bar	The second line shows various menu names.
Drive Icons	The third line shows the current directory, which is in turn related to one of the drives shown in the fourth line. The current drive is also highlighted.
Directory Tree	The first of the three windows in the middle of the screen, this area lists all the subdirectories of the current directory.
File List	This window (with the C:*.* title) displays all the files in the current directory (C:\). The contents here change as the current directory on the left is changed.
Program List	The bottom window (titled Main) lists all the programs that can be run from the Shell.
Status Line	This last line on the screen shows two shortcut keys and the current time; various messages will appear here when you use some commands.

Moving Around the Screen

Besides the menus, there are four areas which you can make active and manipulate the items inside. These are: Drive Icons, Directory Tree, File List, and Program List.

In the beginning, the Drive Icons area is active. The active drive is also highlighted. At this point, you can select another drive by clicking it, or pressing → or ← to highlight a drive and pressing Enter. The new active drive's contents (directories and files) will then be displayed below.

To make another area active with the mouse, you can just click an item in that area. To do it from the keyboard, you need to press Tab (forward) or Shift-Tab (reverse). The active area's title bar is highlighted and a right-pointing arrow (also known as the selection cursor or simply cursor) also marks the current (selected) item in the area, as shown in the Program List area in Figure 10.1.

When the selection cursor is on an item, the item is highlighted and marked with → on the left. The File List area also has a symbol marking a selected file. When → is moved to this area, the current file is marked with →▶ as well as highlighted. If you select multiple files, each will be marked with ▶ as well as highlighted, but only one file will be marked with →.

Figure 10.1

The initial Shell screen

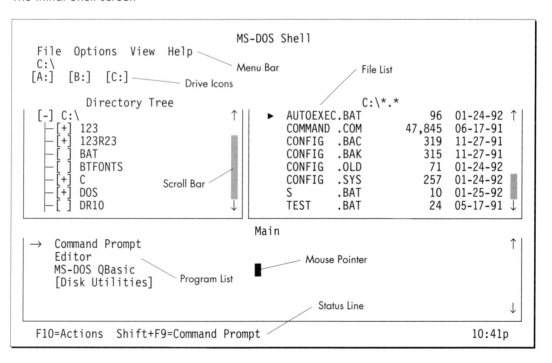

Scroll Bars

The right side of an area containing a list of items has a vertical bar known as the **scroll bar**, which can be used by the mouse to manipulate the list. The top of a scroll bar is marked with ↑ and the bottom with ↓. You can click one to scroll the displayed list up or down by one item at a time; this is comparable to pressing a corresponding arrow key on the keyboard when a particular area is active.

A scroll bar also contains a **scroll box**. This is the blank area between the two arrow keys. The scroll box serves three purposes:

- It shows the proportion (percentage) of the displayed files compared to all the available files. In Figure 10.1, the scroll box in the Directory Tree area shows about 1/5 of the available items displayed in that window, the one in the File List area about 60%, and the one in the Program List area 100%.

- It shows the position of the displayed items. If the scroll box is located in the middle, for example, the middle portion is shown in that window.

- It can be dragged with the mouse up or down to scroll the display. If you drag it upward, for example, the upper portion will be displayed.

From the keyboard, you can scroll the displayed items one screen at a time by pressing PgUp or PgDn. As you do, the scroll box of the area will move up or down accordingly. Use Home (or Ctrl-Home) to go to the top or End (or Ctrl-End) to the bottom.

TIPS AND TRICKS

MOVING THE CURSOR WITH A LETTER

When an area is active, you can press a letter key on the keyboard to quickly move the cursor to the right item. This technique may be speedier than using the mouse or the cursor-movement keys.

Suppose the current directory is C:\DOS and the cursor is in the File List area. You now want to move the cursor to a file starting with R. Pressing R moves the cursor to the first of several files starting with the letter. Pressing it the second time moves the cursor to the second file, and so on.

This technique can be used where there is a scroll bar. It is most useful when there are many files in a directory and you happen to know the first letter of a file name.

ACCESSING THE SHELL'S MENUS

■ *Click a menu to open it and click one of the available commands to use it. From the keyboard, press Alt or F10 to activate the menu bar, press a highlighted key to open that menu, press a highlighted key to use that command.*

After you select an item on the screen, you need to select a command to do something to the item. A command is accessed by opening a menu.

To open a menu with the mouse, just click the right menu in the menu bar, File for example. A box containing all the commands appears, as shown in Figure 10.2.

To open a menu from the keyboard, follow these steps:

FOLLOW THESE STEPS

1. Press Alt or F10. The menu bar is activated and all the key letters are highlighted (underlined in graphics mode).

2. Press one of the highlighted key letters. Alternatively, you can press → or ← to highlight a menu and press Enter to open that menu.

After a menu is open, you can click another menu or press → or ← to close the old one and open a new one.

To close a menu, simply press the Esc key or the right mouse button (or click the menu name).

Figure 10.2

The File menu

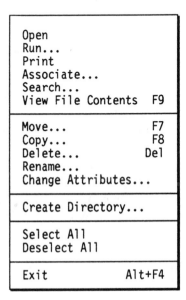

```
Open
Run...
Print
Associate...
Search...
View File Contents   F9

Move...               F7
Copy...               F8
Delete...             Del
Rename...
Change Attributes...

Create Directory...

Select All
Deselect All

Exit                  Alt+F4
```

Figure 10.2 shows all the commands in the File menu. Each command has its key letter highlighted.[2] You can use a command by clicking it, pressing its key letter, or highlighting it (pressing ↓ or ↑) and pressing Enter.

Notice the shortcut keys in the File menu. You can thus open this menu and select Delete to delete a selected item or simply press the Del key on the keyboard to do the same thing. Or you can press Alt-F4 (or F3) to exit rather than selecting File and then Exit.

A command with an ellipsis (...) leads to a **dialog box**, where you will be required to type something so that the command can do its job properly. In a dialog box, you can click any item or press Tab or Shift-Tab to each item and enter any required information.

SEEKING HELP

■ *Press F1 when doing something to get context-sensitive help.*

■ *Open the Help menu to get hypertext help frames.*

The Shell comes with a lengthy file named DOSSHELL.HLP. It provides comprehensive context-sensitive and hypertext help. This help can be accessed via two ways:

- When you are performing a task. For example, when you open the File menu and highlight the Open command, you can press F1 to show what this command is supposed to do. This is known as **context-sensitive help**.

- By selecting the Help menu with hypertext capability. The Help menu opens up as shown in Figure 10.3. From this menu you can roam through a vast number of connected topics and explanation for each.

Figure 10.3

The Help menu

```
Index
Keyboard
Shell Basics
Commands
Procedures
Using Help

About Shell
```

When a help window appears, the center of your screen displays a box with explanatory text. A scroll bar/box also shows the amount of the available material currently displayed on the screen. You can use the cursor-movement keys or the scroll bar with the mouse to display more text as explained earlier. From the keyboard, you can press PgUp or PgDn to scroll by one screen at a time, or Home or End to move to the beginning or the end of the text frame.

As you scroll a help window, you may see a highlighted item (also marked with →); stop scrolling and press Tab or Shift-Tab to see whether you can highlight other items. You can press Enter (or double click) on a highlighted item to display more related information. This

---

2. Depending on your video system and various selections from the Options menu, some commands may be dimmed, invisible, or without a highlighted key letter. These commands cannot be used at this time.

kind of connection is known as **hypertext**, which allows you to move to other text frames to see more details of related subjects.

You can also click or tab to one of these items shown at the bottom of a help window to do more things:

```
Close  Back  Keys  Index  Help
```

Select Close to close the help window or Back to return to the previous help frame; you can always press Esc to get rid of a help window and return to the Shell screen.

MANAGING DIRECTORIES

■ *Expand or collapse directories by using –, +, *, or Ctrl-*.*

■ *Create, remove, or rename a directory by using the File menu.*

You can do many things to manage directories, including creating, removing, and renaming them. You can also display directories in a variety of ways.

You can quickly display a drive's directories, a directory's subdirectories, and the files in a directory. To change to another drive, select another drive (click it or highlight it and press Enter) in the Drive Icons area. This drive's directories then appear in the Directory Tree area. Select any directory (clicking it or moving the cursor there) in this area to display its files in the File List area. As you select another directory, another list of files appears.

If a drive's contents have been read, clicking the drive icon will display the contents without activating the drive. Suppose both drive A and C have been read, clicking A or C will display each drive's contents without reading the drive again. This can speed up screen display. If you want to read a drive again so that its newly added items will also be shown, double click it or highlight it and press Enter.

Notice the [+] and [–] signs in the Directory Tree area in Figure 10.1. A directory thus marked contains one or more subdirectories; one without either sign has no subdirectory.

You can expand or collapse a directory containing subdirectories. Notice the [–] in front of C:\. This directory is known as expanded, which means all its first-level subdirectories are displayed. To collapse this directory, follow either step below:

1. Click the – sign; or

2. Select the directory and press the – (minus) key.

After either step, the – is changed to + and the directory has become current.[3] A collapsed directory is marked with [+], and all its subdirectories disappear from the display.

To expand a directory (and make it current), follow the above steps, except using + instead of –.

When a directory is expanded with +, only one level of subdirectories is shown. If you want to expand all the levels, use * instead of +. If you want to expand all the levels of all the directories, instead of the current directory alone, press Ctrl-*. If you do not remember these keys, open the Tree menu to see all the keys discussed so far. You can press one of these keys from the keyboard or select a menu option.

To create a new directory, follow these steps:

1. Select a drive or directory where you want to create a subdirectory.

2. Open the File menu, shown in Figure 10.2.

3. Select Create Directory. A dialog box appears with these two lines in the middle:

```
Parent name: C:\
New directory name. . [·········]
```

You are now to enter a directory name which will become a subdirectory of C:\.

To delete a directory, select it and press Del or select Delete from the File menu. This message appears:

```
Delete C:\XYZ
```

You can now select Yes, No, or Cancel (click it or tab there and press Enter). If you select the Yes **button** (a button is an option for an action), the directory will be deleted. If the directory is not empty, a message appears telling you that you cannot delete a non-empty directory. Selecting the No or Cancel button will negate your action.

To rename a directory, select the directory and select Rename from the File menu. The old directory name appears and you are prompted to enter a new name. The new name replaces the old in the Directory Tree area.

P R A C T I C E   1 0 - 1

☐   1. Create in A:\ a directory named ABC.

☐   2. Create in A:\ABC a subdirectory named XYZ.

---

3. If you click a directory in any place other than the selection box containing + or –, the directory becomes current, but the sign is not changed.

☐   3. Expand and collapse A:\ABC.

☐   4. Rename ABC as CAB. Restore the original name.

> *(Keep these directories for later use.)*

D R I L L

____   1. To exit the Shell, you need to:
  a. press F3
  b. press Alt-F4
  c. select Exit from the File menu
  d. any of the above

____   2. This key lets you move the cursor from one area of the Shell screen to another:
  a. Esc
  b. Tab
  c. Enter
  d. Space bar

____   3. The cursor can be moved to all these areas except:
  a. Drive Icons
  b. Directory Tree
  c. File List
  d. Program List
  e. Status Line

____   4 This act opens a menu:
  a. press F10
  b   press Alt
  c. click a menu name
  d. none of the above

____   5. This expands all levels of all directories:
  a. +
  b. –
  c. *
  d. Ctrl-*

____   6. A directory name can be changed from the Shell but not on the command line. True or false?

____   7. A non-empty directory can be deleted (removed) from the Shell but not on the command line. True or false?

MANAGING FILES

■ *Highlight a file and press F9 to view its contents.*

■ *Use the Search option from the File menu to show only matching files.*

■ *Use the File menu to move, copy, delete, rename files or change their attributes.*

This section provides concrete steps for using the File menu to manipulate files. Some commands in this menu were covered earlier, and some others are used to run programs and will be covered in the next section.

Viewing File Contents

You have learned to use TYPE to display a file's contents. This command can display all the characters in an ASCII file but can hardly show anything in other types of files. The Shell can do much better.

To show a file's contents, follow these steps:

FOLLOW THESE STEPS

1. Select a file in the File List area. The selected file is preceded with →▶ and highlighted.

2. Open the File menu.

3. Select View File Contents. You can also press F9 after step 1 above.

The file's contents are now displayed in a separate screen. You can click PgUp, PgDn, ↑, or ↓ appearing near the top of the screen; or press comparable keyboard keys to scroll the text.

The top of the screen shows the Display, View, and Help menus. You can use Display to view the file in ASCII or Hex (you can also press F9 to switch between the two)[4], View to repaint the screen (to restore the Shell screen after running some TSR programs) or return to the previous screen (Esc will also work), and Help to access the Help Index.

File Searching

Searching for files is very easy. Just select Search from the File menu and enter a search string. When the command is selected, a dialog box appears as shown in Figure 10.4.

---

4. If a file contains only ASCII characters, it is displayed by default in the ASCII format, otherwise in Hex.

Figure 10.4

The Search File dialog box

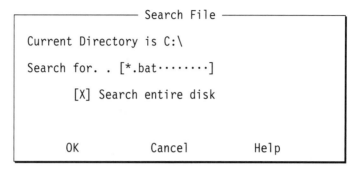

You can enter a search string with wild card characters. In our case, we want to search for any file with the BAT extension. If you do not want to search the entire disk (search only in the current or specified directory), click the selection box or tab there and press the space bar; the X will disappear (you can select it by clicking it or pressing the space bar again). If necessary, enter a directory path such as C:\BAT to limit the search to that particular directory.

All the files found are displayed in a separate screen. You can select one and press F9 to show its contents. You can select some or all (see below) and use a menu to do something. Press Esc to return to the original screen.

Move, Copy, Rename, and Delete

Moving, copying, renaming, and deleting a file are very similar to one another. Just select a file, open the File menu, and select an appropriate command (or press a shortcut key). You will be asked to choose Yes or No in case of deletion, enter a new name in case of renaming, and enter a target in case of moving or copying.

WARNING: The Delete command from the File menu will delete read-only files. When such a file is encountered, a warning appears. If you approve, the file will be deleted.

Using the mouse to move a file is most convenient. Just drag a file to a directory. A little bullet appears for you to drag. You will also be asked to confirm the move.

File Attributes

When you select Change Attributes from the File menu, a separate box appears showing the file name and the file's attribute(s), such as:

```
    Hidden
    System
 ▶ Archive
    Read only
```

You can click one of the attributes to select or deselect. From the keyboard, you can use Tab and ↓ or ↑ to move to the right item and press the space bar to select or deselect. Select the OK button to accept. If you select Hidden or System, the selected file disappears. To display a hidden file, use the Options menu explained below.

Can you change the attributes of a directory, such as making it invisible? Although some third-party programs will let you do that, the Shell does not permit that. When a directory is selected, the Change Attributes option is not available from the File menu.

P R A C T I C E   1 0 - 2

☐   1. Search in all the directories in drive C for all the files with the TXT extension.

☐   2. Copy the README.TXT file from the C:\DOS directory to the A:\ABC directory.

☐   3. Move the same file from A:\ABC to A:\ABC\XYZ.

☐   4. Show the contents of README.TXT in A:\ABC\XYZ.

☐   5. Delete README.TXT in A:\ABC\XYZ.

D R I L L

____   8. When a selection box of [X] appears, you can select or deselect the item by:
     a. tabbing to it and pressing the space bar
     b. clicking the box
     c. both a and b
     d. neither a or b

_____ 9. By dragging a file from the File List area to another directory, you are:

    a. moving it

    b. copying it

    c. deleting it

    d. renaming it

_____ 10. You can use the Change Attributes option from the File menu to make a directory invisible. True or false?

Use the following to answer questions 11–14:

Each key below is used to:

a. F7 b. F8 c. F9 d. F10

_____ 11. Copy a file.

_____ 12. Move a file.

_____ 13. Show a file's contents.

_____ 14. Activate the menu bar.

SELECTING MULTIPLE FILES

■ *Select (highlight) a group of files to apply a command to them.*

■ *To select a group of files with the mouse, combine clicking with Shift or Ctrl-Shift.*

■ *To select a group of files with the keyboard, combine cursor keys with Shift or Shift-F8.*

So far we have worked with a single file at a time. This section demonstrates how to work with multiple files at one time. To do that, you need to do the following:

• Select multiple files.

• Use a command by opening a proper menu or pressing a shortcut key.

You can select files that are in sequence, those that are not in sequence, or those that are stored in various directories. You can then use a command to work on all the selected files.

Mouse Techniques

FOLLOW
THESE
STEPS

To select a group of sequential files:

1. Click the first file.

2. Click the last file while holding down Shift.

All the selected files from the first to the last are then highlighted and each marked with ▶. Clicking a file or directory at this time deselects them, and the highlight disappears.

To select individual nonsequential files, hold down Ctrl and click each file. Each selected file is highlighted and marked with ▶. To deselect a file, click it while holding down Ctrl.

FOLLOW
THESE
STEPS

To select multiple groups:

1. Select the first group as explained above.

2. Move the mouse pointer to the first file of the next group. Hold down Ctrl and click it.

3. Move the mouse pointer to the last file of this group. Click the file as you hold down Ctrl and Shift simultaneously.

4. Repeat steps 2 and 3 with another group.

Keyboard Techniques

FOLLOW
THESE
STEPS

To select a group of sequential files:

1. Go to the first file.

2. Hold down Shift and move the cursor to the last file.

To select individual nonsequential files:

FOLLOW
THESE
STEPS

1. Go to the first file.

2. Press Shift-F8. The word ADD appears in the status line.

3. Move to another file and press the space bar to select or deselect it.

4. Press Shift-F8 after all the files are selected. ADD disappears from the status line.

To deselect a file, just move to the file and press the space bar when ADD appears. If ADD does not appear when you press the space bar, all the files except the current are deselected.

FOLLOW
THESE
STEPS

To select multiple groups:

1. Go to the first file. Hold down Shift and move the cursor to the last file.

T I P S   A N D   T R I C K S

I N V I S I B L E   S E L E C T E D   F I L E S

You may have two or more files selected but are not aware of it. For example, if you click an item in the File List area, that file is automatically selected (marked with ▶). If you now click another directory and then click another file in the new directory, you have two files selected, one shown on the screen and the other not shown. This phenomenon can also happen if you use the keyboard to move the cursor to the File List area of different directories.

When two or more files are selected, you cannot show a file's contents by pressing F9. If you get a beep while trying to show the current file, chances are that you have another file selected somewhere. Press Ctrl-\ to deselect them all and press F9 again; the highlighted file will then be displayed.

When you copy, move, delete, rename, or associate files, the selected files will all appear. Pay attention to the displayed names. When deleting, you will also be asked to confirm each.

---

2. Press Shift-F8 to display ADD in the status line.

3. Go to the first file of the next group and press the space bar to select this file.

4. Hold down Shift and move the cursor to the last file of the group.

5. Repeat steps 3 and 4 as many times as necessary.

6. Press Shift-F8 to end.

Other Selections

To select files in multiple directories:

FOLLOW THESE STEPS

1. Open the Options menu.

2. Select Select Across Directories. A ♦ (diamond) appears before the command. (If you select this command another time, it is deactivated and the diamond disappears.)

3. Follow the previously explained methods to select files.

4. Go to another directory and repeat step 3.

When a directory is made current and the selected files in it are shown in the File List area, they will be marked and highlighted. When the directory is not current, its selected files are not shown.

> **Table 10.1**
>
> *Selecting Multiple Files*
>
> | Keystroke | Purpose |
> |---|---|
> | *These keys are used with the keyboard:* | |
> | Ctrl-/ | Select all the files in the current directory |
> | Ctrl-\ | Deselect all the selected files in all directories |
> | Shift-F8 | Begin ("Add" appears) or end multiple selections |
> | Space bar | Select or deselect a file when "Add" appears |
> | Shift-↑/↓ | Select a block of files. |
> | *These keys are used with the mouse:* | |
> | Shift | Define the end of a block |
> | Ctrl | Define the beginning of another block |
> | Ctrl-Shift | Define the end of the current block |

To select all the files in the current directory:

FOLLOW THESE STEPS

1. Go to the right directory and make the File List area active.

2. Open the File menu and select Select All; or press Ctrl-/.

3. To select all the files in another directory, select another directory and repeat step 2. (You need to make Select Across Directories in the Options menu active in order to select files in multiple directories.)

To deselect, either press Ctrl-\ or select Deselect All from the File menu. All the selections in all directories, regardless of whether they are displayed or not, are deselected.

The different procedures of selecting multiple files are summed up in Table 10.1.

P R A C T I C E   1 0 - 3

☐   1. Select EDIT.COM and DOSSHELL.COM in C:\DOS.

☐   2. Copy the above two selected files to A:\ABC.

☐   3. Move the above two files to A:\ABC\XYZ.

━━ *T I P S   A N D   T R I C K S* ━━

THE ADD MODE

The Shift-F8 key toggles between the ADD and regular modes. In the ADD mode, the ADD message appears in the status line when the File List area is active. This does not affect the mouse, but it surely changes the keyboard. In this mode, pressing the space bar selects or deselects the current file; it does not work that way when ADD is not displayed.

If you exit the Shell with the ADD mode on, it remains on after you start the Shell next time. In this case, there is no preselected file in the active directory and no ▶ appears on the screen. If you use the keyboard to go to the File List area of different directories, you can use a cursor key to move to different files and no file will be preselected. This is not the case when ADD is not displayed. Each time you move the cursor to the File List area of a directory, one file (marked with ▶) will be preselected. You could thus have several files selected and not know it.

☐   4. Make the above two files invisible.

☐   5. Delete all the files in A:\ABC\XYZ.

☐   6. Remove the two directories (A:\ABC and A:\ABC\XYZ).

CUSTOMIZING THE SCREEN

■ *Use the Options and View menus to customize screen colors, modes, and the items to be displayed.*

Various options of the Options and View menus can be used to customize the screen appearance and the way the Shell interacts with you.

If you work with a computer in your school lab, you should not change some of these options. If you do change them, you should restore their original conditions before you exit. When you exit, changes are saved to the DOSSHELL.INI file. When the next user restarts the Shell, the changes made by you will return and thus affect another person.[5]

---

5. One way to restore the original settings is to save the original DOSSHELL.INI file to a floppy disk or another directory. After you exit the Shell, copy this file to the C:\DOS directory to replace the one modified by you. The next user will then start with the original file.

Figure 10.5

The Options menu

```
Confirmation...
File Display Options...
Select Across Directories
Show Information...
Enable Task Swapper
Display...
Colors...
```

The Options Menu

When you open the Options menu, the available options appear as shown in Figure 10.5.

If you select Confirmation, you are given three choices:

```
[X] Confirm on Delete
[X] Confirm on Replace
[X] Confirm on Mouse Operation
```

By default, all the shown operations lead to your discretion, letting you choose Yes, No, or Cancel before an act is carried out. Unless you have a good reason to do otherwise, you should keep these default settings for safety.

Should you decide to change, click any X to select or deselect an item. From the keyboard, tab to this area and press ↑ or ↓ to the right item and press the space bar to select or deselect. Finally, select OK to accept any change or Cancel to restore the original.

Selecting the File Display Options leads to the display shown in Figure 10.6. This box lets you determine how files are to be displayed in the File List area.

If you want to display only certain files, those with the TXT extension for example, you can click or tab to the ellipsis and make changes. If you start typing, the existing text will disappear. If you want to edit it, press an arrow key to the second *, press Del to delete it, type TXT and press Enter.

If you want to display files in descending order and/or hidden/system files, click a proper selection box or tab to it and press the space bar to display X.

If you want files displayed in an order other than file names, click one of the options. Or tab to the area and press ↑ or ↓ to move the bullet to another area. If you choose DiskOrder, the files will be displayed in the same order as when you use DIR alone.

Figure 10.6

Various options for displaying files

```
┌──────────────── File Display Options ──────────────┐
│                                                     │
│  Name:     [*.*··········]                          │
│                                                     │
│                                 Sort by:            │
│                                                     │
│  [ ] Display hidden/system files    (●) Name        │
│                                     ( ) Extension    │
│                                     ( ) Date         │
│                                     ( ) Size         │
│  [ ] Descending order               ( ) DiskOrder    │
│                                                     │
│                                                     │
│           OK            Cancel          Help        │
│                                                     │
└─────────────────────────────────────────────────────┘
```

Figure 10.7

The Disk Information window

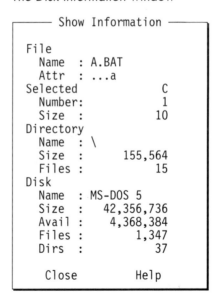

```
┌────── Show Information ──────┐
│                              │
│  File                        │
│    Name  : A.BAT             │
│    Attr  : ...a              │
│  Selected          C         │
│    Number:         1         │
│    Size  :        10         │
│  Directory                   │
│    Name  : \                 │
│    Size  :    155,564        │
│    Files :        15         │
│  Disk                        │
│    Name  : MS-DOS 5          │
│    Size  :  42,356,736       │
│    Avail :   4,368,384       │
│    Files :       1,347       │
│    Dirs  :          37       │
│                              │
│     Close        Help        │
│                              │
└──────────────────────────────┘
```

The Show Information option leads to a display shown in Figure 10.7. It shows information related to the current file, selected file(s), the current directory, and the current drive.

The Enable Task Swapper option is related to running programs; it will be explained in the next section.

The Display and Colors options let you switch among a variety of text and graphics modes and choose a color for text. Among the available options, you can click one or move the cursor up or down and press Enter to select one. Before you select the OK button to accept the new arrangement, select the Preview button to see what it will look like. Press Esc to return from the preview screen and continue to make your choice.

If you choose graphics mode, the rectangular mouse pointer becomes an arrow and various icons appear in front of each displayed item. Programs (with COM, EXE, and BAT extensions) are marked with one type of icons and other files with another type. A program item (see below) is marked with an empty folder and a program group with a filled folder. Finally, menu key letters are underlined as well as highlighted. Graphics mode requires more memory and works slower than text mode.

The View Menu

The View menu lets you alter the ways files are displayed on the screen. It provides the options as shown in Figure 10.8.

The Program/File Lists option is the default. As shown in Figure 10.1, both files and programs are shown. The Single File List option eliminates the Program List area, with its space taken up on the left by Directory Tree and on the right by File List. The Dual File Lists option splits the Single File List arrangement horizontally, thus permitting concurrent display of two separate directories. The Program List option, on the other hand, eliminates the Directory Tree and File List areas and uses the space for listing programs.

Figure 10.8

The View menu

```
┌─────────────────────────────┐
│  Single File List           │
│  Dual File Lists            │
│  All Files                  │
│  Program/File Lists         │
│  Program List               │
├─────────────────────────────┤
│  Repaint Screen  Shift+F5   │
│  Refresh         F5         │
└─────────────────────────────┘
```

The All Files option splits the screen vertically, with the right side displaying all the files in the current directory and the left side showing information pertinent to the current file, similar to the one shown in Figure 10.7.

The last two options of the View menu redraw the screen (to erase some screen remnants of a TSR program), and updates the screen by rereading the current disk so that newly created files or directories can be displayed.

P R A C T I C E   1 0 - 4

1. Change file display options to show only files with the BAT extension and sorted according to date with most recent files first.

2. Restore the original file display options.

3. Select the option to show two directories. Show C:\DOS in the top window and A:\ in the bottom.

4. Restore the default view options.

D R I L L

15. Multiple files can be selected only in a single directory, but not in multiple directories. True or false?

16. This key combination deselects all the files in all the directories:
    a. Ctrl-/
    b. Ctrl-\
    c. Shift-F8
    d. Shift-space bar

17. To display the contents of two directories, you need to select this from the View menu:
    a. Single File List
    b. Dual File Lists
    c. All Files
    d. Program/File List
    e. Program List

MANAGING PROGRAMS

■ *Start a program by double clicking it or highlighting it and pressing Enter.*

■ *Start a program by opening a data file already associated with the program.*

■ *Associate a program and a data file by highlighting either and entering a file name extension or program name.*

■ *Launch several programs and use available keys to switch from one to another.*

■ *Create or modify a program item or program group so that the Shell can launch a program with all the required information.*

Besides the many things discussed so far, the Shell is also a program launcher and task switcher. You can use it to launch multiple programs and switch from one to another. While you work with one active program, the others stay dormant in the background, ready for you to make active by pressing a couple of keystrokes.

Starting a Program

Before we explore various ways of starting a program, let us run a few programs so that you can get a feel of how easy it is. Follow these steps:

FOLLOW THESE STEPS

1. Open Command Prompt (double click or highlight it and press Enter) in the Program List area. The command prompt appears. You can now enter any DOS command or run another program.

┌─────────────── *T I P S   A N D   T R I C K S* ───────────────┐

P R I N T I N G   F I L E S

You can use the Print command from the File menu to print files. As files are being printed, you can continue to work with the Shell.

The Shell uses an external program named PRINT.EXE to manage printing. You must run this program before you can print files. The program can be run from the Shell just as any other program. Chapter 7 provides details related to this program.

After PRINT.EXE is put in memory, you can begin to send files to its print queue. Just select files and select Print from the File menu.

└──┘

2. Enter EXIT. The Shell reappears.

3. Open [Disk Utilities]. A list of names appears, including [Main]. You can open any of these to execute a command.

4. Open [Main]. The Main group reappears in the Program List area.

5. Open Editor. You are asked to enter a file to edit. Press Enter for editing no file.

6. A welcome message appears. Press Esc to clear it. You are now in the DOS Editor.

7. Open the File menu (press Alt and F) and select Exit. You are back to the Shell.

There are four ways to start a program. These are:

- From the Program List area, open a program, as demonstrated in the above steps. This is the most straightforward way. You can also use the Open command in the File menu to run a highlighted program.

- From the File menu, select the Run command and enter a program name. This is similar to selecting Command Prompt and then entering a program name on the command line. The only difference is that you press any key rather than enter EXIT to return to the Shell.

- From the File List area, open an executable program (one with a COM, EXE, or BAT extension). You can double click a program or highlight it and press Enter.

- From the File List area, open a data file which has previously been associated with a program. This is explained below.

Associating Files and Programs

Many application programs, such as a spreadsheet or a word processor, allow you to enter the program name and a file name at the same time; as soon as the program is loaded, the named data file is retrieved. This can also be done from the Shell. This requires associating one or more files with a program. Once the association is established, you can open a matching data file to simultaneously load the program and retrieve the file.

There are two ways to associate a program with some data files. You can work with a program or with a file. Follow these steps to work with a program:

FOLLOW THESE STEPS

1. Select the C:\DOS directory.

2. Highlight EDIT.COM in the File List area.

3. Open the File menu and select Associate. A box titled Associate File appears, showing these two lines:

```
Filename.  .  EDIT.COM
Extensions. .  [·······]
```

4. Enter TXT. The box disappears.

5. Repeat step 3 to show the newly entered extension. Press Esc to continue.

6. Scroll the File List area until README.TXT appears. Highlight it.

7. Repeat step 3. The screen shows a similar Associate File box with these two lines:

```
".TXT" files are associated with:
[C:\DOS\EDIT.COM····]
```

8. Press Esc. The box disappears.

9. Double click or press Enter on the highlighted README.TXT file. The Editor is loaded and the file is retrieved.

10. Select Exit from the Editor's File menu.

If you now open any file with the TXT extension, the Editor will be loaded and that particular file retrieved for you to edit.

TIPS AND TRICKS

EDITING BATCH FILES

If you write batch files often, it will be most convenient if you can just open a batch file to load the Editor and retrieve that file simultaneously.

You cannot start the association process by highlighting a batch file. If you do that, you are asking the Shell to associate this batch file (which is treated as an executable program) with one or more data files.

Since you want your batch files treated as data files, not as program files, you must highlight EDIT.COM (or EDLIN.EXE) and enter the BAT extension as the kind of data files you want to associate with the program. After that, you can simply open any file with a BAT extension to load the Editor and retrieve that batch file.

After the above association, you can no longer open a batch file to execute it. To enable you to execute a batch file, you must dissociate BAT from EDIT.COM. Highlight EDIT.COM and select Associate from the File menu. Erase BAT and select OK.

In step 4 above, you can enter multiple extensions separated with a space. For example, you can enter this:

Extensions. . [**txt doc dat wk1**·····]

You can even enter a single period (.). That means any file will be considered matching. Anytime you open a file with or without an extension, the Editor will be loaded and that particular file will be retrieved.

Instead of working with a program and associating files with it, you can work with a file and associate a program with it. You highlight a data file and select Associate from the File menu. After the dialog box appears, as shown in step 7, enter a program name with a proper directory path. Both methods produce the same result.

If you want to disassociate a program from its files, just erase the program or file extension(s) when they appear (as shown in step 7). Then press Enter or select OK.

Switching Among Programs

The Shell allows you to load two or more programs and switch from one to another. To do this job, the Shell relies on the DOSSWAP.EXE program. To activate this program, you need to open the Options menu and select Enable Task Swapper. A ♦ (diamond) appears before it. After that, the Program List area is split into two, one titled Main and the other Active Task List, as shown in Figure 10.9.

After the Task Swapper is enabled, follow these steps to run two programs:

FOLLOW THESE STEPS

1. Run Editor by double clicking it or highlighting it and pressing Enter. Type something in the screen.

Figure 10.9

The Program List window is split into two after the Task Swapper is enabled

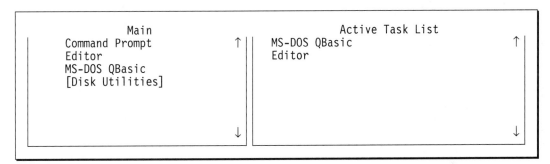

Table 10.2

Task-Switching Keys

Keystroke	Purpose
Ctrl-Esc	Return to the Shell
Alt-Tab	Switch from one program to another
Alt-Esc	Go to the next program
Shift-Alt-Esc	Go to the previous program
Shift-Enter	(Or Shift-double click) Place a program in the Active Task List;

2. Press Ctrl-Esc to go to the Shell screen. Notice Editor appearing in the Active Task List.

3. Run MS-DOS QBasic. Type something in this screen.

4. Repeat step 2. Notice another addition in the Active Task List.

The two programs are now in memory. You can switch from one to the other or to the Shell by using one of the key combinations in Table 10.2.

If you forget these keys, open the Help menu, select Index and then Active Task List Keys to show a list of keys and how each is used.

To cycle from one program to another in the Active Task List, hold down Alt and press Tab without releasing Alt. After a while, a program name appears in a separate screen. If this is the program you want to go to, release Alt. If not, press Tab to display the name of the next program.

To place a program in the Active Task List, highlight its name in either the File List or Program List area and press Shift-Enter or hold down Shift and double click the name. Once placed in this list, you can use the key combinations shown in Table 10.2 to reach it.

As long as there is at least one program in the Active Task List, you cannot exit the Shell by selecting Exit from the File menu. A warning message appears instead. You can go back to each active program and exit properly. You can also highlight a program and press Del. A warning message appears. If you then select OK, the program is deleted from this list (but not from the disk).

Figure 10.10

The File menu of Program List

```
New...
Open            Enter
Copy
Delete...       Del
Properties...
Reorder

Run...

Exit            Alt+F4
```

The Program List's File Menu

When the Program List area is active, opening the File menu leads to a display shown in Figure 10.10. This menu is different from the one shown in Figure 10.2, which appears when the File List area is active. It is used to manage programs rather than files.

Open, Run, Delete, and Exit work the same way as their counterparts on the File menu of the File List. You can use Copy to copy from one group to another. Suppose you want to copy Editor to the Disk Utilities group. First, highlight Editor, and then select Copy from the File menu. The status line displays this message:

> Display the group to copy to, then press F2. Press Esc to cancel.

Now open the [Disk Utilities] group (double click or highlight it and press Enter) and move the cursor to the desired place in the list. Press F2 and Editor enters the cursor location. You can now delete either one by highlighting it, pressing Del, and selecting OK.

Reorder is used to rearrange the order of the programs shown in the Program List area. To do that, highlight the name you want to move to another place, open the File menu and select Reorder, and finally double click another location or move the cursor there and press Enter.

New and Properties are used to add a program item or a program group to the Program List. A **program item** contains all the necessary information to launch a program. A **program group** is a group of program items. As shown in [Disk Utilities], it contains a number of program names. You can create a new group like that or add new items to or remove old items from an existing group.

Adding a Program Item

The steps below add a new program item to the Program List. We assume that you want to use the Shell to run Lotus 1-2-3:

FOLLOW
THESE
STEPS

1. Move the cursor to a desired location in the Program List area.

2. Open the File menu and select New. Two choices appear:

   ```
   ( ) Program Group
   (•) Program Item
   ```

3. Choose Program Item, which is the default; you can click the other box or press ↑ or ↓ to move the bullet. A dialog box titled Add Program appears as shown in Figure 10.11.

4. Type entries as shown. After you complete each area, press Tab/Shift-Tab or ↑/↓ (not Enter) to go to each ellipsis area. In the Shortcut Key area, hold down Ctrl-Shift and press 1. Press Enter or select OK after all the entries are made. The dialog box disappears and the program title you have supplied appears in the Program List area.

If you now open Lotus 1-2-3, the startup directory becomes the current directory and the program specified in the Commands box is loaded; the 1-2-3 screen appears after a while (assuming 1-2-3 files are stored in the C:\123 directory). You can press Ctrl-Esc to return to the Shell screen. If Enable Task Swapper in the Options menu has been selected, the program item's name will also appear in the Active Task List. You can also press the shortcut key (Ctrl-Shift-1) to return to 1-2-3.

Figure 10.11

The entries (properties) to add a program item

```
┌─────────────────────── Add Program ───────────────────────┐
│                                                            │
│  Program Title . . . . [Lotus 1-2-3······················] │
│                                                            │
│  Commands  . . . . . . [c:\123\123·······················] │
│                                                            │
│  Startup Directory . . [c:\123···························]  │
│                                                            │
│  Application Shortcut Key      [CTRL+SHIFT+!        ····]   │
│                                                            │
│  [X] Pause after exit      Password . .  [123··········]   │
│                                                            │
│         OK          Cancel          Help        Advanced...│
│                                                            │
└────────────────────────────────────────────────────────────┘
```

Managing Properties

If you select Properties from the File menu after the above steps and with Lotus 1-2-3 still highlighted, you will be required to enter the exact password (123). After that, Figure 10.11 reappears. You can now make any changes.

You can enter a title up to 23 characters (including spaces), a command up to 255 characters, a startup directory up to 66 characters, and a password up to 20 characters. When the limit is reached, your PC beeps and no more characters are accepted. You can use Home, End, →, or ← to move the cursor to different parts of a long string.

There are restrictions in entering a shortcut key. Do not use C, H, I, M, [, or 5 (on the numeric keypad) in combination with Ctrl or Shift-Ctrl; these may lead to no response or to an immediate action. A single key alone, such as a letter or function key, cannot be used; pressing such a key leads to no response on the screen. Combining Ctrl, Alt, and/or Shift with a function, letter, or number key is a good choice. When you are ready to get rid of a shortcut key, move to the box and press Del or Backspace; (none), the default, reappears.

A command can include one or more replaceable parameters. You can even enter multiple commands in the Commands box, like these:

```
edit %1 ; copy %1 a: ; del %1
```

Each command must be separated from another with a semicolon, which in turn must be preceded and followed by one or more spaces. In our example, you will be required to enter a file name when EDIT is run. This file will be saved to the current directory when you exit EDIT, copied to drive A, and deleted from the current directory. You can also use CALL to nest batch files, like this:

```
call bat1 ; edit %1 ; call bat2
```

In this case, BAT1.BAT will be executed before EDIT and BAT2.BAT after it.

If you supply replaceable parameters in the Commands box, a dialog box named Program Item Properties will appear as many times as the number of replaceable parameters; Figure 10.12 shows an example; notice the %1 near the top. You are then asked to supply more related information. This information appears when you try to use a program item.

Have you ever used the Backup Fixed Disk item in the [Disk Utilities] group? A screen pops up to solicit parameters, as shown in Figure 10.13. Do you know where this screen comes from? Do you know how to create such a screen? If you study Figure 10.13 carefully, you will find the information shown here comes from Figure 10.12. When you use this program item (Backup Fixed Disk), the default parameters are displayed and highlighted; you can press Enter to accept

Figure 10.12

The dialog box showing program item properties

```
─────────────────── Program Item Properties ───────────────────
┌──────────────────────────────────────────────────────────────┐
│  Fill in information for % 1    prompt dialog.                 │
│                                                                │
│  Window Title  . . . .    [Backup Fixed Disk················]  │
│                                                                │
│  Program Information .    [Enter the source and destination ] │
│                                                                │
│  Prompt Message  . . .    [Parameters . . .················]   │
│                                                                │
│     Default Parameters . .    [c:\*.* a: /s················]   │
│                                                                │
│           OK               Cancel              Help            │
└──────────────────────────────────────────────────────────────┘
```

Figure 10.13

The default parameters when using a program item

```
─────────────────── Backup Fixed Disk ───────────────────
┌─────────────────────────────────────────────────────────┐
│  Enter the source and destination drives.                │
│                                                           │
│  Parameters . . .    [c:\*.* a: /s··················]     │
│        OK               Cancel              Help          │
└─────────────────────────────────────────────────────────┘
```

them. This can save you time if the parameters are relatively fixed. You can, however, change the parameters before Enter is pressed.

Advanced Properties

Have you noticed the Advanced option in the Add Program dialog box, as shown in Figure 10.11? Selecting it leads to Figure 10.14.

In the Help Text box you can enter up to 255 characters (including spaces). You can also insert ^M (caret, then m or M) to force a new line in the displayed help message. When this program item is highlighted in the Program List area, you can press F1 to display the help text you have entered.

The second and third lines let you enter memory numbers in kilobytes. These numbers are ignored unless the Task Swapper is enabled. Do not enter

Figure 10.14

The Advanced option from the Add Program dialog box

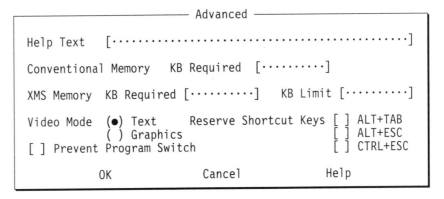

numbers here unless your programs require them. XMS is for extended memory; specifying a limit prevents a loaded program from taking all the available extended memory.

Video Mode can be switched from the default Text to Graphics by clicking either box or using an arrow key to move the bullet. Graphics mode requires more memory and runs slower.

You can check Prevent Program Switch by clicking it or pressing the space bar to display X. This prevents you from switching to the Shell or another program; you must then exit the program to return to the Shell.

Reserve Shortcut Keys shows three key combinations used by the Shell to switch tasks. If you check any of them, the Shell can no longer use it. This may be necessary if your program uses it for another purpose and you want to use the key for that purpose.

Adding and Deleting a Program Group

To create a program group, select Program Group in step 2 in the Adding a Program Item section discussed earlier. A dialog box like the one shown in Figure 10.15 appears. Type the title. Tab to the Help Text area and type help text. Enter a password if you wish. Pressing Enter or selecting OK completes the job and add [Disk/Memory Check] to the Program List area.

To add a program item to this new program group, open the group (select Open from the File menu, double click it, or highlight it and press Enter). Then follow the four steps discussed earlier to add program items.

You can also highlight a program item or program group and select Properties in the File menu to display its properties. If a password has been added, you will

Figure 10.15

The dialog box for adding a program group

```
┌──────────────────── Add Group ────────────────────┐
│                                                    │
│   Required                                         │
│                                                    │
│    Title . . . .      [Disk/Memory Check···]       │
│                                                    │
│   Optional                                         │
│                                                    │
│    Help Text . .      [are two programs in·]       │
│                                                    │
│    Password  . .      [···········]                │
│                                                    │
│                                                    │
│         OK            Cancel          Help         │
│                                                    │
└────────────────────────────────────────────────────┘
```

not be allowed to view its properties unless a matching password (including case and spelling) is supplied. You can also alter the displayed entries by clicking or tabbing to a proper box and make changes. Choose OK to save the changes or Cancel to abort.

You can also delete a program item or program group. To delete an item, highlight it and press Del. Select OK to accept. After all the items are deleted, you can then delete a group. If a group is not empty, you cannot delete it, just as you are not allowed to remove a non-empty directory.

T I P S   A N D   T R I C K S

THE EDITOR AND REPLACEABLE PARAMETER

Whenever you start the Editor from the Shell, you are first required to enter a file name to edit. If you enter nothing (pressing Enter alone), the Editor will greet you with a welcome message and ask you to press Enter for a survival guide or Esc to get a blank screen.

Is there a way to go directly to the blank screen without all the hassle? Yes. The key lies in the Add Program screen (see Figure 10.11). Replace the replaceable parameter in the original entry of EDIT %1 with a file name. For example, you can supply EDIT UNTITLED and select OK to accept the change. When you open the Editor next time, you will be taken straight to its blank screen—unless a file named UNTITLED exists, in which case it will be retrieved and displayed on the screen.

The program items or groups you create will be saved when you exit. They will be displayed when you use the Shell in the future. If the Task Swapper was enabled in the previous session, the Active Task List window will also appear. This arrangement is convenient if you use the Shell as a task switcher.

P R A C T I C E   1 0 - 5

☐   1. Place the DOS-TA disk in drive A and print the SAMPLE.TXT file.

☐   2. Create a program group named MYGROUP.

☐   3. Add a program item to MYGROUP. It should be named CHECK DISK A. Drive A should be checked when this item is opened.

☐   4. Use CHECK DISK A.

☐   5. Place [MYGROUP] at the top in the Program List area.

☐   6. Delete MYGROUP.

☐   7. Associate EDIT.COM with files of the TXT extension.

☐   8. Open SAMPLE.TXT in drive A for editing. Exit the Editor.

D R I L L

Each key combination below is used to:

a. Ctrl-Esc b. Alt-Esc c. Alt-Tab d. Shift-Enter

____   18. Switch from one program to another.

____   19. Return to the Shell screen.

____   20. Switch to the next program.

____   21. Place a program in the Active Task List.

____   22. If a name in the Program List area appears in a pair of brackets, it signifies a:
   a. program item
   b. program group
   c. replaceable parameter
   d. password protection

U S I N G   T H E   D O S   E D I T O R

The DOS Editor, available since version 5, is a full-screen text editor. A full-screen editor is much easier to use than a line editor such as EDLIN, which is available with all versions of DOS before 6.0.

The Editor's screen closely resembles that of the Shell, including the menu bar at the top, the status line at the bottom, and the scroll bar and box.

There are a few exceptions. First, there is also a scroll bar/box at the bottom of the screen. Second, the right bottom corner of the screen shows two numbers (for line and column) indicating the cursor position. Third, you can access the menus only with Alt, but not F10. Fourth, you can no longer exit by pressing F3 or Alt-F4.

Pay occasional attention to a small area in the status line between the bottom scroll bar and the cursor-position numbers. It may display C (when Caps Lock is on), N (when Num Lock is on), ^K, ^P, and ^Q; one of the last three appears when a corresponding key is pressed while holding down Ctrl.

The Editor is a text editor, not a word processor. It can produce only ASCII text, which contains no formatting characters. There is no word wrap at the end of each line, so you must press Enter to end a line. A line can be up to 255 characters long.

STARTING AND EXITING THE EDITOR

■   *Start the Editor by entering EDIT with or without an accompanying data file name. Exit by selecting Exit from the File menu.*

If you have become thoroughly familiar with the Shell, you should have an easy time learning to use the Editor. If you have used the text editor in QuickC or QuickBasic, there is no need for you to learn anything new.

You can start the Editor from the Shell, as amply illustrated in previous sections. If you want to bypass the Shell, you can start it on the command line, like this:

```
C:\DOS>edit filename
```

The Editor needs the QBASIC.EXE program to work. Unless you have provided a search path to this program's directory, you must run EDIT.COM from the directory where QBASIC.EXE is stored.

If a file name is entered as an argument, this file is retrieved if it exists. If the file does not exist, no retrieval is done and only the name is displayed in the title bar. If no file name is provided, the title bar displays "Untitled". If you save (using the Save command), you will be asked to enter a name.

The program can be started with one of the four switches: /B, /G, /H, and /NOHI. See the online help (EDIT /?) for their uses.

Exiting the Editor requires you to select Exit from the File menu; F3 and Alt-F4 are not available for this purpose. If you have added text that has not been saved, you will be asked Yes or No to save the alteration; you can press Y or N as a shortcut.

USING THE EDITOR'S MENUS

■ *Activate the menu bar by pressing Alt. Other techniques used in the Shell also apply here.*

The menus of the Editor also resemble those of the Shell; the only difference is that you can press only Alt but not F10 from the keyboard to activate the menu bar. This section gets you familiar with the menus and the next will let you get into action with these commands.

The menu bar shows these options:

```
File  Edit  Search  Options  Help
```

The File menu leads to Figure 10.16. As you highlight each command, notice the status line showing a brief message for it; you can also press F1 to show a more detailed explanation. New clears the screen without saving. Open retrieves a file, replacing any existing contents. Save saves the current text using the existing name shown in the title bar. Save As lets you save the current text to another file name. Print lets you print text. And Exit lets you leave the Editor.

The Edit menu contains the commands as shown in Figure 10.17. These are used to delete selected text (Clear), to copy, or to **cut and paste**. Copy saves to

Figure 10.16

The File menu

```
┌─────────────────┐
│ New             │
│ Open...         │
│ Save            │
│ Save As...      │
├─────────────────┤
│ Print...        │
├─────────────────┤
│ Exit            │
└─────────────────┘
```

Figure 10.17

The Edit menu

```
┌──────────────────────┐
│ Cut      Shift+Del    │
│ Copy      Ctrl+Ins    │
│ Paste    Shift+Ins    │
│ Clear         Del     │
└──────────────────────┘
```

Figure 10.18

The Search menu

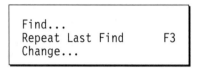

```
Find...
Repeat Last Find        F3
Change...
```

Figure 10.19

The dialog box for changing display options

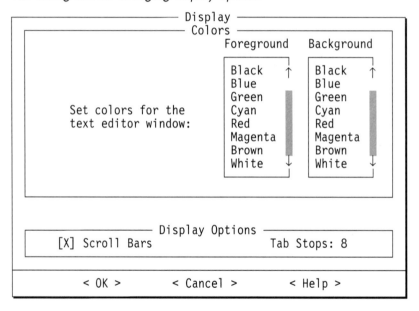

the **clipboard**[6] a copy of the selected text without deleting it. Cut deletes the text and saves it to the clipboard. After Cut or Copy, you can move the cursor to another location and paste the text. Cut-and-paste in effect moves text from one location to another.

The Search menu provides three options as shown Figure 10.18. They can be used to search for text strings or replace one string with another.

The Options menu has two options: Display and Help Path. The latter lets you enter a directory path to the EDIT.HLP file; do nothing if it is stored in the same directory as EDIT.COM. The Display option leads to Figure 10.19.

---

6. This is a memory buffer used to store temporary data. While some programs have multiple buffers, the Editor has only one. It also lacks undo or undelete buffers available in many software packages.

In this screen, you can click or tab to different areas to make changes. You can change the default white foreground and blue background colors; as you make changes, the left side shows what the screen will look like. If you deselect Scroll Bars, the scroll bars disappear. If you change Tab Stops to another number, 5 for example, pressing Tab moves the cursor by that many (5) characters.

CURSOR MOVEMENT

■ *Use numerous available cursor-movement techniques to speed up your work.*

When you have a large file, you can use some special keystrokes to move the cursor quickly to the desired location. Some of the keystrokes used in DOSKEY can be used here also. The most useful keystrokes are shown in Table 10.3.

If you are used to WordStar's cryptic key combinations, you can use most of them in the Editor. Go to the Help screen, select Keyboard, and then look into Cursor-Movement Keys and Text-Scrolling Keys for examples.

Table 10.3

Cursor-Movement Keys

Keystroke	Move the Cursor to
Ctrl-→	One word right
Ctrl-←	One word left
Ctrl-PgUp	One screen left (scrolling text)
Ctrl-PgDn	One screen right (scrolling text)
Home	Beginning of the current line
End	End of the current line
Ctrl-Home	Top of the file
Ctrl-End	End of the file
Ctrl-Enter	Beginning of next line
Ctrl-Q, E	Top of the current window
Ctrl-Q, X	Bottom of the current window

TIPS AND TRICKS

BOOKMARKS AND CURSOR MOVEMENT

You can insert in various text areas invisible numbers of 0-3 known as bookmarks. You can then quickly move the cursor to a specific location by entering a matching number.

To insert a bookmark, move the cursor to the desired location in the text, press Ctrl-K (^K appears in the status line), type a number 0-3 (^K disappears). The number does not appear on the screen.

To move the cursor to a bookmark location, press Ctrl-Q (^Q appears in the status line) and type a number matching the bookmark location (^Q disappears). The cursor immediately goes to the specified bookmark location.

You can have up to four active bookmarks. When an old number is reassigned, it is identified with the new location.

If you have a mouse, use the arrows and scroll boxes on the right and at the bottom to scroll up and down or left and right. The techniques you learned in the Shell can also be applied here.

MANAGING HELP

- *Press F1 if you want help related to the current task.*
- *Open the Help menu if you want to explore various topics.*
- *Press F6 to switch between a help window and the regular editing screen.*

Getting help from the Editor is just as easy as from the Shell. Press F1 to see more information about the current task or open the Help menu to explore various topics.

If you press F1, a pop-up window appears in the middle of the screen. Press Esc or select the OK button to erase it when you are done. The Editor's context-sensitive help, unlike its counterpart in the Shell, lacks hypertext capabilities. Each help frame is a separate entity which is not linked to other frames.

The Help menu, on the contrary, has hypertext capabilities, although more limited than the Shell's. An item that can lead to other related frames is enclosed between ◄ and ►. You can double click it or press tab (Tab/Shift-Tab) to it and press Enter.

A help window (from the Help menu only) and the regular text screen can be displayed simultaneously, with the former at the top and the latter at the bottom. If you find a help window useful and want to display it while you edit text, press F6 to switch between the editing screen and the help window. (Pressing Esc will erase the help window.) You can also press Alt-– (minus) to reduce the current window's size or Alt-+ (plus) to enlarge it. As you reduce the current window's size, the other window appears or is enlarged.

Veteran users of Microsoft's QuickC or QuickBasic should know this trick: text from a help window can be copied to the regular screen. To do so, select the portion you want to copy and send it to the clipboard (Ctrl-Ins). Return to the regular screen and paste it (Shift-Ins); see below for techniques of selecting and pasting text.

You can also print help text by a selected portion or the entire current frame. To do so, move the cursor to a help window, open the File menu, and select one of the two options. If you choose to print the whole frame, the whole frame, including the title and any undisplayed portion, is printed. If you want to print only selected text, select text first and then open the File menu.

The above steps can also be applied to printing the text in the regular screen. Unlike in the Shell, here you do not need to run PRINT.EXE before printing text.

You can move quickly to different help frames by pressing the keys shown in Table 10.4.

Table 10.4

Help Keys

Keystrokes	Effect
Tab	Move to next help topic
Shift-Tab	Move to previous help topic
Character	Move to next frame matching the first character
Shift-Char	Move to previous frame matching first character
Alt-F1	Show the previously viewed help frame
Ctrl-F1	Show the next help frame in the Help file
Shift-Ctrl-F1	Show the previous frame in the Help file
Ctrl-+/–	Enlarge/reduce the current window
F6	Switch between a help window and editing screen

OPENING A FILE

■ *If no data file accompanied the EDIT command, you can use the Open*
option from the File menu to retrieve an existing file to edit.

When you are ready to open (retrieve) an existing file to edit, open the File
menu and select Open. The current directory's contents appear as shown in
Figure 10.20.

Notice the current directory and the default file name pattern. All the files
matching *.TXT in the C:\DOS directory are displayed in the Files box. This box
has a scroll bar/box that allows you to scroll left or right to show more
undisplayed files; you can also press Ctrl-PgUp or Ctrl-PgDn. The right box
shows available drives and any subdirectories of the current directory; you can
scroll up or down to view undisplayed items.

At the outset, the cursor stays in the File Name box, where you can type a new
name. As you type, the existing name disappears. You can also edit it by
pressing Backspace or an arrow key.

You can move the cursor to another box by pressing Tab (forward) or Shift-Tab
(reverse). Once in a box, you can use ↑, ↓, PgUp, PgDn, Home, or End to show
more items or highlight an item. If you highlight a new drive or directory and
press Enter, all the matching files will be displayed in the Files box. If you then
select OK, the drive or directory will become current. If you select Cancel
instead, the previous arrangement will not change.

Figure 10.20

The dialog box for opening a data file

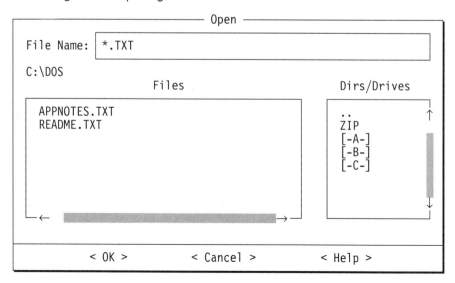

If you have a mouse, just click a file or drive to highlight it. Double click it to open.

Follow these steps to open a file from drive A:

1. Place the DOS-TA disk in drive A.

2. Open the File menu and select Open.

3. Press Backspace to delete TXT and type *; this box now has *.* remaining.

4. Double click [-A-]; or tab to Dirs/Drives box, press ↓ to highlight [-A-] and press Enter. All the files in drive A are now displayed.

5. Double click SAMPLE.TXT; or tab there, highlight the name, and press Enter.

Instead of going through all the above steps, you can simply enter A:SAMPLE.TXT at step 3 to open the file and make A the current drive.

Our sample text now appears on the screen as shown below:

```
This is a sample text file. It is to be used for
demonstrating some DOS commands.

This file has no importance. It can be copied,
altered, and deleted after you have made use
of it.

You will learn in later chapters how to create
and alter a file like this.
```

TIPS AND TRICKS

MERGING FILES

The text editor in Microsoft's Quick language series has a Merge option in the File menu. It is not available in the DOS Editor. This option lets you bring multiple files to the current document. Without this option, you can use Open to bring only one file to memory, which in turn replaces the old file.

What if you want to bring a new file to memory without erasing the one already there? One thing you can do is to use the COPY command to combine files before opening them for editing; this was discussed in Chapter 6.

Another way is to use the clipboard to store the old file. Select the portion you want to store in the clipboard and then press Shift-Del or Ctrl-Ins. Open another file. While the old file in the regular screen is cleared, the clipboard still holds a copy you have put there. Now move the cursor to a proper location in the new file and paste (Shift-Ins) the old file there. The two files are now merged.

SEARCH AND REPLACE

■   *Use the Search menu to find matching strings or replace them with something else.*

With the SAMPLE.TXT file on the screen, we are ready to manipulate the text. Follow these steps to search for strings:

FOLLOW THESE STEPS

1. With the cursor still at the beginning of the file, select Find from the Search menu. The Find dialog box (similar to Figure 10.21, minus the Change To box) appears. The current word "This" also appears in the Find What box.

2. Type "file" and press Enter; or type the word and select <OK>. The first matching word is highlighted.

3. Press F3 repeatedly to move the cursor to the next matching word.

To replace strings, you need to supply a search string and a replace string. After selecting Change from the Search menu, two boxes require your entries, as shown in Figure 10.21.

Here you need to type the first string (do not press Enter unless you have already supplied a replace string), tab to the box below and type the second string and press Enter to start the default action as highlighted below. If you enter the strings as shown in Figure 10.21, you intend to replace all "file" strings with "document".

The <Find and Verify> action is the default and highlighted. When a matching string is found, you will be asked to choose Change, Skip, or Cancel. To change, you can press C or Enter; to skip (no change), press S.

Figure 10.21

The dialog box for replacing strings

```
┌──────────────────────── Change ────────────────────────┐
│                                                         │
│  Find What: ┌─────────────────────────────────────────┐ │
│             │ file                                    │ │
│             └─────────────────────────────────────────┘ │
│                                                         │
│  Change To: ┌─────────────────────────────────────────┐ │
│             │ document                                │ │
│             └─────────────────────────────────────────┘ │
│                                                         │
│     [ ] Match Upper/Lowercase        [ ] Whole Word     │
│                                                         │
├─────────────────────────────────────────────────────────┤
│  < Find and Verify > < Change All > < Cancel > < Help > │
└─────────────────────────────────────────────────────────┘
```

If you want to change all the matching strings, select <Change All> after typing the required strings. You will not be asked to confirm each change.

If you want to delete a string, just leave the Change To box blank. Combine this operation with the <Change All> action with care. You can delete many entries without meaning to. Since there is no undo feature, your action is irreversible.

If you want an operation to be case sensitive, check the Match Upper/Lowercase. In that case, "File" will not match "file".

If you want to match whole words, check the Whole Word box. In that case, "defile" or "filer" will not match "file".

SELECTING TEXT

■ *Hold down Shift as you move the cursor to select and highlight text lines.*
Delete, cut, or copy the selected lines.

When you need to manipulate a portion of text, you need to select it. The selected text can then be deleted, copied, or moved.

FOLLOW
THESE
STEPS

To select text, you need to:

1. Move the cursor to one end.

2. Hold down Shift.

TIPS AND TRICKS

INDENTING TEXT LINES

The Editor, culled from Microsoft's Quick language series, is intended for programmers. Programmers like to indent the program lines in the same group to a uniform level to make the code more readable. The Editor's indenting behavior is intended to make it easy to keep the same group together.

As an illustration, place the cursor at the beginning of a blank line and press Tab once or press the space bar several times. If you now press Enter after typing something, the cursor does not return to the left margin. Instead, it stays in the same vertical position as the beginning of the previous line. If you want to return to the left margin, you need to press Backspace.

After you have entered lines, you can also quickly indent a group of consecutive lines to any position. Just select the lines and press Tab as many times as necessary.

A group of indented lines can also be made flush left. Just select the lines and press Shift-Tab. All the lines will now begin from the left margin.

3. Move the cursor to the other end.

After text is selected, use a shortcut key or menu option to do something. Selected text becomes highlighted. Moving the cursor causes the highlight to disappear.

With a mouse, you can drag the mouse pointer from one line to another to select text lines.

EDIT, COPY, AND PASTE

■   *Use Shift-Del to cut, Ctrl-Ins to copy, and Shift-Ins to paste.*

The Edit menu can be used to delete, copy, or move text. All the options in this menu have shortcut keys, which are easier to use than opening the menu.

Some of the keystrokes used in DOSKEY for editing text can be applied to the Editor. Use Backspace to delete one character to the left and Del to the right. Use Ins to toggle between the default insert mode and typeover mode; the cursor will be enlarged in the latter state.

With the SAMPLE.TXT file retrieved, follow these steps to demonstrate copying, cutting/pasting, and deleting text:

FOLLOW THESE STEPS

1. Move the cursor to the beginning (Ctrl-Home).

2. Hold down Shift and press ↓ three times (or click the blank line). The first paragraph is now selected and highlighted.

3. Press Shift-Del or select Cut from the Edit menu. The first paragraph disappears.

4. Go to the end (Ctrl-End) and press Enter to create a new line.

5. Press Shift-Ins or select Paste from the Edit menu. The cut paragraph reappears at the new location.

If you press Ctrl-Ins in step 3, the paragraph will not disappear. A copy, however, will still be saved to the clipboard. You can then move the cursor to a new location and press Shift-Ins to duplicate it. With either method, the clipboard still holds the text. You can thus make as many duplicates as you wish. When a new copy is sent to the clipboard, it replaces the old.

If you select a block of text and press Del (or select Clear from the Edit menu), its contents are not stored in the clipboard. You can no longer bring it back. There is no undo (or undelete) feature like the one you find in many other software packages.

You can also use Ctrl-Y to move the entire current line to the clipboard, or Ctrl-Q and Y to do the same thing for the text from the cursor to the end of the line. The text can then be pasted somewhere else.

If a block of text is selected, pasting (Shift-Ins) replaces the highlighted text with the contents from the clipboard. The replaced text can no longer be brought back.

SAVING A FILE

■ *Use Save from the File menu to save over the existing file and Save As to write to a new file.*

There are three ways to save a file. If you select Exit from the File menu, you will be prompted to choose Yes or No to save. This happens if you have made alterations that have not been saved. If you choose Yes, the latest version is saved before exit; if you choose No, the previous version is kept.

Beware of the difference between Save and Save As in the File menu. Save lets you save the latest version using the existing file name, thus erasing the file's

T I P S   A N D   T R I C K S

I N S E R T I N G   S P E C I A L   C H A R A C T E R S

To insert ASCII 0–31 characters in a document, you need to press Ctrl-P (^P appears in the status line), and then press Ctrl-?, where ? is a letter shown below:

A B C D E F G H I J K L M N O P Q R S T U V W X Y Z [\ ]

To insert a diamond, for example, hold down Ctrl and press P and D.

Ctrl-J (◙), Ctrl-M (♪), and Ctrl-U (§) do not produce the characters as they are supposed to. To get ♀, you need to press Ctrl-P and then Alt-12 (using the numeric keypad).

Use Alt-30 and Alt-31 to insert ▲ and ▼. Press Ctrl-P and then Ctrl-Del (or Backspace) to obtain △ (ASCII 127).

The ASCII characters from 128 to 254 can be obtained by using Alt and a proper number on the numeric keypad. See Appendix B for the characters and their corresponding numbers.

previous contents. This is done without pause or warning. You could thus inadvertently save a messed up version over the original one. This also happens if you choose Yes when exiting.

Save As lets you enter a new name, unless you press Enter to accept the existing file name. If you want to save two versions, you can enter a new name to save the current version while keeping the old version intact.

A MENU DISPLAY FILE

As the final project in this chapter, you are going to create a text file that will be used in Chapter 11. This file should be named MENU.TXT and will be used as the initial screen display for a menu. It should initially look like this:

```
==================================================
!                                                !
!                                                !
!                Press A Letter:                 !
!                                                !
!                                                !
!                D - dBASE IV                     !
!                                                !
!                L - Lotus 1-2-3                  !
!                                                !
!                W - WordPerfect                  !
!                                                !
!                                                !
!                                                !
==================================================
```

It is not particularly attractive. Change the box to a double-line rectangle by following these steps:

1. Press Ins once. Move the cursor to the first = in the first line, hold down Alt and type 201 on the numeric keypad.

2. Move the cursor to the last = in the first line. Enter Alt-187.

3. Go to the bottom left corner and enter Alt-200.

4. Go to the bottom right corner and enter Alt-188.

5. Replace all = with = (Alt-205).

6. Replace all ! with ‖ (Alt-186).

The graphic signs and their ASCII values are shown in the ASCII table in Appendix B.

The result is an attractive menu shown below:

```
┌─────────────────────────────────────────┐
│                                         │
│                                         │
│        Press A Letter:                  │
│                                         │
│                                         │
│        D - dBASE IV                     │
│                                         │
│        L - Lotus 1-2-3                  │
│                                         │
│        W - WordPerfect                  │
│                                         │
│                                         │
│                                         │
└─────────────────────────────────────────┘
```

You are through with this chapter. Select Save As from the File menu and save the file to drive A. Exit and you are done.

P R A C T I C E   1 0 - 6

1. Run EDIT and open the MENUB.BAT file in drive A (from the DOS-TA disk).

2. Merge MENUB.BAT with SAMPLE.TXT (also in drive A), with MENUB.BAT placed at the beginning of the combined file.

3. Move MENUB.BAT to the end of SAMPLE.TXT.

4. Delete the SAMPLE.TXT portion.

5. Convert all errorlevel strings to uppercase.

6. Clear the screen.

7. Type the following lines:
   What's the matter? Never mind.
   What's mind? No matter.
   Mind or matter, what does it matter?

8. Reverse the first two lines. Restore their original order.

☐ 9. Save the file to drive A as MATTER.

☐ 10. Exit the Editor and delete MATTER.

D R I L L

____ 23. A help window in the Editor can stay on the screen while you edit text, but a help window in the Shell disappears when you return to the regular screen. True or false?

____ 24. You can press F3 to exit the Shell as well as the Editor.

Answer questions 25–28 with the items below; each key or key combination moves to a specific location.

a. End b. Ctrl-Home c. Ctrl-PgUp d. Ctrl-Q, E

____ 25. Top of the document.

____ 26. Top of the current window.

____ 27. One screen left.

____ 28. End of the current line.

____ 29. The key combination of Ctrl-Ins is the same as selecting this command from the Edit menu:
   a. Cut
   b. Copy
   c. Paste
   d. Clear

____ 30. If you select a few text lines and press Tab, the lines are:
   a. indented
   b. deleted
   c. copied to the clipboard
   d. saved to disk

S U M M A R Y   A N D   R E V I E W

Check each item as you review and understand the following highlights of the chapter:

☐   1. The DOS Shell is a file/directory manager and program launcher/switcher. It provides a graphical user interface and allows you to use the mouse or keyboard to automate many tasks with little or no typing.

☐   2. Start the Shell by entering DOSSHELL. Press F3 or select Exit from the File menu to exit. To start the Editor, launch it from inside the Shell or enter EDIT on the command line. To exit, select Exit from the File menu.

☐   3. The initial Shell screen consists of six parts: Menu Bar, Drive Icons, Directory Tree, File List, Program List, Status Line. You can move the cursor to all except the last and make alterations. To move the cursor from one part to another, click it or press Tab or Shift-Tab.

☐   4. A window may contain a scroll bar and scroll box. You can click the arrows or drag the box to scroll the contents. The box also moves up and down as you press various keyboard keys to scroll the items in the window.

☐   5. Open a Shell or Editor menu by clicking a menu name or pressing Alt to activate the menu bar and pressing a highlighted key. Once a menu is open, click a displayed command or press a highlighted letter. Press Esc to close a menu.

☐   6. Get help from the Shell or Editor by pressing F1 when doing something. This leads to a context sensitive help. You can also open the Help menu and get hypertext help frames where one item can lead to one or more related items.

☐   7. The Shell displays in the Directory Tree window all the directories of the current drive. A directory containing subdirectories can be collapsed by pressing or clicking − and expanded by pressing or clicking +. Press * or Ctrl-* to fully expand the current directory or all the directories.

☐   8. You can use the File menu to move, copy, delete, view, rename, and print files or change their attributes. Just highlight one or more files and select a command from the File menu. You can also use the shortcut keys shown in the menu. You can also use the menu to create, delete, or rename directories. You can use the Search command to display only the files meeting certain conditions and then do something to them.

☐   9. When you want to do something to a group of files, you can select (and highlight) them first and then apply a command to them. Hold down Shift while you move the cursor to select sequential files. To select nonsequential files, hold down Ctrl and click each file, or press Shift-F8 and then press the space bar on each file.

10. Use the Options and View menus to set screen colors and modes, change the way items are displayed, enable/disable the Task Swapper (for task switching), and customize other items.

11. To open (launch) a program, just double click it or highlight it and press Enter. You can also open a data file, which has been associated with a program, to launch the program and at the same time retrieve the data file. To associate a program and a data file, highlight the program or data file and select Associate from the File menu, and enter file name extensions or a program name.

12. When the Task Swapper is enabled, you can run several programs and go from one to another by pressing certain key combinations. An Active Task List window opens up to display a list of active programs. You can place a program in this list by highlighting it and press Shift-Enter or hold down Shift and double click the name.

13. You can create a program item or program group, which will put it in the Program List window. A program item contains all the information (properties) necessary to launch a program. A program group contains a number of program items. To create or change a program item or program group, first make the Program List window active and/or highlight an item there. Then select New or Properties from the File menu. Enter the required information in the ensuing dialog boxes.

14. If you are handling a large file in the Editor, use one of the keys shown in Table 10.3 to speed up cursor movement. You can also insert up to four (0-3) bookmarks by pressing Ctrl-K and typing a number. To move the cursor to a bookmark, press Ctrl-Q and type a number.

15. You can use the Search menu to find or replace text strings. After a search string is supplied, press F3 to search (and highlight) each subsequent matching string. You can use the Change option from the Search menu to replace anything or replace something with nothing, which in effect erases the matching strings.

16. Some of the editing keys available in DOSKEY are also available in the Editor. To maneuver text lines, highlight them by holding down Shift and moving cursor keys or the mouse pointer. Press Del to delete the highlighted lines, Ctrl-Ins to copy, Shift-Del to cut, and Shift-Ins to paste.

17. If you did not include a file name when starting the Editor, you can open a file by selecting Open from the File menu. A dialog box appears for you to select a file. If you want to save a file over its original copy, select Save from the File menu. If you want to save to a different name, select Save As and enter a new name. If a file has not been saved, selecting Exit from the File menu will lead to a prompt for Yes or No to save the file before exiting.

R E V I E W   Q U E S T I O N S

Write an answer for each question below:

1. How do you start and exit the Shell and the Editor?

2. Mention some of the things you can do with the Shell.

3. Describe the initial Shell screen.

4. How can you move from one area of the Shell screen to another? In each area, how can you move from one item to another?

5. How can you expand or collapse a directory?

6. How do you rename a directory? Can you do the same thing on the command line?

7. How can you view a file's contents?

8. How can you change a file's attributes?

9. How can you select a group of sequential files?

10. How can you launch a program?

11. How can you associate a program and a data file?

12. What are program items and program groups? How can you create or modify them?

13. Cite the keystrokes in the Editor to move the cursor to: top of the file, end of the file, beginning of the current line, end of the current line, one screen right, and one screen left.

14. How do you move paragraph 1 to after paragraph 2?

15. What's the difference between the Save and Save As options in the File menu?

11 Programming Batch Files

C O M M A N D S   C O V E R E D

ECHO, PAUSE, REM, SHIFT, FOR..IN..DO, IF, GOTO, EXIST, CALL, COMMAND/C, DOSKEY, CHOICE, CONFIG, MENUCOLOR, MENUDEFAULT, MENUITEM, SUBMENU, INCLUDE

N E W   T E R M S   A N D   S Y M B O L S

debugging, @, :, %, replaceable parameter (dummy variable), looping, label, branching, nesting , exit codes, errorlevel, clean boot, multiple configurations, menu block, configuration block

QUICK START

For a summary of batch commands:

> See Table 11.1.

To hide all batch execution, put this in the first line:

> `@echo off`

To create an empty line on the screen during batch execution:

> `echo/`

To add remarks in a batch file:

> Place remarks after REM or :.

To display a message and pause batch execution:

> `echo Turn on the printer and`
> `pause`

To maneuver more than 10 parameters:

> Use SHIFT to shift to each following parameter.

To loop a command a number of times (% on command line, %% in a batch file):

> `A>for %x in (file?) do type %x`

To do unconditional branching:

> `goto LABEL`
> `. . .`
> `:LABEL`

To test parameter existence and do conditional branching:

> `if .==.%1 goto HELP`
> `. . .`
> `:HELP`

To test the existence of an environment variable:

> `if .==.%path% goto . . .`

To test a file's existence:

> `if exist %1 echo %1 is here`

To test an exit code of a command:

```
if errorlevel 2 goto END
```

To have a clean boot (skipping CONFIG.SYS and AUTOEXEC.BAT):

Press F5 at the beginning of booting.

To have a selective configuration (executing some commands in the CONFIG.SYS file):

Press F8 at the beginning of booting.

To show a [Y/N]? prompt for executing a command during booting:

```
device?=...
```

You have been exposed to batch files before. But you have not been introduced to the batch commands that can make batch files more intelligent and useful. This chapter explores these commands. If you can skillfully utilize them, you can create powerful batch files that resemble simple computer programs.

For quicker action, you can use macros. Creating macros, however, is laborious and repetitious. You can use a batch file to create a series of macros to save you lots of work. Macros and batch files will be compared and contrasted near the end of the chapter.

You can use COPY CON, EDIT (Chapter 10), EDLIN (Appendix H), or another text editor to create a batch file. If you use a word processor such as WordPerfect, make sure to save it as ASCII text. The batch files in this chapter are shown as they appear in EDLIN for the simple reason that the line numbers can be used for referencing in the text discussion. Do not include these line numbers if you are using another editor.

DOS 6 includes the CHOICE command, which can be used in a batch file to handle user interaction, and a number of ways to manage startup. These are discussed at the end of the chapter.

BATCH COMMANDS

■ *Batch commands are summarized here.*

About a dozen commands and symbols, as shown in Table 11.1, are used in programming batch files. FOR..IN..DO is often entered on the command line. Others can also be entered on the command line. They are, however, mostly meaningless unless put in batch files. All these batch commands are internal, except CHOICE. There is no need to worry whether DOS can access them.

Table 11.1

Batch Commands

Command	Purpose
@	Hide a line during execution
:	Mark a label
%	Replaceable parameter (dummy variable)
CALL	Execute another batch file and return
CHOICE	Handle user interaction
ECHO	Turn on/off display; show message
EXIST	Check existence of a file
FOR..IN..DO	Repeat execution of a command
GOTO	Go to a label
IF (IF NOT)	Decision making for conditional branching
PAUSE	Halt execution
REM	Remark
SHIFT	Shift to the next parameter

Most of these commands are used to control the flow of batch files so that they can be structured like computer programs. These programming commands are rather limited when compared to a full-fledged computer language like C. Nevertheless, this relatively simple programming device can be a useful productivity tool. While it is not as capable as a programming language, it is much easier to learn. When skillfully used, it can save you time in automating many DOS tasks.

CONTROLLING SCREEN DISPLAY (ECHO, PAUSE, @, REM, :)

- *Use ECHO to display a message on the screen.*
- *Use PAUSE to halt a batch file's execution.*
- *Use ECHO on/off to display/hide execution of commands.*
- *Put @ before a command to suppress its display.*
- *Use REM (or :) to add remarks to batch file lines.*

Three commands (ECHO, PAUSE, and REM) and one symbol (@) are used to provide remarks to batch files and control the screen display—pausing execution and displaying messages.

ECHO and PAUSE

Normally, a batch file is executed with the default of ECHO on. Every single line is displayed on the screen as it is executed. This arrangement is useful in **debugging** (identifying and eliminating errors) a batch file. Each command or error message, if any, is displayed on the screen, allowing you to spot errant lines. You can pause the screen display or echo the display to the printer to examine the error messages.

In a long batch file, you can selectively insert ECHO ON and ECHO OFF in crucial places to identify bugs. The trouble-free portions will not be displayed, and only those that have potential problems will be echoed to the screen for your view.

After a batch file is completely debugged and error free, you should turn off ECHO. Then the batch file's execution will not clutter the screen and distract the user.

Although execution of commands is not displayed when ECHO is off, messages are not suppressed. You can still use ECHO to display a message and use PAUSE to halt batch execution to wait for a user response. The following batch file[1] will display a two-line message and pause for a response from the keyboard:

```
1: echo off
2: echo Turn on the printer and
3: pause
4: copy *.txt prn
```

After running this batch file, the screen will pause and show these two lines:

```
Turn on the printer and
Press a key to continue...
```

The first line of the message comes from ECHO in line 2, and the second line comes from PAUSE.

If you want to replace the message produced by PAUSE, you can do something like this:

```
1: echo off
2: echo Turn on the printer
3: echo Press a key to print or ^C to abort
4: pause > nul
5: copy *.txt prn
```

---

1. All the batch file listings in this and the next chapters simulate the way they appear in EDLIN. If you use EDIT, COPY CON, or a word processor to create them, do not use line numbers.

Lines 2 and 3 will produce a two-line message, and line 4 will only pause. The default message of PAUSE will be discarded (redirected to NUL).

Note: While you can suppress PAUSE's built-in message, you cannot alter it by using the PAUSE command alone. For example, you may consider the following:

```
pause Turn on the printer
```

Your message will be ignored and the original message will be shown instead. If you redirect the original message like this:

```
pause Turn on the printer > nul
```

nothing will be shown during the pause.

Using @ to Hide Display

The above batch file will not display the execution of the commands in lines 2–5, but the execution of line 1 will still be displayed. To remedy this situation, you can use @ to suppress a line's execution. We can thus modify line 1 of our batch file this way:

```
1: @echo off
```

After this modification, only messages, if any, are displayed, and all other actions are hidden.

T I P S   A N D   T R I C K S

E C H O   A N D   E M P T Y   L I N E S

Different DOS versions have different ways of creating empty lines. If you use version 4 or later, put one of the following characters immediately after ECHO, leaving no space between a sign and ECHO:

```
:  ;  ,  .  "  +  /  \  [  ]
```

If there is an intervening space, a sign will be echoed to the screen, instead of creating an empty line. If you use version 3.xx, take out comma (,) and semicolon (;) from the above list.

Some versions will work with ASCII 0 (^@; press F7 to insert) and 255 (hold down Alt and type 255 on the numeric keypad); other versions will not work. Consistency has not been a virtue of DOS.

This book uses / immediately after ECHO to create an empty line. This will work with all versions since 3.xx.

The @ symbol can be put in front of any line to suppress its display. For example, if you want to hide only line 5, you can do this:

```
5: @copy *.txt prn
```

Displaying Empty Lines

Sometimes you want to insert empty lines to make your batch message more readable. There are a number of ways to do that. The simplest way is to put a slash (/) immediately after ECHO:

```
1: @echo off
2: echo/
3: echo Turn on the printer
4: echo Press a key to print or ^C to abort
5: echo/
6: pause > nul
7: copy *.txt prn
```

After this alteration, the message will be preceded and followed by an empty line.

A batch file's ECHO ON/OFF command will not affect the state of ECHO on the command line. However, the opposite is not true. When you run a batch file, the command line ECHO should be kept in the default ON state. Chapter 12 will elaborate more on this.

Using REM or : for Remarks

The REM command is placed at the beginning of each remark line to document a command above or below it. Such a remark can later remind you or others of

---

T I P S   A N D   T R I C K S

E C H O   A N D   C H A R A C T E R S

ECHO and a message are normally separated by a space. You can also use one of these characters in lieu of a space:

```
:  ;  ,  .  "  +  /  \  [  ]  =  (tab)
```

ECHO understands piping and redirection signs (¦, >, <, and >>) and will interpret them as taking certain actions. To display them on the screen, you need to put them in double quotes, such as:

```
echo "¦", ">", "<", and ">>" are redirection symbols.
```

what a tricky line is supposed to do. Without such remarks, you or others may be puzzled and have difficulty using or modifying a batch file.

DOS commands placed after REM are not executed. For example, you may have this batch line:

```
rem echo dir is most useful
```

Neither ECHO nor DIR is executed.

Remarks are not completely ignored during batch execution. If ECHO is on, entire remark lines (including the beginning REM) are displayed; if off, they are suppressed.

If you insert piping and redirection symbols (>, <, >>, and |) without enclosing them in double quotes, they will be interpreted as performing actions, not just displaying signs. For example, a batch line like this:

```
rem A is > B
```

will create a 0-byte file named B—regardless of ECHO's state. On the other hand, this line will do nothing:

```
rem A is ">" B
```

Instead of REM, you could place a colon (:) at the beginning of a line. Anything after the colon, including redirection and piping symbols without quotes, is completely ignored. They are also not displayed regardless of the state of ECHO.

A colon is also used to identify a label for branching. If you use it for remarks, make sure the first word after a colon is not identical to a label you want the batch file to branch to. See another section below for discussions of label and branching.

P R A C T I C E   1 1 - 1

1. Use EDLIN or EDIT to create the following batch file named DEMO.BAT; run it after exiting.

     1: rem DEMO.BAT
     2: echo This batch file is to demonstrate
     3: echo the use of ECHO, REM, PAUSE, @.

2. Add a line to DEMO.BAT to hide its entire execution.

3. Modify DEMO.BAT to pause display after the first line of message.

4. Replace the above PAUSE message with your own.

☐   5. Add an empty line before and after the first line of message.

☐   6. Modify DEMO.BAT so that the text lines will be displayed at the beginning of a clear screen.

D R I L L

_____   1. All the batch commands are internal. True or false?

_____   2. If you do not include any ECHO ON command in a batch file, all the commands being executed will be displayed. True or false?

_____   3. When ECHO is off, remarks are displayed. True or false?

_____   4. If @ECHO OFF appears in the second line of a batch file, which of the following is hidden?
       a. only the first line
       b. the first two lines
       c. all the lines after the second
       d. all the lines from the second

_____   5. A command, such as DIR, placed in the same line after REM will be executed. True or false?

_____   6. If ECHO is entered alone in a separate line in a batch file, it will
       a. display ECHO on/off
       b. create an empty line
       c. do nothing
       d. do various things depending on the version

_____   7. The "pause Turn on the printer > nul" command in a batch file will pause execution and display
       a. "Turn on the printer"
       b. "Press any key to continue . . ."
       c. nothing
       d. will not pause or display anything

_____   8. The line below will create an empty line. True or false?
          echo/

REPLACEABLE PARAMETERS (SHIFT, %)

■ *Use %# as a place holder for a parameter.*

■ *Use SHIFT to shift to each successive parameter.*

Every programming language allows you to maneuver variables. A **variable** is a letter or text string which can be used to represent different values, which can be numbers or text strings. Variables make programs versatile and useful.

DOS provides something akin to variables. Officially they are called **replaceable parameters**. Unofficially some people call them variables and others refer to them as **dummy variables** (or dummy arguments). They are not true variables because you cannot maneuver them as those found in a programming language; you cannot, for example, assign numeric values to them or make them do arithmetic calculations. These dummy variables, a term more suitable to their nature, are used to maneuver only parameters entered on the command line.

The percent sign (%), followed by a number, is used to represent a replaceable parameter. It is a place holder reserving a place for a parameter (argument) that is expected from the command line. The first item entered on the command line (parameter 0, batch file name) is placed in %0, the second (parameter 1) in %1, etc. up to %9. Here is an example:

```
1: @echo off
2: echo batch file name: %0
3: echo parameter 1: %1
4: echo parameter 2: %2
```

Suppose you name this batch file NAME.BAT. You can now enter the following to demonstrate how replaceable parameters work:

```
A>Name Laurel Hardy
batch file name: Name
parameter 1: Laurel
parameter 2: Hardy
```

If you enter more parameters than available replaceable parameters, the extras are ignored and not displayed. If you enter fewer parameters, some replaceable parameters are not assigned any value:

```
A>Name Laurel
batch file name: Name
parameter 1: Laurel
parameter 2:
```

Normally you can use only 10 replaceable parameters, %0 to %9. You can, however, use the SHIFT command to maneuver more. Every time this command is encountered, the next parameter entered on the command line is assigned to the same replaceable parameter. This provides some degree of mobility and versatility resembling the use of a true variable. This phenomenon is demonstrated below:

```
1: @echo off
2: echo %1
3: shift
4: echo %1
5: shift
6: echo %1
```

Suppose you name the above NUMBER.BAT. If you enter the first line below, the three lines after that are displayed:

```
A>number one two three
one
two
three
```

SHIFTING PARAMETERS

If you are puzzled as to how replaceable parameters and parameters are affected by SHIFT, the batch file below may help:

```
1: @echo off
2: rem PARADEMO.BAT--demonstrate parameter shifting
3: echo %0; %1; %2; %3
4: shift
5: echo %0; %1; %2; %3
6: shift
7: echo %0; %1; %2; %3
8: shift
9: echo %0; %1; %2; %3
```

Running this batch file with the four parameters after it shows this result:

```
A>parademo 1 2 3 4
parademo; 1; 2; 3
1; 2; 3; 4
2; 3; 4;
3; 4; ;
```

In the first round, %0 represents the batch file name. In the second, the same replaceable parameter has the value of 1, and so on.

Even though we use only one replaceable parameter, all the three parameters entered on the command line are echoed to the screen. Each time SHIFT is executed, DOS moves to the next parameter. The same replaceable parameter then holds a new value, the next parameter.

One practical use for shifting parameters is this simple batch file:

```
1: @echo off
2: rem TYPALL.BAT
3: :LOOP
4: type %1
5: pause
6: shift
7: if not .==.%1 goto LOOP
```

It allows you to enter a list of files on the command line to show one after another, like this:

A>**typall file1 file2 file3 file4**

After FILE1 is shown, line 5 pauses execution. Line 6 shifts to the next parameter (FILE2). Line 7 checks the existence of another parameter (explained below). If one exists, it is shown; if not, execution ends. If you have long files, you can use MORE to replace TYPE in line 4.

One problem with TYPALL.BAT is that no wild card is allowed in a parameter. If you do, line 4 will be executed this way:

A>**type file?**

Since TYPE accepts only one file at a time, this will not work. One way out is to use FOR to convert wild cards to actual file names, as explained below.

Shifting parameters is a valuable technique that can be used to construct simple but powerful batch files. The following is an example:

```
1: @echo off
2: rem A2B.BAT--copy files from A to B
3: :LOOP
4: copy a:%1 b:
5: shift
6: if not .==.%1 goto LOOP
```

You can use it to copy multiple files with one command. This single command will copy two files:

A>**a2b file1.txt test2.doc**

When the batch file is executed the first time, line 4 treats %1 as FILE1.TXT and copies it. Line 5 shifts the parameter to the next file, namely TEST2.DOC. Line 6 detects the existence of another parameter and branches to line 3. Then the new file placed in %1 is copied. When line 6 next tests false, the batch file ends.

Since COPY accepts wild cards, you can also use wild card characters to copy all the matching files, such as:

```
A>a2b file?.txt test?.doc
```

LOOPING (FOR..IN..DO)

■ *Use the FOR..IN..DO command in a batch file (or enter it on the command line) to repeat an action a number of times.*

Syntax and Usage

In computer programming, the technique of making a program perform a task a number of times until certain conditions are met is known as **looping**. DOS provides a simple looping command. It has this befuddling syntax:

```
FOR %%variable IN (set) DO action %%variable
```

It performs a function similar to BASIC'S FOR-NEXT command. In format, however, it resembles this C looping command:

```
for (i=1; i<=10; i++)
```

In the C command, the variable i is to begin with the value of 1, the looping is to stop when i reaches 10, and i is to increase its value by 1 after each loop. In DOS, a variable (another dummy) is any letter, which is placed after % (on the command line) or %% (in a batch file). The set is a list of files or commands enclosed in a pair of parentheses and separated from one another with delimiters such as a space, comma, or semicolon. And a DOS command is to follow DO. Here is an example:

```
1: @echo off
2: for %%x in (file1.txt, file2.txt) do copy %%x b:
```

The replaceable parameter of x (which can be any letter) is to successively hold each of the files after IN and enclosed in parentheses. It holds a different value each time the loop is repeated. When the command (COPY) after DO is executed, it will first copy the first file, then the second, and so on until all the files in the list are copied.[2]

2. If you want to see how DOS translates this line to actual commands, add REM in front of the first line and run the batch file.

Wild cards can be used with this command, such as:

```
2: for %%x in (*.txt) do copy %%x b:
```

All the matching files found in the current directory will be copied to drive B.

You can also designate a directory path inside the set, such as:

```
2: for %%x in (c:\wp\work\*.txt) do copy %%x a:
```

The FOR..IN..DO command can be entered on the command line, which is rather elaborate and thus often unnecessary. If you do that, you must use a single %, such as:

```
A>for %x in (*.txt) do copy %x b:
```

A less complicated way of doing the same thing is this:

```
A>copy *.txt b:
```

Note: A single % will work on the command line, but it will not work in a batch file; you must use %% in a batch file. In a batch file, a single % will lead to a "Syntax error" message.

Furthermore, variable letters have to be in the same case. Thus, the following command will fail:

```
A>for %x in (*.txt) do copy %X b:
```

DOS will interpret your intention as copying a file named %X, not the files matching the *.TXT pattern.

WARNING: Use the DEL and FOR..IN..DO combination with great caution, such as this:

```
A>for %x in (*.*) do del %x
```

This command will delete all the files in drive A's current directory without warning. Since the command works on one file at a time, it does not trigger the Y/N prompt as this command does:

```
A>del *.*
```

Showing Files

The looping command is most useful with commands, such as TYPE, that do not allow wild card characters. If you want to display the contents of all the matching files one after another, try this:

```
A>for %x in (file?.txt) do type %x
```

The FOR command will convert a wild card character to an actual matching file name, which will become a parameter for TYPE. This arrangement, however, cannot be applied to MORE. These two will not work:

```
A>for %x in (file?.txt) do more < %x
A>for %x in (file?.txt) do type %x ¦ more
```

The first will be executed this way:

```
A>more < file?.txt
```

Since MORE does not accept a wild card, a "File not found" message will appear instead. The second command will completely ignore MORE and execute the rest.

In order for these two commands to work properly, you need to make the batch file call another batch file. This technique will be explored in the Chaining and Nesting section below.

Comparing and Copying Files

The looping technique can be useful in comparing files on two disks, such as:

```
1: @echo off
2: for %%x in (*.*) do if not exist b:%%x echo %%x
```

Suppose you name it COMPFIL.BAT and run it when drive A is the default:

```
A>compfil
```

The screen will show all the files found in drive A but not in drive B. This lets you quickly find out the discrepancies between two disks or directories—the current directory in the current drive and the current directory in drive B.

If you frequently need to back up files, to create duplicate files for safe keeping, the above batch file could be modified to include copying as well. The batch file below will do it:

```
1: @echo off
2: rem SHOWBACK.BAT--show files before copying
3: echo These files exist in source but not target:
4: for %%x in (c:\bat\*.bat) do if not exist a:%%x echo %%x
5: echo Press a key to copy, or ^C to abort.
6: pause > nul
7: for %%x in (c:\bat\*.bat) do if not exist a:%%x copy %%x a:
```

After displaying the discrepancies, the batch file pauses and awaits your response. If you press any key other than Ctrl-C (or Ctrl-Break), copying begins.

Running Multiple Commands

Besides using FOR to maneuver multiple files, as we have demonstrated so far, we can also use it to run multiple commands. Here is an example:

```
1: @echo off
2: rem MOVEFIL.BAT--to copy and delete
3: for %%x in (copy del) do %%x %1
```

Suppose you run this batch file this way:

```
C:\BAT>movefil a:file?
```

The matching files in drive A's current directory will first be copied to the current directory (C:\BAT) and then deleted. The commands inside the parentheses are executed one after another, like this:

```
C:\BAT>copy a:file?
C:\BAT>del a:file?
```

If you are an overly cautious person, always fearful of deleting files, the batch file below may make life less miserable for you:

```
1: @echo off
2: rem TYPDEL--show a file before deletion
3: echo Press a key to delete -- %1 --, or ^C to abort
4: for %%x in (type pause del) do %%x %1
```

When a file is slated for deletion, its name and contents will be shown and you will be prompted to press a key. This gives you an opportunity to press Ctrl-C to abort. This batch file will not work if you use a wild card. The error message below appears if the batch file is executed this way:

```
A>typdel file?
Press a key to delete -- file? -- or ^C to abort
Invalid filename or file not found
Press any key to continue...
```

The error is the result of TYPE being given multiple files to handle. The first command in the batch will thus be executed like this:

```
A>type file?
```

After the pause, if you press a key other than Ctrl-C, the matching files will be deleted because the last command will be executed this way:

```
A>del file?
```

Can this problem be fixed? One remedy for this situation is to loop another FOR. Doing this is not as easy as in other programming languages. This technique will be explored in the Chaining and Nesting section below.

P R A C T I C E   1 1 - 2

1. Write a batch file that will echo to the screen all the parameters entered on the command line. Use a single SHIFT command in the batch file.

2. Modify the COMPFIL.BAT file discussed in the text so that it will display all the files found in both drives A and B.

3. Modify SHOWBACK.BAT to allow source file pattern and target drive to be controlled by parameters entered on the command line.

4. Use DOSKEY to create a macro named DT (DIR and TYPE). DT should allow the user to enter a parameter. It should first show the directory entries based on the parameter and pause for a key press. It then should show the contents of each matching file one after another.

5. Use the DT macro to show all the batch files in drive A.

6. Use the DT macro to show all the TXT files in the C:\DOS directory. Break the display.

D R I L L

9. Replaceable parameters can be used to maneuver (add, subtract, etc.) numeric values. True or false?

10. Suppose DONE.BAT is a batch file. In the following command, DONE is treated as %0. True or false?

    A>done file1 file2 file3

The batch file below, named COPYFIL.BAT, is used to answer questions 11–12:

```
1: copy %1 b:
2: copy %2 b:
3: copy %3 b:
```

11. The following command will produce an error message: 0 File(s) copied. True or false?

    A>copyfil file1 file2

12. The following command will copy all the entered files. True or false?

    A>copyfil file1 file2 file3 file4

13. Without using SHIFT, you cannot use more than 10 parameters in a batch file. True or false?

_____ 14. Assuming TEST.BAT has these lines:

    1: echo %1
    2: shift
    3: echo %1

The command below will cause line 3 to display "line 2" message. True or false?

    A>test line 1 line 2

_____ 15. The following command will:

    A>for %n in (*.txt) do type %n

    a. produce an error message
    b. display contents of all matching files in A
    c. display n number of files
    d. display matching files in drive B

_____ 16. The above command line, without any change, is legal if put in a batch file. True or false?

_____ 17. The following command will produce a warning and display a Y/N prompt. True or false?

    A>for %x in (*.*) do del %x

BRANCHING (IF/IF NOT, GOTO, :, ==)

■ *DOS recognizes a label as a new line beginning with a colon, followed by a text string.*

■ *Use GOTO followed by a label to branch (unconditionally) batch execution to a label.*

■ *Use IF (or IF NOT) and GOTO to do conditional branching.*

■ *Use the common equation of IF .==%1. GOTO . . . to test the existence of a parameter entered on the command line and do conditional branching.*

A batch file, like a computer program, normally runs from top to bottom. Each line is executed sequentially. You can, however, make it run more intelligently by using branching, chaining, and nesting. Branching is explained in this section; chaining and nesting will be covered later.

There are two kinds of **branching**, conditional and unconditional. Unconditional branching may resemble this scenario: execute line 5 and then continue in line 10. Conditional branching could be: Execute line 1 and, if the user enters no parameter on the command line, go to line 20.

Labels are used to mark lines to guide batch execution.[3] A **label** is simply a text string preceded by a colon (:), which is placed at the beginning of a line. It is nothing more than a place marker, marking a particular place where DOS is to branch when instructed to do so.

DOS uses the IF command to do conditional branching. Compared to other programming languages' counterparts, DOS's IF command is very limited. It can be used to test only three conditions:

1. Equality of two strings; can be used to test the existence of a parameter (command-line argument) or an environment variable

2. Existence of a file on disk

3. Exit codes of certain DOS commands and all the ASCII characters

These are covered in the following sections. We will provide various examples of conditional branching—after we have more discussion on labels.

Label Conventions

A label must be legal and unique. If not, either batch execution will end unexpectedly or branching will be done incorrectly. You cannot use just anything as a label. These are the rules you must observe:

- There must be a matching label for a batch file to branch to. Otherwise, the batch file will terminate prematurely.

- Do not use characters that cannot be used in a file name. This will cause premature termination of batch execution.

- Do not use a space in a label. Space signifies the end of a label; the characters after it are ignored. This rule also applies to other delimiters such as a comma or semicolon.

- Uppercase and lowercase are not distinguished.

- Only the first eight characters are significant; other characters after the eighth are ignored.

- DOS searches for a label from top to bottom. If several identical labels exist, only the first (top) can be reached.

---

3. Unlike BASIC, a batch file does not use line numbers; you cannot use a line number for branching batch execution.

You can enter a label in uppercase or lowercase. However, if you have two labels of identical spelling but not in the same case, only the first can be reached, such as the following:

```
1: goto PLATO
2: echo test plato
3: :plato
4: echo 1st label
5: goto end
6: :PLATO
7: echo 2nd label
8: :END
9: echo end
```

Line 1 leads to line 3 (not line 6), and then line 5 leads to lines 8 and 9. Line 2 is skipped, and lines 6 and 7 cannot be reached because another label of the same spelling precedes it. To make labels more readable and more easily identified, using uppercase consistently is a good idea.

To illustrate how DOS does branching, let us modify our batch file as shown below:

```
1: goto plato%1
2: echo test plato
3: :PLATO1
4: echo 1st label
5: goto end
6: :PLATO2
7: echo 2nd label
8: :END
9: echo end
```

Suppose we named this file PLATO.BAT and enter this command:

```
A>plato 2
```

The first line leads to the 6th, thus skipping lines 2–5. If we use anything other than 1 or 2 as a parameter, including no parameter, a "Label not found" message appears and the batch file terminates prematurely.

Suppose we insert a space in our label, as shown below:

```
1: goto plato %1
2: echo test plato
3: :PLATO 1
4: echo 1st label
5: goto end
6: :PLATO 2
7: echo 2nd label
```

```
8: :END
9: echo end
```

Entering the command below:

```
A>plato 2
```

or specifying any parameter will always lead to line 3. The characters after the space are completely ignored.

If you use redirection symbols, you are going to cause yourself trouble. Suppose you insert > after each PLATO occurrence. The first line will create a 0-byte file using the name entered as a parameter. The "Label not found" message will also appear.

DOS cannot distinguish labels that share the first eight characters. Consider this batch file:

```
1: goto platonic%1
2: echo test plato
3: :PLATONIC1
4: echo 1st label
5: goto end
6: :PLATONIC2
7: echo 2nd label
8: :END
9: echo end
```

Line 1 will always lead to line 3 no matter what parameter you enter on the command line. Since the label in line 3 is the first label whose first eight characters match those in line 1, other labels are no longer accessible.

Parameter Testing

When a batch file expects parameters, you must provide for a way to test parameter existence and for branching to a label according to the test result. This mechanism requires the use of IF (or IF NOT) and GOTO.

A wide variety of expressions can be used to test the existence of parameters entered on the command line. The variations shown below are all legal:

```
if !==!%1 goto HELP
if x==%2x goto OOPS
if ""=="%3" goto NONE
if .%1==.lotus goto LOTUS
if %1.==wp. goto WP
if not x==x%1 goto GO
```

The double equal sign, instead of a single one, is used to test the equality of two values (strings), as in C but not in BASIC or Pascal.

There must be at least one (the same) dummy character (any character) before and after ==. If not, a "Syntax error" message appears but batch execution continues.

The decimal number after the % sign depends on the number of parameters you expect the user to enter. For example, if you expect three parameters after the batch file name, use %3.

In each line, the existence of a parameter may make a statement true or otherwise. In the first line, for example, if the user enters no parameter with the batch file name, the statement becomes:

```
if !==! goto HELP
```

This statement then becomes true and batch execution branches to the HELP label. On the other hand, if the user enters FILE with the batch file name, the same statement becomes:

```
if !==!file goto HELP
```

The statement is no longer true and the command after it is ignored. Batch execution then continues with the line immediately below it.

In the last example, if the user enters a parameter, batch execution branches to the GO label because the statement that the two strings are not equal is true. Otherwise, the statement that the two strings are not equal is not true and the line immediately below is executed.

If both sides of an equation have something other than the dummy character, you have to put the dummy in a uniform place. In our fourth example, we place both periods before the strings; in the fifth example, we place both after. Either will work. However, do not put one before and one after, as shown below:

```
if %1.==.lotus goto LOTUS
if .%1==wp. goto WP
```

Suppose the user enters a parameter this way:

```
A>batname wp
```

The second test line will become this:

```
if .wp==wp. goto WP
```

The statement is false because the two strings are not equal, and batch execution will not branch to WP as you may expect.

Displaying and Deleting Files

Here is an example of branching according to the result of parameter testing:

```
1: @echo off
```

```
 2: rem KILL.BAT--display files before mass deletion
 3: rem if no parameter (filename) is entered
 4: if .==.%1 goto HELP
 5: dir %1
 6: echo/
 7: echo Press a key to delete these files, or ^C to abort.
 8: pause > nul
 9: del %1
10: goto END
11: :HELP
12: echo/
13: echo You must enter a parameter, such as: %0 *.txt
14: echo/
15: :END
```

This batch file is intended to provide a safeguard when you use wild card characters to delete files. It displays all the names of the matching files slated for deletion and pauses for you to press Ctrl-C to abort or another key to begin deletion.

Line 4 tests whether or not a parameter has been entered on the command line. If no parameter is entered, in other words only the batch file name is entered, the equation in line 4 becomes:

```
.==.
```

That means the IF statement is true. Execution then branches to the HELP label in line 11. The message in line 13 is displayed like this:

```
You must enter a parameter, such as: kill *.txt
```

In addition to the regular text, line 13 also converts %0 to "kill", the name of the batch file.

After the message is displayed, the batch file runs out of lines to execute and stops. (Keep in mind that a label like :END does nothing except marking a place for branching.)

If line 4 does not test true, namely a parameter is entered on the command line, the action after the equation is not taken. Instead, the line immediately below is executed.

Line 5 displays all the files matching the pattern entered on the command line. Line 7 displays a message, and line 8 pauses batch execution. If you press any key other than Ctrl-C or Ctrl-Break, the displayed files are deleted.

Line 10 branches to line 15, where the batch file ends its execution as there is nothing else to execute. Line 10 is an example of unconditional branching. No test is made; the flow of execution is simply directed to a label. If line 10 did not exist, lines 11–14 would be executed, displaying an unnecessary and misleading message.

Moving Files

KILL.BAT discussed above can be modified so that it can be used to move files from one directory to another:

```
 1: @echo off
 2: rem MOV.BAT--move files from one dir to another
 3: if .==.%1 goto HELP
 4: if .==.%2 goto HELP
 5: dir %1 /p
 6: echo/
 7: echo These files are to be moved to %2
 8: pause
 9: copy /v %1 %2
10: echo/
11: echo Press a key to delete the original files.
12: pause > nul
13: del %1
14: goto END
15: :HELP
16: echo/
17: echo Enter filename and target drive, such as:
18: echo    %0 file? b:
19: :END
```

Line 3 and 4 test to see whether two parameters follow the batch file name. If not, execution branches to the HELP label, where an example is provided and batch execution ends.

If at least two parameters are entered after the batch file name, the matching files to be moved are displayed (line 5). After you press a key, line 9 copies them (with Verify on) to the target. After another pause, line 13 deletes all the matching files.

You can use wild card characters, such as:

A>**mov file? b:**

This moves the matching files from A to B. If you want to move from B to A, try this:

A>**mov b:file? a:**

You need to specify both the source and target, or the HELP message will show up.

Printer Enhancement

The opposite of IF-GOTO is IF NOT-GOTO. It can be used to test the nonexistence of a condition. We will use it to construct a routine to let you enhance your dot-matrix printer:

```
 1: @echo off
 2: rem EPSON.BAT--set various print enhancements
 3: if not .==.%1 goto %1
 4: echo Options:
 5: echo 1 = NLQ  2 = Compressed  3 = Expanded
 6: echo 4 = Elite  5 = Double strike  6 = Reset
 7: goto END
 8: :1
 9: echo ^[x1 > prn
10: goto END
11: :2
12: echo ^O > prn
13: goto END
14: :3
15: echo ^[W1 > prn
16: goto END
17: :4
18: echo ^[M > prn
19: goto END
20: :5
21: echo ^[G > prn
22: goto END
23: :6
24: echo ^[x0^R^[W0^[P^[H > prn
25: :END
26: shift
27: if not .==.%1 goto %1
```

The ^[character represents the Esc character (ASCII 27). In EDLIN, Press Ctrl-V and then [to insert it. In EDIT, press Ctrl-P and then Esc to show the ← character. Both ^[and ← will be accepted by DOS as ASCII 27.

Two tests are conducted by the batch file, in lines 3 and 27. If no parameter is entered, line 3 tests false and lines 4–7 are executed, displaying the available options. So, if you just enter the batch file name alone, you get the instructions:

```
A>epson
Options:
1 = NLQ  2 = Compressed  3 = Expanded
4 = Elite  5 = Double strike  6 = Reset
```

If a parameter is entered, such as:

```
A>epson 1
```

line 3 tests true and batch execution branches to a particular label matching the parameter, and your printer is set to the Near Letter Quality mode. Make sure your printer is turned on. If a control code is registered, the roller will move up by one line.

If you enter multiple parameters, such as:

A>**epson 3 5**

line 3 will branch execution to line 14 to set the expanded mode. Then line 27, detecting the existence of another parameter, will branch batch execution back to line 20 to activate double strike.

Note: Keep in mind that some of these control codes are not compatible with one another. For example, if you enter 1 and 3, only 1 will be accepted and 3 will be ignored. You may also need to cancel all the existing codes, by specifying the 6 parameter, before you enter another one; or turn the printer off and on again to reset.

These codes are valid with an Epson dot-matrix printer. You are free to add other options such as italic and superscript. Your printer may have different control codes; if so, use those control codes instead.

MANEUVERING ENVIRONMENT VARIABLES

■ *Use the environment to reduce typing, pass arguments, convert a string to uppercase, and so on.*

Environment variables were discussed in Chapter 9. Here we explore various ways of using batch files to maneuver these variables.

As explained in Chapter 9, you can use SET on the command line or with macros to create environment variables and assign values to them. However, only batch files (and programs) can access and manipulate these variables in other ways, such as retrieving the assigned values or passing arguments.

Shorthand Expressions

Many programs take advantage of the environment for many purposes; your batch file can do the same. One thing you can do is to store a long string to a short environment variable and use the variable to substitute for the value, much like the way you use a macro to save typing. Here is an example:

```
1: @echo off
2: rem KEYCODE.BAT--display key exit code
3: set n=in (0 1 2 3 4 5 6 7 8 9)
```

```
 4: set n1=in (0 1 2 3 4 5)
 5: set d=do if errorlevel
 6: echo Press a key to show its exit code; Esc to end:
 7:
 8: :TOP
 9: key
10: if errorlevel 27 if not errorlevel 28 goto END
11: echo    (Character)
12: for %%x in (0 1) %d% %%x00 set code=%%x
13: for %%x %n% %d% %code%%%x0 set code=%code%%%x
14: for %%x %n1% %d% 2%%x0 set code=2%%x
15: for %%x %n% %d% %code%%%x set code=%code%%%x
16: for %%x %n1% %d% 25%%x set code=25%%x
17: echo %code%  (Exit code)
18: goto TOP
19:
20: :END
21: for %%x in (n n1 d code) do set %%x=
```

The purpose of this batch file will be fully explained in Chapter 12. Here we use it as an example of using environment variables to shorten a batch file.

Lines 3–5 define three variables. These variables are then repeatedly used in lines 12–16 to reduce typing and shorten some of the lines. When lines 12–16 are executed, each variable will be replaced with its assigned value. Line 13, for example, will be executed this way:

```
for %%x in (0 1 2 3 4 5 6 7 8 9) do if errorlevel %code%%%x0
set code=%code%%%x
```

These variables could clutter the environment and interfere with other batch files. They need to be cleaned up when a batch file is through. In our example, when the user presses Esc to end, line 21 erases all the variables created in lines 3–5.

Passing Arguments

Another thing you can do is to use the environment to pass arguments. In the following example, arguments can be passed from the command line to the environment and then to the FOR command:

```
1: @echo off
2: rem TYP.BAT--show files using environment variable
3: set var=%1
4: if .==.%1 set var=*.bat
5: for %%x in (%var%) do type %%x
6: set var=
```

If the user enters no parameter with the batch file name, line 4 assigns the default value to VAR and uses it as the parameter. All the files matching *.BAT will be displayed. This can save you the trouble of having to repeatedly enter the same file specifications to display files. If a parameter is entered, line 3 assigns it to VAR and line 4 is not executed. This allows you to use the batch file to display other files as well.

Uppercase Conversion

The environment can also be used to convert command-line arguments to uppercase, as shown in this batch file:

```
 1: @echo off
 2: rem UPPER.BAT--convert parameter to uppercase
 3: if .==.%1 goto HELP
 4: :LOOP
 5: set path1=%path%
 6: path=%1
 7: echo %path%
 8: set path=%path1%
 9: set path1=
10: shift
11: if not .==.%1 goto LOOP
12: goto END
13:
14: :HELP
15: echo/
16: echo Enter a string as a parameter, like this:
17: echo/
18: echo %0 bugs bunny
19: :END
```

Running the batch file with these parameters shows the result below:

```
A>upper what's up, doc?
WHAT'S
UP,
DOC?
```

Line 5 assigns the existing path list to another variable. Line 6 assigns the first command-line parameter to PATH. Line 7 shows this parameter in uppercase. Line 8 restores the original path list. And line 9 erases the extra variable.

Line 10 shifts to the next parameter and line 11 checks to see whether there is another parameter. If so, execution branches back to :LOOP for another round. If not, execution ends.

Checking Variable Existence

Sometimes you want a batch file to check to see whether an environment variable exists and branch execution based on the finding. This simple batch file will do the trick:

```
1: @echo off
2: if .==.%path% echo No path
3: if not .==.%path% echo Path = %path%
```

If the PATH variable is not in the environment, line 2 tests true but not line 3. If the variable exists, line 3 shows it. This technique can be applied to PROMPT, APPEND, DIRCMD, and your own variables.

In a real batch file, you will need only one of these two test lines. Add GOTO and a label in the test line to branch to depending on the test result. This is demonstrated below.

Password Protection

We are going to use the environment to provide for a password. The batch file below uses IF-GOTO to test the existence of a parameter and IF NOT-GOTO to test whether the password entered on the command line is equal to the one in the environment:

```
1: @echo off
2: rem PASS.BAT--demo batch use of environment
3: if .==.%1 goto NOPAR
4: if not %password%.==%1. goto NOGO
5: echo You have entered the correct password.
6: rem Enter your program here.
7: rem . . . .
8: goto END
9: :NOGO
10: echo You have failed to enter the correct password.
11: goto END
12: :NOPAR
13: echo You have not entered a password.
14: echo To use this program, you have to follow this:
15: echo %0 password
16: :END
```

Before you run this batch file, you need to create an environment variable and assign a value to it, such as:

A>**set password=tora**

P A T H   A N D   U P P E R C A S E

There are various ways of assigning values to environment variables. Here are some examples:

```
A>path c:\dos
A>path=c:\dos
A>set path=c:\dos
A>set mypath=c:\bat
```

The first two examples will enter the PATH=C:\DOS (all uppercase) string into the environment. The last two will respectively enter these strings instead:

```
PATH=c:\dos
MYPATH=c:\bat
```

In the fourth example, SET is mandatory because MYPATH is not a recognized variable. In the third example, SET is optional. The addition of this command causes the assigned value to be exactly the way you typed it—in contrast to the first two examples where the assigned values are converted to uppercase. This conversion can be used to convert a parameter to uppercase, as shown in UPPER.BAT.

If a user now runs the batch file without a parameter, line 3 branches execution to line 12 and this error message is displayed:

```
A>pass
You have not entered a password.
To use this program, you have to follow this:
     pass password
```

If a parameter is entered, line 4 tests to see whether it matches the one in the environment. If not, this is the result:

```
A>pass nincompoop
You have not entered the correct password.
```

If the two match, line 5 is executed and your program is run.

A savvy user can use the SET command to see the password. To foil such a person, try this command:

```
A>set password=<Alt-255><Alt-255>
```

After the = sign, you are to hold down Alt and type 255 on the numeric keypad; repeat it another time.[4] This enters ASCII 255 (blank character) twice. If you enter SET command alone, you see only this:

```
PASSWORD=
```

Nothing is displayed after the = sign. To enter a correct password after this move, you need to do this:

```
A>pass <Alt-255><Alt-255>
```

That is to enter ASCII 255 twice after typing the batch file name and pressing the space bar once; nothing else will work.

To use the batch file to automatically enter the password into the environment, add this line between lines 2 and 3:

```
set password=<Alt-255><Alt-255>
```

Also add this at the very end to erase the variable (assign nothing to it):

```
set password=
```

If you now use ATTRIB to make your batch file invisible (hidden), you have a fairly fool-proof system.

P R A C T I C E   1 1 - 3

☐ 1. Use EDIT or EDLIN to create a file named PHONE containing 10 lines, each resembling this:

    Dixon, Dick   299-3298

Create a batch file named LOOK.BAT which will allow a user to enter a file name and a person's name (or number) on the command line to display records (lines) found. Use it on the PHONE database. Use the FIND command to do the search. Provide branching to a help line if two parameters are not entered.

☐ 2. Modify MOVEFILE.BAT to allow for multiple files with dissimilar names to be moved with a single command from the current directory to a target entered on the command line. For example, this command will move to drive A all the listed files:

    C:\WP\REPORT>movefile a: report.90 budget.txt propose.doc

(*Hint:* use %1 for target drive/directory and make it an environment variable to freeze it—so it cannot be shifted. Use %2 to hold file list and SHIFT to change its value. Use IF to test the existence of another parameter for looping.)

☐ 3. Modify EPSON.BAT in the text to include an option for italics. (If your printer uses different codes, create a batch file like EPSON.BAT that can control the printer.)

---

4. If your keyboard does not respond to Alt-255, run KEYB.COM with the US parameter, like this:

```
C:\DOS>keyb us
```

4. In PASS.BAT, change IF to IF NOT and IF NOT to IF. (Hint: Use EPSON.BAT as a model for rearranging batch lines.)

5. Modify PASS.BAT so that if the user enters ABRACADABRA as the fourth parameter it will say that a correct password has been entered. The batch file should do nothing if no correct password is provided.

6. Move the test line (11) in UPPER.BAT to the beginning of the loop and modify other lines accordingly.

7. Create a batch file named ENECHO.BAT. It should display as a single line the entire text line (up to nine words) you enter.

8. Modify ENECHO.BAT to display all the words entered on the command line, with each line up to nine words.

D R I L L

18. If there are three lines marked by three labels of :label, :Label, and :LABEL, the "goto Label" batch command will branch to:

   a. whichever is located closest to the command

   b. :Label, due to exact matching in case

   c. :LABEL, for a label must be in uppercase

   d. the one located nearest the top of the batch file

19. A batch file can have line numbers like those found in a BASIC program. True or false?

20. The following command means:

        if m==%3m goto HELP

   a. no more than three parameters are expected

   b. branch to HELP if parameter %3 is absent

   c. both a and b

   d. is a meaningless test

FILE EXISTENCE AND EXIT CODES (EXIST)

■ *Use IF or IF NOT with EXIST to test the existence of a file on disk before taking an action with it.*

■ *Use IF or IF NOT with ERRORLEVEL to test an exit code of some DOS commands and branch batch execution accordingly.*

The IF command can test three items, as explained in the Branching section. Testing the existence of a parameter was explained there as well. This section explains the other two: file existence and exit codes.

File Existence and Copying

IF or IF NOT is used with EXIST to test the existence of files in any drive or directory. Such a test is a straightforward operation. If a specified file exists, then the IF statement is true, otherwise false.

The DUPE.BAT batch file below tests to see if the target drive or directory has duplicate files. If there are no duplicates, copying begins immediately. If duplicates exist, their names are displayed and action is halted. You can then decide whether to go ahead with copying or break the batch execution.

```
 1: @echo off
 2: rem DUPE.BAT--warn before overwriting targets
 3: if .==.%1 goto HELP
 4: if .==.%2 goto HELP
 5: if exist %2\%1 goto WARN
 6: :DO
 7: copy %1 %2
 8: goto END
 9: :WARN
10: echo These files exist in target drive:
11: dir %2\%1 /p
12: echo/
13: echo Press a key to copy, or ^C to abort.
14: pause > nul
15: goto DO
16: :HELP
17: echo You must enter two parameters, such as:
18: echo/
19: echo %0 a:file? b:
20: echo %0 *.txt b:\myfile
21: echo/
22: :END
```

The IF command first tests to see whether two parameters follow the batch file name. If not, the HELP message is shown, where an example is provided.

When correct parameters are entered, they are used by IF to check the existence of duplicate files in the target. Suppose you enter this command:

```
A>dupe *.bat b:\bat
```

The replaceable parameters in line 5 will treat your entry as:

```
b:\bat\*.bat
```

If matching files are found to exist, execution branches to the WARN label in line 9. Line 10 echoes the message, and line 11 executes the DIR command with this parameter:

```
dir b:\bat\*.bat /p
```

Line 14 pauses the action. If you press a key other than Ctrl-C or Ctrl-Break, execution is branched to the DO label in line 6. Line 7 then performs this command:

```
copy *.bat b:\bat
```

After copying, execution branches to the END label and the batch file ends.

Exit Codes and Disk Formatting

Some DOS commands return **exit codes**, some of which are shown in Table 11.2. These are the decimal numbers indicating different conditions of execution. These numbers can be tested by IF for branching.

The IF command can be used with ERRORLEVEL to test each exit code by checking whether it is greater than or equal to an error level. The labels can be in any order. However, you need to arrange the testing (IF) lines from higher to lower numbers, as shown below:

```
 1: @echo off
 2: rem FORMT.BAT--format and report outcome
 3: c:\dos\format a:
 4: if errorlevel 5 goto EL5
 5: if errorlevel 4 goto EL4
 6: if errorlevel 3 goto EL3
 7: echo Formatting is successful
 8: goto END
 9: :EL3
10: echo Aborted due to pressing ^C
11: goto END
12 :EL4
13: echo Aborted due to an error
```

```
14: goto END
15: :EL5
16: echo Aborted due N response
17: :END
```

If no error occurs, the message in line 7 is displayed at the end of formatting. If an error occurs, such as no available disk to format, a proper message is displayed without formatting.

Since FORMAT has two switches (/AUTOTEST and /BACKUP) that lead to no pause, you can take advantage of them in case you need to format many disks one after another with little human intervention. Our modified batch file looks like this:

Table 11.2

Exit Codes

Command	#	Meaning
FIND	0	Successful search, at least 1 match
	1	Successful search, no match found
	2	Unknown error
FORMAT	0	Successful action
	3	Aborted due to ^C
	4	Aborted due to error
	5	Ended due to N response
XCOPY	0	Successful action
	1	Source files not found
	2	Aborted due to ^C
	4	Assorted initiation error
	5	Aborted by user due to read/write error

(Note: Other commands reporting exit codes include: DISKCOMP, DISKCOPY, GRAFTABL, KEYB, REPLACE, RESTORE, and SETVER)

```
 1: @echo off
 2: rem AUTOFMT.BAT--format one after another
 3: :TOP
 4: echo Insert disk in drive A
 5: echo press Enter to begin or ^C to end
 6: pause > nul
 7: c:\dos\format a: /backup /v:abc%1
 8: if errorlevel 3 goto END
 9: echo Formatting is successful
10: shift
11: goto TOP
12: :END
13: echo Aborted or error
```

The /BACKUP switch will normally prompt you for a volume label. In our batch file, the /V switch supplies the ABC label, plus a parameter supplied from the command line. You may, for example, run the batch file this way:

```
C>autofmt 1 2 3 4 5
```

The first disk will have the volume label of ABC1, the second ABC2, and so on. If no parameter is supplied, then all the disks will have ABC as the volume label.

If you do not want a volume label or a display of formatting results, replace the /V and /BACKUP switches with /AUTOTEST in the original line 7.

The batch file, in lines 3–11, contains an infinite loop. After each disk is successfully formatted, batch execution loops back to the beginning. A pause then lets you abort or replace a disk.

If an error occurs or if you press Ctrl-C during formatting, then line 8 tests true. Batch execution branches to line 12 and the message in line 13 is shown.

If you want to be alerted when it's time to insert a new disk, add this line after line 10:

```
11. echo ^G^G^G
```

See the next section on how to insert ^G.

Using XCOPY to Backup Files

XCOPY returns exit code 4 if there is not enough memory, insufficient disk space, or invalid syntax or drive name. This value can be used to prompt you to swap disks, as shown below:

```
 1: @echo off
 2: rem XCPY.BAT--use XCOPY to back up
```

```
 3: :LOOP
 4: xcopy %1 /m a:
 5: if errorlevel 4 if not errorlevel 5 goto FULL
 6: goto END
 7: :FULL
 8: echo ^G^G^G
 9: echo Disk is full; replace it and
10: pause
11: goto LOOP
12: :END
```

In EDLIN, press Ctrl-G to insert ^G. In EDIT, press Ctrl-P and Ctrl-G to insert •. Both ^G and • will be interpreted by DOS as ASCII 7, which, combined with ECHO, causes your PC to beep.

You can use the batch file like this:

```
C:\123\WORK>xcpy report?.wk1
```

All the matching files from the current directory will be copied to drive A. The copied source files will have their A attributes removed. If copying is successful, batch execution ends with no error message. If other errors are encountered, a message is displayed and batch execution ends.

If exit code 4 is returned, however, the "Insufficient disk space" message is displayed by DOS and the FULL label is executed. Your PC beeps three times and the batch file pauses with a message shown in line 9. After you press a key, batch execution branches to line 3 and copies the matching files that still have A attributes. Those without A attributes are ignored. This arrangement lets you back up a large number of files and allows you to swap disks to complete a long job. This may be more useful than MSBACKUP in some situationss.

ERRORLEVEL Conventions

When ERRORLEVEL is used to test an exit code, DOS compares the exit code number returned by a command with the number specified after ERRORLEVEL. If the former is equal to or greater than the latter, the IF statement is true. This phenomenon requires you to arrange your test order from higher to lower values.

In our FORMT.BAT example, if FORMAT returns 5 or higher, then line 4 is true. Since the highest exit code number returned by FORMAT is 5, there is no possibility of error here. If 4 is returned, line 4 is first tested; since it is not true, no branching is done. Then line 5 tests true and execution branches to EL4. Line 6 is skipped.

If we reverse the order shown in lines 4-6, with 3 at the top and 5 at the bottom, any exit code higher than 3 will always branch batch execution to EL3 and all the other lines will have no chance.

Beware of the difference between IF ERRORLEVEL and IF NOT ERRORLEVEL. The former tests exit codes in descending order, but the latter does it in ascending order. For example, IF ERRORLEVEL 5 tests true if the expected exit code is 5 or higher. This is comparable to this C language statement:

```
if (x >= 5)
```

On the other hand, IF NOT ERRORLEVEL 5 tests true only if the expected exit code is less than 5. It is thus comparable to this C statement:

```
if (x < 5)
```

Under some circumstances, you may need to combine both statements, such as this line in XCPY.BAT:

```
5: if errorlevel 4 if not errorlevel 5 goto FULL
```

The IF statement will match 4 or higher, and the IF NOT statement any number lower than 5. As a result, only 4 and nothing else will match. See various menu batch files below for more examples of using this combination.

D R I L L

Answers for 21–24:   a. if not errorlevel   b. if not x==%x   c. if not exist.

_____ 21. Test existence of a parameter.

_____ 22. Test existence of a file.

_____ 23. Test exit codes.

_____ 24. Used with a limited number of DOS commands.

_____ 25. The lines testing error levels should be arranged in a reverse order, with higher numbers placed before lower numbers. True or false?

CHAINING AND NESTING (CALL, COMMAND/C)

■ *Use CALL in a batch file to execute another batch file and return.*

■ *Execute another batch file from within a batch file to chain the new batch file; control does not return to the original batch file.*

Among the common programming techniques, we previously discussed branching and looping. This section explains the other two techniques of chaining and nesting.

Chaining vs. Nesting

The two techniques work differently. **Chaining** transfers control to another batch file. **Nesting** calls another batch file (or program). Chaining does not return control to the original batch file. Nesting always returns control to the original (calling) batch file.

When you run a computer program, including a DOS external command, from inside a batch file, the program is nested. When you run another batch file (instead of a program), however, it is chained. Consider this example:

```
1: rem nesting
2: cd\dos
3: edit x.bat
4: cd\
```

This batch file first changes directory to \DOS and runs EDIT with the file X.BAT. Upon exiting EDIT, line 4 is executed and the root directory is restored.

If you run another batch file, the outcome will be quite different. Suppose you have 2ND.BAT as shown below:

```
1: rem 2ND.BAT
2: echo 2nd batch, the only line
```

Suppose you now run 1ST.BAT as shown below:

```
1: @echo off
2: rem 1ST.BAT chaining 2ND.BAT
3: echo 1st batch, line 1
4: 2nd
5: echo 1st batch, line 2
```

The result below may surprise you:

```
A>1st
1st batch, line 1
2nd batch, the only line
```

By running 2ND.BAT in line 4, control is transferred to 2ND.BAT. Line 5 is thus not executed.

If you want 1ST.BAT to nest (not chain) 2ND.BAT, you need to change line 4 to this:

```
4: call 2nd
```

If you run the modified 1ST.BAT, this is the result:

```
A>1st
1st batch, line 1
2nd batch, the only line
1st batch, line 2
```

When CALL is used, 1ST.BAT nests 2ND.BAT. After 2ND.BAT is finished, control is returned to 1ST.BAT.

The CALL command is akin to a subroutine call (GOSUB-RETURN) of BASIC or function call of C. The only difference is that in a batch file the called (nested) subroutine is outside of the calling batch file and stored in a separate batch file. You can use COMMAND /C in lieu of CALL. The former technique is the only way you could call another batch file in versions before 3.3. Using COMMAND /C loads another copy of COMMAND.COM, but using CALL does not. The latter can run faster and is thus preferable.

Notice that we include @ECHO OFF in 1ST.BAT but not in 2ND.BAT. By using 1ST.BAT to nest or chain 2ND.BAT, the latter's execution is not echoed to the screen because @ECHO OFF is inherited from 1ST.BAT. However, if you run 2ND.BAT alone or have a macro call it, the screen will display each line as it is executed.

You can also use chaining or nesting to pass parameters from the parent batch file to the child batch file, such as these examples:

```
2nd %1 %2            (chaining)
call 2nd %1 %2       (nesting)
```

Two parameters entered on the command line will one by one (not together) be passed to 2ND.BAT. See below for concrete examples.

A batch file can call (or chain) itself. This could create an infinite loop. You must provide a way out. Otherwise, your computer could lock up. If the batch file writes to the screen, you can use Ctrl-C to break it. If not, you may have no choice but to reboot.

Nesting is a useful technique in a long batch file. Smaller routines can be stored in separate batch files and called by the main batch file. This makes it easier to organize a complex batch file. Another benefit is that some of the small batch files can be recycled (called or chained by several batch files), thus saving programming time.

FOR Nesting FOR

Having one batch file nest another is a relatively simple technique, but having a FOR command nest another is not. We are going to use this technique to circumvent the limitations involving TYPE and MORE that we encountered earlier. We start with this simple batch file:

```
1: @echo off
2: rem TYPE1.BAT--show one file after another
3: if .==.%1 goto HELP
4: for %%x in (%1) do type %%x
5: goto END
6:
7: :HELP
8: echo/
9: echo Use this batch file like this:
10: echo/
11: echo %0 file?
12: :END
```

Suppose you now enter this command:

A>**type1 *.bat**

All the matching files with the BAT extension will be displayed one after another. You can pause the scrolling by pressing Pause or Ctrl-S.

We can improve our batch file to show one file at a time—to pause after each file is displayed. To do that, we can make the batch file call another batch file. The first step is to modify line 4 as shown below:

```
4: for %%x in (%1) do call type2 %%x
```

This line will call TYPE2.BAT and pass arguments (parameters) to the new batch file. When TYPE2.BAT is called each time, a new parameter (file name) will be passed to it so that it can do something to the specified file. TYPE2.BAT is shown below:

```
1: rem TYPE2.BAT--called by TYPE1.BAT
2: cls
3: echo -- %1 --
4: for %%x in (type pause) do %%x %1
```

Line 2 clears the screen and line 3 shows the file name. Line 4 nests another FOR command. Suppose TYPE1.BAT passes MYBAT.BAT as the parameter to TYPE2.BAT. Line 4 will be executed this way:

```
type mybat.bat
pause mybat.bat
```

The first command will display the file. The second will pause with the standard message. Since anything after PAUSE is ignored, the file name has no effect.

Line 4 in TYPE2.BAT is an example of FOR nesting another FOR. Another comparable technique is to eliminate TYPE2.BAT and change line 4 in TYPE1.BAT to:

```
4: for %%x in (%1) do command /c for %%y in (type pause) do %%y %%x
```

This requires loading another copy of COMMAND.COM to run another FOR command. Another problem with this is that you cannot break the screen display. Pressing Ctrl-C will break only the current file's display and does not stop the display of subsequent matching files.

The CALL command in line 4 of TYPE1.BAT is important. If we omit it, we are asking the first batch file to chain, not nest, the second. In that case, the second batch file does not return to the first and only the first matching file is shown.

If the files you want to display are relatively long, TYPE2.BAT could be modified this way:

```
1: rem TYPE3.BAT--called by TYPE1.BAT
2: cls
3: echo -- %1 --
4: more < %1
5: pause > nul
```

In this arrangement, MORE pauses the scrolling after the screen is full. PAUSE is necessary to display a file or its fraction that is less than a screenful.

We can also modify our system to print a series of files. Change line 4 of TYPE1.BAT to this:

```
4: for %%x in (%1) do call type4 %%x
```

Also, modify TYPE3.BAT as shown below:

```
1: rem TYPE4.BAT--called by TYPE1.BAT, to print
2: echo -- %1 -- > prn
3: echo/ > prn
4: type %1 > prn
5: echo/ > prn
```

Line 2 sends the file name to the printer. Lines 3 and 5 send extra empty lines to the printer before and after a file's contents. And line 4 redirects a file's screen display to the printer.

MACROS AND BATCH FILES

■ *Macros and batch files are compared and contrasted.*

■ *Avoid using branching techniques in macros.*

■ *Use macros for speed. Use a batch file to quickly create commonly used macros.*

Now that you have mastered both macros and batch files, it is a good time to compare and contrast the two. The two share many similarities. There are also significant differences. You can mix the two to maximize your productivity with DOS.

Similarities and Differences

The similarities and differences between macros and batch files are summarized below:

- Macros stay in RAM and are erased when power is shut off; they must be created in each session. Batch files are permanently stored on disk. Macros can run faster because there is no need to access a disk.

- Each command in a batch file occupies one line; all the commands in a macro must stay in one line but separated from one another with $T.

- A batch file's size is limited by disk space; a macro can be no longer than a single line and 127 characters. If a macro line spills over to another line on the screen, you can move the cursor to all the typed characters and edit them.

- Pressing Ctrl-C (or Ctrl-Break) terminates all the remaining lines in a batch file; you will be asked Y/N. The same key combination breaks only the current command in a macro, not subsequent commands in the same macro. You need to press Ctrl-C once to break each command in a macro.

- A macro recognizes $1–$9 as replaceable parameters; the equivalents in a batch file are %1–%9. You can use $* in a macro to represent all the replaceable parameters entered on the command line; there is no equivalent for this in a batch file. SHIFT cannot manipulate macro parameters as it can batch parameters. %0 can be used to represent the batch file name, but $0 is not recognized by a macro.

- Redirection symbols (<, >, >>, and |) can be directly used in a batch file; you must use equivalent metastrings in a macro. Using such symbols while defining a macro will lead to an immediate action rather than creating a macro.

- You cannot use echo off to hide a macro's execution as you can in a batch file. @ECHO OFF is not recognized. ECHO OFF will turn off ECHO on the command line; it has the same effect as entering the command on the command line.

- A macro can define an environment variable but cannot use it; a batch file can both define and use an environment variable. A variable defined by a macro can be used by a batch file.

- You cannot use GOTO to branch to a subsequent command in a macro as you can in a batch file. All macro commands are executed sequentially one after another. No branching is permitted.

- A macro can call (nest) a batch file. However, a macro cannot be called by itself, another macro, or a batch file. In a macro, you can call a batch file by using the batch file's name alone or precede it with the CALL command.

- A batch file can chain another batch file and transfer control to the new file. A macro can only call but not chain a batch file. All the subsequent commands in the macro will be executed regardless of what the called batch file does.

Macro Limitations

The biggest limitation about a macro, as compared to a batch file, is its inability to handle branching. Suppose you want to simplify the process of showing a command's online help message. You can define a macro like this:

```
C>doskey h=$1 /?
```

You can now enter something like this to get a command's help:

```
C>h xcopy
```

Suppose you now want to make this macro more sophisticated—to handle a situation when no parameter is supplied by the user. You might consider this:

```
C>doskey h=if .==.$1 goto END $t $1 /? $t :END
```

You might think that if no parameter is entered with the macro, it will branch to :END and gracefully terminate itself. It does not work because GOTO is not recognized, nor is a label.

ECHO and PAUSE work in a macro; they can be used to display your own message and pause for a keyboard response. Consider this example:

`C>doskey kill=echo Deleting Files...$t dir $1 $t pause $t del $1`

There are two problems with this macro, however. First, the displayed message is hard to read because you cannot use ECHO OFF to suppress other lines. Second, your idea of using PAUSE to allow you to prevent file deletion may not work. Pressing Ctrl-C after the macro pauses does not prevent the execution of subsequent commands.

Whether or not you can prevent the deletion of files will depend on the parameter you enter with the macro. If the parameter leads DOS to delete files without writing to the screen, you cannot use Ctrl-C to prevent it, such as this example:

`C>kill file?`

This command will eventually lead to this:

`C>del file?`

Execution of this command does not result in writing to the screen. Pressing Ctrl-C cannot stop this command. On the other hand, this command is a different matter:

`C>kill *.*`

It leads to this result:

```
C>del *.*
All files in directory will be deleted!
Are you sure (Y/N)?
```

This allows you to press Ctrl-C to prevent DEL from doing its job.

When it comes to environment variables, a macro behaves very much like a command entered on the command line. Both can use SET to define environment variables but neither can use them. Consider this example:

`C>doskey b=set bat=c:\dos\bat $t dir %bat%`

After running the B macro, the environment will contain the BAT=c:\dos\bat string. You might expect the DIR %BAT% command from the macro or command line to show the C:\DOS\BAT directory. It does not work. If you put DIR %BAT% in a batch file, it will work. On the command line or in a macro, %BAT% is not recognized as an environment variable, as explained in Chapter 9.

Mixing Macros and Batch Files

Within the limitations discussed above, you can make macros and batch files interact with each other. One example is this macro:

```
A>doskey t=for %x in ($*) do call type2 %x
```

This macro uses FOR to nest a batch file containing another FOR; the batch file was shown earlier.

As a more elaborate example, we are going to devise a file-protection scheme that involves two macros and a batch file. Our scheme uses a macro to move files you intend to delete to a special directory. This delays actual deletion of files and gives you extra time to change your mind. When you are ready to delete the files, another macro will quickly do the job. These two macros are shown below:

```
A>doskey del=copy $1 \junk $t del $1
A>doskey killjunk=dir \junk /p $t pause $t echo y $b del \junk
```

Before you can use these macros, you must have a directory named \JUNK as a subdirectory of the root directory.

The first macro redefines the DEL command. When you use this command, as shown below:

```
A>del file*
```

the macro is executed this way:

```
A>copy file* \junk
A>del file*
```

The matching files are actually moved to another directory. You can still use them if you change your mind.

When you are ready to clean up the \JUNK directory, just use the KILLJUNK macro, like this:

```
A>killjunk
```

The macro will be translated to these actual DOS commands:

```
A>dir \junk /p
A>pause
A>echo y | del \junk
```

The matching files slated for deletion will be displayed for your view. After you press a key to end the pause, the last command will automatically delete all the files in the directory. If you want to prevent the deletion of the displayed files, hold down Ctrl-C until the DOS prompt reappears. If you change your mind after deletion, you must undelete them before you write to the same disk.

USING A BATCH FILE TO START DOSKEY

As I use WordPerfect to write this book, I frequently have to leave WordPerfect in RAM and go to the command line to test numerous DOS commands. In the case of DOSKEY, this process creates extra problems. I have to load the TSR program in the upper memory area; otherwise, I cannot return to WordPerfect because my PC will freeze. Furthermore, every time I go back to WordPerfect, DOSKEY will be erased from RAM (together with all the macros I have previously created) and I have to load it another time. As the old saying goes, necessity is the mother of invention; my invention in this case is this simple batch file:

```
C:\BAT>copy con k.bat
lh doskey /insert
doskey k=doskey $*
^Z
```

Now, when I go to the command line, I simply enter K. The batch file will load DOSKEY high and set insert mode as the default. It will also create a macro named K. If I want to create a macro, I type K instead of DOSKEY.

Wouldn't the K macro and the K batch file conflict with each other? No. When there is no existing macro, which is the case when DOSKEY is not loaded, entering K runs the batch file. After the batch file creates the K macro, the latter has priority. You can still run the batch file if you enter K.BAT instead of just K.

As macros are erased when your PC is shut off and must be recreated each time, you can use a batch file to do the job quickly. The following command will create this batch file:

```
A>echo doskey del=copy $1 \junk $t del $1 > junk.bat
A>echo doskey killjunk=dir \junk /p $t pause $t echo y $b del
\junk >> junk.bat
```

The first command will save everything between ECHO and > to JUNK.BAT. The second command (typed as one line) will append the string between ECHO and >> to JUNK.BAT.

When you want to create the macros, just run JUNK.BAT. It will automatically create two macros. This can save you the trouble of having to manually create lengthy macros.

If you use macros often, it is a good idea to assemble your favorite and often used ones in a single batch file named MACROS.BAT or whatever name you fancy. As you create a macro and want to save it, use ECHO to append to it. You may also want to retrieve it to EDLIN or EDIT to clean it up by erasing old and repetitive ones. Your productivity with DOS could improve greatly if you skillfully use this technique.

P R A C T I C E   1 1 - 4

1. Modify the LOOK.BAT file created earlier so that it will report two conditions: (1) when no matching line is found and (2) when an error occurs.

2. Create a batch file that tests the existence of a file (whose name is entered on the command line) in two drives (A and B) and, if it exists in both, use FC to compare them.

3. Enter two commands on the command line, one to test whether a file exists in the current directory and another command to test a file's existence in another directory. Do not use DIR.

4. Modify AUTOFMT.BAT so that volume labels will be piped in from an ECHO command rather than from the /V switch.

5. Use DOSKEY to create a macro named T. This macro should allow the user to enter two parameters, one for file names and the other 3 or 4 to call TYPE3.BAT or TYPE4.BAT. Use T to call TYPE3.BAT to show all the files with the BAT extension.

6. Modify the above system so that the screen display becomes more readable and less cluttered with lines produced by the macro and batch file.

D R I L L

26. After a batch file runs an external program, exiting the program always returns you to the DOS prompt. True or false?

27. If you have A.BAT and B.BAT, line 2 of the following batch file will never be executed. True or false?
```
1: a
2: call b
```

28. If batch file A calls (using CALL) batch file B, control returns to A after B runs its course.

29. This statement is not true:
    a. a batch file can call another batch file
    b. a batch file can call a macro
    c. a macro can call a batch file
    d. a batch file can chain another batch file

_____ 30. If the following batch file is named X.BAT, it will run indefinitely. True or false?

```
1: echo one
2: x
```

BUILDING MENUS

■ *Use a simple batch file to display all the available options. The option routines can be included in the menu batch file or stored in separate batch files.*

■ *To speed up access to a menu option, let the user enter a parameter corresponding to a menu option. A parameter can be a number or an alphabetic letter.*

■ *Use a simple assembly program to provide for interactive mechanism and incorporate it into a menu batch file to make it more automated.*

For our final projects in this chapter (it's been a long chapter, but the end is near), we are going to build a series of menus with minor variations. We start with a simple and crude one that will do nothing other than show available options and end with one that will display the available options and allow you to press a single key to start a program.

A Simple Menu

Our first menu batch file is shown below:

```
 1: @echo off
 2: rem MENU0.BAT--display options only
 3: cls
 4: echo/
 5: echo/
 6: echo/
 7: echo ------------------Menu Options--------------------
 8: echo/
 9: echo                      1.  DOS Editor
10: echo/
11: echo                      2.  Gorilla
12: echo/
13: echo                      3.  Nibbles
14: echo/
15: echo/
```

This batch file simply displays all the available options and does nothing else. You also need to create the following three more batch files:

```
A>copy con 1.bat
c:
cd\dos
edit untitled
cd\
^Z

A>copy con 2.bat
c:
cd\dos
qbasic gorilla
cd\
^Z

A>copy con 3.bat
c:
cd\dos
qbasic nibbles
cd\
^Z
```

The user can now enter a corresponding number to start a batch file and run a program.

(After starting a program, select File Exit to exit—unless you intend to do something. After you enter 2 or 3, press F5 to compile the program; instructions will appear after a while. If you play Gorilla, enter the angle and velocity based on which to hurl your banana to demolish your opponent. In the case of Nibbles, use cursor keys to steer the worm to capture a displayed object while avoiding the sides or roadblocks. Press Ctrl-Break to end a game. Select File Exit to exit EDIT or QBASIC. These QBASIC programs were included in version 5, but not version 6. They are, however, likely to remain in the C:\DOS directory of your hard disk.)

An Integrated Menu

Instead of maintaining four separate files as we did above, we can integrate them into a single file. We will also modify our batch file to let the user enter a number to run a program, as shown below:

```
1: @echo off
2: rem MENU1.BAT--all options in 1 file
3: if %1.==1. goto EDIT
4: if %1.==2. goto GORILLA
5: if %1.==3. goto NIBBLES
6: echo Invalid choice; enter 1, 2, or 3:
```

```
 7: goto MENU
 8:
 9: :EDIT
10: c:
11: cd\dos
12: edit untitled
13: cd\
14: goto END
15:
16: :GORILLA
17: c:
18: cd\dos
19: qbasic gorilla
20: cd\
21: goto END
22:
23: :NIBBLES
24: c:
25: cd\dos
26: qbasic nibbles
27: cd\
28: goto END
29:
30: :MENU
31: echo/
32: echo ------------------Menu Options-------------------
33: echo/
34: echo                    1.  DOS Editor
35: echo/
36: echo                    2.  Gorilla
37: echo/
38: echo                    3.  Nibbles
39: echo/
40: :END
```

You can now enter the batch file's name followed by a number as a parameter to start a program. If you enter no parameter or an invalid one, batch execution branches to the MENU label and displays all the options.

Branching with FOR

Instead of using three test lines for branching as shown in lines 3–5, you can use a single FOR command. It can be done this way:

```
for %%x in (1 2 3) do if %1.==%%x. goto LABEL%%x
```

This limits user choices to only those listed. In this arrangement, you can also put letters instead of numbers inside the parentheses. That will allow the user to enter a letter to run a program. This technique is shown below:

```
 1: @echo off
 2: rem MENU2.BAT--uses FOR and letter options
 3: if %1.==. goto MENU
 4: for %%x in (E e G g N n) do if %1.==%%x. goto OPTION%%x
 5: goto MENU
 6:
 7: :OPTIONE
 8: c:
 9: cd\dos
10: edit untitled
11: cd\
12: goto END
13:
14: :OPTIONG
15: c:
16: cd\dos
17: qbasic gorilla
18: cd\
19: goto END
20:
21: :OPTIONN
22: c:
23: cd\dos
24: qbasic nibbles
25: cd\
26: goto END
27:
28: :MENU
29: echo/
30: echo ------------------Menu Options--------------------
31: echo/
32: echo                    E - DOS Editor
33: echo/
34: echo                    G - Gorilla
35: echo/
36: echo                    N - Nibbles
37: echo/
38: echo Enter the batch file name with a letter, such as
39: echo        %0 e
40: echo/
41: :END
```

In MENU2.BAT, lines 3 and 5 respectively handle no parameter or an invalid parameter. When these happen, batch execution branches to the MENU label to display the available options.

If an option letter is entered, line 4 tests to see whether it matches (including case) any in the list and, if so, branches execution according to the parameter. Suppose the user enters the command this way:

```
A>menu2 e
```

Line 4 is now executed this way:

```
if e.==e. goto OPTIONe
```

The IF statement is now true and execution branches to the OPTIONE label.

An Interactive Program

A typical menu displays all the options and lets the user press a single key to select an option. The mechanism of pressing a single key to start an action was not available until the CHOICE command, newly available in version 6. We will save CHOICE for later in this chapter. In the meantime, we will create a program of our own and find some use for it. We need to enlist a tool used mostly by computer programmers, a mini-assembler called DEBUG.COM. It is available in the DOS package. We will use it for an interactive mechanism in this chapter and to show scan codes for keyboard keys in Chapter 12. You do not need to understand DEBUG; just follow the procedure below. Here are keystrokes to create the program:

```
A>debug
-a
26FB:0100 mov ah,1
26FB:0102 int 21
26FB:0104 mov ah,4c
26FB:0106 int 21
26FB:0108
-rcx
CX 0000
:8
-n key.com
-w
Writing 0008 bytes
-q
```

Actually, what you really need to type, after DEBUG is loaded, are the following keystrokes:

```
a
mov ah,1
int 21
mov ah,4c
```

```
int 21
rcx
8
n key.com
w
q
```

Everything else not shown above is automatically entered by DEBUG. This creates an assembly program that is 8 bytes long and named KEY.COM. Check your disk to see its existence.

Note: If you do not want to go to the DEBUG screen, use COPY CON to create the above file and name it KEY.SCR (or any name) and then enter this command:

A>**debug < key.scr**

This will redirect the input file and automatically create KEY.COM without your having to go to the DEBUG screen.

Note: The KEY.COM file is included on the DOS-TA disk. It is used by the MENUB.BAT batch file also on the disk. This batch file is a more complex version of MENU4.BAT discussed below. It can be used to run the Drill lesson files. It runs more slowly than the MENU.EXE program, also included on the disk. If you wish, you can retrieve MENUB.BAT to EDLIN or EDIT and modify it for your own purposes.

A Menu with Number Options

We can now use our interactive program to improve MENU1.BAT, as shown below:

```
 1: @echo off
 2: rem MENU3.BAT--press a number key to start
 3: if %1.==1. goto EDIT
 4: if %1.==2. goto GORILLA
 5: if %1.==3. goto NIBBLES
 6:
 7: goto MENU
 8:
 9: :EDIT
10: c:
11: cd\dos
12: edit untitled
13: cd\
14: goto END
15:
```

```
16: :GORILLA
17: c:
18: cd\dos
19: qbasic gorilla
20: cd\
21: goto END
22:
23: :NIBBLES
24: c:
25: cd\dos
26: qbasic nibbles
27: cd\
28: goto END
29:
30: :MENU          TYPE MENU. TEXT
31: echo
32: echo ------------------Menu Options------------------
33: echo
34: echo                    1.  DOS Editor
35: echo
36: echo                    2.  Gorilla
37: echo
38: echo                    3.  Nibbles
39: echo
40: echo Press a number (1, 2, or 3)
41: :MORE
42: key
43: if errorlevel 52 goto NO
44: if errorlevel 51 goto NIBBLES
45: if errorlevel 50 goto GORILLA
46: if errorlevel 49 goto EDIT
47: :NO
48: echo ^G^G^G INVALID CHARACTER
49: goto MORE
50: :END
```

We have erased line 6 (MENU1.BAT) and added lines 40–50. If no parameter is entered with the batch file name, line 7 leads to line 30 to display the available options. Line 42 executes KEY.COM. This program pauses batch execution and waits for a keystroke. When a key is pressed, it is displayed on the screen, and the real action begins!

Lines 43–46 check the key pressed and do branching accordingly. Each key on the keyboard has a corresponding exit code based on its ASCII value. The keys of 1, 2, and 3 have the corresponding ASCII values of 49, 50, and 51 (see Appendix B). If any of these keys is pressed, execution will branch to a proper label.

If you scrutinize lines 43–46, you will notice the reverse order of the numbers. As explained earlier, ERRORLEVEL considers the exit code of the key you press to be matching the number specified in a test line if the former is equal to or greater than the latter. Thus, branching will not proceed accurately if we arrange the numbers in an ascending or random order.

Based on the arrangement in lines 43–49, if the exit code of the key you press is lower than 49 or higher than 51, execution will branch to the NO label in line 47. Line 48 causes the PC to beep three times and line 48 branches execution back to the MORE label to run KEY.COM another time. Here you can also branch to the MENU label to display the menu and run KEY.COM another time.

Line 43 is crucial in trapping a key that has an exit code higher than 3 (ASCII 51). Without this, pressing 4 or an alphabet key will lead to line 44 being tested true. This will not happen after adding line 43 because it branches execution to line 47.

A Menu with Letter Options

MENU3 traps keystrokes whose exit codes are sequential. What if you want to trap nonsequential keys? This situation occurs when you allow the user to press an alphabetic letter to start a program.

Our final menu assumes that you use dBASE, Lotus 1-2-3, and WordPerfect. It will let you press one of the three letters in uppercase or lowercase to start a program:

```
 1: @echo off
 2: rem MENU4.BAT--press an alphabetic key to start
 3: cls
 4: echo Select: W (WordPerfect), L (Lotus), D (dBASE)
 5: echo/
 6: key
 7: if errorlevel 119 if not errorlevel 120 goto WP
 8: if errorlevel 108 if not errorlevel 109 goto LOTUS
 9: if errorlevel 100 if not errorlevel 101 goto DBASE
10: if errorlevel 87 if not errorlevel 88 goto WP
11: if errorlevel 76 if not errorlevel 77 goto LOTUS
12: if errorlevel 68 if not errorlevel 69 goto DBASE
13: goto NONE
14: :WP
15: wp.bat
16: :LOTUS
```

```
17: 123.bat
18: :DBASE
19: db.bat
20: :NONE
21: echo Not a valid selection
```

Line 4 displays the available options. Line 6 runs the KEY.COM program and pauses for a keystroke. The key pressed from the keyboard is now checked for its exit code. Each letter has an exit code, which is its ASCII value. The letter "w", for example, has the ASCII value of 119. So line 7 intercepts the key press and branches execution to the WP label in line 14. Line 15 then runs a batch file named WP.BAT. MENU4.BAT is finished, and control is transferred to WP.BAT.

Notice that we include the BAT extension in each batch file to be chained. You can exclude this extension if you wish. However, if a batch file and your application program have the same name and stay in the same directory, the latter (with a COM or EXE extension) takes precedence; it will be executed instead of your batch file. By adding the BAT extension, the specified batch file will be run instead.

WP.BAT may contain something like the following, depending on where you store your files:

```
1: cd\wp51
2: \wp
3: cd\
```

In this arrangement, C:\WP51 is designated as the current directory and WP.EXE is started from it. When you exit WordPerfect, line 3 changes back to the root directory. Instead of storing them in a separate batch file, these lines can be, if you wish, inserted in MENU4.BAT as we did in MENU3.BAT.

Lines 7–12 of MENU4.BAT require a little elaboration. Each of these lines is intended to isolate a particular letter and branch execution to a proper line. The first three lines intercept lowercase w (119), l (108), and d (100); the last three lines uppercase W (87), L (76), and D (68). When any one of these letters is pressed, execution is branched to a proper line. When any other key is pressed, execution will branch to NONE and the batch file will end, after displaying the message in line 21.

Using IF ERRORLEVEL and IF NOT ERRORLEVEL in the same line can prevent a mismatch. Let us examine line 7 as an example. If you do not use IF NOT ERRORLEVEL, any exit code equal to or higher than 119 will be considered matching. So if the user presses "z," for example, batch execution will branch to WP. By adding IF NOT ERRORLEVEL 120, only 119 is matching. In this arrangement, you no longer need to adhere to a descending order as shown in MENU3.BAT. You can rearrange the order of lines 7–12 in any manner you want and the batch file will still work.

Line 4 of MENU4.BAT displays a one-line menu at the top of a clear screen. If you want to have a more attractive menu, first change it to:

```
4: type menu.txt
```

Then set out to create another file named MENU.TXT. If you created this file in Chapter 10 (using EDIT), the modified line 4 can use it without your doing anything.

From now on, whenever you run MENU4.BAT, the MENU.TXT screen will greet you. If you want it displayed as soon as DOS is booted, change MENU4.BAT to AUTOEXEC.BAT and store it (as well as MENU.TXT and KEY.COM) in the root

---

TIPS   AND   TRICKS

CREATING   A   Y/N   PROMPT

You can use KEY.COM and ERRORLEVEL to create a Y/N prompt. There are several ways you can handle this situation. You can branch execution to YES if the user presses Y and to NO if any other key is pressed. You can branch to NO if N is pressed and to YES if any other key is pressed. Or you can branch to YES if Y is pressed, to NO if N is pressed, and to reprompt the user if any other key is pressed. We will simulate the first situation:

```
 1: @echo off
 2: rem YESNO.BAT--to show Y/N prompt and branch
 3: echo/
 4: echo Do you want to continue (Y/N)?
 5: key
 6: if errorlevel 89 if not errorlevel 90 goto YES
 7: if errorlevel 121 if not errorlevel 122 goto YES
 8: echo/
 9: echo You have chosen N. Goodbye!
10: goto END
11: :YES
12: echo/
13: echo You have chosen Y.
14: echo Press a key to end.
15: pause > nul
16: rem . . .
17: :END
```

Lines 6 and 7 trap a keystroke. If Y (ASCII 89) or y (ASCII 121) is pressed, execution branches to YES. If any other key is pressed, no branching is done and execution continues with the lines immediately below.

directory of the boot disk. You can also make your AUTOEXEC.BAT call MENU4.BAT to show the menu.

CHOICE FOR USER INTERACTION

■ *Handle user interaction in a batch file using the external command CHOICE.COM.*

DOS 6 has a new external program called CHOICE.COM that can be used in a batch file to handle user interaction. This program can replace KEY.COM discussed in the previous section. Keep in mind that CHOICE is an external program—quite unlike the other batch commands. If you use it in a batch file, you must copy it to your floppy disk or provide a path for DOS to find this program.

Basic Rules

We will first discuss and demonstrate how this command works on the command line. Then we will apply it to the last menu batch file discussed in the previous section.

Entering CHOICE /? on the command line leads to this syntax:

```
CHOICE [/C[:]choices] [/N] [/S] [/T[:]c,nn] [text]
```

Notice that all the parameters are optional, enclosed in brackets.

If you enter CHOICE alone, this is the result:

```
C:\DOS>choice
[Y,N]?
```

The default [Y,N]? prompt appears and a pause begins. If you press Y, y, N, or n, the pause ends and the DOS prompt reappears. Pressing anything else leads to a beep and no budge in the cursor.

You can use the /C (or /C:) switch, followed by the characters that will end the pause. This arrangement limits the choices to the characters placed after /C:. The following two commands are identical and legal:

```
C:\DOS>choice /c:abcde
[A,B,C,D,E]?A
```

```
C:\DOS>choice /cabcde
[A,B,C,D,E]?A
```

Notice that the colon makes no difference, but it does enhance readability. In either case, when a permissible key is pressed, the pause ends. Otherwise, a beep is heard and the pause continues.

Notice that the choices are displayed in uppercase. If you include the /S (sensitive in case) switch anywhere after CHOICE, the choices will be displayed in the specified case, lowercase in our case. In that case, only pressing a permissible letter in the right case will end the pause; a corresponding letter in the other case will no longer be acceptable.

If you use /N (no prompt), the choice prompt and the ending question mark will not be shown during the pause. This allows you to substitute the standard prompt with one designed by yourself. You can also add your own message to the standard prompt. Here are two examples:

```
C:\DOS>choice Here are the choices--/s/c:abc
Here are the choices--[a,b,c]?c
```

```
C:\DOS>choice Here are the choices--a, b, c--/n /c:abc /s
Here are the choices--a, b, c--b
```

In the first example, the standard prompt is augmented with an extra message; in the second, it is totally replaced due to the addition of the /N switch. The /S switch causes the standard prompt in the first case to display the choices in lowercase; user responses, c and b in the above examples, are also displayed in lowercase.

Your message text can be placed anywhere, as long as it is separated from switches. Here we place it at the end and use numbers as options:

```
C:\DOS>choice /c:123 Make a choice:
Make a choice:[1,2,3]?1
```

You can use /T (time) to automatically supply the default choice after a specified number of seconds (0 to 99). Here is an example:

```
C:\DOS>choice Here are the choices--/s/c:abc /t:a,5
Here are the choices--[a,b,c]?a
```

If no response is supplied after 5 seconds, a is automatically provided as the default. You must use /C to provide choices if you have /T. This example will thus lead to an error:

```
C:\DOS>choice /ta,2
CHOICE: Timeout default not in specified (or default) choices.
```

You can use /C to supply the choices before or after the /T switch. Either arrangement below is legal:

```
C:\DOS>choice /cabc /ta,2
[A,B,C]?A
```

```
C:\DOS>choice /ta,2 /cabc
[A,B,C]?A
```

B E   S E N S I T I V E   T O   Y O U R   C A S E S

If you use the /S switch, you restrict legal responses to the characters of the specified case. If you use it alone, the default prompt is displayed in uppercase, like this:

```
C:\DOS>choice /s
[Y,N]?
```

The legal responses are now limited to Y or N, but not y or n. What if you want to limit to lowercase characters? Specify them with the /C switch, like this:

```
C:\DOS>choice /s /c:yn
[y,n]?
```

If you take out the /S, the default prompt will reappear in uppercase, so all the parameters become redundant.

Can you use /S with choices consisting of numbers, like this?

```
C:\DOS>choice /s /c:123
[1,2,3]?
```

Yes, but you are wasting your time because numbers are not case sensitive.

You can make the displayed options different from the legal responses by using different cases. This may prevent another person from using your menu batch file (see below) to access a program. On the command line, it may look like this:

```
C:\DOS>choice Make a choice--a, b, c: /n /s /c:ABC
Make a choice--a, b, c: A
```

Even though the displayed choices are a, b, or c, the only legal choices are A, B, or C.

If the user presses a key not included in the choice list, the pause becomes indefinite; the specified time is no longer valid.

CHOICE and Batch Files

A user choice corresponds to an errorlevel number, the first being 1, the second 2, and so on; this number is different from an ASCII value expected by KEY.COM. These numbers can be used for branching in a batch file. We can now modify (and simplify) our last menu batch file this way:

```
1: @echo off
2: rem MENU5.BAT--use CHOICE for user interaction
3: cls
4: echo Select: W (WordPerfect), L (Lotus), D (DBase), None
```

```
 5: echo/
 6: c:\dos\choice /c:wldn /t:n,10
 7: if errorlevel 4 goto NONE
 8: if errorlevel 3 goto DBASE
 9: if errorlevel 2 goto LOTUS
10: if errorlevel 1 goto WP
11: :WP
12: wp.bat
13: :LOTUS
14: 123.bat
15: :DBASE
16: db.bat
17: :NONE
```

T I P S   A N D   T R I C K S

U N U S U A L   C H O I C E   C H A R A C T E R S

CHOICE recognizes extended ASCII characters shown in Appendix B. You can use them to encrypt your menu options. Lines 4 and 6 of MENU5.BAT can thus be modified this way:

```
4: echo Select: WordPerf (201), Lotus (202), DBase (203)
5: echo/
6: c:\dos\choice /n /c:╔╦╗ /t:╠,10
```

The four characters shown after /C: are obtained by holding down Alt and pressing a number shown in line 4. These characters are not displayed because of the /N switch. Thus a user has to press Alt-201 in order to run WordPerfect. This could deter an amateur from using your menu.

If you want to use some fun characters, try the following on the command line:

```
C:\DOS>choice /c^A^B^D^E^L
[☺,☻,♣,♠,♀]?☺
```

To enter the characters on the command line as well as in response, press Ctrl and a proper character, or Alt with a proper number on the numeric keypad where Alt-1 equals Ctrl-A, Alt-2 equals Ctrl-B, etc.

Here is another example:

```
C:\DOS>choice Quo Vadis /c^X^Y^Z
Quo Vadis [↑,↓,→]?
```

These characters are Ctrl-X (Alt-24), Ctrl-Y (Alt-25), and Ctrl-Z (Alt-26). Alt-27 (←) is Esc and cannot be used here.

After running MENU5.BAT, line 4 displays a one-line message and line 5 shows the [W,L,D,N]? prompt. If no key is pressed in 10 seconds, the pause ends because the default option of N will be chosen and line 7 will branch batch execution to line 17.

CHOICE and Redirection

Have you wondered whether CHOICE can have its input or output redirected? After experimenting for a while, I can give you a definite yes. Here is an example:

```
C:\DOS>echo y ¦ choice
[Y,N]?Y
```

Y is automatically supplied and no pause awaits you. The output, however, is displayed on the screen. We can hide the output this way:

```
C:\DOS>echo n ¦ choice > nul
```

This command in effect does nothing. N is automatically piped in where an answer is expected and the output is redirected to the NUL device.

An expected response can also be supplied by a redirected input. If a legal choice is provided, CHOICE will not pause to wait for a response. If you have a file named Y which contains nothing but a Y character, this is what happens:

```
C:\DOS>choice < y
[Y,N]?Y
```

Is there a practical use for any of these? Maybe. One thing I can think of is using redirection to record the outputs produced by your menu batch file by using a mechanism like this:

```
C:\DOS>choice >> record
```

This shows no prompt during the pause. An illegal response leads to no noticeable response from DOS, not even a beep. A legal response, Y or N, is sent to the file named RECORD.

You can use the following batch file to record the selections made by anyone using the menu.

```
1: @echo off
2: rem MENU6.BAT--to record menu selections
3: cls
4: echo Select: WordPerfect, Lotus, DBase, None
5: echo Press--W, L, D, or N
6: c:\dos\choice /c:wldn >> record
7: if errorlevel 4 goto NONE
8: if errorlevel 3 goto DBASE
```

```
 9: if errorlevel 2 goto LOTUS
10: if errorlevel 1 goto WP
11: :WP
12: wp.bat
13: :LOTUS
14: 123.bat
15: :DBASE
16: db.bat
17: :NONE
```

After using this batch file a few times, you can examine what has been saved to RECORD. You can also add the date-time stamp by adding these lines after line 2:

```
3: echo/ ¦ date ¦ find "C" >> record
4: echo/ ¦ time ¦ find "C" >> record
```

The RECORD file may include lines like these to indicate the date, time, and selection:

```
Current date is Tue 05-11-1993
Current time is  8:10:12.82a
[W,L,D,N]?W
```

MANAGING STARTUP

As PCs become more powerful and versatile, more and more TSR programs and device drivers are now being loaded by your CONFIG.SYS file. Things become so complicated that DOS 6 now provides a variety of ways and tools to manage your PC's startup. You can now:

- Have a clean startup—bypassing the CONFIG.SYS and AUTOEXEC.BAT files.

- Select certain lines in the CONFIG.SYS file to skip or execute.

- Program the CONFIG.SYS file to let the user choose one of multiple configuration blocks to execute.

- Tie the AUTOEXEC.BAT file to the selection made by the user during the CONFIG.SYS file's execution.

Some of these items can be understood and implemented by a novice, but most require considerable computer savvy. For that reason we have saved the beginning issue to be covered at the end, after you have gained some knowledge of programming.

Clean Boot and Selective Configurations

When your PC starts, it races to execute the CONFIG.SYS and then AUTOEXEC.BAT files. The latter can be aborted if you hold down Ctrl-C. But the former cannot be stopped. If you want a different configuration, you have to edit the CONFIG.SYS file, adding REM before certain lines to prevent their execution. After saving the file, you can then reboot to get a new configuration.

You no longer have to do those in DOS 6. You can do a clean boot or select certain configuration commands to skip. To have a clean startup, press F5 or hold down Shift when the following message appears at the beginning of booting:

```
Starting MS-DOS...
```

This message appears after a while:

```
MS-DOS is bypassing your CONFIG.SYS and AUTOEXEC.BAT files.
```

This approach may help you identify some problems related to your PC or TSR programs. Since device drivers and programs are not loaded, don't expect your PC to behave the same way. The following variables, however, are automatically entered into the DOS environment:

```
PATH=C:\DOS
PROMPT=$P$G
COMSPEC=C:\COMMAND.COM
```

Instead of F5, you can press F8 to let you determine which lines to execute. You will see a prompt like this:

```
DOS=HIGH [Y,N]?
```

You can press Y to execute the line, or N to skip it. During a pause, you can press Esc to execute all the remaining lines or F5 to skip all of them.

After all the configuration lines are taken care of, this final prompt appears:

```
Process AUTOEXEC.BAT [Y,N]?
```

You can now press Y or N to execute or skip the file.

You can also use ? in certain lines in your CONFIG.SYS file, like this:

```
device?=c:\dos\ramdrive.sys
```

When this line is slated for execution, you will be prompted with [Y,N]. Lines without a ? are executed automatically.

Normally, when DOS is booted, there is a 2-second delay to wait for you to press F5 or F8. If you want no delay, include SWITCHES=/F command in your CONFIG.SYS file. You can also disable these keys by using /N. In the following example (it can be placed anywhere in your CONFIG.SYS file),

```
switches=/f /n
```

the startup is not delayed and the user cannot use F5, F8, or Shift to halt or abort execution.

After discussing all the confusing keystrokes and techniques, a summation is in order. The following table can serve as a quick reminder:

F5/Shift	Clean boot
F8	Selective boot
Esc	Execute all remaining
F5	Bypass all remaining
device?	Prompt for [Y,N]
switches=/n	No bypassing

Multiple Configurations

There are occasions when a PC needs to be configured differently—to run different programs or be used by different persons. Each person or program may require different configuration commands for the PC to run efficiently. For example, when you do not intend to use a RAM disk, you may want to skip loading the program so as not to waste memory. In addition to the techniques discussed in the previous section, you can now get your CONFIG.SYS file to display a menu so that the user can choose a block of items to execute and skip the rest. Using a configuration menu is a preferred approach if the CONFIG.SYS file becomes complicated. A CONFIG.SYS file may look like this:

```
device=c:\dos\himem.sys
dos=high
files=30
buffers=20
numlock=off
device=c:\dos\setver.exe

rem--This is a menu block:--
[menu]
menuitem=ram,Create a RAM disk
menuitem=ansi,Load ANSI.SYS

rem--This is a configuration block:--
[ram]
device=c:\dos\ramdrive.sys

[ansi]
device=c:\dos\ansi.sys
```

After running the above file, this menu appears:

```
MS-DOS 6 Startup Menu
=====================

    1. Create a RAM disk
    2. Load ANSI.SYS

Enter a choice: 1
```

The bottom of the screen also tells you that you can press F5 to bypass execution or press F8 to toggle between [Y] and [N] for selective execution. [N] is the default. If [Y] is selected, you will be prompted with [Y,N] before a selected line is executed.

The first option in the menu is also highlighted. You can press 1 or 2 to highlight an option. When you press Enter, the highlighted option is executed.

Let us now discuss our CONFIG.SYS file. The first four lines have been explained in previous sections. NUMLOCK is a new configuration command that lets you specify ON or OFF to determine the beginning state of the Num Lock key. Loading SETVER.EXE lets you use previous DOS programs; without this I cannot use EDLIN from version 5 (version 6 no longer includes EDLIN).

The remainder of the file contains three blocks, each beginning with a block header and ending with another header or the end of the file. The first block is known as a **menu block** and always headed with the [menu] header. It serves the same purpose as the main() function in C. It contains menu items which are used to display messages and branch execution to a selected block. The last two blocks are known as **configuration blocks**. Each is like a function in C to be branched to when a selection is made.

The MENUITEM command contains two items separated by a comma. The first must match the header of a configuration block, and the second provides the text string for display. If the second item is missing, the first is used for display as well. Each item can have a string up to 70 characters long. MENUITEM can be included only in a menu block, not a configuration block.

You can use the INCLUDE command to include one configuration block in another. This can serve as a shortcut to repetitive typing. You can also use the [common] header to mark a configuration block, which tells DOS to always execute the lines included in such a block. In our example, the beginning lines are executed before [menu] is encountered. You can include them in a [common] block and place them in any part of the file. You can have multiple [common] blocks placed in various parts of the file. They will be executed in the order of their locations from top down.

This modified file includes examples of INCLUDE and [common]:

```
device=c:\dos\himem.sys
dos=high

[menu]
menuitem=ram,Create a RAM disk
menuitem=ansi,Load ANSI.SYS
menuitem=both,RAM disk & ANSI

[ram]
device=c:\dos\ramdrive.sys

[ansi]
device=c:\dos\ansi.sys

[both]
include=ram
include=ansi

[common]
files=30
buffers=20
numlock=off
device=c:\dos\setver.exe
```

The third menu item includes all the commands from both [ram] and [ansi]. Even though [common] is placed at the end, it will be executed regardless of what option the user chooses.

A menu block can contain up to nine menu items. If you need more, you can use the SUBMENU command to provide for more choices. This is comparable to branching to a subroutine, which in turn branches to another. Here is an example:

```
device=c:\dos\himem.sys
dos=high

[menu]
menuitem=ram,Create a RAM disk
menuitem=ansi,Load ANSI.SYS
submenu=ems,Choose EMS or No EMS

[ram]
device=c:\dos\ramdrive.sys

[ansi]
device=c:\dos\ansi.sys

[ems]
menuitem=win,No EMS--to run Windows
menuitem=dos,EMS--to run DOS
```

```
[win]
device=c:\dos\emm386.exe noems

[dos]
device=c:\dos\emm386.exe ram

[common]
files=30
buffers=20
numlock=off
device=c:\dos\setver.exe
```

The menu block now contains a SUBMENU item. It will be displayed as the third option when the menu is shown. When option 3 is chosen, another menu appears with two options. If the user chooses 1, the [win] block is executed and no expanded memory is created. (Most DOS applications use expanded memory but Windows needs extended memory.)

We have so far discussed [menu], [common], MENUITEM, SUBMENU, NUMLOCK, and INCLUDE. Let us now cover the other available commands: MENUDEFAULT and MENUCOLOR.

MENUDEFAULT is placed in a menu or submenu block to automatically supply the default choice after a specified time elapses—similar to the /T switch in CHOICE discussed earlier in this chapter. MENUCOLOR sets values for text and background colors. Consider this example:

```
[menu]
menuitem=ram,Create a RAM disk
menuitem=ansi,Load ANSI.SYS
submenu=ems,Choose EMS or No EMS
menucolor=1,8
menudefault=ansi,10
  . . .
```

The background will be changed to gray and text to blue. If no selection is made after 10 seconds, [ansi] will be executed.

In setting colors, the first value is for text and the second (optional) for background. You can choose among these values:

0	black	8	gray
1	blue	9	bright blue
2	green	10	bright green
3	cyan	11	bright cyan
4	red	12	bright red
5	magenta	13	bright magenta
6	brown	14	bright brown
7	white	15	bright white

If you specify no color, the default is white on black. If you use the same value for both text and background, the display becomes invisible.

Integrating CONFIG.SYS and AUTOEXEC.BAT

If you use a menu for multiple configurations, DOS 6 creates an environment variable called CONFIG. This variable has the value of the header of the configuration block selected by the user. This value can be used by the AUTOEXEC.BAT file to branch to a line to automatically load a selected program. This arrangement can keep your CONFIG.SYS and AUTOEXEC.BAT in sync.

Suppose you use Windows and WordPerfect for DOS. The configuration for each is different. You can set up a menu in the CONFIG.SYS file to let you choose to run either package. If you choose to run Windows, the related configuration block will be executed. Then the Windows section in the AUTOEXEC.BAT file will be run.

The CONFIG.SYS file may look like this:

```
device=c:\dos\himem.sys
dos=high,umb

[menu]
menuitem=wp,Start WordPerfect
menuitem=win,Start Windows

[win]
device=c:\dos\emm386.exe noems

[wp]
device=c:\dos\emm386.exe ram

[common]
files=30
buffers=20
numlock=off
devicehigh=c:\dos\setver.exe
```

The AUTOEXEC.BAT file may resemble this:

```
@echo off
lh c:\dos\smartdrv.exe
prompt $p$g
path=c:\dos
goto %config%

:WP
cd\wp
wp
goto END
```

```
:WIN
lh c:\mouse\mouse.com
cd\win
win

:END
```

We have added UMB in the first file so that we can access the UMA, and SEVER.EXE is loaded to the area. The second file uses LH to load SmartDrive (for disk caching) and MOUSE.COM (newer mouse drivers have the COM extension and are loaded from AUTOEXEC.BAT) to the UMA.

After the first file is executed and a menu displayed, you can choose between *Start WordPerfect* and *Start Windows*. If you choose the first, the [wp] block is executed to create expanded memory and the CONFIG=wp variable enters the environment. This variable is then used by the second file to do automatic branching. The *goto %config%* command in line 5 is translated to *goto wp* when executed. WordPerfect will then be loaded.

If you choose Windows when the menu is shown, the [win] block is run to configure the RAM differently and *goto %config%* becomes *goto win*. Windows will run after the mouse driver is loaded.

This arrangement of integrating your CONFIG.SYS and AUTOEXEC.BAT can achieve a high degree of automation. If your system is set up properly, a user needs to do little work during the startup and the system will be optimally configured. Setting up such a system or altering it, however, requires considerable savvy and effort.

Here is one more complication. If you use multiple configurations with MemMaker, you need to go through these elaborate steps to optimize your memory use for each configuration:

1. Retrieve your CONFIG.SYS file to a text editor.

2. Save each configuration block (together with all the commands to run a program) as a separate file, maybe CONFIG.1, CONFIG.2, and so on; these files should not contain any commands used in menu display or branching—just plain configuration commands.

3. Change CONFIG.SYS to something else and CONFIG.1 to CONFIG.SYS.

4. Run MemMaker.

5. Repeat steps 3 and 4 with another configuration file until all are covered.

6. Combine all the configuration files into one.

If you are willing to go through that, as suggested in the DOS 6 printed manual, you deserve an award for dedication.

Here is probably a better idea. Edit your CONFIG.SYS file and add REM before all the lines except the block you want MemMaker to optimize. Run MemMaker to optimize the resaved CONFIG.SYS. Repeat with each new block. After each block is tested, make a final arrangement in the CONFIG.SYS file. This is still an elaborate procedure, but it is less complicated than the previous.

P R A C T I C E   1 1 - 5

- [ ] 1. Modify MENU0.BAT so that if no parameter is entered with the batch file name, 1.BAT will be executed. If other parameters are entered, the batch file should do nothing but display the options.

- [ ] 2. Modify MENU1.BAT so that when the user enters a number, a corresponding batch file saved on disk will be chained.

- [ ] 3. Add a Quit option to MENU4.BAT. The user should be allowed to press Q or q to end the batch file. If an unavailable option is chosen, the menu is to be displayed again.

- [ ] 4. Create a batch file that will provide help for three DOS commands each in a separate screen; the text for each help screen should be stored in a separate file. The batch file should provide for these scenarios:
     1. No parameter entered
     2. Available option
     3. Unavailable option
  Use the DOS.EXE program included on the DOS-TA disk as a model.

- [ ] 5. Modify YESNO.BAT to branch to NO if N or n is pressed. Execution is to continue below if any other key is pressed.

- [ ] 6. Modify YESNO.BAT to branch to YES if Y or y is pressed and to NO if N or n is pressed. No other key should be accepted.

- [ ] 7. Modify TYPEn.BAT files discussed earlier in the text so that the screen will display a file name and the user prompted with Y/N. If Y or y is supplied, the file should be displayed. If another key is pressed, another matching file name should be displayed and the user prompted again.

- [ ] 8. Modify the above so that a file name will be displayed and the user will be prompted Y/N to print the file.

- [ ] 9. Create a batch file named TESTKEY.BAT. It should run KEY.COM and contain two test lines using ERRORLEVEL. The first line should display "–100" if a key pressed has an exit code below 100. The second line should show "100+" if a key pressed has an exit code of 100 or higher.

- [ ] 10. Use TESTKEY.BAT to test c, d, and e (all lowercase) and report the results.

S U M M A R Y   A N D   R E V I E W

Check each item as you review and understand the following highlights of the chapter:

☐   1. There are about a dozen batch commands and symbols that can be used in batch files to make them behave similar to computer programs. Use these commands in batch files to make them more intelligent and to make you more productive.

☐   2. Keep the default ECHO on when debugging a batch file. Turn it off after it is debugged. Put the @ECHO OFF command in the first line to hide the entire batch file's execution. Or put @ in front of selected lines to hide their execution.

☐   3. Use REM (or :) to add remarks. They can remind you of what some tricky lines are supposed to do. They are useful if you need to revise a batch file.

☐   4. Replaceable parameters (dummy variables) allow you to handle parameters entered on the command line. There can be up to 10 such variables at one time.

☐   5. Use the SHIFT command to handle more than 10 parameters. The command can make replaceable parameters more mobile and versatile.

☐   6. GOTO and : go in tandem. The former is used to branch batch execution to a text string preceded by the latter, which is known as a label. A label marks a place to which GOTO directs batch execution.

☐   7. When doing branching, make sure there is a proper label to branch to. If no matching label is found, batch execution will terminate prematurely.

☐   8. Labels can be in uppercase or lowercase. As long as the spelling is identical, two labels of different cases will be considered matching. In searching for a label to match, DOS begins from the top of the batch file and goes down from there. If there are several identical labels, only the topmost will be matched and the rest are not accessible.

☐   9. Only the first eight characters are significant in a label. If there are several labels which all share the same first eight characters, only the topmost will be accessible. A label containing a delimiter such as a space, comma, or semicolon will have all the characters after the delimiter ignored by DOS.

☐   10. The IF command is used for conditional branching. It can test: (1) the existence of a parameter or an environment variable, (2) the existence of a file on disk, and (3) an exit code of certain DOS commands and all the ASCII characters.

☐   11. Use the common expression IF .==.%1 to test the existence of a parameter entered on the command line. Change the number to the number of parameters expected. Use IF .==.%PATH% to test the existence of an environment variable.

☐   12. Use the FOR..IN..DO command for looping operations. It is a compact command that can pack a number of activities in a simple line. It will convert wild cards to actual file names, and is thus useful in applying some commands such as TYPE to multiple files.

13. A FOR command normally cannot nest another FOR command. You can, however, use COMMAND /C to run another copy of FOR in the same line. You can also make one FOR call another batch file to nest another FOR.

14. Take advantage of the environment space to pass arguments from the command line to a batch file or from one batch file to another. Use environment variables to shorten some long and repetitive batch lines.

15. When a batch file executes a program, control is returned after the program exits. On the contrary, when a batch file executes another batch file, control is not returned. This is a chaining operation.

16. If you want control to return after executing another batch file, use CALL followed by a batch file name. This becomes a nesting operation.

17. If you want to pass an argument to the nested or chained batch file, add a parameter after the calling or chaining batch file's name.

18. For a long and complex batch file, break it down to smaller modules and nest or chain them. This is easier to organize and debug. Some of the modules can be recycled, thus saving you programming time.

19. Use the external CHOICE command to handle user interaction. Branch batch execution with IF and ERRORLEVEL. The first user choice returns exit code 1, the second 2, and so on. This mechanism is easier to handle than ASCII values.

20. Use clean boot (F5) or selective configurations (F8) to manage startup. Create a startup menu so that you can select an option to execute a group of configuration commands. This lets you make better use of your memory.

R E V I E W   Q U E S T I O N S

Write an answer for each question below:

1. If you don't want a line's execution displayed, what can you do? If you want to hide an entire batch file's execution, what can you do?

2. How do REM and : differ?

3. What message does the PAUSE command display? How can you pause a screen display and display your own message instead?

4. What is a label? How does DOS recognize a label?

5. Are labels case sensitive? If there are several labels of the same spelling, which one is recognized?

6. What is a replaceable parameter (dummy variable) and how is each replaceable parameter related to a command-line parameter?

7. What does the SHIFT command do?

8. Explain the differences among looping, branching, nesting, and chaining.

9. What can the IF command test?

10. Mention the major rules concerning batch labels.

11. What is the difference between a batch file calling (using CALL) another batch file and running another batch file?

12. What is the difference between a batch file running another batch file and running a program?

13. What are exit codes and cite a few commands that use them?

14. Cite the commands used to:
    a. Test a file's existence
    b. Test an exit code
    c. Test a parameter's existence
    d. Test the existence of an environment variable

15. What does the FOR..IN..DO command do?

12 Using ANSI.SYS

C O M M A N D S   C O V E R E D

PROMPT, ECHO, DOSKEY

N E W   T E R M S   A N D   S Y M B O L S

ANSI, ANSI escape sequence, $e[, ^[[, ←[, extended keys

513

QUICK START

To enter an ANSI command on the command line:

> A>prompt $e[7m

To enter an ANSI command from a batch file:

> echo ^[[7m   (EDLIN)
> echo ←[7m   (EDIT)

For various ways of locating the cursor on the screen:

> See Table 12.1.

To place the cursor at a particular position:

> A>prompt $e[row#;col#H

For various screen attributes:

> See Tables 12.2 and 12.3.

To set black foreground (text) and white background:

> A>prompt $e[30;47m

To define F10 to enter DIR by just pressing it:

> A>prompt $e[0;68;"dir";13p

To define F12 to display "prompt $e[" (for quick use of PROMPT):

> A>prompt $e[0;134;"prompt $$e["p

For single-number key codes:

> See Table 12.4.

For extended key codes:

> See Table 12.5.

To show the key codes of a keyboard key:

> Run KEYCODE.BAT and press the desired key.

To quickly enter an ANSI command:

> Run ANSI.BAT with proper parameters.

To create a macro for a quick entry of an ANSI command:

A>**doskey p=prompt $$e[$*$$p$$g**

To quickly write a memo:

Use the MEMO.BAT or MEMO1.BAT batch files

To quickly write a phone message:

Use the MSG.BAT batch file and the accompanying key definitions.

As explained in Chapter 9, ANSI.SYS is a special device driver included in your DOS package. It must be installed before you can follow the chapter material. To install it, you simply include this line in the CONFIG.SYS file before booting:

device=c:\dos\ansi.sys /x

This line tells DOS to go to the C:\DOS directory to load ANSI.SYS stored there. If you store it somewhere else, you need to provide a different path. Do not include the /X switch if you are not using an enhanced keyboard (101 keys). If you have such a keyboard, the /X switch allows you to define the extra keys available on your keyboard.[1]

When it comes to keyboard input and screen output, the original DOS is really a Dumb Operating System. The keyboard cannot be redefined, nor does it have any macro capability (storing multiple keystrokes in one key) unless DOSKEY is loaded. The cursor cannot be freely moved to any part of the screen. Screen colors or display modes cannot be changed.

ANSI.SYS has changed all that. After you have it installed, you can do the following:

- Locate the cursor anywhere on the screen

- Erase a displayed line or the whole screen

- Set screen display modes and colors

- Redefine keyboard keys

- Assign multiple characters to a key

The ability to do all these things is what makes learning DOS more fun. After studying this chapter, you will no longer view DOS as the Dull Old Stuff.

---

1. The /X switch may not affect your keyboard. On the enhanced keyboard connected to my 386 PC, I can define F11 and F12 with or without the switch.

This chapter explains the ANSI features in this order: ANSI escape sequences, controlling the cursor, setting graphics modes/colors, and redefining keys. After these basics are covered, we will use them in a few batch files to let you quickly write memos and take telephone messages.

ANSI ESCAPE SEQUENCES

■ *Put $e[after PROMPT to enter an ANSI escape sequence.*

■ *Put ^[[(in EDLIN) or ←[(in EDIT) after ECHO or PROMPT to enter an escape sequence.*

ANSI (American National Standards Institute) has adopted a set of rules to enhance input and output functions. To tap into the installed ANSI.SYS driver to extend keyboard and screen functions, you need to use the proper DOS commands to enter ANSI commands.

An ANSI command consists of the following components:

- Esc (escape) character (ASCII 27)

- Left bracket ([, or ASCII 91)

- One or more characters or decimal numbers

- Ending with a specific letter

An ANSI command starts with the Esc character, followed by a series of characters. Such a sequence of characters is often referred to as an **ANSI escape sequence**. The two terms, ANSI command and ANSI escape sequence, are thus synonymous.

To send an ANSI escape sequence to the computer, you need to use a proper DOS command that can understand and convert an ANSI escape sequence into action. It may be the following, which sets the screen display to reverse video:

A>`prompt $e[7m`

The escape character (here shown as $e), often referred to as Esc or ESC, is not the same as your typing these three letters or pressing the Esc key on the keyboard. DOS will understand it only if you send the ASCII 27 (1B hex) value.

How do you tell DOS to go by ASCII 27? There are two ways, depending on what DOS command you use. These are shown below:

$e	Used with PROMPT only; entered from the command line, EDLIN, EDIT, or COPY CON
^[or ←	Used with PROMPT, ECHO, COPY, MORE, TYPE; entered in EDLIN, EDIT, or another text processor

When used with PROMPT, DOS interprets $e (escape) as ASCII 27. When this string is followed by [, DOS expects an ANSI parameter. Other commands, however, treat $e[as pure and simple text without any special meaning. An ANSI command entered on the command may look like this:

A>**prompt $e[0;66;"dir "p**

You can enter $e on the command line, COPY CON screen, EDLIN, or EDIT; ^[or ←, however, can be entered only in EDLIN, EDIT, or another text processor, not on the command line or COPY CON screen.[2]

To enter an escape character in EDLIN, you need to press Ctrl-V to insert ^V and then left bracket ([); the screen then shows ^V[. When you use the L command to list text lines, you see ^[. After ^[(ASCII 27), you need to add an extra [, as required by ANSI. With an escape character and a left bracket, you can then enter parameters to form a meaningful ANSI escape sequence. An ANSI command entered in EDLIN may look like this:

echo ^[[0;66;"dir "p

In EDIT, you can press Ctrl-P (the bottom right corner of the screen shows ^P) and then Esc or Ctrl-[. The result on the screen is the ← sign. If you now add [, DOS knows that you intend to enter an ANSI escape sequence. An ANSI command entered in EDIT may look like this:

echo ←[0;66;"dir "p

In WordPerfect, you can insert ^[by holding down Ctrl and pressing V and [. Ctrl-V lets you insert an uncommon character and Ctrl-[enters ASCII 27. You can also press Ctrl-V and then press Esc to show ^[. You can also enter ASCII 27 by holding down Alt and typing 27 on the numeric keypad. The result is a ← sign. Both are recognized by DOS as ASCII 27.

Keep in mind that DOS treats ^[and ← the same and both as ASCII 27. If you import a file with ^[to EDIT, it is changed to ←. If you import a file with ← to EDLIN, it becomes ^[.

If ANSI.SYS is not installed, these escape sequences are displayed as text or special characters and not converted to any action. These commands are meaningless to plain old DOS.

In the examples below, we use EDLIN screen displays to explain entering ANSI commands mainly because its line numbers are useful for referencing. You can use EDIT or another text editor to enter these commands. If you use these editors, keep the following two points in mind. First, do not enter line numbers.

---

2. On the command line or COPY CON screen, Esc or Ctrl-[leads to an immediate action, namely canceling the current line. There is no way to enter this character (ASCII 27) in a text line.

Second, the escape character may appear different in each editor. The different ways Esc is handled in EDLIN and EDIT are summarized below:

	EDLIN	EDIT
Display	^[	←
Keystrokes	Ctrl-V [	Ctrl-P Esc

PROMPT OR ECHO

■ *In a batch file, ECHO is better than PROMPT for entering ANSI escape sequences.*

The most common ways to enter ANSI escape sequences are through PROMPT and ECHO. PROMPT is used most commonly on the command line, and ECHO in batch files.

On the command line, you have no choice but to use PROMPT. From a batch file, however, you can choose to use PROMPT or ECHO. These two behave quite differently. PROMPT will alter the DOS prompt. When ECHO is off, PROMPT will work haphazardly. ECHO, on the other hand, will not change the DOS prompt and will work well whether ECHO is on or off.

The following are a few examples of the differences between PROMPT and ECHO in entering ANSI commands. All the examples are intended to assign "dir" to the F8 key, "type" to F9, and "copy" to F10. Redefining (reassigning or remapping) keys will be explained later. For now, we use these examples to illustrate ECHO and PROMPT.

PROMPT and $e[

The first example uses PROMPT with $e[:

```
1: @echo off
2: prompt $e[0;66;"dir "p
3: prompt $e[0;67;"type "p
4: prompt $e[0;68;"copy "p
```

Lines 2 and 3 will fail, and only line 4 will result in redefinition; the previously assigned values of F8 (line 2) and F9 (line 3), if any, will remain. If line 1 is deleted, all redefinitions will be successful. Line 4 (the last of the list) will also be in the environment regardless of the ECHO status. If you enter the SET command, a list, including the following, will appear:

```
PROMPT=$e[0;68;"copy "p
```

The previous PROMPT line in the environment, if any, is replaced by this line. The familiar A> prompt also disappears. If you enter PROMPT alone, the default A> prompt reappears, and the environment PROMPT disappears.

PROMPT and ^[[(or ←[)

In order to see how PROMPT's behavior is affected, let us modify the above batch file by replacing each $e[with ^[(or ← if you use EDIT). In the batch file below, you are to press Ctrl-V to display ^V, and then follow it with [(press Ctrl-P and Esc in EDIT). When you use the L command, the escape character becomes ^[, as shown below:

```
1: @echo off
2: prompt ^[[0;66;"dir "p
3: prompt ^[[0;67;"type "p
4: prompt ^[[0;68;"copy "p
```

This batch file will work (or fail) the same as the earlier one. The only difference is that the environment will show this line:

```
PROMPT=
```

The escape sequence after PROMPT is not displayed.

T I P S   A N D   T R I C K S

S A V I N G   T H E   P R O M P T

Whenever the PROMPT command is entered, either on the command line or from a batch file, the DOS prompt disappears. This could be disorienting to novices. To prevent this, you can add necessary metastrings to automatically bring back the prompt, such as:

```
A>prompt $e[7m$p$g
A:\>
```

After setting the reverse video, the PG strings display the current directory of the current drive, plus the > sign.

In the future, you can also add these or similar strings after setting cursor location, changing screen colors, or defining keys, such as:

```
A>prompt $e[0;68;"dir";13p$n$g
A>
```

This command defines F10 as "dir" plus a carriage return. After the definition, the A> prompt is restored. Without the two metastring characters at the end, the prompt would disappear.

If you use TYPE to show the batch file, the escape character (^[or ←) and all the data after them are also invisible, unlike $e[, which are visible like any text string.

ECHO and ^[[(or ←[)

Let us now replace every PROMPT with ECHO:

```
1: @echo off
2: echo ^[[0;66;"dir "p
3: echo ^[[0;67;"type "p
4: echo ^[[0;68;"copy "p
```

This batch file, unlike those before, will work well. All the key definitions will succeed. The DOS prompt will not change. And the environment's PROMPT, if any, will not be affected.

The above examples show that using ECHO is preferable over PROMPT when in a batch file. Since ECHO can be turned off, the screen remains uncluttered when keys are being redefined.

Note: If you need to use metastrings, however, you must use PROMPT. ECHO does not recognize them. This will be demonstrated shortly.

From now on, we will use ECHO in a batch file when an escape sequence is to be sent. On the command line, however, we will continue to use PROMPT in combination with $e[, because the escape character recognized by ECHO (^[or ←) cannot be entered from the command line.

D R I L L

____ 1. DOS will accept and implement an ANSI escape sequence with or without ANSI.SYS installed. True or false?

____ 2. To enter Esc in an ANSI escape sequence, you can press the Esc key on the keyboard. True or false?

____ 3. The following command entered on the command line will change your screen display to reverse video. True or false?

A>echo ^V[[7m

____ 4. If you enter the command below, the DOS prompt will disappear. True or false?

A>prompt $e[7m

____ 5. The command in question 4 will cause the following line to be included in the DOS environment. True or false?

PROMPT=$e[7m

____ 6. Both ECHO and PROMPT will work with metastrings. True or false?

____ 7. In the batch file below, both PROMPT commands will be successfully implemented. True or false?

```
@echo off
prompt $e[0;68;"dir"p
prompt $e[7m
```

CONTROLLING THE CURSOR

■ *Use a cursor-control escape sequence to position the cursor on the screen or erase a screen display.*

The ANSI escape sequences for controlling the cursor are listed in Table 12.1. You can send an escape sequence appearing on the left to achieve a special effect described on the right.

Table 12.1

ANSI Escape Sequences—Cursor and Erasure

Cursor Control	Purpose
Esc [#;#H	Cursor row-col position; default: 1,1
Esc [#;#f	Same as Esc [#,#H
Esc [#A	Cursor up by # lines; default 1
Esc [#B	Cursor down by # lines; default 1
Esc [#C	Cursor forward (right) by # columns; default 1
Esc [#D	Cursor backward (left) by # columns; default 1
Esc [6n	Device status report
Esc [s	Save cursor position
Esc [u	Restore cursor position
Display Erasure	
Esc [2J	Erase display; clear screen
Esc [K	Erase from cursor to end of line

The # character in the table should be replaced with a decimal number representing a row or column position on the screen. Where there are two such characters, the first is for row number and the second column number.

WARNING: Beware of case. Each letter must be entered as shown in the table. If you use a different case, DOS will not understand your instruction and thus will fail to implement your wish.

Let us try some concrete examples. Follow these steps:

1. Move the cursor to the middle of the screen:

    A>**prompt $e[12;40H**

The cursor now goes to the center of a 25 × 80 screen; the familiar DOS prompt, as usual, disappears. This new location will not interfere with your giving instructions to DOS.

2. Display directory entries:

    A>**dir**

The screen should be full, but the cursor remains in the middle of the screen instead of at the usual bottom of the screen.

3. Clear the screen:

    A>**cls**

The screen is cleared, but the cursor remains in the same place.

4. Display the contents in the environment:

    A>**set**

In addition to whatever is previously stored in the DOS environment, you will find this line:

    PROMPT=$e[12;40H

This is what causes the cursor to stay in the same place. Unless this value is changed, the cursor stays where it is no matter what you do.

5. Clear the environment PROMPT:

    A>**prompt**

Entering the PROMPT command alone or in combination with parameters will cause the PROMPT line in the environment to disappear or change its value. The cursor position will be controlled by either nothing or a new value. After the above command, the cursor now goes back to the left margin and begins to behave normally.

6. Clear the screen:

    A>**prompt $e[2J**

The screen is cleared and the cursor goes to the top left corner of the screen. The line below also enters the environment:

```
PROMPT=$e[2J
```

7. Display directory entries:

```
A>dir
```

The display is immediately erased. As long as this PROMPT value remains in the environment, the screen will continue to behave this way.

8. Clear the environment PROMPT:

```
A>prompt
```

Instead of erasing the whole screen, you may want to erase the current line from the cursor location to the end. This command will do just that:

```
A>prompt $e[k
```

Most of the escape sequences shown in Table 12.1 have default values. If you do not enter a number in place of #, DOS assumes that you want 1. For example, if you want to park the cursor at the top left corner of the screen, you can simply enter this command:

```
A>prompt $e[H
```

The missing row and column values are defaulted to 1. The same thing is true when you want to move the cursor up, down, left, or right. If no value is entered, 1 is presumed.

Sometimes it is useful to save a cursor position and then return to it. When "Esc [u" is encountered, the cursor returns to where it was after "Esc [s" was most recently executed. This technique will be used in a batch file in the next section.

ESCAPE SEQUENCES AND BATCH FILES

■ *On many occasions, it is preferable to enter ANSI escape sequences by using a batch file rather than typing on the command line.*

Entering ANSI escape sequences is quite laborious, requiring numerous keystrokes. To save time, you can enter the necessary keystrokes in a batch file. When the batch file is run, all the stored keystrokes will be quickly replayed.

Combining Metastrings and ANSI Commands

In Chapter 5, you learned to use the PROMPT command and metastrings to do a variety of tricks with the DOS prompt. We can now combine that knowledge with what has been discussed so far in this chapter to do something fancy.

Use EDLIN or EDIT to create a file named SHOWTIME.BAT. Then enter the following lines:

```
1: @echo off
2: cls
3: prompt $e[s$e[7m$e[1;67H$d$e[2;67H$t$e[0m$e[u$n$g
```

Double check your typing. When everything is correct as shown, save the file and exit. Run the batch file:

A>**showtime**

The upper right corner of the screen displays in reverse video something like the following:

```
Mon 06-22-1992
19:42:08.74
```

The cursor also stays at the top left corner, after the default DOS prompt.

The items in line 3 of the batch file are separately explained below:

$e[s	Save cursor position at execution time
$e[7m	Turn on reverse video
$e[1;67H	Position cursor in row 1, column 67
$d	Display the current date
$e[2;67H	Position cursor in row 2, column 67
$t	Display the current time
$e[0m	Turn off all colors; restore white on black
$e[u	Restore cursor position saved by $e[s
$n	Display current drive letter
$g	Display greater than sign (>)

Note: Notice that you can combine lots of escape sequences and mix them with metastrings. Each ANSI parameter has to be placed after $e[, and each metastring preceded by $. Also, the PROMPT in the above batch file cannot be replaced with ECHO, which cannot manipulate metastrings such as DT.

There are numerous ways you can create fancy prompts by combining metastrings and ANSI commands. Here is another example:

```
1: @echo off
2: rem FLAG.BAT
3: cls
4: prompt $e[44;5m * * $e[41m█████$_$e[44;5m * * $e[41m█████$e[K$e[m$p$g
```

Enter line 4 as a single line (do not break it up). The solid bar is made up with ASCII 223 characters (hold down Alt and type 223 on the numeric keypad). When you run this batch file, a blinking colorful flag will become your prompt style. If you do not understand the various numbers, consult the metastring table in Chapter 5 and various tables in this chapter.

Displaying a Message

Another trick you could use in your batch file is to build a routine to clear the screen and display whatever message you intend for yourself or another user. The following fragment could be put in your longer batch file:

```
1: ^[[2J
2: ^[[12;34HWarning!
3: ^[[14;26HYour message is put here.
```

If you write this as a separate file and name it MESSAGE, you can use the following command to display the message:

```
A>type message
```

The screen will be cleared and the text displayed in the middle. The above command can be included in a batch file, such as the following:

```
1: @echo off
2: type message
3: echo ^[[24;1f
4: pause
5: rem . . . .
```

This batch file will clear the screen and display the message. After that, the PAUSE message will be displayed at the bottom of the screen, namely line 24, column 1. The "f" in line 3 can be changed to H if you wish; they are interchangeable.

Saving the Original Prompt

Every time you use PROMPT to do something, you are likely to cause the DOS prompt to disappear, unless you add some laborious metastrings. You can use a batch file to save the old prompt while you use the PROMPT command for other purposes; after you are done, the batch file will restore the original prompt. Here is an example:

```
1: @rem PROM.BAT--save and restore old prompt
2: set prompt1=%prompt%
3: prompt $e[%1
4: set prompt=%prompt1%
5: set prompt1=
```

The existing prompt, if any, is assigned to PROMPT1 in line 2. Line 3 converts your command-line parameter to an ANSI escape sequence. Line 4 restores the original prompt. Line 5 erases PROMPT1.

T I P S   A N D   T R I C K S

E C H O   O N / O F F

When ECHO is off on the command line (showing no prompt), using PROMPT to enter an ANSI command will not work immediately. Consider the following sequence of commands:

```
A>echo off
prompt $e[7m
```

This will send the second line to the environment, but not affect the screen color right away. If ECHO is now turned on, the screen will be changed to reverse video. If ECHO is then turned off, the reverse video remains.

This observation also applies to metastrings such as $D and to other ANSI actions such as redefining a key.

You can turn ECHO on/off at will to enable/disable a PROMPT command in the environment intended to control the cursor. When ECHO is off, a cursor-control PROMPT, such as PROMPT $e[2J, has no effect and the cursor behaves normally.

You can use PROM.BAT to enter any single parameter. Here are some examples:

A>**prom 5m**	(blinking text)
A>**prom m**	(normal, black on white)
A>**prom 46m**	(cyan background)
A>**prom 1h**	$(40 \times 25$ color)
A>**prom 3h**	$(80 \times 25$ color)
A>**prom 2J**	(clear screen)
A>**prom K**	(erase current line)

Notice that we do not include @ECHO OFF in PROM.BAT. Consequently, all the lines except the first are written to the screen. This is necessary for PROMPT to produce any effect. For the same reason, the command line ECHO should also remain on.

P R A C T I C E   1 2 - 1

☐   1. Use the PROMPT command to position the cursor at row 1, column 1 and at the same time clear the line after the default DOS prompt.

☐   2. Use the PROMPT command to position the cursor at the bottom left corner of the screen. The default prompt must also be displayed.

☐   3. Use the PROMPT command to clear the screen and at the same time position the cursor at the top left corner of the screen. Then restore the default prompt and the regular screen behavior.

☐   4. Use the PROMPT command to display the current time in reverse video in row 1, column 35. Then restore the regular DOS prompt.

☐   5. Use PROMPT to set the screen to reverse video and display the current directory and >.

☐   6. Use EDLIN or EDIT to create a batch file that will display in the middle of a clear screen the message "Hello, World." No prompt shall be displayed and the cursor located at the bottom left corner. Restore the default DOS prompt.

☐   7. Modify PROM.BAT to allow up to five parameters entered on the command line.

D R I L L

Which of the following letters should replace ? in questions 8–11:

a. A   b. B   c. C   d. D

_____   8. Cursor right—Esc [#?

_____   9. Cursor left—Esc [#?

_____   10. Cursor up—Esc [#?

_____   11. Cursor down—Esc [#?

_____   12. The following command will:

     A>prompt $e[H

    a. cause the DOS prompt to disappear
    b. move the cursor to the top left corner
    c. both a and b
    d. neither a nor b

_____   13. The following command will:

     A>prompt $e[2J$d/$t

    a. clear the DOS prompt
    b. clear the screen and display date/time
    c. both a and b
    d. do nothing

____ 14. What happens if you have a file named X, which contains the following, and you enter the TYPE × command?

    ^[[7m

   a. The computer beeps

   b. An error message is shown

   c. The screen is changed to reverse video

   d. Nothing happens

____ 15. After the following two commands, the current directory's entries will stay on the screen. True or false?

    A>prompt $e[2J
    dir

SETTING SCREEN COLORS AND MODES

■ *Set colors or display modes by specifying attributes and ending with "m"*
(for monitor).

ANSI.SYS allows you to set your monitor with a variety of attributes, most notably colors and the number of lines and characters displayed. Tables 12.2 and 12.3 show the formats and attributes. (Your monitor may not be capable of accepting the available attributes.)

As with cursor control, explained in the previous section, you need to send escape sequences to your computer. Here is an example:

A>**prompt $e[30;47m**

This command sets the text color to black and the background color to white, achieving the same effect as reverse video on both color and monochrome monitors. Do not forget the "m" at the end; it has to be lowercase.

Instead of using PROMPT with $e[to set screen colors, you can use ^[[(or ←[) with ECHO, TYPE, MORE, or COPY CON, such as this batch file:

```
1: @echo off
2: ^[[30;47m
```

Suppose you name this file COLOR.BAT. You can enter this command to set colors:

A>**type color.bat**

Table 12.2

ANSI Escape Sequences—Colors

Esc [#;...;#m

Parameter	Effect
0	Normal; black on white
1	Bold; high intensity
4	Underline; mono only
5	Blink
7	Reverse video
8	Concealed; invisible
30	Black foreground
31	Red foreground
32	Green foreground
33	Yellow foreground
34	Blue foreground
35	Magenta foreground
36	Cyan foreground
37	White foreground
40	Black background
41	Red background
42	Green background
43	Yellow background
44	Blue background
45	Magenta background
46	Cyan background
47	White background

Table 12.3

ANSI Escape Sequences—Monitor Modes

Set Mode
    Esc [=#h

Parameter	Effect
0	40×25 monochrome (text)
1	40×25 color (text)
2	80×25 monochrome (text)
3	80×25 color (text)
4	320×200 4-color (graphics)
5	320×200 monochrome (graphics)
6	640×200 monochrome (graphics)
7	Wrap at end of line
13	320×200 color (graphics)
14	640×200 color (16-color graphics)
15	640×350 monochrome (graphics)
16	640×350 color (16-color graphics)
17	640×480 monochrome (graphics)
18	640×480 color (16-color graphics)
19	320×200 color (256-color graphics)

Reset Mode
    Esc [=#l

Same as SM, except 7, which turns off wrap; in a long line, the screen shows only one line.

The TYPE command can also be replaced with MORE or COPY CON, such as:

```
A>more < color.bat
A>copy color.bat con
```

If you run this batch file, such as:

```
A>color
```

you will get an error message. DOS does not consider the second line as a valid command. The following change will rectify the problem:

```
1: @echo off
2: echo ^[[30;47m
```

If you need to change the screen mode, you can use a command like this:

```
A>prompt $e[=1h
```

This command sets the screen to 40×25 color. The "h" can be replaced by "l" with the same effect. To get back to 80×25 color, enter this:

```
A>prompt $e[=3h
```

Normally, when you enter a long line, DOS automatically goes down to the beginning of a new line for you to continue. If for some reason you do not want to wrap, try this:

```
A>prompt $e[=7l
```

After that, the cursor continues to stay in the same line at the right margin. DOS continues to accept your typing, but each new character replaces the old one displayed. To restore the default, this command will do:

```
A>prompt $e[=7h
```

Armed with this knowledge, you can now spruce up the message display explained in the previous section (name it MESSAGE.BAT) and make it flashy:

```
 1:*@echo off
 2: echo ^[[2J
 3: echo ^[[=1h
 4: echo ^[[5;31;43m
 5: echo ^G^G^G
 6: echo ^[[11;17HWarning!
 7: echo ^[[13;8HYour message is put here.
 8: echo ^[[22;1H
 9: echo ^[[0m
10: pause
11: echo ^[[=3h
```

When you run this batch file, the computer beeps and the message in lines 6-7 appears in large size and blinking in bright colors. The PAUSE message appears at the bottom in white on black.

You can understand most of the lines by referring to Tables 12.2 and 12.3. Line 2 clears the screen. Line 3 sets 40×25 mode and line 11 sets it back to 80×25 when it is over. Line 4 sets blinking red foreground and yellow background. Line 5 causes a beep three times. Line 8 locates the cursor near the bottom of the screen. Line 9 turns off all color attributes.

P R A C T I C E   1 2 - 2

☐ 1. Modify PRACTICE 12-1 question 6 by displaying green text in yellow background; restore the default value at the end. If you have a monochrome monitor, make the text blink and underlined.

☐ 2. Modify the above to display the word HELLO vertically and nothing else on a black-on-white screen.

☐ 3. Use the modified PROM.BAT to set 320 × 200 color graphics mode and clear the screen.

☐ 4. Use the modified PROM.BAT to set 80 × 25 color text mode and clear the screen.

D R I L L

____ 16. The following command will:
        A>prompt $e[5
   a. cause text to blink
   b. turn off the prompt
   c. generate an error message
   d. do nothing

____ 17. The following command will:
        A>prompt $e[7;m
   a. turn on reverse video
   b. turn on high intensity
   c. turn off all attributes
   d. do nothing

____ 18. The following command will produce:
        A>prompt $e[1;5;7m
   a. high intensity, blink, reverse video
   b. reverse video only
   c. high intensity only
   d. none of the above

____ 19. The following command will produce:

A>prompt $e[m;7m

a. reverse video

b. blink

c. default attribute

d. an error message

REDEFINING KEYS

◼ *Most of the keyboard keys can be redefined (reassigned).*

◼ *Redefine a key by entering an escape sequence containing the first item as the original key, the second item as the new key, and ending with a lowercase p.*

◼ *Use a batch file to show the exit code of each key pressed so that you can use the number for key redefinition.*

With ANSI.SYS installed, you can redefine almost all the keys you see on your keyboard and their many combinations. Since many keys or key combinations are either unused by DOS or rarely used, you can redefine them to speed up much of your work.

Redefinition Methods

Table 12.4 shows a number of ways you can redefine keys. To redefine a key, simply use an ANSI command to enter the original value, its replacement value, separating each value with a semicolon and always ending with a lowercase p.

Table 12.4

ANSI Escape Sequences—Key Definition

Esc [#;#p	Assign value (2nd #) to key (1st #)
Esc [#;"string"p	Assign a string to a key
Esc [#;"dir";13p	Assign "dir" and Enter to a key
Esc [0;#;"string"p	Extended keys with 0 as 1st number
Esc [224;#;"xxx"p	Gray keys with 224 as 1st number

Table 12.5

Single Number Key Codes

1–26	Ctrl-A–Ctrl-Z
3	Break; ^C
7	Beep; ^G
8	Backspace, Shift-Backspace
9	Tab
10	Ctrl-Enter
13	Enter; ^M
27	Esc; ^[

If you want to redefine a key appearing on the keyboard, just put the original and its new definition in quotes, such as:

`A>prompt $e["[";"{"p`

After this, pressing the [key will always show {. To restore its original definition, try this:

`A>prompt $e[91;91p`

This restores [to its original ASCII value of 91.

Some keys, such as Esc or ^C, have no literal existence like the visible keys appearing on the keyboard; these are shown in Table 12.5. To redefine such a key, you need to enter its ASCII value, such as:

`A>prompt $e[27;"Escape"p`

This assigns the "Escape" string to the Esc key. If you press Esc now, "Escape" appears. To restore its original definition, try this:

`A>prompt $e[27;27p`

After this command, pressing Esc sends ASCII 27 to your PC and displays the usual \ sign.

WARNING: Do not assign another value to the Enter key (ASCII 13, which is also the value of ^M), such as this example:

`A>prompt $e[13;"dir"p`

D I S A B L I N G   T H E   E N T E R   K E Y

Do you work in an office and are often annoyed by coworkers snooping around your hard disk while you are temporarily away from your PC? The system described here may thwart those snoopers. You need two batch files, as shown below:

```
1: @echo off
2: rem NOCR.BAT--disable Enter
3: echo ^[[10;"yecr";13p
4: echo ^[[13;3p
```

```
1: @echo off
2: rem YECR.BAT--enable Enter
3: echo ^[[13;13p
```

After running NOCR.BAT, pressing Enter is the equivalent of pressing Ctrl-C. This allows no command to be registered. Pressing Ctrl-Enter (ASCII 10) runs YECR.BAT to return ASCII 13 to the Enter key. So, after the system is set up, run NOCR.BAT before your coffee break and press Ctrl-Enter after your return.

In line 4, you can also add ASCII 255 to the Enter key, like this:

```
4: echo ^[[13;255;13p
```

Pressing Enter after this will cause the addition of the invisible character and prevent any command from being entered. This system requires installing KEYB.COM (KEYB US).

After this command, you can no longer use the Enter key for its original purpose. Every time you press Enter or Ctrl-M, "dir" will show up. Unless you have assigned ASCII 13 to another key, you can no longer enter ASCII 13 to register a DOS command. The only way out is to reboot.

Extended Keys

There are also **extended keys**, which require you to enter two numbers to redefine them. The first number for most of them is 0 and the second is based on those shown in Appendix C, ASCII Key Codes; the key codes for all the function keys are also shown in Table 12.6. Here is an example:

```
A>prompt $e[0;68;"prompt $$e["p
```

23.6

Extended Key Codes

Key Name	Code for... Key Alone	Shift-Key	Ctrl-Key	Alt-Key
F1	0;59	0;84	0;94	0;104
F2	0;60	0;85	0;95	0;105
F3	0;61	0;86	0;96	0;106
F4	0;62	0;87	0;97	0;107
F5	0;63	0;88	0;98	0;108
F6	0;64	0;89	0;99	0;109
F7	0;65	0;90	0;100	0;110
F8	0;66	0;91	0;101	0;111
F9	0;67	0;92	0;102	0;112
F10	0;68	0;93	0;103	0;113
F11	0;133	0;135	0;137	0;139
F12	0;134	0;136	0;138	0;140

This command redefines F10 as "prompt $$e[". The two dollar signs are to display the second dollar sign; without two, none will be displayed. After this command, pressing F10 will show this:

```
A>prompt $e[
```

You can now enter numbers and characters to complete an escape sequence. This will save you a lot of time as you experiment with ANSI commands.

You can assign multiple values to a key, such as:

```
A>prompt $e[0;93;"dir";13p
```

This assigns to Shift-F10 "dir" plus a carriage return (ASCII 13 has the same effect as pressing Enter from the keyboard). If you now press Shift-F10 (without pressing Enter), the current directory's entries will be immediately displayed.

If you have an enhanced keyboard, you can take advantage of F11 and F12 and their various combinations. Here is an example:

```
A>prompt $e[0;134;"cls$_"p
```

After this command, pressing F12 will immediately clear the screen.[3] The "$_" metastring, as explained in Chapter 5, has the effect of pressing the Enter key. You can thus use this metastring or ASCII 13 as used in the previous command.

Version 5 or 6 has new codes for the gray keys in the middle of an extended keyboard. Each of these cursor keys has two numbers. The first number is always 224. The second number is the same as its counterpart on the numeric keypad. For example, the Home key on the numeric pad has the values of 0;71, but the same key on the cursor pad has 224;71. This distinction allows you to redefine the two keys for different purposes. See Appendix C for all the key code numbers.

Showing Key Codes

Instead of having to look up each key code, we can create a batch file to show the code for each key pressed on the keyboard. This batch file is shown below:

```
 1:*@echo off
 2: rem KEYCODE.BAT--display key exit code
 3: set n=in (0 1 2 3 4 5 6 7 8 9)
 4: set n1=in (0 1 2 3 5)
 5: set d=do if errorlevel
 6: echo Press a key to show its exit code; Esc to end:
 7:
 8: :LOOP
 9: key
10: if errorlevel 27 if not errorlevel 28 goto END
11: echo    (Character)
12: for %%x in (0 1) %d% %%x00 set code=%%x
13: for %%x %n% %d% %code%%%x0 set code=%code%%%x
14: for %%x %n1% %d% 2%%x0 set code=2%%x
15: for %%x %n% %d% %code%%%x set code=%code%%%x
16: for %%x %n1% %d% 25%%x set code=25%%x
17: echo %code%     (Exit code)
18: goto LOOP
19:
20: :END
21: for %%x in (n n1 d code) do set %%x=
```

KEYCODE.BAT requires KEY.COM (line 9), which was introduced in Chapter 11. The program pauses batch execution to wait for a key press. The batch

---

3. If your keyboard does not respond as defined, you may need the short TSR program listed in *PC Computing* (June, 1990, p. 242).

file then checks the ERRORLEVEL of the key to determine its exit code. This is the result:

```
A>keycode
Press a key to show its exit code; Esc to end:
a         (Character)
097       (Exit code)
A         (Character)
065       (Exit code)
          (Character)       (F1)
000       (Exit code)
;         (Character)
059       (Exit code)
          (Character)       (Shift-F10)
000       (Exit code)
]         (Character)
093       (Exit code)
╙         (Character)       (Alt-211)
211       (Exit code)
╞         (Character)       (Alt-198)
198       (Exit code)
A>_                         (Esc)
```

If a key has a single number, its key code is shown below the displayed key (see the first two examples). If a key has two numbers (F1 for example), four lines are displayed. The first line shows a corresponding symbol (if any) and the second line shows the number of 000. The third line shows a character whose ASCII value is shown in the fourth line. The gray keys on an extended keyboard also return 000 as the first number. If you redefine these keys, keep in mind to use 224 as the first number.

Since each key's ASCII value and its corresponding character are shown by KEYCODE.BAT, you can use either to redefine a key. For example, you can use either 93 or "]" as the second number to redefine Shift-F10.

This batch file will also show extended ASCII characters. For example, if you want to know what character corresponds to the value of 211, hold down Alt and type 211 on the numeric keypad. The character and the number will be displayed.

If you want to see how KEYCODE.BAT works, delete line 1 or add REM at the beginning and run it. Press Pause at crucial points to see how the numerous environment variables are assigned what values.

Lines 12-16 check the exit code of a pressed key. To save typing, we have used lots of shorthand expressions. Each variable enclosed in a pair of %, such as %N%, represents a string defined in lines 3-5. When lines 12-16 are executed, each variable will be substituted with its assigned value. See Chapter 11 for more details.

Line 12 checks to see whether the pressed key has an exit code lower than 100. If so, CODE is assigned 0; if not, it is given 1. This number is used as the first of the three digits for a code that is below 200.

Line 13 tries to identify the second digit. Depending on what is produced by line 12 (1 or 0), this line goes through sequential numbers of 100 (000), 110 (010), 111 (011), and so on. If the exit code matches a number, CODE is assigned a number which consists of the number produced by line 12 and the value of the × variable. Suppose the exit code is 123. CODE will be given the value of 12.

Line 14 checks an exit code that is 200 or higher and assigns a value accordingly. Line 16 screens numbers 250-255. In our example, these lines will not change the value of CODE, which remains 12 after line 14 is executed and 123 after line 16 is executed.

Line 15 determines the third digit. It goes through the value of CODE in combination with 0, 1, 2, etc. When a number matches the exit code of the key, the last digit is added to CODE. In our example, CODE will have the value of 123 after this line is executed.

Line 17 displays the value of CODE and line 18 branches execution back to the LOOP label to prompt you to press another key. This will happen if the pressed key has a single number. If the key has two numbers, however, execution will resume in line 12 and down. Another number will be produced after lines 12-16 are executed another time.

P R A C T I C E   1 2 - 3

1. Redefine the Esc key on the keyboard so that when you press it alone the current directory's entries will immediately appear.

2. Restore the Esc to its original state.

3. Redefine the Home key (on the numeric keypad) so that you can press it alone to display the root directory's entries.

4. Redefine the Alt-Esc key combination so that when you are editing a line in EDLIN you can press this key combination to cancel the line and exit EDLIN (and save the file) at the same time.

5. Modify the NOCR.BAT and YECR.BAT system so that pressing Alt-Enter (instead of Ctrl-Enter) will restore the original value of the Enter key.

☐   6. Modify the NOCR.BAT and YECR.BAT system so that you can press F11 to disable Enter and F12 to restore it.

☐   7. Modify KEYCODE.BAT so that when Enter is pressed the batch file will end.

☐   8. Modify KEYCODE.BAT to allow the user to press Ctrl-A to end the batch file.

☐   9. Modify KEYCODE.BAT to allow the user to press Q or q to end the batch file.

☐   10. Modify KEYCODE.BAT so that the user cannot press Ctrl-C to abort the batch file.

D R I L L

_____ 20. The following command will define:

        A>prompt $e[0;1;3p

    a. ^A as ^C

    b. ^A as 3

    c. Alt-Esc as ^C

    d. nothing

_____ 21. The following command will define:

        A>prompt $e[26;8p

    a. ^Z as Backspace

    b. ^A as ^Z

    c. Alt-P as ^Z

    d. nothing

_____ 22. The following command, entered from a batch file, will redefine "b" as "B". True or false?

        echo ^[["b";"B"p

_____ 23. The following will restore the above key to its original definition. True or false?

        echo ^[[98;98p

_____ 24. The following command will define:

        A>prompt $e[0;16;"dir"p$e[0;17;"type"p

    a. Alt-Q

    b. Alt-W

    c. both a and b

    d. neither a nor b

USING ANSI.BAT TO SET ANSI VALUES

■ *Use a batch file to speed up setting screen colors and/or redefining keys.*

Using the PROMPT command on the command line to set screen colors/modes or redefine keyboard keys, as shown in previous sections, requires a great deal of repeated typing. Furthermore, the DOS prompt disappears every time you enter the PROMPT command. These problems can be remedied with a batch file like this:

```
1:*@echo off
2: rem ANSI.BAT--set ANSI color and key definition
3: if .==.%1 goto HELP
4: echo ^[[%1;%2;%3;%4;%5
5: goto END
6: :HELP
7: echo/
8: echo You forgot to enter parameters, such as:
9: echo   %0 7m (for reverse video)
10: echo   %0 30;47m (black text, white background)
11: echo   %0 0;68;"dir"p (define F10 as "dir")
12: echo/
13: :END
```

If you just enter the batch file name alone, namely ANSI, line 3 becomes true and line 6 is executed. The error message in lines 8-11 is displayed. Lines 7 and 12 create empty lines to make the error message more readable.

If a parameter is entered after ANSI, line 3 is ignored and line 4 is executed. Each replaceable parameter is replaced by a parameter entered on the command line. For example, you could enter this command:

A>ansi 0;68;"dir/p";13p

In this command, four parameters separated by semicolons follow the batch file name. DOS responds by executing line 4 this way:

```
echo ^[[0;68;"dir/p";13p;
```

This causes F10 to be defined with "dir/p" plus a carriage return.

You can, if you wish, use a space instead of a semicolon as a parameter separator, such as:

A>ansi 0 68 "dir¦sort" 13p

This will assign "dir¦sort" plus a carriage return to F10. Pressing F10 after this command will display sorted directory entries.

The arrangement in line 4 allows five parameters to be entered on the command line. If fewer are entered, the screen displays the extra semicolons and no harm is done. If more are entered, your command may not be executed. If you need to enter more parameters, you can increase the number of replaceable parameters up to nine.

Since the batch file does not use the PROMPT command, running it will not cause the DOS prompt to disappear or change the value of PROMPT, if any, in the environment.

Note: This batch file can also be used to set screen modes/colors or control cursor positions; just make sure to end each command with a proper letter. It is a simple and versatile ANSI companion; don't use ANSI without it.

ANSI AND DOSKEY

Both ANSI and DOSKEY give you macro capabilities, the arrangement in which you can assign a long string to a short one to save you time and typing. There are, however, significant differences between them. They are compared and contrasted below:

- ANSI lets you assign a string to a key or key combination on the keyboard; you press the key to replay the string. DOSKEY lets you assign a string to a

---

TIPS   AND   TRICKS

THE   GHOST   OF   PROMPT

If you use ECHO to redefine a key (or change screen colors), it will not negate an identical command entered with PROMPT. Suppose you have most recently entered this command to redefine F10:

```
A>prompt $e[0;68;"dir"p
```

If you try to redefine F10 with a batch file command like this:

```
echo ^[[0;68;"type "p
```

the key will not be redefined. The reason is that this line still stays in the environment:

```
PROMPT=$e[0;68;"dir"p
```

If you enter PROMPT alone or in combination with other parameters, the above line will either disappear or change its value. If you then redefine F10 (or any other key) with ECHO, there will be no obstacle to your move.

name consisting of one or more characters that can be legally used in a file name; you enter the name from the keyboard to replay the string.

- Use 13 or $_ to assign ASCII 13 (carriage return) to a key; use $T in a macro as the equivalent of a carriage return. If a key has ASCII 13 assigned to it, pressing that key alone will register the assigned command and carriage return. In a macro, you must type the name and press Enter to execute it.

- If a function key used by DOSKEY is redefined, the string assigned by you preempts the original assignment. Restore its ASCII value if you want to return a key to its original purpose.

- A redefined key can be used in EDLIN. The value assigned by you preempts the original value. When in EDIT, its assignments preempt yours. When you exit EDIT or go to the command line, your assignments return. This remark applies to other programs such as Lotus 1-2-3 and WordPerfect.

- DOSKEY and ANSI can interact with each other. A key can be redefined to execute a macro. A macro can also be used to redefine a key.

Since the Esc character cannot be entered on the command line, you can use EDLIN or EDIT to create a macro that contains an escape character. For example, you can create a batch file containing a line like this:

```
doskey e=echo ^[[$*        (EDLIN)
doskey e=echo ←[$*        (EDIT)
```

After running this batch file, the macro will enter the DOSKEY buffer. You can show it with this command:

```
A>doskey /m
E=echo ^[[$*
```

Regardless of which editor you use, the escape character appears as ^[[. In contrast, if you use TYPE or COPY CON /B to show the batch file, the escape character (^[[or ←[) does not appear.

After the E macro is created by a batch file, you can use it to enter ANSI escape sequences, like these:

```
A>e 7m                    (reverse video)
A>e m                     (default video mode)
A>e =3h                   (80 × 25 color text mode)
A>e 0;67;"dir"p           (F9 redefined as DIR)
A>e 0;67;0;67p            (F9 restored)
```

Since we use $* in the macro, you can enter as many parameters as you wish and they will all be accepted; if you use $1, only the value before the first semicolon will be accepted. This is more versatile than a batch file having to use a number of replaceable parameters (%1, %2, etc.), each of which can accept only a single parameter.

If you do not want to use a batch file (created with EDLIN or EDIT) to create a macro, you need to use PROMPT instead of ECHO, like this:

A>**doskey p=prompt $$e[$*$$p$$g**

Each pair of $$ is to produce a single $ when the macro is executed, and the $* is to accept all the command-line parameters. For example, if you enter 7m as the parameter, the macro will be executed this way:

```
A>p 7m
A>prompt $e[7m$p$g
```

The screen is set to reverse video and this string also enters the environment:

```
PROMPT=$e[7m$p$g
```

If ECHO is off on the command line, the string enters the environment but it has no effect until ECHO is on again. As long as ECHO is on, you can use the P macro to redefine keys, such as this:

A>**p 0;67;"dir"p**   (F9 redefined as DIR)

After a key is defined or monitor mode set, the PROMPT value can change without affecting previous changes.

In our P macro, we add pg at the end to prevent the prompt from disappearing. Since using ECHO does not affect the prompt, there is no need for this extra trouble in the E macro.

P R A C T I C E   1 2 - 4

1. Use ANSI.BAT to redefine the PgUp key so that when you press it the parent directory's entries are displayed.

2. Use ANSI.BAT to redefine x as Y and then restore the original.

3. Use ANSI.BAT to redefine Ctrl-F10 as "dir ¦ sort ¦ more", plus a carriage return.

4. Restore Ctrl-F10 to its original value.

5. Modify the P macro so that the screen will be cleared as soon as an action is taken.

6. Use the P macro to change the monitor to 320 × 200 four-color graphics mode. Change it to 80 × 25 color text mode.

USING MEMO.BAT TO WRITE MEMOS

■ *Use a batch file for quick writing of memos.*

If you know how to redefine keys, you can take advantage of the knowledge to simplify and speed up your work. For example, if you often write short memos while working with DOS, you can use the batch file as below to quickly do the work:

```
1:*@echo off
2: rem MEMO.BAT--using COPY CON to write memos
3: if .==.%1 goto HELP
4: echo ^[[0;50;"                    MEMO";13;13;"To: "p
5: echo ^[[0;33;"From: "p
6: echo ^[[0;32;"Date: "p
7: echo ^[[0;31;"Subject: "p
8: cls
9: echo ^[[7m
10: echo Alt-M to start memo; Alt-F = From, Alt-D = Date, Alt-S = Subject
11: echo The file being created is: %1. Press F6 and Enter to save file.
12: if exist %1 echo %1 already exists. It'll be replaced if you continue.
13: if exist %1 echo Press ^C if you wish to abort.
14: echo ^[[0m
15: copy con %1
16: goto END
17: :HELP
18: echo/
19: echo You must enter a file name after MEMO. Try again.
20: echo/
21: :END
```

You must run this batch file with a file name, such as:

A>**memo carl**

The file named CARL will be created in the end. If no file name is entered, this message appears and the batch file ends:

A>**memo**

```
You must enter a file name after MEMO. Try again.
```

A>_

After the batch file starts, a two-line message appears:

```
Alt-M to start memo; Alt-F = From, Alt-D = Date, Alt-S = Subject
The file being created is: carl. Press F6 and Enter to save file.
```

The message also appears in reverse video, which is turned on by line 9 and off by line 14.

If the file name you enter matches one in the current directory, you will be warned of that fact. If you proceed, the new one will replace the old. If you do not want that to happen, press Ctrl-C to abort the batch file and start again with a new name.

You can now utilize any of the four keys already defined by the batch file to speed up your work. If you press Alt-M, the first two lines shown below appear and the cursor is positioned for you to enter a name.

```
                MEMO
     To: Carl
     From: Tim
     Date: 6/22
     Subject: Sales
```

After you type the first line and press Enter, you can press Alt-F, Alt-D, and then Alt-S and enter each line. After that, you can type whatever message below. Press F6 and Enter to save the memo.

Lines 4-7 redefine the four keys to be used in writing a memo. After the memo is finished, these definitions remain. If you wish, you can use them for whatever purpose. If you want to restore their original definitions, add a simple routine between lines 15 and 16.

P R A C T I C E   1 2 - 5

☐   1. Modify MEMO.BAT by replacing all the Alt keys with Ctrl. (Use ^N for Alt-M. Do not redefine ^M, which is the same as Enter. If you did, you would no longer be able to enter another command.)

☐   2. Use the modified batch file to write a memo.

☐   3. Print the memo by using COPY.

USING MEMO1.BAT TO WRITE MEMOS

■ *Use a batch file to load EDLIN for quick writing of memos.*

If you feel COPY CON is too restricting in typing text, you can modify the batch file to let you use EDLIN. Our modified batch file, named MEMO1.BAT, is shown below:

```
 1:*@echo off
 2: rem MEMO1.BAT--using EDLIN to write memos
 3: rem EDLIN must be in the current dir
 4: if not exist edlin.com echo EDLIN not found in the current directory.
 5: if not exist edlin.exe goto END
 6: if .==.%1 goto HELP
 7: cls
 8: echo ^[[7m
 9: echo Alt-M to start memo; Alt-F = From, Alt-D = Date, Alt-S = Subject
10: echo The file being created is: %1
11: if exist %1 echo %1 already exists. It'll be replaced if you continue.
12: if exist %1 echo Press a key to continue or ^C to abort.
13: if exist %1 pause > nul
14: echo ^[[0m
15: echo ^[[0;50;"                MEMO";13;13;"To: "p
16: echo ^[[0;33;"From: "p
17: echo ^[[0;32;"Date: "p
18: echo ^[[0;31;"Subject: "p
19: edlin %1
20: echo/
21: goto END
22: :HELP
23: echo/
24: echo You must enter a file name after MEMO1. Try again.
25: echo/
26: :END
```

Lines 4-5 handle the situation when EDLIN.EXE is not found in the current directory. A message is displayed and the batch file ends. If EDLIN is found, a message similar to MEMO.BAT appears, showing the redefined keys available for use. If no matching file exists, EDLIN is started immediately, and the screen displays "New file" message. You can enter I to start the first line. Pressing Alt-M will start the beginning lines of a memo. Other steps are the same as in MEMO.BAT.

If an old matching file exists, this message appears:

```
Alt-M to start memo; Alt-F = From, Alt-D = Date, Alt-S = Subject
The file being created is: carl
carl already exists. It'll be replaced if you continue.
Press a key to continue or ^C to abort.
```

If you press Ctrl-C, EDLIN is not started and the batch file is ended. Pressing any other key will start EDLIN and display the "End of input file" message. You can then enter the L command to show the file and make necessary changes.

MEMO1.BAT has one advantage over MEMO.BAT. It allows you to edit lines after pressing Enter. Use it if your memos are fairly elaborate and require editing. For short memos, MEMO.BAT is quick and easy.

WRITING PHONE MESSAGES

■ *Use a series of batch files to quickly take, save, and print phone messages.*

Imagine that you are working with DOS, a database, and/or a spreadsheet program. Suddenly, the phone rings and you need to take a message. If you are in DOS, you can use the batch files below to quickly complete the task. If you are somewhere else, go to DOS without exiting your program, and use the batch files.

To do that, you need to create three batch files. It sounds complicated. It may be a little elaborate. But once you have the system set up, everything becomes automated and you can save a lot of time.

Basically, we intend to set up a system in which you can press F10 to immediately go to the COPY CON screen where you can start typing right away. After you exit, you can, if you wish, press Shift-F10 to print the message just created; or you can print several related files altogether at a later time.

The first batch file is a simple one:

```
1:*@echo off
2: rem F10.BAT--define F10 and Shift-F10
3: echo ^[[0;68;"msg m0 m1 m2 m3 m4 m5 m6 m7 m8 m9";13p
4: echo ^[[0;93;"printit";13p
```

It redefines two keys, F10 and Shift-F10. Shift-F10 will run a batch file as explained below. F10 will enter the following command:

```
A>msg m0 m1 m2 m3 m4 m5 m6 m7 m8 m9
```

It runs the batch file named MSG.BAT, which is explained below, plus 10 parameters. These parameters are used as file names. In the beginning, the first file created (message taken) will be saved as M0. After that, the next file will be named M1, and so on. This arrangement allows 10 separate messages to coexist at any time.

The MSG.BAT file resembles in part MEMO.BAT explained earlier. Two keys are defined. The Date item is eliminated; date and time data will be automatically added by the batch file.

Line 5 provides a safeguard. When all the ten parameters are used up, you can no longer create files. When all the files named M0-M9 are detected, %1 is assigned no value and COPY CON cannot create a file. At this point, batch execution branches to the HELP messages and ends.

```
 1: echo off
 2: rem MSG.BAT--using COPY CON to take messages
 3: :AGAIN
 4: if exist %1 goto NEXT
 5: if .==%1. goto HELP
 6: echo ^[[0;50;"                    MESSAGE";13;13;"To: "p
 7: echo ^[[0;33;"From: "p
 8: cls
 9: echo ^[[7m
10: echo Alt-M to start message; Alt-F = From
11: echo The file being created is: %1
12: echo Press F6 and Enter to end, or ^C to abort.
13: echo ^[[m
14: copy con %1
15: echo | more | date | find "C" >> %1
16: echo | more | time | find "C" >> %1
17: goto END
18: :NEXT
19: shift
20: goto AGAIN
21: :HELP
22: echo/
23:*echo You have run out of available parameters
24: echo You must erase some of M0...M9 files.
25: echo You can press Shift-F10 to print and erase them.
26: echo/
27: :END
```

Line 4 is a little tricky and requires explanation. It tests to see whether a particular file exists in the current directory. If M0, the first parameter entered on the command line, does not exist, then line 4 is ignored and M0 is used in line 12 as the name of the file to be created by COPY CON.

When you run the batch file another time, line 4 will detect the existence of M0 and branch to line 18. Line 19 then shifts to the next parameter, namely M1, thus assigning M1 to %1. Line 4 again tests M1's existence. Since it does not already exist, it becomes the next file to be created.

After you exit the COPY CON screen, lines 15-16 add the date and time data to the end of the file just created. This saves you the trouble of having to add them when you are busily taking a message.

As explained in Chapter 8, MORE will have the effect of pressing the Enter key after DATE/TIME is entered, thus obviating the need to press this key manually.

FIND will look for the string starting with "C". Finally, ECHO will append the found string to the named file.

When you press F10 to start, the screen displays in reverse video the top three lines shown below. You can then press Alt-M to begin your work. After entering the first line, press Alt-F to begin the second line. When you finish taking the message, the screen resembles what is shown below:

```
Alt-M to start message; Alt-F = From
The file being created is: m2
Press F6 and Enter to end, or ^C to abort.
                 MESSAGE
To: George
From: Garage
Your car has been fixed. Call 909-AUTO.
^Z
        1 File(s) copied
```

If you use the TYPE command to display the file just created, it shows something like this:

```
                 MESSAGE
To: George
From: Garage
Your car has been fixed. Call 909-AUTO.
Current date is Thu 06-25-1992
Current time is  3:39:44.97p
```

Since the files are named M0, M1, M2, etc., it is difficult to determine what message is for whom. You can use the command below to display them successively on the screen:

```
A>for %x in (m?) do type %x
```

If this command is too laborious to type, you can define a key for it. The following assigns the long command to Ctrl-F10:

```
A>prompt $e[0;103;"for %x in (m?) do type %x";13p$n$g
```

If you do not want the trouble of redefining this key repeatedly, you can put this line in F10.BAT:

```
5: echo ^[[0;103;"for %%x in (m?) do type %%x";13p
```

After defining the key either way, pressing it will display all the matching files one after another. Use the Pause (or Ctrl-S) to halt the scrolling or Ctrl-C to break it.

The F10.BAT definition of the F10 key limits 10 message files at one time. This number should be sufficient for most circumstances. After this number is reached, MSG.BAT will no longer be able to create a file. If you find this number inadequate, you can increase it in the F10.BAT file and adjust other related items.

Whenever you are ready to print the saved messages, you can simply press Shift-F10, which is defined by F10.BAT to activate this batch file:

```
 1:*@echo off
 2: rem PRINTIT.BAT--print and delete all M? files
 3: echo/
 4: echo Get the printer ready and press a key to start.
 5: pause > nul
 6: echo Printing . . .
 7: copy m? prn
 8: echo/
 9: echo Press a key to delete printed files, or ^C to stop.
10: pause > nul
11: del m?
```

Line 4 displays a message and line 5 pauses the batch file; line 5 echoes the message of PAUSE to the NUL device, namely not showing it on the screen. Line 6 copies each matching file to the printer.

After the matching files are sent to the printer (or printer buffer), line 9 displays a message and lets you decide whether to delete the files, which is executed in line 11. These files named M0, M1, etc. need to be periodically deleted. If not, no file will be saved after M9 is reached.

When you have the three batch files ready, you need only to manually enter this on the command line:

A>**f10**

This defines F10 and Shift-F10. If you want these keys automatically defined each time you power up, include the batch file lines in your AUTOEXEC.BAT file or put "f10" in the last line to run (chain) F10.BAT. After these keys are defined, the rest is just a matter of pressing a single key to do a complex job.

P R A C T I C E   1 2 - 6

1. Create the entire system described in the text, except using F9 instead of F10. Your system should enable you to press F9 to start writing a phone message, Shift-F9 to print and delete all the accumulated messages, and Ctrl-F9 to display one after another all the existing messages. (Use F12 if you have an enhanced keyboard.)

2. Use the completed system to simulate writing five messages, display them, and then print/delete them.

☐   3. Create a separate batch file that will allow you to display one message at a time and then press a key to go to the next. Assign this batch file to Ctrl-F9.

☐   4. Add to the above batch file a function that will show the name of the displayed file and allow the user to select Y/N to delete it.

D R I L L

____ 25. The second command, entered from a batch file, will succeed in redefining the F10 key. True or false?

   A>prompt $e[0;68;"dir"p
   echo ^[[0;68;"type "p

____ 26. The following batch line will assign:

   echo ^[[0;50;"MEMO";13;13;"To: "p

   a. three lines to two keys
   b. three lines to one key
   c. two lines to one key
   d. one line to one key

____ 27. If ANSI.BAT is the batch file discussed in the text (containing this key line: echo ^[[%1;%2;%3;%4;%5), the following command will generate an error message. True or false?

   A>ansi f

____ 28. The following command entered on the command line will work. True or false?

   A>echo ^V[[0;68;"dir"p

____ 29. The following command will succeed in defining a key. True or false?

   A>prompt $e[1;"for %x in (*.*) do type %x";13png

____ 30. The following command contains two carriage returns. True or false?

   echo ^[[0;50;"MESSAGE$_";13;"To: "p

S U M M A R Y   A N D   R E V I E W

Check each item as you review and understand the following highlights of the chapter:

☐   1. Install ANSI.SYS before entering ANSI escape sequences. Include the /X switch if you have an enhanced keyboard. The switch allows you to redefine many more keys.

☐ 2. An ANSI escape sequence consists of Esc (ASCII 27), the left bracket ([), followed by one or more decimal numbers, and ending with a specific letter. Enter Esc in EDLIN by pressing Ctrl-V and then [or in EDIT by pressing Ctrl-P and then Esc.

☐ 3. You can send an escape sequence to the computer with a number of DOS commands, the most common being PROMPT and ECHO.

☐ 4. On the command line, you can use only PROMPT in combination with $e[. The DOS prompt will disappear unless you include metastrings such as NG to restore it.

☐ 5. The most recent escape sequence or metastring sent with PROMPT will enter the DOS environment and stay there until another PROMPT command is entered. This may affect what you do in the future.

☐ 6. When ECHO is off, the PROMPT command will not work properly or immediately in sending an escape sequence. This is true regardless of whether you use PROMPT with $e, ^[(EDLIN), or ← (EDIT) to represent the escape character.

☐ 7. Under most circumstances, it is preferable to use ECHO and ^[[(or ←[) to enter ANSI escape sequences from a batch file. This will not affect the DOS prompt or change anything in the environment.

☐ 8. Each ANSI parameter ends with a letter. This letter must be correct in case. You cannot substitute lowercase for uppercase where the latter is required.

☐ 9. To control the cursor position or erase screen display, end an escape sequence with one of these letters: A, B, C, D, f, H, K, S, U, and 2J.

☐ 10. Change screen colors with an escape sequence ending with "m" and change screen modes with "h" or "l".

☐ 11. Redefine keys with an escape sequence ending with "p". For single keys that appear on the keyboard, redefine them by either putting them in double quotes or entering their ASCII values.

☐ 12. To redefine extended keys, two numbers are necessary. The first is 0 or 224 (gray keys) and the second based on a number assigned to a particular key or key combination. Check Appendix C for the numbers or use KEYCODE.BAT discussed in the text to display them on the screen.

☐ 13. Entering an ANSI command with possibly a long string of characters can be simplified with a batch file. ANSI.BAT, discussed in the text, can be used to quickly enter such a command.

☐ 14. Macros created with DOSKEY can be used to quickly enter a long ANSI escape sequence. Use EDLIN or EDIT to create a batch file that combines ECHO and an

☐ escape character, which cannot be entered on the command line or in COPY CON. Run the batch file to create one or more macros.

☐ 15. You can assign a number of keystrokes to a key to save time and speed up your work. After a key is redefined, pressing it will retrieve all the keystrokes stored there. You can use this technique to enter phrases that are repeatedly used, or quickly execute a DOS command or run a batch file.

☐ 16. The MSG.BAT file and related files involve extensive use of redefining some keys for quick action. They represent efficient utilization of this macro capability available in ANSI.SYS. Adapt them to your work with DOS and you will make yourself more productive.

REVIEW QUESTIONS

Write an answer for each question below:

1. What are ANSI escape sequences? What does such a sequence consist of?

2. What DOS commands can be used to enter an ANSI escape sequence?

3. Describe the two methods of entering the Esc character.

4. How do PROMPT and ECHO differ in entering an ANSI escape sequence?

5. How is the DOS environment affected by ECHO or PROMPT?

6. If ECHO is turned off in a batch file, can you enter multiple PROMPT commands to enter ANSI escape sequences? Explain what will happen.

7. If ECHO is turned off on the command line, will a cursor-control PROMPT command affect the cursor behavior? Illustrate with some examples.

8. Explain what each of the following cursor-control escape sequences does:
   A>prompt $e[H
   A>prompt $e[2J
   A>prompt $e[22C

9. What does each of the following batch lines do?
   echo ^[[0;1;5m
   echo ^[[0;1,5;m

10. What does this command do?
   A>prompt $e[0;30;"All men are created equal";13p

11. What does this batch file do?
    ```
    echo ^[[5m
    echo/
    echo This is a test.
    echo/
    echo ^[[m
    ```

12. What does this batch line do?
    ```
    ^[[97;65p^[[98;66p
    ```

13. What DOS commands can be used to send the above to the computer?

14. What is the purpose of this command?
    ```
    A>prompt $e[0;68;"memo m0 m1 m2 m3 m4 m5 m6 m7 m8 m9";13p
    ```

15. What does this batch line do?
    ```
    echo ^[[0;32;"echo│more│date >> notes";13p
    ```

Appendix A: Glossary

(Note: If a term within a definition appears in **boldface**, it is explained separately.)

A

Adapter See controller card.

Allocation unit See cluster.

Alphanumeric characters **ASCII** characters which may be alphabetic or numeric. Each one, letter or number, has a specific value; see Appendix B.

ANSI American National Standard Institute—an organization that determines standards for various computer-related activities, including **ANSI escape sequence** and **ASCII**.

ANSI escape sequence An ANSI command to extend PC input and output, including screen colors and keyboard redefinition. To use an ANSI escape sequence, you must first install **ANSI.SYS**.

ANSI.SYS A special file that comes with a DOS package. This file must be included in your **CONFIG.SYS** file before DOS can implement an ANSI escape sequence.

Application software A computer program intended to handle a specific task. Examples include word processors, spreadsheet programs, and database management systems. It is often contrasted with **system software**.

Archive An attribute given to a file. A file normally carries an archive bit. This attribute is shown when you use the ATTRIB command to display a file. Some commands such as BACKUP and XCOPY can maneuver this archive bit in backing up a file. ATTRIB can add or remove this archive bit.

Argument Also known as command-line argument; see parameter.

ASCII American Standard Code for Information Interchange, a common standard for converting characters to numerical values, which a computer can understand and maneuver. There are 256 ASCII characters. The first half (0–125), including all the **alphanumeric characters**, are standardized. The second half (126–255), known as extended ASCII characters, contain various drawing characters and are not standardized. The table in Appendix B shows the extended characters adopted by IBM.

ASCII file A file that contains only ASCII characters. A file created with COPY CON, EDIT, or EDLIN is an ASCII file. Various DOS commands can handle such a file. A file created with an application program such as a word processor usually contains various formatting characters and is thus not a pure ASCII file. Most word processors, however, allow you to create an ASCII file.

AT   Originated from IBM PC-AT. AT stands for Advanced Technology. The original IBM AT, introduced in 1984, was based on the Intel 80826 **CPU**. Today, an AT-class PC can be any non-IBM computer based on 80286, 80836, or 80846 CPU. IBM's new products are renamed **PS/2**.

AUTOEXEC.BAT   Automatic executable batch file. It can contain various DOS commands, such as setting DOS paths and loading a program. It must have the exact name and be stored on the booting disk. After DOS is booted, it looks for **CONFIG.SYS**, if any, to execute, and then this **batch file**, if any.

AUX   AUXiliary device or **serial port**; can be COM1, COM2, COM3, or COM4 (versions before 3.3 can handle only COM1 and COM2).

B

Batch file   A user-created file that can contain a series of DOS commands. When a batch file is executed, all the commands in it will be executed one by one. A batch file can be written to behave like a simple computer program, with branching, looping, and other techniques. A batch file must be **ASCII** text and have a BAT extension in its file name.

Baud   Transmission rate for **modem** and other devices. A baud is 1 **bit** per second (bps). Most modems sold today are 9600-baud models.

Binary   A base 2 numerical system. A binary system has only two digits, 0 or 1.

BIOS   Basic Input-Output System, instructions (computer code) stored in a ROM chip to control input and output devices. BIOS is the first step in booting DOS.

Bit   A binary digit. A bit is either 0 (off) or 1 (on). This is the smallest unit a computer can maneuver.

Boot record   A disk record (program) created by formatting. This record is used to load the two system (hidden) files in the booting process.

Boot disk   Or bootable disk, a disk containing two hidden system files and COMMAND.COM, which can be used to start DOS. The /S switch of FORMAT can be used to create a boot disk. The DISKCOPY and SYS commands can transfer the hidden files to a new disk to make it bootable. Other commands do not recognize the hidden files.

Boot   To start DOS or to make it pull itself up from its bootstraps.

Branching   A programming technique that forces program or batch execution to interrupt the top to bottom routine and go to another routine to continue execution. In batch files, GOTO is used for unconditional branching and IF-GOTO for conditional branching.

Buffer   A memory area for storing temporary data. The BUFFERS command in a **CONFIG.SYS** file can increase the default of 2 or 3 disk buffers to an optimal number of 20–30. A DOS or EDLIN command is also stored in a buffer called the **template**.

Bug   An error in a computer program or **batch file**.

Bus   Also known as data bus, a circuitry inside a PC used to transmit information from one part to another. See MCA and EISA.

Byte   8 **bits** constitute 1 byte. A byte is used to form a character. If a file contains a single character and nothing else, it is 1-byte long.

C

CD-ROM   Compact Disc–Read-Only Memory. A **ROM** compact disc resembles an audio CD and can store huge amounts of data. The data stored on a ROM disc cannot be erased. A special player is needed to retrieve stored data.

CGA   Color Graphics Adapter, IBM's first color graphics card used to run an **RGB** monitor.

Chaining   A programming technique which transfers control from one program to another without returning to the first program. See also nesting.

Chip   A small device made of silicon containing integrated circuit. Chip examples include **RAM**, **ROM**, and **CPU**.

Clean boot Starting DOS without executing the CONFIG.SYS and AUTOEXEC.BAT files. Press F5 to have a clean boot at the beginning of booting.

Clones See compatibles.

Cluster Also known as allocation unit, a cluster is the smallest disk space DOS can work with. The size of a cluster varies from one type of disk to another. On a floppy disk, a cluster can be 1 or 2 **sectors**, namely 512 **bytes** or 1**KB**. A file as small as 1 byte can thus take up as much space as 1KB because DOS is not capable of utilizing a smaller disk space.

CMOS Complementary metal oxide semi-conductor. It consumes little power and is thus often used in laptops or in desktop PCs to store configuration data.

Code page A set of special characters belonging to a national language. If you want DOS to handle some unique characters belonging to a foreign language, you must tell it to use another code page number.

COM1 The first serial communications port. Version 3.3 and later can handle up to COM4; those before, only COM1 and COM2.

Command See DOS command.

Command line The line on the monitor screen where a DOS command (instruction) is to be entered.

Compatibles PCs that are compatible to IBM models. An IBM compatible PC can use parts and run software intended for an authentic IBM PC.

Computer virus A computer program that is designed to damage computer **files**.

CON Short for console, which is a combination of keyboard and monitor. CON is recognized by DOS as a device representing the standard input (keyboard) and standard output (monitor) devices.

CONFIG.SYS A **file** you create to define various PC hardware. This file must be put on the booting disk. As soon as DOS is booted, it looks for this file, if any, to execute. Common directives and driver files included in a CONFIG.SYS file are BUFFERS, FILES, ANSI.SYS, MOUSE.SYS (it comes with a mouse package), and RAMDRIVE.SYS.

Configuration block A block of items in a CONFIG.SYS file starting with a block header. The block contains a group of items that will all be executed if the user chooses this block from a configuration menu.

Context-sensitive help Help information corresponding to a task you are doing. Both the DOS Shell and Editor can provide context-sensitive help; press the F1 key to show related help information.

Control characters The first 32 (0–31) **ASCII** characters. These are used to control computer hardware and software.

Controller card A computer device inserted into an expansion slot and connected to other devices such as a printer and disk drive.

Conventional memory The first 640KB memory based on the 8088 or higher CPU. This 8088 chip can address up to 1MB memory, but IBM reserves the area between 640KB to 1MB for system use. This forces DOS to limit itself to the first 640KB. See also expanded memory and extended memory.

CP/M Control Processor/Micro, a popular **operating system** for **micros** before DOS. It has largely been displaced by DOS.

CPU Central processing unit. The brain of a computer, the CPU performs arithmetic and logic functions, and controls other parts of a computer. Most PCs today use a line of Intel CPU chips ranging from 8086/88 to 80486.

Current directory The active **directory**, the place where DOS is supposed to access when not directed to do otherwise.

Current (default) drive The active disk drive, whose letter is shown in the **DOS prompt**, such as A> or C>.

Cursor A little blinking underscore character on the screen to designate the location where a character is to be displayed.

CVF Compressed volume file, a file created by DoubleSpace to contain all the compressed data.

Cylinder A **track** of a hard disk **platter**.

D

Daisy-wheel printer A printer using a daisy wheel to produce printed characters. A daisy wheel resembles the typing elements (keys) of an electrical typewriter. Such a printer produces fully formed characters, but is not capable of printing graphics. Once popular, daisy-wheel printers have mostly been replaced by **dot-matrix printers**.

DAT Digital audio tape, a magnetic tape resembling an audio cassette tape. It can store huge amounts of data and also provide random access like a diskette.

DEBUG A DOS program that can be used to write small assembly programs, or identify and correct errors in a program.

Debug Identify and correct errors, an essential and tedious process in writing computer programs.

Device A piece of computer equipment which DOS can recognize and maneuver. DOS recognizes them via **reserved words** such as **AUX, COM1, CON,** and **PRN**.

Device driver A compiled computer file intended to maneuver a computer device. A device driver, once installed, can extend DOS's ability to handle an unusual computer device. The DOS package contains a number of such drivers, which usually have a file name extension of SYS.

Directory An indexing system used by DOS to manage files. A directory can have a parent directory, one level above it; or one or more subdirectories, one level below it. Each disk has a root directory, which is created by DOS in the formatting process. Other directories may be created or removed by the user.

Directory entries The information related to files and directories. The DIR command is used to show directory entries.

Disk Magnetically coated storage media. Two commonly available types are floppy and hard (fixed) disks.

Disk buffer See buffer.

Disk drive A device used to maneuver disks for storing and retrieving data.

DOS editing keys Certain keys on the PC keyboard used for editing DOS and EDLIN commands. These include Esc, Ins, Del, Backspace, and some function keys.

DOS command An instruction you can give which DOS can understand and execute. There are dozens of DOS commands, some are **internal** and others are **external**.

DOS device name A special term treated by DOS as a computer device. **PRN**, for example, is considered to be a printer. See reserved words for other names.

DOS environment A memory area set aside for DOS to maneuver certain data. Normally, PATH, PROMPT and APPEND (if installed with /E) strings are entered into the environment. These strings determine how DOS is to display its system prompt or search for executable and data files. The environment has limited space; it can be expanded if necessary. See also environment variable.

DOS prompt Also known as system prompt. It marks the location where a DOS command is to be entered. The DOS prompt by default contains the letter of the default drive and the > sign. It can be changed with the PROMPT command.

Dot-matrix printer A printer that prints characters by using a matrix of pins (wires). Currently 9-pin and 24-pin models are common. The more pins a printer has, the more fully formed characters it can produce.

Dummy variables See replaceable parameter.

E

EGA Enhanced Graphics Adapter. An EGA card is needed to drive an EGA monitor. The duo was introduced with the AT in 1984. While still popular, the EGA standard is mostly replaced by **VGA**.

EISA Extended Industry Standard Architecture. This is a bus structure designed by a consortium of IBM rivals to counter IBM's **proprietary MCA** bus. A PC based on this bus can utilize existing AT parts while an MCA-based PC cannot.

EMS Expanded memory specification; see expanded memory.

Enhanced keyboard A keyboard introduced with the **PS/2** line of PCs. It has 101 keys and 12 function keys. An additional cursor pad is also added.

Environment See DOS environment and operating environment.

Environment variable Also known as named parameter, an alphanumeric string entered into the **DOS environment**. Use SET to assign a value to a variable and enter both into the environment. Use a batch file to maneuver environment variables enclosed in a pair of %, such as %var%.

Errorlevel Used with IF in a **batch file** to respond to an **exit code**. For example, if BACKUP cannot find a source file to back up, it returns errorlevel 1. You can thus use a batch file to respond to this situation. DOS also treats a character as an errorlevel number which is identical to the character's ASCII value. This phenomenon can be used to construct a menu batch file.

Executable file A file which DOS can execute. It could carry a COM, EXE, or BAT extension. If there are three files with same file name but with these separate extensions, the COM file has priority over the EXE file, which has priority over the BAT file.

Exit codes Numbers returned by DOS in response to the outcome of some commands. FORMAT, for example, can output exit codes depending on whether formatting is successful. These codes can be maneuvered with an **errorlevel** in a batch file.

Expanded memory Additional memory installed on a PC conforming to the LIM (Lotus Intel Microsoft) specifications. Such memory can be used by many DOS-based application programs. DOS can use up to only 640KB of conventional memory, but it can take advantage of as much as 8MB of expanded memory. Expanded memory is slower than **extended memory**.

Expansion slot A slot on the **motherboard** to which a **controller card** can be inserted. The controller card can then be connected to a device such as a printer or disk drive.

Extended key codes Used in **ANSI.SYS** to redefine keyboard keys. Some keys, such as function keys, require two numbers (the first number is mostly 0, but 224 for the gray keys in the middle of an extended keyboard) if you want to redefine them. These numbers are known as extended key codes.

Extended memory Memory installed in a 286 or higher PC beyond the 1MB boundary. DOS cannot use such memory (except **HMA**). OS/2, UNIX, and Windows can use such memory. Some programs (such as Quarterdeck's QEMM) can convert the memory beyond the 1MB area to **expanded memory**. DOS 5 can use EMM386.EXE to convert extended memory to expanded memory in a 386 or higher system.

External command A DOS command that is not included in COMMAND.COM. It is stored on a disk. To use such a command, it must be located in the **current directory** of the **current drive**, or DOS must be told where to access it (using the PATH command).

Environment software See operating environment.

F

FAT File allocation table, a table created by formatting and used by DOS to keep track of disk space usage, and find files to read and space to store data. Two FATs are maintained on each disk.

File handles   The number of files DOS can handle at one time. The FILES command included in a **CONFIG.SYS** file can be used to increase the default of 8 file handles to an optimal number of 20–30.

File   A collection of related data. A file has a unique name which is different from another. DOS recognizes some files by their extensions such as COM, EXE, BAT, and SYS.

Filter   A DOS command that can sieve through information going to the screen and produce output in a specified way. FIND, MORE, and SORT are DOS filter commands.

Firmware   A device which is a combination of software and hardware. It is usually a **chip** (which is hardware) containing computer instructions (software). When power is on, the instructions are acted upon; when power is off, they do nothing. A **BIOS** chip is an example of firmware.

Function keys   The keys on the PC keyboard marked as F1, F2, etc. DOS uses only the first 6 keys for editing. DOSKEY uses some other keys. If **ANSI.SYS** is installed, these keys and their various combinations can be defined for your own use.

G

Gigabyte   One billion or 2^30 bytes.

GUI   Graphical user interface, an operating environment that provides the user a screenfull of icons which can be manipulated with a mouse. The user can use the GUI to run multiple programs and switch from one to another. Windows is a good example. The Shell in DOS 5 is a less capable version.

H

Hercules   A monographics card allowing graphics to be displayed on a monochrome monitor. Most mono monitors today are equipped with cards that are compatible to the Hercules standard.

Hexadecimal   Base 16, or 2-byte, numerical system. Hex digits consist of 0, 1, 2, 3, 4, 5, 6, 7, 8, 9, A, B, C, D, E, and F. Hex is often used in writing computer programs. **DEBUG**, for example, can recognize only hex numbers.

HMA   High memory area, the 64KB memory beyond the 1MB area in a 286 or higher PC. You can use HIMEM.SYS and DOS=HIGH in version 5 to load DOS in this area so that more conventional memory will be available for your application programs.

I

Index hole   A round hole near the center of a 5.25-inch disk to control the disk's reading and writing. On a 3.5-inch disk, a rectangular hole on the backside of the disk called sector notch serves the same purpose.

Internal command   A DOS command included in COMMAND.COM. When DOS is booted, COMMAND.COM stays in memory. Since an internal command is in **RAM**, it can be used regardless of what the default drive or current directory is. DOS does not need to go to a disk to access it.

Installable Device Driver   See device driver.

K

KB   Kilobyte, 1024 or 2^10 bytes.

L

Label   A marker for branching batch execution. A label in a batch file is a text string preceded with a colon (:).

Laser printer   A printer using laser beam and photocopy technology. It produces printout by using a large number of dots. Today, the low-end models output 300 by 300 dots per inch. High-end models used in typesetting have much higher resolutions.

LIM-EMS   Lotus Intel Microsoft Expanded Memory Specification; see expanded memory.

Logical drive A drive which DOS can recognize and manipulate. Normally DOS can handle four drives of A, B, C, and D. If you want it to handle more, you need to put the LASTDRIVE=x command in your **CONFIG.SYS** file. After that, X becomes the last (highest) drive DOS can maneuver. If a logical drive is not paired with a physical drive, an error may result.

Looping A programming technique that forces execution of a routine a number of times. The FOR..IN..DO command is the most commonly used looping command.

LPT1 The (line) printer connected to the first **parallel port**.

M

Macro An arrangement that allows a series of keystrokes or commands to be stored in one key or a name. When that key is pressed or the name entered, all the stored keystrokes will be replayed. You need to install **ANSI.SYS** to assign multiple keystrokes to a key and **DOSKEY** to assign multiple commands to a name.

Mainframe A large-scale computer.

MB See megabyte.

MCA Micro Channel Architecture. This is a **proprietary** bus structure introduced with the **PS/2** line of PCs. An AT add-in card cannot be plugged into the motherboard of this system. See EISA.

MDA Monochrome Display Adapter, the card used to drive IBM's mono monitor. This system produces crisp screen characters, but cannot handle graphics. It is mostly displaced by **Hercules** cards, also known as MGA (monographics adapter).

Megabyte One million or 2^20 bytes.

Menu A screen display of options available in a computer program or batch file.

Memory See RAM.

Menu block The block of commands in a CONFIG.SYS file starting with the [menu]

header. The block contains items for a menu display and branching mechanism to handle a user selection.

Metastring A text string placed after the PROMPT command (or in a macro) to maneuver the DOS prompt (or parameters). Such a text string usually consists of a special character put after a $ sign.

Microcomputer Or micro, a tiny computer. This term was popularly used in the 1970s to mean any small computer below the minicomputer. Today it is mostly used for a small computer primarily for playing games.

Minicomputer Or mini, a small-scale computer. It is between a **mainframe** and a PC. Most minis use **UNIX** as the **operating system**. Today's high-end (386 and 486) PCs are replacing minis.

Modem MOdulator DEModulator, a communications device used to send data between a PC and another PC, a bulletin board, or a commercial database like CompuServe. Modem speeds are measured by **bauds**. When modems first became popular, 300-baud models were common. They were quickly replaced by 1200-baud models. Today, 2400-baud models are most common.

Motherboard Also known as main board or system board, a flat device placed at the bottom of a **system unit**. All the vital parts of a PC, such as **CPU, RAM, controller cards**, etc. are placed on it or connected to it.

Mouse An input device that resembles an animal of the same name. A mouse can be used to control the cursor, maneuver objects on the screen, or execute a program. Character-oriented programs generally have little use for this device, but graphics-oriented programs often cannot be run without it. A mouse can be used with the DOS Shell and Editor in version 5.

MPC Multimedia PC, a PC that has a ROM-disk player. A MPC combines a PC with CD-quality sound and HDTV-quality animation. This exciting technology is still at a developmental stage.

MS-DOS   Microsoft Disk Operating System. A DOS marketed by a vendor other than IBM is generally known as MS-DOS. MS-DOS and PC-DOS are practically identical.

Multitasking   Doing several jobs at the same time. **UNIX** and **OS/2** are examples of multitasking **operating systems**. Windows 3.x can also be set up to do multitasking.

N

Nesting   A programming technique that branches execution to a routine and then returns. In a **batch file**, nesting means using the CALL command to execute another batch file and then return to the original batch file. See also chaining.

NLQ   Near Letter Quality, said of print quality. Some **dot-matrix printers** allow you to select this mode to produce more fully formed characters.

O

Octal   Base 8 numerical system. Its digits range from 0 to 7.

Online help   Help information available on the command line. Use HELP and a command or a command followed by /? to get the help message pertinent to the command. Enter HELP alone for a list of commands that can give you more help.

Operating Environment   A kind of computer program that provides an interface between the user and compatible application programs. Some can be character-based and others graphics-based. The Shell program in WordPerfect Library is an example of the former. Microsoft Windows, a graphical operating environment resembling the Mac, has become a popular package in recent years.

Operating system   Or OS, a computer program that maneuvers mostly computer hardware such as CPU, RAM, printer, and monitor. DOS,

OS/2, and **UNIX** are popular operating systems for the PC.

OS/2   Operating System/2. A new operating system created by Microsoft and now solely developed by IBM. It can be run only on a PC with 80386 or higher **CPU**. It is primarily a multitasking operating system. With additional equipment and software, it can also be a multiuser system like UNIX.

P

Parallel port   An interface for a parallel device, such as a printer. A parallel device, unlike a serial device, transmits data 8 bits (1 byte or character) at a time.

Parameter   An argument or qualifier that can be used with a DOS command or is expected by a batch file. To copy a file, for example, you need to have a **source** and a **target**; these are considered parameters. A batch file may also expect one or more files; these are also parameters.

Parent directory   A **directory** which is one level above the current one.

Partition   A unit in a hard disk system. The FDISK command is used to create partitions. Before a hard disk can be used by DOS, it must be partitioned and then formatted.

Path   The specific trail which DOS is supposed to search for a file to execute or to read. A predetermined path can be entered into the **DOS environment** by using the APPEND or PATH command.

PC   Personal Computer. It originated from IBM PC. Today it has become a generic term applied to any serious computer below the **minicomputer**. It is a large umbrella under which there are subcategories such as **XT, AT, PS/2**, etc. Most PCs use Intel CPUs and are compatible with IBM models.

PC-DOS   Personal Computer–Disk Operating System. A DOS marketed by IBM is known as PC-DOS. Those marketed by other vendors are known as MS-DOS. Both are practically identical.

Peripheral   An external computer device, such as a printer.

Pipe   A connector of two DOS commands. The ¦ sign is used to pipe two commands, such as:

```
A>type filename ¦ more
```

Pixels   Dots displayed on the screen. Characters and graphics images are formed with pixels. The more pixels, the better-looking displays.

Platter   A disk inside a hard drive. A hard disk unit usually contains a number of platters.

Print queue   A list of files lined up to be printed one after another. The PRINT command can add files to or delete them from a print queue.

Printout   A printed (hard) copy of a **file**.

Prompt   A cue or signal for user response. The **DOS prompt** invites you to enter a command. Some DOS commands prompt you to swap disks and others to enter Y or N.

PRN   A **reserved word** treated by DOS as the standard printer.

Proprietary   Controlled by one company, as a contrast to open standard. Large vendors like IBM, Apple, and Compaq like to sell proprietary products because they are highly profitable and competitors cannot market compatible products. Consumers, however, like open-standard products because they have more choices of good-quality and low-priced parts that are interchangeable with one another.

PS/1/2   Personal System/2 is a line of small IBM computers introduced in 1987. It replaces the original PC-XT and PC-AT. This new line is a hodge-podge combination of several products based on a variety of CPUs ranging from 80386 to 80486; the low-end products, based on lower CPUs, are known as PS/1. Most of the higher priced models use a new **proprietary bus** structure called **MCA**. Rival vendors have produced models based on the extended AT bus structure called **EISA**.

Q

Queue   See print queue.

R

RAM   Random access memory, or computer memory. It's called random access because any part of the memory can be accessed at will. RAM is volatile. When power is on, it can be used; when power is off, the data in it is erased.

RAM disk   A memory area set aside to simulate a real disk. A RAM disk (or drive), also known as virtual disk, can temporarily store data. When power is off, the stored data is wiped out.

Read-only   An attribute marking a file. Such a file can only be read but cannot be altered or erased. The ATTRIB command is used to add or remove this attribute.

Read-write opening   A disk area that is opened for reading and writing. On a 5.25-inch disk, this area is exposed. On a 3.5-inch disk, it is covered with a shutter, which is automatically opened when a disk is inserted into a drive.

Redirection   Redirecting input or output from the standard device. Normally, DOS expects an input from the keyboard when you issue a command like this:

```
A>del *.*
```

You can, however, supply the expected input of Y or N from a file. A normal output also goes to the screen. It can also be redirected. This command redirects output to a disk file:

```
A>dir > dirfile
```

Replaceable parameter   A macro or batch file place holder reserving a place for a command-line parameter. It is represented with $ (macro) or % (batch), followed by a number, such as $1 or %1. A batch file name entered on the command line is considered parameter 0, or %0; the first item after the macro or file name is treated as parameter 1, $1 or %1; and so on. Batch (but not macro) parameters can be maneuvered with the SHIFT command. You can use the "if .==.%1" equation to test whether an expected parameter is entered with a batch file.

Reserved words   Words that are used by DOS (or another computer language) for special purposes. Such words, including **AUX** (serial port), **COM1** (1st serial port), **CON** (console), NUL (dummy, nonexisting, device), **PRN** (parallel port) and **LPT1** (1st parallel port), cannot be used as file names.

RGB   Red Green and Blue, used to designate the first color monitor marketed by IBM. To run an RGB monitor, you need to equip your PC with a **CGA** graphics card. The combination produces dotty characters and crude graphics. Today, many low-end PCs still use this combination; more expensive models, however, are equipped with the **VGA** system.

ROM   Read-only memory. It is usually a chip containing computer instructions that, unlike **RAM**, cannot be erased. A PC includes a number of ROM chips, one of which contains **BIOS**.

Root directory   The highest-level **directory**. Every disk, even though not divided into any subdirectory, has a root directory, which is created by FORMAT. This directory is used to keep track of the files stored on a disk.

S

Scanner   A device that can read printed text or graphics and feed the data into an application program. Some models are equipped with software that can recognize and maneuver printed words; others simply treat any scanned object as an image that cannot be maneuvered.

Sector   A subunit of a **track**. Each sector has the storage capacity of 512 bytes. A track can be divided into 8 or 9 sectors for a 5.25-inch, double-density disk, 15 sectors for a 5.25-inch quad-density disk, 9 sectors for a 3.5-inch, double-density disk, and 18 sectors for a 3.5-inch quad-density disk.

Sector notch   See index hole.

Selective configurations   Selecting certain configuration lines to execute and others to skip. Press F8 at the beginning of booting and answer Y or N for each line.

Serial port   An interface for a serial device, such as a mouse or modem. A serial device transmits data one bit at a time, in contrast to a **parallel device**.

Source   The original object for DOS to act on. Some commands, COPY for example, expect a source and a **target**.

Standard input   The device where raw data is normally entered. The keyboard is the standard input device.

Standard output   The device to which a computer output is normally sent. The screen is the standard output device.

Subdirectory   A **directory** that is one level below the current one.

Surge protector   A device to control a sudden surge in the electrical current and prevent it from harming your computer. It usually comes with an on-off switch and multiple electrical outlets.

Switch   An option used with certain DOS commands. To format a bootable disk, for example, you need to use the /S switch.

System prompt   See DOS prompt.

System unit   A rectangular metal box containing the vital parts of a PC, including **motherboard, CPU, ROM, RAM, disk drives**, etc.

System software   See operating system.

T

Target   Opposite of **source**. A target drive of the COPY command, for example, is where the files in a source drive will be duplicated to.

Template   A memory area (**buffer**) where the most recently entered DOS (or EDLIN) command is stored. This stored line can be copied to the screen and maneuvered with **DOS editing keys**.

Toggle   Used with certain keys for switching between two modes. The Ins key, for example, is a toggle key. It can toggle (switch) between insert and typeover modes. Normally this key operates in insert mode. Pressed once, it goes to typeover mode. Pressed another time, it goes back to insert mode, and so on.

Track   A concentric ring of a disk created by formatting. Currently, a floppy disk can be divided into 40 (5.25-inch double density) or 80 (5.25-inch quad-density and 3.5-inch) tracks.

TSR   Terminate and Stay Resident. Some computer programs, such as DOSKEY, are memory resident once loaded. You can press a certain key combination to activate it. When these keys are not pressed, the program stays dormant.

U

UMA/UMBs   Upper memory area and upper memory blocks. The memory area in a 8088 CPU between 640KB to 1MG is known as the upper memory area and is reserved for system use (not available for DOS). Different blocks are used by hardware devices such as the monitor. Others that are not used are known as upper memory blocks. DOS 5 can use EMM386.EXE to load some device drivers such as **ANSI.SYS** and **TSR** programs such as DOSKEY in these available blocks; this applies only to 386 or higher PCs.

UNIX   A multiuser **operating system** initially developed by the Bell Lab of AT&T. It is a popular operating system with mini-computers and widely used in colleges. It is being adapted to run on 386/486 PCs.

Undelete   To recover data from a deleted file. Use the UNDELETE command newly available in version 5 to undelete files before you write files to the same disk space.

Unformat   To recover a disk from inadvertent reformatting. Use UNFORMAT alone or in combination with MIRROR to recover such a disk as soon as a mistake is made.

V

VGA   Video Graphics Array. A video card introduced with the **PS/2**. It is used to drive a VGA monitor. This duo is the current video display standard, providing displays that are more attractive than previous systems. There are now super VGA (SVGA) systems that have resolutions much higher than the standard VGA.

Video graphics card   A controller card inserted into an expansion slot to control a monitor. The most common cards today are **Hercules, CGA, EGA** and **VGA**.

Volume label   An optional text string (up to 11 characters) you can use to identify a disk. FORMAT, LABEL, and VOL can create and/or display volume labels.

W

Wild card characters   The ? and * characters. A question mark is used to represent any character in a particular position in a file name. An asterisk can represent any number of characters from a certain position.

Write-protect notch/switch   A device on a floppy disk to prevent writing to a write-protected disk. On a 5.25-inch disk, this is a cut-out rectangular hole. When this hole is covered, the disk is write-protected. On a 3.5-inch disk, a built-in switch can be pushed to the edge, thus showing a see-through hole, to write-protect the disk.

X

XMS   Extended memory specification; see extended memory.

XT   Extended Technology. It originated from IBM PC-XT. Today an XT-class PC is an entry-level PC equipped with 8086/8088 **CPU**.

Appendix B: ASCII Characters

The ASCII character set contains 256 characters, numbered from 0 to 255. To find the number of a particular character, first find the character in the table, then use the row and column numbers to determine the numercial value. The ¿, for example, is in row 16, column 8, and so its corresponding number is 168.

(handwritten, left margin) represents code # for character

	0	1	2	3	4	5	6	7	8	9
00		☺	☻	♥	♦	♣	♠	•	◘	○
01	◙	♂	♀	♪	♫	☼	►	◄	↕	‼
02	¶	§	▬	‡	↑	↓	→	←	∟	↔
03	▲	▼		!	"	#	$	%	&	'
04	(	)	*	+	,	–	.	/	0	1
05	2	3	4	5	6	7	8	9	:	;
06	<	=	>	?	@	A	B	C	D	E
07	F	G	H	I	J	K	L	M	N	O
08	P	Q	R	S	T	U	V	W	X	Y
09	Z	[	\	]	^	_	`	a	b	c
10	d	e	f	g	h	i	j	k	l	m
11	n	o	p	q	r	s	t	u	v	w
12	x	y	z	{	|	}	~	⌂	Ç	ü
13	é	â	ä	à	å	ç	ê	ë	è	ï
14	î	ì	Ä	Å	É	æ	Æ	ô	ö	ò
15	û	ù	ÿ	Ö	Ü	¢	£	¥	₧	ƒ
16	á	í	ó	ú	ñ	Ñ	ª	º	¿	⌐
17	¬	½	¼	¡	«	»	░	▒	▓	│
18	┤	╡	╢	╖	╕	╣	║	╗	╝	╜
19	╛	┐	└	┴	┬	├	─	┼	╞	╟
20	╚	╔	╩	╦	╠	═	╬	╧	╨	╤
21	╥	╙	╘	╒	╓	╫	╪	┘	┌	█
22	▄	▌	▐	▀	α	ß	Γ	π	Σ	σ
23	µ	τ	Φ	Θ	Ω	δ	∞	φ	ε	∩
24	≡	±	≥	≤	⌠	⌡	÷	≈	°	·
25	·	√	ⁿ	²	■					

(handwritten, bottom) ALT # ____ exp (ALT 202) 1st 30 doesn't always work

569

Note: 0 is a null character; 32 is a space, the same as pressing the space bar; 255 is a blank. To enter a character, hold down Alt and type a corresponding number on the numeric keypad. 1–31 are not supported by DOS; e.g., Alt-1 or Ctrl-A shows ^A, not ☺.)

Appendix C: ASCII Key Codes

Key Name	Code for... Key Alone	Shift-Key	Ctrl-Key	Alt-Key
F1	0;59	0;84	0;94	0;104
F2	0;60	0;85	0;95	0;105
F3	0;61	0;86	0;96	0;106
F4	0;62	0;87	0;97	0;107
F5	0;63	0;88	0;98	0;108
F6	0;64	0;89	0;99	0;109
F7	0;65	0;90	0;100	0;110
F8	0;66	0;91	0;101	0;111
F9	0;67	0;92	0;102	0;112
F10	0;68	0;93	0;103	0;113
F11	0;133	0;135	0;137	0;139
F12	0;134	0;136	0;138	0;140
Home	0;71	55	0;119	—
↑	0;72	56	0;141	—
PgUp	0;73	57	0;132	—
←	0;75	52	0;115	—
→	0;77	54	0;116	—
End	0;79	49	0;117	—
↓	0;80	50	0;145	—
PgDn	0;81	51	0;118	—

Key Name	Code for... Key Alone	Shift-Key	Ctrl-Key	Alt-Key
Ins	0;82	48	0;146	—
Del	0;83	46	0;147	—
Home (gray)*	224;71	224;71	224;119	224;151
↑ (gray)	224;72	224;72	224;141	224;152
PgUp (gray)	224;73	224;73	224;132	224;153
← (gray)	224;75	224;75	224;115	224;155
→ (gray)	224;77	224;77	224;116	224;157
End (gray)	224;79	224;79	224;117	224;159
↓ (gray)	224;80	224;80	224;145	224;154
PgDn (gray)	224;81	224;81	224;118	224;161
Insert (gray)	224;82	224;82	224;146	224;162
Delete (gray)	224;83	224;83	224;147	224;163
Print Scrn	—	—	0;114	—
Pause/Break	—	—	0;0	—
Backspace	8	8	127	0
Enter	13	—	10	0;28
Tab	9	0;15	0;148	0;165
a	97	65 (A)	1	0;30
b	98	66	2	0;48
c	99	67	3	0;46
d	100	68	4	0;32
e	101	68	5	0;18
f	102	70	6	0;33
g	103	71	7	0;34
h	104	72	8	0;35
i	105	73	9	0;23
j	106	74	10	0;36

*gray = the cursor keypad on an extended keyboard

Key Name	Code for... Key Alone	Shift-Key	Ctrl-Key	Alt-Key
k	107	75	11	0;37
l	108	76	12	0;38
m	109	77	13	0;50
n	110	78	14	0;49
o	111	79	15	0;24
p	112	80	16	0;25
q	113	81	17	0;16
r	114	82	18	0;19
s	115	83	19	0;31
t	116	84	20	0;20
u	117	85	21	0;22
v	118	86	22	0;47
w	119	87	23	0;17
x	120	88	24	0;45
y	121	89	25	0;21
z	122	90 (Z)	26	0;44
1	49	33 (!)	—	0;120
2	50	64 (@)	0;3	0;121
3	51	35 (#)	—	0;122
4	52	36 ($)	—	0;123
5	53	37 (%)	—	0;124
6	54	94 (^)	30	0;125
7	55	38 (&)	—	0;126
8	56	42 (*)	—	0;127
9	57	40 (()	—	0;128
0	48	41 ())	—	0;129
–	45	95 (_)	31	0;130
=	61	43 (+)	—	0;131

Key Name	Code for... Key Alone	Shift-Key	Ctrl-Key	Alt-Key
[	91	123 ({)	27	0;26
\	92	124 (¦)	28	0;43
]	93	125 (})	29	0;27
;	59	58 (:)	—	0;39
'	39	34 (")	—	0;40
,	44	60 (<)	—	0;51
.	46	62 (>)	—	0;52
/	47	63 (?)	—	0;53
'	96	126 (~)	—	0;41
Enter (key)*	13	—	10	0;166
/ (key)	47	47	0;142	0;74
* (key)	42	0;144	0;78	—
– (key)	45	45	0;149	0;164
+ (key)	43	43	0;150	0;55
5 (key)	0;76	53	0;143	—

---

*key = numeric keypad

To remap a key, you must install ANSI.SYS first. You can then use a command like the one below to reassign a new defination to a key:

```
C>prompt $e[0;104;"dir"p
echo ^[[0;104;"dir"p
```

Either command will assign DIR to Alt-F1. The first can be entered from the keyboard or in a batch file. The second must be implemented from a batch file. See Chapter 13 for details.

Your keyboard may not recognize remapping of some keys, particularly key combinations on the cursor keypad (gray keys) of an extended keyboard. You may increase your chances of being able to remap more keys if the /X switch is included in your CONFIG.SYS file, like this:

```
device=c:\dos\ansi.sys /x
```

Appendix D: DOS Versions

DOS versions are usually shown with two or three digit numbers. The first digit indicates a major release, and the second a minor revision. The third digit, if any, signifies a bug-fix release (e.g., 4.01) or a special version (e.g., 2.11) for a less compatible system such as PC Junior and Sanyo MBC-550. Use the VER command to show what DOS version you are currently using.

Each new version provides a few new commands to enable DOS to perform more sophisticated tasks. Some old commands also have new added functions to handle newly available hardware such as a hard disk and a 3.5-inch floppy disk.

The list below shows each version's new commands (and device driver files) and old commands' enhancements. If a command provides no explanation, related information is available in Appendix E.

VERSION 1

Original Commands

CHKDSK

COMP

COPY

DATE

DEBUG

DEL (ERASE)

DIR

DISKCOMP

EDLIN

FORMAT (initially one side, and then two sides up to 320KB)

MODE

PAUSE

REM

REN

SYS

TIME

TYPE

VERSION 2

New Commands and Drivers

ANSI.SYS	IF
ASSIGN	GRAPHICS
BACKUP	MD (MKDIR)
BREAK	MORE
CD (CHDIR)	PATH
CLS	PRINT
COMMAND (to load another copy of COMMAND.COM)	PROMPT
	RD (RMDIR)
CTTY (to change standard input/ output device)	RECOVER
	RESTORE
DEVICE (configuration command to specify a driver file)	SET
	SHELL (to load another command processor)
DISKCOPY	
ECHO	SHIFT
EXIT (to exit an extra copy of COMMAND.COM)	SORT (no adjustment for upper and lower cases, placing "Z" before "a")
FC (MS-DOS version of COMP)	
FDISK	TREE
FILES	VER
FIND	VERIFY
FOR	VOL
GOTO	

Enhancements

- This version can format a 5.25-inch floppy disk up to 360KB.
- Support for hard disks and installable device drivers.
- Support for piping (|), filtering (FIND, MORE, SORT), and input-output redirection (<, >, >>).
- EDLIN: C, M, P and T commands added.

VERSION 3.0

New Commands and Drivers

ATTRIB (to add or remove only R attribute)

COUNTRY (configuration command for setting country-specific date-time format)

FCBS (configuration command for specifying the number of file control blocks that can be currently open)

KEYBxx (to set country-specific keyboard layout)

GRAFTABL (to display some characters on CGA monitor)

LABEL

LASTDRIVE

SELECT (for country-specific keyboard layout and date-time format)

SHARE (for file sharing and locking)

VDISK.SYS (configuration command to create RAM disks)

Enhancements

- A directory path can be specified before an external command, such as:

  A>c:\dos\format a:

- FORMAT: can format a 1.2MB floppy disk; has a new parameter of /4 to format a 360KB disk in a 1.2MB drive; a new warning message for formatting a hard disk.

- BACKUP and RESTORE: can back up files to a hard disk or from a floppy to another floppy.

- DISKCOMP and DISKCOPY: can handle 1.2MB disks.

- DATE: can support mm-dd-yy or dd-mm-yy formats.

- GRAPHICS: can support color printing.

- SORT: upper and lower cases adjusted, placing "a" before "Z".

VERSION 3.1

New Commands and Drivers

JOIN

SUBST

Enhancements

- This version begins support for networking.
- LABEL: a new prompt before deleting a volume label.
- SHELL: a new switch of /E:size to expand the size of the environment; size is the number of 16-byte blocks.
- TREE: a new /F switch to display files.

VERSION 3.2

New Commands and Drivers

DRIVER.SYS (to permit assigning a letter to a floppy drive)

RAMDRIVE.SYS (MS-DOS version of VDISK.SYS)

REPLACE

XCOPY

Enhancements

- ATTRIB: a new switch of /A to set or remove the A attribute.
- FORMAT: can format 3.5-inch, 720KB disks.
- DISKCOMP and DISKCOPY: can handle 720KB disks.
- SHELL: the size in the /E:size switch is changed to bytes.

VERSION 3.3

New Commands and Drivers

APPEND

CALL

CHCP (to change code pages)

DISPLAY.SYS (to display language-specific characters)

FASTOPEN (to speed up disk access)

NLSFUNC (national language support function; to specify a country driver file before changing code pages)

PRINTER.SYS (to print language-specific characters)

Enhancements

- Support for 1.44MB disks and up to four (instead of two) serial ports (COM4).
- ATTRIB: /S switch added.
- BACKUP: new switches of /F, /L and /T; target disk need not be preformatted.
- Batch files: @ to suppress batch execution and %var% to maneuver environment variables; CALL available for the first time to replace COMMAND.COM/C.
- DATE/TIME: changes the system's calendar.
- FDISK: divides a large hard disk (more than 32MB) into multiple drives.
- FORMAT: new switches of /N and /T.
- MODE: can handle code pages.
- KEYB: replaces KEYBxx of version 3.2.
- RESTORE: new switches of /B, /E, /L, and /N.
- SHELL: default environment size increased from 128 to 160 bytes.

VERSION 4

New Commands and Drivers

MEM

SHELL.BAT (to start DOS Shell environment)

SMARTDRV.SYS (disk cache)

XMAEM.SYS (to use 386 extended memory to simulate expanded memory)

XMA2EMS.SYS (to use LIM expanded memory)

Enhancements

- Disk serial numbers are created and displayed by various commands.
- A new (optional) user interface that resembles Microsoft Windows.
- ANSI.SYS: new switches of /X, /K and /L for enhanced keyboard and EGA/VGA monitors.
- APPEND: adds new switches of /X:ON, /X:OFF, /PATH:ON, /PATH:OFF.
- BACKUP: needs access to FORMAT.COM and automatically formats target disk if necessary.
- CHKDSK and FORMAT: show allocation unit (cluster) information.
- DEL (ERASE): a new /P switch.
- FDISK: can create a larger partition.
- FORMAT: adds /F and /V:diskname switches.
- MODE: can speed up keyboard and increase display lines for EGA and VGA.
- REPLACE: a new /U switch.
- REM: remarks permitted in a CONFIG.SYS file.
- SYS: can specify a source drive other than where SYS.COM is stored.
- TIME: can use 24-hour format or "a" or "p" in 12-hour format.
- TREE: displays diagram (not list); has a new /A switch; can analyze a directory as well as a whole disk.

VERSION 5

New Commands and Drivers

DEVICEHIGH

DOS

DOSKEY

DOSSHELL

EDIT

EMM386

EXPAND

HELP

HIMEM.SYS

INSTALL (to install TSR programs without environment variables)

LOADHIGH (LH)

MIRROR

QBASIC

SETVER (to specify an earlier version number so that your program may run with DOS, if it can't work with version 5)

UNFORMAT

UNDELETE

Enhancements

- ANSI.SYS: can now be used to remap the gray keys (the extra cursor keys in the middle) of an extended keyboard.

- ASSIGN: a new switch, /STATUS, to show drive assignment status.

- ATTRIB: can use +/–H and +/–S to handle hidden and system file attributes.

- COMP: five new switches: /A, /C, /D, /L, and /N.

- DIR: five new switches are added: /A, /B, /L, /O, and /S. /A can be used to show hidden system files and /O to sort items numerous ways.

- FIND: new /I switch for case insensitive search.

- FORMAT: two new switches: /Q for quick formatting and /U for unconditional formatting; you can now use the /F switch to format a 3.5-inch floppy disk to 2.88MB.

- MEM: a new switch, /CLASSIFY, to show high-memory use.

- RESTORE: a new switch, /D, to display files available for restoration.

- SYS: will now copy COMMAND.COM as well as the two hidden system files.

VERSION 6

New Features

- File Compression (DBLSPACE): This is the most widely advertised addition, licensed from Vertisoft. The program, known as DoubleSpace, can compress files to fit more data on the same disk, hard or floppy. This can nearly double a disk's capacity. File compression is done at the system level and transparent to the user; you won't notice it.

- MOVE: This new command lets you move files and rename directories.

- DELTREE: This new command can be used to delete files and directories (together with files and subdirectories).

- CHOICE: This new command can be used in a batch file to handle user interaction.

- DEFRAG: This disk defragmenter is a slimmed down version of Norton SpeedDisk. It brings fragmented files together so that your disk access time can be reduced.

- Anti-Virus: Licensed from Central Point Anti-Virus, Microsoft Anti-Virus can detect and clean viruses from your memory or disks. A memory-resident program can also monitor any virus-like (shall we say virulent?) activity and alert you.

- Memory Optimizing: The new memory optimizer called MemMaker can analyze and alter your CONFIG.SYS and AUTOEXEC.BAT files so that more memory-resident programs can be loaded to the upper memory area. This can free up more conventional memory for your applications.

- Startup: When booting DOS, you can now have a clean boot (bypass both CONFIG.SYS and AUTOEXEC.BAT) and selective boot (answer Y or N to execute a line in CONFIG.SYS). Your CONFIG.SYS file can now be written in such a way to show a menu which will let you select an option to execute only a block of configuration commands. In addition, the option selected by the user can pass value to the subsequent AUTOEXEC.BAT execution.

- Diagnostics: MSD (Microsoft Diagnostics) can show lots of information related to your system, including memory maps and peripheral data. You can use it to print a comprehensive report about various parts of your system.

- INTERLNK: If you have a laptop computer, you can use the INTERLNK.EXE program and a parallel or serial cable to link up between the laptop and your desktop PC. You can also use POWER.EXE to save power on your laptop.

Enhancements

- Online Reference: Online help was first introduced in version 5; this program is still available in version 6. But there is a new full-screen, menu-driven online reference. This electronic reference has replaced the bulky printed manual that used to accompany each previous version. Consequently, the manual that comes with version 6 is much skimpier (and using much less paper) than its previous incarnations. DOS has turned green—ecologically green.

- Backup: The previous BACKUP and RESTORE to back up and restore files have been discarded and replaced with Microsoft Backup, a new program licensed from Norton Backup. It has many new features and works much better.

- UNDELETE: This old command has absorbed MIRROR, available in version 5. It also offers a new level of protection against file deletion.

- Windows: If you are using Windows 3.0 or 3.1, the SETUP program lets you install the Windows flavor of UNDELETE, Anti-Virus, and MS Backup. You can access these features by clicking an icon on the Windows screen.

Deletions

The following files were included in version 5, but removed from version 6. They are available from Microsoft on a supplementary disk:

ASSIGN.COM

BACKUP.EXE

COMP.EXE

EXE2BIN.EXE

EDLIN.EXE

GRAFTABL.COM

JOIN.EXE

MIRROR.COM

QBASIC sample programs

RECOVER.EXE

Appendix E: DOS Commands

B = batch (internal) command   I = internal command

C = configuration (internal) command   M = memory resident (TSR)

D = device driver file   U = user-created

E = external command

Command		Purpose
ANSI.SYS	D	Special driver to enhance input/output
APPEND	EM	To set/display path for text files
ATTRIB	E	To set or remove A and R file attributes
BATCH	U	To store and execute a series of commands
BREAK	CI	On/off to determine DOS's check on ^C
BUFFERS	C	To set the number of memory buffers
CALL	B	To call (nest) another batch file
CD	I	To change to another directory
CHKDSK	E	To check a disk for various information
CHOICE	E	A batch command to respond to a user selection
CLS	I	To clear the screen
COMP	E	To compare files (PC-DOS only)
CONFIG.SYS	U	To configure (define) the system

Command		Purpose
COPY	I	To copy, combine, and create files
COPY CON	I	To create files (copy from console to disk)
DATE	I	To display and/or change PC clock date
DBLSPACE	E	To compress files and manage compressed disks
DEFRAG	E	To defragment a disk
DEL	I	To delete file(s)
DELTREE	E	To remove files and directories
DEVICE	C	To load a device drive in conventional memory
DEVICEHIGH	C	To load a device driver in upper memory blocks
DIR	I	To show disk directory information
DISKCOMP	E	To compare two floppy disks
DISKCOPY	E	To duplicate a disk (copy by tracks)
DOS	C	To load DOS in the HMA and access UMBs
DOSKEY	EM	To let you edit and recycle commands
DOSSHELL	E	To load the Shell, a graphical user interface
ECHO	BI	To display ECHO on/off or batch message
EDLIN	E	A line editor to create text files
EMM386	DE	To manage UMBs and convert XMS to EMS
ERASE	I	To erase files, same as DEL
EXIST	B	To test existence of a file or errorlevel
EXPAND	E	To decompress compressed files with _ extension
FASTHELP	E	To show abbreviated online help
FC	E	To compare files (MS-DOS only)
FDISK	E	To partition a hard disk
FILES	C	To set the number of file handles
FIND	E	To find text lines matching a search string
FOR	I	To loop a command a number of times
FORMAT	E	To prepare a disk for use
GOTO	B	To branch to a batch label
GRAPHICS	EM	TSR, to print a screen graphics display
HELP	E	To show online help
HIMEM.SYS	D	To manage XMS and access the HMA

Command		Purpose
IF	B	To test parameter, file, and errorlevel
KEYS	–	Keys commonly used by DOS
LABEL	E	To display/change disk volume label
LASTDRIVE	C	To set the last logical drive
LOADHIGH	I	To load a TSR program in the upper memory area
MD	I	To make (create) a directory
MEM	E	To show memory use
MEMMAKER	E	To load more programs to the upper memory area
MODE	E	To check/set monitor, printer, and keyboard
MORE	E	To filter text lines
MOVE	E	To move/rename files; rename a directory
MSAV	E	To detect and clean up viruses
MSBACKUP	E	To backup, compare, and restore files
MSD	E	A diagnostic program to show system information
PATH	I	To display/set path for executable files
PAUSE	B	To pause batch execution
PRINT	EM	To print text files in the background
PROMPT	I	To set prompt, enter meta-string & ANSI commands
RD	I	To remove directory
REM	B	To add remarks in a batch file
REN	I	To rename a file
REPLACE	E	To replace (update) files
RESTORE	E	To restore files created by BACKUP
SET	I	To set/display environment variables
SHELL	C	To increase environment size
SHIFT	B	To shift parameters
SORT	E	To filter and sort text lines
SUBST	E	To substitute a drive for a directory
SYMBOLS	–	Signs and Symbols used by DOS
SYS	E	To transfer system (hidden) files
TIME	I	To display/change system time
TREE	E	To display directory structure

TYPE	I	To display a file
UNDELETE	E	To undelete a file deleted by DEL
UNFORMAT	E	To restore previous directory and FAT
VER	I	To show DOS version
VERIFY	I	To verify writing after copying file(s)
VOL	I	To show a disk's volume label
VSAFE	EM	To monitor virus activities
XCOPY	E	To copy source files to memory and then to target

DETAILED REFERENCE

ANSI.SYS   *external/device driver*

A special device driver file to enhance input (keyboard) and output (monitor) functions. This file must be included in your CONFIG.SYS before you can do the following.

Examples:

A>prompt $e[7m	Set reverse video
A>prompt $e[2J	Erase entire screen
A>prompt $e[0;68;"dir/p"p	Define F10 as "dir/p"
echo ^[[5;31;43m	Set blinking red text, yellow background
echo ^[[0m	Turn off all color attributes
echo ^[[0;133;"cls$_"p	Define F11 as "cls" with carriage return

Remarks:

ANSI escape sequences (commands) are mostly entered via PROMPT with $e[and ECHO with ^[[(EDLIN) or ←[(EDIT). The former is entered on the command line, and the latter can be entered only from a batch file created with EDLIN, EDIT, or another text editor. To define the extra keys on an enhanced keyboard, you must install ANSI.SYS with the /X switch. See Chapter 12 for details and Appendix C for key codes to define keyboard keys.

APPEND   *external, TSR*

Make DOS search for nonexecutable (data) files through a path list.

Syntax:

```
A>append list
```

Switches:

/E	Store paths in DOS environment; can then be changed by the SET command
/PATH:ON	Search both command-line and environment paths; default
/PATH:OFF	Ignore environment path if command-line path specified
/X or /X:ON	Act like PATH; search for COM, EXE, BAT
/X:OFF	Not search for executable files; default
;	Placed after APPEND to clear path list

Examples:

C:\DOS>append /e	Enter into environment
A>append c:\xyz/x	Search for both executable and data files in C:\XYZ
A>append;	Clear path list

Remarks:

APPEND stays in RAM after running. It could collide with other TRS programs and crash your computer. You can install it (use it the first time) with /E to put it in the environment and maneuver with SET. See Chapter 5 for APPEND and Chapter 9 for SET.

ATTRIB   *external*

Set or remove file attribute.

Syntax:

```
A>attrib +r +a filename
```

Switches:

+/−A	Set/remove archive
+/−R	Set/remove read–only
+/−H	Set/remove hidden
+/−S	Set/remove system
/S	Subdirectories

Examples:

C>attrib +r file? /s	Set R for all matching files in the current directory and subdirectories
A>attrib +a +r file?	Set A and R for all matching files
A>attrib -a b:*.*	Remove A attribute for all files in B
A>attrib *.* ¦ sort	List all files, sorted & with attributes
C>attrib /s *.* ¦ find "FILE"	List files matching FILE

Remarks:

A new or modified file automatically carries the A attribute. Some commands such as BACKUP and XCOPY can remove it after a file is copied. The R attribute prevents deletion, modification, and overwrite. H and S are available since version 5. See details in Chapter 7.

BATCH   *user-created*

A batch file is an executable file that can contain a series of DOS commands, or be programmed to behave like a computer program. It must have the BAT extension in the file name. It can be created with COPY CON or in EDLIN. The following commands, all internal, can be used in a batch file to make it behave like a computer program:

@	Hide a line during execution
:	Mark a label
%	Replaceable parameter (dummy variable)
==	Test existence of parameters
CALL	Execute another batch file and return
CHOICE	Handle user interaction
ECHO	Turn on/off display; send data to a device
FOR..IN..DO	Repeat execution of a command
GOTO	Go to a label
IF (IF NOT)	Decision making for conditional branching
EXIST	Check existence of a file
PAUSE	Halt execution
REM	Remark
SHIFT	Shift to the next parameter

Remarks:

See ECHO and FOR, which are often used on the command line. See IF for an example of using @, :, %, ==, ECHO, GOTO, IF, EXIST, REM and SHIFT. Chapter 11 provides much more details of programming batch files and how to use each batch command.

BREAK *see CONFIG.SYS*

BUFFERS *see CONFIG.SYS*

CALL *see BATCH*

CD (CHDIR) MD (MKDIR) RD (RMDIR) *all internal*

Change directory; make directory; remove directory

Examples:

A>md b:temp	Make directory named TEMP in drive B
A>cd b:temp	Make TEMP the current directory in drive B
C:\WP>md misc	Make subdirectory named MISC, below C:\WP
C:\WP>cd misc	Change directory to MISC
A>rd b:temp	Remove TEMP directory in B, must be empty
C:\WP\MISC>cd\	Change to root directory, namely C:\
C:\WP\MISC>cd..	Change to parent directory, namely C:\WP
C:\WP>del misc	Delete all files in MISC subdirectory
A>cd	Display the path to the current directory

Remarks:

A directory must be empty before it can be removed. You can remove only a directory lower than the current one. Use PROMPT PG to show a default drive and current directory prompt; see PROMPT for details. Chapter 5 provides more details.

CHKDSK *external*

Check a disk's formatted size, number of files and their total size, available disk space, allocation units, and available memory.

CHKDSK *(continued)*

Switches:

/F   Fix errors

/V   Verbose; list files and their directory paths

Examples:

A>chkdsk b:	Check the entire disk in B
A>chkdsk b:file?	Check matching files' contiguity; file names displayed if not contiguous
A>chkdsk b:*.*	Check contiguity of all files
C>chkdsk /v ¦ sort	List all files in drive C, sorted
C>chkdsk /v ¦ find "FILE"	List files matching FILE

Remarks:

Volume label (if any) and serial number are shown for disks formatted with version 4 or later. If files are messed up, /F will create files named FILEnnnn.CHK, where nnnn is a number starting from 0000 and increasing as needed. See Chapter 3 for more details.

CLS   *internal*

Clear the screen and place the cursor at the top left corner. See Chapter 1.

Syntax:

A>cls

CONFIG.SYS   *user-created*

Configuration commands are those commands that you put in a CONFIG.SYS file, which DOS will execute during booting. There are more than a dozen commands which you can selectively put in your CONFIG.SYS file. You can also put device drivers in your CONFIG.SYS to expand the PC's capabilities. These drivers usually have SYS as their file extension. ANSI.SYS is a good example and is covered separately in this appendix.

Your CONFIG.SYS may look like this:

```
break=on
buffers=20
files=30
device=c:\dos\ansi.sys
device=c:\dos\ramdrive.sys
```

CONFIG.SYS *(continued)*

Remarks:

Chapter 9 explains what these and other configuration commands will do.

Version 6 includes a host of new tools which you can use to manage your PC's startup. You can have a clean boot (bypassing the CONFIG.SYS and AUTOEXEC.BAT files) if you press F5 at the beginning of booting. You can also have a selective configuration by pressing F8 instead; you can then select Y or N to execute each line.

Version 6's new configuration commands include: MENUCOLOR, MENUDEFAULT, MENUITEM, SUBMENU, INCLUDE, and DEVICE?—plus a new environment variable called CONFIG. The end of Chapter 11 explains how to use them.

COPY *internal*

Copy and combine files; copy files to devices PRN, CON, COM1, and NUL.

Syntax:

`A>copy source target`	From source to target
`A>copy source`	Target is the default drive/directory

Switches:

/V	Verify target file
/A	ASCII, default for combining; read up to 1st ^Z and add ^Z to target
/B	Binary, default for copying; read entire source and add no ^Z to target

Examples:

`A>copy *.* b:`	Copy all from A to B, no file name change
`C:\DOS>copy a:*.*`	Copy all from A to current directory
`A>copy f1+f2+f3`	Append f2 and f3 to f1, ^Z added to f1
`A>copy file?? file.all`	Copy matching files to last, no ^Z added
`A>copy file+,,`	Stamp current date-time on file, add ^Z
`A>copy f1/b f2/a`	Read entire f1, add ^Z to f2
`A>copy/b file*.* b:+`	Binary and current date, add ^Z
`A>copy/b prog*.* .+`	Stamp current date-time, binary, no ^Z
`a>copy/b . . +`	Stamp current date-time on all, no ^Z
`A>copy f1+f2 prn`	Copy disk files to printer

COPY   *(continued)*

Remarks:

Details in Chapter 6; see also COPY CON.

COPY CON   *internal*

Copy to or from the screen; create or add to a file.

Examples:

```
A>copy con file1                    (Create a file; copy from
This creates a file named FILE1.     screen to file)
^Z

A>copy file1 + con                  (Add to a file; add from screen
This line is added to FILE1.         to file)
^Z

A>copy /b prog.exe con              Display file in binary format

A>copy file?? con                   Display all the matching files
```

Remarks:

To end file creation, press F6 and Enter. The /B switch, which can be placed at the end of a command, uses the binary format to do copying. Without this switch, COPY CON will work the same as TYPE, stopping when the first ^Z is encountered. See also COPY.

DATE   *internal*

Display and/or set date. See Chapter 1.

Examples:

```
A>date              Show the current date and/or enter new one

A>date 6/6/92       Enter a new date with /

A>date 07-07-92     Use – to set date
```

DBLSPACE   *external*

Create and manage compressed disks, hard or floppy.

Examples:

```
C:\DOS>dblspace              Load DoubleSpace

C:\DOS>dblspace a: /mount    Mount drive A disk
```

```
C:\DOS>dblspace /?        Show abbreviated help

C:\DOS>help dblspace      Show comprehensive help
```

Remarks:

DoubleSpace can increase your disk space by about 70%; your disks will also slow down. Use an option in DoubleSpace to compress a disk. Once compressed, a hard disk (drive C) can be used as usual. You need to use the /MOUNT switch to make DOS recognize a compressed floppy disk. See Chapter 7 for details.

DEFRAG   *external*

Defragment a disk in order to bring together fragmented files.

Syntax:

```
C:\DOS>defrag a:      Defragment drive A
```

Remarks:

Once DEFRAG is loaded, you can choose a drive and various ways of sorting files and defragmenting. A defragmented disk runs faster and increases chances of recovery from file deletion. See Chapter 6 for details.

DEL   *internal*

Delete named or matching files, which can be recovered with UNDELETE; it can't delete files marked R by ATTRIB.

Syntax:

```
A>del filename
```

Switches:

/P   Prompt for Y/N, available in v. 4.0 or later

Examples:

```
A>del fil                      Delete FIL in drive A
A>del *.*                      Delete all in drive A
A>del .                        Same as above
A>echo y ¦ del .               Delete all, no prompt; dangerous to use
A>for %x in (*.*) do del %x    Same as above
A>del b:fil*.txt               Delete matching files in B
```

DEL *(continued)*

`A>del ??? /p`	Delete files with 3 letters or less, prompt
`C:\TEMP>del .`	Delete all files in current directory
`C:\>del misc`	Delete matching file or entire subdirectory

Remarks:

It's dangerous to use DEL with wildcards. You can wipe out files you may intend to keep. Use /P switch when wildcards are used. In the last example, if MISC is a file, it is deleted immediately. If it's a subdirectory, you'll be prompted for Y/N before all the files are deleted. See Chapters 2, 4 and 5.

DELTREE   *external*

Delete files and directories.

Switches:

/Y   Show no [yn] prompt

Examples:

`A:\>deltree \smith`	Delete a file or directory
`A:\>deltree . /y`	Delete all files and directories, no prompt— dangerous to use

Remarks:

DELTREE can delete files like DEL. It can also delete a directory full of files. When a matching name (file or directory) is encountered, you will be prompted with [yn], unless you use the /Y switch. See Chapter 5 for details.

DEVICE   *see MEMORY MANAGEMENT*

DEVICEHIGH   *see MEMORY MANAGEMENT*

DIR   *internal*

Display directory information.

Syntax:

`A>dir filename/directory`

Switches:

/P   Pause after a screen is full

/W   Wide format, only file names, not sizes or dates

/A: Attributes (what kind of files to display), including A (archive files only), D (directories only), H (hidden files only), R (read-only files only), S (system files only); use – before each value to negate each attribute; default: /A alone means any of the attributes

/B   Bare format; file and directory names only; will negate /W if used together

/C   Compression ratio (version 6)

/L   Lower case used to show information

/O: Order (what order to display) according to D (date/time in ascending order), N (names of files and directories mixed and sorted in alphabetic order), E (extensions in alphabetic order), G (group directories before files, both unsorted), or S (size in ascending order); use – before each value to reverse the default order; default: /O is the same as /O:GN

/S   Subdirectories's files are also displayed

Examples:

`A>dir`	Current directory of default drive
`A>dir file?`	Matching files
`A>dir b: /p`	B's current directory, one page at a time
`A>dir ¦ sort`	Sort by file name
`A>dir ¦ sort/+14`	Sort by file size
`C:\BAT>dir..`	Parent directory
`C:\BAT>dir..\dos`	Show C:\DOS
`C:\>dir bat`	A single file or subdirectory
`C:\WP\REPT>dir ¦ find "SMITH"`	List all SMITH files
`C>dir /b`	Only files and directories
`C>dir b:\*.txt /s`	All directories in drive B matching *.TXT files
`C>dir /b /l`	Display in bare format and lower case
`C>dir a: /a:hs`	Drive A, hidden and system files only
`C>dir /a:-h /p`	Non-hidden files, pause

DIR   *(continued)*

C>dir \ /a:d /s	Directories only in entire drive C
C>dir \ /s /a:r	Read-only files in all directories in drive C
C>dir /a:-r	Excluding read-only files
C>dir /o /p	Directory/file names in alphabetical order, pause
C>dir /a /o	Directories and all files in alphabetical order
C>dir /o:-d /w	Most recent dates first, wide
C>dir /o:-s /p /w	Largest files first, pause, wide
C>dir a: /o:e	Drive A, sort extensions small to large
C:\DOS>dir \ /o:d /s /p ¦ find "REPORT"	Find REPORT in all drive C, sorted in reverse date, pause

Remarks:

DIR can now show hidden and system files. Do not use colon (:) after /A or /O when either is used alone. The last five of the seven switches are added in version 5. You can also use the DIRCMD environment variable to set the default parameters for the command. See Chapter 2 for details.

DISKCOMP   *external*

Compare two floppy, not hard, disks and report any discrepancies.

Syntax:

A>diskcomp disk1 disk2

Switches:

/1   Compare one side only

/8   Compare the first 8 sectors

Examples:

A>diskcomp a: b:	Compare disks in drive A and drive B
C>\dos\diskcomp a: a:	Load command from C:\DOS, 1-drive operation
A>b:diskcomp a: b:	Load command from drive B

Remarks:

If you have only one floppy drive, any of the above examples will work. You'll be prompted to swap disks. DISKCOMP is useful to compare the original and a copy produced with DISKCOPY. Comparison may not be meaningful if copy is produced by COPY or XCOPY. Details in Chapter 6.

DISKCOPY   *external*

Duplicate disk's contents track by track. Target disk need not be formatted and its contents, if any, will be destroyed. Can be used to duplicate a system (bootable) disk without formatting it with the /S switch. You can't diskcopy a hard disk. You'll be prompted to swap disks, if necessary.

Syntax:

```
A>diskcopy source target
```

Switches:

/1   Copy first side only

Examples:

`A>diskcopy a: b:`	Copy from A to B
`A>diskcopy`	Copy from A to A
`A>c:\dos\diskcopy b: a:`	Load command from C:\DOS, copy B to A

Remarks:

If no parameter is provided, one-drive copying will be performed. Files in target will be erased. Source should be write-protected. Don't diskcopy a fragmented diskette, use: A>copy *.* b:. See Chapter 6 for details.

DOS   *see MEMORY MANAGEMENT*

DOSKEY   *external and memory resident*

TSR program that allows you to recyle and edit commands, enter multiple commands, and create macros.

Syntax:

```
A>doskey /bufsize=1000 /insert
```

Switches:

`/BUFSIZE`	Buffer size, default 512KB
`/HISTORY`	Display all the commands in the buffer
`/INSERT`	Set insert mode as default
`/MACRO`	Display macros in the buffer

DOSKEY *(continued)*

/OVERSTRIKE	Set typeover mode as default	
/REINSTALL	Install another copy and delete existing one	

Examples:

C>md practice ¶ cd practice	^T to get ¶; multiple commands
C>doskey mov=copy $1 a: $t del $1	Create a macro
C>mov file?	Use macro to move files
C>doskey p=prompt $$e[$*$$p$$g	Create the P macro
C>p 0;59;"dir"p	Use P to remap F1 as "dir"
C>doskey del=del /p	Macro to customize a command
C>doskey /m	Show macros in the buffer
C>doskey /h	Show commands in the buffer

Remarks:

After DOSKEY is installed, commands you enter can be recycled and edited. See the end of Chapter 4 for the keys (to edit and recycle commands) and different metastrings that can be used on the command line and in macros. See the end of Chapter 11 for differences between macros and batch files. See Chapter 12 for a comparison of DOSKEY and ANSI.SYS. Enter DOSKEY /? on the command line to show highlights of using the command.

DOSSHELL   *external*

To start the DOS Shell, an environment program that shields the user from the command line and its cryptic commands.

After DOSSHELL is started, the screen is divided into 5 areas: Menu Bar, Drive Icons, Directory Tree, File List, and Program List. You can use the mouse to click any area or item on the screen to select the item and make the area active. From the keyboard, press Tab to move to different areas and other cursor keys to select items.

The Shell can be used to manage files and directories, launch multiple programs, and switch from one program to another. See the first half of Chapter 10 for details.

ECHO   *internal and batch*

Display ECHO state; echo text and control characters to devices.

Examples:

A>echo	Show ECHO on or off
A>echo on	Turn on ECHO
A>echo off	Turn off ECHO
A>echo y | del *.*	Supply Y to delete all; use with caution
A>echo print this line > prn	Send one line to the printer
@echo	Hide execution of batch lines
echo/	Create an empty line in a batch file screen display
echo ^L > prn	Send formfeed character to printer
echo ^[[0;68;"dir/p"p	Define F10 as "dir/p" in ANSI command
echo Turn on the printer	Echo message to the screen

Remarks:

ECHO is used mostly in batch files and ANSI escape sequences; see Chapters 8, 12, and 13 for much more details of using this versatile command.

EDIT   *external*

The full-screen text editor available since version 5. EDIT.COM needs QBASIC.EXE to run. This DOS Editor is copied from Microsoft's Quick language series. See the second half of Chapter 10 for details.

EDLIN   *external*

Line editor available in all DOS versions, including 5. Must be loaded with a filename following it.

Commands:

.	Current line		M	Move lines
#	Last line		P	Page display
A	Append lines		Q	Quit, no save
C	Copy lines		R	Replace string
D	Delete		S	Search string
E	Exit and save		T	Merge text
I	Insert lines		W	Write lines
L	List lines		n	Enter n to edit line n

EDLIN *(continued)*

Enter   Press Enter alone to edit the line below current

–/+   Before and after the current line

?   Placed before R/S to show Y/N in search or replace

^Z   Separate search and replace strings

Remarks:

An old file is renamed with BAK extension. Control characters can be entered in EDLIN, not with COPY CON. ^Z is added at the end of each file. See Appendix H for details. See also KEYS for using editing keys.

EMM386   *external and device driver*

Expanded-memory manager newly available in version 5. It can be used with 386 or higher PC to access upper memory blocks and convert extended memory to expanded memory. See MEMORY MANAGEMENT for loading this device driver.

To access UMBs (between 640KB and 1MB), EMM386.EXE must be loaded with the RAM or NOEMS switch. The former provides access to both EMS and the UMA. The latter provides access to the UMA but does not convert XMS to EMS.

You can also specify the amount of EMS with or without the RAM switch, such as these examples:

```
device=c:\dos\emm386.exe 256
device=c:\dos\emm386.exe 1024 ram
```

If no number is specified, 256KB is presumed. If RAM is not specified, no access to UMBs is provided.

EMM386 can be entered on the command line with the ON, OFF, or AUTO switch. ON or OFF turns on or off access to EMS; AUTO lets your program determine access to EMS. If no switch is specified, EMM386 shows EMS status. The end of Chapter 9 has more details.

ERASE   *see DEL*

EXIST   *see BATCH and IF*

EXPAND and SETUP   *both external*

Use SETUP to install version 6 on a hard disk. Use EXPAND to decompress individual files that come with the DOS package.

To run SETUP, insert DISK 1 in drive A and enter this:

```
A>setup
```

Follow the screen instructions to complete installation.

To expand an individual file, enter this:

```
C:\DOS>expand a:ega.sy_ ega.sys
```

This expands the compressed file in drive A and copies it to the current directory.

See Appendix F if you have problems relating to installation or expanding individual files.

FC   *external*

Compare two files line by line, unless /B is used.

Switches:

/A	Abbreviated; only first and last lines shown
/B	Binary comparison; byte by byte; no resynchronizing
/C	Case difference ignored
/L	Line comparison; ASCII text; resynchronize; default
/LBn	Line buffer (default n=100); maximum lines of errors compared; comparison ends when buffer is full
/N	Number; line numbers displayed in ASCII comparison
/T	Tabs are not expanded to spaces for comparison
/W	White spaces and tabs are compressed for comparison
/nn	Number (default nn=2) of consecutive lines must match for the two files to be considered resynchronized.

Examples:

```
A>fc file1 file2 /n              Show line numbers
A>fc file*.txt b:file*.bak /a    Show first and last lines
```

Remarks:

FC will compare two files of unequal lengths. If differences are detected, lines will be displayed. FC in version 5 or 6, unlike previous versions, allows wild cards. See details in Chapter 6.

FDISK   *external*

Partition a hard (fixed) disk so that DOS can use it to store data.

Syntax:

A>fdisk

Remarks:

A hard disk must be partitioned before it can be used by DOS. Version 3.3 and before can create a partition up to 32MB capacity; version 4 and later can go much higher. After the program is loaded, you will be prompted with a series of screens. You have numerous options to partition your hard disk. This needs to be done only on a new disk or when a hard disk crashes. Using FDISK will destroy any data on a hard disk. See Chapter 3 for more details.

FILES   *see CONFIG.SYS*

FIND   *external*

A filter command used to search for ASCII text lines. Can be used with ATTRIB, CHKDSK, DIR, MORE, SORT and TYPE to find text lines or file names.

Syntax:

A>find "string" filename

Switches:

/C   Count number of lines found

/I   Case insensitive search

/N   Number; a number precedes each found line

/V   Void; show lines not containing search string

Examples:

A>find "string" file	Display lines in FILE containing "string"
A>find /c "one" file	Count number of lines containing "one"
A>find /n "two" file	Display found lines with numbers
A>dir ¦ find /v "<"	Display directory without subdirectories
A>dir ¦ find "SMITH"	Find SMITH files and directories
C:\>chkdsk /v ¦ find "SMITH"	List all SMITH files and directories

FIND *(continued)*

```
C:\DOS>dir \ /o:d /s /p ¦ find "REPORT"
```
        Find REPORT in all drive C, sorted in
        reverse date, pause

```
A>find "no" file ¦ find "no"
```
    Suppress display of file name

```
A>echo ¦ more ¦ time ¦ find "C" >> file
```
        Append current time to FILE

```
A>for %x in (*.*) do find "string" %x
```
        Find "string" in every file

Remarks:

When /C is specified, it can negate other switches. Details in Chapter 8.

FOR..IN..DO   *internal and batch*

A looping command to repeat a command a number of times.

Syntax:

```
A>FOR %variable IN (file-list) DO command %variable
```

Examples:

```
A>for %a in (c:\wp\*.doc c:\ss\*.wk1) do copy %a b:
```
        Copy all the matching files to B

```
A>for %x in (fil?) do type %x
```
    TYPE all the files matching FIL?

```
A>for %m in (*.*) do del %m
```
    Delete all the files, no warning

```
for %%x in (type pause del) do %%x %1
```
      (batch)
        Show a file before deleting; ^C to prevent
        deletion

Remarks:

FOR can make a command do lots of work. You place a character (any character) after % as a variable. You then list in parentheses all the files you want to work on. Finally specify a command and the variable. Some DOS commands, e.g. TYPE, do not accept wild card characters. The FOR command can bypass that limitation, such as the 2nd example. FOR is used most often in batch files; in that case, you must use %% before a variable. As shown in the last example, you can put several commands inside the parentheses and make them run one after another. See Chapters 8 and 11 for details related to this command.

FORMAT   *external*

Prepare floppy and hard disks for booting and file storage.

Syntax:

```
C>format b:
```

Switches:

/1	1 side only
/4	Format 360K in a 1.2MB drive
/8	8 sectors per track
/B	Blank space for later transfer of system files
/F:n	Disk capacity; n = 160, 180, 320, 360, 720, 1.2 (or 1200), 1.44 (or 1440), 2.88 (or 2880)
/N:n	Number of sectors per track, used with /T
/Q	Quick formatting; no scanning for bad sectors
/S	System files transferred
/T:n	Tracks per side, used with /N
/U	Unconditional formatting; no recovery; used on new disks
/V:1	Volume label; if omitted, you'll be prompted

Examples:

```
A>format b: /f:360 /s     Format B, 360K in 1.2MB drive, system
A>format b: /n:9 /t:80     720KB in a 1.44MB drive
```

Remarks:

If no parameters are specified, a disk is formatted according to the drive's default capacity, such as 1.2MB. Formatting creates a new directory and two FATs; the old ones, if any, are saved so that UNFORMAT can use them to recover previous data. Details in Chapter 3.

GOTO   *see BATCH and IF*

GRAPHICS   *external*

Load GRAPHICS.COM; the program stays in the memory after that. You can then press Shift-PrtSc to print a graphics display. If the program is not in RAM, a graphics display will not be printed. See Chapter 2.

Syntax:

```
A>graphics
```

HELP   *external*

Comprehensive online help program that has hypertext capabilities.

Examples:

`C:\DOS>help`	Show the initial screen
`C:\DOS>help copy`	Show help for COPY command
`C:\DOS>fasthelp`	List of commands
`C:\DOS>fasthelp copy`	Abbreviated help for COPY command
`C:\DOS>copy /?`	Same as above

Remarks:

You can search for a string to move to a pertinent screen. You can print or save a help screen. A great deal of information is provided for most commands. You can also use a mouse to maneuver many things. In each screen, you may find items that will give you more related help. If you want an abbreviated help, use FASTHELP instead. See Chapter 1 for details.

HIMEM.SYS   *see MEMORY MANAGEMENT*

IF ECHO EXIST GOTO
REM SHIFT @ % : ==   *(all internal batch commands)*

IF is used to test the existence of a parameter (line 4), of a file on disk (line 5), and errorlevels available with XCOPY, FORMAT and other commands. GOTO branches batch execution to a label marked by :. SHIFT shifts to the next parameter entered on the command line. @ hides batch execution.

```
        1: @echo off
        2: rem TESTFILE.BAT--test existence of files
        3: :LOOP
        4: if .==.%1 goto END
        5: if exist %1 echo %1 exists
        6: shift
        7: goto LOOP
        8: :END
A>testfile jim jane jack
jim exists
jane exists
A>_
```

IF ECHO EXIST GOTO REM SHIFT @ % : == *(continued)*

Remarks:

When this batch file is run, all the files placed after the batch file name will be tested. If a file is found, a proper message is shown; if not, nothing is shown. This batch file is created with EDLIN. If you use COPY CON to create it, take out the numbers and the colons right after them.

KEYS   *Commonly Used DOS Keystrokes*

F1	Copy from template 1 character a time, same as right arrow
F2	Copy BEFORE 1st typed char; press F2, then a character
F3	Copy all remaining characters (from cursor to end)
F4	Copy FROM the 1st typed character; end with F3
F5	Save line to template; command is not executed
F6	Insert ^Z (end of file) character
F7	Insert ^@ (null, ASCII 0) character
Esc	Abandon edited line
Backspace	Delete 1 character to the left, same as left arrow
Del	Skip 1 character in template
Ins	Insert characters before copying from template
Ctrl-C	Terminate an action
Ctrl-P	Echo every move from console to printer
Ctrl-S	Halt screen display, same as Ctrl-Num Lock
Shift-PrtSc	Print screen display
Alt-Ctrl-Del	Reboot

Remarks:

The template is a memory area storing the most recently entered command. See Chapter 2 for the last five and Chapter 4 for the rest. When DOSKEY is installed, you can use many other keys to edit and recycle commands. Use DOSKEY /? on the command line to show these keys.

LABEL   *external*

Display and/or change a disk's volume label.

Syntax:

```
A>label drive
```

Examples:

```
A>label b:        Show/change drive B's volume label

A>label disk2     Change drive A's volume label to DISK2
```

Remarks:

Version 4 or later will also display the serial number of a disk, which cannot be changed. See Chapter 3 for more details.

LASTDRIVE *configuration*

To designate the highest drive letter DOS can handle. Up to Z can be specified. If no LASTDRIVE is specified, DOS can handle only up to drive E. This is covered in Chapter 9. To let DOS use all the possible drive letters, put this in your CONFIG.SYS file:

```
lastdrive = z
```

LOADHIGH *see MEMORY MANAGEMENT*

MD (MKDIR) *see CD*

MEM *external*

Show memory use. Available in version 4 and later.

Switches:

```
/DEBUG            /MODULE

/PROGRAM          /PAGE

/CLASSIFY
```

Examples:

```
A>mem              Show total and available memory

A>mem /program    Show above, plus programs already in memory

A>mem /debug      Show above, plus input-output devices

A>mem /c          Show high-memory use and available UMBs
```

MEM *(continued)*

Remarks:

MEM, without any switch, shows memory use just like CHKDSK. The two switches will show amount of memory used by each program and their beginning and ending addresses. See Chapter 9 for more details.

MEMORY MANAGEMENT

If you have 286 PC, you can use HIMEM.SYS and DOS=HIGH to load DOS in the high memory area (the 64KB beyond the 1MB boundary). If you have a 386/486, you can combine the above with EMM386 to load device drivers (e.g., ANSI.SYS) and TSR programs (e.g., DOSKEY) in the upper memory area (between 640KB and 1MB) and/or convert extended memory (XMS) to expanded memory (EMS). Enter the first two (286) or all the lines (386) in your CONFIG.SYS file:

```
device=c:\dos\himem.sys
dos=high
dos=umb
device=c:\dos\emm386.exe ram
devicehigh=c:\dos\ansi.sys
devicehigh=c:\mouse\mouse.sys
```

HIMEM.SYS is the extended-memory manager; it must be loaded first. DOS=HIGH loads portions of DOS in the high memory area. If you have a 286 system, these are the only things you can do.

In a 386/486 system, DOS=UMB opens up the unused portions in upper memory blocks (between 640KB and 1MB) for use. The fourth line loads the expanded-memory manager (see EMM386 for details). The last two lines attempt to load device drivers in UMBs. If DOS fails, the drivers will go to conventional memory. To load a TSR program in UMBs, try this:

```
C>lh doskey
```

You can also use LOADHIGH instead of LH; this is an internal command. Use MEM /CLASSIFY to see what UMBs are still available before loading programs there. See the end of Chapter 9 for memory varieties and management.

MEMMAKER   *external*

A memory-optimizing program.

Syntax

```
C:\DOS>memmaker
```

Remarks:

MemMaker will search for various upper memory blocks to load your TSR programs and device drivers; this may leave more conventional memory for other programs. Your CONFIG.SYS and AUTOEXEC.BAT will be altered to achieve this goal. What MemMaker maps out for you may not work and may actually freeze your PC. You can use the /UNDO switch to negate what it has done. See Chapter 9 for details.

MODE   *external, partially TSR*

Set or report devices.

Syntax:

A>mode

Examples:

A>mode con rate=32 delay=1	Set highest keyboard speed, if supported by BIOS
A>mode co40	Set color, 40-column mode for CGA
A>mode bw80	80-column black and white for CGA
A>mode lpt1 132, 8	To print 132 columns and 8 lines per inch
A>mode lpt1 80, 6	Restore the default mode
A>mode lpt1=com1	Reroute printing to serial port
A>mode con	Report console status
A>mode	Report status of all devices

Remarks:

If you have EGA or VGA, you can display 43 lines on the screen. You need to specify the /L switch when installing ANSI.SYS (see ANSI command), and then enter this on the command line: A>mode con lines=43. See Chapter 9.

MORE   *external*

A filter command to output ASCII text a screenful at a time. Can be used with ATTRIB, CHKDSK, DIR, FIND, SORT and TYPE.

Syntax:

A>more < filename

MORE *(continued)*

Examples:

A>more < filename	Display ASCII text one screen at a time
A>type fil ¦ more	Same as above
A>more > prn	Print each text line entered on the screen.
A>dir ¦ more	Display directory a screenful, like DIR/P
A>type fil ¦ find "Smith" ¦ sort ¦ more	
	Show Smith lines, sorted, a screen at a time
A>echo ¦ more ¦ date ¦ find "C" >> file	
	Append current date to FILE

Remarks:

MORE is useful in sending each line typed on the screen to the printer, like the 3rd example. The last example can be put in a batch file to insert the current date in a file. See Chapter 8 for details.

MOVE   *external*

Move and rename a single file; move but not rename multiple files; rename but not move a directory.

Examples:

A:\ABC>move file1 \xyz\filex	Move and change name
A:\>move \abc\file1,\abc\file2 \xyz	Move two files
A:\>move \xyz\f* \new\one	Create directory and move files
A:\>move \old \new	Change directory name

Remarks:

MOVE can rename one directory at a time. It can move and rename one file. It can move (but not rename) several matching files (with wild cards or separated by commas) to a directory, which can be created if not existing. It cannot combine files. See Chapter 5 for details.

MSAV   *external*

Detect and clean viruses.

Syntax:

C:\DOS>msav

Remarks:

You can use MSAV (Microsoft Anti-Virus) to detect and clean viruses. You can also show a list of known viruses which MSAV can handle. It has a comprehensive online help. See Chapter 6 for details.

MSBACKUP *external*

Back up, compare, and restore files.

Syntax:

```
C:\DOS>msbackup
```

Remarks:

MSBACKUP (Microsoft Backup) is a menu-driven program replacing the BACKUP and RESTORE commands of version 5 and before. You can use it to do full, incremental, or differential type of backup. You can use a setup file to quickly do a backup. It has extensive online help that obviates the need for a printed manual. See Chapter 7 for details.

MSD *external*

A system diagnostic program.

Syntax:

```
C:\DOS>msd
```

Remarks:

MSD (Microsoft Diagnostics) will show a great deal of information about your system and memory use. You can use it to customize a report, which can be printed or saved as an ASCII file. See Chapter 9 for details.

PATH *internal*

Make DOS search a list of paths for executable files (command path). After a path list is entered, you can run an external command in any drive/dir without specifying a path prefix. DOS will go through the list to search for and execute the command.

Syntax:

```
A>path list
```

PATH   *(continued)*

Examples:

`A>path a:\;b:\;c:\bat`	Search A:\, B:\, C:\DOS
`A>menu`	Go to above list to execute MENU.BAT
`C:\>path=c:\dos;c:\bat`	Search C:\DOS and C:\BAT
`C:\>tree`	Go to above list to execute TREE.COM
`A>path`	List existing paths
`A>path;`	Clear path list

Remarks:

PATH guides DOS to search for files ending with COM, EXE or BAT extensions. Others are ignored. For these nonexecutable files, use APPEND to search for them. Use SET to see the current path list in the environment. See Chapter 5 for details.

PAUSE   *see BATCH*

PRINT   *external, partially TSR*

Print ASCII files in the background.

Syntax:

`A>print file?`

Switches:

`/B:size`	Buffer size in bytes, default 512
`/D:dev`	Device, such as COM1, default PRN
`/M:max`	Maximum number of clock ticks, 1–255, default 2
`/Q:num`	Queue; maximum number of files put in print queue
`/S:slice`	Time slices, 1–255, default 8
`/U:wait`	Wait clock ticks, 1–255, default 1
`/C`	Cancel printing files
`/P`	Print files
`/T`	Terminate all printing

Examples:

`A>print /t`	Terminate all printing; clear print queue
`A>print f1/c f2`	Cancel both files
`A>print f1/c f2/p`	Cancel F1, print F2
`A>print`	Show print queue

Remarks:

/C, /P, /T can be specified any time; others only the first time. See Chapter 7 for details.

PROMPT   *internal*

Change the DOS prompt with text or metastrings shown below.

Switches (Metastrings):

e	Esc		l	Less-than sign (<)
p	Current drive/directory		b	Bar (¦)
g	Greater-than sign (>)		q	Equal sign (=)
n	Default drive		h	Backspace
d	Date		–	New line
t	Time		$	Dollar sign
v	Version of DOS			

Examples:

`C>prompt $p$g`	Display current directory, default drive, & >
`A>prompt $n$g`	Default, showing A>
`A>prompt $t$g`	Display time and >

Remarks:

Can be used with ANSI.SYS to maneuver cursor position and screen colors. See ANSI and Chapter 5 for more details.

RD (RMDIR)   *see CD*

REM   *see BATCH and IF*

REN   *internal*

Rename a file; give a new name to an existing file.

Syntax:

```
A>ren oldname newname
```

Examples:

A>ren file.txt file.doc	Change FILE.TXT to FILE.DOC
A>ren file.txt *.doc	Shorthand of above
A>ren b:file?.txt file?.doc	Change all matching files in drive B

Remarks:

A new file name cannot be the same as that of another file in the same directory. See Chapter 2. REN cannot rename a directory. If you want to rename a directory, run DOSSHELL and select Rename from the File menu.

REPLACE   *external*

Replace old files with new ones of the same names. Read the syntax below as "putting source files in target."

Syntax:

```
A>replace source target
```

Switches:

/A	Add files which are in source but not in target
/P	Prompt for Y/N to replace old files
/R	Read-only files are also replaced
/S	Subdirectories in target; files there replaced
/U	Update old files with new
/W	Wait for a key press before acting

Examples:

A>replace b:*.*	Replace all in A with those in B if matching
A>replace *.* c:/s	Replace in C, including subdirectory, with those from A
A>replace file? b:/a	Replace B with A; add if not in target

Remarks:

Good for replacing old DOS files with new ones. /R can overwrite a source marked with R attribute; COPY and XCOPY can't. Details in Chapter 7.

RESTORE *external*

Restore file(s) from a backup file created by BACKUP.

Syntax:

```
C:\WP\WORK>restore a: file?
```

Switches:

/A:date	After; restore files backed up on or after date
/B:date	Before; restore files changed on or before date
/E:time	Earlier; files changed at or before specific time
/L:time	Later; files changed at or after specific time
/M	Modified; restore modified or deleted files
/N	None; restore files not in the target
/P	Prompt before replacing a changed file
/S	Subdirectory files are restored

Examples:

`C:\SS\BUDGET>restore a: budget1`	Restore a file to current dir
`C:\>restore b: file? /s`	Restore matching files to C and subdirectories

Remarks:

Must have a space after drive spec; must use original file names and directory, which was used as source by BACKUP. See Chapter 7.

SET *internal*

Display environment strings or enter environment variables.

Examples:

`A>set`	Display all the strings in the environment
`A>set dircmd=/o /a`	Set default parameters for DIR
`A>set var=one`	Put in environ VAR as var & ONE as its value

SET   *(continued)*

`set pa=%path%`	Assign existing PATH value to new variable PA
`set path=%pa%`	Assign PA to PATH
`set pr=%prompt%`	Assign existing PROMPT value to new variable PR

Remarks:

The DOS environment automatically contains PATH, PROMPT, and APPEND (if installed with /E); these can be entered without SET. You can use SET to enter your variables from the command line. Other uses, such as the last three lines above, must be done via batch files. See Chapters 9 and 11.

SETUP   *see EXPAND*

SHELL   *see CONFIG.SYS*

SHIFT   *see BATCH and IF*

SORT   *external*

A filter command that can sort alphanumeric strings. Can be used with ATTRIB, CHKDSK, DIR, FIND and TYPE to display output in sorted order.

Switches:

/R   Reverse (descending) order

/+c   Column number where c is the nth column from left margin

Examples:

`A>sort < file /r`	Sort FILE in reverse order
`A>sort < file > file.srt`	Save sorted file to a new file
`A>sort < file /+10`	Sort by the 10th column
`A>dir ¦ sort`	Sort directory by file name
`A>dir ¦ sort ¦ more`	Show sorted directory a screenful at a time
`A>dir ¦ sort /+30`	Sort directory by year

Remarks:

To sort items entered from the keyboard, run SORT without parameter, enter items, and press F6 and Enter to sort. SORT can't accurately sort numerals of unequal lengths. See Chapter 8 for details.

SUBST *external*

Substitute a drive for a directory.

Examples:

A>subst z: c:\wp\wk	Substitute Z (logical drive) for directory
A>subst	Show list of substitution
A>subst z: /d	Delete substitution

Remarks:

Don't use this command with: BACKUP, DISKCOPY, DISKCOMP, FDISK, FORMAT, PRINT, RESTORE. See Chapter 9 for more details.

SYMBOLS *Symbols used by DOS for special purposes*

<	Redirect input	==	Test equality in batch file
>	Redirect output	+	Combine files
>>	Append to a device	*	Match remaining
¦	Pipe DOS commands	$	Metastring
.	Current directory	$e	ANSI command (also ^[[)
¶	End of command (DOSKEY)	$T	Macro command separator
..	Parent directory	@	Hide batch command
\	Root directory	:	Batch label
/	Switch	%x%	Environment variable
?	Match 1 character	%1	Batch replaceable parameter
=	Assignment	$1	Macro replaceable parameter
←	Esc in EDIT	^Z	End of file

Examples:

A>dir > file	Create FILE to store directory entries
A>dir >> file	Append to FILE
A>type file > prn	Redirect output to a printer
A>dir ¦ more	Pipe DIR output to MORE to display a screenful
A>sort < file	Redirect FILE as an input file to be sorted
A>del .	Delete all in current directory

SYMBOLS   *(continued)*

A>del file?	Delete matching files
C:\WP\X>cd..	Move up directory one level

Remarks:

See Chapter 2 for /; Chapter 4 for ?, *, ¶, $1, and $T; Chapter 5 for ., .., \ and $; Chapter 6 for + and ^Z; Chapter 8 for <, >, >>, < and ¦; Chapter 9 for = and %x%. Chapter 11 for @, :, % , %% and ==; Chapter 12 for $e[and ^[[. EDLIN uses a separate set of symbols; see EDLIN and Appendix H for details. See also Chapter 10 for the special characters you can enter in EDIT.

SYS   *external*

Transfer system (hidden) files.

Examples:

A>sys c: Transfer system files from A to C

Remarks:

The SYS command is used mostly to transfer a new DOS version's hidden system files from a floppy to a hard disk. SYS in version 5 or 6 will also copy COMMAND.COM. See Chapter 8 for more details.

TIME   *internal*

Display and/or set time. Version 4 or later will accept A (am) and P (pm); earlier versions will accept only the 24-hour format.

Examples:

A>time	Show current time
A>time 0	Set time to midnight
A>time 12:30	Set time to half past noon

TREE   *external*

Display directory structure.

Switches:

/F	List files, in addition to directories
/A	Use ASCII characters, instead of graphic characters, to display diagram; for speedier screen display

Examples:

A>tree b:	Display directories in B
A>tree /f	List files, plus directory, in A
C:\DOS>tree c:\misc	Analyze C:\MISC directory and subdirectory

Remarks:

See Chapter 5 for details.

TYPE   *internal*

Display a file's contents.

Examples:

A>type filename	Display on the screen
A>type filename > prn	Redirect to the printer
A>type fil ¦ sort ¦ more	Show text, sorted, one screen at a time
A>for %x in (file?) do type %x	Show all files matching FILE?

Remarks:

TYPE works in the ASCII mode. It stops reading when a ^Z (end of file) character is encountered. If you want to display a binary file on the screen, use COPY CON. TYPE can work with only one file at a time; no wild card character is allowed. You can bypass that by using the FOR command as shown in the last example. See Chapter 2 for details.

UNDELETE   *external and TSR*

Load Delete Tracker or Delete Sentry; undelete files.

Switches:

/ALL	Recover all files
/DOS	Use DOS directory to recover files
/DS	Use Delete Sentry to recover files
/DT	Use Delete Tracker to recover files
/LIST	List recoverable files
/LOAD	Load memory-resident portion with default values
/PURGE	Clear the contents of SENTRY directory

UNDELETE   *(continued)*

/S	Load memory-resident portion for Sentry
/STATUS	Show protection status
/T	Load memory-resident portion for Tracker
/UNLOAD	Unload memory-resident portion

Examples:

C:\DOS>undelete /sa	Load Sentry for drive A
C:\DOS>undelete /status	Show protection status
C:\DOS>undelete a: /ds /all	Undelete all
C:\DOS>undelete /unload	Unload memory-resident portion

Remarks:

Delete Tracker saves FAT entries when a file is deleted; these entries allow UNDELETE to recover a deleted file stored in noncontiguous sectors. Delete Sentry saves deleted files to a hidden SENTRY directory; the files are deleted when the directory is full or the specified time is up. See Chapter 6 for details.

UNFORMAT   *external*

Restore an inadvertently reformatted hard or floppy disk.

Syntax:

C>unformat a:

Switches:

/J	Test to see whether a disk can be recovered with a mirror file
/L	Lists files and directories
/P	Print output
/PARTN	Use PARTNSAV.FIL to restore corrupted partitions
/U	Unformat without using a mirror file
/TEST	Test to see whether disk can be recovered without using a mirror file

Examples:

C>unformat a: /test	Testing without recovery or using a mirror file
C>unformat a:	Use a mirror file if available

Remarks:

Use UNFORMAT to recover a disk before writing files to it. UNFORMAT cannot restore a disk if reformatted with the /U switch. UNFORMAT will use a file created by MIRROR. If it is not available, it will use information stored in the FAT and root directory. Switches should be placed after other parameters.

VER *internal*

Show DOS version.

Syntax:

```
A>ver
```

VERIFY *internal*

Display and turn on/off Verify.

Examples:

A>verify on	Turn on Verify.
A>verify off	Turn off Verify.
A>verify	To see VERIFY ON/OFF state

Remarks:

Verify is off by default. When turned on, writing to disk is verified. It has the same effect as using the /V switch with COPY. See Chapter 6.

VOL *internal*

Show volume label of a disk; version 4 or later also shows a disk's serial number. Change a volume label with the LABEL command.

Examples:

A>vol	Show drive A's volume label

VSAFE *external and TSR*

Monitor virus activities and alert you for action.

Syntax:

```
C:\DOS>vsafe
```

VSAFE *(continued)*

Remarks:

After the program is loaded, press Alt-V to pop up a menu which lets you make alterations. Press Alt-U if you want to unload. See Chapter 6 for details.

XCOPY *external*

Read source file(s) to available memory, then copy to target.

Syntax:

```
A>xcopy source target
```

Switches:

/A	Archive, only marked files copied
/D:mm-dd-yy	Date, copy files on or after date
/E	Empty, copy empty directories, used with /S
/M	ReMove archive bit in source after copying
/P	Prompt for Y/N before copying each file
/S	Subdirectory, copy subdirectory from source to target
/V	Verify target file
/W	Wait for a key press before copying

Examples:

A>xcopy *.* b:	Copy all from A to B, no file name change
C:\DOS>xcopy *.* b:/s	Copy C:\DOS and subdirectories to B
A>xcopy file??.* /p	Copy matching files, prompt Y/N
A>xcopy *.* b: /a	Copy all marked with 'A'

Remarks:

XCOPY is improved COPY. It works faster with large files, can handle subdirectories and backup dated files. See Chapter 6 for details.

Appendix F: Installing Version 6

Unlike version 5, DOS 6 is sold in only upgrade but not standard package. You can purchase it in either 3.5-inch or 5.25-inch disk format; both are on high-density disks. If you have only double-density drives, you can fill out a coupon inside the package and wait for Microsoft to mail you the proper disks.

Each package contains on Disk 1 a file named PACKING.LST telling you all the file names in the package. You can use the TYPE command to read it. If you have unusual hardware or software or encounter problems using DOS 6, make sure to read README.TXT on Disk 1.

If your hard disk has no previous version of DOS installed, start the PC with Disk 1 in drive A. The AUTOEXEC.BAT file will run the BUSETUP.EXE program to begin the installation procedure. If this program detects the existence of a previous version of DOS, it will advise you to choose an option to abort or let you choose the other option to replace the existing files with new ones.

If you are using a previous version of DOS, the standard installation procedure involves these steps:

1. Have ready one or two (if 360KB) formatted and unused disks. You should label these Uninstall #1 and Uninstall #2.

2. Start your PC without memory-resident programs.

3. Run the SETUP.EXE program on Disk 1, which can be in drive A or B, depending on the disk format you have.

Step 1 is to safeguard against a failed installation. The disks will be used by the SETUP program to store the previous version of DOS. If the installation is not successful, you can use them to start and restore the previous DOS. After you have completed the installation, these files can be erased—or restored in case you don't like DOS 6.

Step 2 is to avoid conflict between the SETUP program and the programs automatically loaded by your CONFIG.SYS and AUTOEXEC.BAT. To start your PC without these programs, use a text editor such as EDLIN or EDIT and add REM to the beginning of each pertinent line; save the edited files over the old ones and restart your PC. After you have completed installation, edit CONFIG.SYS and AUTOEXEC.BAT and take out the REM commands, resave the files, and restart the PC.

Step 3 involves making drive A or B current, inserting Disk 1 in that drive, and running SETUP.EXE. The initial screen appears, showing you that you can press F3 to exit, F1 for more information, and Enter to continue.

Most of version 6's original files are compressed; these are shown with an underscore (_) at the end. To make them useful, you must use the SETUP program to decompress and then copy to a target disk. You can also use the provided EXPAND program to decompress one file at a time, as explained below.

After the SETUP program is started, you will be asked to insert the first blank disk (Uninstall #1) in drive A. If you are installing from drive A, take out Disk 1 and put in your disk. The old DOS information will be copied to your disk. If there is not enough space, you will be prompted to insert Uninstall #2.

You are now instructed to insert each sequential disk. The screen shows a series of options and asks for your approval. If you agree with the choices made by the program, just press Enter to proceed. At the beginning, you will be asked these options:

Setup will use the following system settings:

```
DOS Type:          MS-DOS
MS-DOS Path:       C:\DOS
Display Type:      VGA
```

The settings are correct.

The last line in the box will be highlighted. If you agree to the options the program has chosen, just press Enter. If not, press ↑ or ↓ to highlight a desired line and press Enter. You will then be asked to enter your desired item. After this screen is taken care of, the next screen shows the programs to be installed:

```
Backup:            MS-DOS only
Undelete:          MS-DOS only
Anti-Virus:        MS-DOS only
```

Install the listed programs.

The right side of each program shows the number of bytes (not shown here) required of your hard disk. The bottom of the screen also shows the available hard disk space and the total bytes required. The above display appears when the SETUP program does not find Windows installed on your hard disk. If Windows is detected, the *MS-DOS only* message will be replaced by *Windows only*. If you agree with the selections, just press Enter to accept. If not, press ↑ or ↓ to highlight the option and press Enter. You will be given these choices:

```
Windows and MS-DOS
Windows only
MS-DOS only
None
```

As you move the cursor up and down, the right side and the bottom of the screen show different numbers. If you choose *Windows and MS-DOS*, you can later access these features from both Windows and the DOS command line; you will also need lots of disk space. You cannot install the Windows version of these programs unless Windows has previously been installed. If you install Windows after running SETUP, you can use the SETUP /E command to install the Windows version. After installing the Windows version, a group called Microsoft Tools will be created. You can later click this group icon to access these features; their proper icons will appear for you to click.

SETUP now begins to copy files from each floppy to the hard disk. When a floppy disk is completed, you will be prompted to insert the next disk. The middle of the screen shows the percentage of completion and the bottom displays each file being read and written. While you are waiting and idle, you can read the top part of the screen telling you some of the new features in the new version.

After all the files (more than 100) are copied, you are given a final message and instructed to press Enter to start the new version. Remove the disk in drive A, if any, and press Enter to start DOS 6.

If installation fails or if you just want to return to the previous version, you can insert the Uninstall #1 disk in drive A and press the Reset button on your PC (or press Ctrl-Alt-Del). This disk saves all the information about the old version with a series of files with the DAT extension. If you no longer need the old version, you can delete these files.

The SETUP program also creates a directory named OLD_DOS.1 (may be other directories with 2 or 3 as its extension) and saves the old DOS files in the C:\DOS directory to this directory. An ASCII file named README.NOW is also created. It tells you that these files can be deleted with the DELOLDOS command entered on the command line; you can also use the DEL command to do the job. Most of these external commands can no longer be used; if you try to run them, you will likely get the *Incorrect DOS Version* message.

The C:\DOS directory may still contain some old files. EDLIN and sample BASIC programs, both of which came with version 5 but are no longer included in version 6, are good examples. You can keep these files or delete them as you see fit.

The CONFIG.SYS and AUTOEXEC.BAT files will also be modified by the SETUP program. The old ones are changed to the BAK extension and the new ones may have additional lines added at the beginning or end of the file. If necessary, you can modify these files.

Many of the files decompressed and copied to your hard disk by the SETUP program are not essential. If you need to use the disk space for other purposes, you can erase many of them. If you need to use any of them in the future, you can use the EXPAND program to decompress them.

For example, if you do not have an EGA system, you can erase the two related files this way:

```
C:\DOS>del ega.*
```

This deletes EGA.SYS and EGA.CPI. Should you need those files later, you can place the right disk in drive A and enter these two commands:

```
C:\DOS>expand a:ega.sy_ ega.sys
C:\DOS>expand a:ega.cp_ ega.cpi
```

These commands run the program (EXPAND.EXE) in the current directory, decompresses EGA.SY_ and EGA.CP_ stored in drive A, and sends the decompressed files with proper extensions to the current directory. If you are not sure what extension you should provide for a decompressed file, check the PACKING.LST file.

The EXPAND program does not accept wild card characters. You cannot use * or ? in either the source or the target. If you enter EXPAND alone (no parameter), you will be prompted to enter a source and a target.

To convert another hard disk (perhaps the one in your home or office), you can copy version 6's SYS.COM to a boot disk (formatted with /S). Take this disk to the new computer and boot the system with the floppy in drive A; your PC is now running DOS 6. Then enter this command:

```
A>sys c:
```

This will transfer the three hidden files (IO.SYS, MSDOS.SYS, DBLSPACE.BIN) and COMMAND.COM to your hard disk; the old files of the same names will be replaced. If you now reboot with drive A's door open, the new version will be booted from the hard disk. If you need to transfer some external DOS commands to the new PC, use EXPAND as explained earlier.

If you have an existing floppy disk formatted (with or without the /S switch) by a previous version, you can also use SYS to transfer DOS 6's system files to it, like this:

```
C:\DOS>sys a:
```

You can use SETUP /F to install a minimal version of DOS 6 on a floppy disk. SETUP has 9 switches all together. You need to insert Disk 1 in drive A and enter SETUP /? from drive A to show them. SETUP.EXE is not copied to C:\DOS during the installation and you cannot show the switches from this directory; nor can you show anything pertinent from the HELP program.

Appendix G: Basic Computer Math

A computer may appear intelligent, but at its basic level it can "understand" only whether power is on or off. To give it an instruction, we need to go by 1 (on) or 0 (off). The two digits of 1 and 0 then form the basis of binary (base 2) math.

The building block of binary math is the bit, which is a contraction of two words—binary digit. A bit can have the value of either 1 or 0.

When you read binary numbers, read from right to left. When a digit goes beyond 1, the excess is carried to the next number on the left. Consider the following examples of equivalent binary and decimal (base 10) numbers, and the methods for converting the former to the later:

Binary	Decimal	Calculation
1	1	1
10	2	2+0
11	3	2+1
100	4	4+0+0
101	5	4+0+1
110	6	4+2+0
111	7	4+2+1
1000	8	8+0+0+0
1001	9	8+0+0+1
1010	10	8+0+2+0

Each bit has the value of 2 to a certain power. The first (rightmost) is 2 to the power of 0 (by definition, $2^0 = 1$), the second 1, the third 2, etc, as shown below:

Decimal		128	64	32	16	8	4	2	1
2^n	n =	7	6	5	4	3	2	1	0

Based on the above table, 2 to the power of 7 is 128.

Depending on whether a bit is on or off, the following binary number:

00111001

can be translated to its decimal equivalent this way:

$0 + 0 + 32 + 16 + 8 + 0 + 0 + 1 = 57$

By putting 8 bits together, as in the above example, you will get a byte and up to 256 variations (11111111 in binary equals 255 in decimal; that and 0 add up to 256 possible combinations). The 255 ASCII values, as shown in Appendix B, are based on this principle. The following table shows some examples of decimal, binary, and ASCII equivalents:

Decimal	Binary	ASCII Character
49	00110001	1
50	00110010	2
51	00110011	3
...		
65	01000001	A
66	01000010	B
67	01000011	C
...		
97	01100001	a
98	01100010	b
99	01100011	c

Bytes can go up to thousands, millions, billions, and more. For simplicity, programmers use KB (kilobyte), MB (megabyte), and GB (gigabyte). These numbers coincide with some unique numbers as shown below:

Power of 2	Abbreviation	Decimal
2^{10}	KB	1024
2^{20}	MB	1048576
2^{30}	GB	1073741824

Thus, 1KB is 2 to the power of 10 (2 multiplied by itself 9 times or $2 \times 2 \times 2 \times 2 \times 2 \times 2 \times 2 \times 2 \times 2 \times 2$), 1MB the power of 20, and 1GB the power of 30.

Binary numbers are difficult to maneuver, so programmers use octal (base 8, 1 byte) and hexadecimal (base 16, 2 bytes). An octal digit can be 0 to 7, and a hex digit can be any of the following 16:

Hex	0	1	2	3	4	5	6	7	8	9	A	B	C	D	E	F
Decimal	0	1	2	3	4	5	6	7	8	9	10	11	12	13	14	15

Hex numbers are marked with H or h at the end, such as:

3B8D2H

3b8d2h

The following shows how this number can be converted to decimal value:

Hex number	3	B	8	D	2	
Calculation	3×16^4 +	11×16^3 +	8×16^2 +	13×16^1 +	2×16^0	
Decimal	196608 +	45056 +	2048 +	208 +	2	= 243922

When you use MEM /CLASSIFY to show upper memory use, the numbers are displayed in hex. Use the above method to calculate how much memory in an upper memory block before loading another TSR program there.

Appendix H: Using EDLIN

EDLIN is a line editor program which was regularly bundled with DOS before version 6. The regular version 6 package does not include this program. You can, however, ask Microsoft to supply it to you in a supplementary package. Also, the program that was included in version 5 is likely to remain in the C:\DOS directory because version 6's SETUP program does not erase it.

Three major categories of software packages are used to maneuver text, namely word processor, text editor, and line editor. A full-feature **word processor** such as WordPerfect and Microsoft Word provide all imaginable features to manipulate text. A **text editor** is less sophisticated. The editor in DOS 5 and 6 is a good example. It has full-screen editing capabilities. But there is no capability to format text output—only plain ASCII text is produced. A **line editor** like EDLIN also produces only ASCII files, but it can handle only one line at a time, not the whole screen.

EDLIN has a number of pluses and minuses. Let us look at the disadvantages first:

- There is no word wrap. You must press Enter at the end of each line. A line can be no more than 253 characters long.

- You cannot move the cursor up and down. Since EDLIN is a line editor, not a full-screen editor, you can move the cursor or make corrections only in the current line.

- There are limited cut-and-paste capabilities. Although you can easily move and copy entire lines, you need to go through rather elaborate steps to maneuver characters inside a line or across lines.

- There is no undo feature. If you make a mistake, you cannot undo it as you can in other packages.

Here are the advantages:

- It is easily available. Since it comes with the DOS package, you need not spend extra money to acquire it.

- It is easy to learn. Since there are few complicated features to learn, you can quickly master it.

- It is compact. Its small size will enable you to work with a computer with limited memory and disk space.

- It is convenient for some occasions. Since it outputs only ASCII text, it can be used conveniently to create and edit a DOS batch file or language code.

EDLIN is particularly useful for creating and editing a long batch file. For a short batch file, you can use COPY CON. For a longer one, it is more convenient to use EDLIN. For batch files containing control characters, you have to use EDLIN (or EDIT) because you cannot enter these characters through COPY CON.

Version 5 or later comes with a new full-screen editor named EDIT, which is covered in Chapter 10. EDIT is more versatile because you can move the cursor to anywhere on the screen. It has one big disadvantage, however, and that is its large size. You need to run EDIT.COM, which in turn loads QBASIC.EXE. The latter is 254,799 bytes in size. In contrast, EDLIN.EXE is only 12,642 bytes. For shorter files such as most batch files, EDLIN is quick and nimble.

A QUICK TOUR THROUGH EDLIN

Using EDLIN requires some simple steps. Let us try a quick tour through it. We will run it, create a simple file, and exit. If the environment contains the PATH=C:\DOS string, you are ready to go. Follow these steps:

FOLLOW THESE STEPS

1. Put in drive A a disk to save a text file.

2. Start the program:

    ```
    A>edlin twain
    ```

If this is a new file or TWAIN is not found in drive A, the screen shows the following:

```
A>edlin twain
New file
*
_
```

The asterisk (*) is the **EDLIN command prompt**, comparable to the > sign for DOS. When it appears at the left margin of the screen, you are to enter one of the available commands to instruct EDLIN to do something.

3. Since we intend to insert text, enter the I command. The screen displays the following:

```
A>edlin twain
New file
*i
        1:*_
```

The cursor stays after the * of line 1. The * in a text line denotes the current line (explained below). EDLIN is now ready for you to enter text in line 1.

4. Type the following lines and press Enter at the end of each:

```
1:*East is East, and West is West,
2:*and never the twain shall meet.
3:*_
```

5. Press Ctrl-C (or Ctrl-Break). The cursor moves down and left, and a new * prompt appears. The screen now shows this:

```
A>edlin twain
New file
*i
        1:*East is East, and West is West,
        2:*and never the twain shall meet.
        3:*^C

*_
```

6. Enter E to save the file and exit.

The screen shows the A> prompt again. You have now exited EDLIN and created a new file. To verify that, enter the following command:

```
A>type twain
```

The screen shows the two lines of text you have entered, minus the numbers, asterisks, and indentation.

Note: If anything went wrong when you followed these steps, one of two things may have happened. First, you may not have entered a required file name. If you do not enter a file name after the program name, EDLIN will not load. You will get this error message instead:

```
File name must be specified
```

Second, you may not have provided the path for DOS to find the program. This situation will lead to this message:

```
Bad command or file name
```

If this happens, you must direct DOS to the drive or directory storing EDLIN.EXE.

You can specify a directory to load EDLIN and another to save your file, like the following:

```
A>c:\dos\edlin twain
B>c:\dos\edlin twain
C:\DOS>edlin a:twain
C:\DOS>edlin b:twain
```

The first two will load EDLIN from the C:\DOS directory and save your file in the current drive (A or B). The last two will load EDLIN from the current directory and save the file to the specified drive.

If you do not want to save a file, enter the Q command instead of E. You will be asked this:

```
Abort edit (Y/N)?_
```

If you press Y, the DOS prompt appears and the file is not saved. If you press any other key, you are back to EDLIN, with the file still in memory.

EDLIN will automatically insert a ^Z marker at the end of any file it saves. This is in contrast to COPY CON, which by default does not add such a marker to the end of a file it creates. EDLIN can edit a file created with COPY CON. However, a ^Z character will be added to the end, even though it was not present in the original.

EDLIN COMMANDS

Now that you know the rudimentary steps of using EDLIN, let us explore its other features. Table H.1 shows what command to enter to accomplish a specific purpose.

A glance at Table H.1 should convey the impression that an EDLIN command consists of one letter (in uppercase or lowercase), plus optional parameters (numbers and signs) placed mostly before but sometimes after the letter.

As EDLIN commands are cryptic, you may need to refer to this table frequently to enter correct commands. Each command's details will be explained more thoroughly in this appendix.

INSERTING LINES

Let us now retrieve the file we just created and make some additions:

FOLLOW THESE STEPS

1. Run EDLIN to edit an existing file:

```
A>edlin twain
End of input file
*_
```

The message tells you that the entire file has been retrieved to the memory, and the * prompt is ready for your input.

Table H.1

EDLIN Commands

Command	Format	Purpose
A	nA	Append from disk n lines to the file in memory being edited
C	m,n,p,qC	Copy m through n lines to pth line q times; pth becomes current
D	D	Delete current line
	nD	Delete nth line
	m,nD	Delete lines m through n
	,nD	Delete from current to nth lines
E	E	Exit with file saving
I	I	Insert at current line
	nI	Insert at nth line
	#I	Insert at end of file
L	L	List current plus 11 above & below
	nL	List 23/24 lines, from nth line
	m,nL	List lines m through n
	,nL	List current to nth line
M	m,n,qM	Move lines m through n to qth
P	P	Page from below current line
	m,nP	Page m through n
	,nP	Page from below current through n
Q	Q	Quit without saving file
R	m,n?Rstring1^Zstring2	Search m to n lines and replace string 1 with string 2; optional ? displays O.K.?
S	m,n?Sstring	Search m to n lines for string; ? displays O.K.? prompt
T	nTdrive:filename	Transfer (merge) file on disk to memory, enter at nth line
W	nW	Write n lines in memory to disk
n	n	Enter number n to edit nth line
Enter	Enter	Press Enter alone to edit one after current line

(The following are used with other commands.)

.	.	Current line
#	#	End of file, after last line
?	?S	Used with S & R to display a prompt
−/+	−5,+5L	# of lines before/after current one
^Z	Rs1^Zs2	Separate search and replace strings

(Note: m, n, p, and q denote line numbers.)

2. Enter the L (List) command to display the file:

```
A>edlin twain
End of input file
*l
          1:*East is East, and West is West,
          2: and never the twain shall meet.
     *
     _
```

Notice that the first line is preceded with an *. It tells you that this is the current line. The **current line** is always line 1 when a file is first retrieved. The current line changes as different commands are issued. Many commands will be applied to the current line by default.

3. Enter the I command to insert a new line at the current line, namely the first line; you can also use 1I for inserting at line 1.

4. Type "Rudyard Kipling" and press Enter two times, the first to end the line and the second to create an empty line and move the cursor to a new line.

5. Press Ctrl-C to end inserting. The screen should look like the following:

```
A>edlin twain
End of file input
*l
          1:*East is East, and West is West,
          2: and never the twain shall meet.
     *i
          1:*Rudyard Kipling
          2:*
          3:*^C
     *
     _
```

6. Use the L command to list the lines:

```
     *l
          1: Rudyard Kipling
          2:
          3:*East is East, and West is West,
          4: and never the twain shall meet.
     *
     _
```

Notice that the original lines have been moved down and renumbered. Also, the third line has become the current line (marked with *), due to the fact that the previous editing ended at that point. If you now issue the I command alone, this particular line will appear.

7. Issue the #I command to insert at the end (you can also enter 5I):

```
    *1
                    1: Rudyard Kipling
                    2:
                    3:*East is East, and West is West,
                    4: and never the twain shall meet.
    *#i
                    5:*_
```

8. Add the additional lines as shown below:

```
                    1: Rudyard Kipling
                    2:
                    3: East is East, and West is West,
                    4: and never the twain shall meet.
                    5:
                    6: Bible
                    7:
                    8: Do unto others what you want
                    9: others to do unto you.
                   10:
                   11: Confucius
                   12:
                   13: Do not do unto others what you
                   14: do not want others to do unto you.
                   15:
                   16: Kipling, the old British imperialist was
                   17: right. The two civilizations will travel
                   18: different paths. Just look at the popular
                   19: quotes from the Bible and the Chinese sage
                   20: Confucius. The former implores people to go out
                   21: and convert the infidel, and the later
                   22: counsels people to leave others alone.
                   23: Even the simplest idea of being kind to
                   24: your fellow men can take such different
                   25: paths.
```

If you break (pressing Ctrl-C) at line 26 and then use the L command to display the lines, the * showing the current line will not be seen anywhere. The reason is that the line below the last line is designated as the current line. Since that line does not exist, it is not displayed, nor is the *. Details of displaying lines will be discussed later.

9. Enter the E command to save the file and exit.

The new TWAIN file now contains the above 25 lines of text. What happened to the old file? It has been renamed TWAIN.BAK. The contents are unchanged; only the name is altered. If the original file name has an extension, such as

TWAIN.DOC, the extension will be replaced with BAK. EDLIN always does this whenever you save an existing file.

EDITING LINES

When you want to edit a line, you need to enter that particular line's number. The line is displayed and a blank line appears below for you to edit. Suppose you want to edit line 16. You can enter that number to get the following:

```
*16
            16:*Kipling, the old British imperialist was
            16:*_
```

You can now do a number of things. If you press Enter without typing any text, the original line is kept and editing is terminated. This line (16 in our example) has also become the current line. This is what you can do if you want to designate a particular line as the current line. To designate the end of the file, the line below the last existing line, as the current line, use a # in lieu of a number.

You can use DOS editing keys to speed up your work. Chapter 4 explains how these keys work.

If something you want to change lies near the end of a line, you can edit it this way: enter the line number, press F3 to display the whole original line, press Backspace or the ← key a number of times, type the new characters, and press Enter.

If errors lie somewhere else, you may try some other ways. These may seem a little complicated at first. But if you can master them, it is less time-consuming than retyping the whole or most of a long line.

TIPS AND TRICKS

E D L I N ' S   T W O   B U F F E R S

EDLIN maintains two separate buffers, one for the text line (as explained in the text) and the other for the command line.

On the command line, when the cursor is after the * at the left edge of the screen, you can also use the DOS editing keys to maneuver characters previously entered on the command line.

Most of the time you do not need to resort to this because most EDLIN commands consist of one character. However, when a long string is involved, such as a replace operation explained in the next section, this knowledge comes in handy.

MOVING, DELETING, AND COPYING LINES

Moving, deleting, and copying lines are simpler than changing words inside a line. Being a line-oriented editor, EDLIN makes it relatively easy to maneuver lines, whether singly or in a block

To demonstrate the steps of using M (Move), C (Copy), and D (Delete) commands, let us retrieve the TWAIN file and follow these steps:

FOLLOW THESE STEPS

1. Display the first 15 lines:

   ```
   End of input file
   *1,15l
           1:*Rudyard Kipling
           2:
           3: East is East, and West is West,
           4: and never the twain shall meet.
           5:
           6: Bible
           7:
           8: Do unto others what you want
           9: others to do unto you.
          10:
          11: Confucius
          12:
          13: Do not do unto others what you
          14: do not want others to do unto you.
          15:
       *
       _
   ```

2. Move lines 5–9 to line 15, and display the new lines:

   ```
   *5,9,15m
   *1,15l
           1: Rudyard Kipling
           2:
           3: East is East, and West is West,
           4: and never the twain shall meet.
           5:
           6: Confucius
           7:
           8: Do not do unto others what you
           9: do not want others to do unto you.
          10:*
          11: Bible
          12:
   ```

```
            13: Do unto others what you want
            14: others to do unto you.
            15:
    *
    _
```

The 5,9,15M command tells EDLIN to move lines 5–9 to the location of line 15. The Confucius quote moves up to fill in the vacated lines, occupying lines 5–9. Notice that the new current line is the beginning of the moved block, namely line 10.

3. Delete line 16 through the end, and redisplay the file:

```
    *16,#d
    *1l
```

The pound sign (#), you will recall, designates the end of the file. The bottom half of the file has disappeared. The new file contains only the lines shown above, minus the current line marker. The current line is after the last line and is thus not shown.

If you enter L alone (instead of 1L) at this point, you will display only lines 5–15, not all the 15 lines. The reason for this will be explained in the next section.

4. Delete line 1 and redisplay the remaining lines:

```
    *1d
    *1
```

Every line is renumbered. There are now 14 lines left. The current line is line 1, after the previously deleted line. If you enter D alone at this time, line 1 (the current line) will be deleted.

5. Delete the current line through line 9, and display the remaining lines:

```
    *,9d
    *1
            1:*Bible
            2:
            3: Do unto others what you want
            4: others to do unto you.
            5:
    *
    _
```

If you do not specify the number before the comma, EDLIN assumes that you want to begin at the current line. If the current line is not line 1 and you intend to delete lines 1-9, you must enter the following:

```
    *1,9d
```

You can also mark so many lines before and after the current line by using - and +. If you enter this command:

```
    *-1,+2d
```

you instruct EDLIN to delete four lines—the current line, one line above (-1), and two lines below (+2).

WARNING: One important precaution to keep in mind when deleting lines is that the line numbers below are immediately renumbered. You should then use the L command to show the new line numbers before deleting more lines. If you do not, you may end up deleting wrong lines.

6. Copy the current line (1) to the 7th line three times and display the new lines:

```
*,,7,3c
*l
        1: Bible
        2:
        3: Do unto others what you want
        4: others to do unto you.
        5:
        6: Bible
        7:*Bible
        8: Bible
  *
  _
```

Note: Notice that EDLIN starts filling in the first line after the last existing line, namely line 6. Line 7 is designated as the current line as you have ordered. What happens if you want to copy to line 7 only once? Only line 6 will be filled. Line 7 is still the designated current line, but it is not shown because it does not exist.

You can enter up to four numbers before the C command, each separated by a comma. The first two are for the beginning and ending line numbers. If no number is entered before and after the first comma, the current line is assumed. If there is only one line to be copied, you need to enter the same number, such as:

```
*5,5,10,1c
```

These numbers tell EDLIN to copy line 5 alone to line 10 once. The third number (the destination line) must be entered; otherwise, an error message will be displayed. If you do not specify the last number, EDLIN assumes that you want to copy only once. If line 5 is the current line, the above command could be simplified to this:

```
*,,10c
```

7. Finally, terminate editing without saving file:

```
*q
Abort edit (Y/N)?y
A>_
```

The earlier file which you retrieved at the beginning of this session remains intact. The mutilated file on the screen is abandoned. If you use the E command at the end, this mutilated file will be saved, and the original file will be renamed with a BAK extension.

WARNING: A final word of caution. Before you delete lines, make sure that is what you intend to do. After you press Enter to register your command, the lines are gone forever. You can no longer get them back, unless you go back to the old file still saved on disk. Some word processors, such as WordPerfect, allow you to undelete (retrieve from the buffer) up to three previous deletions. EDLIN, however, lacks that capability.

DISPLAYING LINES

So far you have learned to use only the L (List) command to display text lines on the screen. There is also the P (Page) command. They behave differently. This section explains how to use both of them.

Using the L Command

The L command alone is used to display lines around the current line. Under normal circumstances, it will display the current line in the middle and 11 lines above and 12 lines below. The top portion can be no more than 11 lines, while the bottom part may be more.

When a file is newly retrieved, with the first line designated as the current line, issuing the L command will display the current line, plus 23 lines below, thus filling the screen with 24 lines. The number of lines below the current line depends on the lines above it. If the above lines are fewer than 11, the bottom part is proportionally increased.

If you use L alone, EDLIN will not display more than 11 lines above the current line. For example, if there are 15 lines and line 15 is the current line, using the L command alone will display only lines 4-15.

You can designate a specific range of lines around the current line to display. For example, if you issue this command:

    *-5,+5l

you tell EDLIN to display five lines above and five lines below the current line.

If you want to display from the current line, use a period (.). For example, this command

    *.l

will display the current line at the top, followed by 23 lines below.

You can use numbers to display a specific range of lines. For example, this command

    *5,10l

will display lines 5–10 regardless of where the current line is. The second number must be higher than the first. Otherwise, an error message will be displayed.

You can omit either of the two numbers. If you omit the first, such as:

    *,15l

EDLIN assumes that you want to display from 11 lines before the current line and end with the specified line.

If the second number is omitted, the display starts with the first number and ends with 23 lines below.

You can combine editing a line with displaying a range of lines. For example, this command

    *15;-5,+5l

will let you edit line 15 and, when you press Enter after finishing it, display the edited line, plus five lines above and five lines below.

Notice the semicolon (;) separating the two separate commands. If nothing is entered before the semicolon, the line after the current line is made available for you to edit. If you want to edit the current line, put a period (.) before the semicolon.

What happens if you enter a large number of lines to display on the screen? Suppose you enter this:

    *1,50l

The screen will display 24 lines at one time. If there are more lines to be displayed, the scrolling will pause and this message will be displayed at the bottom:

    Continue (Y/N)?_

If you press N, the scrolling is terminated. If you press Y, another screenful of lines are displayed, forcing the earlier lines to scroll out of sight.

When a long text line spills down to the line below, the above phenomenon may also occur. You may want to display only 24 lines, but the actual display may have 25 or more lines. You may thus be prompted with Y/N.

Using the P Command

All that is said so far about the L command can be applied to the P command, with two major exceptions. First, P behaves slightly different from L. Second, P changes the current line.

Normally, the P command alone displays 23 lines starting after the current line, except when the current line is 1. When line 1 is the current line, entering P will display lines 1–23. If the current line is 5, however, P will display lines 6-28, or the end of file if there are fewer lines.

Every time P is used, the current line is changed to the last displayed line. Thus, if the current line is 1 and you continue entering P alone, you can page through the whole file 23 lines at a time.

When a range is specified, P behaves exactly like L, displaying only a specified range of lines. Up to 24 lines are displayed and a "Continue (Y/N)?" prompt appears if there are more. If you press Y, another 24 lines are shown. If you press N, scrolling ends. The last line of the specified range also becomes the current line even if you press N to discontinue scrolling.

SEARCH AND REPLACE

EDLIN allows you to search for or replace a string. These features are easy to use and quite speedy.

Searching for Matching Lines

Let us demonstrate how to search for a string in our file. Retrieve the TWAIN file and use the L command to show the first part. Then follow the steps shown below:

```
*snot
        13: Do not do unto others what you
*s
        14: do not want others to do unto you.
*s
Not found
*
```

The first command, "snot", tells EDLIN to search for the string of "not". After that command is entered, line 13 appears. This line becomes the current line.

The second command, S alone, continues to search from below the current line for the same string last entered. This search results in the display of line 14.

The third command, also S alone, results in displaying the "Not found" message. The current line is not changed from the previous search.

Now enter 1 to designate line 1 as the current line and try another way to search for the same string. Enter other commands as shown below:

```
*1
        1:*Rudyard Kipling
        1:*
*?s
       13: Do not do unto others what you
O.K.? n
       14: do not want others to do unto you.
O.K.? n
Not found
*
  _
```

The ?, placed before the S command, tells EDLIN to pause and display the "O.K.?" prompt for user input. If this is the line you are looking for, you are to press Y or Enter. The search then stops. If you press anything else, including the space bar, the search continues.

If you want to search in a specific range, place the line numbers before the S command, such as:

```
*5,20snot
```

If the first number is omitted, the default is the line below the current line. If the second number is missing, the last line is assumed. If you want to search the entire file with prompt, enter 1 as the only number before S, such as

```
*1?snot
```

EDLIN's search is case sensitive. EDLIN will only identify strings that literally match the search string you enter. If anything does not match, case or spelling, EDLIN cannot find what you want. Thus the following search strings are not the same:

```
*1?sbible
*1?sBible
```

A search string can be anything, including spaces and control characters as explained below. For example, you can have the following as a search string:

```
*1?sBritish imperialist
```

The string between S and the place where Enter is pressed is what EDLIN will search for in your file.

Replacing Strings

Replacing a string follows the same rules as a search operation, with the exceptions of substituting R for S and adding a replace string. The search string is placed ahead of ^Z (Ctrl-Z or F6), and the replace string after it.

To demonstrate replace operations, enter the following two commands:

```
*16,16rimperialist^Zcolonialist
        16:*Kipling, the noted British colonialist was
*16,16rnoted ^Z
        16:*Kipling, the British colonialist was
*
 _
```

Both commands limit operations to line 16. The first replaces "imperialist" with "colonialist", and the second replaces "noted " with no string, thus erasing it. Notice that the "noted " string has an extra space. Without it, an extra space will be left after the deleted word.

A replace operation may seem complicated. It is actually very simple. First you specify a range of numbers, which is optional (if no number is specified, the replace range is from below the current line to the end of the file). Then enter the R command, then the search string, and then the ^Z character. Finally, enter the optional replace string. If no replace string is specified, the search string, when found, is deleted.

You have the option to insert spaces before R for easier reading. After R, however, space and no space are treated differently. The following are the same:

```
*1 rBible^Zbible
*1RBible^Zbible
```

These two, however, are not the same:

```
*1rBible^Zbible
*1rBible^Z bible
```

The second command inserts an extra space to the original string, besides converting the first letter to lowercase.

Like a search string, a search-replace string is saved in the buffer. If you use R alone after a replace operation, EDLIN will repeat the previous operation. This may produce unexpected results, possibly mutilating your file beyond recognition.

After a replace operation, you can also use S alone to search for the search string entered in the replace operation. For example, if you did this:

```
*6,6rBible^Zbible
```

you can use S alone to search for "Bible".

If you need to alter a long search or replace command, try one of the DOS editing keys explained earlier. This can save you time in entering a long command.

WARNING: Doing a global replace operation, from line 1 to the end and without a prompt, is dangerous. Your file could be ruined. Fixing such a file will be a heck of a headache. It is thus advisable to use a prompt (?) when doing a replace operation in a large range of lines, such as the following:

```
*1?rBible^Zbible
         6: bible
O.K.? n
         19: quotes from the bible and the Chinese sage
O.K.? y
*
_
```

EDLIN will show you what the altered line will look like and let you choose yes or no. If you press Y or Enter, the displayed line will be registered. If you press any other key, the original line will be kept.

HANDLING CONTROL CHARACTERS

Control characters, those special ASCII codes numbered 0 to 31, can be entered in a batch file to control different parts of a computer system, particularly the printer. What these characters do will be further explained in Chapters 11 and 12. This section mostly illustrates how you can enter them in EDLIN.

The control characters can be entered only in EDLIN (EDIT or other software packages), but not COPY CON. This in turn makes it valuable in creating useful batch files. Table H.2 shows the most commonly used control characters.

Entering most of these characters requires special steps. For example, ^@ cannot be entered in any other way except by pressing the F7 key (when DOSKEY is not installed). Others can be entered by holding down Ctrl and pressing an appropriate letter, such as Ctrl-G.[1]

Characters that cannot be entered by combining Ctrl with a letter can be entered by inserting Ctrl-V before them. Follow these steps to enter ^H:

FOLLOW THESE STEPS

1. Use the I command to begin inserting in line 1.

2. Hold down Ctrl, press v, and release Ctrl to get ^V on the screen. Hold down Shift and press h to get H; you must use uppercase here. Press Enter to complete the line.

---

1. ^G is the only control character that can be entered on the command line or in COPY CON.

Table H.2

Control Characters

ASCII	Display	Purpose	Key(s) Pressed
0	^@	Null character	F7
7	^G	Beep	Ctrl-G
8	^H	Backspace	Ctrl-V H
9	^I	Horizontal Tab	Ctrl-V I
10	^J	Linefeed	Ctrl-V J
11	^K	Vertical Tab	Ctrl-V K
12	^L	Formfeed	Ctrl-V L
13	^M	Carriage Return	Ctrl-V M
27	^[	Escape character	Ctrl-V [

T I P S   A N D   T R I C K S

EDLIN, ANSI.SYS AND CONTROL CHARACTERS

As explained in Chapter 13, the "Esc [7m" command instructs your monitor to display text in reverse video. To enter the escape character (Esc), you need to press Ctrl-V, followed by typing [[. The ^V and [combination is treated as ^[by EDLIN and as the escape character (Esc) by DOS. The next [is required by ANSI. After these preliminaries, DOS can interpret the 7m as ordering reverse video. The steps below for creating this file are similar to those enumerated before:

```
*i
   1:*prompt ^V[[7m
   2:*cls
   3:*prompt
   4:*^C

*e
```

After creating this batch file, you can run it to display a color or monochrome monitor in reverse video. If your CONFIG.SYS file does not include ANSI.SYS, the first line will be treated as a meaningless text string, which will be displayed and cleared (by line 2) without changing the monitor display. Line 3 restores the default DOS prompt.

3. End insertion by pressing Ctrl-C.

4. Use the L command to display ^H on a VGA monitor (H^ on a Hercules monographics screen).

5. Use L to list lines; ^H appears. The screen shows the following after all these steps:

```
    *i
            1:*^VH
            2:*^C

    *l
            1: ^H
    *
     _
```

Some of the control characters are used to control the keyboard. That is why you need to use ^V to enter them into a file. If you press Ctrl-H, for example, the cursor will erase to the left, behaving like the Backspace key. To tell EDLIN to put these keystrokes in the text file, you need to enter ^V and then H.

The same is true for ^C. If you press ^C in a line, you terminate editing immediately. What if you want to put the character in the text without terminating editing? You put a C after ^V.

In ANSI.SYS, explained in Chapter 12, you can use $e[as the escape character. This character is placed before certain instructions to the computer to perform a specific act. You can enter this in EDLIN or use the alternative of ^[[.

HANDLING LARGE AND SPECIAL FILES

EDLIN is suitable for handling small and medium files, particularly batch files that are rarely large. If you must handle a large file with EDLIN, you need to be aware of some commands in case you get in a jam.

Working with Large Files

With a large file and/or limited memory, EDLIN retrieves only up to 75% of the available memory. If you do not see the "End of input file" message, that means the entire file is not retrieved.

After editing a file that is not completely retrieved, use the W command to save earlier lines, thus freeing some memory. You can specify a number of lines to be written to disk by putting a number before W, or let EDLIN free up 25% memory by using W alone.

After memory is made available, use the A command to append more text lines from disk to memory for editing. You can specify a number before A to append that many lines, or let EDLIN append to fill up to 75% of memory.

Another important precaution while working with a large file is that you have enough disk space to save the edited file. If there is not enough space when you use the E command to exit EDLIN, only a portion will be saved and the file will be given the $$$ extension; the rest is lost. The original file is not changed in name or contents.

You can also use the T command to transfer or merge a file on disk to the file being edited in memory. The entry point of the new text can be specified in a line number before T, or at the current line if no number is specified.

Editing Binary Files

Some versions of DOS (including version 5) allow you to use the /B switch with EDLIN to edit a binary file, such as:

```
A>edlin filename.ext /b
```

Without the switch, EDLIN will operate in ASCII mode and retrieve from the file only the part before the first ^Z; the rest is ignored.

Other versions, due to bugs, will ignore the /B switch and refuse to retrieve after the first ^Z encountered. One way to remedy this is to retrieve the file, delete it, and merge the original file. After the file you want to edit is retrieved, use the L command to show it. If it does not show the entire file, then enter these commands:

```
*1,#d
*tb:filename.ext
```

The first command deletes everything in memory. The second retrieves from drive B the whole file, including all the ^Z characters. This works with all versions of PC-DOS and MS-DOS.

WARNING: Most of the time you should avoid using EDLIN to edit a non-ASCII text file. If you retrieve a compiled program, such as MORE.COM, the screen shows mostly strange characters. If you retrieve a regular WordPerfect file, you find some ASCII characters, plus many incomprehensible codes. If you try to edit such a file, you risk the possibility of locking up your computer.

EDLIN, MACROS, AND BATCH FILES

If you use EDLIN often, you can use a couple of batch files to speed up your work. This arrangement is particularly useful if you use EDLIN to experiment with a series of batch files.

Suppose you have a batch file named X.BAT, which you need to repeatedly edit and run. You could use a batch file named E.BAT with which you can quickly load EDLIN and retrieve X.BAT for you to edit. Then, when you exit EDLIN, the original batch file will automatically run the edited batch file. All you need to do is to create a batch file like this:

```
A>copy con e.bat
edlin x.bat
x
^Z
```

Running E.BAT will automatically load EDLIN and retrieve (or create) the X.BAT file for you to edit. When you exit EDLIN, the edited X.BAT file will automatically be executed.

If you want to keep the contents of X.BAT, you can rename it or copy it to another disk. Otherwise, the edited version will replace the old one on the same disk. The X.BAT file will continuously change as you continuously use it to experiment with new batch files.

When you are ready to experiment with another batch file, run E.BAT, delete the contents of X.BAT (1,#D will delete everything), enter new batch lines, and exit to automatically run X.BAT. This arrangement can save you a lot of time when you work with lots of batch files.

If you plan to work with different files, this batch file may be more versatile:

```
A>copy con e.bat
edlin %1.bat
^Z
```

This arrangement lets you specify a file name on the command line to edit or create. The BAT extension is already in the batch file; all you need to do is to enter E followed by a file name without the BAT extension. If you now want to edit X.BAT, for example, just enter two letters, like this:

```
A>e x
```

Instead of using E.BAT as shown above, you can create a macro named E to do the same thing, like this:

```
A>doskey e=edlin $1.bat
```

This macro will let you enter a file name as a parameter and load EDLIN with the specified file name.

A MENU DISPLAY FILE

As the final project, you are going to create a text file that can be used in Chapter 11. This file should be named MENU.TXT and will be used as the initial screen display for a menu. It should initially look like this:

```
 1:
 2:
 3:
 4:            ===================================================
 5:            !                                                 !
 6:            !                                                 !
 7:            !              Press A Letter:                    !
 8:            !                                                 !
 9:            !                                                 !
10:            !              D - dBASE IV                       !
11:            !                                                 !
12:            !              L - Lotus 1-2-3                    !
13:            !                                                 !
14:            !              W - WordPerfect                    !
15:            !                                                 !
16:            !                                                 !
17:            !                                                 !
18:            ===================================================
```

When you use the TYPE command to show this file, the contents will be displayed in the middle of the screen. It is not particularly attractive. Let us change the box to a double-line rectangle by following these steps:

1. Go to line 4. With the cursor at the first =, hold down Alt and type 201 on the numeric keypad.

2. Press F3 and then ← to locate the cursor at the last character of the line. Enter Alt-187.

3. Go to the beginning of line 18 and enter Alt-200.

4. Go to the end of line 18 and enter Alt-188.

5. Replace all = (equal) with = (Alt-205) with this command:

   *1r=^Z=

6. Replace all ! with ‖ (Alt-186) with this command:

　　*1r!^Z‖

The graphic characters and their corresponding ASCII values are shown in the ASCII table in Appendix B.

The result is an attractive menu shown below:

```
 1:
 2:
 3:
 4:
 5:
 6:
 7:
 8:
 9:
10:
11:
12:
13:
14:
15:
16:
17:
18:
```

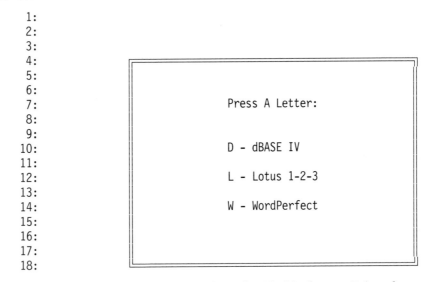

```
┌──────────────────────────────────┐
│                                  │
│         Press A Letter:          │
│                                  │
│                                  │
│         D - dBASE IV             │
│                                  │
│         L - Lotus 1-2-3          │
│                                  │
│         W - WordPerfect          │
│                                  │
│                                  │
│                                  │
└──────────────────────────────────┘
```

After you see the above display, you are through with this chapter. Exit and save the file.

Appendix I: Further Reading

Note: Most of the following PC-related periodicals are available in many bookstores, computer stores, college libraries, and public libraries. If you don't find them there, contact the publishers in the provided addresses or phone numbers. The computer press is highly volatile. Some of these publications may no longer exist by the time the book is published; new ones may appear.

Academic Computing

This monthly publication (no publication for June, July, August and December) contains mostly articles written by professors and administrators dealing with computer use in colleges and universities. Software vendors like to announce here their special discounts for college students. The annual subscription fee is $40. Write to: Academic Computing, P.O. Box 840, McKinney, TX 75069; or call 214 548-2101.

Byte

Published by McGraw-Hill, this monthly provides comprehensive coverage for small computers of all kinds. One of the few surviving publications that accompanied the onset of the PC revolution, it recently celebrated its 15th anniversary. Byte has adapted to the rapidly changing world of micro-computers. As the PC has become more popular, Byte has concentrated more on it, shifting from earlier emphasis on Apple, Atari, and Commodore. You can find tidbits about new products, reviews of individual products, questions to the editors and their answers. It operates BIX (Byte Information Exchange) online service for members who pay extra fees. You can also find frequent ads by various book clubs soliciting members; joining a book club is an inexpensive way to acquire the books you really need. To subscribe, contact Subscription Department, P.O. Box 558, Highstown, NJ 08520-9409. Annual fee: $24.95.

Compute

This magazine thrived during the first wave of the micro revolution by covering popular Z80 and 6502 machines such as TRS-80, Apple, Atari, Commodore, etc. As these machines went bust, so did the magazine. It was recently resurrected to concentrate on the IBM-standard machines. There is limited coverage of popular hardware and software news and reviews. There is still a great deal of emphasis on games and entertainment programs for the PC; the magazine is old in age but still young at heart. Annual subscription: $35; $12.97 in a recent promotion. Write to COMPUTE, P.O. Box 3244, Harlan, Iowa 51593.

Home Office Computing

Previously known as Home and Office Computing, the skimpy (about 100 pages) monthly is primarily intended for people who use their homes as offices. Most articles provide advice for people who use PCs to produce incomes at home. Coverage of PC and Mac hardware and software items commonly used in the home office settings. Published by Scholastic Inc., 730 Broadway, NY, NY 10003. Annual subscription costs $19.97.

InfoWorld

This weekly resembles PC Week in contents and appearance. For subscription, contact InfoWorld, P. O. Box 5997 Pasadena, CA 91117; or call 818 577-7233. The annual fee is $100.

PC Computing

Aimed at individual and business users of the PC; there is occasional coverage of the Mac. Brief news about new or updated products, and half-page reviews of some recently released popular products. Half a dozen columns by PC veteran writers. There are tips and hints provided by experts and readers on various popular applications such as dBASE, Lotus 1-2-3, and WordPerfect. Every issue includes some help or hints for DOS. If you have tenacious bugs or problems with your hardware or software, you can write to them. If their staff cannot solve them, readers will be offered $50 to come up with solutions. Published once a month by Ziff-Davis. For subscription, write to PC/Computing, P.O. Box 58229, Boulder, CO 80321-2770; or call 800 365-2770. Annual subscription fee: $24.97 for 12 issues. The fee is lower during periods of promotion, $14.97 in a recent campaign. The company also offers software giveaways to entice subscribers.

PC Magazine

Published twice a month, 22 issues for one year, by Ziff-Davis. This is a substantial (about 400 pages) and comprehensive magazine. It has typical new and updated software and hardware news, and columns by veteran PC writers. Each issue has one or two kinds of products (software and hardware), such as laser printers, thoroughly tested and compared. Those designated as PC Magazine Editor's Choice are frequently cited by vendors in their advertisements. You should consult these comparisons and test results before you buy an expensive item. Each issue contains some tutorial material related to DOS and other popular programs. If you have questions, you can ask the Tutor. If you know some neat tricks, you may be paid $50 for your contribution. For subscription, contact PC Magazine, P.O. Box 54093, Boulder, CO 80322; or call 800 289-0429. The annual fee is $44.97. In a recent promotion, the fee was $29.97, plus a bonus of two utility diskettes. The company also operates PC MAGNET online service, from which members can download existing programs.

PC Week

Latest news about hardware and software products and companies in the PC industry—with emphasis on corporate use and development of PC products. Useful weekly Buyer's Guides comparing one kind of products, such as dot-matrix printers, with charts supplying detailed specifications for each. Opinions of those who have used or tested new or updated products. Several weekly columns written by veteran writers. Occasional coverage of non-PC products such as Macs and workstations. Published by Ziff-Davis. For subscription, write to: Consumer Service Department, PC Week, P.O. Box 5970, Cherry Hill, N.J. 08034; or call 609 428-5000. Annual subscription fee: $160. Free subscription available to qualified persons and institutions.

PC Novice

Billed as "the magazine for computer newcomers," this is a relatively new and skimpy (about 100 pages) monthly. It features some reviews of software packages for beginners and annotated glossary of some commonly used PC terms. For subscription, contact Peed Corporation, 120 West Harvest Drive, Lincoln, NE 68502. Annual fee: $19.

PC World

This is a slightly smaller (about 250 pages) and less comprehensive version of PC Magazine. Published monthly by PCW Communications, Inc. For subscription, contact Subscriber Service, P.O. Box 55029, Boulder, CO 80322-5029. In a recent promotion, the annual fee was $19.97, plus a free calculator.

OTHER PUBLICATIONS

There are other publications that are less general in nature. They include Computer Language, Dr. Dobb's Journal, Microsoft Systems Journal, PC Tech

Journal, and Programmer's Journal for programmers; Computer Shopper and Computer Buyer's Guide for bargain hunters; Desktop Communications, Personal Publishing, and Publish! for desktop publishing; AI Expert, Computerworld, and Information Week for computers at large. Many of these are available in a college library.

OTHER SOURCES

Besides print media, there is a variety of electronic media which can supply you PC-related news more quickly. These include TV shows, bulletin boards, and fee-based databases.

Some TV broadcasts are available on cable and, from time to time, PBS. They provide relatively shallow coverage.

Most large cities have bulletin boards run by individuals, computer clubs, or public colleges. These contain lots of free (shareware or public domain) DOS games, graphics, applications, and utilities that can be downloaded to your disk by using a modem.

Information providers such as CompuServe, Source, GEnie (General Electric), and Prodigy (a consortium of IBM and Sears) have special interest groups (SIGs) devoted to all kinds of specialties such as DOS, Lotus, WordPerfect, etc. You need a modem and pay various amounts of fees to access them; their subscription packages are readily available in computer stores and frequently advertised in computer publications.

University of Washington maintains a nation-wide system called ISAAC (Information System for Advanced Academic Computing); it is financed by IBM. Qualified academicians will be given a password and a disk containing Kermit (communications program) for accessing the system via a toll-free (800) number. There is no fee (other than buying a modem) for using the system. Contact the following for details: ISAAC, m/s FC-06, University of Washington, Seattle, WA 98195.

Appendix J: Solutions

CHAPTER 1: PC AND DOS

Drill

1.e; 3.b; 5.d; 7.c; 9.d; 11.e; 13.d; 15.a; 17.b; 19.c; 21.S; 23.S; 25.S; 27.T; 29.F.

Practice 1-1

1. Press the Reset button on the front panel of the system unit. If your PC has no such a button, press Ctrl-Alt-Del.

3. Type something and then press Esc. The cursor goes down one line where a new command can be entered.

5. Enter the VER command.

7. Enter the TIME command. When the prompt for new time appears, type the same hour, then colon, and then the new minute. Press Enter to register the command.

Review Questions

1. PC (Personal Computer) is the term used by IBM when it first introduced its small computers. XT (Extended Technology) is an improved PC. AT (Advanced Technology) was used when IBM first introduced its 286-based PCs. PS/1 and PS/2 are the names IBM has given to its current crop of PCs.

3. If it's 8080 or 8086, it is the slowest and most limited. 80286 is in the middle range. 80386 is in the top range. 80486 is rare and very powerful.

5. CGA-RGB is the crudest color system. A Hercules monographics system is the most popular non-color system. EGA is still widespread, but VGA is rapidly becoming the most popular graphics system. It can accommodate both monochrome (analog) and color monitors to display high-resolution characters and graphics.

7. PC, AT (larger Enter key and some lighted panels) or Enhanced (12 function keys on top, extra cursor keys, etc.).

9. Restart your PC (warm boot), just like the Reset button available on newer PCs.

11. DOS for Intel lines of CPUs. It's a single-user, single-tasking system. OS/2 for Intel CPU of 80386 or higher. It is basically a multitasking system. UNIX, originated from AT&T's Bell Lab, is basically a multiuser system; it runs on 80386 or higher CPUs.

13. It does if date and time are kept up to date. It maintains power supply to the calendar and keeps it up to date even when power is off.

15. Simply enter the DATE or TIME command on the command line to change the numbers.

CHAPTER 2: A QUICK TOUR THROUGH DOS

Drill

1.T; 3.T; 5.F; 7.b; 9.d; 11.a; 13.d; 15.c; 17.a; 19.T; 21.F; 23.F; 25.e; 27.d; 29.c.

Practice 2-1

```
1. A>b:
   B>a:
```

```
3. A>dir b: /w
```

```
5. A>dir c:\dos\*.txt /o:s
```

Practice 2-2

```
1. A>copy sample.txt b:myfile.doc
```

```
3. A>type b:file2.txt
```

Practice 2-3

```
1. B>ren myfile.doc newdoc
```

```
3. A>b:
   B>del file2.txt
```

Practice 2-4

    1. A>`dir`
       (Press Shift-Print Scrn after entering the command.)

    3. A>`type sample.txt`   (do not press Enter)
       Press Ctrl-P.
       Press Enter.

    5. A>`copy sample.txt prn`

Review Questions

    1. A collection of related data. COM is a command file, EXE is an executable file, and BAT is a batch file. DOS can run all three of them. SYS is a device driver that can define or alter your system or allow it to drive some unusual devices.

    3. Where a command or file will automatically be accessed. To change it, simply enter a drive letter followed by a colon, such as B:.

    5. /P to pause after a screen is full; /W to display wide format; /A to display files of certain attributes; /O to determine the sorted order of displayed items.

    7. A switch is specific with each command. Some commands have no switch while others have more than half a dozen. A switch is placed after a backslash. A parameter is a command-line argument (which could include a switch) telling DOS how to do a job such as specifying a different target drive.

    9. Yes, if you store different copies in separate directories. Otherwise, you must use a different name.

    11. If a file is recoverable, you will first be asked to supply Y or N. Then you'll be asked to provide the first character of the file name.

    13. A echoes every keystroke to the printer. B halts a screen display. C prints a screen display.

    15. Prints a file named FILENAME. Actually, a disk file is copied to the printer. The screen also shows "1 File(s) copied" message.

CHAPTER 3: MANAGING DISKS

Drill

    1.b; 3.a; 5.F; 7.T; 9.F; 11.tracks; 13.512; 15.F; 17.c; 19.d; 21.T; 23.F; 25.T; 27.T; 29.F.

Practice 3-1

1. A>vol

3. C>label a:
   If a volume label is not shown: Enter a name.
   If a volume label is shown: Press Enter, N, Enter.

Practice 3-2

1. A>c:\dos\chkdsk a: (a: can be omitted; \dos\ can be omitted if
   DOS is the current directory in drive C)

3. C>chkdsk a:*.*

5. C>format a: /q

Review Questions

1. CD-ROM stands for Compact Disk Read Only Memory. It resembles an audio compact disk. Huge amounts of data can be stored on it. The data normally cannot be erased by the user. DAT stands for Digital Audio Tape. This is a relatively new storage media. It can store large amounts of data and also provide for slow random access. It is erasable.

3. A 1.2MB drive can format a disk to 360KB or 1.2MB, and can read and write to either. A 360KB drive can read only a 360KB, but not 1.2MB disk. A 1.44MB drive can format both 1.44MB and 720KB disks as well as read and write to them. A 720KB drive cannot handle a 1.44MB disk.

5. A disk is divided into a number of circular rings called tracks. Each track is divided into a number of sectors. Each sector has the storage capacity of 512 bytes.

7. The smallest unit DOS can use to save a file. A cluster can be one, two, or more sectors (512 bytes). When a file is saved, no matter how small, it takes up a whole cluster.

9. This is available with version 4.0 or later. It allows you to specify byte size to format a disk.

11. Volume label, serial number (version 4 or later), number of files (including hidden), cluster size, available disk space and memory.

13. This command will show all the fragmented files:
    A>chkdsk *.*

15. Just like a series of floppy disks stacked together. Each disk is known as a platter, which is divided into a number of tracks known as cylinders.

CHAPTER 4: CREATING AND NAMING FILES

Drill

1.F; 3.c; 5.d; 7.T; 9.a; 11.F; 13.c; 15.b; 17.a; 19.a; 21.F; 23.a; 25.g; 27.b; 29.d.

Practice 4-1

```
1. A>copy con quote
   Live simply so others may simply live.
   ^Z
```

```
3. A>ren quote quotes
```

Practice 4-2

```
1. A>copy con quota
   Those who do not learn from history are doomed to repeat it.
   ^Z
```

```
3. A>del quot* /p
```

Practice 4-3

```
1. A>copy con filename
   You can't be all things to all people.
```

3. Press F4, then e, then Ins, then B, and then F3.

Practice 4-4

```
1. A>copy con f.bat
   c:\dos\format a:
   ^Z
```

```
3. A>copy con ck.bat
   c:\dos\chkdsk %1:
   ^Z
```

```
5. C>doskey ql=c:\dos\label a:$1
   C>ql diskname
```

Review Questions

1. You ask DOS to copy what you type from the console to the named file in the current directory. In effect, this creates a new file.

3. Press Ctrl-C or Ctrl-Break. A ^C character appears and the file is not saved to disk.

5. Space, period, comma, <, >.

7. No. ? is ignored and characters after * are discarded.

9. Yes for REN, no for TYPE. TYPE is directed at a specific file. It is not capable of displaying a group of files.

11. You abandon the command, and DOS will not execute it. The cursor goes down to the beginning of the line below for you to enter another command. If DOSKEY is installed, the cursor does not go down; only the existing entry disappears.

13. To give the user more flexibility. It can be replaced with any parameter entered from the keyboard. One batch file can thus be used to do a number of tasks, depending on the parameter entered.

15. Yes. Use ¶ (Ctrl-T) on the command line and $T in a macro. Both are the equivalent of your pressing Enter. The two, however, are not interchangeable.

CHAPTER 5: MANAGING DIRECTORIES

Drill

1.F; 3.F; 5.d; 7.a; 9.b; 11.d; 13.d; 15.a; 17.e; 19.c; 21.F; 23.F; 25.T; 27.F; 29.T.

Practice 5-1

```
1. A>copy con computer
   Those who are low in computer skill cannot expect to thrive in
   a high-tech world.
   ^Z
```

```
3. A>copy \computer
```

```
5. A>rd temp
```

```
7. A>direct                    (run macro; enter below)
   doskey direct=cd\ $t del \temp\x.bat $t rd temp
   ^Z                          (save X.BAT)
   A>dir                       (show new directory)
   A>type \temp\x.bat          (show new batch file)
```

```
9. A>direct                    (run macro)
   A>dir                       (TEMP directory is gone)
```

Practice 5-2

```
1. A>md alpha
   A>md beta
   A>md gamma
```

```
A>md delta
A>cd alpha
A>md a1
A>md a2
A>md a3
A>cd \delta
A>md d1
A>md d2
A>md d3
```

3. `A>copy computer \delta\d3`

5. `A>dir\`

7. `A>doskey c=copy $1\computer $2`

Practice 5-3

1. `A>prompt $p$$`

3. `A>prompt $t$h$h$h$h$h$h$g$g`

5. `C>doskey ps=prompt $$$1`
   ($$ to display $; $1 to accommodate a parameter. If you enter PS T, the actual DOS command becomes PROMPT $T.)

7. `C>echo doskey k=doskey $* > a:kp.bat`
   `C>echo doskey p=prompt $* >> a:kp.bat`
   `C>k p=`   (delete the P macro)
   `C>k k=`   (delete the K macro)
   `C>doskey /m`   (you can no longer use K; deleted above)

9. `C>doskey timeprom=prompt $$t$$h$$h$$h$$h$$h$$h $$p$$g`
   `C>timeprom`   (run macro)
   `C>doskey timeprom=` (delete macro)
   `C>doskey /m`   (verify deletion)
   `C>prompt`   (restore default prompt)

Practice 5-4

1. `C>tree a: /a`

3. `C>tree a:\delta`

5. `A>append /x`
   `A>append a:\delta`
   `A>append`

7. `C>ap c:\dos;c:\bat;a:\`
   `C>ap /x:on`   (the above list is not affected)
   `C>ap /x:off`

Review Questions

1. Different persons can use the same disk without undue interference on one another. Related files can be put in a directory for easier remembrance and access. Different software packages can coexist and not interfere with one another. It takes a shorter time to display available files in a directory. Being a separate unit, a directory can be managed more efficiently. Files of same names can be stored on the same disk, different directories.

3. The active directory, where all actions can be taken without telling DOS where to apply them to. Thus, when you use the command DIR alone, the current directory's files are displayed.

5. This command will do:

```
A:\SPORTS\SHOPS>md \runner
```

The \ sign tells DOS to create a directory just below the root directory.

7. Use the CD.. command.

9. The screen displays the default prompt, which includes the current drive letter, followed by the greater-than (>) sign.

11. `PROMPT $D$_$N$G`

13. You ask DOS to go to C:\DOS to run the TREE program. In version 3.3 or before, the screen shows a list of directory names of the entire disk in the current drive (A). Version 4 or later displays the tree structure (diagram) of the current directory and those below.

15. To display on the screen the previously entered path specifications. To clear a path list, put a semicolon (;) after PATH or APPEND.

CHAPTER 6: COPYING AND COMPARING FILES

Drill

1.b; 3.b; 5.d; 7.d; 9.c; 11.d; 13.d; 15.F; 17.F; 19.T; 21.F; 23.d; 25.E; 27.I; 29.E.

Practice 6-1

```
1. A>copy con test1
   This is test1.
   ^Z
   A>copy con test2
   This is test2.
   ^Z
3. A>copy test3 + test1 + test2
5. A>copy test? . +
```

Practice 6-2

1. A>copy /b test1 con   (change 1 for other files)

3. A>copy test2 + test3 prn

5. A>cpy 3 prn

Practice 6-3

1. A>md testdir
   A>cd testdir
   A>copy test1 testdir
   A>del test1

3. A>b:
   B>dir
   A>dir testdir
   Three test files were copied if you have selected Y when prompted. A directory was also created and the file in the original source directory was also copied to the new directory.

5. A>del test? ¶ del \testdir\test? ¶   rd testdir

Practice 6-4

1. C:\DOS>diskcomp a: b:

3. **A>c:\dos\fc test1 test2 /b**

5. Enter this command to show the UNDELETE.INI file:

   > A>type c:\dos\undelete.ini

   It should contain the following values:

   > [mirror.drives]
   > A=
   > d.tracker=TRUE

7. A>c:\dos\defrag a: Press Enter to begin optimizing.

Review Questions

1. Copies all the files with DOC extensions from drive B to drive A and changes the extensions to BAK. This is a binary operation, and no ^Z is added to target files.

3. Appends all the files in the current directory of drive B to the named file. An extra ^Z is added to the target file.

5. Binary mode for copying. Everything in the source is read and written to the target. In file combination, ASCII mode is default. A source file is read until a ^Z is encountered. A target file has an additional ^Z added. The /A and /B switches can be used to counter these default settings.

7. The first copies each of the files from drive A to B. The fragmented pieces of each file are put together before writing to drive B. The target disk needs to be formatted and has enough space to hold the incoming files. The second physically duplicates in drive B the disk in drive A. A fragmented original produces an equally fragmented copy. The target disk need not be formatted. A bootable disk can also be duplicated this way.

9. A>copy filename prn

11. Duplicates in the target drive the directory structure of the source. If target directories do not exist, they are created before copying files.

13. No to both.

15. It stores the default values for the memory-resident portion of UNDELETE. When you use UNDELETE with the /LOAD switch, these values govern how your deleted files will be protected. You can use a text editor to change the values. When you use UNDELETE with a switch to specify a value different from a comparable one stored in UNDELETE.INI, this file's contents will be changed.

CHAPTER 7: MAINTAINING FILES

Drill

1.T; 3.F; 5.d; 7.F; 9.F; 11.T; 13.T; 15.c; 17.c; 19.T; 21.a; 23.d; 25.d; 27.F; 29.T.

Practice 7-1

1. ```
   A>copy con test1
   This is test1.
   ^Z
   A>copy con test2
   Here is test2.
   ^Z
   A>replace test? b:
   ```

3. ```
   A>copy test1 + con
   This line is added.
   ^Z
   A>replace test? b: /u
   ```

5. `C:\DOS>dir a: /a:hs`

Practice 7-2

1. `A>attrib test?`

3. `A>replace b:test? /r`

5. A>attrib -r test?
   A>del test?
   A>replace b:test?

7. A>del test?
   File not found   (DEL cannot see S and/or H files.)

Practice 7-3

1. A>print test?

3. A>print test1 test2

5. A>print c:\dos\readme.txt

Review Questions

1. To transfer hidden system files—IO.SYS, MSDOS.SYS, DBLSPACE.BIN—and COMMAND.COM. You can use it to make a disk bootable without using FORMAT /S or DISKCOPY.

3. All the files in drive C and all its subdirectories will be replaced with identical files found in A.

5. FILE1 in A will be replaced with FILE1 from B. The /R switch can replace a file with the R attribute. Without this switch, the file will not be replaced.

7. Remove the A attribute of a source file after copying. If you use /M again to copy, such a file will not be copied, unless it is modified, which restores the A attribute.

9. Backs up selected files, those with A attributes, and removes their A attributes. If you do another incremental backup in the future, these files will not be selected because they no longer have the A attribute. If you select an entire directory to back up, only the new and modified files will be marked as selected. This type of backup is good to use if you keep creating new files. You should keep the full and all the subsequent incremental backup copies.

11. The file name can be interpreted this way:

C	The first source drive
D	The last source drive
3	Year, 1993
12	Month, December
13	Date, 13th
A	Sequence of the day; could be A/B or A to Z
001	The first target disk

13. New or modified files, those with A attributes, will be automatically selected for backup. If you perform incremental backups periodically,

only new and modified files will be backed up and those that have been backed up will be ignored.

15. Cancel the first two files and print the last.

CHAPTER 8: REDIRECTING FILES

Drill

1.d; 3.b; 5.a; 7.d; 9.a; 11.F; 13.F; 15.F; 17.F; 19.F; 21.T; 23.T; 25.T; 27.F; 29.c.

Practice 8-1

1. A>copy con xyz
   Line 1.
   This is line 2.
   Here goes line 3.
   ^Z

3. A>type xyz > nul
   A>type xyz > prn

5. A>copy con cr
   ^Z
   A>copy con t.bat
   time < cr
   ^Z

Practice 8-2

1. A>more > prn
   He who knows others is learned;
   He who knows himself is wise.
   ^C

3. A>more fool > prn

5. A>doskey m=more$1$1 $t pause $t type 1g prn
   A>m fool

Practice 8-3

1. A>copy con address
   Drake, Daffy   123 Kwack Ave., Fun City   CA   94000
   Bunny, Bugs   999 Doc Road, Mud Town   OK   74037
   . . .

   ^Z
   (Use spaces to separate different fields.)

3. A>sort < address /r

5. A>sort < address /+55 > prn
   (Count the position of the Zip field, including spaces.)

Practice 8-4

1. A>find "CA" address

3. A>find "CA" address ¦ find "Smith" address

5. A>copy con seeadd.bat
   find "%1" address
   ^Z

Practice 8-5

1. Change DIARY.BAT in the text to NOTE.BAT and DIARY.TXT to NOTES. Use ECHO/ as shown in DIARY.BAT.

3. A>copy con nt.bat
   doskey nt=note
   ^Z

5. A>doskey sm=sort $1 $1 $b more

Review Questions

1. Keyboard is standard input, and monitor standard output. The former is used to enter raw data, and the latter to output processed data.

3. 1. Saves directory entries to FILENAME.
   2. If existent, FILENAME ignored; if not, command aborted.
   3. Appends to FILENAME.

5. 1. Line is echoed to NUL, not duplicated on the screen.
   2. Line is printed.
   3. Line is saved.
   4. Line is appended.

7. MORE is run without any parameter. After exiting MORE by entering ^Z, DIR is executed.

9. Those of equal lengths. SORT treats each character as an ASCII value, except adjusting for uppercase and lowercase. Numbers and letters are sorted according to their ASCII values, not numeric ones.

11. A>dir ¦ find "3-" ¦ find "-90"
    Will search for all the files containing "3-" and "-90", namely March, 1990.

13. A>dir ¦ find "FILE.*" ¦ sort /+14

15. ECHO sends MORE's carriage return to the DATE command, thus causing both Date lines to be output automatically. FIND filters the line with C and redirects it to DATEDATA.

CHAPTER 9: CONFIGURING THE SYSTEM

Drill

1.F; 3.a; 5.d; 7.T; 9.T; 11.F; 13.T; 15.T; 17.d; 19.F; 21.F; 23.d; 25.d; 27.a; 29.b.

Practice 9-1

1. A>mode con rate=32 delay=1

3. A>mode lpt1 132
   A>echo This is in tiny print. > prn
   A>mode lpt1 80
   A>echo Back to normal again. > prn

5. A>doskey pm=mode lpt1 $1 $2

7. A>pm /sta
   A>pm 80 6

9. A>mm 40 25
   A>mm 80 50
   A>mm 80 25

Practice 9-2

1. Add the following line in your CONFIG.SYS and reboot:

   lastdrive=x

   You can add a line to your CONFIG.SYS like this:

   A>copy config.sys + con
   lastdrive=z
   ^Z

3. A>prompt pg
   A:\>x:
   X:\>

5. X:\>a:
   A:\>

7. A:\>rd xyz
   Attempt to remove current directory - XYZ

   A:\>deltree xyz
   Delete directory "xyz" and all its subdirectories? [yn] y
   Deleting xyz...

   Nothing happens. Use DIR XYZ or SUBST alone to show that the directory still exists.

9. `A:\>subst x: /d`
   `A:\>subst`

The directory is changed to ABC. Use DIR ABC or DIR XYZ to prove it.

Practice 9-3

1. `A>break`
   `A>break on`
   `A>break off`

3. `F>md temp`
   `F>copy a:ramcopy.bat \temp`

5. `A>fc ramcopy.bat`

Practice 9-4

1. `A>append /e`
   `A>copy con addappnd.bat`
   `@echo off`
   `set append=%append%;%1`
   `^Z`

3. First, add a new line to ENVPROM.BAT:
   `A>copy envprom.bat + con`
   `set pc=Enter a command:`
   `^Z`
   Second, add a new line to SETPROM.BAT:
   `A>copy setprom.bat + con`
   `if %1.==c. prompt=%pc%`
   `^Z`
   Finally, run ENVPROM.BAT and set the new prompt style with this:
   `A>setprom c`

5. `A>doskey cd=c $1`   (run C.BAT with a parameter)
   `A>cd d1`   (run CD macro with a parameter)

7. `A>copy con oldprom.bat`
   `set prompt=%prompt1%`
   `^Z`

Review Questions

1. Keyboard (CON), monitor (CON), parallel printer (LPTn), serial printer (COMn), and modem (COMn).

3. 6/8 lines per inch and 80/132 columns.

5. You can substitute a nonexisting drive for an existing directory. The drive letter can be determined by the number of drives installed or set higher by you.

7. It will analyze your system and alter your CONFIG.SYS and AUTOEXEC.BAT files in order to load more programs in the upper memory area. You can use the /UNDO switch to restore your original files.

9. An area of memory treated as a disk drive. Include this line in your CONFIG.SYS file:

    ```
    device=c:\dos\ramdrive.sys
    ```

11. PATH, PROMPT, and APPEND (if installed with /E). Use the SET command to enter an environment variable, such as:

    ```
    A>set var=value
    ```

13. Two memory-management programs are provided. HIMEM.SYS is the extended-memory manager and EMM386.EXE is the expanded-memory manager. The former can utilize the 64KB of the initial extended memory (high memory area) and load DOS there to free up some conventional memory. The latter can do two things with a 386/486 PC: loading some TSR programs in the upper memory area (between 640KB and 1MB area) and converting extended memory to expanded memory.

15. It will analyze your CONFIG.SYS and AUTOEXEC.BAT files and alter them if necessary. The objective is to put as many programs and device drivers as possible in the upper memory area so that more conventional memory will be made available for use by other programs.

CHAPTER 10: DOS SHELL AND EDITOR

Drill

1.d; 3.e; 5.d; 7.F; 9.a; 11.b; 13.c; 15.F; 17.b; 19.a; 21.d; 23.T; 25.b; 27.c; 29.b.

Practice 10-1

1. Make A the current drive by clicking it or highlighting it and pressing Enter. Open the File menu. Select Create Directory. Enter ABC.

3. Select the ABC directory. Press – or click the – sign to collapse. Press or click + to expand.

Practice 10-2

1. Make C:\ the current directory. Open the File menu. Select Search. Enter *.TXT.

3. Make A:\ABC the current directory. Select README.TXT. Open the File menu and select Move (or press F7). Enter \ABC\XYZ. You can also drag the file to the new directory.

5. Select README.TXT and press Del. Select Yes to confirm.

Practice 10-3

1. Click the first file, and click the second while holding down Ctrl. From the keyboard, highlight the first file and press Shift-F8; move to the second file and press the space bar. Press Shift-F8 again.

3. Make A:\ABC the current directory. Select all the files by pressing Ctrl-/. Select Move from the File menu and enter A:\ABC\XYZ.

5. Make A:\ABC\XYZ the current directory. Make sure all hidden files are displayed. If not, select Files Display Options from the Options menu and check the selection box. Select all the files in the directory by pressing Ctrl-/. Press Del and confirm each deletion.

Practice 10-4

1. Select File Display Options from the Options menu. Enter *.BAT in the Name box. Select Descending Order. Drag the bullet to Date. Select OK.

3. Select Dual File Lists from the View menu. Make C:\DOS the current directory in the top window. Tab to the bottom window and make A:\ the current directory.

Practice 10-5

1. Go to the C:\DOS directory and run PRINT.EXE (double click or highlight it and press Enter). Press Enter to accept PRN as the print device. Press Enter to return to the Shell screen. Go to drive A. Highlight SAMPLE.TXT. Select Print from the File menu.

3. Open MYGROUP (double click it or press Enter when it is highlighted). Select New from the File menu. Enter the program title. In the Commands box, enter C:\DOS\CHKDSK A:. Enter other optional information and select OK.

5. Open MAIN to return to the Program List screen. Highlight [MYGROUP]. Select Reorder from the File menu. Double click the first item or highlight it and press Enter.

7. Make C:\DOS the current directory. Highlight EDIT.COM. Select Associate from the File menu. Enter TXT. Select OK.

Practice 10-5

1. Enter this on the command line:

```
C:\DOS>edit a:menub.bat
```

From the Shell, associate EDIT.COM with BAT and open MENUB.BAT in drive A.

3. Hold down Shift and move the cursor to highlight the top portion. Press Shift-Del to cut. Move the cursor to the end and press Shift-Ins to paste.

5. Open the Search menu and select Change, type errorlevel as the search string and ERRORLEVEL as the replace string, and select <Change All>.

7. Type the lines as shown after the screen is cleared.

9. Select Save As from the File menu and enter A:MATTER.

Review Questions

1. Start the Shell by running DOSSHELL. Start the Editor by running EDIT. Exit by selecting Exit from the File menu (or pressing F3 or Alt-F4 in the Shell).

3. The top shows a menu bar. Then comes a drive-icons line. The bottom line is known as the status line. The middle is divided into three windows, Directory Tree, File List, and Program List. These windows also contain scroll bars and boxes.

5. When a directory is expanded, a – sign appears in front of it. To collapse it, click the – or press – with the directory highlighted. To expand it, use + instead. To expand all the subdirectories, use *. To expand all the directories to the fullest, press Ctrl-*.

7. Highlight the file and press F9. Scroll up and down to view more. Press Esc to return to the Shell. If you get a beep after pressing F9, press Ctrl-\ to deselect other files and then press F9 again.

9. Move to the first file, hold down Shift, and move to the last file. All the files will be highlighted. You can do something to all of them, such as copying or moving.

11. Highlight a program or a data file and select Associate from the File menu. Enter a file name extension or a program name.

13. Ctrl-Home, Ctrl-End, Home, End, Ctrl-PgDn, Ctrl-PgUp.

15. Save saves the current contents to the existing file, replacing the original contents. If no file name has been specified, you will be prompted to enter one. Save As allows you to enter a new file name to save the current contents; you can use this option to save multiple copies of the same file.

CHAPTER 11: PROGRAMMING BATCH FILES

Drill

1.T; 3.F; 5.F; 7.c; 9.F; 11.F; 13.T; 15.b; 17.F; 19.F; 21.b; 23.a; 25.T; 27.T; 29.b.

Practice 11-1

1. A>edlin demo.bat
   Enter I and type the lines as shown. In line 4 press Ctrl-C. Enter E to exit.

3. Insert this in line 4:
   pause

5. Insert a line like this before and after each message line:
   echo/

Practice 11-2

1.
```
1: @echo off
2: :AGAIN
3: echo %1
4: shift
5: if not .==%1. goto AGAIN
```

3.
```
1: @echo off
2: echo These files exist in source but not target:
3: for %%x in (%1) do if not exist %2:%%x echo %%x
4: echo Press a key to copy, or ^C to abort.
5: pause > nul
6: for %%x in (%1) do if not exist %2:%%x copy %%x %2:
```

5. A>dt a:*.bat

Practice 11-3

1.
```
1: @echo off
2: rem LOOK.BAT--to look up strings in a file
3: if .==%1. goto HELP
4: if .==%2. goto HELP
5: find "%1" %2
6: goto END
7: :HELP
8: echo/
9: echo You forgot to enter two parameters, like this:
10: echo     %0 string filename
11: echo/
12: :END
```

3. First, change line 5 to this:
```
5: echo 0 = Italic  1 = NLQ  2 = Compressed  3 = Expanded
```
   Second, insert these after line 7:
```
8: :0
9: echo ^[4 > prn
10: goto END
```
   Finally, add ^[5 to the existing line 24:
```
24: echo ^[5^[x0^R^[W0^[P^[H > prn
```

5.
```
1: @echo off
2: rem PASS3.BAT
3: if %4.==ABRACADABRA. goto PASS
4: goto END
5: :PASS
6: echo You have entered the correct password.
7: :END
```

Run the batch file like this for line 3 to test true:

```
A>pass3 x x x ABRACADABRA
```

7.
```
1: @echo off
2: rem ENECHO.BAT--echo typed words up to 9
4: set env=%1 %2 %3 %4 %5 %6 %7 %8 %9
5: echo %env%
```

Practice 11-4

1.
```
1: @echo off
2: rem LOOK2.BAT--to look up strings in a file
3: if .==%1. goto HELP
4: if .==%2. goto HELP
5: find "%1" %2
6: if errorlevel 2 goto EL2
7: if errorlevel 1 goto EL1
8: goto END
9: :EL1
10: echo Search successful; no match found
11: goto END
12: :EL2
13: echo An unknown error has occurred
14: goto END
15: :HELP
16: echo/
17: echo You forgot to enter two parameters, like this:
18: echo      %0 string filename
19: echo/
20: :END
```

3. A>if exist autoexec.bat echo found here
   C:\>if exist \dos\format.com echo It's here

5. A>doskey t=for %x in ($1) do call type$2 %x
   A>t *.bat 3

Practice 11-5

1. Change line 4 to:
   ```
   4: if %1.==. 1
   ```

```
3.       1: @echo off
         2: rem MENU3.BAT--show available options
         3: :MENU
         4: cls
         5: echo Select: W(ordPerfect), L(otus), D(Base), Q(uit)
         6: key
         7: echo/
         8: if errorlevel 119 if not errorlevel 120 goto WP
         9: if errorlevel 113 if not errorlevel 114 goto END
        10: if errorlevel 108 if not errorlevel 109 goto LOTUS
        11: if errorlevel 100 if not errorlevel 101 goto DBASE
        12: if errorlevel 87 if not errorlevel 88 goto WP
        13: if errorlevel 81 if not errorlevel 82 goto END
        14: if errorlevel 76 if not errorlevel 77 goto LOTUS
        15: if errorlevel 68 if not errorlevel 69 goto DBASE
        16: goto MENU
        17: :WP
        18: wp.bat
        19: :LOTUS
        20: 123.bat
        21: :DBASE
        22: db.bat
        23: :END

5.       1: @echo off
         2: rem YESNO1.BAT--to branch to NO if N pressed
         3: echo/
         4: echo Do you want to continue (Y/N)?
         5: key
         6: if errorlevel 78 if not errorlevel 79 goto NO
         7: if errorlevel 110 if not errorlevel 111 goto NO
         8: echo/
         9: echo You have chosen Y.
        10: echo Press a key to end.
        11: pause > nul
        12: goto END
        13: rem . . .
        14: :NO
        15: echo/
        16: echo You have chosen N. Goodbye!
        17: :END
```

7. Change line 4 of TYPE1.BAT to this:

```
        4: for %%x in (%1) do call type3 %%x
```

Modify TYPE3.BAT as shown below:
```
 1: rem TYPE3.BAT--called by TYPE1.BAT
 2: cls
 3: echo %1
 4: echo/
 5: echo Do you want to show this file? (Y/N)
 6: key
 7: if errorlevel 89 if not errorlevel 90 goto SHOW
 8: if errorlevel 121 if not errorlevel 122 goto SHOW
 9: goto END
10: :SHOW
11: more < %1
12: pause
13: :END
```

9.
```
1: @echo off
2: key
3: if not errorlevel 100 echo -100
4: if errorlevel 100 echo 100+
```

Review Questions

1. Put @ before a command; put "@echo off" in the first line.

3. "Press any key to continue..." The following two lines will do it:
```
echo Turn on the printer!!!!
pause > nul
```

5. No. The topmost is always executed. DOS starts looking for a matching label from the top of a batch file. If one matching the spelling is found, all those below are ignored.

7. To assign the next parameter to the same dummy variable. If %1 holds the first parameter the first time, after SHIFT, it holds the second parameter.

9. 1. A file's existence:
```
IF EXIST FILENAME GOTO . . .
```
2. The existence of a parameter or environment variable:
```
IF .==%1. GOTO . . .
IF .==.%path% GOTO . . .
```
3. An exit code:
```
IF ERRORLEVEL 3 GOTO . . .
```

11. CALL nests another batch file and returns execution to the calling batch file. Running batch 2 in the middle of batch 1 transfers control to batch 2 and batch 1 is through. Both can pass parameters and @ECHO OFF to a child batch file.

13. They are responses to a command's various states of execution, such as successful formatting or certain error conditions. BACKUP, FORMAT, REPLACE, and RESTORE use exit codes.

15. It is a looping command. FOR specifies a variable, IN includes a list of files or commands, and DO acts on the matching files or runs the listed commands.

CHAPTER 12: USING ANSI.SYS

Drill

1.F; 3.F; 5.T; 7.F; 9.d; 11.b; 13.c; 15.F; 17.c; 19.c; 21.a; 23.T; 25.F; 27.F; 29.T.

Practice 12-1

1. `A>prompt $e[1;1H$n$g$e[K`

3. `A>prompt $e[2J`
   `prompt`

5. `A>prompt $e[7m$p$g`

7. Change line 3 to this:
   `3: prompt $e[%1;%2;%3;%4;%5`

Practice 12-2

1.
```
1: @echo off
2: echo ^[[2J
3: echo ^[[32;43m
4: echo ^[[13;34HHello World
5: prompt $e[25;1H
6: echo ^[[0m
```
For mono, change line 3 values to "4;5".

3. `A>prom =13h 2J`

Practice 12-3

1. `A>prompt $e[27;"dir";13p`

3. `A>prompt $e[0;71;"dir\";13p`

5. Change line 3 of NOCR.BAT to:
   `3: echo ^[[0;28;"yecr";13p`

7. Change line 10 to:
   `10: if errorlevel 13 if not errorlevel 14 goto END`

9. Change line 10 and add line 11:

```
10: if errorlevel 81 if not errorlevel 82 goto END
11: if errorlevel 113 if not errorlevel 114 goto END
```

Practice 12-4

1. `A>ansi 0;73;"dir..";13p`

3. `A>ansi 0;103;"dir¦sort¦more";13p`

5. `A>doskey p=prompt $$e[$*$$p$$g$t cls`

Practice 12-5

1. Change 0;50 to 14 (^N), 0;33 to 6 (^F), 0;32 to 4 (^D), and 0;31 to 19 (^S). Also change instructions where appropriate.

3. `A>copy filename con`

Practice 12-6

1. Use 67 (F9), 92 (Shift-F9) and 102 (Ctrl-F9) to replace the numbers in the text.

3. First, define Ctrl-F9 as below, plus carriage return:

```
showmsg m0 m1 m2 m3 m4 m5 m6 m7 m8 m9
```

Second, create this batch file:

```
 1: @echo off
 2: rem SHOWMSG.BAT--show one message after another
 3: :AGAIN
 4: cls
 5: if .==%1. goto END
 6: if not exist %1 goto NOTEXIST
 7: echo/
 8: echo -------------------- %1 --------------------
 9: echo/
10: type %1
11: echo/
12: pause
13: shift
14: goto AGAIN
15: :NOTEXIST
16: shift
17: goto AGAIN
18: :END
19: echo/
20: echo That's all.
21: echo/
```

Finally, press Ctrl-F9 to show one file at a time.

Review Questions

1. They are commands adopted by the American National Standards Institute. They are used to extend screen and keyboard functions. Each ANSI command (escape sequence) consists of Esc (ASCII 27), [(left bracket), a series of numbers, and ending with a letter.

3. $e is used with PROMPT exclusively. ^[(EDLIN) or ← (EDIT) is entered in a file and then sent to the computer with ECHO, COPY CON, TYPE, or MORE.

5. The latest PROMPT command will go to the DOS environment, which may affect your future activities. An ECHO command does not go to the environment.

7. A PROMPT command has no effect until ECHO is turned on again. A command such as "prompt $e[2J" will erase every screen display when ECHO is on. Its feature is disabled when ECHO is off.

9. First, set monitor to high intensity, blink. Second, set to default attributes; "m" alone is same as "0m".

11. Shows blinking message preceded and followed by a blank line. Blinking is turned on and off by the first and last lines.

13. Use TYPE, COPY, or MORE to send the file to the screen, such as:

    ```
    A>type filename
    ```

15. Assigns to Alt-D the string inside the quotes, plus a carriage return. Pressing Alt-D then appends two-line date data to a file named NOTES.

Appendix K
New Features in Version 6.2

This appendix is intended for users of versions 6.20, 6.21, and 6.22. It describes what's new in the new versions and explains how to use them.

You will find some page numbers in the following pages. They refer to the pages in *The DOS 6 Coursebook*. You may want to glance through this appendix without learning the details—just remember what's available in the new versions. At proper places in the Coursebook, you might then refer to this appendix so that you can tie everything together.

VERSION VARIATIONS

There is a proliferation of numbers in DOS brands and versions. A little background information may help clear the foggy air.

There are now three DOS brands: MS-DOS, PC DOS, and Novell DOS.[1] MS-DOS and PC DOS used to be identical. Both were written by Microsoft; one was marketed by Microsoft and the other by IBM. This IBM-Microsoft marriage ended after DOS 5. After the divorce, IBM began to market its own PC DOS.

Novell DOS came from DR DOS. DR (Digital Research) was the vendor of the popular CP/M operating system that started the microcomputer revolution. DR is now part of Novell, the network software giant. Novell has since

---

[1]The February 1994 issue of *PC Computing* contains a fairly thorough article comparing these three operating systems.

changed DR DOS to Novell DOS. (Novell also took over WordPerfect Corporation and purchased Borland's Quattro Pro spreadsheet program in mid-1994.)

These three software giants have been engaging in a numbers game, with each weaker one using a higher number to gain a marketing advantage. As a result, there is a continuous escalation of numbers. Shortly after Microsoft began to market MS-DOS 5, DR DOS 6 was rolled out. Currently Microsoft is selling DOS 6.2x and Novel is marketing DOS 7.

MS-DOS 6 brought Microsoft macro-hard problems in its DoubleSpace (p. 274). The numerous bugs forced Microsoft to release 6.2 barely half a year after the debut of 6.0. Where is 6.1? Between 6.0 and 6.2, IBM shipped its new PC DOS 6.1. To avoid confusion or to be higher than its rival, Microsoft called the new release 6.2. As of this writing (6/94), IBM is marketing 6.3.

DoubleSpace might as well be called DoubleTrouble. Besides the famous bugs, it also brought a lawsuit in which Microsoft lost $120 million. Microsoft licensed the technology from a little known company called Vertisoft. If Microsoft's lawyers tried to use this ploy to shield the company from a patent-infringement lawsuit, it did not work. A jury in early 1994 agreed with Stacker, the most popular commercial file-compressing program, that Microsoft infringed on its patent. The aforementioned sum was to compensate Stacker for the MS-DOS copies already sold. Microsoft was left no choice but to release 6.21, which is 6.2 minus DoubleSpace. The company began to ship 6.22 in June, 1994. DoubleSpace is now replaced by Drive-Space, which is written by Microsoft's own programmers; everything else remains unchanged.

This appendix uses 6.2 for discussion. If you use 6.21, what is said about DoubleSpace does not apply to you. If you use 6.22, what is said about DoubleSpace can be applied to DriveSpace as well.

NEW FEATURES

If you want to know what's new in 6.2, as compared to 6.0, a good place to start is the online help.[2] Enter this on the DOS command line:

---

[2]The full DOS 6.2 package comes with the old 6.0 manual. The 6.2 Stepup package contains one disk and no manual. New features are explained only in the online help.

```
C>help whatsnew
```

This executes the HELP.EXE file and brings up a frame explaining the new features in 6.2.

You can also launch the online help first, like this:

```
C>help
```

The resulting display resembles Figure 1.6 on p. 32 (see Coursebook). The main difference is this new item at the top:

<What's New in MS-DOS 6.2?>

The cursor also rests on this item. If you press Enter, this topic will be brought up for your view.

DOS 6.2's few features can be grouped into these categories:

- ScanDisk, the full-screen utility to check and repair disks

- Copy improvements: preventing COPY, XCOPY, and MOVE from overwriting matching target files; one-pass diskcopy in one drive

- Safeguards against the hazards of DoubleSpace/DriveSpace

- Improved memory management

- Mechanisms to step through the AUTOEXEC.BAT and an ordinary batch file

The remainder of this appendix discusses the above items in the displayed order.

MANAGING DISKS WITH SCANDISK

ScanDisk is a full-screen utility like DEFRAG (p. 234) and MSBACKUP (p. 261). A series of screens offer a number of options to let you check and repair a variety of drives, including hard drives, floppy drives, RAM drives, and DoubleSpace drives. It can do much more than CHKDSK. In fact, if you use CHKDSK, a message appears to urge you to use ScanDisk instead.

To check a specific drive (disk), specify it as the parameter. You can also specify multiple drives or the /ALL switch; ScanDisk will check them all. To check drive A, enter a command like this:

```
C:\DOS>scandisk a:
```

Figure 1 appears and scanning on drive A begins right away. The middle of the screen shows the items completed (marked by √) and the one in progress (marked by »). Three buttons are displayed at the bottom. If you choose Pause (the leftmost), the button is changed to Continue, as shown in Figure 1. During the pause, you can choose More Info to show a brief explanation. You can choose Exit at any time to quit.

```
Microsoft ScanDisk
───────────────────────────────────────────────────────────────────

ScanDisk is now checking the following areas of drive A:
     √      Media descriptor
     √      File allocation tables
     √      Directory structure
     »      File system
            Surface scan









 ◄ Continue ►    < More Info >    < Exit >
───────────────────────────────────────────────────────────────────
You paused ScanDisk. To continue checking this drive, choose Continue.
```

Figure 1   The initial ScanDisk screen

ScanDisk's commands (option buttons) are flanked by <> and the current selection by ◄►. If you press Enter, the current selection is activated. You can use Tab, Shift-Tab, or a cursor key to make another selection and then press Enter to activate it. Each button also contains a highlighted letter; you can hold down Alt and press that letter to activate that option.

If no drive is specified with the SCANDISK command, the current drive is checked. This command checks drive C:

        C:\DOS>**scandisk**

If a drive has been compressed by DoubleSpace and is mounted, you will be asked whether you want to check it first, as shown in Figure 2. You can also specify to check a host drive with a command like this:

```
C:\DOS:>scandisk h:\dblspace.000
```

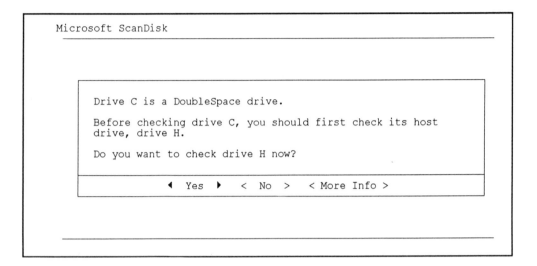

Figure 2   Checking a DoubleSpace drive

If no error is encountered after checking a drive, ScanDisk offers to scan the disk's surface and gives you an estimated time to complete the job. You can choose Yes or No. If you choose Yes, a new screen appears; it resembles the one produced by DEFRAG (Figure 6.1, p. 235).

After ScanDisk completes its job or is aborted by you, the screen shows a View Log button. You can choose it to report the result, as shown in Figure 3. You can press the PgUp/PgDn keys or click the displayed up/down arrows to scroll the text.

When an environment program such as Windows or DOS Task Swapper is loaded, you can run ScanDisk only with the /CHECKONLY switch. This will only check but not repair the specified drive. The reason for this restriction is to prevent rearrangement of disk space, which may be used by the loaded program.

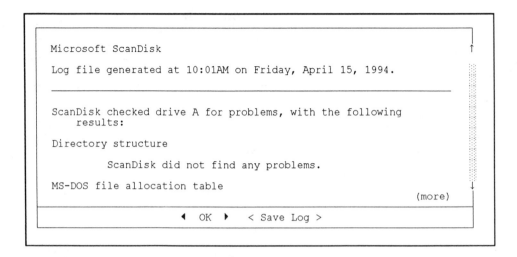

```
Microsoft ScanDisk                                              ↑

Log file generated at 10:01AM on Friday, April 15, 1994.
_____


ScanDisk checked drive A for problems, with the following
     results:

Directory structure

          ScanDisk did not find any problems.

MS-DOS file allocation table                                   ↓
                                                       (more)
```
◄   OK   ►   < Save Log >

Figure 3   Viewing the result of ScanDisk

The default ScanDisk settings are specified in SCANDISK.INI, an ASCII file. It contains numerous comments. You can use the TYPE command to read or print it.

If problems are found, a screen titled Problem Found appears with a number of option buttons. The list below appears when lost clusters are found:

<Save>   <Delete>   <Don't Fix It>   <More Info>

If you need a more detailed explanation, choose More Info. If you choose Don't Fix It, the problems are left unrepaired. (Some problems may lead to a Fix It button.) If you choose Delete, the lost clusters (disk data not connected to any existing file name) are deleted. If you choose Save, the lost clusters are saved to one or more files named FILEnnnn.CHK (FILE-0001.CHK, FILE0002.CHK, etc.) in the root directory of the disk being checked. These ASCII files share the same name as those created by the CHKDSK command. You can use TYPE or a text processor to read them and then decide what to do with them.

When problems require disk alterations, a screen titled Create Undo Disk appears to direct you what to do. You are given the following options:

<Drive A>   <Drive B>   <Skip Undo>   <More Info>

If you choose Skip Undo, ScanDisk proceeds to correct the problems without saving undo data. This option leaves no room for reversing the action. If something goes wrong with ScanDisk's action, there is no recourse.

To be on the safe side, you can choose either drive. You need to insert in the specified drive a disk with some space for saving data. ScanDisk will save a file named SCANUNDO.DAT. If something goes wrong, you should undo what ScanDisk did before you do anything to the modified disk. Use a command like this:

```
C:\DOS>scandisk /undo a:
```

This assumes that the undo disk is in drive A. ScanDisk will restore the original condition of the target drive (C in our example).

If ScanDisk causes no trouble, you can erase the SCANUNDO.DAT file. This file is given the R attribute. You need to use the ATTRIB command to remove it before you can delete the file.

COPY IMPROVEMENTS

Version 6.2 contains improvements in these old duplication commands: COPY, XCOPY, MOVE, and DISKCOPY.

In previous versions, the COPY, XCOPY, and MOVE commands would overwrite a matching target file. You could thus inadvertently erase files and not know it. To prevent such a potentially disastrous consequence, version 6.2 gives these commands the following new switches:

/Y   Automatic overwrite without pausing for user consent

/-Y   Pauses to let the user choose one of three options

By default, version 6.2 prompts you to make a choice when a matching target file is found. Suppose you have two files both named X, one stored in the current directory in drive C and the other in drive A. This is what happens when you try to copy one to the other:

```
C:\X>copy x a:
Overwrite A:X. (Yes/No/All)?n
         0 file(s) copied
```

If you enter Y, the matching file is overwritten. If you enter N as shown above, no copying is done. If your command includes a wild card character and there are other matching files, you will be prompted to overwrite each matching file. If you enter A when prompted, all the matching files will be overwritten without further prompting.

What happens if you supply a character other than Y, N, or A? The character you type does not appear and the cursor does not budge. This is also true when you press Enter without typing anything. As usual, you can press Ctrl-C or Ctrl-Break to break a command or prompt.

In the following command, we try to copy from drive A to the current directory in drive C two files named X1 and X2:

```
C:\X>copy a:x?
Overwrite C:X1. (Yes/No/All)?y
Overwrite C:X2. (Yes/No/All)?y
        2 file(s) copied
```

In the following command, we try to copy from drive B to the current directory in drive C. By supplying A at the prompt, all the matching files are copied without further pause:

```
C:\X>copy b:x?
Overwrite C:X. (Yes/No/All)?a
B:X1
B:X2
        2 file(s) copied
```

If you use COPY CON (p. 115) to create a file, you will also be prompted to overwrite an existing matching file. In the following command, no file is created (copied) when you enter N at the prompt:

```
C:\X>copy con x1
Overwrite X1 (Yes/No/All)?n
        0 file(s) copied
```

In the following command, supplying Y lets you proceed to create a file. After you enter ^Z, the new file writes over the existing matching one:

```
C:\X>copy con x1
Overwrite X1 (Yes/No/All)?y
xxx^Z
        1 file(s) copied
```

If you find this new feature bothersome, you can change the default by using the new environment variable named COPYCMD. Use this variable as you do DIRCMD (p. 363). To overwrite matching files without a prompt, enter this command:

```
c:\X>set copycmd=/y
```

If you now enter the SET command alone, you will see, among other strings, this particular line:

```
COPYCMD=/y
```

If you now use COPY as shown in the above examples, no prompt appears and all the matching files will be automatically overwritten.

If you want to restore the default, enter this command to clear the variable from the environment:

```
c:\X>set copycmd=
```

When you use COPY in a batch file, the command maintains its old habit of overwriting matching files without prompting you for a response. If you want a prompt, enter the /-Y switch in the environment. This can be done on the command line as shown above or via a batch file. Here is a sample batch file:

```
@echo off
rem SAFECOPY.BAT--prompt for overwrite
set copycmd=/-y
copy *.txt a:
set copycmd=
```

The third line assigns the /-Y value to COPYCMD. The fourth copies matching files from the current directory to drive A. And the fifth clears the environment variable. After the third line is executed, copying will lead to a prompt if a matching target is located.

You can also assign the /A switch to COPYCMD. It has the same effect as /-Y. Both will prompt you when a matching target file is found. This happens either on the command line or via a batch file.

What has been said about COPY can all be applied to MOVE and XCOPY. The same prompt and options will appear.

DISKCOPY has also seen some improvements. It is now possible to do same-drive copying in one pass. If you have used this command to diskcopy in one drive, you already know that you need to swap disks several times to complete the job. The reason for that is that DOS copies from the source disk to the available conventional memory and then from there to the target disk.

If your memory is limited and/or your disk capacity is large, you have to repeatedly switch the two disks.

The new version uses your hard disk (the directory specified in the environment variable named TEMP) to temporarily store the source disk's data. Since your hard disk is likely to have enough room to store the entire source disk, you need to insert the source disk once and then replace it with the target disk.

If you like the old way (using the available conventional memory rather than the hard disk as the interim storage device), you can use the new /M switch. If one pass cannot complete the job, you will be prompted to swap disks as in previous DOS versions.

Here are some examples:

```
C:\DOS>diskcopy a: a:
A:\>diskcopy a:
A:\>diskcopy /m
```

All the above commands diskcopy from drive A to drive A. In the first command, both parameters are necessary. If you specify one or none, the hard disk (default drive) will be the presumed target; an error will result. The second command specifies drive A as the source; the presumed target is the current drive (drive A). In the third example, DOS assumes that both source and target are the default drive; the optional /M switch precludes the hard disk in the copying operation.

DOUBLESPACE REMEDIES

Microsoft has taken numerous steps to ensure the safety of DoubleSpace. The following are the major ones:

- Before setting up a compressed disk, DoubleSpace runs ScanDisk to scan the disk's surface and sets aside unusable sectors. This can reduce data loss that can cause DoubleSpace to malfunction.

- If a disk contains stored data, DoubleSpace runs DEFRAG to rearrange the data before compressing them. This can improve speed and reduce chances for errors.

- SMARTDrive is now by default set to read caching only. In version 6.0, both read and write caching were enabled by default. This can improve your PC's performance. The write cache temporarily stores data in RAM and writes to disk only when the CPU is not so busy. If something happens to your PC in the meantime, the data may be lost, thus corrupting the disk and data. Taking out the write cache may slow down your PC, but it reduces the chances of ruining your disk.

- The /DOUBLEGUARD switch is new and on by default. It constantly checks the system's memory. If it is corrupted, the PC is shut down to prevent writing corrupted data to disk. This can protect disk files, but it can also lead to loss of data that has not been saved. You can use this switch to disable this feature (/DOUBLEGUARD=0). This feature can be set to off by default; run DBLSPACE on the command line and choose Options from the Tools menu.

- A compressed floppy disk is now automatically mounted. In version 6.0, swapping a disk required the /MOUNT switch to make Double-Space recognize its existence (p. 279). There is no need for this extra step in the new version. If you want to unmount, use the /UNMOUNT switch. Use /MOUNT to remount. This feature can also be set to off by default the same was as /DOUBLEGUARD explained above.

- You can now use the /UNCOMPRESS switch to reverse the course of compression. This may not be practical when a hard disk is involved because you need a great deal of disk space to store the uncompressed files. If you really want to do that, you may be required to delete some of the files to free up enough space; you will be told how much space you need.

- You can press Ctrl-F5 to bypass DoubleSpace at startup. A message appears telling you that DoubleSpace, CONFIG.SYS, and AUTO-EXEC.BAT are not loaded. You can also press Ctrl-F8 to bypass DoubleSpace and then step through CONFIG.SYS and AUTO-EXEC.BAT. You can change the switches in the DBLSPACE.INI file to alter the default settings. See the online help on this file for details.

There are many other switches as well. A good place to learn more details is the online help program. It used to provide skimpy help for only the DBLSPACE.SYS item. It now contains two additional items in the initial screen—<Dblspace> and <Dblspace Tips>. Each of these in turn leads to more hints and new switches. Microsoft used to be niggardly in giving out details as if their trade secrets might be stolen by somebody. Now users are deluged with tons of minutiae on DoubleSpace. Their new attitude seems to be: We're telling you everything; if you still mess up, it's no longer our fault.

Is DoubleSpace safe to use? The new features have made it much less likely to wreak havoc. Some critics, however, maintain that it is still unreliable. They point out that if you use third-party (non-Microsoft) disk utilities, many things can potentially go wrong. If you find yourself in this situation, you might want to spend sometime perusing the lengthy README.TXT file. It addresses the potential pitfalls and remedies for using the packages from other vendors.

If you have not used DoubleSpace, you may not want to start now. Hard disk prices have fallen dramatically in the past few years. It may make more sense to buy a larger drive or an additional drive than to compress an existing one.

If you have two PCs, you might want to do what I do. My old 386 PC has a 40MB hard disk. I use it most for old DOS programs and files. To extend its life, I use DoubleSpace to compress the hard disk. I use my new 486 PC mostly for Windows programs. The 500MB hard disk has more than enough capacity to accommodate the half a dozen programs I use regularly. There is no need for me to compress it. I don't compress my floppies so that I can use them on either PC. With DSHD floppy disks selling for barely above 50 cents each, compressing them seems to make little sense.

If your hard disk is not compressed when you boot DOS from it, DBL-SPACE.BIN is not loaded. This frees up about 50KB of RAM. If your hard disk was compressed when you install a new version, the new file compressor will be installed and loaded. If you install version 6.22 from a Stepup disk (it retails for about $10 and can be used to update previous versions 6.2x), it will automatically convert DoubleSpace files to DriveSpace counterparts.

Is DriveSpace safe? It's too early to tell. Some people say they never trust Microsoft's version x.0 products because each new major release is full of bugs. DriveSpace is a brand new product and hastily rushed to fill the void created by a lawsuit. If you plan to use it, it may be wise to regularly read some of the popular weekly and monthly computer publications to see what bugs their readers and experts might discover and how these bugs can be fixed. DriveSpace should become safer when it is bundled with MS-DOS 7. This version may be available in early 1995 when Windows 4, aka Chicago, is rolled out.

MEMORY MANAGEMENT

A number of minor improvements in memory management appear in version 6.2. Some are related to DoubleSpace, as discussed in the preceding section; others are not.

DoubleSpace's new safety features come at a price: higher memory consumption. DBLSPACE.BIN now takes up 10KB more RAM than its predecessor. Disabling the automounting feature (using /UNMOUNT) frees up about 5KB.

MemMaker no longer scans the upper memory area aggressively. Aggressively claiming this memory area for DOS could lead to conflict with some hardware devices and freeze your PC. If you want MemMaker to scan this area to possibly increase usable RAM, you can choose a proper option from the MemMaker screen. Read section 2 of the README.TXT file for details.

SMARTDrive is now by default set to read-caching only. If it was previously set to both read and write caching, that setting is not altered by the SETUP program. To find out what SMARTDrive is doing, enter this command:

```
C:\DOS>smartdrv
Microsoft SMARTDrive Disk Cache version 5.0
Copyright 1991,1993 Microsoft Corp.

Cache size:  2,097,152 bytes
Cache size while running Windows:  2,097,152 bytes


          Disk Caching Status
drive   read cache   write cache   buffering
---------------------------------------------
  A:        yes          no           no
  B:        yes          no           no
  C:        yes          yes          no
Write behind data will be committed before command prompt
returns.


For help, type "Smartdrv /?".
```

If the MSCDEX (Microsoft Compact Disk Extension) command appears before SMARTDRV in your AUTOEXEC.BAT file, SMARTDrive will also provide read cache for your CD-ROM drive to speed up reading data. In that case, the above display will also show that drive.

The HELP program supplies a great deal of information about SMARTDrive. If you want to change the default settings determined by the SETUP program, carefully study the various switches. One advice is worth repeating here. Before you shut off your PC or press the Reset button, you should enter this command to flush any unsaved data that might still linger in the write cache:

```
C:\DOS>smartdrv /c
```

If you press Ctrl-Alt-Del to restart your PC, according to the online help, the cache will be automatically flushed first; so there is no need to enter the above command.

If you use Windows, you can run the SMARTMON.EXE (SMARTDrive monitor) program by choosing the Run option from Program Manager's File menu and entering the program name. A separate screen will appear to show SMARTDrive's settings. The program's online help provides plenty of information. This program was also available in version 6.0 but not documented anywhere.

At startup, HIMEM.SYS now automatically checks your RAM. That is why this line appears at the beginning of booting:

```
HIMMEM is testing extended memory...
```

If the memory is sound, the word "done" appears at the end of the above line. If defects are found, a message appears. In that case, you may need to check or replace some RAM chips. If you want no testing (testing can delay startup), add the /TESTMEM:OFF switch after the HIMEM.SYS command in the CONFIG.SYS file. This device driver includes quite a few new switches. Check the online help for details.

If you encounter the *Stack Overflow* error, you may want to increase the numbers for the following CONFIG.SYS command:

```
STACKS=9,256
```

This line was put in my CONFIG.SYS file by the DOS SETUP program. The first number is for the number of stacks, which can be 0-64. The second is the byte size of each stack, which can be 0-512. If your PC works with the 0,0 values, you can free up some memory. If errors result, you need to increase the numbers.

DEBUGGING BATCH FILES

New features in version 6.2 allow you to step through the AUTOEXEC.BAT file as well as an ordinary batch file. This makes debugging batch files much easier than before.

DOS 6 introduced the feature of letting you press the F8 key at startup. As discussed on p. 501, you can use this method to step through only the lines in the CONFIG.SYS file. After this file is through, you are asked whether or not to process the entire AUTOEXEC.BAT file; you have no option of stepping through individual lines.

This has been changed in version 6.2. After you supply Y to process the AUTOEXEC.BAT file, you are prompted with [Y/N] to execute each line.

To step through an ordinary batch file, you need to load an extra copy of COMMAND.COM. The COMMAND command's online help now shows these three additional switches:

/Y   Steps through the batch program specified by /C or /K.

/C *command*   Executes the specified command and returns.

/K *command*   Executes the specified command and continues running.

If you enter COMMAND alone, a copy is loaded and a copyright message is displayed. The same thing happens when you use COMMAND with the /Y switch alone.

The difference between /C and /K is that the former loads COMMAND.COM and exits but the latter retains the program. If a program name follows the switch, the program is executed; if not, nothing else happens.

To unload each additional copy of COMMAND.COM, just enter EXIT on the command line. After all the extra copies are unloaded, entering EXIT does nothing. If a shell program such as Windows has been loaded, the last EXIT will return you to that program's screen.

To step through a batch file, follow this syntax:

```
c:\DOS>command /y /c batname.bat
```

Replace /C with /K if you want to keep the newly loaded copy of COMMAND.COM in memory. The /Y switch must be placed before the /C switch. Otherwise, an error will result. The two switches can be together or separated by a space.

The batch file name immediately follows the /C switch. The BAT extension is optional. However, if there is a matching command with the COM or EXE extension, it may be executed instead. In that case, the whole program is executed at once, not in single-step mode as when a batch file is run.

The command to step through a batch file is rather lengthy. We can shorten it with a batch file like below:

```
@echo off
rem STEP.BAT--to step thru a batch file
command /y/c %1
```

We can now use this batch file to step through the SAFECOPY batch file shown in an earlier section. This is what happens:

```
C:\X>step safecopy
safecopy [Y/N]?Y
echo off [Y/N]?Y
rem SAFECOPY.BAT--prompt for overwrite [Y/N]?N
set copycmd=/-y [Y/N]?Y
copy *.txt b: [Y/N]?Y
Overwrite B:X1.TXT (Yes/No/All)?
```

At the outset, you are prompted to execute the specified batch file (or program). If we had entered a compiled program as the argument, this would have been the only prompt. Since we specify a batch file, you are prompted before each line is processed.

The following keys are useful. They appear on p. 502. They can be used here as well:

Esc   Execute all remaining

F5   Bypass all remaining

If you press Esc in the middle of stepping through lines, all the remaining lines will automatically be executed. If you press F5 instead, batch execution ends without executing another line.

The above rules apply when a [Y/N] prompt is displayed. However, when you are prompted to overwrite a file as shown in the last line, these keys do not work. You need to press Ctrl-C to terminate or choose one of the available options.

If you intend to debug an errant batch file, you might want to add ECHO OFF and ECHO ON at proper places to see what each line does.

If you use DoubleSpace or DriveSpace, the table on p. 502 can be augmented by the following:

F5	Load DBLSPACE.BIN, but skip CONFIG.SYS and AUTO-EXEC.BAT
Ctrl-F5	Skip everything
F8	Load DBLSPACE.BIN; step through CONFIG.SYS and AUTOEXEC.BAT
Ctrl+F8	Skip DBLSPACE.BIN; step through CONFIG.SYS and AUTOEXEC.BAT

Index